The Status of the Individual in East and West

East-West Philosophers' Conference, 4th, Univ. of Hawaii, 1964.

The Status of the Individual in East and West

EDITED BY CHARLES A. MOORE
WITH THE ASSISTANCE OF ALDYTH V. MORRIS

UNIVERSITY OF HAWAII PRESS HONOLULU 1968

Copyright 1968 by the University of Hawaii Press
Manufactured in the United States of America
Library of Congress Catalog Card Number 67-14717

Dedicated

To the cordial spirit of these Conferences

To the outstanding participants who have made
them significant

To the many contributors—of time and/or funds—
who have made them possible

Contents

Foreword

This volume is the last book edited by Senior Professor Charles A. Moore—Professor of Philosophy at the University of Hawaii since 1936, Chairman of the Department until 1954, Director of the 1939, 1949, 1959, 1964 East-West Philosophers' Conferences, and Editor of *Philosophy East and West* from its inception in 1951 until his death, April 14, 1967.

If time and events bear out Bertrand Russell's surmise that the next major infusion of ideas into the history of Western philosophy may likely come from Asia, there is no philosopher of our time more appropriately to be termed the foremost pioneer in the "New Frontier" than Charles Moore. The promotion of cultural rapprochement by way of philosophical understanding between the people of East and West was his mission; to that end he gave his life.

Every care has been taken by those responsible for the publication of this volume to ensure that the high standards set by Professor Moore have been scrupulously adhered to. In the completion of this task special recognition and appreciation must be accorded to those who so generously and painstakingly gave of their knowledge and time: Chung-ying Cheng, Kenneth K. Inada, Walter H. Maurer, S. K. Saksena, Yukuo Uehara, and Beatrice T. Yamasaki.

WINFIELD E. NAGLEY

Honolulu
December 1967

Preface

This volume is the "official" Report of the work of the Fourth East-West Philosophers' Conference, held at the University of Hawaii during the summer of 1964. The volume is composed primarily of the papers presented at the formal meetings of the Conference (plus some of the Public Lectures). The essence of the work of the Conference was provided by these formal papers, and so this volume presents the substance of the Conference in its essentials. It contains also—in the form of questions and answers —some of the substantial and extensive, and also enlightening and frequently controversial, discussion that took place at formal meetings, informal and special coffee hours, five receptions, and six weeks of constant personal interchange among the some 125 members of the Conference. Of course, no volume of this type could do full justice to a Conference which involved so much constant give-and-take discussion and formal and informal intellectual encounter and dialogue.

This Conference was like the three preceding East-West Philosophers' conferences, except that, this time, the work was centered around one basic problem—namely, the comparative status of the individual in the major philosophical and cultural traditions of Asia and the West. As at the earlier Conferences, the work of the 1964 Conference was divided into six "Sections," in each of which one special aspect of the over-all problem was presented in formal papers and discussed extensively and in depth for an entire week—such discussion involving, as already said, not only that which took place at the formal meetings, but also that which occurred at informal coffee hours (which, by the way, were unanimously considered of great value), and that at informal—and practically continuous— personal discussions. This division of the work into six major Sections, each dealing with one of the basic aspects of the problem, provided the opportunity for concentrated explanation and discussion—although, as is stated in the Introduction to this volume, such rather strict demarcation, calling for possibly artificial divisions of the problem, was questionable and may have been somewhat misleading for the members from Asia.

In format, this fourth Conference resembled the previous Conferences. This consisted of (1) formal Conference meetings (four nights per week), at each of which, on most occasions, one formal paper was read in its entirety by its author and then discussed, first and primarily by the Panel Members, and then by the general membership (unfortunately, for too short a period of time); (2) daily coffee hours, at which the paper presented at the formal meeting the night before was discussed by the full membership in informal fashion and in much more detail than was possible at the formal meeting alone; (3) one Public Lecture by a Panel Member each of the last five weeks of the Conference; and (4) a few special coffee hours, at which supplementary papers or lectures (or papers which could not be included in the formal program because of the time factor) were presented and fully discussed.

The format of this volume, in general, conforms with that of the Conference, and the order of the papers follows the order of their presentation at the formal meetings of the Conference and in the Conference program—Section by Section. (Professor William Ernest Hocking's paper—sent to the Conference and read by his son, Dr. Richard Hocking, because of Professor Hocking's inability to follow through on his original intention of participating in the Conference—is included in Section I, because it deals primarily with the metaphysical aspect of the problem.) At the end of most papers there are some Questions and Answers to represent what the authors considered the most important items in the discussion of their papers. Following the formal papers are some of the Public Lectures. (The lectures by Dr. Chan and Dr. Tara Chand are not published herein, since these two Conference members have formal papers in the earlier Sections of the book.)

One of the rather serious difficulties of organizing and editing this volume has been the matter of the length of the individual papers. This has been at times a rather delicate matter in some cases. The "rules of the game" called for papers of such length that they could be read at the formal Conference meetings within a 45-minute time limit—so as to provide the writer ample time for the presentation of basic pertinent ideas and also to provide for significant discussion. It was very difficult in some cases for the writer to restrict himself to this limit—and some did not do so. Accordingly—and unfortunately—the papers in this volume are of unequal length. In fairness to those who kept the length of their papers within prescribed limits, some attempt has been made to edit a few of the papers so as to bring them more into line with the "required" limits of length. This was most difficult, sometimes unsuccessful, and at times practically impossible.

The technical problems of editing a volume like this are immense, because of the very nature of its contents, in terms of the variety of language and cultural perspectives, the necessity for Asian members to express themselves in sometimes difficult English terminology, the variety of styles which the several authors individually prefer in such matters as italics, capitals, hyphenation, personal names, transliteration, translations of the same words or titles from Asian languages, dates, etc. While consistency of style in all such matters is clearly the ideal—for the sake of clarity in reading—the editor has not felt that consistency throughout the volume is of such importance as to justify ignoring or rejecting the technical stylistic preferences of the outstanding scholars whose papers comprise this volume. This is not to say that the volume presents a carelessly permissive miscellany of styles. Consistency of style is sought as far as feasible, and consistency within each paper has been achieved.

An attempt was made to achieve uniformity or consistency of style in the transliteration in the papers on the Far East without violating the expressed professional preferences of the authors. This attempt was unsuccessful. It was decided, therefore, to leave names and titles—including capitalization and hyphenation—in the papers and in the footnotes as the authors presented them. Uniformity of style will be achieved in the index, in spite of necessary conflict between entries there and the corresponding items in the text.

Capitalization and hyphenation have been constant causes of concern to the perhaps overzealous editor. In neither case has precise uniformity been insisted upon or achieved, except within the several papers.

Hyphenation has been used rather abundantly—wherever it seemed advisable for ease of reading on the part of those not too familiar with Asian languages, but not at the cost of technical accuracy. Technically, there is no precisely correct style of hyphenation, nor, in many cases, any consistent system of uniformity, in any of the Asian languages. "Correct" hyphenation in titles of books and articles proved next to impossible of achievement in the uniformity of styles preferred by authors. This was especially true in the footnotes. In some papers, hyphenation (and capitalization) was not changed at all in the editing process. Also, in some cases, footnotes were left unedited.

Capitalization is decidedly "inconsistent" in the volume as a whole, and occasionally within individual papers. These differences are not inaccuracies. The capital and the lower case, in most instances, are used to indicate different meanings or statuses of the words underlined—metaphysical status usually calling for the capital, empirical status for the lower-case letter. Examples are numerous: Heaven or heaven, *Nirvāṇa* or *nirvāṇa*, *Dharma* or *dharma*, the Buddha and *buddha*-nature (and related terms), *Śūnyatā* or *śūnyatā*, Soul and/or Self (*Ātman* and *ātman*), State, Nature, Moral Law, etc.

Following the wishes of authors of papers in this volume, italics for emphasis have been generally retained.

Sometimes technically inaccurate styles have been used, for ease of reading and in deference to common usage; for example, the formation of plurals of Sanskrit words by the terminal "s" (e.g., *brāhmaṇas*); and such terms (very occasionally) as *"brāhmin"* instead of the correct *"brāhmaṇa"*; also e.g., *ātman* and *karma* (instead of *karman*).

It has not been considered the prerogative of the editor—in this case, possibly less than sufficiently "strict"—to insist upon any mandatory or arbitrary style for the volume as a whole, partly because in many cases there is no "correct" style, but primarily out of respect for the judgment of the outstanding authorities responsible for the papers that make up this volume, and also because of the very nature of the volume, a symposium of papers by representatives of various traditions and cultures who do not think or write or express themselves in any one restricted manner.

However, the editor assumes full responsibility for revising usage employed by some Chinese authors—and common usage—in cases of published items—called *"chuans"*—which are in fact articles or chapters or parts of standard works. These are enclosed within quotation marks and are not italicized.

It should probably be mentioned that, since this book is in English, an effort has been made in the editing to make it as readable and intelligible as feasible, without committing too-gross violations of accuracy. For example, the aforementioned general Western practice of adding a final "s" to form plurals of Asian terms has been employed, although it is not technically accurate. Also, as mentioned, common usage has been followed occasionally. Also, there is some inconsistency in the matter of italicizing foreign words —sometimes common Asian words are italicized, sometimes not. These are matters of individual preference, complicated by an editor's somewhat obligatory reliance upon English dictionaries in the case of terms which have become matters of common usage in English. It is not felt, however, that any of these discrepancies will cause serious confusion—in fact, the opposite has been the purpose of the editing practices adopted.

Small superior letters, comparable to footnote numbers, will be encountered frequently in articles by representatives of China and Japan. These letters indicate Chinese and/or Japanese characters which are provided at the end of the respective articles. Sanskrit, Pali, Chinese, Japanese, and Arabic terms, especially in cases where there is any possible doubt of translation, will be found within parentheses after the English (or the English will be in parentheses after the Asian terms, if the author prefers that style). Both in the text and in the footnotes, English equivalents of all terms, titles, and expressions in Asian languages will be given.

In many instances—for the sake of clarity and historical perspective—dates are provided for some historical periods and outstanding thinkers in the Asian fields.

Recognition—and sincere thanks—should be given here to those who have been so significantly helpful in the preparation of the papers and of the volume for publication, and there are many who deserve special mention and commendation.

Without going into detail concerning specific ways in which they were helpful—and most co-operative—the editor personally wishes to express his appreciation to Professor Wing-tsit Chan, the editor's constant guide and advisor, Professor Kenneth K. Inada, Professor S. K. Saksena, Professor Chung-ying Cheng, Professor Richard P. Haynes, and to Professor Beatrice Yamasaki (who assumed responsibility for preparation of the Who's Who items found in the Appendix)—for specific and valuable help with editing chores; to Mr. Thomas Nickerson, Director of the University of Hawaii Press; to Mr. Robert Sparks, Managing Editor of the University of Hawaii Press; and to those authors of papers and lectures who co-operated so well in the editing of their contributions. Dr. Inada went far beyond "the call of duty," examining, with the editor, almost innumerable detailed and specific problems in the Asian papers during a final re-checking of all papers just before publication. He has been extremely helpful and deserves and hereby receives the editor's enthusiastic appreciation. (The editor, of course, assumes sole responsibility.)

A special expression of appreciation must go to Mrs. Aldyth V. Morris, the "very special assistant" to the editor of this volume—as she was also of the volumes from the two preceding conferences (*Essays in East-West Philosophy*, 1949; and *Philosophy and Culture —East and West*, 1959). An attempt to recognize her unusually significant contribution has been made by citing her on the title page.

The editor's secretary, Mrs. Floris Sakamoto, must also be included in this list and thanked for her industriousness, co-operative spirit, and patience throughout the long and difficult and confusing, and at times frustrating problems of typing and re-typing parts of the manuscript, and the many other chores involved—and there were many.

To all who have been helpful, my sincere appreciation. To those who may find the editing too far short of perfection, my apologies. The editor assumes full responsibility for all errors for which editors are responsible—but not for discrepancies which were more or less beyond his control. To take one's work as editor as a very serious responsibility and at the same time to recognize the high scholarly stature of those whose work constitutes the body of a volume—that is a rather precarious predicament.

CHARLES A. MOORE

Honolulu
September 1, 1965

Video and audio tapes and 16-mm. films of many of the activities of the Conference are available for purchase—at cost. These include the reading of the formal papers, the discussion at formal meetings, the public lectures, and weekly summaries (plus an introductory statement and an over-all summary). For detailed information, please write to University of Hawaii Communications Center, University of Hawaii, Honolulu.

Greetings

THOMAS H. HAMILTON
President, University of Hawaii

Whenever one is asked to participate in the opening of a conference such as this, he inevitably tries to reflect on what may be its central significance. This is difficult, because gatherings like this result in important ends in a number of ways—some of which can be predicted, others of which cannot. But it seems to me that certainly one of the central essentials of this Conference being held here at this time is its appropriateness. And it seems to me appropriate in a number of ways.

First, physically it is being held in these Islands, which lie geographically almost half way between the great land masses of North and South America and the continent of Asia. It is, in short, symbolically appropriate from this geographical point of view that there would be a place where those from the West and those from the East could convene to discuss their philosophical traditions as they relate one to the other.

It is appropriate, too, that this Conference is held here because of the unusual composition of our citizenry. Over half of our citizens can trace their cultural and ethnic lineage directly back to the continent of Asia, while an almost equally large group were born of the intellectual tradition which stretches from Plato and Aristotle through St. Thomas, Rousseau, Locke, Mill, and Thomas Jefferson. There is, as far as I know, no place on earth where there live together in harmony groups with these diverse cultural affinities.

It is appropriate, too, that this Conference is being held on a university campus. As we develop historical perspective, it becomes increasingly evident to us that ideas have consequences in the affairs of men. And it is ideas to which this Conference is devoted, and trafficking in ideas is the primary business of a university. As John Erskine has said so well, "We believe that the virtues wait upon intelligence—literally wait, in the history of the race. Whatever is elemental in man—love, hunger, fear—has obeyed from the beginning the discipline of intelligence. We are told that to kill one's aging parents was once a demonstration of solicitude; about the same time men hungered for raw meat and feared the sun's eclipse. Filial love, hunger, and fear are still motives to conduct, but intelligence has directed them to other ends. If we no longer hang the thief or flog the schoolboy, it is not that we think less harshly of theft or laziness, but that intelligence has found a better persuasion to honesty and enterprise.

"But the lover of intelligence must be patient with those who cannot readily share his passion. Some pangs the mind will inflict upon the heart. It is a mistake to think that men are united by elemental affections. Our affections divide us. We strike roots in immediate time and space, and fall in love with our locality, the customs and the language in which we were brought up. Intelligence unites us with mankind, by leading us in sympathy to other times, other places, other customs, but first the prejudiced roots of affection must be pulled up. These are the old pangs of intelligence.

"Yet, if intelligence begins in a pang, it proceeds to a vision. Through measureless time its office has been to make of life an opportunity, to make goodness articulate, to make virtue a fact. But all that intelligence has accomplished dwindles in comparison with the vision it suggests and warrants. Beholding this long liberation of the human spirit, we foresee, in every new light of the mind, one unifying mind, wherein the human race shall know its destiny and proceed to it with satisfaction, as an idea moves to its proper conclusion; we conceive of intelligence at last as the infinite order, wherein man, when he enters it, shall find himself." [1]

Thus, it is my pleasure to welcome you on behalf, not only of the University of Hawaii, but of the East-West Center, to this singularly appropriate Conference.

NEAL S. BLAISDELL
Mayor of the City of Honolulu

It is indeed a privilege to welcome this distinguished group to the Fourth East-West Philosophers' Conference in Honolulu. We know that you citizens of the world of ideas feel very much at home here —as one of your Conference members has said, "In Hawaii no one is a stranger or foreigner"—and we are proud that you have chosen Honolulu as an appropriate meeting place during the period of our most significant development as a microcosm of East-West rapprochement.

However, it might be even more appropriate for you to welcome the people of Honolulu and Hawaii to the world of the ideas you bring to our academic center, which is still rather remote from the periphery of our workaday world. You may observe here in Honolulu the processes of acculturation which have taken place almost instinctively and inevitably, the way a child gradually develops without being conscious of the process.

[1] John Erskine, "The Moral Obligation to be Intelligent." *Hibbert Journal*, vol. 12, 1913–14, pp. 184–185.

We, on the other hand, are only beginning to observe, analyze, and direct those processes as our economic, political, and social activities are studied by professors and researchers. Probably very few of us have had the time, the training, or the tendency to view our own way of life from the objective and universal viewpoints you bring to this Conference. And so, we are, in a way, strangers in our own society, while you are visiting a community which is familiar to you as a significant point between the past and the future of man.

One of your speakers at the 1959 Conference, Professor Gray L. Dorsey, of the Washington University Law School, traced the influence of philosophy on law and politics in Western civilization. He said that from the earliest beginnings of Western civilization a central purpose of society has been power, whereas the central purpose of Chinese society was the establishment and maintenance of universal harmony. Here in Honolulu we can trace these two concepts as they gradually approach and include each other. We can see in the history of Hawaii, during the past century, the introduction of Western technology and the corporate system, concurrent with the introduction of Oriental hand-labor and the family system of thrift. We see those systems merging to produce that segment of our community—Americans of Chinese ancestry—which now has the highest per capita income in Hawaii, and still retains its close-knit family structure in modern business enterprises.

Professors of religion and philosophy from Japan, in 1959, analyzed the factors which have contributed to the complex character of the Japanese people, such as the ancient codes of concord in all human relationships, the avoidance of dissent and self-assertion, the strong attachment to both family and state, and the preoccupation with immediate, tangible pursuits. As Professor Nakamura, of Tokyo University, said, Japan alone among Asian nations made rapid progress in modernization because of this emphasis on practical affairs.

Here in Hawaii, we have observed their characteristic of non-involvement modified by the rapid political ascendancy of the Nisei, who now constitute a majority in our state and local governments. And this has been accomplished without any appreciable loss of their socially mature qualities of courtesy, self-control, and concern for the feelings of others—qualities greatly needed in Western political life.

Dr. S. K. Saksena, Head of the Department of Philosophy at Lucknow University, pointed out that in the West the term "practical" refers to man's control of his environment, whereas in India it has the opposite meaning of mastery of one's own self. He said it was heartening that one of America's great sociological thinkers,

City Planner Lewis Mumford, was advocating as much emphasis on individual redevelopment as on urban redevelopment. This more advanced concept is now a recognized necessity for our rapidly growing metropolitan area. At a recent Urban Renewal Conference in Honolulu, special interest was shown in the discussions of social planning for individual enrichment.

And so, in the day-to-day life of our multi-racial community, we are receptive to the philosophical ideas first propounded at conferences such as this one. We are overwhelmingly involved in the economic or political or social obstacles to the accomplishment, and, indeed, we may never see the fulfillment of advanced ideas in one lifetime.

But, since you have walked and talked among us, we in Honolulu and Hawaii are more aware of our singular role in the long evolution of civilization, which was summed up at your 1959 Conference by Chancellor Radhakrishnan, of Delhi University, when he said, "History is not made by the tumult and uproar, but it is made in silence by changes in the minds of men."

We are grateful to those among us who have made it possible for you to come here every five years, so that ideas and action may accelerate together in a harmonious environment conducive to progress.

JOHN A. BURNS
Governor, State of Hawaii

Mr. Mayor, President Hamilton, Dr. Moore, and distinguished participants in the East-West Philosophers' Conference, my fellow Americans.

We in Hawaii are distinctly pleased, we are heartened in our endeavor to meet our challenges, we are overwhelmed by our opportunity to be your hosts at this most meaningful Conference. I would perhaps take a small exception to President Hamilton's placement of the relationship of ideas. It seems from the course of history that we can remove intelligence from man and have him act like an animal. But we can never make him act as a totally intelligent being would. We all hope this day can change, and perhaps the beginning of the change is with the confrontation of those who are possessors and proponents of ideas as they meet here to exchange those ideas with one another and offer the exchange for public consideration. Diverse as ideas and presentations may be, we gain by the very diversity with a special dividend of strength and development in this time of battle for the minds of men.

As we approach the twenty-first century, nothing is more important than the development of an ability to accommodate, to reason together, as our great President Lyndon Baines Johnson has so frequently said. If we are to carry forward the heritage and the civilization that we have today, we must find a means of reconciling different ideas, different philosophies. We must be able to move forward with strength born of the very diversity that binds us together.

I want to take this opportunity to acknowledge the very great debt the State of Hawaii owes to Dr. Charles Moore. It was my privilege to experience his energetic persuasiveness and his steadfast persistence prior to the last East-West Philosophers' Conference when he sought to have a certain gentleman, now the President of India, His Excellency, Mr. Radhakrishnan, participate in the Conference. I know and I think we should all know that Dr. Moore, laboring against overwhelming odds, has been the father, the Godfather, and the midwife of the East-West Conferences.

I think we ought to acknowledge contributions of others, too, who have stimulated these meetings held in the hope and confidence that the minds of men can be brought to understand philosophies held by others. Proper recognition should go to Dr. Hung Wo Ching, who determined after attending the last Philosophers' Conference that ten years was too long to wait for another. As a consequence of his initiative and persistence, with the co-operation of Dr. Moore, we have let only five years elapse between East-West Philosophers' Conferences.

To all participants, we extend our heartiest Aloha. May you not only find exhilaration and experience a contribution to your thinking, but may you also find in Hawaii the true spirit of Aloha, the true brotherhood of man, and may you return whence you came heartened by the evidence that a brotherhood of man can be made to work, not only in Hawaii, but throughout the world. We are delighted to have you with us. We hope that you not only labor productively here during the Conference, but that you also learn to know something of Hawaii and our people.

Mahalo and God bless you.

The Status of the Individual in East and West

CHARLES A. MOORE

Introduction: The conference, the problem, the program*

Now that you outstanding philosophers from many parts of the world have been welcomed by the President of the University, by the Mayor of Honolulu, and by the Governor of the State of Hawaii —in that order—may I on behalf of the Steering Committee of the Conference and the Department of Philosophy, and for myself as Conference Director, welcome you, thank you for joining us in our work, and express the hope that you will enjoy your stay here and find the Conference a rewarding personal and philosophical experience.

And, on behalf of the Steering Committee of the Conference, the Department of Philosophy, and myself, I welcome this happy opportunity to express our enthusiastic appreciation for the fine co-operation we have received from the Administration of the sponsoring University of Hawaii and, particularly, its able and philosophically oriented President, Dr. Thomas Hale Hamilton.

This Introduction is essentially a "work paper" to describe the background, the purposes, and the program of the Conference; to suggest some of the many problems which are significantly pertinent for our consideration; and, if I may, to set the tone of our deliberations.

The University of Hawaii has conducted East-West Philosophers' Conferences at ten-year intervals over the last quarter of a century —1939, 1949, and 1959. This is the fourth such Conference. This one is being held after only five years, thanks to the voluntary co-operation and generosity of some 100 individuals, business organizations, and Foundations in Hawaii—under the leadership of Dr. Hung Wo Ching—who provided all the funds necessary to finance the Conference. The raising of these funds and the donations themselves reflect the spirit of these Conferences and the spirit of Hawaii, dedicated as both are to the attempt to enhance and to embody mutual understanding between the peoples of Asia and the West. We cannot begin this Conference without calling attention to this truly remarkable and completely multiracial achievement and

---

* The substance of this introduction is a revised combination of part of a paper distributed at the public ceremony opening the Conference and remarks made at that meeting.

without thanking all those who have thus made this Conference possible.

All of these Conferences originated and have continued with three ideas and ideals in mind: (1) to help develop greater mutual understanding between the peoples of Asia and the West at the level of philosophical conviction; (2) to encourage total or global perspective in philosophy; and (3) the conviction that provincialism is both philosophically unsound and dangerous, possibly tragic, in the contemporary world.

These are philosophy conferences, but they are unique in several ways and for several reasons.

For one thing, we have never been concerned exclusively with the purely intellectual or academic or technical examination of philosophical concepts and problems as such—or with philosophy in the abstract, or with its problems in a vacuum. We have been concerned, rather—and here we may reveal evidence of learning from the East—with the significance of philosophy as the ground or foundation for living and for culture, in the conviction that genuine understanding can be achieved only by an understanding of the fundamental ideas and ideals and attitudes of peoples and cultures.

These Conferences are unique also in the sense that we have deliberately sought, not only mutual understanding among peoples, East and West, but also the generic philosophical goal of total perspective—and in this we claim genuinely unique philosophical status.

Also, we have insisted that the philosophies of the several major peoples and cultures with which these Conferences have been concerned must be represented by scholars from and within those philosophical and cultural traditions. They understand their cultures better and therefore can very probably explain them to others better than "outside" (although perhaps more objective) scholars and interpreters. We have worked on the premise that understanding can come only through seeing and understanding others as they see themselves.

These Conferences are unique also—up to this one, at least—in the sense that the underlying attitude has been almost exclusively that of trying to understand and comprehend and even "feel with" the other fellow. Mutual understanding is, in our judgment, based upon openmindedness and cordiality to alien ideas, rather than mutual criticism (the trademark, alas, of much of scholarship). Unphilosophically perhaps, we have not so much sought solutions of philosophical problems by mutual criticism as we have sought the deepest possible mutual understanding and respect. I think we can say that this *spirit* of these Conferences is unique.

And, further, these Conferences have been unique in the specific delimitation of the area or areas under special consideration, namely, East and West. Of course, East and West comprehend the whole of mankind, but, in the light of the now recognized profound significance of the great philosophical traditions of Asia and because of Hawaii's special interest in and qualifications for the search for mutual understanding between these traditions and the West, we have resisted—even in our search for total perspective in philosophy —the attempt to become an all-comprehensive international conference. That work is done by others. Perhaps this East-West delimitation also emanates from the conviction that Asia has great philosophical wisdom to offer to the total perspective of philosophy, but, tragically, that it has been widely ignored by the West. It has been our purpose to work in the direction of overcoming this unphilosophical lack of total perspective.

We have one other uniqueness, and that is the six-week length of the Conferences. This has been one of the happiest aspects of the program: the chance to become really acquainted personally and philosophically. This long opportunity for personal and informal talks, chats, and discussions—and arguments on occasion—has been unanimously and strongly cited in the past as one of the chief advantages of these Conferences, and the major factor in producing genuine understanding and mutual respect—as well as lasting personal and professional friendships. These friendships have carried the spirit and the substance of our work into succeeding years in many ways and with many valuable results, such as collaborative projects, professional correspondence, visiting professorships, etc., as well as the warmth of personal respect and of respect for the traditions which these new friends represent.

Another unusual and valuable—though supplementary—feature of these Conferences has been the offering of a number of special and especially related courses in the Summer Session of the University of Hawaii. These courses—usually some eight in number—deal with Chinese, Indian, Buddhist (and Japanese), and East-West Comparative Philosophy. Courses at the elementary and at the advanced level are offered in each of the major traditions of Asia. "Seminars" are offered in East-West philosophy. In these seminars topics and problems encountered at Conference meetings are frequently brought up for discussion in the context of the course. These courses are all taught by authorities in their field, all Conference members. These special courses are in addition to the several regular courses in Western philosophy offered by the Department of Philosophy of the University.

I recommend that in our deliberations we keep constantly in mind three major lessons from our past Conferences. First, there is the great significance of *historical perspective* (in our descriptions, in our judgments and interpretations, and in our comparative evaluations) as so forcefully emphasized in 1959 by Dr. Hu Shih. Second, there is the frequently cited unsoundness and injustice of the common practice of disparagingly comparing one's own *ideals* with the *practices* of others. And, third, there is the constant danger of falling into the colloquial trap or cliché of thinking of *"the East"* and *"the West"* in utter violation of the great philosophical and cultural complexity and variety in and among all the areas and traditions that are our special concern.

The problem of the present Conference is more specific than that examined by any of our preceding Conferences. But, even so, our problem requires clarification so as to prevent our wandering afield. Formally, our problem is "The World and the Individual in East and West." In the revised Brochure announcing the Conference, I have taken the liberty of adding a clarifying subtitle, namely, "The status of the individual in reality, thought, and culture in East and West." We shall still be vitally concerned with the basic purposes of all of our past Conferences, namely, mutual understanding and the broadening of perspective in philosophy, but we shall now be directly and primarily concerned with this one specific problem of the individual.

To quote from the official Brochure:

"The status of the individual has been a constant and basic problem in the history of philosophy in both Asia and the West and in practically all the major philosophical and cultural traditions within each of these areas. The [at least alleged] varying status of the individual has also been the basis of serious mutual criticism and misunderstanding between East and West, and is a most crucial problem in the contemporary world—socially, politically, religiously, and philosophically.

"In view of the profound and far-reaching significance of this problem, the Conference will study its philosophical aspects in depth and as comprehensively as time and circumstances permit. The Conference will consider concepts, theories, attitudes, and practices —*past and present*—in the major philosophical and cultural traditions of East and West. It will examine—and attempt to overcome —common pertinent misunderstandings and antagonisms which exist between East and West. It will thus come to grips, philosophically, with one of the most fundamental problems facing the contemporary and changing world of Asia and the West."

The general belief here—call it a cliché—has been widespread, and serious, on both sides, namely, that in the East (the entire East) there is no respect or dignity or even autonomy for the individual, who is lost, sometimes said to be annihilated, in an Absolute, in nothingness, in the family, in the state, or in social tradition, whereas in the West, on the other hand, the individual is every-thing, and the group, no matter what it is, is of relative insignifi-cance. The cliché in the West is that the group exists for the indi-viduals. We hear of Western democracy and "Oriental despotism." We hear of Western individualism and that life is cheap in the Orient. We hear of personal immortality in the West and ultimate absorption or annihilation in the East, and on and on and on, but all to the same effect. And that effect is the basis of fundamental mutual criticism and disrespect—and frequently mutual antagonism —because the alleged gap is so great and the issue so vital.

The six Sections of our agenda correspond to the six specific areas of concentrated attention with which we will attempt to bring into focus for special consideration the six major aspects of the over-all problem. The point to note here is that our problem is fraught with many difficulties, great complexity, and much confusion. We must be willing to have our claims and counterclaims examined thor-oughly if we are to achieve either mutual understanding or greater philosophical knowledge and perspective.

There are certain negative aspects of our problem—what our problem is *not*.

For one thing, the cold war and the political East-West orien-tation. This is not a conference on communism versus democracy or the free world versus the communist world—although what we say and do here could have clear implications for that relationship. We are concerned here and now—as at all these Conferences—with the traditional, the philosophical and cultural, East and West.

Also, we are not here concerned directly—certainly not primarily —with the *nature* of the individual, except insofar as that problem is inseparable from the many-sided problem of the *status* of the individual. Nor will we be concerned directly with "individualism" or "the meaning of humanism." The Conference is based upon the thought that the status of the individual is a sufficiently distinct and significant problem to be examined in its own right. We are con-cerned with the status of the individual human being regardless of how the respective traditions interpret the essence or nature of that individual human being. It is of vital importance that we limit our-selves to this specific problem; otherwise, our work will not be done and we will vastly increase the difficulties we will have to face. I suggest that we will have our hands full, first, trying to determine what we mean by significant status—freedom, equality, equality of opportunity, independence, self-responsibility, or whatever—*and* in determining the acceptance and recognition of these marks of a genuine individual in the areas and traditions with which we are concerned.

Again, we are not to limit ourselves, this time, to explanatory description, which has been the general mode heretofore because of our dominant and almost exclusive interest in understanding each other. We are again seeking deeper understanding of the several traditions, East and West, but, this time, also the way for possible advance in both theory and practice with reference to the status of the individual. To this end, we must engage in mutual examination, comparative evaluation, and both philosophical and ordinary criticism, in the hope of achieving such theoretical and practical progress.

In the course of our work this time—especially in the areas devoted to social thought and practices and to legal and political thought and institutions—we shall encounter sensitive problems and situations, matters which because of current prominence are fraught with emotion. It is incumbent upon us all to realize the fundamentally philosophical nature of this Conference and to avoid every temptation to ignore or to destroy the spirit and character of our approach to the specific problems at hand—and to avoid emotional reactions. Specifically, we are not here to fight the cold war or the battle of civil rights in their political and emotional ramifications —this is not a conference on race relations, discrimination, or integration versus segregation, although many of us in the United States are acutely aware of and concerned about these problems.

In this procedure, involving mutual questioning, thorough examination, comparative evaluation, and forthright presentation of the facts, it is hoped that the spirit of our earlier Conferences will be maintained, namely, the attitude of cordiality, openmindedness, and friendliness of discussion—expressed in the Brochure in the words "frank but cordial" examination of each other's points of view. Criticism as such is not our purpose. But we must resort to "the kind of face-to-face dialogue which is necessary in such cases," to use the words of a UNESCO publication. We will assume that, as someone has said, "instead of widening differences, candor [may] bridge them."

The plan of work has been formulated by the Steering Committee in a manner intended to produce both comprehensive and detailed examination and understanding. The main feature of this plan is the division of the problem into six major Sections. In these special areas we shall attempt to understand and evaluate—mutually—the status of the individual in what seem to be the six major aspects of the problem. Let me identify these six areas and illustrate each— and its importance—by one concise example or problem.

First, we shall consider the metaphysical—or the ontological—status (or statuses) of the individual in the several major traditions as perhaps the most fundamental aspect of our problem, because here we shall be concerned with ultimates. The cliché here, of course, refers to the *monistic* East and the *pluralistic* West.

Second, we will investigate the question as to whether or not the several traditions emphasize—generally or exclusively—certain epistemological approaches to knowledge or certain methodological idiosyncrasies or ways of thinking and philosophizing which either indicate or determine that tradition's basic attitude toward the status of the individual. For example, we will investigate the cliché that the mystical East obviously must and does downgrade the individual, or denies him or ignores him, whereas the empirical and scientific West must obviously recognize the individual and belittle the universal or Absolute, or its equivalent.

Third, in the area of religion, we shall be concerned with both the empirical and the ultimate status of the individual. Here the cliché is one of extreme dichotomy, to the effect that the West is dominated by the concept of a personal God, the infinite value of the individual spiritual human being, personal and individual immortality, and never, except in heterodoxy, the loss or denial of such individual status in any form of substantial identity with God or a mystic One. On the contrary, the East—and that is the phrase the cliché uses—is dominated by mysticism or Absolutism, which, of course, ignores or transcends or absorbs—and perhaps, in one special form, annihilates—the individual in the ultimate reaches of spiritual achievement.

Fourth, we shall examine the problem of the status of the individual in the area of ethics. Our primary concern here will be the question as to whether or not the individual has the right of personal, or private, or individual conscience or moral convictions which may stand up against or at least challenge social or traditional morality —or whether the individual has no choice in attempting to be ethical but to submit to the rules and regulations of the moral code of his tradition, whether they come from God, from society, or from history. Here, too, the cliché sets the East over against the West. The common interpretation is that in the East the individual has no right of private conscience or moral right to challenge the tradition or group morality, especially the family, perhaps; whereas, in emphasis at least, the ethical autonomy of the individual and the right of conscience are mandatory and fundamental in the tradition of Western ethics.

In the fifth Section, entitled "Social Thought and Practices," we may wander somewhat from the strict domain of technical philosophy by being concerned with practices as well as social philosophy as such, but it is an indispensable part of our work to attempt to determine, under the guidance of our social philosophers, not only the status of the individual in the social thought-pattern of the respective traditions, but also whether or not these social philosophies, taken somewhat as ideals, are borne out in practice insofar as the status and importance of the individual are concerned. The cliché here also divides East from West, in both theory and practice, since it is thought widely that in both social thought and practice in the East the individual is dominated by and subservient to the grouping to which he belongs, primarily the family but also the social structure as a whole, and, perhaps especially in Japan, the state; whereas in the West the individual is thought to have prior or primary significance in social philosophies and societies, the emphasis being that society exists for the individuals and that the individual is not required to submit to social conditions or social practices to anything like the degree to which such subservience dominates the Eastern traditions.

The sixth and last area of our work is that of legal and political thought and institutions—certainly a comprehensive and complex area. The political problem—in our cliché context—may be thought of as "Oriental despotism" and political authoritarianism in the East, as opposed to democracy and liberalism and political individualism in the West, such that all Western totalitarianisms, past and present, are untypical. Here, as everywhere in our work, we must consider *both* traditional and idealistic theories *and* contemporary realities. And specifically, for example, we must face the alleged lessening of genuine democracy in the contemporary West and the problem of the authenticity, as it were, of the newly developed democracies of Asia. The legal part of our problem may be expressed in the contrast of the scientific and rationalistic legal philosophy characteristic of the West—a legal philosophy sometimes called by Northrop "law of contract"—as contrasted with the legal philosophy of Asia, the "law of status." In this Western concept, all men are "equal before the law," "enjoy equal protection under the law," or are a part of "our tradition of freedom under law." In the East, on the other hand, one's legal status seems to be determined primarily by one's biological or family status, and mediation or avoidance or compromise of the law is the rule—in serious contrast to the more rationalistic, more mechanical, more absolutist, and more universalistic legal philosophy of the West. Equality of individuals before the law is the crux of the matter, and in this interpretation it again *seems* that East is East and West is West.

Our work is thus divided into six specific areas. There is possibly a serious defect here. This is that any such departmentalizing of the problem is unsound—certainly and fundamentally to our Asian colleagues. This division of the problem into six separate topics or areas is a falsification of the actual unification or unity of life in its many aspects. The falsity of our analysis thus lies in virtually forcing Easterners to think in Western terms. To the Asian, the six-way approach may seem to make it impossible even to clarify the issues. In fact, some of our Asian representatives have had great difficulty preparing their papers for the Conference because of this division of work, which must seem to them artificial and perhaps even arbitrary. There is some overlapping among the papers from Asia, Section by Section, because of this intrinsic Asian attitude toward the wholeness of life and experience and thought.

Part of our work could be—and perhaps should be—what may be called "unfinished business." That is, the problem of this Conference was anticipated, if not necessitated, by a number of observations that have been made by members of previous Conferences —but never followed up or challenged. For their suggestiveness, let me cite a few such statements, both for their explanatory value and also for the problematic character of the interpretations implied. In this way, we can look more fully and perhaps more critically, so as to see more clearly and possibly to ask some questions. (Every one of the following statements was made by a member of one or more of these Conferences.)

"Rigidity and conservatism, the inherent tendencies of every legal system, were accentuated in the case of the *sharī'a* ["a formalized code of conduct extending over all of life"]. . . . The most important implication of all this . . . was the danger it brought to the autonomy of ethical action. Is there a question of ethical action if individuals are expected merely to perform what is obligatory and avoid what is prohibited? Would ethics not become merely a catechism?"

"Just as religion was the basis of the ethical thinking of the Indians, family the basis of the practical morals of the Chinese, so the State was the basis of all thought in Japan. The Japanese way of thinking is undergoing a change, but their thinking is an inheritance, a tradition."

"He [the Japanese] holds onto the traditions of the past with one hand and with the other reaches for the future. . . ."

"Science demands individuality in the sense of freedom of thought on the part of the individual—and . . . personal moral integrity."

In India, ". . . man, the embodied self, is conceived of as possessing potentiality for infinite perfection. . . . It is the duty of the ideal State to create conditions and opportunities that will gradually help man overcome his ignorance, selfishness, and immoral tendencies, so that a harmonious community may evolve in which every individual can advance toward the supreme goal of *spiritual* freedom. . . ."

"Asians are not especially fond of the law because of its rigidity and its impersonality, but no one [from the East] denies the significance of universal or absolute law in matters of great importance."

"Each of the major areas [considered at the 1959 Conference] considers itself decidedly democratic in basic political philosophy, in spite of obvious differences in detail both in theory and in practice in the course of history."

"The nationalistic spirit [in Japan] . . . produced a national unity that produced the idea of a strong centralized State. . . . Confucianism produced in China and in Japan diametrically opposed results."

"The Japanese have learned to attach unduly every importance to their human nexus in disregard of the individual."

"Every nation has a way of living and thinking which is more or less peculiar to it, constituting, as it were, its distinctive spirit. . . . For instance, the American way of life is marked by the spirit of democracy and fair play. The spirit may not be fully realized in actual practice, but that makes no difference. . . ."

"To love freedom is an elementary human trait on which Americans have no monopoly."

"Do those traditions where mysticism is prominent or prevalent mean by freedom, not freedom of man in Nature and in society, but freedom *from* them?"

"The Chinese never went behind sensed objects to postulated objects [as compared with the West which always goes behind sensed objects to postulated objects or principles]."

"I have not run across any of this [religious domination] in accounts of Eastern thought, which was in general individualistic. . . ."

"Freedom is inherently individualistic. . . . Freedom pertains primarily to an individual mind and world."

"Emphasis on the importance of the individual is common to all the Indian systems of philosophy."

"The individual's right to life and freedom of development is recognized [in Indian philosophy] as the fundamental right."

"Confucians consider the family as the foundation of society."

"Respect for individual dignity, the worth of the individual personality, the belief that man is sacred, himself an end and not to be used as means—these were identified as universal ideas and not confined to either East or West." (From a Seminar Report in 1949.)

"The Orient has never proposed individualism as a primary principle, nor the sacredness of personality."

"We have tried to instill into the Orient a disposition to fight injustice, and to reform its institutions in the interest of individual freedom of action. . . . And the modern Orient . . . finds the germ of individual, aggressive effort in its own philosophy and fans these into new life."

"The ethical world has to be a world of plurality."

"Oriental philosophy as a whole has been believed to allow no reality for the individual. The individual is nothing more than a drop of water in the ocean, it is believed. In the ultimate sense this is true in Hinduism, Taoism, and Buddhism. . . . Taking all Oriental philosophies together . . . there is undoubtedly the fact that the Many are definitely subordinate to the One, on which it depends for its ultimate reality. In other words, Oriental philosophy is at bottom monistic. . . ."

"The West has always felt the same longing for an all-embracing unity. It achieved it in the reason which permits unequivocal communication and does not dissolve the particular. . . . In the East, the ultimate unity is realized through *elimination* of every distinction; in the West, the distinctions are carefully emphasized, and the unity has to be achieved through their *harmonization*. . . . The Western search for unity discovers the *totality* which maintains individual and personal distinctions. . . ."

"The Chinese political authority may be summed up in a few words. Political authority is a trust conferred by the Mandate of Heaven upon the government for the welfare of the people. The government is created for the people. . . ."

These striking statements and interpretations indicate the complexity and the difficulty of the problem and its vital significance both for philosophy and for mutual understanding.

We who are and have been connected with these Conferences are happy about the purposes behind the Conferences, the work done at them, the spirit embodied in our deliberations, and the results achieved. Some of these results are quite tangible and direct—books, articles, seminars, conferences, courses, etc.—while others are intangible and indirect—such as a greater recognition of and respect for the philosophies of Asia. While it would be immodest and inappropriate here to enlarge upon this aspect of our work, let us hope that these Conferences have contributed significantly to the enhancement of total perspective in philosophy—what Professor E. A. Burtt has called "world philosophizing"—and to greater mutual understanding between the peoples of Asia and the West.

One final matter, a question. Why hold these Conferences in Hawaii time after time? To answer this, let me mention four specific items. First: At the end of the 1959 Conference I politely suggested that we might consider holding the next Conference somewhere in Asia, at New Delhi, or Tokyo, or Taipei, or elsewhere. The reaction was one of strong and unanimous disapproval springing from the apparently unanimous conviction that only in Hawaii could such a conference be held in the spirit in which such a conference must be held, namely, the spirit of cordiality, openmindedness, and the deliberate attempt to understand each other, as is so well exemplified in the life of multi-racial Hawaii and in its famous racial harmony. Second: The fact that at the end of the last Conference one Asian member told the Chairman of the Board of Regents of the University of Hawaii, "This is the first international conference my Oriental colleagues and I have ever attended where we felt on an equal footing with everybody else." Third: A fellow Asian representative supplemented that by saying, "In Hawaii nobody feels like an outsider or a foreigner." And, fourth: This particular Conference is being held here—partly, at least—for the practical reason that it is directly the result of local support and generosity and of the spirit of mutual understanding that pervades the life and thought of Hawaii, as evidenced by this voluntarily proffered support.

Speaking now to our outstanding guests: we in Hawaii consider these Conferences—and the purposes underlying them—most fitting to Hawaii because of the cordial, harmonious, interracial, and intercultural spirit which pervades and characterizes these Islands. We also consider it a great opportunity to undertake the work of these Conferences. We further consider it a special responsibility, one which derives from our extreme interest in and our unique qualifications for this particular undertaking. May I, as Conference Director and as representative of all those responsible for this Conference, and on behalf of all who are here tonight and thousands besides, welcome you to the Conference and request that all of you join us in the responsibility of carrying it out successfully and significantly—together.

It seems appropriate to list here the personnel of the Conference.

The donors whose generosity made this Conference possible will be listed in my "Concluding Remarks."

The following is a list of the members of the Conference—with their academic institutional affiliations (the names are printed in Western style). Apologies are hereby extended to any members whose names are not included—the reason for this being admitted lack of certainty concerning attendance, etc. Relatively brief Who's Who items about the Panel Members are included later in the volume.

STEERING COMMITTEE

Wing-tsit Chan, *Dartmouth College, Hanover, New Hampshire*
Cornelius Kruse, *Emeritus, Wesleyan University, Middletown, Connecticut*
Sterling M. McMurrin, *University of Utah, Salt Lake City, Utah*
Charles A. Moore, *University of Hawaii, Chairman*
Hajime Nakamura, *University of Tokyo, Tokyo, Japan*
S. K. Saksena, *University of Hawaii*
W. H. Werkmeister, *University of Southern California, Los Angeles*

ADVISORY MEMBERS

Willard Wilson, *Secretary of the University of Hawaii*
John M. Allison, *Deputy Acting Chancellor, East-West Center*
Shunzo Sakamaki, *Dean of Summer Session, University of Hawaii*

HONORARY MEMBERS

William Ernest Hocking, *Emeritus, Harvard University, Cambridge, Massachusetts* (by paper, in absentia)
F. S. C. Northrop, *Emeritus, Yale University, New Haven, Connecticut* (unable to attend)
Sarvepalli Radhakrishnan, *President of India* (unable to attend)
Gregg M. Sinclair, *President Emeritus, University of Hawaii*
D. T. Suzuki, *Emeritus, Otani University, Kyoto, Japan*

PANEL MEMBERS

Kalidas Bhattacharyya, *Viśva-Bharati University, Santiniketan, West Bengal, India*

Wing-tsit Chan, *Dartmouth College, Hanover, New Hampshire*

Tara Chand, *Indian School of International Studies, New Delhi, India*

Mrs. Surama Dasgupta, *Lucknow University, Lucknow, India*

Thomé H. Fang, *National Taiwan University, Taipei, Taiwan, China*

John N. Findlay, *King's College, University of London, London, England*

Max H. Fisch, *University of Illinois, Urbana, Illinois*

Tesshi Furukawa, *University of Tokyo, Tokyo, Japan*

Ichirō Hori, *Tohoku University, Sendai, Japan*

Yu-wei Hsieh, *New Asia College, Hong Kong*

Takeyoshi Kawashima, *University of Tokyo, Tokyo, Japan*

Masaaki Kōsaka, *President, Tokyo Gakugei University, Tokyo, Japan*

Cornelius Krusé, *Emeritus, Wesleyan University, Middletown, Connecticut*

G. P. Malalasekera, *Emeritus, University of Ceylon, Peradeniya, Ceylon* (by paper, in absentia)

Harold E. McCarthy, *University of Hawaii*

Richard P. McKeon, *University of Chicago, Chicago, Illinois*

Sterling M. McMurrin, *University of Utah, Salt Lake City, Utah*

Y. P. Mei, *State University of Iowa, Iowa City, Iowa*

Shōson Miyamoto, *Emeritus, University of Tokyo, Tokyo, Japan*

Charles A. Moore, *University of Hawaii*

T. R. V. Murti, *Banaras Hindu University, Varanasi, U.P., India*

Winfield E. Nagley, *University of Hawaii*

Hajime Nakamura, *University of Tokyo, Tokyo, Japan*

Raymond Polin, *The Sorbonne, Paris, France*

Karl H. Potter, *University of Minnesota, Minneapolis, Minnesota*

Fazlur Rahman, *Central Institute of Islamic Research, Karachi, Pakistan* (by paper, in absentia)

P. T. Raju, *The College of Wooster, Wooster, Ohio*

Miguel Reale, *São Paulo University, São Paulo, Brazil* (by paper, in absentia)

Constantin Regamey, *Lausanne University, Lausanne, Switzerland*

S. K. Saksena, *University of Hawaii*

John E. Smith, *Yale University, New Haven, Connecticut*

Edward W. Strong, *University of California, Berkeley, California*

Chün-i T'ang, *New Asia College, Hong Kong*

Yoshifumi Ueda, *Nagoya University, Nagoya, Japan*

W. H. Werkmeister, *University of Southern California, Los Angeles, California*

John C. H. Wu, *Seton Hall University, South Orange, New Jersey*

GENERAL MEMBERSHIP

B. L. Atreya, *Emeritus, Banaras Hindu University, Varanasi, U.P., India*

Paul J. Braisted, *President, Edward W. Hazen Foundation, New Haven, Connecticut*

Cecil C. Brett, *Monmouth College, Monmouth, Illinois*

D. Mackenzie Brown, *University of California, Santa Barbara, California*

Robert W. Browning, *Northwestern University, Evanston, Illinois*

Jane Cauvel, *The Colorado College, Colorado Springs, Colorado*

Te Chen, *New Asia College, Hong Kong*

Chung-ying Cheng, *University of Hawaii*

John W. Clifford (The Rev.), *National Taiwan University, Taipei, Taiwan, China*

Robert A. Cornett, *Randolph-Macon Woman's College, Lynchburg, Virginia*

Charles L. Crowe, *Sweet Briar College, Sweet Briar, Virginia*

D. H. Daugherty, *American Council of Learned Societies, New York City, New York*

Richard J. DeMartino, *Otani University, Kyoto, Japan*

Ryōsetsu Fujiwara, *Ryukoku University, Kyoto, Japan*

Edwin N. Garlan, *Reed College, Portland, Oregon*

Wallace Gray, *Southwestern College, Winfield, Kansas*

Floyd A. Harper, *Institute for Humane Studies, Stanford, California*

Philomène Harrison, *South Pasadena, California*

Kyosho Hayashima, *University of Tokyo, Tokyo, Japan*

Richard P. Haynes, *University of Hawaii*

Maylon H. Hepp, *Denison University, Granville, Ohio*

Teikichi Hiraoka, *Kagoshima University, Kagoshima City, Japan*

Grimsley T. Hobbs, *Earlham College, Richmond, Indiana*

Richard Hocking, *Emory University, Atlanta, Georgia*

Clarence S. Howe, *Humboldt State College, Arcata, California*

Siu-chi Huang, *Beaver College, Glenside, Pennsylvania*

Ronald M. Huntington, *Chapman College, Orange, California*

Félix C. Ilárraz, *University of Idaho, Moscow, Idaho*

Kenneth K. Inada, *University of Hawaii*

Yuho Kasuga, *The Japan Defense Academy, Tokyo, Japan*

Charles Landesman, *University of Kansas, Lawrence, Kansas*

Leta Jane Lewis, *Fresno State College, Fresno, California*

Shu-hsien Liu, *Tunghai University, Taichung, Taiwan, China*

Ryoen Minamoto, *Nihon Women's University, Tokyo, Japan*

Prem Nath, *Panjab University, Chandigarh, India*
N. A. Nikam, *Macalester College, St. Paul, Minnesota*
Jennings G. Olson, Jr., *Weber State College, Ogden, Utah*
Troy Organ, *Ohio University, Athens, Ohio*
Tze-yau Pang, *Christian Study Center, Hong Kong*
Herta Pauly, *Upsala College, East Orange, New Jersey*
John C. Plott, *Honolulu*
Joseph Politella, *Kent State University, Kent, Ohio*
William L. Reese, *University of Delaware, Newark, Delaware*
Hugo Reimann, *Goetheanum, Dornach, Switzerland*
Michael D. Resnik, *University of Hawaii*
Dale Riepe, *State University of New York at Buffalo, Buffalo, New York*
Dorothy (Mrs. W. C.) Roberts, *Honolulu*
Mary Edith Runyan, *Elmira College, Elmira, New York*
Mitsuyoshi Saigusa, *Kokugakuin University, Tokyo, Japan*
Hiroshi Sakamoto, *Otani University, Kyoto, Japan*
Herbert L. Searles, *Emeritus, University of Southern California, Los Angeles, California*
B. B. Singh, *University of Gorakhpur, Gorakhpur, U.P., India*
Bhek Pati Sinha, *The City College of the City University of New York, New York City, N.Y.*
Malcolm F. Stewart, *Illinois College, Jacksonville, Illinois*
Fred G. Sturm, *Western College for Women, Oxford, Ohio*
Franklin S. Takei, *Clarion State College, Clarion, Pennsylvania*
S. M. Tewari, *University of Gorakhpur, Gorakhpur, U.P., India*
T. K. Venkateswaran, *Colorado Woman's College and University of Denver, Denver, Colorado*
William S. Weedon, *University of Virginia, Charlottesville, Virginia*
Donald A. Wells, *Washington State University, Pullman, Washington*
James E. Whitehurst, *Illinois Wesleyan University, Bloomington, Illinois*
Beatrice Yamasaki, *California State College at Los Angeles, Los Angeles, California*
Tokuryu Yamauchi, *Ryukoku University, Kyoto, Japan*

STUDENT MEMBERS (AUDITORS)

Robert S. Anderson, *University of British Columbia, Vancouver, Canada*
John S. Barbour, *University of Hawaii*
Anne Berens, *University of Hawaii*

Harold A. Bassford, *University of Hawaii*
Charles Bush, *University of Hawaii*
Fred Burian, *University of Hawaii*
David K. Coe, *University of Hawaii*
Douglas D. Dayne, *University of Wisconsin, Madison, Wisconsin*
Kuang T. Fan, *University of Hawaii*
Arnold M. Hall, *Claremont Graduate School, Claremont, California*
Bruce Halverson, *University of Hawaii*
David Ishizaki, *University of Hawaii*
Charles J. Jones, *University of Colorado, Boulder, Colorado*
W. Michael Kavanaugh, *University of Hawaii*
John M. Koller, *University of Hawaii*
Rhoda P. LeCocq, *University of Hawaii*
Michael J. Makibe, *University of Hawaii*
Ashok Malhotra, *University of Hawaii*
Jeffrey L. Masson, *Harvard University, Cambridge, Massachusetts*
Bimal Krishna Motilal, *Harvard University, Cambridge, Massachusetts*
Anne Pic'l, *University of Hawaii*
Gerald Poliks, *University of Hawaii*
Douglas Price, *University of Hawaii*
Paul S. Rosenberg, *University of California, Berkeley, California*
Melvin Sakaguchi, *University of Hawaii*
Norman Steffenson, *DePauw University, Greencastle, Indiana*
Gerald Walker, *University of British Columbia, Vancouver, British Columbia, Canada*
Robert E. Walters, *University of Hawaii*
John A. Young, *University of Hawaii*

ASSOCIATE MEMBERS (AUDITORS)

John M. Allison, *Acting Deputy Chancellor, East-West Center, University of Hawaii*
George Chaplin, *Editor,* The Honolulu Advertiser, *Honolulu*
Hung Wo Ching, *President, Aloha Airlines, Honolulu*
Mrs. George P. Conger, *University of Minnesota, Minneapolis, Minnesota*
Robert C. Elliott, *Honolulu*
William H. Ewing, *Editor,* Honolulu Star-Bulletin, *Honolulu*
Erich Kraemer, *University of Hawaii*
Joseph Krimsky, *Marshall University, Huntington, West Virginia*
Samuel Lambert, St. Louis Post-Dispatch, *St. Louis, Missouri*

The Rt. Rev. Robert Mackey, *President, Chaminade College, Honolulu*

Richard K. Morris, *Trinity College, Hartford, Connecticut*

Harold S. Roberts, *University of Hawaii*

Joseph R. Royce, *University of Alberta, Edmonton, Alberta, Canada*

Shungo Sakamaki, *University of Hawaii*

Willard Wilson, *Secretary, University of Hawaii*

Paul C. Domke, *Department of State, Honolulu*

Metaphysics

THOMÉ H. FANG[a]

The world and the individual
in Chinese metaphysics*

I

The trends of Chinese metaphysical thought, taken in its entire range, may be roughly likened to the bar-lines across the stave. At regular or irregular intervals, different modes of speculation are marked out in bars, each running in compound triple time with beats in varying accentuation. From time immemorial to the middle of the twelfth century B.C., the metaphysical moods would be the chords sounded in the triad of myth, religion, and poetry. Thenceforward, until 246 B.C., for a creative period of more than nine hundred years, there came to be the articulation of primordial Taoism, Confucianism, and Moism[b]. This period was followed by a long epoch (246 B.C.–A.D. 960) of fermentation and absorbent creation, tending to bring forth eventually a type of highly creative speculation in Chinese Mahāyānic Buddhism. From A.D. 960 down to the present day, we have had a re-awakening of metaphysical originality in the form of Neo-Confucianism somewhat imbued with the spirit of Taoism and Buddhism. In this period of regeneration, there have come into prominence three trends of metaphysics: (a) Neo-Confucianism of the realistic type; (b) Neo-Confucianism of the idealistic type; and (c) Neo-Confucianism of the naturalistic type.

Apropos the systems of Chinese metaphysics, two essential points must be noted. (1) The world is not taken for what it is in natural regard; it awaits to be transmuted into a moral universe for the Confucians, into an aesthetic realm for the Taoists, and into a religious domain for the Buddhists. The world, philosophically considered, should be a *transfigured world*, taken in its ideal regard. The task of Chinese metaphysics is an analysis of facts issuing in an understanding of destiny. The transfigured world is nothing less than a teleological system of axiological importance. (2) The individual is a very complicated concept; its richness of meaning is not exhausted by a simplified unitary procedure of approach. The status of the individual is not a problem to be posed once and for all; its answer is not to be found ready-made once and for all. The question about it has to be continually asked. In different epochs of time and

---

* In this paper (except in some of the notes) the author's capitalization has in the main been retained—Editor's note.

in various contexts of thought, the answer would be radically different. Throughout the history of Chinese philosophy, Yang Chu^c (521?–442? B.C.) was the only one who spoke audaciously for the actual individual. But all other things have looked askance at him. To the Confucians, the individual should be ceaselessly edified; to the Taoists, he should be constantly liberated; and, to the Buddhists, he should be perpetually purified before his status can be firmly established in the transfigured world of moral and aesthetic and religious perfection.

II

Let us now proceed with a discussion of the three major systems of Chinese metaphysics in successive order.

Two important features may be discerned in the metaphysical system of Confucianism. The first asserts the creative power of the heavenly *Tao,* whereby the dynamic world of all beings comes into existence; the second emphasizes the intrinsic value of human nature in congruence with the cosmic order. These two, together, constitute the architectonic structure of Confucianism from classical antiquity to the present day. The most important embodiment of this mode of thought is found in *The Book of Change*^d to be supplemented by *The Book of Mencius*^e and *The Works of Hsün Tzu*^f, which, apart from re-enforcing a set of original metaphysical ideas, elucidate the cardinal doctrine of a philosophical anthropology.[1]

The Book of Change is a formidable historical document. There are involved in it (1) a very complicated stratified historical frame, (2) a complete system of symbolic constructions based upon strict rules of logic, and (3) a set of interpretations making out the meanings of these symbolic constructions, expressible in the systematic syntax of language. All these three are the prelude to a theory of time conducive to the working out of a set of metaphysical principles explanatory of the cosmic order.

The revolutionary philosophy of change, initiated by Confucius (551–479 B.C.) himself and, upon the evidences[2] of Ssu-ma T'an^g and Ssu-ma Ch'ien^h, further elaborated by Shang Chüⁱ (b. 522 B.C.) and others, was really a long evolutionary product. Its new features might be diversified into four different forms: (1) A new philosophy of enlivened Nature permeated with the dynamic confluence of Life. Nature is power or vital impetus, creative in advance and conducive to the fulfillment and consummation of Life capable of being partaken of by all beings.[3] (2) An exposition of intrinsic moral goodness in human life adorned with beauty. Such a moral-aesthetic perfection was characteristic of the unique human personality.[4]

(3) A general theory of value in the form of the Supreme Good assimilating into it all the relative ranks of values prevalent in the entire universe.[5] (4) The final formulation of a value-centric ontology asserting the fullness of Being in its entirety.

The archetypal time-man, represented by the Confucians, deliberately chooses to cast everything—whether it be the life of Nature, the development of an individual, the frame of society, the achievement of value, the attainment to the fullness of Being—into the mold of time in the order of its authentic existence.

The question is, What is time?[6] The essence of time consists in change; the order of time proceeds with concatenation; the efficacy of time abides by durance. The rhythmic process of epochal change is wheeling round into infinitude and perpetually dovetailing the old and the new so as to issue into an interpenetration which is continuant duration in creative advance. This is the way in which time generates itself by its systematic entry into a pervasive unity which constitutes the rational order of creative creativity. The dynamic sequence of time, ridding itself of the perished past and coming by the new into the present existence, really gains something over a loss. So, the change in time is but a step to approaching eternity, which is perennial durance whereby, before the bygone is ended, the forefront of the succeeding has come into presence. And, therefore, there is here a linkage of being projecting itself into the prospect of eternity. Hence, in the nexus of the dynamics of time, *"The Book of Change* contains the measure of heaven and earth, enabling us to comprehend the all-pervasive *Tao*[j] and its order."[7]

Based upon the concept of time, three metaphysical principles may be set out.

(1) The principle of extensive connection. Three essentials are involved in its formulation. Logically, it is a system of consistent deduction demonstrated rigorously.[8] Semantically, it is a syntax of language in which the rules of formation and transformation of significant statements indicate unerringly a relation of co-ordination and a relation of dovetailing and mutual relevance so as to discriminate what is licit from the illicit and to change the latter into the former.[9] Metaphysically, the philosophy of change is a system of dynamic ontology based upon the process of continuant creativity in time, as well as a system of general axiology wherein the origin and development of the idea of the Supreme Good is shown in the light of comprehensive harmony. Thus, the principle of extensive connection asserts at the same time that the confluence of life permeating all beings under heaven and earth partakes of the creative nature of time and achieves, as a consequence, the form of the Supreme Good.

(2) The principle of creative creativity. Confucius in *The Book*

of Change—the philosophical part of it designated as the *chuans* —and his followers in *The Book of Propriety*[k]—including *The Doctrine of the Mean*[l]—diversified the all-pervasive *Tao*[10] into (a) the *Tao* of Heaven as the primordial creative power, giving rise to all creatures, comprehending them in the cosmic order of dynamic transformation conducive to a perfectly harmonious fulfillment, and issuing in the attainment of the Supreme Good; (b) the *Tao* of Earth, which, as the power of procreation, is a continuation and extension of the creative origination, sustaining all forms of existence; and (c) the *Tao* of man, who, with an assured status at the center of the universe, in communion with the creative and procreative power of Heaven and earth should come to the full awareness of the Spirit and thereby become co-creative agents in the perpetual continuance of Life as a whole. With the Confucians, this spiritual awareness has given rise to a sense of individual moral excellence, a fellow-feeling of the intrinsic worth of other forms of existence, as well as a rational insight into the identifiable unity of the equitable Being of all beings.

(3) The principle of creative life as a process of value-realization. In the "Hsi-tz'u"[m] we find a theory set out by Confucius that "what is called *Tao* operates incessantly with the rhythmic modulation of dynamic change and static repose, thus continuing the creative process for the attainment of the Good and completing the creative process for the fulfillment of Nature, which is Life. . . . It manifests itself in the rational sentiment of humanity but conceals its great function unawares, propelling all beings in a swing of vitality without inciting the anxieties of the holy. Its richness of virtue, its grandeur of enterprise is of all things the most sublime. Superabundance is what is called the deed-act; forevermore creativeness is what is called the supreme value. . . . The unfathomed mystery underlying the rhythmic modulation of the dynamic energy and of peaceful repose is what is called the Divine."[11] Elsewhere Confucius said: "Embracing all in its comprehensiveness and investing each with its magnificence, it ensures that anything and everything will enjoy the concordant bliss of well-being."[12] "Of all values, the Good exhibited in the primordially creative-procreative is towering in its supremacy. Concordance in the sport of bliss is the convergence of all that is beautiful. Benediction in the realm of Life is the pervasiveness of all that is righteous. Consummation in the deed-act is the fundamentum of the world of enterprise."[13]

In the light of the above principles, the objective order of the universe is constituted by the superabundant power of creativity in the dynamic process of time. The human individual is thus confronted with a creative world. He must be equally creative in order to fit in with it. And, therefore, the Confucian dynamic value-centric ontology, once completed, evoked a system of philosophical anthropology. It was averred in *The Doctrine of the Mean* that the most truthful and sincere man in all the world, after completely fulfilling his own nature in the course of life, would extend his boundless sympathy by doing the same with other men, as well as with all creatures and things. In doing so, he could participate in the cosmic creation through the process of transformation and thereupon become a *co-creator* with Heaven and Earth.[14]

As the natural and moral order of life was initiated by the creative power of Heaven, so man can cope with the most high in creative potency. In some such way the Confucians developed a homocentric conception of the world as a prelude to the value-centric conception of man. This is why Mencius (372–289 B.C.) maintained that the spiritual stream of a superior man's life was concurrent with that of Heaven and Earth. He went further in asserting that a real man, relying upon his own intrinsic goodness, could, in virtue of his beautiful endowment, develop himself to the utmost into a great man. This greatness of character, enhanced by a subtle touch of spiritual exaltation in the process of transformation, would make him, first, a sage and, finally, a holy man invested with inscrutable magnificence.[15]

Not only Mencius. Even Hsün Tzu (313–238 B.C.), who started with the empirical observation of the ill nature of man, ventured to assert that man through a course of perseverent endeavor of cultivation could come to achieve greatness. Among the primordial Confucians, Hsün Tzu was the only one who seemed to be "fed up" with the value-centric conception of Heaven. Just for this reason, he wanted to set up the supremacy of man apart from unnecessary complication with Nature, which is nothing more than a neutral order[16] with physical energies in store for human utilization. According to Mencius, man, by virtue of his inborn goodness, is spontaneously great. In the opinion of Hsün Tzu, man's greatness is cultured in the best sense of the word. Allowing this difference between them, man is ultimately great just the same.

What, after all, is the *rationale* of human greatness? In *The Book of Propriety*,[17] compiled by Senior Tai Te[n], Confucius is reported to have said, in reply to the queries of Duke Ai of Lu[o], that there are five types of men in a rational linkage of development. Among (1) the common run of men, the individual can be educated to be (2) a learned and enlightened person who, with an insight of knowledge and with sagacity in action, issuing in the noble art of life, will become (3) a superior man, adorned with beauty of character and balance of mind. Through further edification he can come to be (4) a man of excellence. His choices and forsakings are in accord with the high standard of values acceptable to mankind as a whole. He always tries to act in the right without sacrificing the least part of the fundamental principles. His utterance of truth sets a good standard to the world without the loss of his own integrity. Finally, he becomes (5) a sage, or holy man. With perfect wisdom at his command, he acts in congruence with the ways of the great *Tao,* adapting himself to any circumstance of life in the flux of change without confronting any crises of danger or encumbrance. This he does because he thoroughly understands the true nature and disposition of all things. In virtue of such perfect understanding, all his decisions of value are made in accordance with the great function of reason. And, therefore, the achievement of greatness knowingly keeps abreast of Heaven and Earth in creativity. This development of man from the natural capacity to the ideal perfection by way of the function of reason is the Confucian rationale of human greatness. In the light of this rationale man copes with the most high in potency.

All of this leads to the natural conclusion that the world and the individual must be always in reciprocal communion.[18] In such a communion, the cosmic status of the individual is firmly established for the reason that the full capacities constitutive of his personality are, now, developed to the utmost.

To the Chinese, the Confucian type of man is near and dear, like an ideal figure who has been cut by his own noble art of life in a set of expanding spheres representing gradually enlarged and qualitatively perfected humane relations, and toward whom all other persons, intimate in spiritual linkage and sympathetic in moral aspirations, are subtly attracted in such a way that there is always an interfusion and interplay of exultation in the influence of exalted personality. This is what makes of the Chinese world and Chinese society a natural domain of moral democracy incessantly leveling up to a higher plane of ethical culture which has sustained the Chinese national state ever since Confucianism came into vogue.

III

But, when we come to a consideration of the Taoists, we are suddenly transferred to a different world—a visionary dream-world. The Taoists make the best type of space-man. They are wont to take flights into the realms unfrequented by the common run of people, in which they uplift us, level after level, each more exalted and mysterious than the last. From their vantage point at a height, unafraid, they gaze disinterestedly upon the stratified world below in which the tragi-comic persons are involved in the regressive lapse into folly and wisdom, illusion and truth, appearance and reality, all falling short of supreme Perfection, the Truth, and Reality.

Tao is the supreme category in the system of Lao Tzu[p] (561?– 467? B.C.). It may be diversified into four cardinal points.

(1) Ontologically, *Tao* is the infinite ontic substance which was multifariously characterized by Lao Tzu (a) as the fathomless unity of all beings, prior in existence even to God;[19] (b) as the fundamental root of heaven and earth, infinite in nature, invisible in shape, but really great in function because all creatures are begotten from it;[20] (c) as the primordial One having ingression into all forms of beings;[21] (d) as the unique pattern of all kinds of activities, discursive but wholesome, twisted around but straightforward, emptying out but remaining full, worn out but forever renovating, eventually comprehensive of all perfection;[22] (e) as the Great Form[q], or the receptacular Matrix, wherein all creatures are embraced, free of harm, and full of peace, like babies held close to the bosoms of their mothers;[23] and (f) as the final destiny whereto all creatures, after emptying out every kind of "quixotic" energetic activities in the course of life, will return for the ease and peace of rest, conceived under the form of eternity and achieved in the spirit of immortality[24]—thus, on the score of eternity, consciously discerned, all come to be complaisant, equitable, noble, natural, and spontaneous, in full accord with the imperishable *Tao*.

(2) Cosmogenetically, the infinitely great *Tao* is the all-pervasive function with an inexhaustible store of powerful energy exerting itself in two different ways. On the one hand, being invisibly subsistent up in the transcendental realm of Nothingness[r] and deeply sheathed back in the noumenal realm of unfathomed Mystery, it darts itself out and down into the realm of Being[s]. Thus we can say that in the beginning there was Being, and Being was with Nothingness.[25] Henceforward, the *Tao* is the primordial begetter of all things. On the other hand, the supplied energy, within the bounds of Being, may be spent and exhausted through dispersion and waste. The immanent world of Being, in a state of urgent want, will resort to the transcendental world of *Tao* for a fresh impartation of energy. Hence, Lao Tzu has every reason to lay emphasis upon "the reversal of procedure in the dynamic transformation of *Tao*."

The function of *Tao* is dyadic in track. Progressively, the fundamental Nothingness in *Tao* gives rise to the being of all forms in the world,[26] whereas, regressively, the immanent Being in the whole world depends upon the Nothingness of the transcendental *Tao* for the performance of adequate function. Hence the pronouncement:

"The fulfillment of Being leads to eudaemonia, whereas the attainment to Nothingness fulfills the performance of function."[27]

(3) Phenomenologically, the attributes of *Tao* can be classified under two headings, namely, natural attributes and arbitrary attributes. The natural attributes are discerned as so many properties inherent in the *Tao* conceived under the form of eternity. They may be enumerated as follows:

1) Integrity of *Tao* revealing itself as substance in the realm of Nothingness and as function in the realm of Being;
2) Conformation of non-action in which nothing is left undone[t];
3) The primordial incentive in the begetting of all things with no claim of origination;
4) Accomplishment of work on the cosmic scale with detachment[u];
5) Sustenance of all things without domination[v];
6) Creation without possession[w];
7) Energizing activity with no egocentric claim of merit.

On the contrary, the arbitrary attributes are those which are affirmed from the subjective viewpoint of men and inappropriately portrayed in terms of the inadequate human language. Apart from these, the *Tao* conceived *per se* is the really real Reality, or, what is the same thing, the mysteriously mysterious Mystery intelligible only to men of supreme wisdom like the sage.

(4) Characterologically, the supreme excellences, manifested as the natural attributes, originally pertain to the nature of *Tao* but will come in ingress into the integrity of the sage, who is really the exemplar of the *Tao* in this world. The sage, as an ideal man, has transcended all limitations and weaknesses by reason of his exalted spirit and by virtue of his assessment of ever higher worth. He knows how to gain a world of love and reverence by employing himself generously for the world. Having lived for the benefit of other men, he is richer in worth; having given all he has to other men, he is more plentiful in being. "And, therefore, the sage is always skillful and whole-hearted in the salvation of men, so that there is no deserted man; he is always skillful and whole-hearted in the rescue of things, so that there is no abandoned thing."[28] Thanks to Lao Tzu, we have come to the consciousness that the essence of each individual man, when realized in full, consists in an endeavor to attain to the ideal of the sage. Man's mission is constantly to make a campaign for the realization of this ideal. Thus the "wages" of winning a sure status in the world is his own inward sageliness.

Many perplexities in the system of Lao Tzu came to be cleared away by Chuang Tzu[x] (b. 369 B.C.) in an attempt to push through the nullifying process far back into mystery after mystery, so that there would be no final Nothingness in the serial regress. Similarly, what was posited in the being of Being could be infinitely iterated, back and forth, thus forming a set of endless bilateral processes of progression and retrogression. The original antithesis between Nothing and Being was theoretically reconciled inasmuch as both Being and Nothing should merge into the profound mystery in such a way as to form an interpenetrative system of infinite integral Reality.[29] Finally, Chuang Tzu brought out the chief tenet of Lao Tzu as positing both the eternal Nothing and the eternal Being[y] predominated over by the supreme unity, thus affirming the authentic Reality in the form of vacuity, which would not destroy the reality of all things[z].[30] For the same reason and in the same sort of way, the discrepancy between eternity and temporality was dissolved.[31]

Chuang Tzu could accomplish so much because, besides being a great Taoist, he was also much influenced by Confucius and Mencius,[32] as well as by his bosom friend, Hui Shih[aa], from the logico-analytical camp. In the philosophy of change, Confucius thought of time as though it had a definite beginning in the past but an indefinite progression into the future. Chuang Tzu, however, accepted the indefinite stretch into the future but denied the definite origination in the past through the agency of creation. This is because he knew how, on the basis of "the reversal of procedure" in the function of Tao[ab], to probe mystery after mystery[ac] without coming to a standstill in the remote past. Thus, time is literally infinite in respect to the past as well as to the future. Time is a long-enduring natural process of transformation without any beginning and ending. Hence, the Confucian assumption of the primordial power of creation—in fact, all necessity for the cosmic creation—is theoretically extirpated.

Not only is time infinite in span; space, likewise, is infinite in scope. Furthermore, with the metaphysical acumen of his poetic vision, he transformed, by a subtle touch of imagination, the obstructive mathematico-physical space into the infinite "painterly" space as a liberated realm of spiritual exultation whereunto he is to infuse "the wondrous proceeding of the Tao" in order that his own exalted "soul" may reach the most sublime for its ultimate acquirement. In a word, the metaphysics of Chuang Tzu is an elaboration of the great Tao, projected into the frame of infinite Space and Time, into a way of exalted spiritual life.

Such is the metaphysical import implied in the story of "A Happy Excursion"[ad] described in poetico-metaphorical language. Like the great magic bird, p'eng[ae], Chuang Tzu could lift himself up into an intellectual solitude unafraid and exulting insofar as the greatness of his liberated nature would partake of the omnipotent with the support of the infinite Tao.

The "most fantastic" story of "A Happy Excursion" has been variously interpreted by different thinkers. The true meaning should be made out in the light of the philosophy of infinity under discussion by following up the clues indicated by Chuang Tzu himself in the context of the relevant chapters.

(1) It is asserted that the supreme man should lead his own spirit up to the primordial in its infinite regress, reposing blissfully in the realm of Nowhere, doing away with all petty knowledge about lowly things and getting entirely free from the bother of their burdens.[33] (2) At the culmination in the realm of perfect truth and in abidance by the fundamentum of the eternal *Tao*, his elevated spirit, being thus estranged from the physical world and disencumbered of all material allurings, would become independent and free from all restraint.[34] (3) Upon entering the gate of infinitude, and having an excursion in the realm of supreme bliss, he would immerse his unique spirit in the exuberant light of the celestial and lose his identity in the eternal harmony of cosmic order.[35] (4) At the attainment to sagehood, he would abandon himself to the vast concord of all perfection. He is, now, the archetype of man in the full capacity of the omnipotent (*Tao*) to be cast into the mold of cosmic life as a whole wherein he gains nothing in particular and loses nothing in full. He forgets himself and forgets that he is really immersed in the bliss of *Tao*, just as fish swim in the river and sea and forget all about it.[36] (5) The perfected and perfect man is now what he is by virtue of his identifiability with the "Creator," imparting his potency to all the world without becoming the center of fame, the contriver of plans, the director of works, and the claimer to knowledge. He embraces infinity within the range of his experience and rambles in the realm of the infinite with levity and freedom.[37] He fulfills all that is natural in him without a sense of gain. In the spirit of vacuity, he employs his mind and heart like a mirror, impartially reflecting all that there is in the world without showing a trace of lure, dejection, or injury. It is then, and only then, that the final status of his exalted individuality is firmly established in the infinite world of *Tao*.

All these spiritual modes of life are, as it were, the rockets that launch the Taoistic type of space-man into the realm of the infinite, in which he is to find a vantage point called by Chuang Tzu "the acme of the Celestial"[af] whereon he can survey the World-All from height to height, from width to width, and from depth to depth. The happy excursion into the realms of the infinite all along embodies Chuang Tzu's philosophy of spiritual liberation in the course of life. This is the Taoist temper of mind, which has incited the best of Chinese poetry as an expression of inspiration.

The exalted individual, once achieved, becomes a true sage who, upborne by the wondrous procedure of *Tao,* can penetrate in insight into the Very One Truth comprehending the entire universe. All the partial appearances, viewed from different angles in varying heights, will be facet-symbols for beauty susceptible of being interfused into the integral whole of reality. All differences in viewpoints will be reconciled in the over-all perspective which forms a complementary system of essential relativity, going anywhere and anywhen, as well as everywhere and everywhen, with the full swing of the all-pervasive *Tao.*

This is the pivotal point of his theory of *leveling up all things.*[38] Thus it is that the system of essential relativity is an all-inclusive system in which everything can find a place of its own fitness and in which no one thing can claim to have an especially privileged position so as to impose its surreptitious importance upon all others. At the same time, the system of essential relativity is an interpenetrative system wherein all entities come to be what they are by interlacing their own essences with one another so that nothing in it can stand alone in complete isolation. It is a system of interrelatedness and mutual relevance in which any one thing has its own intrinsic importance that will bear out valuable results as unique contributions to the make-up of any other. Furthermore, it is a system in which the infinite *Tao* operates as the unconditioned that will embrace all the conditions originally uncontrollable by any one individual outside the system. Especially the human individuals before their entry into this infinite system have suffered limitation, restraint, and bondage. Now that they, through the spirit of liberation, being aware of what ridiculous figures they have cut within the bounds of contracting narrowness, have discovered the authentic sagely Self by sharing the nature of *Tao,* they must cry for joy in writing with the Ineffable and Inscrutable in the realm of the infinite, which breaks forth entirely from the limitations of any arbitrary scheme of thought, feeling, and action in life. As a result of all these characteristics exhibited in the infinite system of essential relativity, Chuang Tzu has set out a great theme: "The universe and I sustain a relation of co-existence; I and all beings have the same entry into the One."[39] Thus, being most inward with the Infinite, the individual in the exalted mode of life has well established himself in the world in congruence with all others.

IV

For an epoch of some five hundred years (241 B.C.–A.D. 240) China in the Asian world was not unlike Rome in the West. People of all ranks were busy doing work in the conquest of the practical world. Speculative interest waned in the intellectual realm.

The real revival of metaphysical contemplation dated from the year 240, when Ho Yen[ag] (190–249) and Wang Pi[ah] (226–249) made an attempt to reconcile the differences between Confucius and Lao Tzu by laying importance upon the category of Nothingness for the interpretation of *Tao*.[40] Historically, Ho Yen was primarily a Confucian in that he tried to absorb Taoism into the system of Confucianism,[41] whereas Wang Pi was essentially a Taoist with an intention of assimilating Confucianism into the system of Taoism. What was common in them consisted of an attempt to bring forth the unity of infinite substance as the core of metaphysical inquiry.

In his Commentary on the *Lao Tzu*, Wang Pi elucidated the central theme that all things considered as Being, taking shape in manifolds subject to limitation, should be, in the last resort, redeemable by the integral *Tao*, which, though designated as Nothing, is really everything transmuted into infinite perfection. It is in this light that he came to see the import of the philosophy of change. The whole world of dynamic being, begotten by the creative power exhibited in a plenitude of incessant change and variegated transformation, must revert to the fundamentum of *Tao* for its primordial unity, which, reposing in the form of Reason and in the spirit of eternity, will prevail over all multiplicities. Confucianism, as understood by Wang Pi, reveals only the origin of all things in the world of Being, while Taoism helps it to see into the ultimate destiny in which all of Being in every mode of change is brought back to a final consummation of perfection which is Nothing, that is, *nothing in particular but everything in full*.[42] It is the end result of all changes, borne out by the inexhaustible richness of function, that should be grasped as the infinite substance.

The spirit of Buddhism encompasses two alternative realms of thought: one conceived under the form of incessant change and the other conceived under the form of eternity. Should we include Hīnayāna Buddhism, we would find more causes to fight against the fluctuating mundane world, in which bigoted individuals plunge themselves into the deep waters of miserable blunders and sufferings. The vehicle of deliverance would have to bear them up through the fluctuations of time before reaching the other shore. In this sense, the Buddhist is a time-man, and he is such not in the blessed spirit of a Confucian. But, if we should take Mahāyāna Buddhism into consideration, the enlightenment it attained would illuminate before us an upper world of *Dharma*[ai] and *Dharma*-fulfillment in which the tragic sense of life in the process of time would be superseded by the bliss of eternity.[43] So, in this way the liberated spirit of a Mahāyānist would undertake a happy excursion into the poetically inspired space-world with the Taoist. He could, now, afford to forget the tragic sense of life enmeshed in the wheel of changing time. Under this circumstance, the spirit of a Buddhist was quite congenial with that of a Taoist.

V

It had taken a long epoch of more than seven centuries (67–789) for Chinese Buddhism to run its course of full development, which was, of course, conditioned by the continual works done in translation[44] and by the creative works done in system-building. From 789 onward until 960, the Buddhist tradition only went on and slid down in elaboration. Chiefly in the sixth century, the forerunning sects were to be formed and eventually in the period of Sui-T'ang[aj] (581–960) the ten different schools of Chinese Buddhism were completed. I cannot here attempt to outline their systematic theorizings which, because of their doctrinal complexity and elaborateness, should form an independent study by themselves.[45] The most I can do now is to select some features of Buddhism as ways of expressing the singular power of the Chinese mentality.

Upon being first introduced, Buddhism could have taken deep root in the Chinese mind only by coming under the dominant influence of Chinese thought. It goes without saying that Chinese Buddhistic metaphysics was evoked and re-enforced by the spirit of Taoism and not vice versa.[46] The Taoists all along had claimed fundamental Nothingness to be a supreme category in their own system. And Buddhists like Lokākṣin[ak] (resident in China during 176–189), Chih Ch'ien[al] (192–252), and K'ang Seng-hui[am] (d. 280) continually laid extreme importance upon the category of fundamental Nothingness, which they took to be equivalent to Tathatā[an] (thusness).[47] During the fourth century, the impact of Taoism upon the philosophy of Prajñā[ao] was most obvious in the school of Tao-an[ap] (312–385) and his contemporaries.

As regards the controversies about wu and yu (Nothingness and Being), there were, then, six or seven schools[48] diversified into twelve trends[49] of thought discriminating the genuine truth from mundane creeds. On the evidences successively given by the monks Tan-chi[aq] (ca. 473), Seng-ching[ar] (302–475), Hui-ta[as] (ca. 481), and Yüan K'ang[at] (ca. 649) and on the further evidence[50] of Chi-tsang[au] (549–623), the above set of theories may be tabulated as follows:

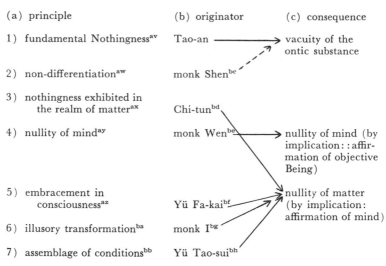

(a) principle	(b) originator	(c) consequence
1) fundamental Nothingness[av]	Tao-an	vacuity of the ontic substance
2) non-differentiation[aw]	monk Shen[bc]	
3) nothingness exhibited in the realm of matter[ax]	Chi-tun[bd]	
4) nullity of mind[ay]	monk Wen[be]	nullity of mind (by implication::affirmation of objective Being)
5) embracement in consciousness[az]	Yü Fa-kai[bf]	nullity of matter (by implication: affirmation of mind)
6) illusory transformation[ba]	monk I[bg]	
7) assemblage of conditions[bb]	Yü Tao-sui[bh]	

In the above tabular scheme, (1) is more fundamental than the other six, which are all derived therefrom. According to Tao An, "the fundamental Nothingness is the prius of all transformations, and vacuity is the beginning of all the visible world." All modes of the true *Dharma* are by nature vacuous and pure, spontaneously ensured from, and essentially identifiable with, the *Bhūta-tathatā* (Thatness of being)[bi] denuded of any contamination by defiled elements. The trends of thought in the seven schools of Chinese Buddhism during the fourth and fifth centuries were centered around the metaphysical thesis which advocated the importance of Nothingness. From now, the Buddhists would join hands with the Taoists and form a united front against traditional Confucianism.

The influence of Chuang Tzu is even more prominent in the school of Kumārajīva (343–413). His contribution lay in the field of the philosophy of *Śūnyatā* (Emptiness)[bk]. Ultimate Reality is that which has emptied out all fantastic whims so as to show its own purity of essence in the form of Thusness. Among a great number of his pupils, Seng-chao[bl] (384–414) and Tao-sheng[bm] (374?–434) stood out as the twin stars never waning in their spiritual illuminancy.

The synoptic visions of Seng-chao are diversified into three cardinal theses: (1) correlative motion and rest; (2) reconcilable Being and Nothing, or inseparable substance and function; and (3) the dovetailing of knowledge and "no-knowledge" transmuted into supreme wisdom.

(1) I have no time here to go into his penetrative arguments in this regard except to call attention to the two conclusions he arrived at. (a) Men of the world, engulfed in the flux of change, would have no sense of assurance, inasmuch as life in a shifting course of

action would lead to death likely to destroy everything achieved in life. They are always sick of life and sick for unattainable *nirvāna*[bn]. (b) The man of wisdom can discern permanence in the midst of change. He knows how to remain non-active in a state of spiritual repose and yet will not dispense with the world of action. It is only he who, being immortal in spirit, can plunge into the deep waters of life with no danger of annihilation. In his approach to *nirvāna,* he has attained it, and yet he will not stand attached to it, out of keeping with the changing world.

(2) Tao-an and his associates relied too much upon the fundamental Nothingness by asserting the vacuity of the ontic substance, or the nullity of matter, or the illusiveness of mind. Seng-chao, however, dissented strongly from all of them. Generally, in the usage of linguistic expressions or "ostensible names," we talk about an "objective" which is neither simply real as posited in Being nor simply unreal as denied in Not-Being or Nothing. The said "objective" may be either, and it may be both. In the light of the *Mādhyamika-śāstra*[bo], to be or not to be: that is the *one-sided* question. It takes a man of supreme wisdom to discern Nothing in all modes of Being and to observe Being in the midst of Nothing. The ontic Substance and the complete truth thereof cannot be rent into grotesque pieces.

(3) Seng-chao's metaphysics is a philosophy of the supreme wisdom which is concerned with Ultimate Reality, *Nirvāna, Dharmakāya* (lit., Law-body)[bp], *Bhūta-tathatā,* and *Dharmatā* (Reality as such)[bq]. All of these are to him different names of the same "objective." In order to avoid misunderstanding, however, a distinction should be made between supreme wisdom *per se* and wisdom in the form of *upāya-kauśalya*[br], i.e., expedient wisdom. The power of the former penetrates deep into the objective, whereas the function of the latter adapts itself to all beings in the changing world. In virtue of wisdom *per se,* we are to illuminate the nature of the Void, while, by means of expedient wisdom, we are to launch into the world of fluctuating Being. In dealing with Being in full, we shall have no misgivings with the nature of the Void. And, therefore, we can encounter the realm of Being without attachment. That being the case, we can illuminate what is essentially vacuous without falling back upon it tenaciously. In the midst of knowledge in acquaintance with the world we shall arrive at a wondrous state of the liberated spirit with no knowledge whatever. The reason is that, if you know something in particular, there will be numberless other things that you do not know. Just because the spirit of the divine is with no knowledge in particular, there will be nothing that it does not know, freely and all-pervasively. Hence, the knowledge of no-knowledge embraces all that there is to be known. This may sound quite per-

plexing, but men of great genius, e.g., Shakespeare in the West, have understood it quite well.

> O, out of that "no hope"
> What great hope have you! No hope that way is
> Another way so high a hope that even
> Ambition cannot pierce a wink beyond,
> But doubt discovery there.[52]

The objective of the knowledge of no-knowledge is intent on the spirit of the divine. The divine spirit reposed in a state of vacuity, having no fumblings to get rid of, can be said to possess no knowledge. No knowledge that way is not the same as the supposed knowledge about Nothingness, which is something nullified into nothing. It is far above mere knowledge correlative with the limited modes of being. It is completely denuded of nescience, which is sheer ignorance. In a word, it is Enlightenment[bs] and *Prajñā* fused into the One. Enlightenment shades off what is extrinsic to itself and is essentially inner light in the form of no-knowledge, while *Prajñā* is an out-pouring of the inner light over the world-all by denuding it of fallaciousness.

I have mentioned Seng-chao and Tao-sheng as the twin stars in the ethereal sky of Chinese Buddhistic speculation. But there is a difference between them. Seng-chao formulated a system of principles explanatory of the nature of wisdom, whereas Tao-sheng turned the Mahāyānic theory into a way of spiritual life wherein human nature is fulfilled to the extent that it can partake of *Buddha*-nature[bt].

Hitherto, Chinese Buddhists had looked upon the mundane world as a case of malady and thought about the actual individual as a source of blunder. Any acceptance of the world in its illusory appearances and any affirmation of the individual in his fantastic grimaces would indicate a silliness of view. But the monk Hui-yüan[bu] (334–416) had a different turn of mind. The world could exist in the form of permanence constitutive of Ultimate Reality. The human being could come to the possession of a real Self in intimacy with the Buddha. This line of thought had quite an influence upon Tao-sheng in formulating his philosophy of *Buddha*-nature. For brevity's sake, his fundamental ideas[53] in this regard may be enunciated as follows:

(1) The all-pervasive function of *Prajñā* and the substantial nature of *Nirvāṇa* are inseparable in the make-up of Ultimate Reality, which will embody the true *Dharma* and the perfect *Buddhatā* (*Buddha*hood) in the unity of *Buddha-dharma*[bv].

(2) The ideal of *Nirvāṇa* is realizable in the midst of fluctuating life and death. Hence, the pure land of the Buddha is not different

from the existent realm of all creatures. By way of moral purification, all creatures dwelling in the defiled world of blunders will be
reinstated in the world of the noble and sublime, won over through
the employment of Reason. Abidance in the enlightening Reason of
the Buddha enables each and all to see every facet of the world as
pure· as it can be.

(3) The conquest of the darkened mind by the potency of Reason
is the only way to emancipation. In pursuance of this, the real self
of spontaneous freedom is achieved by the righteous mind which has
been restored to the original purity of nature through the exertion
of Reason. Thus all human beings—not even excepting the *icchan-
tika* (forsaken one), endowed with intrinsic Reason, can come to
share equally the ubiquitous *Buddha*-nature and to unfold the illuminating Buddha-wisdom implicit in their own conscience. In this
sense, human individuals are spiritual comrades, equal in cosmic importance with the Buddha.

(4) As the light of supreme wisdom has a most direct penetration
into his own rational essence, each man through devout devotion
can come to a *sudden awakening*[bw] of the *Buddha*-nature within
the inner constitution of his own nature and achieve *Buddha*hood on
his own accord. This is the chief tenet of Mahāyāna Buddhism.

Tao-sheng's philosophy of *Buddha*hood is of great importance
for several reasons. (a) It evoked a number of interpretations of
Buddha-nature during the fifth and sixth centuries. (b) His emphasis on the perfectibility of human nature after the model of *Buddha*-
nature is quite congenial with the Confucian theory of the original
goodness of man. This is evidenced by the fact that the poet-
philosopher, Hsieh Ling-yün[bx] (385–433), in hearty sympathy with
Tao-sheng's idea of sudden awakening, made a very favorable comparison of the spiritual achievement of Confucius with that of the
Buddha.[54] (c) His theory of sudden awakening by reverting to the
inmost nature of the mind anticipated the later philosophy of
Ch'an[by] (Zen). (d) His concept of the importance of Reason in
gaining an insight into Ultimate Reality even anticipated the Neo-
Confucianism of the Sung Dynasty[bz] (960–1279). In short, Tao-
sheng was, on the one hand, the culmination of the line of thought
in the linkage of Buddhism with Taoism, and, on the other, a bridge
over which several schools of Buddhism were to make headway in
alliance with some schools of Confucianism.

In the epoch of Sui-T'ang (581–960) ten different schools of
Buddhism flourished in China. "A beggar of time" like me, finally,
cannot refrain from mentioning, in particular, the categorical
scheme of Hua-yen[ca]—the Avataṁsaka school—as a powerful expression of Chinese comprehensive harmony. Theoretically, if not

entirely historically, the Hua-yen school may be made the line of convergence along which many systems of Buddhistic thought would have their confluence.

The categorical scheme of Hua-yen[55] was an attempt to integrate all the differentiating worlds, all the noble deed-acts, and all the achieved end results of the *Buddhas* in the past, present, and future into a sum total of the True Realm of *Dharma* in the form of supreme perfection with a view to showing that each human being, inherently possessed of wondrous excellences, could awaken in himself, all at once, *Buddha*-nature, adequately, spontaneously, and congruently. The one real Realm of *Dharma*[cb] is not far from this actual world of man, if everyone knows thoroughly how to live and act wisely by way of participation in the fundamental wisdom of the Buddha. *Buddha*-nature *in toto* has the potentiality of coming in ingress into the perennial spiritual constitution of man. This is the equality and equanimity of *Dharma*. The spiritual sun sheds its exuberant light over and into all living beings, and all living beings, in turn, assimilate and reflect and interfuse and re-enforce this spiritual light uniquely and reciprocally. Thus, all modes of the spontaneous function of reason, manifesting themselves in infinite varieties, would, at the same time, be actuated into a concert of life activities, in unison with the One True Realm of *Dharma,* equanimous in essence. In the midst of enriched varieties, the light of *Tathatā* (Thusness) radiated by the Buddha and witnessed and shared by all men alike will gladden the differentiating minds and the differentiating worlds into the non-differentiation of Reality perfectly embedded in the integral truth, which is Enlightenment, inherent in each and interpenetrative into all.

Taken in its all-inclusive unity, this One True *Dharma-dhātu* (Realm of *Dharma* or Law) evinces the omnipresence and omnipotence of Mind constitutive of the noumenon of all the phenomenal worlds, diversifying itself into (a) the differential Realms of Events, (b) the integrative Realm of Reason, (c) the interpenetrative Realm of Reason and Events, and (d) the interlacing Realm of all Events.

The theoretical formulation of the categorical scheme,[56] initiated by Tu-shun[cc] (557–640), developed by Chih-yen[cd] (602–668), elaborated by Fa-tsang[ce] (643–720), and further expounded by Ch'eng-kuan[cf] (760–820) and Tsung-mi[cg] (d. 841), embraces three grand views,[57] i.e., (1) of the true Void[ch], (2) of the congruence of Reason and Events[ci], and (3) of the dovetailing of all Events in the form of universal coherence[cj].

In the first view, an attempt is made to show (a) that the worlds of physical properties can be dissolved into the nature of the Void, just as phenomena are transmutable into the noumenon; (b) that the Void as the Ultimate Reality is constitutive of, and identifiable with, the assemblage of purified physical phenomena; (c) that the Void and the physical are mutually congruent; and (d) that, eventually, after the impenetrable inertia of the physical is explained away in terms of the efficacy of mental and spiritual transmutations and through the insinuation of the ontic essence—the true nature of the Void—into the physical, all one-sided characterizations in respect of the physical and the Void are transcended in the highest integral truth of the middle path.

In the second view, it is maintained that reason and events can be melded in a perfect manner. Reason is the wondrous function deeply rooted in *Bhūta-tathatā* and has its efficacy anytime anywhere in virtue of the omnipresence of the Buddha. This can be accounted for in the following ways: (a) Reason as a whole, denuded of any specification, is universally present in all the worlds of events, however differentiated the latter may be, inasmuch as the *Dharmatā* is manifesting itself incessantly without limitation. And, therefore, even the minutest event-particles are immersed in the integral truth and imbued adequately with Reason. (b) The items of events which, as such, are differentiated must be restored into unity in the integration of Reason, just as the wavicles, spreading forth far and away, are losing their own unique momenta and can be re-enforced and saved only by taking up continually with the oceanic ingratiation. Hence, it may be asserted that events, each and all, are constituted according to the Reason which is exhibited thereof. Though they are interrelated, the truth, however, is not simply events which, once constituted, would overshadow the Reason inherent in them, and the events are not simply the truth which, if verified, would supersede the events limitative in their differentiation.

In the third view, it is asserted that the dovetailing of all events will vindicate the universal coherence of truth. This can be shown as follows: (1) Reason operates for the sake of events. It makes the events what they are in the mode of existence, in the way of differentiation, qualitatively as well as quantitatively, and in the process of change and transformation. Hence, the function of Reason issuing in truth will come in ingress into all the differentiating worlds of events. (2) The events, each and all, abide by Reason in virtue of which they would go through the process of change in incessant successions and remain permanent in the realm of eternity. And, therefore, the events in observance of Reason would permeate all modes of *Dharma*. (3) The events, as implied in Reason, would bring forth the following modes of implication: (a) one implicates another; (b) one implicates every other; (c) one implicates all others; (d) all others implicate one; (e) all others implicate every other one; and (f) all others implicate all others. Thus, the whole and the parts, the one and the many, as well as the universal and the particular, will be intertwined.

The above consideration brings into prominence the principle of mutual implication, the principle of mutual relevance, and the principle of all-pervasive coherence. All these principles, taken together, are explanatory of the integral infinite *Dharma-dhātu*. In the way of mutual implication, any one *dharma* can gather up any other one unto itself and enter into the constitution of that one; any one can gather up all others unto itself and enter into the constitution of that one; all others can gather up all others unto themselves and enter into the constitution of those others. Hence, the principle of mutual relevance needs no further elucidation. Furthermore, the principle of all-pervasive coherence holds on the following conditions: (a) one *dharma* gathers up another one into itself and enters into that one; (b) one gathers up all other *dharmas* into itself so as to enter into that one; (c) one gathers up another one so as to enter into all others; (d) one gathers up all others in order to enter into all others; (e) all other *dharmas* gather up one so as to enter into another one; (f) all other *dharmas* gather up all others so as to enter into any one; (g) all others gather up one so as to enter into all others; and (h) all others gather up all others in order to enter into them all. When all of these are melded together, the ultimate result is the integrity of the infinitely perfect *Dharma-dhātu*. If the above conditions are fulfilled, then the ten approaches to the metaphysical profundity and the six characteristics of all *dharma* will be clear in the light of day without further elucidation. In view of such a philosophy, if any person is to gain a firm footing in the One Real *Dharma-dhātu*, he must live and have his being in the spirit of infinity.

VI

In the above I have tried to depict tersely the ways in which the Chinese contemplative minds have been fascinated with the world and the human individual, which are taken, however, not so much in natural as "in dramatic regard."[58] The world and the individual, taken "in natural regard," would be the exhibitions of related facts, definite in content, determinate in nature, specific in conditions, articulate in forms, full in being, or substantial in essence. All of these, characteristic of scientific explanations, are, of course, very important for the understanding of man and the world. But Chinese philosophers choose to take a step further than this in their modes of contemplation. From their viewpoints, the world, taking shape in

Ultimate Reality, must transcend the limitations of these relatively specific characterizations before all of its complete nature can come to the light of day. The actual world, strictly philosophically conceived, should be transformed into an ideal pattern adorned with the axiological unity of supreme perfection. The Chinese always aspire toward the transfigured world of liberating art, of edifying morality, of contemplative truth, and of religious piety. Any other world short of these will be a realm of anxiety making us look pale and tired. This is why Confucians have craved so much for the continually creative potency of the heavenly *Tao* in the shaping of the cosmic order as a whole. This is why the Taoists have wholeheartedly cherished the ideal of Nothingness for its coming to the rescue of all things relative in the realm of Being. And this is also why Chinese Buddhists have vehemently struggled for the partaking of the *Buddha*-nature embedded in the integral truth of the ultimate spiritual Enlightenment.

As to the nature and status of man, the Chinese, either as a unique person or as a social being, takes no pride in being a type of individual in estrangement from the world he lives in or from the other fellows he associates with. He is intent on embracing within the full range of his vital experience all aspects of plenitude in the nature of the whole cosmos and all aspects of richness in the worth of noble humanity. Anything different from this would be a sign of the impoverishment in the inner constitution of personality which is miserably truncated in development. This accounts for the concerted efforts of Chinese philosophers to advocate the exaltation of the individual into the inward sageliness and the outward worthiness which together make up the intrinsic greatness of man as Man.

[1] Cf. my *Chinese View of Life* (Hong Kong: The Union Press, 1957), chap. 3, pp. 87–115, especially pp. 99–115.

[2] In the *Shih chi*[ck] (General History, Royal Library edn., 1746), Vol. 67, p. 8, and Vol. 130, p. 2, Ssu-ma Ch'ien clearly stated that his father, Ssu-ma T'an, learned the philosophy of change from Yang-ho,[cl] whose intellectual heritage was traced back to Confucius through an unbroken lineage of eight generations.

[3] This cardinal doctrine was set forth by Confucius in the "Tuan" *chuan*[cm] (Compendiums), in the "Hsi tz'u" *chuan* (Conspectus), and in the early section of the "Shuo kua" *chuan*[cn] (Scholia on the Hexagrams).

[4] This idea was first formulated by Confucius in the "Wen yen" *chuan*[co] (Corollaries of the Hexagrams "Ch'ien" and "K'un") and more systematically in the "Shang" *chuan*[cp] (Symbolics).

[5] The idea of value and the consequential value-centric ontology are developed in the "Hsi-tz'u."

[6] I attacked this problem in *Sheng-ming chīng-tiao yü mei-k'an*[cq] (The Sentiment of Life and the Sense of Beauty), National Central University Monograph on Art and Literature, Vol. 1, No. 1, 1931, pp. 173–204, especially pp. 192–203.

[7] The "Hsi-tz'u," chap. 4.

[8] Cf. my essay, "Logical Formulations of the Philosophy of Change," in the *I-hsüeh tao lun chi*[cr] (Joint Studies on The Book of Change). (Changsha: Commercial Press, 1941), pp. 31–54.

[9] Cf. Chiao Hsün[cs], *I-t'u lüeh*[ct] (Logical Structure and Syntactical Scheme Exhibited in *The Book of Change*) (8 vols., 1813), Vol. I, p. 4, Vol. II, pp. 13–14; *I hua*[cu] (Talks on the Philosophy of Change) (2 vols., 1818), Vol. I, pp. 3, 12; *I-t'ung shih*[cv] (General Commentary on *The Book of Change*) (20 vols., 1813); and *I chang-chü*[cw] (*The Book of Change: A Study in Syntax*) (12 vols., 1815).

[10] Cf. the "Tuan," the "Wen yen," and the "Hsi tz'u," chaps. 5, 7; *Doctrine of the Mean*, 22. See also Tai T'ung-yüan[cx], *Yüan-shan*[cy] (Treatise on the Good), chap. 1.

11 The "Hsi tz'u," chap. 5.
12 The "Tuan."
13 The "Wen yen."
14 Cf. *Doctrine of the Mean*, 22.
15 Cf. *Book of Mencius*, VIIB.25.
16 Cf. *Works of Hsün Tzu* (Chekiang: Chekiang Book Co., 1876), Vol. 11, chap. 17, pp. 11–16, 18.
17 Cf. Tai Te's version of *The Book of Propriety*, edited by Lu Chien-tseng[cz], 1758, Vol. 1, pp. 4–6.
18 Cf. the "Wen yen" in *The Book of Change*.
19 *The Book of Lao Tzu* (Chekiang: Chekiang Book Co., 1875), chap. 4.
20 *Ibid.*, 6.
21 *Ibid.*, 39.
22 *Ibid.*, 5, 22.
23 *Ibid.*, 35, 28.
24 *Ibid.*, 16.
25 *Ibid.*, 40–41, 45.
26 Cf. *ibid.*, 40.
27 *Ibid.*, 11.
28 *Ibid.*, chap. 27.
29 Cf. *The Works of Chuang Tzu*, Vol. I, chap. 2, p. 24; Vol. V, chap. 12, pp. 6–7; Vol. VI, chap. 17, pp. 9–12; Vol. VIII, chap. 23, pp. 9–10.
30 Cf. *ibid.*, Vol. X, chap. 33, p. 25. Also cf. Ma Hsü-lun[da], *Chuang Tzu i-cheng*[db] (Verifications of Meanings in Chuang Tzu). (Shanghai: Commercial Press, 1930), Vol. 33, pp. 18–19.
31 Cf. *ibid.*, Vol. III, chap. 6, pp. 7, 10; Vol. VI, chap. 17, p. 10; Vol. VII, chap. 21, p. 24; Vol. VII, chap. 22, pp. 36, 39; Vol. VIII, chap. 23, p. 9; Vol. VIII, chap. 25, p. 34.
32 Cf. *ibid.*, Vol. VIII, chap. 24, p. 22; Vol. X, chap. 31, p. 9 (Kuo Hsiang's notes). The monk Te-ch'ing[dc], in the Ming Dynasty (1368–1643), in a commentary on the *Chuang Tzu*, said emphatically that Mencius had a tremendous influence upon this great Taoist.
33 Cf. *The Works of Chuang Tzu*, Vol. X, chap. 32, p. 12.
34 Cf. *ibid.*, Vol. V, chap. 13, p. 24.
35 Cf. *ibid.*, Vol. IV, chap. 11, p. 26.
36 Cf. *ibid.*, Vol. III, chap. 6, pp. 7, 9–10, 15–16.
37 Cf. *ibid.*, Vol. III, chap. 7, pp. 22–26.
38 Cf. Chang T'ai-yen[dd], *Ch'i-wu lun shih*[de] (Commentary on the Theory of Leveling All Things), pp. 1, 3, 11, 14, 18–19, 21–25, 51–55.
39 *The Works of Chuang Tzu*, Vol. I, chap. 2, p. 25.
40 The *Chin shu*[df] (History of the Chin Dynasty), (Shanghai: Commercial Press, 1934), Vol. 43, p. 8.
41 Cf. Chang Chan's[dg] citations from Ho Yen in the commentary on *The Works of Lieh Tzu*[dh] (Chekiang: Chekiang Book Co., 1876), Vol. I, chap. 1, pp. 4–5; Vol. IV, chap. 4, pp. 4–5.
42 Cf. Wang Pi and Han K'ang-po[di], Commentaries on *The Book of Change* (Shanghai: Chung Hua Book Co., 1922): (a) Wang's portion in Vol. III, p. 4; Vol. I, pp. 2, 5–6; Vol. II, p. 11; Vol. IV, pp. 2–3; (b) Han's portion in Vol. VII, pp. 3–4, 6–9; Vol. VIII, pp. 5–6. See also Wang Pi, *Chou-i lüeh-li*[dj] (Sketchy Exemplifications of the Principles of Change) in the same edn., Vol. X, pp. 1–3, 6–8.
43 Cf. the *Mahā-parinirvāṇa-sūtra*[dk] in Chinese trans. (Shanghai: 1913, 1926), Vol. 2, chap. 2, pp. 11, 19; chap. 3, pp. 23–5, 28; Vol. 3, chap. 4, pp. 11, 15; and the *Mahā-prajñā-pāramitā-sūtra*[dl] in Chinese trans., portion 16 (published in Ssuch'uan, 1940), Vol. 596, pp. 4–6.
44 Cf. *Liang jen-kung chüan-chi*[dm] (Collected Essays of Liang ch'i-ch'ao), 1st series (Shanghai: Commercial Press, 1923), pp. 1–23; 81–134; 155–254.
45 See Junjirō Takakusu, *The Essentials of Buddhist Philosophy* (3rd edn., Honolulu: Office Appliance Co., 1956), and Chiang Wei-ch'iao, *Fo-hsüeh kai-lun* (Introduction to Buddhism)[do] (Shanghai, 1930).
46 T'ang Yung-t'ung has given ample evidences to demonstrate this fact in the *Han-Wei Liang-Chin Nan-pei-ch'ao fo-chiao shih*[dp] (History of Chinese Buddhism During the Period of 67–588) (2nd edn., Taipei: Commercial Press, 1962), Pt. I, chap. 6, pp. 89–111.
47 Cf. the Tathata-parivarta of the *Daśa-sahaṣrika* (*Prajñā-pāramitā-sūtra*)[dq] in different Chinese translations by Lokākṣin and Chih Ch'ien. See the Taishō edn. of the Buddhist Tripiṭaka in Chinese. No. 224, p. 453; No. 225, p. 374.
48 Cf. Hui-ta, *Chao-lun hsü*[dr] (Preface to *Seng-chao's Discourses*). See the Taishō edn. of the Buddhist Tripiṭaka in Chinese, No. 1858, p. 150.
49 Cf. Yüan K'ang, *Chao-lin su* (*Commentary on Seng chao's Discourses*). See *ibid.*, No. 1859, pp. 162–163.
50 Cf. Chi-tsang *Chung-kuan lun shu*[dt] (Commentary on the *Mādhyamika-śāstra*). See *ibid.*, No. 1824, p. 29.
51 Cf. his "*Wu pu-ch'ien-lun*," "*Pu-jen-kung-lun*," "*Pan-jo wu-chih-lun*"[du] (Discourses On the Perennial, On the Non-Vacuous, and On the *Prajñā* as No-Knowledge). See the Buddhist Tripiṭaka in Chinese, No. 1858, pp. 150–7.
52 *The Tempest*, Act 2, sc. i.
53 Tao-sheng's ideas are scattered in the commentaries on the *Saddharma-puṇḍarīka-sūtra*, on the *Mahā-parinirvāṇa-sūtra*[dv] and on the *Vimalakīrti-nirdeśa-sūtra*.[dw]
54 Cf. Hsieh Ling-yün, *Pien-cheng lun*[dx] (Essays on the Discrimination of Doctrines) in the Further Collection of Essays on Buddhism, Vol. 18, pp. 13–19.

55 Cf. Chieh-huang, *Hua-yen ching yao-chieh* (Essentials of the *Avataṁsaka-sūtra*)dz compiled in 1128. Nanking Centre for Buddhist Publications, 1872.

56 For the important literature on the Hua-yen school, see the *Taishō* edn. of the Buddhist Tripiṭaka in Chinese. No. 1836, pp. 71–76; Nos. 1866–1890, pp. 477–792.

57 Here I am utilizing Tsung-mi's *Chu Hua-yen fa-chieh kuan-men* (Elucidations of the Hua-yen View of the *Dharma-dhātu*), which is essentially more systematic than the earlier expositions by Tu-shun and Fa-tsang, (*ibid.*, No. 1884, pp. 684–692).

58 Cf. C. Lloyd Morgan, *Mind at the Crossways* (London: Williams & Norgate, 1929), pp. 2–4, 13–14, 20–21, 224–227, 230–235, 267–272.

a	方東美	am	康僧會
b	墨家哲學	an	如來
c	楊朱	ao	般若
d	易經	ap	道安
e	孟子	aq	曇濟
f	荀子	ar	僧鏡
g	司馬談	as	慧達
h	司馬遷	at	元康
i	商瞿，子木	au	吉藏
j	道	av	本無
k	禮記	aw	本無異
l	中庸	ax	即色
m	繫辭傳	ay	心無
n	戴德	az	識含
o	魯艾公	ba	幻化
p	老子	bb	緣會
q	大象	bc	琛法師
r	無	bd	友遁，道林
s	有	be	濕法師
t	無爲而無不爲	bf	于法師
u	爲而不恃	bg	喜法師
v	長而不宰	bh	于道師
w	生而不有	bi	眞如
x	莊子	bj	鳩摩羅什
y	建之以常無有	bk	空性
z	以空虛不毀萬物爲實	bl	僧肇
aa	惠施	bm	道生
ab	反者道之用	bn	涅槃
ac	玄之又玄	bo	中觀論
ad	逍遙遊	bp	法身
ae	鵬	bq	法性
af	寥天一	br	漚和（拘舍羅）方便善巧
ag	何晏	bs	菩提
ah	王弼	bt	佛性
ai	法	bu	慧遠
aj	隨唐	bv	一闡提
ak	支婁迦讖	bw	頓悟
al	支謙	bx	謝靈運

by 禪

bz 宋朝

ca 華嚴宗

cb 一眞法界

cc 杜順

cd 智儼

ce 法藏

cf 澄觀

cg 宗密

ch 眞空觀

ci 理事無礙觀

cj 周遍含容觀

ck 史記

cl 楊何

cm 彖傳

cn 說卦傳

co 文言傳

cp 象傳

cq 生命情調與美感

cr 易學討論集

cs 焦循

ct 易圖略

cu 易話

cv 易通釋

cw 易章句

cx 戴震，東美

cy 原善

cz 盧見曾

da 馬叙倫

db 莊子義證

dc 釋德清，憨山

dd 章炳麟，太炎

de 帝物論釋

df 晋書

dg 張湛

dh 列子書

di 韓康伯

dj 周易略例

dk 大般涅槃經

dl 大般若經第十六分

dm 梁任公全集

dn 蔣維喬

do 佛學概論

dp 漢魏西晋南北朝佛教史

dq 道行經

dr 肇論序

ds 肇論疏

dt 觀論疏

du 物不遷論，不眞空論，般若無知論

dv 大般若經

dw 維摩詰所說經

dx 辨言論

dy 戒環

dz 華嚴經要解

ea 註華嚴法界觀門

The status of the individual
in Indian metaphysics*

I. INTRODUCTION

Regarding the Indian attitude toward the individual, Westerners hold certain views which are not wholly correct. They are:

(1) In Indian metaphysics there is no place for a plurality of individuals. Plurality of individuals is ultimately an illusion: the ultimate reality is one ineffable Absolute (called *Brahman*).

(2) This metaphysics has so influenced the general Indian mind that in formulating the ideal of life it has ignored what concerns, or should concern, individuals as individuals. The ultimate aim of life, for the Indians, is complete merging in the Absolute.

(3) It is because of this neglect of the individual that Indians could never develop systematic ethics and social philosophy, and the only spiritual religion they have developed is a mystical form of pantheism, which, according to many Westerners, is no religion at all and borders dangerously on a life which is thoroughly irreligious and irresponsible.

(4) Even where they have admitted individuals, as, for example, on the empirical (*vyāvahārika*) plane, they have systematically deprived them of freedom of will. Westerners hold that the Indian doctrine of *karma* is a direct denial of freedom of individuals.

Of these four views, the last one is wholly incorrect, and the first, second, and the third are correct only insofar as they represent the standpoint of the Advaita Vedānta. But the Advaita Vedānta is only one of the Indian systems of philosophy. There are other systems, such as the Nyāya, the Vaiśeṣika, the Sāṃkhya, the Yoga, the Mīmāṃsā, and non-Advaita Vedāntic systems, none of which is of less significance to Indian life in general than the Advaita. There are also lesser philosophers, such as the Śaivas, Śāktas, and Grammarians. Add to the list the three great heterodox systems (Buddhism, Jainism, and the philosophy of the Cārvākas), and we have all kinds of Indian views of the individual. Except for a few Śaivas and Grammarians and the philosophers of one or two schools of

---

* Because of continued serious illness, the author was unable to supply the full documentation he had intended to provide—*Editor's note.*

Buddhism, none denied plurality of selves, none recommended the liquidation of individuals, and none spoke of the Absolute as the only reality or preached pantheism of the Advaita brand.

In fact, there is no *one* Indian view of the status of the individual. There are many views, each upheld by substantial Indian thinkers and by a large section of the Indian people. The Cārvāka system apart—which somehow could not stand repeated onslaught by every other system—if there is anything common to the different Indian views of the individual, it is (1) that every individual has a spiritual side, (2) that his spiritual side is, from the valuational point of view, more essential than his material side, (3) that its autonomy has to be fully realized, and (4) that this realization is possible through progressive detachment (*vairāgya*) from the less essential sides of our being. Detachment from these has not always meant their dismissal.

II. INDIVIDUALS AS FREE AGENTS

To show now that the last one of the four views of the Indian attitude on the individual is wholly incorrect:

By the word "individual" we mean throughout this paper a human being who is not entirely an item of Nature, accepting unquestioningly what Nature offers and submitting blindly to its forces, but one who often resists it and initiates new actions, one, in other words, who is as much above Nature as in it. This over-natural status of man is called "freedom."[1] We are told that in this sense of the word "freedom" Indians have never admitted free individuals. Their Law of *Karma,* we are told, is a direct disavowal of such freedom.

This, however, is entirely wrong.[2] Movements made by an individual have been classified by Indians into three groups—*tāmasika, rājasika,* and *sāttvika. Tāmasika* movements are those over which the individual, whose movements they are, has no control, the individual remaining in a state of stupor, as it were. These movements are absolutely unfree. Movements which are blindly biological belong to this group. *Rājasika* movements are those of which the individual is conscious, though unreflectively, as *his* actions—actions, viz., for which he is prepared to take full responsibility, but which are still not free, because they proceed through, and are determined by, emotions and sentiments, the keynote of which is positive attachment (*rāga*) or repulsion (*dveṣa*). These unfree movements are as much biological and blind as the *tāmasika* ones, and yet they are claimed by the individual as *his* actions only because he can, and often does, follow, though unreflectively, quite a large number of subtle varieties of *rāga* and *dveṣa,* which animals and men-in-stupor cannot. There is an important reason, again, why the individual is prepared to take responsibility for these actions. It is always possible for the individual, though this requires a good amount of effort, not to yield entirely to the operating *rāgas* and *dveṣas*, but either to keep his actions confined within his mind, preventing them from maturing into physical actions, or to channelize them into moral contexts, maintaining all through an over-all control over them.

So far, this over-all control is only possible. As and when, however, it becomes actual, the actions that result have risen to the level called *sāttvika*. The guiding principle at this level is detachment (*vairāgya*), which, however, admits of degree. Short of absolute detachment, it leads to actions which are socio-moral (*dharma*) at the lower stage and spiritual (*ādhyātmika*) at a higher. At the moral level, noted in the last paragraph, actions proceeding through *rāga* and *dveṣa* were only channelized, and in more austere forms of *dharma* attempts are made to render these two motive forces more and more inoperative. Attempts at channelizing ordinary actions or preventing them from maturing into physical movements, practiced again and again, lead in their turn to an accumulation of corresponding dispositions which, as they grow stronger and stronger, sap, in proportion, the life-force of the germs of action that could mature through *rāga* and *dveṣa*. This entire course of progressive sapping constitutes the spiritual life of the individual, and, with sapping concluded, he reaches a stage which is the last doorway to liberation (*mukti*). Activities prior to that liberation, beginning with the first actual control, are *sāttvika;* and, when liberation is attained, one finds oneself in a new dimension altogether, beyond all *tamas, rajas,* and *sattva.* Through all stages, *sāttvika* actions are free in the sense that one so acting has so far detached himself from Nature.

This account is given explicitly in the Sāṃkhya, and, somehow or other, with minor variations here and there, it has also been accepted in most other systems.[3]

Also, the Law of *Karma,* properly understood, is *not* against freedom of action. It is true that according to this law my present life is somehow determined by the merits and demerits of what I did in my previous life, that life, again, by the merits and demerits of what I had done in a life still previous, and so an ad infinitum, but this does not mean that everything of a particular life is determined. It has been explicitly stated that only three things in a life are determined. They are (1) the bodily and mental make-up and social position at the time of birth in that particular life (*jāti*), (2) the span of that life (*āyuḥ*), and (3) particular experiences with all the hedonic tones that they have in that life and all that is necessary as objects or direct or indirect causes of those experiences (*bhoga*). Among these direct and indirect causes are included my physiological movements and actions which proceed through *rāga* and *dveṣa*, but not actions at the moral and spiritual levels. Moral and spiritual actions have been excepted on the following grounds:

(1) We are definitely told that with the results yielded in a particular life the merits and demerits of actions done in the previous life get exhausted, and these results as experiences with appropriate hedonic tones are meant as rewards or punishments. It follows that, if the results as experiences in the present life could in their turn yield further results with hedonic tones—whether in this life or in the next—that would be the grossest form of injustice. It would amount to rewarding or punishing an individual for all eternity. That would also go against the accepted theory that merits or demerits of actions get exhausted in their results.

(2) It would also speak against all possibility of betterment of the individual, and equally against all conscious effort for liberation (*mukti*), unless, of course, the betterment and the effort in question are results of good actions in the life preceding the present one. But, then, even in the case of the latter alternative, the goodness of these previous actions has to be explained, and, should one say that it, too, is similarly the result of good actions done in a life preceding the previous one, it would follow that an individual once good in one life is good in all lives, and similarly with individuals who are bad; and that, in turn, would mean that bad individuals could never become good and the good never bad—a thesis which no Indian system would ever allow. Perhaps it would also follow that a bad soul should continually grow worse than before—a doctrine more severe than that of eternal damnation and never acceptable to Indians. It would also follow that, if as a result of non-meritorious actions an individual is born in the next life as a tree or a sub-human animal, he would lose all chance as much of betterment as of worsening, for the actions (movements) of these latter, as not proceeding through attachment (*rāga*) and repulsion (*dveṣa*) could never acquire merit or demerit—they are completely amoral.

(3) If the Law of *Karma* is understood as a theory of complete determination, this would go against the very spirit of scriptural or, for the matter of that, any, prescription or prohibition. If one is bound to do what one does, why should there be prescription or prohibition?

So, Indians never meant that everything of the present life is determined by what one did in the preceding life. Add to this the fact that they have distinguished moral and spiritual actions from actions that are biological, and it will follow that there is nothing against these actions being considered free. To repeat: Spiritual actions, which proceed from detachment (*vairāgya*), have maximum freedom, because there is no submission to *rāga* and *dveṣa;* moral actions as channelizing, according to prescriptions and prohibitions, normal biological activities are free in the sense that in their case there is no blind submission; and actions which proceed consciously through *rāga* and *dveṣa* and are consequently accompanied by an I-feeling are free only in the sense that in their case there is always a possibility of not having submitted to them.

III. PLURALITY OF INDIVIDUALS

It is only in one Indian system, viz., the Advaita Vedānta, along with a few sub-schools of Śaiva philosophy and the philosophy of Grammar, that the plurality of individuals has been denied an ultimate status. All other schools and sub-schools have recognized plurality as an ultimate truth. Most of these schools and sub-schools have taken this for granted; only a few have come forward to meet the Advaita thesis on logical grounds.

The Advaita Vedāntist has denied the ultimate status of individual persons principally on three grounds. They are:

(1) The individual as we ordinarily understand him is a complex consisting of a body, a mind (*ahaṁkāra* = ego),[4] and a self. Of these three constituents, the self is the most important; it is the essence of the individual. Normally, this essence remains fused—one might even say confused—with the mind and the body, but, since in itself it is an autonomous essence, the individual, whose ultimate duty is to realize himself, will have to distinguish this essence. He will have to dissociate it from the mind and the body, which are only accidents. This dissociation of the self has been understood by the Advaita Vedāntist in an extreme sense. He understands it as the severance of all its relations with the mind and the body, even of the slightest relation called "reference," and from this he concludes, a little too easily, that therefore this dissociate self cannot be many, for it is only the bodies and minds (*ahaṁkāras*) that are many, and, if the dissociate self—the self-in-itself—has no need of even referring to these, there is no reason why it should be many. To admit plurality of selves over and above that of minds and bodies would unnecessarily multiply entities.

(2) Often, again, the Advaita Vedāntist has denied the plurality of selves on the *ipsi dixit* of the scriptures, particularly of the Upaniṣads.

(3) Later Advaita thinkers have attacked the very concept of plurality (difference). They have pointed out inconsistencies in that concept.

The Advaita Vedāntist thus holds that ultimately there is only one self, and, as the self is the essence of the individual, all individuals must be essentially one. This one essence—the Absolute, or *Brahman* as it is called—is in no need of even referring to minds and bodies. It follows that the many individuals we normally are in this world are due only to illusory identification of this Absolute with different mind-body complexes.

However, other Indian systems[5] have rejected this Advaita doctrine. They have not indeed denied that the self constitutes the essence of the individual or that it is the duty of the individual to realize his self as the autonomous essence. What they have refused to do is to interpret this autonomy as rejection of all its relations, even the relation of reference, to the mind and the body.

The Sāṃkhya, the Yoga, and a number of Śaiva thinkers hold that the self, even in its full autonomy, constantly refers to—in the language of Indian philosophy, reveals or witnesses—mental states and, through these, as the occasion arises, objects that are nonmental. Mere reference (revealing or witnessing) need not affect the freedom of the self. One may keep oneself aloof from certain things and just witness their behavior. The self as just witnessing the mind and its states is what is actually found in self-consciousness. As the self, while witnessing the mind and its states, can yet retain its autonomy, there is no need to reject this witnessing. The autonomy of the self need not, therefore, transcend its witnessing or reference function. The free self as just witnessing the mind and its states is called in the Sāṃkhya and the Yoga, and even in the Advaita Vedānta, *sākṣin* (witness) or *sākṣi-puruṣa* (witness-self); and, since it thus refers, of its own nature, to a particular mind (ego), which reference it has no need to transcend or abjure, it follows that the self as *sākṣin* is particular. Since, again, no *sākṣin* can refer in this way to another particular mind (ego), it follows, further, that selves, even as autonomous, are many.

Free reference of the *sākṣin* to the particular mind corresponding to it may indeed imply that it might not have exercised that reference and is, therefore, capable of withdrawing it. But this may well be an impotent capability, just wishful thinking, not capable enough to mature into actuality. One may be reminded here of Kant's Ideas of Reason. A possible need not be a possible actual. The Advaitist has not shown that this possible withdrawal of reference is a possibility of actual withdrawal.

The Advaita has indeed attributed this reference at the *sākṣin* stage to the last vestige of nescience (*ajñāna*). But what exactly is meant here by "last vestige" and how it can possibly disappear have never been clearly stated in Advaita texts. The Advaitists have only expressed their conviction that it should disappear.

We may note in this connection that the doctrine of *jīvan-mukti*, (liberation in one's lifetime), to which the Advaitist, along with many others, has subscribed, is not very consistent with his denial of individuality. The Adyaitist admits that some individuals may realize their autonomous essences and, therefore, their complete identity with the Absolute, even in their lifetime, still retaining their minds (and bodies). These are the *jīvan-muktas*. If, now, these *jīvan-muktas,* who have retained their minds (and bodies), can yet be completely free (liberated), it is difficult to believe that they have ceased to be individuals. If their activities were merely biological, and nothing more, we could somehow imagine them as wholly identical with *Brahman,* for it is not difficult to conceive that these activities are not appropriated by the self. But the Advaitist has, as a matter of fact, attributed to them actions which are also moral and spiritual.

The plurality of individuals was denied only by the Advaita, not even by other schools of the Vedānta. The Rāmānujists and Mādhvas, for example, have resolutely held that even pure selves are many. They have replied to all the Advaita charges against the concept of difference and interpreted the so-called monistic scriptural texts along different lines; and, as regards the autonomy of the self, they have distinguished it from the body only, the mind (*ahaṁkāra* = ego) and the self being the same thing in their systems. This is equally the view of Nyāya-Vaiśeṣika thinkers and the Mīmāṁsakas.

That there are many individual selves in addition to many bodies is for all these thinkers an obvious truth to start with,[6] and, if the Advaitist has argued against this obvious truth, they have offered counter arguments. Their main point is that, even if the ultimate realization of the self amounts to severance of all connection with the body[7] that the individual had, even then the distinctive individuality of the self need not disappear. Appeal to the law of parsimony would be useless here, for parsimony is relevant only in the context of hypotheses, not with regard to obvious facts.

Some hold even that at no stage is there complete freedom from the body. Even God, for them, has an eternal body made of a pure stuff, and so has the self that at liberation severs connection with the gross (and subtle) body.

With the exception of the Rāmānujists, these philosophers are all deists, holding that God is one of the many selves, though infinitely superior to others in many respects. They understand God in such a way that his infinity is not in any way jeopardized by the independence of others.

The Rāmānujists and Vedāntists of a few other schools, on the other hand, have preferred theism. The Rāmānujists hold that the individual selves, distinct from one another and from God, are all still adjectival to God, and believe that God and all these adjectival selves have formed one grand unity. Of this grand unity, God forms the central part—he is the substantive to which these selves, and the world, too, cling as adjectives. The Rāmānujists warn, however, that the relation between God, on the one hand, and the individual selves and the world, on the other, is no form of identity-in-difference. Much along the lines of the Nyāya-Vaiśeṣika, they hold that, if two things are identical, they cannot be different at the same time, and vice versa, though they admit at the same time that this does not preclude the possibility of these factors forming a unity. In the case, for example, of a man with a stick in his hand, the man and the stick, though each a distinct thing, have formed a unity, viz., the man-with-the-stick. Such unities may sometimes be very close (*apṛthaksiddhi,* inseparability), as in the case of a blue flower, where the flower and the blue color, each distinct from the other, form such a close system that it is impossible to divorce one of them from the other. The example of loose unity (*pṛthaksiddhi,* separability) is the man-with-the-stick. The unity that God and the individual selves have formed is a close one, according to the Rāmānujists. Often, indeed, Rāmānuja has compared the relation between God and individual selves with that between a master and his servants or that between a king and his subjects, or that between the soul and the body, etc., almost suggesting that the unity formed need not be a close one. But this is only a loose way of speaking. What he means is perhaps that God, the substantival part of the unity, could remain without reference to individual selves but never does remain so, his remaining alone being a mere possibility that never, even from the metaphysical point of view, can mature into actuality. With the Advaitist, on the other hand, this possibility indicates actual metaphysical transcendence.

The Vedāntists of some other schools, viz., the Bhāskarites and Nimbārkists, have argued, however, in favor of identity-in-difference. The notion of identity-in-difference has always troubled the Indian mind. Nyāya-Vaiśeṣika thinkers and the Rāmānujists have openly denounced it as self-contradictory, and those who have favored the concept have always had to defend their case. They have defended it in one of the three following ways:

(1) Logic cannot denounce what is, after all, a patent fact. Is not identity-in-difference evident in the cases of substance and its characters, material cause (stuff) and its effects (modes), parts and their whole, etc.?

If the Nyāya-Vaiśeṣika has, in such cases, proposed to replace identity-in-difference by what it calls inherence (*samavāya*), this is not merely a gratuitous complication of the issue; it involves another difficulty, viz., that the relation of this inherence with that to which something stands in that inherence relation goes unexplained. Rāmānuja's attempt to replace identity-in-difference by what he calls "unity of differents" is no less defective, for he, too, has faltered over clear cases like the relation between a substance and its attributes and could bypass the difficulty only by postulating the hasty notion of close unity (*apṛthaksiddhi*).

(2) Others, less defiant of the Law of Contradiction, have defended identity-in-difference by holding that the two things between which this relation holds are identical in one way (i.e., from one point of view) and different in another (i.e., from another point of view).

(3) The third way of defending identity-in-difference is to argue that, though ultimately (from the *pāramārthika*—ultimate—point of view) identity-in-difference is untenable (because self-contradictory), we in our daily life put up with it, which means that it has provisional, pragmatic (*vyāvahārika*) value.

The first of these three defenses was offered by the Bhāskarites and Nimbārkists, and, to some extent, by the Sāṁkhya. The second way of defense was advocated by the Mīmāṁsakas, and, again, sometimes by the Sāṁkhya. The third was the way of many Advaita thinkers.

The problem of plurality, or otherwise, of individuals and their relation to God or the Absolute is one that concerns only the essence of individuals, i.e., their selves. So long, however, as individuals are understood as body-self or body-mind-self complexes, there is no denial anywhere in Indian philosophy of their plurality and difference from God. Except in metaphysics, again, which concerns the essence of the individual, Indians have not generally underrated the status of the body and the mind. Full compliments are paid to these in *artha-śāstra* (economics and politics), *daṇḍa-nīti* (science of government), *āyur-veda* (medicine), *kāma-śāstra* (science of living and enjoyment), and different other *vidyās* (sciences and arts); and, though the philosophical ideal is always regarded as the highest for the individual, so much so that other ideals have been subordinated to it and placed in proper perspective, in actual life the average Indian has not been nearly so unbalancedly otherworldly as he is believed to be by people in the West. Regarding the philosophical ideal, again, there have been, as we have already seen and shall see more fully later, all kinds of views, of which the Advaita view is just one, and the average Indian's life has not been less influenced by any of these other views than by the Advaita. One must not forget also that materialism, which had for ages been dominant in India in some form or other, has always been a problem for all other Indian thinkers. As we have already said, there has never been *one* Indian view of the status of the individual, except in the sense stated on page one. The systems that have influenced Indian life most are Śaivism, Śāktism, and Vaiṣṇavism in their different forms, and they were mostly for the plurality of individuals and some significant difference somewhere between them and God (or the Absolute).[8]

IV. DOCTRINE OF INACTION AND ITS REFUTATION[9]

The only school of Indian philosophy that has preached inaction as the ultimate goal of life is the Advaita Vedānta, and undoubtedly this doctrine has had some influence on Indian life in general. But there are two points to be noted in this connection. First, no other system has preached this doctrine, and in the whole field of philosophical literature it has more often been opposed than supported. Second, even as the Advaita preaches it, there is always the prefatory warning that this inaction is only for those who have attained liberation. Until that liberation is attained, every man is called upon to perform moral and spiritual action, and it is clearly said in the Advaita that performance of such actions is a necessary prerequisite for earning the right (adhikāra) to inaction, so that the common charge against the Advaita that it has left no scope for morality and religion is so far unfounded.

If, in spite of all this, the doctrine of inaction has sometimes appealed to the lay Hindu public, this can be traced, in most cases, to political debacles. One cannot also deny altogether that, to some extent, the Advaita philosophy itself was responsible for that. It often extended the scope of inaction by prescribing it even for those who are on the path to liberation, not actually liberated. The esoteric exercises (sādhana) which they are to practice have often been designated as cognitive (jñāna-sādhana), as opposed to the performance of moral actions and the worship of God (karma-sādhana). If others have argued that sādhana itself cannot but be an action, the Advaita has gone to the length of saying that it is only a pseudo-action (uidhicchāyā), i.e., something which is really of the nature of cognition, though spoken of (perhaps necessarily) in terms of action. The Advaita idea is that the individual on the way to liberation is only to seek discovery of the Absolute, and discovery, or seeking discovery, is a cognitive affair.

Liberation is freedom from all bondage. The Advaita holds that freedom proper is found only in a knowledge situation which is, or at least tends to be, free from attachment, even to the ego. Knowledge of X is not primarily *I knowing* X; it is equivalent to *X is X* or *it is X*. This is true as much of reflective knowledge as of unreflective knowledge: the I that is evident in reflection is only another X— another object or a self-evident entity; and whatever of subjective I-feeling accompanies reflection—in the form *"I know X"*—and whatever still less might accompany even unreflective knowledge —is what, as unwanted in a cognitive situation, ought to disappear, according to the Advaita Vedānta. Of action, on the other hand, the subjective I-feeling is an integral factor. Action, almost by definition, is some agent acting. Action can never be impersonal; of its very nature it is egocentric; and, unlike what is desirable in cognition, there is no question of this egocentricity's disappearance. Hence, according to the Advaita philosopher, no action is free, and action cannot, therefore, belong to the essence of the individual.

The Advaita alone has held this view. No other system has subscribed to it in this extreme form. Very few of them have, it is true, denied that liberation is a stage of cognition in that the self as the essence of the individual comes to be discovered,[10] but none has said that it is nothing else. They hold that, besides cognitive freedom, there is freedom of action also. For them, therefore, there is no denial of the things of the world, for, in the absence of such things, no action is possible. Every action is some manipulation of things in the world, and free action, as we have seen, is only that type of manipulation which, as not proceeding through attachment (rāga) and repulsion (dveṣa), is not entirely determined by Nature. Free actions, actions, viz., which are moral and spiritual, are thus constructive and forward looking, not acts of mere withdrawal. The best representation of this view is found in the concept of action which is absolutely disinterested (niṣkāma-karma) in the Bhagavad-gītā. Śaṁkara's interpretation of this niṣkāma-karma as but a form of cognition does not appear to be convincing, and no other interpreter (unless he is an Advaitist) has understood it that way.

Indians speak of three approaches to liberation (mukti), viz., cognitive (the way of jñāna, i.e., knowledge), actional (the way of karma, i.e., action), and emotional (the way of bhakti, i.e., love, respect, etc.).[11]

Mukti attained in the cognitive way is only discovery (rediscovery) of the self as the essence of the individual, and beyond this discovery there is nothing else for the liberated individual to know or do. For one who attains mukti through karma, however, there is no cessation of action. He has indeed got entirely beyond the clutches of rāga and dveṣa, but he continues his niṣkāma-karmas, i.e., his duties and spiritual activities—actions, in other words, which are for the sake of duty only and also those which are meant for the well-being of others (including God and gods). In mukti attained by the way of emotion, on the other hand, the purified individual (the self) is placed in proper relation to God, and, through that, to other selves —purified or not. It is only in pure cognitive mukti that the question of the individual's relation to other individuals loses all meaning, the discovery of the self = the Absolute being the sole end. But in mukti attained in other ways there inevitably arises the problem of adjusting oneself to others.

A vital weakness of Indian philosophy should here be frankly admitted. Indian philosophers who advocate *mukti* through action or emotion have not discussed as systematically as they should have the problem of the relation of the liberated individual to other individuals, liberated or not, or, in the light of this, the relations that should bind unliberated individuals to one another. Even Advaita philosophers have manifested this weakness in another way. Normally they should not consider the relation of the liberated individual to other individuals. But sometimes, unable to avoid the problem, they have discussed whether one's own liberation only or others' too, should be the ideal of one's life.

In Indian philosophy this weakness has manifested itself in still another way. Most Indian systems[12] have, uncritically enough, combined all the three approaches. This synthetic view is called "*samuccaya-vāda.*" The weakness here lies in the fact that these systems, somehow conscious of some disparity between cognition, action, and emotion, have, instead of working it out, slurred over it and allowed the three approaches to combine without further ado. For, it is more than evident—and the Advaita and, to some extent, the Bengal Vaiṣṇavas already preferred to depend upon it—that the further one proceeds along the cognitive, the actional, or the emotional path, the further these three diverge: cognition, seeking to discover the self, looks more and more inward; action proceeds more and more outward; and emotion, unable to be at peace with either, alternates between the two. It is not without reason, therefore, that the Advaita doctrine of inaction—a necessary consequence of cognitive *mukti* —has found favor with a large section of educated Indians.

It is interesting to see, again, how with his extreme attitude even the Advaita philosopher has sometimes faltered. We have seen (page 53) how incongruously he has allowed action for the *jīvan-muktas.* His God (as distinct from *Brahman*) also, who is otherwise completely free, acts. He creates, sustains, and destroys the world.

True, according to the Advaita, God, as distinct from *Brahman,* has still retained cosmic nescience (*māyā*), though as wielded by him it cannot bind him; and the *jīvan-muktas,* similarly, we are told, have *māyā* still left in them. But, so far as *māyā* does not bind a self, and, if sometimes the self can behave as even its master, why need the Advaita thinker take so much trouble to get rid of this innocuous *māyā?* The heavens would not fall if even in its fullest freedom the self could retain *māyā* and use it.

The lack of interest on the part of non-Advaita philosophers to keep *jñāna* and *karma* as apart as they really are and their hasty theory of synthesis (*samuccaya*) have done one permanent mischief. It is that the intrinsic outwardness of *karma,* due to which the freer a *karma* is the more outward and encompassing it should be, has been overlooked, not merely by philosophers, but equally by the lay public, for whom the easy theory of *samuccaya* has had a natural appeal. The result is that the lay public, as much as the philosophers in India, has taken it almost for granted that the higher and freer our *karma* becomes the more inward it grows, the highest one being meditation on the self or God or both. *Karma* intended for *mukti* has thus been largely confused with *jñāna;* and the *karmas* that proceed outward—social, political, and moral actions—are not considered as spiritual, i.e., intrinsic to *mukti* (*antaraṅga-sādhana*). The only merit these *karmas* are said to have is that they prepare us —much as measured quantities of food and water do—for undertaking spiritual work. They are taken as extrinsic, though helpful, to spiritual action or liberation—they are called *vahiraṅga-sādhanas* (external discipline), as contrasted with *antaraṅga-sādhana* (internal discipline).

QUESTION: Why did you not consider the Buddhist and Jaina views of the metaphysical status of the individual?

ANSWER: Buddhism is to be considered in detail by others. I did not include Jainism because of space limit.

QUESTION: You say that the Advaita conception of the *jīvan-mukta* and God as absolutely free and yet acting is self-contradictory. But there is nothing of self-contradiction here. God and the *jīvan-mukta* are egoless individuals that are not yet wholly the Absolute (*Brahman*).

ANSWER: This is a possible interpretation. But the idea never occurred to me. Besides, we may discuss it when the questioner (Professor Murti) will himself elaborate the idea in his Conference paper (in Section III).

QUESTION: Is not your use of the term "Absolute" on different occasions in your paper ambiguous?

ANSWER: I believe I have throughout used the term "Absolute" in one sense, viz., in the Advaita sense of *Brahman*. If I have used it in any other sense, it was unintentional. I have always meant that the Absolute is in an important sense different from God, though I have pointed out that with Indian philosophers God, even falling short of the Hegelian Absolute, is omnipotent, omniscient, etc.

QUESTION: You say that there are different views of the status of the individual in the different systems of Indian philosophy and that none of these systems is of less importance in the general Indian life than the Advaita Vedānta. But why, then, is it so widely held in the West that the Advaita Vedānta is the quintessence of philosophic speculation in India?

ANSWER: Four things are responsible for this wrong impression. They are:

1. Modern Indian monks of the Advaita school and some modern Indian philosophical writers have somehow popularized this wrong notion. Of course, the Advaita Vedānta is one of the finest systems of philosophy, but in India there are other systems also, not all of them less important than the Advaita Vedānta.

2. It is often believed, even by many Indians, that the spiritual side of man is the monopoly of the Advaita Vedānta. They have not noted that, except for the Cārvāka, every other system has studied the spiritual side, and in many of these other systems this spiritual side is the dominant topic throughout.

3. Historically, it is Śaṁkara who completely broke the dominance of Buddhism in India and from his time Buddhism has practically ceased to be a living system in India. Śaṁkara is practically the father of systematic Advaita Vedānta. Naturally, the general mass of the Indian people were persuaded to believe that the only dominant system after the disappearance of Buddhism was the Advaita Vedānta. Add to this another historical fact: Madhusūdana Sarasvatī, in his many works, particularly in the *Advaita-siddhi,* almost successfully (for the time being) refuted all the charges that had been brought against the Advaita Vedānta by the dualist Mādhvas, the Vaiśeṣikas, and others. This certainly lent support to the then popular view that the most dominant, if not the only working, system in India was the Advaita Vedānta. But we, in the twentieth century, cannot ignore the fact that, except for Buddhism (and probably also the Sāṁkhya), other systems were then continuing as before and continued for some centuries after that, and there were always large sections of the people attaching themselves to these schools.

4. All the orthodox Indian systems claim descent from the Upaniṣads, and the Upaniṣads are called *"Vedānta."* This naturally confused the Western mind, which thought that therefore all Indian systems are Vedāntic. There was another confusion, even in the minds of Western-educated Indians, viz., that the Advaita was the only form of Vedānta. It is time now to tell Westerners in unambiguous terms (a) that the Upaniṣads, *technically* called "Vedānta," need not be Vedānta in the sense in which other Vedāntic systems are, and (b) that, even inside the Vedāntic fold, there are various (at least six major) sub-schools, often sharply opposed to one another. We should also tell Westerners (1) that, though some major Upaniṣads definitely speak in the Advaita strain, there are other Upaniṣads (and some of them are equally major) which speak either in a full-dualist or half-dualist trend, and (2) that the regular systems of philosophy other than the Advaita Vedānta have interpreted even the apparently monistic statements in the Upaniṣads in their own ways quite as much as the Advaita Vedāntists have interpreted their apparent dualistic (pluralistic) statements in their own way.

QUESTION: The concept of freedom of will has undergone many changes and different formulations in the West. Has there been any such thing in India?

ANSWER: No. The problem of freedom of will has never been systematically discussed in Indian philosophy.

QUESTION: Free will cannot keep itself detached from Nature. It requires involvement. How, then, can you say that freedom is detachment from Nature?

ANSWER: There are both detachment and involvement. There is involvement insofar as free will is, after all, will or action, and there can be no action unless one manipulates a given situation and thus gets involved in it. However, the manipulation is free: a free individual does not manipulate the situation as a sub-human animal does. Behind the entire manipulation there is an attitude of detachment, i.e., the manipulation is not for any personal gain or loss, but just because it is duty.

QUESTION: Is there any emotional involvement in free manipulation?

ANSWER: No, except for one type of emotion, viz., respect for morality or spirit (as in Kant).

QUESTION: *Sāttvika* action is, after all, a part of Nature. How, then, can it be free or over-natural?

ANSWER: It is natural insofar as there is manipulation of items of Nature, but it is over-natural in that it is still free, and between this naturality and over-naturality there is no contradiction. Indeed, over-naturality is some sort of shadow (symbolic representation) in Nature, of the ultimate freedom, which is *mokṣa*.

Or, much as Kant, in his *Religion Within the Limits of Reason,* spoke of a diabolical tendency of the Practical Reason (which in itself is good) to act wrongly, we, in the same way (though in the reverse direction) may speak of an over-natural tendency in Nature (which in itself is only Nature).

QUESTION: Though in his *Critique of Practical Reason* Kant spoke of the Categorical Imperative as detachment from Nature, in his *Perpetual Peace* he regarded good action as the very movement of Nature.

ANSWER: Yes, but when I referred to Kant in my paper I had in mind the Kant of the Second Critique; and, further, I have not altogether denied that there is a movement in Nature toward the good.

QUESTION: What would be the difficulty if the idea of *cognitive liberation* could be rejected altogether in favor of that type of liberation in which the liberated individual goes on acting and acting for the good of the world? At least, that is the dominant Chinese view.

ANSWER: Yes, that is the dominant Chinese view. It is also the dominant Western view. Some Indians, too, have held this view. Yet, the very idea of cognitive freedom is an expression of the typical Indian attitude. While Chinese and Westerners are generally in the attitude of assertion, speaking, motion, and action, the general Indian preference is for provisional submission in listening to others and for seeking peace and stability. These are guaranteed most in cognitive liberation, and few Indian philosophers are against cognitive freedom; only, many of them have *added* action and emotion at the stage of liberation. Submission and listening have not, however, meant blind submission and lethargy in speaking out. They have always prescribed rigorous ratiocination after listening, and, after that, seeing things for oneself. It is in ratiocination and seeing for oneself that there are the elements of assertion and speaking.

QUESTION: Wisdom in the East consists in merging oneself in the great ineffable distinctionless Absolute, whereas Western wisdom lies in differentiating all that can be differentiated. Is this not correct?

ANSWER: I do not agree. I do not like to say anything positively regarding the Western attitude, but what you are saying regarding the Eastern attitude (and by "Eastern" you obviously mean here "Indian") is true only of the attitude of the Advaita Vedāntist. But, even there, the Advaita Vedāntist is never against differentiation in the daily work-a-day life, indeed at any stage prior to liberation, though certainly unity is considered as of more importance than the distinct entities. No other Indian system of philosophy has spoken for elimination of distinctions even at the highest stage, and none has attached more importance to unity than to the distinct entities.

But there is one point in your favor, though that, too, has to be accepted with a good deal of salt. It is in the socio-political life that the Indians have generally subordinated individuals to an over-all socio-political pattern, and to such an extent that it has often amounted to a virtual elimination of individuals. All this is true, but at the same time there have been great and small socio-political reforms at different times, and these were mostly worked out by certain individuals—the heroes of different ages. The idea is that individuals were given the right to assert only after they had acquired that right. Individuals in general were constantly reminded of their limitations, and they were therefore asked to submit to the rules framed by great men. But this does not mean that they were prevented from developing themselves, training themselves, and thereby earning the right to be great men and legislate. This was a unique type of reconciliation of the individual with an over-all unity, though there is seldom anything of this type of reconciliation in their metaphysics. (It may be noted in this connection that, even in ancient days, in some parts of India there were democracies in the literal sense of the term, as, for example, in the eastern part of India.)

QUESTION: How was it possible for India to keep so many different views in peaceful coexistence?

ANSWER: These different views—sometimes exactly opposite to one another—have generally for ages continued in peaceful coexistence (though this does not mean that clashes or syntheses have not taken place). It is the peculiar genius of the Hindus that made this possible. Hindus form a loose family in which the only tie is that they recognize they belong to one grand family. The entire Hindu people is like a big oak tree with its many branches and roots, with birds and reptiles and insects having permanent residence there or just coming there occasionally and perching or crawling over the trunk and branches, and even with travelers taking shelter in its expansive shade—all a loose but a very living unity. Thus, a large number of groups belong to the Hindu fold; and, though the rules for living may be rigid for each group, there are no strict rules—or only a handful—to bind the different groups together. The most living principle that cements them is simply the consciousness that they belong to the grand Hindu fold. This is as much true of the socio-political life of the Hindus through all ages as of their systems of philosophy.

QUESTION: You have distinguished among the knowledge-way, the action-way, and the emotion-way to liberation. You have said that the more one goes up one way the more it is found that it diverges from the other two ways. But why?

ANSWER: I have stated in my paper that, as the knowledge-way means discovery (or rediscovery) of the self, it is necessarily in the inward direction—toward the self—and that the action-way as manipulating things of Nature is necessarily in an outward direction, etc. This is the type of divergence I meant.

QUESTION: But is the knowledge-way necessarily an inward attitude? What, for example, would be the case with knowledge of this table before me?

ANSWER: Knowledge of this table is certainly not an inward attitude; it is clearly an outward attitude.

QUESTION: Do you hold, then, that knowledge may be inward in some cases and outward in other cases? If so, what would be the feature common to the two types of knowledge? And how would you distinguish between knowledge and will?

ANSWER: Yes, knowledge may be inward or outward, as the case may be. The common feature of knowledge is twofold: (1) In knowledge there is always the desired elimination of egocentricity, which elimination is neither possible nor desirable in will, and (2) knowledge is distinguishment—whatever is known is distinguished in itself and from other things.

1 It is because of this over-natural status that man can, in theoretical pursuit, question why Nature behaves as it does and can certify or reject what it offers and thus build science and philosophy.

2 This is mainly the Sāṁkhya doctrine. We find it discussed in the *Gītā*, in Vyāsa's Commentary on the *Yoga-sūtra*, and also in the sub-commentaries on Vyāsa's Commentary.

3 Except in the Cārvāka system, which is frankly materialistic, and also in the Nyāya and the Vaiśeṣika, which never took an interest in these details.

4 The self is distinguished from the mind on the ground that it can keep itself dissociated from certain states and affairs which clearly belong to the mind. For example, one may very deliberately keep oneself undisturbed by insults and worries even while these, as mental affairs, are actually taking place in the mind, quite as much as one may calmly tolerate physical torture.

5 With the exception of a few Śaivas and Grammarians.

6 The famous Sāṁkhya argument to which others have also subscribed, viz., that, if there were only one self for all individuals (*jīvas*), then with the birth or death of one individual other individuals would also be born or die, or that, if one individual were deaf or lame, others, too, would have the same lot, is either pointing to the simple truth that, like individuals, their selves, too, are many, or arguing to its plurality from the *sākṣin*hood of the selves.

7 Severance not as in death. For, according to Indians, death is not the end of the self's journey. There are repeated births and deaths. Hence, severance of all connections means such absolute severance as is calculated to prevent further birth. Again, most Indian thinkers hold that, though an individual is completely liberated, he, even after death, remains with a subtle body which, in complete liberation, is almost a permanent appendage around which different grosser and grosser elements accumulate to form grosser and grosser bodies.

8 Kashmir Śaivism, however, developed along Advaita lines. Indian life was largely influenced by Buddhism also (and probably by Jainism, too), and, though later Buddhism practically disappeared from India, many Buddhist concepts have, in disguise, continued in the Yoga, Śaivism, and Śāktism, and some add, in the Advaita Vedānta also.

9 This section is in answer to the third objection by Westerners to the Indian view of the individual cited at the beginning of this paper.

10 A few schools of Bengal Vaiṣṇavism deny even this. They have denounced cognition as having anything to do with liberation and have relied mainly on sublimated emotion and, secondarily, on good action.

11 The monism of the Advaita Vedānta can be understood only from the point of view of *jñāna-mārga*, and not from the point of view of *karma-mārga* or *bhakti-mārga*. In order to explain this, I here discuss the three *mārgas* and show how those who acknowledge *karma-mārga* or *bhakti-mārga*, with or without *jñāna-mārga*, have been compelled to vote for plurality.

12 With the exception of the Advaita Vedānta and the extreme Vaiṣṇava systems in Bengal already referred to.

G. P. MALALASEKERA

The status of the individual
in Theravāda Buddhist philosophy

One of the most significant features of Buddhism is that its founder, the Buddha, was a man—an extraordinary one, it is true—and died as a man. Everything about him was unequivocally within the domain of Nature. What he had done, every other human being could do also, if he chose to do so and was prepared to make the requisite effort. The whole drama of salvation, as depicted by the Buddha, takes place on this earth, on the stage of life as lived in this world. "Within this fathom-long body," he declared, "are the world and the origin of the world, and the ceasing of the world, and the path leading to its cessation." The world in which the problem is posed and in which the solution is found is none other than the familiar, everyday world, in which our mortal life completes its brief span. To the Buddha, the world is the scene of human endeavor; the significance that attaches to things derives from the meaning of human life. What is man, and what should he make of his life in this world so as to achieve the supreme value that life affords? These are the problems which the Buddha set himself to solve and to which he found the answer.

The Buddha was a ceaseless searcher for the truth about things as they really are. It was this intense desire to find out the truth that drove him from his father's palace, where the indulgence of luxury gave him no peace, to undertake the most austere penances that imagination could conceive. When these, too, failed to give him satisfaction, he turned his mental eye inward, resolved to find therein, in the depths of his own being, that which the outer world had denied him. He had the daring to demand to know of life itself its right to exist. Truthfulness toward oneself, seriousness of search regardless of consequences, an unfailing sense of reality—these were the qualities which brought an end to his quest, the discovery which became for him a unique teaching.

This teaching he gave to the world as a way of life, telling men and women how they should employ this existence in order to achieve supreme happiness. But he recognized that the question of how cannot be satisfactorily answered without a knowledge of the what—the question, What am I? I must know what I am and what are the things and beings outside me. I must learn my relation to the external world. I must apprehend the meaning and significance of life before I can possess a genuine canon and standard for my behavior, for my morality. It is only in virtue of conscious cognition that any act, whether it be in doing or in leaving undone, acquires moral value. There can be no real morality without comprehension, without, in fact, a world conception.

Now, the essence of all cognition is the individual. Every act of cognition is always something individual, personal, pertaining to me alone. Even were all men to cognize alike, the content of the cognition would still be the possession of each and every single person. Thus cognition separates. The realization of this fact in its ultimate sense is in Buddhism called wisdom or insight (*paññā*), the understanding of reality (*tathatā*), i.e., that which it is, a fact.

But, besides cognition, there is another function of human nature which can be summarized as emotion. Considered from this point of view, morality, the good life, is founded upon the right feeling of correlation which finds expression in our attitudes toward others. Its proper cultivation is made manifest in every form of compassion, the instinctive feeling of kinship and identity with all who live and breathe, the perfection of compassion (*karuṇā*). These two qualities, wisdom and compassion, are in Buddhism complementary, and their perfection culminates in enlightenment (*bodhi*), whose embodiment is the Buddha, the Enlightened or Awakened One.

An individual is a being, i.e., something that is, but, in the Buddha's teaching, the individual's being is, in fact, a *becoming*, a coming-to-be, something that happens, i.e., an event, a process. And, whenever there is process, whenever anything happens, there must be adequate cause for it to happen. It is in order to explain the adequate cause that the Buddha formulated his teaching of *kamma* (action), the law of cause and effect. And, since in the Buddha's philosophy every cause is itself the effect of an anterior, prior cause and comes to be only in dependence upon such anterior cause, the Buddha further expanded his teaching of *kamma* into what is known as the doctrine of dependent origination, or conditioned simultaneous arising (*paticca-samuppāda*).

Buddhism includes all things that exist under one term, "*sankhāra*," a term considered the epistemological key word of its philosophy. It means that which is compounded or conditioned, also the compounding and conditioning. All *sankhāras* are processes, divided into two categories, the living and the dead. The living processes are maintained, while the living maintain themselves. Every process which we call existence can be analyzed into the elements of which it is composed, such elements being given the name of *dhammas*, which etymologically means that which has or "bears" certain qualities. Nothing exists apart from *dhammas*.

In this analysis, the human being was found to consist of two parts, *rūpa* and *nāma,* loosely translated as corporeality (matter) and mind, *rūpa* representing the physical elements and *nāma* the mental ones. Matter is composed of the four "elementary" qualities of extension, cohesion, caloricity (temperature), and vibration. The mental elements are similarly divided into four groups: feelings, sensations, or "receptions" (*vedanās*); "perceptions" or ideas (*saññās*); "mental activities," "complexes," "confections," "discriminations," (*sankhāras*); and cognitions, "conceptions," consciousnesses, (*viññānas*). Matter (*rūpa*) and these four divisions of mind (*nāma*) are never found singly but only in conglomerations or aggregates (*khandhas*).

The five aggregates together constitute what is called the "I" or "personality" or the "individual." The aggregates are not parts or pieces of the individual but phases or forms of development, something like the shape, color, and smell of a flower. Even the sense-organs and the organs of the body are likewise really forms of development or manifestations, since they all originate from one common source. There is no "stuff" or substratum as such but only manifestations, energies, activities, processes. In Buddhist thought, to speak of matter as apart from energy would be like speaking of one side of a sheet of paper imagined by itself.

Every living being, since it is a process, is described as a flux, a flowing, a stretching forth, a continuity (*santāna*), or, more frequently, as a combustion, a flame. There is no "substance," no "self" or "soul," underlying the process, unifying it. What we call the "I" or the "personality" or the individual, whatever appears to be unitary, is in reality not an entity but a function. It is like a burning flame in which one may distinguish a number of layers of color, but these layers are not parts laid out after the fashion of pieces in a mosaic, alongside one another. They are a continuity of changes. So, also, with the five *khandhas;* they are a continuous, unbroken process of action, of which it is expressly said that they constitute a burning. In all of them an arising and a passing away are to be cognized; they are forms of action, processes of mental-corporeal "nutrition" or "sustenance" in which the corporeal as well as the mental forms of grasping (*upādāna*) fall together into one conceptual unity. A fire can burn only as long as it lays hold of new fuel; so, also, the process of individuality is a constant arising, an ever-renewed laying hold, a grasping, of the objects of its attachment.

In theistic religions, every living being exists by virtue of the manifestation in him of a universal force, as a transcendent, an Absolute, called God or *Brahman.* In Buddhism, every living being exists by virtue of an individual force, peculiar to him alone. This force is called by the Buddha the *kamma* of each living being. *Kamma* means action, working, activity. It is, in quite a literal sense, an in-force, an energy, by virtue of which a living being manifests activity after its own unique fashion, and in its own unique way reacts upon the external world, thus making him an individuality, a personality. Every living being is a singly determined existence. He is unique by virtue of his actions, his *kammas*. His *kamma* exists, possesses being, solely in dependence upon its material. In the case of *kamma,* the relevant materials are the *khandhas,* or aggregates, already described.

In every moment of the process which is called life or existence, I am the force of *kamma* itself, wholly and entirely the embodiment of my *kammas,* my actions of body, speech, and mind. There is no being, no enduring substantial self or soul, beyond and beneath these happenings, these activities, which constitute my experience. The teaching of "becoming" is the principle which the Buddha emphasized from the very start. He taught a phenomenalistic philosophy very much like that which more than twenty centuries later David Hume expressed in almost identical terms: "I never can catch myself at any time without a perception and never can observe anything but the perception. . . . What we call mind is nothing but a heap or bundle of different perceptions united together by certain relations."[1] There is no enduring entity, no "constant" derived from some external source, but only out-and-out processes constantly in motion, representing at every moment of their existence a fresh biological value. As in a flame there is nothing hidden or concealed, its activity constituting its entire being, so in the I-process there is nothing concealed, nothing standing behind it, no "sub-stance." Its activity constitutes its entire being and this activity in its entirety is disclosed in consciousness to the individual himself and to him only.

Generally speaking, things are so constituted that with them concept and object are separable; it is possible to manipulate the concept apart from the object. But, there is one thing in the world in which, according to Buddhism, no such separation is possible—I myself. That which I conceive myself as, that even I myself am, and every attempt to form a concept is just a form of myself. I myself am the unique, pure reality of the world. This is the basis of the whole teaching of "no-soul" (*anattā*) in Buddhism.

Existence is action itself, in process. Action (*kamma*) is that which gives to the process its coherence and its continuity. As such, it presents itself to me, the individual, as consciousness. Consciousness, however, is not *kamma,* but *kamma* in the course of its self-acting development becomes consciousness. Consciousness is the ultimate value in which at every moment of its existence the form of the energy and the energy itself merge and mingle. Consequently, it is that which gives to the I-process not only conceptual but also actual continuity. It is in this sense that the Buddha says, in one context, that *cetanā* (thinking or consciousness) is *kamma* (action), and *kamma* is *cetanā*. It is in this sense also that the often-recurring formula has to be understood: "In dependence upon individuality (*nāma-rūpa*) arises consciousness (*viññana*); in dependence upon consciousness arises individuality."[2]

The I-process in all its activities, corporeal and mental, is a constant growing-up of life itself, an arising and a perpetual refreshing. It is a self-charging process. In a flame, each moment of its existence represents a specific degree of heat which is the power to set up a succeeding moment of ignition. This continues for as long as inflammable matter, fuel, continues. With the calling into life of a new ignition-moment a new degree of heat is produced which passes anew into living energy, thus forming a repetition of the whole procedure.

The process of life in an individual is likewise a self-sustaining process. *Kamma* (action) does not have to receive an impetus from outside to come into activity; it is activity itself. *Kamma* does not, like a cord of some solid substance, thread itself through this process, constituting what might be called a soul, any more than the lightning in the firmament has a cord to join the flashes together. In life, there is no I that experiences, no I that thinks, speaks, does. I do not have these as my functions, but this doing, speaking, thinking, itself I am. Buddhism does not deny the existence of a personality or a "soul" in the empirical self. What it does deny is a permanent individuality, an unchanging "self." A man's personality is at any given moment a fact (*sacca*), but it does not correspond to any fixed entity in man, something that persists while all else changes. In Buddhism, to be real does not mean to be permanent in that sense.

It is the thirst for life, the craving for it, which upholds life, causing it again and again to spring up anew, and which is life itself. In the flame, it is the heat of the flame which upholds the flame and is the flame itself. This thirst for life (*tanhā*) manifests itself as clinging or grasping (*upādāna*). "Personality, they say. But what does the Exalted One say the person is?" To which the answer is given: "The fivefold form of clinging is the personality, the Exalted One has said—the clinging to body, to sensations, to perceptions, to mental activities, to consciousness." And, when asked how this personality arises, the answer is, "The thirst for life that leads to rebirth, bound up with lust and craving, now here, now there, reveling in delight. This, the Exalted One has said, is the arising of personality."

Thus, in every moment of my life I myself fashion the next

moment with the present life and the life that shall follow it. I am, and I become, in the most literal sense, the architect of my own fate, of my destiny. "The self is Lord of the self, who else is the Lord?"[3] Every individual is a thing unique by virtue of his actions and the result of these actions.

What happens at the death of an individual? In Buddhism, death is nothing but living in a new environment. Whenever an existence disintegrates, the *kamma,* by virtue of which it has been "burning," takes hold anew in a new location, and there sets alight a new I-process that unfolds itself into a new personality which is neither the same as the old one nor yet another but is a continuance from which both absolute diversity and absolute identity are excluded. As fuel is necessary for the flame, so a new existence needs new "fuel." What is the "fuel" when the flame is carried by the wind? The wind itself, says the Buddha. When a being leaves one body and arises in another, so to speak, the "fuel" is the craving for life itself.[4] As the igniting spark becomes the flame by developing itself, so does *kamma* become the new form of existence.

This continuance is, again, a unique process in the case of each individual. The fact of my birth derives, not from parents or from God, but from my own previous dying. Dying is nothing but a backward view of birth, and birth nothing but a forward view of death. I take rise in my parents only in the same sense as the fountain takes its rise in the hill. Heirs of deeds, the Buddha calls living beings, not heirs of father and mother. They spring from the womb of *kamma.* At every moment of my existence I am the final member of a beginningless series in a self-sustaining process. "A world without end is this round of birth and death," says the Buddha. "No beginning can be seen of those beings hindered by ignorance, bound by craving, running the round of birth and death."

Such a process can never have a beginning, because then it would not be a self-sustaining thing but a product of something else. To seek a beginning of life is like chasing after a horizon which ever recedes. But, can we say there is a first beginning to life? Yes, in the same way as we can say the spring welling from the rock is the first beginning of the river. It is the first beginning when one objectifies the river as an identity. It should sound no more strange to say that life is beginningless than to say, as all theistic religions do, that God is beginningless.

Every single moment of existence is something unique. It is a mathematical instant (*khaṇa*), the moment of an action's efficiency. Although the moments that constitute an individual's life are not connected with each other by any pervading stuff, there is, nevertheless, as has already been shown, a connection between them. It is the fact that their manifestations are subject to definite laws, the laws of causation. The flow of life is not a haphazard process. Every single moment in it is a "dependently-originating" moment, i.e., it depends for its origin on the moment that precedes it. Thus, existence becomes dependent existence and is expressed by the formula, "If there is this, there comes to be that."[5] Strictly speaking, there is no causality at all, no production of one from the other. The relation is one of "consecution," in which there is no destruction of one thing and no creation of another, no influx of one substance into another, but only a constant, uninterrupted, infinitely graduated change. In the case of each individual, his individuality persists, and he is a separate personality, his separateness consisting in the individualism of the sequence of his *kamma*—causation.

Discrimination between individuals is recognized by the Buddha when he says: "And I saw, looking at the world with the awakened eye, beings of noble kind and of common kind, acute of mind and obtuse of mind, well endowed and ill endowed, quick to understand and slow to understand. . . ." And he goes on: "It is like some lotus flowers which grow in deep, muddy water, while others push up toward the surface of the water, and yet others emerge from the water and stand up free from the water."[6]

One of the Buddhist texts is called *Puggala-paññatti* (Designation of Human Types) and deals with the various types of individuals that exist in the world. But such discrimination is between different natures, on the basis of achievement and spiritual development, and not on such adventitious things as caste or class. "Not by birth does one become noble or lowly but by actions" was the Buddha's "lion roar."[7]

Not only is man his own master and the master of his fate and destiny, but, in his capacity for attaining the highest spiritual development, that of enlightenment, man is higher than even the gods. It is his sole responsibility to work out his own emancipation from the fetters that bind him. This life has value in itself, independently of any life hereafter or even a belief in it, because it is as a human being in this world that *nibbāna*, the Buddhist goal of supreme happiness, can be won. No man is so debased that he is beyond redemption. Well known is the story of the brigand Angulimāla, who, having committed ninety-nine murders, met the Buddha while on his way to kill his own mother. The Buddha rescued him from his evil ways, and Angulimāla became an *arahant*, a perfect saint, and one of the most famous of the Buddha's disciples. The Buddha, in judging human individuals capable of realizing a perfected humanity, independent of any transcendental outlook, raised life to a very high value. It is the qualitative estimate of life, however, that is emphasized, the life of individuals ever lifting the world to higher insights and nobler issues.

The world into which we are born as individuals is, according to Buddhism, a world full of *dukkha*. *"Dukkha"* is most frequently but misleadingly translated as pain, sorrow, suffering, misery, the opposite of well-being. It is true that there is a very great deal of unhappiness in the world, and that fact has to be accepted by everyone. But the Buddhist conception of *dukkha* involves more than mere suffering and pain. It involves also the element of imperfection, the incompleteness that life exhibits, the conflict between our wishes and our attainments. It is not merely the intermittent frustration of our desires but a quality permeating experience even for the most fortunate of us, the sense of our alienation from the world, what some call "anguish" and what Thoreau describes as "quiet desperation."

But, in accordance with the law of cause and effect, enunciated by the Buddha as a universal principle, *dukkha,* too, has a cause which can be controlled and ultimately eliminated. The cause of *dukkha* is called *tanhā,* generally, but wrongly, translated as desire. *Tanhā* is, rather, what might be called thirst, the craving of the limited, individual, living creature seeking to gratify itself in its separateness and to use the external world as a means to satisfy its self-centered needs. The evil in man's life is man-made, and, therefore, eradicable by man, without outside interference. In Buddhism, there is no such thing as original sin, no innate depravity, and no one is foreordained to be doomed. There is, likewise, no atonement and no forgiveness of sins, because there is no one who can forgive, and because a transgression, once committed, cannot be redeemed. Every cause has its inevitable effect; all we can do is to find out and understand the cause and take steps to remove it, if we want it removed.

The morality of Buddhism consists of the path described by the Buddha. The individual, however, is completely free to follow whatever path he chooses. The Buddha claims no monopoly as guide; he is only a *kaliyāna-mitta* (good friend) to those who seek his advice and are willing to profit by his experience. The need of the four freedoms for human happiness was recognized by the Buddha many centuries before the Atlantic Charter. Freedom of worship, freedom to question the efficacy of any dogma whatsoever, should be a basic human right. He called his own teaching the "come-and-see" doctrine, the teaching which invites investigation before approval. Hence the absence of religious persecution in Buddhist lands. A man should also be free to speak his thoughts, provided his speech is free from hatred and slander, truthful, in proper time and place, and likely to be of profit to himself or to others or to both.

Fear, according to the Buddha, results from the feeling of bondage. Freedom is every man's birthright, freedom from bondage both physical and spiritual. The whole purpose of the Buddha's teaching is, according to him, to teach men how to be free, perfectly, supremely free, in every conceivable way. "Even as the great ocean has but one taste, the taste of salt, so has this doctrine and discipline but one taste, the taste of freedom."[8] The injunction everywhere is for men and women to "get free."

The Buddha was a great believer in democracy. The Order of Monks which he founded is the oldest democratic institution in the world. Every decision taken therein is guided by the votes of those present. No one can be made to suffer a penalty for any offense, even after he is found guilty by a committee of his peers, unless the offender admits his guilt of his own free will. In the Order, the Buddha claimed no greater privilege than was voluntarily afforded to him as teacher. When the time came for him to leave this life, he stoutly refused to appoint a successor, leaving it to the monks themselves to choose their own head, if they so desired.

What does Buddhism have to say regarding free will? The question does not seem ever to have been asked of the Buddha, but, if he had been asked, he would probably have answered that the question does not arise or that it is inaccurately put. There can be no such thing as a free will outside the causal sequence which constitutes the world process. All that can be said in this connection is to ask, when an individual acts, does he do so through deliberate choice or through whim or caprice? Our actions are generally impulsive; desires are often immediately translated into deeds without a thought of the implications involved. What the Buddha would have us do is to act with mindfulness, analyzing motives before allowing them to influence conduct, thus allowing an interval of inactivity between thought and deed, intention and execution. The cultivation of this quality of awareness (*sati*) is one of the basic principles of Buddhist meditation. It is freedom of choice which such awareness will help to achieve that makes us free and enables us to achieve emancipation from all bondage. Self-discipline and mindfulness are the virtues that give to an individual confidence, dignity, and decorum and make him a true nobleman (*ariya*).

Though every individual is, in Buddhism, a unique phenomenon, no individual can be an island unto himself in the sense that he can exist alone, without being a member of the human community. The very word *"kula-putta,"* clansman, used to indicate the layman, is an acknowledgment of this fact. There are four basic needs which have to be supplied for anyone to have even the barest minimum necessary for existence: clothing, food, shelter, and medicine. In normal life, these can be obtained only through communal living. Even the ascetic, living far away from the haunts of men, like the "lone-dwelling rhinoceros," has occasionally to visit human habitation in search of salt and acid foods.

Because of this essential dependence on society, the individual develops social relationships and obligations which he has to honor and satisfy. But, because society is nothing apart from the individuals who constitute it, society has its obligations to the individual, too. Six such mutual relationships are specifically mentioned in a discourse of the Buddha. They are the relationships between parents and children, between the educator and the educated, between husband and wife, between friends, relatives, and neighbors, between employer and employee, between the religious and the laity. To give but one example of such a relationship—that between husband and wife: the husband should always honor his wife and never be wanting in respect to her; he should love her and be faithful to her; he should secure her a dignified position and a comfortable life. The wife, in her turn, should supervise and look after household affairs; she should entertain guests, visitors, friends, relatives, and employees; she should love her husband and be faithful to him; she should protect his interests and safeguard his welfare; she should be skilled and energetic in all her activities. Love between husband and wife is called *"sadāra brahme cariya,"* sacred family life, such a relationship being considered almost religious or sacred.

It should be mentioned in passing that in a truly Buddhist society, though a husband, as head of the household, has certain privileges, there is no discrimination between men and women. There has never been any system of seclusion of women in Buddhist lands. The Buddha declared that what a man can do a woman can do equally well, sometimes even better.[9]

The individual is told that in his actions he should always be mindful of their effects on those around him. Happiness, declares the Buddha, can never be the result of selfishness. "Work for the welfare both of yourself and of others" (*ubhinnam attham caratha*) is a constantly recurring theme. Basic morality consists in abstaining from five wrong actions: killing and hurting life, theft, wrong indulgence in sensual pleasures, speech that is false or otherwise wrong, and intoxicants and drugs that cause heedlessness. All these things are considered evil because of the harm they do, not only to oneself, but also to others. Abstinence from them is called observance of the Five Precepts. This is regarded as the minimum requirement of the good life. The first precept deals with the sanctity of life, both one's own and that of others. The second precept enjoins due regard for the rights of others, with regard to both their property and everything else that is rightfully theirs. The third is to prevent men, not only from overindulgence, but also from being a burden on society by appropriating more than their proper share of the good things of life. The fourth precept calls for the maintenance of trust and confidence and good relationships with others. The fifth is, among other things, to prevent oneself from being a nuisance to others.

Because one has to depend on the community of fellow men for one's welfare, the debt one incurs thereby is immense. The only way of repaying it is by service to humanity. This is a duty enjoined on monk and layman alike. The monk discharges this duty by being an exemplar of the good life and acting as counselor and friend in solving human problems, the layman in various other ways open to him. The good man's life should be a life of dedication, both to himself and to others. When, soon after the Buddha's enlightenment, the Great Brahmā appeared before him to salute him and sing his praises, among the things he said was that the Buddha could now consider himself as being completely free from his "debt" to the world. The path to this "debtlessness" has to be trodden for a long time with unceasing earnest effort. It is not a path already created for someone to tread on. Each step has to be created by the traveler by his own treading.

Religion has sometimes been defined as an estimate of human life based on a hypothesis and suffused by an aspiration. What, then, in Buddhism, is the aspiration of the individual? The ultimate goal of the good life is supreme happiness, to be achieved here on this earth, in this human life, and not after death in some faraway heaven. This goal is called *nibbāna*.

"*Nibbāna*" literally means ceasing to be, extinction, like the blowing out of a candle. Extinction it undoubtedly is, of the fires of lust, hatred, infatuation, and all other passions and torments: what is extinguished is selfish desire and the craving for and the need of continued rebirth. But it does not mean either a state of escape from the unbearable sorrows of life into nothingness or sheer annihilation. It includes the realization that one has achieved an ardently sought emancipation, a hitherto unexperienced freedom. It is a conscious, positive experience, having in it the qualities of peace, joy, insight, and love. The freedom and the joy come from the realization that all bondage has been destroyed. The insight comes from the true understanding of reality made possible by the destruction of cramping desires and attachments. The love is the free and compassionate outpouring of ourselves to others without asking anything in return, an all-embracing love that knows no bounds, love for "all the universe in all its heights and depths and breadth," free from all possessiveness and making no demands on the person or object that is loved, a loving oneness with others with the releasing joy that it brings.[10]

The individual who has attained *nibbāna* is described as "*brahma-*

bhūta" become divine or one with the highest (God) and *"dhamma-bhūta,"* one with the Absolute or with Actuality.[11] *Nibbāna* is the only thing which is not a *sankhāra,* a compound, a complex of elements. It is, therefore, the only thing that is unchangeable and eternal. It is, however, a *dhamma,* and, since the old formula says all *dhammas* are devoid of self (*sabbe-dhammā-anatta*), there is no abiding self either.

What happens to the individual who has attained *nibbāna* when he dies and his body is cremated? He is described as having gone into *pari-nibbāna,* i.e., *nibbāna* without any residue whatsoever of the *khandas,* the aggregates. *Pari-nibbāna* is *nibbāna* without corporeality, the transition of sorrowlessness into timelessness, changelessness, perfect peace. While *nibbāna* is still colored by the last dregs of individuality, *pari-nibbāna* is not so besmirched. It is a condition "where there is neither arising, nor passing away, nor dying; neither cause nor effect; neither change nor standing still."[12] And yet, it is not complete annihilation. When the Buddha was charged with being a nihilist, he said that nihilism was one of the extremes which he emphatically condemned. Even to the man of knowledge it has never been raised—the curtain that conceals the "other side." It is revealed only to him who has gone there. By no stretch of thinking can it be reached, because it lies beyond all thought.

According to the teaching of the Buddha, every man makes his own *nibbāna* and his own *pari-nibbāna.* All indeed lies in us; the entire world, with its arising and its passing away. As the beginning of the world is individual, so also is its ending.

[1] *A Treatise of Human Nature,* Book I, Part 4.
[2] *Saṁyutta-nikāya,* Part II, Book II, chap. XII, secs. 3–4.
[3] *Dhammapada,* 160.
[4] *Ibid.,* Part V, Book II, chap. XLV, sec. 9.
[5] *Majjhima-nikāya,* Part II, sec. 32; *Saṁyutta-nikāya,* Part II, Book II, chap. XII, sec. 23.
[6] *Mahāvagga-vinaya,* Book I, chap. V, secs. 2 ff.
[7] *Dhammapada,* 393.
[8] *Dīgha-nikāya,* Part III, secs. 180–193.
[9] A practical example of this is that the first female prime minister in history comes from the Buddhist country of Ceylon.
[10] *Sutta-nipata,* verse 1076.
[11] See *Udāna,* VIII. 1.
[12] *Ibid.*

UEDA YOSHIFUMI[a]

The status of the individual
in Mahāyāna Buddhist philosophy

I. THE FUNDAMENTAL WAY OF THINKING IN BUDDHIST PHILOSOPHY

There is a unique way of thinking in Buddhist philosophy which is
not found in any other philosophy. Since in early Buddhism this
unique way of thinking existed in an immature, naïve form[1] whose
special characteristic was not clearly distinguishable, it was open to
several differing interpretations. Consequently, it was difficult to
determine which among the various interpretations was the correct
one. It was in Mahāyāna Buddhism that this way of thinking
appeared in a form clear enough not to allow differing interpretations. From the Prajñā-pāramitā Sūtras, through the Mādhyamika,
the Yogācāra, and Zen[b], to the Shin[c] Buddhism of Shinran[d], who
expounded faith in Amida Buddha, all Mahāyāna Buddhist philosophies, with the exception of a few,[2] have followed this way of
thinking. Since they follow this way of thinking, they belong to the
Mahāyāna tradition. If one should take away this way of thinking,
it would not be an overstatement to say that, basically, the whole
point of view had thereby lost its essence as Mahāyāna Buddhist
philosophy. To say that almost all Mahāyāna Buddhist philosophies
follow this way of thinking means that they have all originated in or
have been derived from one and the same concept of ultimate reality
(dharma-kāya, literally, reality-body).[3]

If Aristotelian logic is meant by the word "logic," this Buddhist
way of thinking will probably not be considered logical. However,
this is clearly one way of thinking, and, if we should wish to include
in the broad meaning of "philosophy" a way of thinking that is
unique to many Asian peoples, then we must recognize a type of
logic that is non-Aristotelian. Perhaps we need not necessarily call
it "logic." It is simply that, should we not recognize that we have
here a unique way of thinking and should we immediately decide
that its propositions are not valid simply because they go against
Aristotelian logic, it would be impossible to understand Buddhist
philosophy. This way of thinking is truly difficult to understand for
those who have been trained in philosophies which base their thinking upon Aristotelian logic. And, since we shall follow this way of
thinking in our consideration of the problem, "The Status of the

Individual," we must consider here why Buddhist philosophers had to develop this way of thinking.

The focus of the problems pursued by Buddhist philosophers has been the true self. They pursued the true self to its limits and were finally able to realize it through a unique experience. This way of thinking was born within that experience. It goes without saying that most people and many philosophers think it is possible to know ourselves—through self-reflection. However, if we consider this very carefully, we will see that the self grasped through reflection is a conceptualized self and that our true selves, i.e., the self as it really is, can never be grasped through reflection. Those philosophies which think it is possible to cognize the self through reflection establish self-cognition on an assumption. The problem is whether or not that assumption may be permitted. One of the leading philosophers of Japan during the first half of this century, Hatano Seiichi[e], had the following to say concerning self-cognition.[4]

> Parallel to the cognition of the objective world, the subject also knows itself. As is stated above, objects are expressions of the subject and contain the factor of selfhood which is disclosed in them. The subject does not express itself except as object or in objects. This is the reason why the subject can know its own self. When the objects, that is, the expressions of the subject, become the symbols of the subject: that is, when the subject gets acquainted with its own self, and the hidden self or the center of the knowing act and the disclosed self or the known self are separated and opposed and, at the same time, maintain or realize their identity, the subject knows itself. . . .
>
> Of course, while we talk and think in this manner, we are obliged to stand at the level of reflection. And while distinguishing the factor of the life of experience, i.e., of real existence, from that of reflection, i.e., of ideal content, we establish a relationship of the two. So the former, i.e., the real existence, may also be introduced into the content of conceptual cognition. This is, however, the very difficulty one must face when he seeks for the source of experience. But it is a problem which one can no longer solve at the level of reflection. It is the very basic fact of life, and there is no other way than to be in it and to live through it. A closer observation will show us that, as we have seen in the cognition of the self, all the difficulties in identifying the hidden, really existing subject with the disclosed, ideal subject belong, after all, to the same category. They may all equally be reduced to what we call the transcendental identity of the subject. It is the identity of the subject of basic experience and that of reflection, in other words, the identity of the really existing subject and the subject which is expressed in reference to concepts in their objective phase. That is, it is the identity of the cognizing subject [the really existing subject] and the subject which is cognized [the ideal, conceptual subject]. Thus, as this identity is primarily assumed as a prerequisite of reflection, it is not a matter of comprehension, but is a basic fact of life that should be experienced as we live through it.

The attitude expressed in Hatano's consideration of the problem is sound, and a penetrating insight faithful to the facts is advanced. As long as we take the standpoint of reflection, we cannot help but agree with Hatano. However, if we look at the problem from the standpoint of Buddhist philosophy, we can ascertain whether or not "this identity . . . assumed as a prerequisite of reflection" can be established. The reason we can do so is that Buddhist philosophers have succeeded in "knowing" the really existing subject without transforming it into an ideal, conceptual content, and, since they were able to cognize the true self, they were able to know just what constituted the identity between the subject which knows and the subject which is known in the self-cognition of the true self.

What is the nature of this identity between the subject which knows and the subject which is known in the self-cognition of the true self? In the self-cognition of the true self, since the really existing subject knows itself, what knows and what is known are both the same real self—they are completely one and the same. Nevertheless, since the act of knowing is thereby established, the differentiation of the knower and the known must be established within this one and the same self. The fact that there is one and the same self and at the same time that there is the differentiation of the knower and the known is a logical contradiction, but, in order to establish the self-cognition of the true self, such a contradictory relationship must be capable of establishment. Buddhist philosophers put their greatest effort and endeavor into establishing in reality this kind of experience, and into finding a way of thinking through which this experience can be expressed. When Asaṅga and Vasubandhu spoke of differentiation of non-differentiation, i.e., the subsequently realized wisdom (*tat-pṛṣṭha-labdha-jñāna*), and when Pai-chang Huai-haiⁱ said, "Awaking to the Here-Now," it was of the experience of the realization of the true, real self. Nāgārjuna's "highest wisdom" (*prajñā-pāramitā*) is nothing other than this experience. This experience is established when there is no differentiation of subject and object, i.e., when one has gone through the experience of non-differentiation (*nirvikalpa*). What is realized in this non-differentiated experience is called "fundamental wisdom" (*mūla-jñāna*).[5] When this fundamental wisdom develops further and the differentiation of the knower and the known arises, though without losing its non-differentiation, the realization of the true self is established. This is what Asaṅga called "the subsequently realized wisdom."

Since this simultaneous relationship between the non-differentiation and the differentiation of the knower and the known is logically contradictory, it is completely different in nature from that identity which had to be assumed as a prerequisite of self-cognition from the standpoint of reflection. When it is seen that this non-

differentiation must be a complex structure which includes contradiction, it can be seen that the identity necessarily assumed as a
prerequisite of self-cognition from the standpoint of reflection is not
a true one. In other words, the identity between the ideal, conceptual subject and the really existing subject (known through reflection) cannot be established, and it is clear that the former (the
ideal, conceptual subject) does not manifest the latter (the really
existing subject).

"*Prajñā*" (the term Nāgārjuna uses), or "the subsequently realized wisdom" (Asaṅga's and Vasubandhu's expression), is the wisdom established upon pursuing and realizing the true self. In this
wisdom, one can know, not only the really existing self as it is, but
also each thing in the world as it really is. This is because, when
one realizes the real self, one at the same time touches reality itself;
to know the real self means, at the same time, to know reality.
A thing known as it really exists is nothing other than reality known
as it is. To know reality can be nothing other than to know our
selves and all the things in the world as they really exist and
become. In this manner, the wisdom that can know the real self can
also know everything in the world as it really exists and really
becomes, i.e., it can know things completely objectively. We shall
consider this more in detail in the following.

In the self-cognition of the self, the knower and the known are
the same self, i.e., the same subject. Herein there is only the subject;
there is no object. With this meaning, it is subject-only (*vijñāna-
mātra*).[6] This subject-only has a twofold structure. That is, it has
the aspect of the differentiation of the knower and the known, i.e.,
the affirmation of the subject and the negation of the object, and it
has the aspect of the non-differentiation or identity of the knower
and the known. Although subject-only shows that it is not an object,
i.e., the known, if it were simply a subject, there would not be the
least meaning of "the known." If this were the case, since there
would be the meaning of a knowing subject only and no meaning of
a known subject, it could not be said that the self knows the self.
How can the meaning of a known subject be included in subject-
only? It is the other aspect of subject-only, i.e., it is nothing other
than the known which is included in the non-differentiation of the
knower and the known. However, since this known is identified with
the knower, its meaning is not completely manifest. In order to
manifest completely the meaning of this known, it must be made
clear that it is not the knower—in other words, there must be the
negation of the knower. Accordingly, since the knower is truly the
self, or the subject, the negation of the knower is non-self, or non-
subject, i.e., the object. In this manner, in order that the meaning of
the known, which is included in subject-only, may be completely

manifest, the object must be affirmed and the subject negated. That is, object-only must be established. Only in this manner can the true self first be known as it really exists, i.e., become the known. This is why Vasubandhu said subject-only (*vijñāna-mātra*) is non-subject (= no-mind = *acitta*).[7] That subject-only is object-only he expressed as "subject seen as things in the world" (*artha-pratibhāsaṁvijñānam*).[8] No-mind has the same meaning as non-self (*anātman*).

As to the meaning of object-only, although it means that the true self is known, it is nothing other than reality being known. And reality is not merely the self; it is all things in the world. Object-only means that, besides all things in the world, there is no subject opposed to them. And yet, the fact that this thing is an object shows that this is that which is known. Accordingly, that the subject knows all things reveals the relation of all things (reality) as they are known by themselves. Here, the identity of the knower with the known is included. It is not that the subject is existent outside the object and sees it as an object. Rather, the subject, being non-existent other than as an object, knows all things. The subject, being non-existent, as it were, sees the object. This is nothing other than being free of all subjective and partial views and seeing things just as they are. Seeing the self as it is is not different from seeing things as they are; neither is it anything other than seeing reality as it is. It is only because the self is the knower and things are not the knower that knowing the self as it is is called "subject-only" and that things known as they are are called "object-only." However, since the self as reality is no different from things, subject-only simultaneously includes the meaning of object-only. And, since the self as reality is the knower, the identity of the knower and the known is included in the fact of things' being known. Accordingly, if there is no subject-only, object-only cannot be established, either.

Subject-only, i.e., non-self, is nothing other than the true self, which has realized itself. At the same time, it realizes the world just as it is (object-only). And, on the other hand, in order that things in the world can be known just as each is or becomes (object-only), subject-only, i.e., the non-existence of the object, must be established, too. This is the meaning of Seng-chao's[g] "All things in the world, though real, are formless,"[9] and Zen's "To see the form of the formless." The true self is non-self, and things as they really are are formless forms. The so-called fourfold consideration of Rinzai (Lin-chi,[h] died 867), a famous Zen Master, shows this subject-only and object-only in four phrases:

(i)   Object only
(ii) Subject only
(iii) Both subject and object negated
(iv) Both subject and object affirmed

The true self is this kind of subject, and really existing things are this kind of object. When one knows the self and the things in the world in this unique way, one knows *tathatā* (suchness). *Tathatā* has many synonyms: *śūnyatā* (emptiness), *animittam* (the formless), *dharmatā* (things as they really are), *bhūta-koṭi* (end of reality), *paramārthatā* (objects as known in supreme wisdom), *dharma-dhātu* (realm of things as they really are).[10] In addition to these, the following, which were previously given, are also synonyms: *vijñāna* (=*vijñapti*)-*mātratā* or *citta-mātratā* (subject-only or mind-only) and *acitta* (no-mind).

One of the greatest Buddhist philosophers of Japan, Dōgen[i], had the following to say. "To study Buddhism is to study oneself. To study oneself is to forget oneself. To forget oneself is to realize oneself as all things [in the world]. To realize oneself as all things is to strip off both one's own mind and body and the mind and body of others."[11] Here, what was said before—that Buddhist philosophy began with the problem of knowing one's true self, that the self-cognition of one's true self (subject-only) is non-self, that this is object-only, and that this is freedom—is expounded in a way different from that of Rinzai and in a clearer manner. The first original philosopher to be respected as such after the transplantation of Western philosophy into Japan and whose name is known even in other countries, is Nishida Kitarō[j]. That his thought has something in common with the foregoing thought of Buddhist philosophy can be seen in his words: "Our true self is the basic substance of the universe, and, when we know the true self, we not only unite with the good of mankind, but we merge with the basic substance of the universe and spiritually unite with the divine mind."[12]

That an individual knows his true self means that the universe awakens to itself from itself. The individual's self-cognition is not simply a phenomenon in the consciousness of an individual, but indeed a fact of the universe. When he knows things in the world, it is not merely the individual himself who knows, but the universe; and, when things are known by him, the universe knows itself from within itself. When he knows things, this brings about the self-awakening of the universe from within itself, and this is nothing other than the development and growth of the universe. It is the becoming of the universe.

We have pursued in the foregoing the fundamental way of thinking in Buddhist philosophy. All the problems of Mahāyāna Buddhist philosophy are considered on this base, so that one cannot consider other problems without touching upon it. As we have seen in the foregoing, the relationship between the knower and the known is not simply an epistemological problem but is fundamentally a metaphysical one. "To be" and "to know" cannot be discussed apart from each other. (And, as hinted at the end of the last paragraph, "to be" and "to become" cannot be considered apart from each other.)

Next, let us consider the relationship of the individual and the world from the aspect of the relationship between the one and the many.

II. THE ONE AND THE MANY

In Buddhist philosophy, the logic of the relationship between the individual and the world is grasped as the relationship in which "the one enters the many and the many enter the one" (one is one and not many, many are many and not one, and yet, at the same time, the one is identical with the many, and the many are identical with the one[13]). The one and the many are in a mutually negating opposition at the same time as they are one and the same. This is a case of differentiation of non-differentiation. But why is the relationship between the individual and the world like this? First, the individual, because he is born, lives, and dies in the world, is completely within the world. That the individual is established within the world as a historical product is because the one enters into the world as the many. Second, however, at the same time, the historical world is being built by the creative power emanating from the individual. The world exists, not only as an object seen by the individual, but, at the same time, as something being created by each individual it is in the process of becoming. The individual is not simply a seer, but also an actor. As something being created by this actor, the many are included in the one. This is stated as "the many enter into the one." The individual and the world are mutually created by each other.

That this relationship is established is due to the fact that the individual is not simply one among many but is also the one as a negation of the many, and that the many are not simply a collection of ones but are the many as a negation of the one. To say that the individual is not simply one among many but is the negation of the many means that the individual is the subject. An individual viewed as a speck in society is an objectified individual. A man can survey a society which is made up of many people as an object. In what respect is this man different from the others in this situation? This is due, of course, to the fact that he is a subject who is seeing and creating the society. When he is subject, all the other persons are object; he alone is affirmed as subject, and all the others are negated. This is the aspect in which the many enter into the one, or it is the one as a negation of the many. This one is an affirmed self or the aspect of the existence of the subject, and the aspect of the non-existence of society or the historical world.

To say that the many are not simply a collection of ones but are the many as a negation of the one means that society is established with the negation of the individual. Each individual has to give up his own welfare when the welfare of his whole society requires it. This is the aspect in which the one enters the many, or it is the many as a negation of the one. This one is a negated self or the aspect of the non-existence of the subject (*anātman,* non-self), and the aspect of the existence of society or the historical world.

The Buddhist philosopher who made the framework of this mutual relationship of the one and the many clearest is Fa-tsang[k] (643–712) of the Hua-yen[l] school. He calls this the relationship of mutually becoming a lord and vassals.[14] In the aspect in which the many enter the one, each individual is, respectively the center of the universe. When individual A is the lord, all other individuals and Nature, or the whole world, are the vassals. At the same time, A, with respect to B or C, is a vassal. All individuals are at the same time lords and vassals. In this situation, the world of the many does not refer only to the assembly of men, with Nature unconsidered. There is no thought of a realm of matter severed from spirit or life. The concept of a body separated from mind, or of matter separated from spirit or life, was unknown to the Buddhist philosopher. Material things, too, are grasped as things inseparable from spirit or life. All things are viewed as personal.

When the relationship between the individual and the world is grasped as the relationship in which the many are negated in the one and the one is negated in the many, it is probably the most radical manner of grasping that relationship. The individual does not refer to each respective human being, but to *the subject.* And the very subject is the true life. That the life observed from the outside is not true life is seen in the fact that our own death can never be the same to us as is that of others. In the respect that the one enters the many, this is not monism; and in the respect that the many enter the one, this is not pluralism in the usual sense. Since the establishment at the same time of the mutual negation and identity of the one and the many, in other words, of the relationship of differentiation of non-differentiation between the one and the many, as seen previously, is nothing other than the other aspect of the establishment at the same time of the mutual negation and identity of the subject and object, the opposition of monism and pluralism in the history of Western philosophy is based on a way of thought quite different from that of Buddhist philosophy. In Buddhist philosophy, since subjectivism is transcended due to the concept of the non-existence of the subject, i.e., non-self or no-mind, idealism was not established; and, because of the negation of the concept of a real existence transcending the subject due to the con-

This table shows a detailed analysis of the logical structure of the "differentiation of non-differentiation" stated in part II.

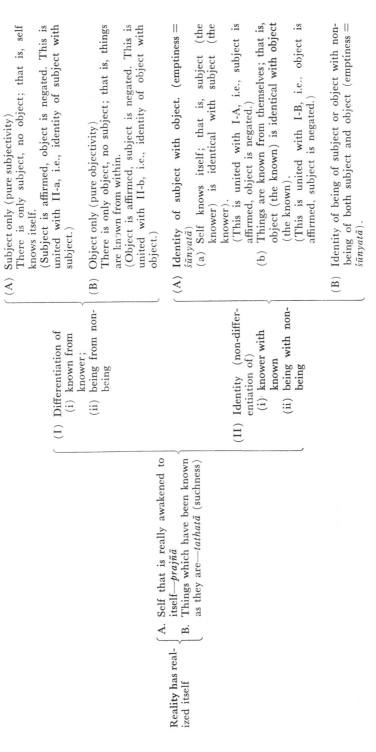

Reality has realized itself

A. Self that is really awakened to itself—*prajñā*

B. Things which have been known as they are—*tathatā* (suchness)

(I) Differentiation of
(i) known from knower;
(ii) being from non-being

(A) Subject only (pure subjectivity)
There is only subject, no object; that is, self knows itself.
(Subject is affirmed, object is negated. This is united with II-a, i.e., identity of subject with subject.)

(B) Object only (pure objectivity)
There is only object, no subject; that is, things are known from within.
(Object is affirmed, subject is negated. This is united with II-b, i.e., identity of object with object.)

(II) Identity (non-differentiation of)
(i) knower with known
(ii) being with non-being

(A) Identity of subject with object. (emptiness = *śūnyatā*)
(a) Self knows itself; that is, subject (the knower) is identical with subject (the knower).
(This is united with I-A, i.e., subject is affirmed, object is negated.)
(b) Things are known from themselves; that is, object (the known) is identical with object (the known).
(This is united with I-B, i.e., object is affirmed, subject is negated.)

(B) Identity of being of subject or object with non-being of both subject and object (emptiness = *śūnyatā*).

cept of the non-existence of the object, realism was not established.

The delineation given above of the framework of the establishment at the same time of the mutual negation and identity between the subject and object follows the interpretation of men belonging to the early Yogācāra, i.e., Maitreya, Asaṅga, Vasubandhu, Sthiramati, and Paramārtha,[15] while the delineation of the framework of the one entering the many and the many entering the one follows the interpretation of Fa-tsang. The reason for this is that these men have best clarified the logic of these relationships. Neither of the two concepts can be established without the other. Fundamentally they are one. This single thought in its naïve form is Nāgārjuna's idea, "Form (rūpa) is emptiness (śūnyatā), and the very emptiness is form." Form and emptiness are identical, yet, at the same time, they stand in mutually negating opposition.

If we desire to delve deeper than this into the logic of the relationship of the individual and the world, or the one and the many, we must enter into a consideration of Buddhist philosophy's most difficult problem, "time and eternity." With a consideration of this problem, the place of the individual as the center of the world of becoming would become even clearer; but, since it would be impossible to give an elucidation of this problem in the time available, I should like to leave it for a later occasion.

QUESTION: I would like to raise two elementary points. First, a point in regard to reflexive relations. In Western logic the notion of a reflexive relation is not regarded as involving a contradiction; at least, by most people it is not regarded as contradictory. The fact that A has a relation to A is not an absurd situation. You appear to be using an argument to the effect that, if A assumes two functions, if the relation were asymmetrical and something assumes two functions in the relation, two places in the relation, it would, as it were, become directed to two distinct entities. Now, this does not follow, any more than it follows that, if I love you and you love me, I assume both the loving and loved position, but it does not follow for that reason that I am two persons. I am one and the same person. If, now, I love myself or know myself, it does not for that reason follow that I am two persons. I am one and the same person. I would be very far from regarding self-knowledge as a very lucid thing and very far from saying that it might not involve very profound difficulties that would lead to contradictory formulae. But the very fact that it is a reflexive relation does not appear to be one of these. That is one point. I would like to raise a second.

The second is: I am profoundly confused as to how, granted that, in knowing the self as object, the self assumes these two positions, both as subject and as object. I am confused as to how the object gets differentiated. The self as object gets differentiated into a great number of distinct objects. Once these distinct objects are there, I can understand the rest of the paper perfectly. But this differentiation appears unclear. Now, there have been other philosophers who have held similar views. St. Thomas thought that God, in knowing himself, knew everything else. But he gave reasons why —because God was in an eminent manner everything else, and so on. And, similarly, people like Hegel have said that all knowledge of things is knowing them in the form of self, in the form of universals. But, again, this depends on a particular view of the self. Now, there does not appear to me to be any sort of mechanism which differentiates the self *qua* object in this system.

Re-phrased: The first question is this: What is contradictory about the same thing being both subject and object? The second is: How can the knower be known?

QUESTION: You say that the Buddhist way of thinking is a unique way of thinking which is not found in any philosophy. I do not see why this is so.

QUESTION: What is the meaning of the expression "to know" when you say "to know the true self"?

ANSWER: These questions will be answered en bloc because of the nature of the problem.

Some of the questions seem to be asked from the standpoint of reflective thinking without paying careful attention to the distinction between that standpoint and the standpoint of Buddhist philosophy. As long as we are standing on the level of reflection, there is no contradiction about the same thing being a subject and an object. The proposition that I can know myself is established without any contradiction. In this case, however, "I" is divided into two parts, the really existing I, or the center of the knowing act, and the conceptual I, or the known I, and, besides, it is only the latter that is known; the former remains unknown. It is in this sense that we say we cannot "know" our really existing self by means of reflection.

Buddhist philosophy, however, does not stand on the level of reflection. It has gone far beyond reflective thinking and stands where it is possible for the really existing self to know itself.

In order to get to this level of thinking, a Buddhist philosopher or a *bodhi-sattva* (one whose essence is perfect knowledge; sometimes translated as would-be *buddha*) passes through two stages. Starting from the level of reflective thinking, he goes into the first stage, where ordinary reflective thinking gradually dies away in his consciousness by being replaced by the thinking which acts in accordance with the way of thinking which belongs to the third stage, that is, the standpoint of Buddhist philosophy. Going through this first stage with strenuous discipline for many years, he reaches *samādhi* (intense contemplation), where there are no thoughts; there is neither the consciousness of the conceptual self nor any concept of objects, nor consciousness of the really existing self or of the subject; there is no subject-object dichotomy. His mind at this stage becomes completely identified with reality or suchness (*tathatā*). This is called literally "reality-body" (*dharma-kāya*). This is explained by Asaṅga as non-differentiation of that which is originated in time (*saṁskṛta*) and that which is not originated and timeless (*asaṁskṛta*). This is the second stage.

From this stage, i.e., *samādhi*, he becomes awakened to the here-now, that is, reality becomes conscious, and the differentiation of *saṁskṛta* from *asaṁskṛta* appears. He sees colors and shapes and hears voices and sounds; he thinks and speaks of anything. This is the third stage. The standpoint of Buddhist philosophy is established here.

These three stages were called by Asaṅga, in sequence, wisdom leading to wisdom-without-differentiation (*prāyogika-nirvikalpa-jñāna*), wisdom-without-differentiation (*nirvikalpa-jñāna*), and subsequently-realized-wisdom (*tat-pṛṣtha-labdha-jñāna*), whereas Nāgārjuna called all these stages with only one name "*prajñā-pāramitā*" (perfect wisdom).

Though a Buddhist philosopher sees or thinks everything at this stage, he no longer sees or thinks of anything as an object which confronts him; in other words, there is no subject which sees anything as an object, and, accordingly, there is no object which stands vis-à-vis the subject. There is no subject except object (non-self, *anātman,* or no-mind, *acitta*), on the one hand. A thing, as it were, is seen from itself, from within. There is seen here an identity of the seer with the seen. This identity means, not only that there is no seer or subject except the seen or object (non-self or no-mind), but also that the seer or subject sees his own self: this latter sense shows the other aspect of non-self or no-mind, namely, that there is no object except subject (mind-only, *vijñpti-mātratā*).

The reason why he is non-self is the reason why he "knows" his true self without conceptualizing it, and, at the same time, it is the reason why he can "know" everything as it is (suchness, *tathatā*).

In order to understand the uniqueness of Buddhist philosophy, it would be helpful for us to notice the uniqueness of the philosophy of Martin Heidegger in the history of Western philosophy. He calls that thinking "*vorstellendes Denken*" (object-thinking) which sets being before oneself and observes it as an object (*Gegenstand*). He says, "The thinking, strictly speaking, is the thinking of being. The genitive 'of' has a twofold meaning: (1) The thinking belongs to being; the genitive 'of,' in this case, means that being is an agent of thinking, and (2) The thinking listens to being; the genitive 'of,' in this case, expresses an objective case."

Here is implied a sense of identity of that which thinks with that which is thought of. We shall be able to see in this idea of Heidegger a logic through which we are able to grasp our really existing self without setting it up as an object before us. If there is no sense of the identity of that which thinks with that which is thought of, he may be said not yet to have transcended his so-called "*vorstellendes Denken*," because, when or if there is no sense of identity, there is nothing other than that there is fundamentally the dichotomy of subject and object. If we suppose that he could make his consideration deeper to that extent where he could state clearly the identity of that which thinks with that which is thought of and, at the same time, the differentiation between the two, we would be able to know or understand the standpoint of Buddhist philosophy. This is why I emphasized the uniqueness of Buddhist philosophy in my paper.

---

1 For example, see Pali Text Society's *Pāli-English Dictionary* edited by T. W. Rhys Davids and William Stede, on the term, *"sankhāra"* as ". . . one of the most difficult terms in Buddhist metaphysics, in which the blending of the subjective-objective view of the world and of happening, peculiar to the East, is so complete that it is almost impossible for Occidental terminology to get at the root of its meaning in a translation."

2 There are a few in later Indian Mahāyāna Buddhism who are not in accord with this way of thinking.

3 The *Mahāyāna-saṁgraha* (*Taishō*, Vol. 31, No. 1595, p. 173b) states: "The correct

teaching of the Mahāyāna is that which has been streamed out of the pure world of reality (*dharma-dhātu*).

[4] Hatano Seiichi, *Time and Eternity*, Suzuki Ichirō[m], trans. (Tokyo: Japanese National Commission for UNESCO, 1963), pp. 29, 35–36. Although the lines quoted here are the same as those quoted in my "Thinking in Buddhist Philosophy," in *Philosophical Studies of Japan* (Tokyo: Japanese National Commission for UNESCO, 1964), Vol. 5, I have cited them again since the latter is still in press. (Now published.)

[5] The substance of fundamental wisdom is the *dharma-kāya*. "The *dharma-kāya's* characteristic is the non-duality of being and nothingness" (Asaṅga, *Mahāyāna-saṁgraha*, *Taishō*, Vol. 31, No. 1595, p. 251b).

[6] This is a term used by Yogācāra philosophers. D. T. Suzuki (Suzuki Daisetz Teitarō)[n] calls it "pure subjectivity." See my above-quoted article, "Thinking in Buddhist Philosophy."

[7] *Triṁśikā-vijñaptimātratāsiddhi*, ed. par S. Lévi, verse 29. See my article, "What Is Idealism in Buddhist Philosophy?" in C. A. Moore, ed., "Idealism in World Perspective" (in preparation) for a more detailed exposition of the theory of *vijñapti-mātratā*.

[8] See my "Thinking in Buddhist Philosophy" for more concerning the meaning of "*artha-pratibhāsaṁ-jñānam*."

[9] *Taishō*, Vol. 45, No. 1859, p. 154c. Although the phrase quoted here is the same as that quoted in my "Thinking in Buddhist Philosophy" (see note 4), I have cited it again since the article is still in press. (Now published.)

[10] Maitreya, *Madhyānta-vibhāga*, ed. par Yamaguchi Susumu[o], p. 49; Asaṅga, *Mahāyāna-saṁgraha*, *Taishō*, Vol. 31, No. 1595, p. 191c.

[11] Dōgen, Shōbōgenzō (Repository of True Buddhist Teachings)[p], chapter on Genjō Kōan[q]; *Taishō*, Vol. 82, No. 2582 p. 23c. Although the lines quoted here are the same as those quoted in my "Thinking in Buddhist Philosophy" (see note 4), I have cited them again since the article is still in press. (Now published.)

[12] Nishida Kitarō, *Zen no kenkyū*[r] (A Study of Good) (2nd ed., Tokyo: Iwanami-shōten, 1924), p. 180.

[13] Fa-tsang, *Hua-yen i-ch'eng-chiao I-fen-chi-cheng*[s] (*Kegon ichijō kyōgi bunzai shō*) (A System of Kegon Philosophy), *Taishō*, Vol. 45, No. 1866, p. 503b.

[14] *Ibid.*, p. 505c, and also, Fa-tsang, *Hua-yen-ching T'an-hsüan-chi*[t] (*Kegongyōtangenki*) (A Commentary on the *Avataṁsaka-sūtra*), *Taishō*, Vol. 35, No. 1733, pp. 123b, 124a.

[15] For details see my article, "What Is Idealism in Buddhist Philosophy?" *op. cit.*

[a] 上田義文

[b] 禪

[c] 眞宗

[d] 親鸞

[e] 波多野精一

[f] 百丈懷海

[g] 僧肇

[h] 臨濟

[i] 道元

[j] 西田幾多郎

[k] 法藏

[l] 華嚴

[m] 鈴木一郎

[n] 鈴木大拙

[o] 山口益

[p] 正法眼藏

[q] 現成公案

[r] 善の研究

[s] 華嚴一乘教義分齊章

[t] 華嚴經探玄記

WILLIAM ERNEST HOCKING

A brief note on individuality
in East and West*

Individuality is a quality everyone vaguely understands but nobody fully understands. The individuality we are here concerned with is a very precious attribute of human personality, a quality or group of qualities that make a person not only different from everybody else, but in some significant way irreplaceable.

There is a kind of individuality no one can help having, for the human being can never be a mere specimen of the *genus homo,* such that any other specimen could be substituted for him without perceptible change. There is an inescapable physical uniqueness, if it is only a uniqueness of position in space and time, which makes every human being, purely by the biological separateness of his body— after the crisis of being born—a center of distinctive experience. The ordinary self-regard of his ego, his capacities for pleasure and pain, for attraction and aversion, for hope, for success and failure —these give him the conditions for a personal history distinct from every other, but not yet for the individuality that concerns us here.

This biological separateness is by no means negligible. We must begin with it. It is this feebly distinguished but promissory biological specimen that receives from its parental stock an *individual name,* coupled usually with a family or clan name. This name—not yet known by its owner—far from implying self-sufficiency, will, nevertheless, indicate a world structure in which the contrast between I and thou is fundamental.

Curiously enough, the first concern of the anxious parents is not with the individuality promised by the given name, but with the *generic completeness* of this incipient *homo.* Is the newborn biologically perfect and typical? Will the newborn, male or female, validly represent, not its individual self, but its forebears, the type from which it emerges? Homo-geneity comes first, including family heredity and race. The raw material for individuality is there—the necessary conditions are present, but not the sufficient conditions. For individuality is not conferred: it has to be achieved.

---

* This paper by Professor Hocking, an Honorary Member of the Conference, was read at a special Coffee Hour by his son Professor Richard Hocking, who also led the discussion of the paper. The author could not attend because of illness.

The stages of this achievement are traced with much insight by the psychologist Gordon Allport, who holds that

> . . . only in the second year of life does [the infant] commence to relate his experiences to himself and begin to act as a reflexly conscious agent. Only when he comes to resent offences against his person, encroachments upon his dignity, is he building up a sense of his own ego as an object of value. This stage in a child's development, marked, as it usually is, by stubbornness and negativism, is unmistakable. From the age of two onward, the most universal of all values resides in the *keen sense of individuality* which constantly demands self-expression, craves power, and feels pride.[1]

THE EMERGENCE OF INDIVIDUALITY

Allport too readily uses the term "individuality" as a synonym for the elementary self-sense which is closely akin, if not equivalent, to the enveloping *egoism* in which human and animal psychology tend to summarize their instinctive unity. That there is such an enveloping instinctive drive there can be little doubt; and, just because it is an effort toward *consensus of all* the fundamental drives, it is less definite in its objective than any specific impulse, such as hunger, pugnacity, need for companionship, sex, will-to-power; and, as indefinite, it easily accepts the label of "subliminal" or "unconscious." In the words of William James suggesting that "a subliminal island of individual being rests upon an ocean floor of universal mind," a certain vagueness claims resident rights in the very nature of individuality. But we may defer this surrender to psychological haze unless truth compels it.

Individuality is not to be achieved through the refinement of our sense of selfhood: it can be achieved only through a social situation in which the ego comes to realize that for every thou with whom it has dealings *it also is a thou*. Then, whatever it claims from others it begins to realize is reciprocally claimed by them from itself: the notion of a "rule" arises. A rule is a demand made upon every ego: its "Thou shalt" is addressed to him, and individuality as a distinction is thereby wiped out. As rule-giver, society, whether through precept or custom or law, does nothing to nourish the uniqueness of the individual ego.

And yet, without that very uniqueness, society fails to elicit a quality which it needs to sustain its life. We face a paradox: for *law-obeying* cannot be universal unless *law-making* has in principle a corresponding universality; and this paradox was, in point of fact, realized in various early societies, by way of what we might define as a *custom providing for the breach of custom*.

The rite of initiation, commonly understood as a revelation to the initiate of the mores of the tribe, typically begins as a forced experience of privation and loneliness, leading to the dreaming of a private dream, winning a private name, gaining private access to some aspect of deity—one's personal fetich or daimon. Only with this achievement of solitary being, standing free and separate before ultimate power, can the initiate be safely trusted with the burden of the mores. Why so? Because, while it is to be his primary duty to revere and follow the customs, it may become his function—official or unofficial—to judge, criticize, perhaps revise them in such light as he—now qualified by his new insight—can achieve.

Individuality is born at that moment—and only at that moment —when the soul in its loneliness sees its life in society—necessarily under a system of rules—as *subject to a goal-seeking beyond these rules.*

This goal is commonly the unspoken treasure of religion, conveyed to the seeker as a privately won vision. The individual is the potential prophet. His experience may be called mystical, not in the sense of a subliminal blur, but in the sense of a directive, seeking embodiment, including the corrective function of the Socratic familiar spirit.

INDIVIDUALITY IN THE EAST

All civilization involves membership in a society under customary rules. All living civilization finds ways of revising its rules under the aegis of persons presumably endowed with a sense of the goal of law. Few are the civilizations that have endeavored to spread this endowment through their membership and thus to develop individuality.

The civilization of India is one of these exceptions. It is an ancient Hindu maxim that "A man's first birth is from his parents; his second birth is from his *guru.*" It is the responsibility of the *guru* to preside over the process we call initiation, but in such a way as to make precise reference to the specific *needs and capacities* of the youth in tutelage. As Allport puts the matter:

> Although other religions provide personal counsel for the initiate at the threshold of maturity, probably none goes to such lengths in making a close analysis of the youthful personality. . . . a rare instance of an institutional religion recognizing the ultimate individuality of the religious sentiment . . . [and taking] more responsibility than a psychodiagnostician in the West would like to assume. . . .[2]

An important part of this individual prescription of the *guru* to his pupil is the sacred *mantras* from the Vedas or the Upaniṣads for his meditation. One cannot but be impressed by the contrast between the behavior of a boys' school at Santiniketan at a period of "recess," each seeking his own silent corner, as I have seen them do, and the behavior of any American group at "recess," to whom an injunction to meditate would induce pure bewilderment.

A further element is the initiate's name for the deity, a name prescribed individually by the *guru*, as "a private instrument for prayer,"[3] constituting a personal bond of union between the initiate and God. This name is presumably kept secret from all others, including friends and spouse, so that "in the last analysis, each person confronts his deity in solitude."[4] Gandhi had his secret of secrets, no doubt, though he told me, when speaking of his cordial relations with a monastic order in Italy, that for him the name *Rama* was the most significant and intimate of names for God.

In this respect, India has long and far outpassed any Western civilization known to me.

But, while India takes first place in implanting the seeds of individuality, it is less adept in identifying the *fruits of that planting* than another Oriental tradition. All religious education seeks to develop the vital attachment of the worshipper to his deity, and, no doubt, incidentally, to the specific cult identified by a historic tradition. It tends to confirm a certain way, and so far to promote similarity. But the fruit of individuality should be *differential* and characteristic of the person.

In this respect, Confucianism seems far in advance of any other cult of East or West. For it is only Confucianism that has called on the individual worshipper to find in that relationship a specific "calling" in which, since it is the *"appointment of Heaven"* (*T'ien-ming*), he must succeed. You will allow me to remind you of the familiar incident in Confucius' own life which so aptly illustrates this conception. The firm and critical political views he had espoused and attempted to promote brought him a harvest of resentment and at times of public hostility. When his disciples had to rescue him from a mob in a certain center, and remonstrated with him for so recklessly exposing himself to injury if not to death, his reply was, "Heaven has commissioned me to teach this doctrine; [and until I have done so] what can the people of K'uang do to me?"[5] This proud sense of mission is essentially individual, not as a planting but as a fruit.

Here Confucius brings to recognition an evident but difficult truth, namely, that individuality in the human being will be unique, not alone in what he is, but in what he does. His life may be expected to yield something significant—not only different—and something which *no one else can do*. In this deed, the individual is realized; and the character of this realization deserves our attention.

The psychology of our time continues to seek a name for the total drive of the human will. The will-to-live, the Darwinian struggle for existence, have given place to more positive but more shadowy conceptions; we linger over the "will-to-power," not in Nietzsche's sense as a power *over* man and Nature, but as a power *for* man, for achievement, the opposite of the primal evil of futility. This will-to-power may be aimed toward realizing some universal good, the essential *creativity*—the favored term of today. And, since all creation involves pain, let us call this total will the *will to suffer in creation.*

Seeing one's way to such a deed may be accompanied by a sense of necessary success, an element of destiny, in which one's personal fulfillment is also a part of human history (as when old Ptah Hotep, about 4000 B.C., finishing his "Instructions," says of them what is valid today, that they "will not perish out of the Land forever, for the quality of Truth is in them"). Such an awareness I have called "the Prophetic Consciousness,"[6] as carrying an individual assurance of lasting effect. Passing beyond the ethical half-goods of Stoicism and altruism, with their consolations for personal failure, this aim rises to a certain partnership with the ultimate world-purpose involving certitude in place of mere hope. It touches destiny, as *T'ien-ming,* the appointment of Heaven.

INDIVIDUALITY IN THE WEST

There are other aspects of individuality affecting and affected by institutions in East and West. Perhaps the most remarkable is the *assumption of potential individuality* in the human being as such, independent of any manifestation of distinctive character or capacity.

It is the peculiarity of the West that it assumes individuality as potentially present in the human infant, and even in the embryo, wholly apart from any manifestation of capacity to contribute an "individual" point of view to the judgment of experience. There is here a paradoxical—I will not say indifference, but—non-differential postulate of germinal individuality in the human being as such, carrying with it a practical summons of respect for the unrealized potency.

Western institutions since Roman times have given various expression to this non-differential demand for respect, based on an idea of the "soul" as having an eternal destiny. In the Christian tradition, "God's love for the soul" established a norm to which the mores must conform; and non-difference has had no limiting effect on individuality, because mankind is in fact all *alike in willing to be different.* To be human is to be capable of considering the world alone, with one's own ideas of value. The love-of-God-for-man operates as a blank check to be realized by efforts necessarily individual.

The West has had a certain leadership in the art of giving legal and political coinage to this non-differential background of individuality. The "rights of man" have sought definitive expression, beginning with the "right to life" and to certain liberties, personal and political. These efforts have had notable effect in improving the common lot over the years, culminating in the Kantian formula of right: "So act as to treat humanity, whether in thine own person or in that of any other, in every case as an end withal, never as means only."[7]

But non-difference pursued without qualification has its perils. If one adopts as a guide the formula "All men are created equal," one must abandon the attempt to evaluate purely potential individuality; for equality cannot be asserted of non-actual entities. Still less can we use the quantitative measure implied in "equality" of the non-quantitative entity, the soul. The "created equal" phrase, close to being literally meaningless, must be interpreted in terms of the all-human *élan vital,* that glint of kinship with the spirit of the whole that leads us on.

That glint of kinship is well expressed in the Buddhist conception that in every human being there lives *"buddha-*nature" deserving our reverence.

REALIZATION

But the Buddhist is not content with the formulation of non-realized possibilities. The strength of the West, in bringing its intimations of potential individuality to effect in the legal and social order, is at the same time a weakness because of its failure to pursue the possibility to its achievement. The West is full of hypocritical equalities and empty respect toward individualities not realized.

It is only in the East that we find a wide and determined pursuit of "realization."

The genius of the West has turned with emphasis to the type of knowledge we call scientific; and its knowledge of the self, of social life, of ethics, of religion, is drawn toward the ideal of objective truth. The genius of the East has turned with even greater emphasis toward a type of knowledge in which the distinction between subject and object yields place to an experience of unity, an immediate awareness of its theme. A recent work, *Philosophy of Hindu Sadhana,*[8] declares, "The essence of religion lies in the immediate experience of the divine," and holds that only the Vedānta has found the way to the unconditional knowledge which Kant sought in his *Critique of Practical Reason.* The older *yoga* was itself a form of disciplined realization. And later, Buddhism, based on the founder's experience of enlightenment, relies for its evidence on an "Eightfold Path" of observance, culminating in exercises in meditation (*sammā-*

samādhi) through which one not only knows but realizes emancipation.

The history of religion in the West is not wholly alien to the search for realization, though it has been inclined to regard such seekers as a separate and somewhat eccentric group, the "mystics," for whom worship is an experience of participation in the ultimate real. We have still much to learn in this matter from the East. And, while Oriental *sādhana* (realization) has at times run into tantric excesses in pursuit of realization, the moment for mutual advance has come; and there are few themes of greater importance and promise.

1 Gordon W. Allport, *The Individual and his Religion* (New York: The Macmillan Company, 1950), p. 14. (Italics mine.)

2 *Ibid.*, p. 11.

3 *Ibid.*

4 *Ibid.*

5 *Analects,* IX.5.

6 W. E. Hocking, *The Meaning of God in Human Experience* (New Haven: Yale University Press, 1934), chap. XXXII, especially p. 521.

7 Or "Act so as to use humanity, whether in your own person or in the person of another, always as an end, never as merely a means." Kant, *Fundamental Principles of the Metaphysic of Morals,* in John Abbott, *The Philosophy of Kant* (Glasgow: Jackson, Willie & Co., 1927), p. 246.

8 Nalini Kanta Brahma, *Philosophy of Hindu Sadhana* (London: Kegan Paul, Trench, Trübner & Co., 1932), p. 13.

SECTION II   **Methodology**

T'ANG CHÜN-I[a]

The individual and the world in Chinese methodology

INTRODUCTION

I shall limit this paper to the four important typical ways of thinking about the individual and the world in Chinese epistemology:

1. To think of the individual as objectively existing as a part of the world.

2. To think of the world as a part of, or the content of, or identical with, the being of the individual subject.

3. To think that both the individual and world must be transcended, and that there is then in reality neither individual nor world.

4. To think that both the individual subject and the objective world are to be asserted positively as existing, yet neither is asserted as a part of, or the content of, or identical with, the other; nor are they asserted as mutually exclusive, because their mutual transcendence and mutual immanence are both accepted.

I. THE INDIVIDUAL KNOWN AS OBJECTIVELY EXISTING AND AS A PART OF THE WORLD THROUGH CLASS NAMES, POINTING, SPATIO-TEMPORAL LOCATION, AND RELATIONAL THINKING

First, the way of thinking of the individual as objectively existing and as part of the world is that way of thinking which *starts* from the world as the objective side of our knowledge (through the temporary forgetting of the individual as a unique knowing or acting subject and the conscious—though not self-conscious—activity of the objectivation of the subject as one of the individual things in the world) and *ends* in the assertion that I, as an individual, and all other individual things co-exist as parts of the world. The problem here—how I as an individual person can be objectively known or conceptually determined as an individual—is included in the general problem as to how any individual thing is objectively known or conceptually determined as an individual. Since individual things are usually thought of objectively by general concepts or class terms, which are universal in meaning, the problems as to how the individuality of a particular individual can be conceptually determined and how the individual can be thought of objectively have been complicated and delicate problems from Plato to the present in Western thought. However, Chinese philosophers have not taken the problem so seriously as has the West, though we are not lacking in answers to the problem. These answers are represented by the Moists[b], the Logicians[c], Hsün Tzu[d] (313–238 B.C.), and the Yĭn-Yang[e] school in classical Chinese thought.

(a) Moists think of the individual objectively merely as a member of a class. They stress the idea of class (*lei*[f]) earlier than Mencius[g] (372–289 B.C.) and Hsün Tzu. Mo Tzu[h] (468–376 B.C.) teaches universal love as based upon the idea that all human beings are of the same kind. He teaches also that one should love the father of another man as he does his own. Thus, Mo Tzu takes my father merely as one member of the class of fathers. So, when Moism is developed into a theory of epistemology and logic in Mo Pien[i], an individual thing is called an individual or an actuality (*shih*[j]), a *shih* genus name. As a proper name is arbitrarily given to a *shih*, conceptual knowledge of a *shih* requires the use of a class name. However, Mo Pien did not discuss the problem as to how an individual can be conceptually determined by the class name, which expresses the universal concept only. In Mo Pien's thought, the use of a class name to denote an individual is a practical matter. If a genus name is not enough to express the peculiarities of an individual, then a species name or sub-species name is required to differentiate one individual from another of the same kind. As the process of using class names with more specified meanings goes on, there is no problem as to how the individual can be conceptually determined and expressed by a class name. Consequently, this problem is not raised and discussed by Moists. However, it has to be raised and discussed, because the process of using names with more specified meanings cannot go on infinitely, since there is no infirm species or lowest subordinative class-name to use; and, even if there were, it would still be a class name, and we could know the individual only as a member of the class.

(b) Another way to know the individual as existing objectively is represented by the *Kung-sun Lung*[k] (498–? B.C.) of the logician school of Pre-Ch'in (Ch'in, 221–206 B.C.) philosophy. This is the way of knowing an individual by pointing to it. Kung-sun Lung is famous for his insistence on the difference of meanings between species name and genus name. Thus, "White horse is not horse" is his slogan. If genus name is different from species name because it has a wider denotation, it is implied that the lowest class-name still can denote more than one individual, and so, individuality cannot be expressed by any class-name as such. Thus, the individual can be pointed out or indicated only by names and not conceptually determined by them. These are the topics of his two other treatises, "Ch'i wulun"[1] (On Pointing and Things) and "Ming-shih lun"[m] (On Name and Actuality), which are less mentioned than his theory of the difference of species and genus as expounded in his treatise "Po-ma lun"[n] (On White Horse). It is quite clear that Kung-sun Lung thinks that the actuality (*shih*) of an individual thing can be pointed to only by names and that the differences between species name and genus name are based upon their different functions in pointing.[1] We use names for pointing out the individual thing, and the individual thing is shown and known to us in the very act of pointing.

It is one thing to use a universal name to point to an individual thing, and another for a person to be understood by others, as when we use a certain universal name to point to a certain individual. If the individuality of an individual is not capable of being determined in some other way, where can one get the guarantee that one shall not be misunderstood? Thus, the third way of knowing the individual, as propounded by Hsün Tzu, needs consideration.

(c) The third way of knowing the individual as existing objectively is that of determining an individual in a spatio-temporal system. When Hsün Tzu discusses how an actuality or an individual thing is determined in his chapter of the *Cheng-ming*[o] (Rectification of Names), he disagrees with the view that an individual is determined by its appearances or attributes, which are usually expressed by universal names. Two things may have the same appearances or attributes but be in different places. Thus, they have to be called two distinct actualities, two individual things. On the other hand, in the process of becoming, "one [individual] thing may have different appearances or attributes [at different times] but must still be called one individual."[2] An actuality, or an individual, is determined by its location in the spatio-temporal system, with emphasis laid on the different spatial locations of different individual things. However, when we differentiate the different things according to their different locations in space and time, we presuppose that the space-time system is already differentiated in its structure prior to the things in it. Here the epistemological problem is: if there are not things related differently to one another in space-time, how can space-time, which is simply extended in spatio-temporal dimensions and is thought to be homogeneous everywhere, be differentiated by itself into different locations. If we cannot find any other answer to this problem, we can look for the principle of individuality only in the different things as differently related to each other.

(d) As things which are similar in appearances or attributes and subsumed under a class name do not usually have the same relations, such as causal relations, with other things, so any two individuals can be differentiated according to their different relations with different things. The Yin-Yang school is representative of this way of thinking: the fourth way of knowing the individual, that of relational thinking, the way of knowing the individual in its many-sided relations with other things. This way, expounded first by the Yin-Yang school, was adopted by many Confucianists after the Han Dynasty (206 B.C.–A.D. 220).

The meaning of *yin*[p] and *yang*[q] are subtle and complicated.[3] Originally, *"yin"* meant what is concealed and unknown to us, and *"yang"* meant what is manifested and known to us. They were originally concepts of attributes of things based on their status relative to other things, and were not originally concepts of substance or force. According to their derivative meanings, anything which is in front of or before other things is called *yang,* and that which is in back of or after other things is called *yin.* Consequently, what is progressive or active or generative is *yang,* and what is retrogressive or passive or degenerative is *yin.* All these meanings are relative. Therefore, according to the Yin-Yang school, everything takes the role of *yin* or *yang* relatively to other things, and anything of the same class can be differently determined as having different relations of *yin* and *yang* to these other things. Even if we limit the meaning of *"yang"* to "active" and *"yin"* to "passive," it is not difficult to determine the things to which a certain individual thing is peculiarly related, actively and passively, and then to differentiate it from the other individual things of the same class, in order that the uniqueness of a certain individual can be expressed through this kind of relational thinking without confusion.

The way of relational thinking of the Yin-Yang school was originally a way of thinking of an individual thing as existing objectively in the natural world. Yet, it is exactly like the Confucian way of thinking of the status of the individual person through his ethical relations in the human world. When an individual person is seen as existing objectively in the human world, his action and personality are regulated and determined by his reciprocal relations with other persons. As there are no two individual persons who have the same ethical relations to the other persons around him, so the unique status of an individual person in the human world can be cognized and conceptually determined through knowledge of his peculiar ethical relations to others.

II. THE INDIVIDUAL AS A SELF-CONSCIOUS MORAL SUBJECT AND THE WORLD AS SEEN BY SUCH A SUBJECT

I myself as a subject am a self-conscious subject. When I am self-conscious, what I am conscious of can be known as the content of my consciousness, and comprehended by my self-consciousness, which therefore transcends the world, and can then include it as a part of itself. If we say that only the self-consciousness which immediately reveals itself to me exists, this is extreme individualism or solipsism; and, if we say that there are different worlds belonging to the different self-consciousnesses of different individuals, this is pluralistic idealism or pluralistic spiritualism, and is a kind of individualism, too.

But, how can we know that self-consciousness is itself an individual reality belonging to me exclusively or belonging to each person separately? It is quite possible that self-consciousness, revealed immediately as a self-conscious subject, is simply a subject without being an individual, or a part of, or an expression of, a universal self-conscious subject, which is the only reality, as objective idealism or absolute idealism contends. Nevertheless, we still have reason to call the self-conscious subject an individual, because the self-conscious subject, since it transcends the world, can differentiate itself from the world. Hence, it is a unique being and capable of being defined negatively as different from everything else in the world and from the world as a whole, and can be called an individual, because any individual thing in the ordinary sense is usually defined as that which is different from everything else. Although we may not be able to define the self-conscious subject positively as an individual in the ordinary sense, we should leave open the question as to whether it is a part of or an expression of a universal self-conscious subject. If it is legitimate to call the self-conscious subject an individual, then any thought which thinks the world-being as the content of, or a part of, or identical with, the subject is a process of thinking of the world subjectively.[3a]

There is no eminent philosophy of pure Chinese origin—other than Buddhist Vijñāna-vāda idealism, which comes from India— which argues for a subjective idealism or for individualism by taking the self-conscious subject as a purely knowing subject and taking the world simply as the object known. However, there is a very important trend of Chinese thought which takes the self-conscious subject as both acting and knowing, and thereupon thinks of the world-being as subjectively included or comprehended as a part of, or the content of, or identical with, the subject.

This trend of thought may be called a kind of ethical idealism. Mencius, Lu Hsiang-shan[r] (1139–1192), and Wang Yang-ming[s] (1472–1528) are the leading philosophers involved. All of them emphasize the self-consciousness of the subject as a moral subject, which is not purely a knowing subject but a subject which knows its moral ideal, acts in conformity with it, and then knows itself self-consciously as a subject of both knowing and acting. There is here the thesis that "the universe (the ten thousand things) is perfectible in myself"[4] and "The universe is my mind, and my mind is the universe"[5] and "Pervading Heaven and Earth, there is just this spiritual light . . . my spiritual light is the master of Heaven, Earth, and deities. . . . leaving my spiritual light, there is no Heaven, Earth, deities, or ten thousand things."[6]

It would be quite misleading, however, to interpret this thesis from the point of view of epistemological idealism or ordinary mysticism. Chinese philosophers who have held this thesis have never stated in a strict sense their epistemological arguments for this kind of idealism, nor have they said that the meanings of their thesis are mysterious as beyond the reason of man.

In ethical idealism, we take those things which ought to be as our ideal. This ideal determines what we ought to do to realize the ideal, and then the realization of the ideal is itself a moral ideal and moral action. The way of thinking in ethical idealism begins, in its first step, with seeing the things of the world as what they ought to be as our ideal prescribes, and then they are seen as full of possibilities or potentialities. It then proceeds, in the next step, to seeing things through our moral ideal and moral action. Henceforth, things are seen as gradually transforming themselves and tending to be what they ought to be; and their possibilities, when realized by our moral action, are found as of the nature of what they ought to be and of the ideal; while, on the contrary, what they are in actual fact is thought of as not so in reality. Therefore, if the moral subject has a moral ideal and moral action which are so high and lofty as to realize the universal *jen* (the utmost goodness in the world through the self-consciousness of our good nature, or our original mind[t], or *liang-chih*[u])—as held by Mencius, Lu Hsiang-shan, and Wang Yang-ming —then all things in the world will be seen through this high and lofty ideal and action of the moral subject, and all things and the whole world will be seen as acted upon by the subject's moral action and as tending to realize its moral ideal, and will be thought of as of the same nature as the moral mind. Consequently, it is quite natural for Mencius to think that the ten thousand things are perfectible by me as a moral subject, for Lu Hsiang-shan to think that the universe is my mind, and for Wang Yang-ming to think of *liang-chih* as the spiritual light of Heaven, Earth, deities, and the ten thousand things.

The expression "see the world through the ideal and action of the moral subject" states a way of thinking by a fully self-conscious moral subject as a moral individual. It is not a way of thinking of the world as an object opposite to the subject. It is a way of thinking which begins by withdrawing the light in the ordinary outward-knowing process back to our inner self; and then throws the light out again, along the very line of the extending of our moral ideal and our moral action; and knows the world as mediated by that very ideal and action, and as the realm for the embodiment of that ideal and action. Here, the seeing "eye" of the moral subject is immanent in the extending of the ideal and moral action, being acted upon by the action and transformed by the action. As the world is itself transformed to conform to the ideal, the "eye" will see the world as absorbed into the action and the ideal of the subject, and will experience it as one in being with the subject. When the subject is self-conscious and knows itself as transcending the world as experienced, the "eye" will see the subject as above the world, and the world will be seen as just a part of, or the content of, the subject as an absolute individual or an absolute I. This is the reason Liu Chi-shan[v] (1578–1645), a great Neo-Confucianist in the late Ming Dynasty (1368–1644), gives so high a place to the idea of tu^w and tu-$chih^x$—the awareness of the solitary individual in absolute morality.[7]

III. THE INDIVIDUAL AND THE WORLD AS TRANSCENDED IN VACUITY AND RECEPTIVITY OF MIND AND IN ENLIGHTENMENT AND SPIRITUALITY

The third typical way of thinking of the individual and the world in Chinese philosophy is to think that both the individual and the world have to be transcended, such that there is in reality neither world nor the I as an individual. This is the same type of thinking as that of Western and Indian mystics and philosophers who think of "before the day of creation," but with different emphasis about the way in which the world and the I, or the self as an individual, are to be transcended.

Chuang Tzu[y] (369–? B.C.), one of the two most important Taoistic philosophers, is representative of this way. He has a spiritual vision which is beyond the sense of self as an individual and of the world as opposite to the self. "Forgetting of myself," "loss of myself," "forgetting the world under Heaven," and "out of the world under Heaven" are pertinent sayings of his. When Chuang Tzu talked about the "upward wandering with the creator [and] downward having friends who are beyond death and life and of no beginning and ending,"[8] he was using a metaphor for the expression of his spiritual vision. His spiritual vision originates from his profound wisdom, aesthetic enjoyment, and inner spiritual cultivation, rather than from his primary belief in the existence of a mystic state.

Chuang Tzu has three ideas about the mind which are closely related to the experience of "forgetting the world and the self as an individual." The first idea concerns the nature of mind as $hs\ddot{u}^z$ and $ling^{aa}$. "$Hs\ddot{u}$" means to be vacuous and receptive. Confucius and Lao Tzu spoke of $hs\ddot{u}$ mainly as a moral teaching. Chuang Tzu, followed by Hsün Tzu and the Neo-Confucianists, takes $hs\ddot{u}$ as one fundamental nature of the mind and connects it with the word *"ling,"* which means knowing freely, spontaneously, and without attachment. When the nature of the mind is seen as both vacuous and receptive, the sense of ego or of self as an individual differentiating itself from other things is uprooted in the depth of the mind.

The mind can be receptive without being a positive receiver. When the mind is vacuous and receptive, all things of the world can be received by it, and then pass through it without meeting any barrier. This self-forgetting can be cultivated and continued in principle. Here, the most important thing is that the mind will be revealed to itself as both vacuous and receptive simultaneously. When it knows, it is receptive. But, if it is not simultaneously vacuous, then what is received is attached to the mind, and the mind is in turn attached to things. This is the ordinary way of knowing with attachment. On the contrary, if the mind is revealed to itself as both receptive and vacuous simultaneously, it can know things without attachment.

Secondly, Chuang Tzu uses the idea of *ming*[ab], which means the lasting actual state of the mind when its nature, as purely vacuous and receptive, is fully realized in its knowing. Literally, *"ming"* means "light." As a state of mind, it is enlightenment of mind. When Western religious thought talks about enlightenment of mind, it usually means that the mind is enlightened by something above. It is not so in Chinese thought. All Taoists, Confucianists, and Buddhists use the word *"ming"* as self-enlightenment or enlightenment without self. For Chuang Tzu, enlightenment is a state of mind which is purely transparent, and this transparency of mind, which comes from that nature of the mind as both purely vacuous and purely receptive, is fully realized in its knowing. Ordinarily, we know things through concepts and names. When the concepts and names are applied to the things coming to our attention, we meet the things halfway. Here the mind is not purely receptive. The only remedy for such ordinary thinking is to transcend and withdraw our ordinary concepts and names and let the vacuity of mind be realized. Then the mind becomes purely receptive, and is willing to welcome things wholeheartedly, and all the things are thus transparent to us. Here we have enlightenment and also self-forgetting. Nevertheless, the enlightenment of the mind is difficult to achieve, because before things come to attention we already have habits from the past, ready concepts or subconsciousness. These are waiting for our use, and, when things come to us, they pour out like fluids and fill the vacuity of mind and sentence it to death, as it were. Chuang Tzu said that the death of the mind is the greatest lamentation.[9]

According to some philosophies and some religious thought, as, e.g., in Buddhism, we must engage in practice of inner meditation and concentration of mind to enlighten what is dark in our foreconsciousness and subconsciousness. It is not clear whether Chuang Tzu has the same point of view. In Chuang Tzu's philosophy, besides the dialectic thinking used for canceling our presupposed judgments, ready concepts, and names and habits of the past, there is a third important idea about the mind, the idea of *shen*[ac] as the function of mind which is complementary to the idea of *ming*. Meeting things with *shen* is Chuang Tzu's way for attainment of the state of self-forgetting and enlightenment. This is quite different from the way of quiet meditation or serious concentration of mind as generally understood. The word *"shen"* originally meant deity or spirituality. *Shen* is usually connected with—sometimes synonymous with—the word *"ling,"* as explained above. Chuang Tzu uses it to indicate a function of the mind which is not a definite psychological process such as willing, feeling, perceiving, imagining, conceiving, or reasoning, but one which is pervading, and meets the things in their changing processes with intuitive and sympathetic understanding but without attachment. *Shen* is a function of the mind when the mind is permeated with fully living life. *Shen* is always characterized by freedom and spontaneity and is never contracted and reflexive. When *shen* is extended and meets things with intuitive and sympathetic understanding, we have self-forgetting immediately, and we transcend any things which fill our mind. Thus, vacuity of mind can be realized, and enlightenment can be attained through the very extending of *shen*.

In view of Chuang Tzu's three ideas of the mind, it is quite clear that self-forgetting is possible of achievement. When such self-forgetting is achieved, the sense of the self as an individual is gone and, since the world is correlated with the individual self, the sense of the world can thus be forgotten also.

As self-forgetting and world-forgetting are both stressed by Chuang Tzu, we call his way that of transcending the sense of both the individual self and the world as dualistically related, and as thinking that there is, in reality, neither world nor individual. We may interpret this as the way of experiencing the two as one. Chuang Tzu says, "I am living with Heaven and Earth; I am one with the ten thousand things."[10] However, experiencing the two as one is not necessarily to be thought of or talked about. If it is thought of or talked about, the very thinking or talking has to be transcended again. Here we have paradoxical thinking and talking. This is because, when the mind is vacuous, receptive, and knowing without attachment, and enlightenment and spirituality of the mind are realized, the concept "one" cannot be used. It, too, has to be enlightened through and passed by the extending of spirituality also, and so the sense of the world and the individual as one has to be transcended, too. Therefore, according to this type of thinking, there is neither world nor individual. The state of mind of this type of thinking is thus neither subjective nor objective. Instead, it resides in the center of subject and object, and, hanging *in vacuo,* escapes from the duality of these two.[11]

When Lin-chi I-hsüan[ad] (785–857?), the Ch'an master, talks about his way of teaching disciples, he says: "Sometimes I cancel the [idea of] 'person' [as subjective], but not [the idea of] world [as objective]; sometimes I cancel the [idea of] 'world' [as objective] but not the [idea of] 'person' [as subjective]; sometimes, I cancel both the 'person' and the 'world'; and sometimes I cancel neither the 'person' nor the 'world.' "[12] His first way of teaching corresponds to the first way of thinking described above, with the difference that the latter positively asserts the individual person as existing in the objective world. His second way of teaching corresponds to the second way of thinking mentioned above, with the difference that the latter asserts positively the being of the objective world as identical with, or part of, or the content of, the being of the individual as subject. His third way of teaching is more like the third way of thinking, as discussed in this section; it is a synthesis of the earlier two, and rightly represents the spirit of Ch'an. Therefore, the way of thinking of Ch'an also belongs to this type. His fourth way of teaching is the negative of the third way in its logical form, and is actually the same in the spirit of negativity. "I cancel neither the person nor the world" is not the same as "I assert positively both the existence of the subjective person as an individual and the objective world." This will be discussed in the next section.

IV. THE INDIVIDUAL AND THE WORLD KNOWN AS MUTUALLY TRANSCENDENT AND IMMANENT THROUGH KNOWLEDGE OF VIRTUOUS NATURE AND SENSE KNOWLEDGE

The fourth way of thinking of the individual and the world—that both exist—is a general tendency of Chinese thought. Even those thinkers who have been classified above as belonging to the other three types never deny this explicitly. However, only the Confucianists take the co-existence of individual and world seriously, and only in Confucianism do we get the philosophical basis of this way of thinking, a view of the mind which is more synthetic than the other three views.

This fourth view takes the mind as both receptive cognitively and active and creative morally, and insists that, when its nature is realized authentically, enlightenment (*ming*) and spirituality (*shen*) can be included. This view originated with Mencius and was developed in *The Doctrine of the Mean* (*Chung yung*[ae]) and the Commentaries on *The Book of Changes* (*I ching*[af]), which can be supposed to be later than Mencius, and was further developed by Neo-Confucianism in the Sung and Ming dynasties (960–1644). It is sometimes neglected by some Confucian thinkers who are more practically oriented.

In this trend of thought, when the mind knows cognitively and becomes intelligent or wise, it should also be as vacuous as it can be. When the mind is vacuous, it is purely receptive and can become transparent and enlightened. In this respect there is no fundamental difference between Confucianism and Taoism. Yet, on the other side, the mind has its activity and creativity, and it can be self-conscious of itself as an acting subject or a creative subject. When the mind knows the objective world cognitively and has no reflection of itself or thinks of its knowing subject or itself as a thing existing in the world objectively, then we have the first type of thinking, which neglects the subject as an individual which is incapable of being objectified as one among the other things in the world. When the mind is self-conscious of itself as a knowing and acting subject, and thinks of the world-being as identical with its own being or as the content or a part of itself, we have the second way of thinking, which neglects the independent and transcendent existence of the objective world. The first way of thinking may lead man to lose the sense of individual dignity and go astray in the myriad things of the world. The second way of thinking may lead man to assert his self as an absolute and in that case may engender the sense of pride, which is contrary to the moral sense of man. The third way of thinking considers the mind as vacuous, and then self-pride is eradicated. The shortcoming of the third way is its neglect of the mind of the individual self as a subject which is active and creative and self-conscious of itself as such. As it is active and creative, it is not simply vacuous as non-being, but is being and existence also. As it is self-conscious of itself, it can know itself as being an existing self-conscious individual self. On the other side, as the mind is receptive and can know things other than itself, the things also can be self-consciously known as existing. As it is possible also for the mind to forget itself as self-conscious, it is not necessary for it to see things existing merely as a part of, or the content of, or identical with, its being, and it is quite possible for the mind in its self-forgetting to assert the existence of the world and to see it as independent existence.

When the existence of the mind of the individual self and the existence of the things of the world are both asserted, we have the fourth way of thinking of the individual and the world. In this fourth way, Confucianists have the idea of enlightenment and spirituality, which are connected with the mind as active and creative more than with the mind as vacuous and receptive.

According to Mencius, the mind is active and creative, because it has moral nature, which is essentially good, with an inner light. When man fully realizes his good nature and has sageliness, which is unfathomable by knowledge, he has spirituality or holiness.[13] As Mencius' thought is developed into the thought of *The Doctrine of the Mean* and the Commentaries on *The Book of Changes,* ideas about enlightenment and spirituality become more important. In the former, the virtue of human nature is called *"ch'eng*[ag]*,"* which means "creating and accomplishing oneself and all the things of the world."[14] *Ch'eng* is *Tao,* the principle of the world as well as of man. The highest *ch'eng,* as it is realized by the sage, is a way of everlastingly creating and accomplishing, which is the same as everlastingly creating and accomplishing Heaven and Earth. When *ch'eng* is realized and is expressed, there is light or enlightenment, and from enlightenment one can also realize *ch'eng* also.[15] Therefore, the "everlastingly creating and accomplishing" is not only a process of continuous activity; it is also a process illuminated by light and transparent from beginning to end; it is the same as the way of the deity, which is a way of spirituality.

In *The Doctrine of the Mean,* one's inner self and outer things are harmonized in the idea of *ch'eng* as a universal principle. This is rightly called the way of thinking whereby both the individual and the world exist in one ultimate harmony[ah], with light illuminated through it. The inner self as subjective and outer things as objective are then mutually reflected, as mutually creating, mutually accomplishing, and interdependent in a common spiritual enlightenment. In the Commentaries on *The Book of Changes,* the principle of Heaven is called *"ch'ien*[ai]*,"* which is a principle of knowing and creating, and the principle of Earth is called *"k'un*[aj]*,"* which is a principle of realization and accomplishment.[16] These two principles are embodied in man as his human nature, in which intelligence or wisdom, and *jen*[ak], generating love, originated. Here intelligence or wisdom is receptive in knowing, and, at the same time, knowing is an act and is creative also. Generating love is creative, and, at the same time is receptive to what is loved. The mind as receptive may be called its *yin* aspect, and as creative may be called its *yang* aspect.[17] As *yin* and *yang* are two principles or two aspects of the one ultimate *Tao,* and are mutually rooted in each other, therefore the creative aspect and the receptive aspects of mind are mutually rooted in its nature, and the mind, as knowing and acting, or as intelligence or wisdom and generating love (*jen*) are mutually implied in their meanings.

In the Commentaries on *The Book of Changes,* the idea of enlightenment (*ming*) and the idea of spirituality (*shen*) are also emphasized. *Ch'ien,* a universal principle of knowing and creating, is also characterized as a "great enlightenment from beginning to end,"[18] and spirituality is taken as "pervading all things of the world" and "without particular direction."[19] Here enlightenment is not merely a static state of mind; it also resides in a dynamic process of changing life; and spirituality is not only meeting things with intuitive and sympathetic understanding and without attachment, but also "pervading in creating and accomplishing all things according to their particularities without remainder."[20] As spirituality and enlightenment exist in man, what should be sought is the "preservation of them in silence and the realization of them in virtuous action."[21] Thus, the "human nature of oneself is realized" and "Heaven's decree is attained or fulfilled."[22] This is a way of thinking which puts emphasis on both oneself as an individual subject and other individual things of the world as objects, and all of them are seen as organically related in one ultimate harmony, a universal principle of man or of human nature and of all things in the world, and the co-existence of the world and the individual was thus established in classical Confucianism.

Its development in the Neo-Confucianism of the Sung and Ming dynasties consists in the clearer elucidation of the thoughts of classical Confucianism with some new interpretations. One new idea agreed to by almost all Neo-Confucianists of the Ch'eng-Chu[al] school is the idea of "one principle (or one reason) participated in by different things," which is a metaphysical idea for the synthesis of the one and the many, identity and difference, and the universal and the particular individual. It is also closely related to a new theory of mind and knowledge. As Chang Tsai[am] (1020–1077) and the Ch'eng brothers classify man's kinds of knowledge into sense-knowledge and knowledge of virtuous nature, the latter is always taken as universal, self-identical, and one, and the former is always taken as particular and as differentiated according to the many sensed objects.

As knowledge of virtuous nature can be expressed through sense-knowledge, we have an example of "one principle participated in by different things." According to Chang Tsai and the Ch'eng brothers, "knowledge of virtuous nature[an]" is quite different from "sense-knowledge." One of the differences is that we can have knowledge of virtuous nature which comprises spirituality and enlightenment,[23] but we cannot attain to spirituality and enlightenment through sense-knowledge alone. The reason knowledge of virtue can comprise enlightenment and spirituality is based upon the fact that knowledge of virtuous nature is not merely knowledge which takes virtuous nature[ao] as its object.

Knowledge of virtuous nature is knowledge through the very virtuous practice of the moral mind. More adequately, it is not knowledge about anything else; it is only self-knowledge of the moral mind as such, or of the moral mind self-conscious of itself as such, or the moral mind as transparent to itself as such, and this is self-enlightenment. As the self-conscious moral mind is active, creative, and pervading all things in the world, it knows no limits in its creative and active extending, and it acts like deity and comprises spirituality. However, sense-knowledge is directed to the sense-object, which is opaque by itself, but can, so to speak, absorb the light radiated from our minds. Therefore, when isolated from the knowledge of the virtuous mind, it does not comprise self-enlighten-ment, and thus we can never attain spirituality through it alone.

Sense-knowledge is distinctly different in kind from self-knowledge of virtuous nature or spiritual enlightenment, but they are not nec-essarily separated in existence and can co-exist. In fact, they ought to co-exist, and the knowledge of virtuous nature can fully exist only through sense-knowledge. This is because the virtuous nature ought to be realized in moral action, and moral action is purposive in creating and accomplishing objective things, which can be known only through the senses. So far as our knowledge of virtuous nature is realized and expressed in the outer world through sense-knowledge about outer things, the knowledge of virtuous nature is taken as one, and sense-knowledge about outer things varies according to the differences of things. We thus have an actual exemplification of "one principle expressed (and participated in) by different things." Since knowledge about outer things is the necessary condition for the expression of our knowledge of virtuous nature, it ought to be sought and stressed even from the point of view of the knowledge of virtuous nature. Since things known by sense-knowledge are all individuals, "investigation of individual things one by one" is in-cluded in the teaching of the "investigation of things" as expounded by Ch'eng I[ap] (1033–1107) and Chu Hsi[aq] (1130–1200).

Furthermore, since these two kinds of knowledge are related and are differentiated only by their directions as outer-oriented and inner-oriented, what is known through them as "I as self-conscious moral subject" and "individual things of the world" should both be posited as really existing. Here we have four points of view about the mutual transcendence and immanence between the world and individual self.

First, when I am known by myself mainly through my sense-knowledge as an individual existence, I then co-exist with other outer things and persons in one objective world, and I as one indi-vidual and all other individuals are immanent in one objective world.

Second, if all outer things, including my body and other persons and things known as outer things, are taken as nothing but those known only through my sense and immanent in my world of sense, and, if I am convinced also that I have knowledge of virtuous nature, which belongs to a higher level about my knowledge of outer things, then I, as an individual self-conscious moral subject, can be taken as transcendent to all things of the world known as outer, and, similarly, can be looked upon as transcendent to the whole outer world.

Third, from a higher point of view, I know also that I am not the only individual self-conscious moral subject, and that other individual persons whom I know through sense of existing in the outer world are each actually having their knowledge of virtuous nature, and each is an individual self-conscious moral subject as well as I am; and I as an individual am known by others through their sense and by being seen by them as existing in their outer worlds also; therefore, I have to acknowledge their transcendence to me and that I am immanent in their sense of the outer world. Thus, I am immanent in the outer worlds of others, which are transcendent to me.

Fourth, from a still higher point of view, we should have the self-conviction that I know all that has just been said. I know that each person has the same self-conscious moral mind and knowledge of virtuous nature. I know also that I have to act toward them with respect and love. I know all of these through the reasoning of my moral mind (also the rational mind), which is based on the knowledge of my virtuous nature. Consequently, nothing is transcendent to this reasoning of my moral mind, which is based on the knowledge of my virtuous nature. Thus, the reasoning of my moral mind is without doubt mine. However, this reasoning leads me to the acknowledgment of others as having the same moral mind, the same outer world, and the same reasoning as mine. It is, then, a transcendental reasoning which leads me to transcend the "very reasoning as only mine," and such reasoning should be taken as self-transcending reasoning and not only as belonging to me but also as revealed to me. Thus it may be taken as heavenly reasoning, or the heavenly principle, as participated in by me and flowing in my mind. As heavenly, the reasoning or principle is universal and of the world as well as mine. It is revealed to me and participated in by me as an individual, as well as revealed to, and participated in by, any different individual who is a self-conscious mind or moral subject, as I am. Hence, we have an ultimate belief in "one principle" or "one reason" participated in by different individuals, which is closely related to the ideas about the nature of moral mind, the knowledge of virtuous nature, and sense-knowledge.

In conclusion, though the world and the individual are either immanent or transcendent to each other from the different points of view of different levels of thinking, they are ultimately included as moments of one idea of an ultimate harmony of mind and Heaven, or one vision of the ultimate harmony of the individual and the world which expresses "one principle expressed by (or participated in by) different things," as in the Ch'eng-Chu school.

As the fourth way of thinking about the individual and the world is not denied explicitly by other schools of Chinese thought, the relation of the individual subject and the objective world is usually thought of by Chinese thinkers as in one ultimate harmony.

The Chinese translation of the words "subject" and "object" of Indian and Western philosophy are "chu[ar]" and "pin[as]," or "jen[at]" and "ching[au]," or "chien[av]" and "hsiang[aw]." Originally "chu" means host, and "pin" means guest; "jen" means man, and "ching" means environment or things in vision; "chien" means seeing, and "hsiang" means what is seen and taking the role of assisting in the seeing. The three pairs of words are reciprocally complementary as in a harmonious whole or a harmonious experience. Taking the subject as host, the object is the guest who is invited and loved by the host (this symbolizes the object's immanence in the subject), and also respected and sent out by the host (this symbolizes the object's transcendence to the subject). On the other hand, the world can be seen also by the poets and philosophers as host, and then the man (or I as an individual) is guest of the world and is entertained by the hospitality of the world. It is quite clear that there is no dualism between host and guest. This metaphor is the best symbol for Chinese thought about the relation of the subjective individual and the objective world as mutually immanent and transcendent in an ultimate harmony.

QUESTION: In Section III of your paper you have quoted the sayings of Lin-chi I-hsüan and have translated the fourth sentence as "I cancel neither the person (as subject) nor the world (as object)." The same sentence is translated by Suzuki as "to make both the subject and the object remain," as quoted in the paper by Ueda Yoshifumi. Which of the two translations is closer to the original, or do they both have the same meaning?

ANSWER: According to the Chinese original, Lin-chi I-hsüan used the word "chü-pu-to[bq]" in the fourth sentence, which means to "cancel neither," as I have translated it. Suzuki's translation has converted the negative sentence into a positive one, as if to "cancel neither" may imply to "assert both." Nevertheless, in the spirit of Ch'an, a double negation does not necessarily imply an assertion; therefore, to "not cancel" or to "cancel neither" may simply imply the negation of canceling, and nothing more. So I think my translation may be closer to the original.

QUESTION: You have classified Chinese thought about the individual and the world according to four types, yet most of your illustrations are taken from the schools of pre-Ch'in philosophy[br]. I would like to know how you classify the different schools of Chinese Buddhism of the Medieval Ages and Neo-Confucianism of the Sung-Ming[bs] and Ch'ing[bt] dynasties according to these four categories.

ANSWER: The reason that most of my illustrations of the categories come from schools of the pre-Ch'in period is that the thoughts of these schools are more original and purer in type and their essential ideas are more easily grasped. As to the classification of Chinese Buddhism and Neo-Confucianism, the problem is somewhat complicated. Roughly speaking, in the different schools of Buddhism, the Mādhyamika school, which takes *śūnyatā* as objectively pervading all individual things, is a way of thinking belonging to the first category in a superseded form; the Vijñānavāda school, which begins with epistemological idealism and ends in a kind of ethical idealism through the transformation of *vijñāna,* has to be classified as beyond the individual and the world, and belongs therefore to the third type. The schools of Hua-yen[bu] and T'ien-t'ai[bv], which are schools of Buddhism created by Chinese monks and which emphasize, not only the teaching of co-existence of the one and the many, of the world and the individual, but also their mutual inclusion and interreflexive relations in a most comprehensive and subtle metaphysical system, may be taken as a Buddhist version of the *Chung yung* and *The Book of Changes,* and thus belongs to the fourth type.

After the Sung Dynasty, the thoughts of Chou Tun-i[bw] and Chang Tsai, who take the cosmological approach to philosophy and see man as part of the objective world which is not pervaded simply by *śūnyatā* but exists objectively, belong to the first category. The *Lu-Wang*[bx] school and the Ch'eng-Chu[by] school are classified as belonging to the second and third type respectively, as explained in my paper. Some thinkers of the Lu-Wang school, such as Yang Chien[bz] and Wang Chi[ca], who emphasize the sense of "beyond the self as individual ego and the world as opposite to the self," and some forerunners of Ch'eng-Chu school, such as Shao Yung[cb], who, in his philosophical poems expresses his pure contemplation of the changes of the universe without recognition of the individual or the world, are all of the third type of thinking.

At the end of the Ming Dynasty and the beginning of the Ch'ing Dynasty, there is Wang Fu-chih[cc], who goes back to Chang Tsai's way of thinking and emphasizes the status of the individual against the background of an objective, natural, historical world. Tai Chen[cd], Yen Yüan[ce], and many scholars of the Ch'ing Dynasty all laid emphasis on the knowledge of individual things as objectively determined by their spatio-temporal locations, their actual functions of and relations to other things of the world, and thus encouraged the study of history, ancient classics, and historical remains. It seems to be that in the later period of the Ch'ing Dynasty, the profound Chinese philosophical wisdom sank to acceptance of what is actually existing in the objective historical world. The reason the historical materialism of Marx and Engels could conquer the mind of recent China is that it takes advantage of this trend of thought, though the other three typical ways of thinking in traditional philosophy will come back again, according to the historical fluctuations of Chinese thought.

1 He begins his treatise "On Pointing and Things" with the statement that nothing is incapable of being pointed to, but that the pointing (with the names we use for pointing understood) is not being pointed to. *Kung-sun Lung,* 3.

2 *Hsün Tzu,* 22, "Rectification of Names." For detailed discussion on Hsün Tzu's theory of names, see my paper "Hsün Tzu cheng-ming yü ming-hsüeh san tsung[ax]" (Hsün Tzu's Rectification of Names and Three Schools of Logicians in Pre-Ch'in Philosophy), *New Asia Journal*[ay], V, No. 2. (August, 1963), 1–22.

[3] For the original meaning and the derivative meanings of the words *"yin"* and *"yang,"* consult my book *Che-hsüeh kai-lun*[az] (A Treatise on Philosophy) (Hong Kong: Mencius Educational Foundation, 1961), Vol. II, Part III, chap. 5, sec. 3, and chap. 9, sec. 1.

[3a] As for individualism, we have Yang Chu[ba] (400–? B.C.) in the Pre-Ch'in period, who insists on the theory of one self (*wei-wo*[bb]), and who is as influential as the Moist school was in the Mencius age. However, we know nothing clear about all his arguments for individualism. He does not expound any solipsism or subjective idealism in the epistemological sense.

[4] *Mencius,* VIIA.4.

[5] *Hsiang-shan ch'üan-chi*[bc] (Complete Works of Lu Hsiang-shan) (Shanghai: Chung Hua Co., 1935), Vol. 36, p. 37.

[6] *Yang-ming ch'üan-shu*[bd] (Complete Works of Wang Yang-ming) (Shanghai: Chung Hua Co., 1935), Vol. III, p. 26.

[7] Liu Ch'i-shan's discussion on the ideas of *tu* and *tu-chih* is available in the last volume of *Ming-ju hsüeh-an*[be] (Anthology and Critical Accounts of the Neo-Confucians of the Ming Dynasty), edited and written by Huang Tsung-hsi[bf] (1610–1695). For a contemporary exposition, see Mou Tsung-san's[bg] article "Liu Chi-shan chih ch'eng-i-chih-hsüeh[bh]" (Theory of Authenticity of Will of Liu Ch'i-shan), *Tzu-yu hsüeh-jen*[bi] (Free Thinker), I, No. 3 (October, 1956), 9–24.

[8] *Chuang Tzu,* 33.

[9] *Chuang Tzu,* 2.

[10] *Ibid.*

[11] The second chapter of the *Chuang Tzu* begins with talking about "loss of ego," which can be rightly explained as getting out of the duality of subject and object.

[12] *Chih-wu-lu*[bj] (Records of the Pointing of the Moon), edited by Chu Ju-chi[bk] (Taipei: Far East Book Co., 1959), Vol. 14, p. 5.

[13] *Mencius,* 7.

[14] The word *"ch'eng"* is sometimes translated as sincerity. This is quite misleading and does not conform to the text of the *Chung yung.* It is better to define it as "creating and accomplishing oneself and all the things of the world" than to follow a literal translation.

[15] *Chung yung,* 21. (Shanghai: Commercial Press edition, 1937), p. 12.

[16] The best exposition of *ch'ien* as principle of knowing and creating and of *k'un* as principle of realization and accomplishment is available in the *Hsü-tan-chih-chüan*[bl] (Looking around the Altar with Straightforward Illustrations) of Lo Chin-ch'i[bm] (1515–1588). See my essay "Lo Chin-ch'i chih li-hsüeh[bn]" (On the Philosophy of Lo Chin-ch'i), Special issue for one hundred issues of *Min-chu p'ing-lun*[bo] (Democratic Review), V, No. 6 (March, 1954), 2–10.

[17] See my book *Che-hsüeh kai-lun*[bp] (A Treatise on Philosophy), Vol. II, Part II, chap. 19, sec. 6.

[18] See "Ch'ien wen-yen[bq]" (Commentaries on *ch'ien* as a Principle of Heaven), in *The Book of Changes.*

[19] Commentaries on *The Book of Changes.*

[20] *Ibid.*

[21] *Ibid.*

[22] *Ibid.*

[23] The ideas of *shen* (spirituality) and *ming* (enlightenment) are two very profound ideas of Neo-Confucianism which are closely related to the knowledge of virtuous nature, but are usually neglected by contemporary scholars of Confucianism. I have given some hints on the significance of these two ideas in Confucianism in Chapter 4 of my book, *Chung-kuo wen-hua chih ching-shen chia-chih* (The Spiritual Value of Chinese Culture). (Hong Kong: Cheng Chung, 1953). Further study of their meanings in Neo-Confucian thought is needed.

a	唐君毅	m	名實論
b	墨家	n	白馬論
c	名家	o	正名
d	荀子	p	陰
e	陰陽家	q	陽
f	類	r	陸象山
g	孟子	s	王陽明
h	墨子	t	本心
i	墨辯	u	良知
j	實	v	劉蕺山
k	公孫龍子	w	獨
l	指物論	x	獨知

y 莊子

z 虛

aa 靈

ab 明

ac 神

ad 臨濟義玄

ae 中庸

af 易經

ag 誠

ah 太和

ai 乾

aj 坤

ak 仁

al 程朱學派

am 張載

an 德性之知

ao 見聞之知

ap 程頤

aq 朱熹

ar 主

as 賓

at 人

au 境

av 見

aw 相

ax 荀子正名與名學三家

ay 新亞學報

az 哲學概論

ba 楊朱

bb 爲我

bc 象山全集

bd 陽明全書

be 明儒學案

bf 黃宗羲

bg 牟宗三

bh 劉蕺山誠意之學

bi 自由學人

bj 指月錄

bk 瞿汝稷

bl 盱壇直詮

bm 羅近溪

bn 羅近溪之理學

bo 民主評論

bp 哲學概論

bq 乾文言

br 俱不奪

bs 前秦

bt 宋明

bu 清

bv 華嚴

bw 天台

bx 周敦頤

by 陸王學派

bz 程朱學派

ca 楊簡

cb 王畿

cc 邵雍

cd 王夫之

ce 戴震

P. T. RAJU

Indian epistemology
and the world and the individual

I. INTRODUCTION

Epistemology[1] can discuss the problem of the world and the individual by answering the two main questions: (1) How are the world and the individual cognized?[2] and (2) Since knowledge is communicated in language, how are the concepts of the world and the individual expressed? Some languages may not have developed a philosophy of themselves, but Sanskrit has its own philosophies, not merely one but many. Of them, the philosophy of the Grammarians is the most pertinent. Our second question has, therefore, to include the question, What place do the world and the individual occupy in the philosophy of language?

II. THE NATURE OF EPISTEMOLOGY

Indian epistemology is generally divided into three topics: (1) the distinct means (*pramāṇas*) of obtaining valid knowledge; (2) the nature of validity (*prāmāṇya*); and (3) the nature and status of the object of illusion (*khyāti*).

Semantics was from the beginning of the systems a part of epistemology, for the word was recognized as a distinct means of valid knowledge by almost all the schools and classified under means of knowledge. When a word is uttered, we "perceive" only noises—as when we listen to an absolutely foreign language—but not its reference to objects. When I see a book, I see a color and a shape. The color and shape mean[3] the book. But they belong to the book, whereas we do not believe that the word "horse" belongs to the object horse. So, verbal knowledge is a distinct kind of knowledge. The wonder that is the word was therefore recognized by Indian thinkers. In addition, the Veda was orally transmitted and was considered to be sacrosanct. How can the words of the Veda contain the mystery of the universe? Hence, also, the philosophical interest in the word. Also, grammar was prescribed as an indispensable subsidiary study to the Veda; it must therefore lead to what the Veda itself teaches, namely, knowledge of the most important reality. Then the philosophy of grammar must be almost as important as the philosophy of the Veda and has to support it. Hence the importance of the philosophy of grammar. But, as the philosophy of the Veda is differently understood by the different schools, they developed different philosophies of grammar also. Thus, the interest in the nature of language, grammar, and semantics was intense from the very beginning.

Right from the time of Gautama (*ca.* 400 B.C.?), the founder of the Nyāya, or perhaps even from an earlier time, it has been recognized that the knowable (*prameya*) is dependent on the means of knowledge (*pramāṇa*), i.e., mctaphysics is dependent on epistemology. But, first, as often done in the West,[4] we can so interpret the same epistemological processes and criteria as to fit a particular metaphysics. The schools need not accept the same metaphysics even when they accept the same sources of knowledge. Second, Indian thought did not start in the Upaniṣads with epistemology, but with a kind of ontology, to which at least nominally all the orthodox schools owe allegiance. Third, even if a school accepts a number of ways of knowing, that does not mean that whatever is known through those ways is also accepted as unmistakably true. This distinction is often overlooked, but it is important. The question is about the ways by which our consciousness can reveal Being and beings. For instance, consciousness reveals something through imagination also. But is what is so revealed to be taken as real? Perception, inference, postulation, etc., can be mistaken; yet, they are accepted as revealing the existence of objects. Now, if every one of them is a means of valid knowledge, how can invalidity come in? And what is then the nature of invalid knowledge? Fourth, if we have several sources of valid knowledge, what are we to do when there is conflict between any two or three? For instance, if perception tells us that the object at a distance is water, but inference tells us that it is a mirage, what are we to do? Śaṁkara says that in such cases perception has to be ignored and inference is to be accepted. Rāmānuja[5] says that both have to be accepted and somehow reconciled. In any case, Indian philosophers have maintained that, with the help of the different sources of knowledge, we have to build up our knowledge and the known world.

III. THE SOURCES OF KNOWLEDGE

The well-known schools of Indian philosophy recognize one or more of the six[5a] ways (means) of knowledge:[6] perception (*pratyakṣa*), inference (*anumāna*), verbal knowledge (*śabda*), comparison (*upamāna*), postulation (*arthāpatti*), and non-apprehension (*anupalabdhi*).[7]

Perception. In perception we observe the individual or individuals. All schools accept—the Cārvāka is not clear—the distinction between indeterminate and determinate perceptions. But many, following the Nyāya, treat indeterminate perception as useless, since it presents only "a being" but not the type of being. It is formless and relationless.[8] But the Mīmāṁsā of Prabhākara and the Vedānta of Rāmānuja say that indeterminate perception is not formless; only, it does not involve memory, and so the form (universal) is not distinguished in it. It is what corresponds to Russell's knowledge by acquaintance. In knowledge by description, in which the What is involved, memory enters. So, real perception is knowledge by acquaintance and is indeterminate and relationless. Although the Buddhist Vijñānavādins do not accept the Vaiśeṣika doctrine of the particular, they say that in perception we cognize only the particular (*apodha*), that which is itself and not anything else (*apoha*). Names, forms, and relations enter our knowledge later, but they have no ultimate reality. The rivals of the Buddhists point out that that factor of perception which is "not anything else" is relational, and perception cannot, therefore, be non-relational.

Now, according to the Nyāya theory, which is generally accepted, that we perceive a determinate individual horse, e.g., means that we perceive an object determined by the universal (form, *prakāra*) horseness. Here the Nyāya has an interesting development. Through the perception of horseness in the individual, we cognize—indeed, perceive—all individual horses. "That is a horse" then becomes "That is a member of the class of horses." Thus the class concept or idea is accepted by the Naiyāyikas, who utilize it for forming universal premises such as "All horses are mortal." To obtain the idea of the class "horses," it is not necessary to perceive many horses.

The Nyāya divides perception into the ordinary and the extra-ordinary. The cognition of the class horses is one form of the extra-ordinary. The second type of the extra-ordinary is the perception of an object of one sense organ by another. I see a rose and say, "That is a sweet rose." The sweet smell is generally perceived by the nose, but here I see it through the eye. The third type belongs to the *yogin*.[9]

Thus, it is recognized that in perception we see the individuals, but it contains factors that enable us to go beyond the individuals and expand our knowledge to cover the rest of the world. Again, what we know in perception is not the abstract individual, but a particular individual, not a mere member of a class, but this or that member.

Inference.[9a] It is recognized by all schools that inference is relational. The relations generally accepted in this context are class membership, class inclusion, causal relation, and spatial and temporal relations. But, until inferential knowledge ends in perception, we stay in the realm of the Whats only, i.e., of description. We may infer the presence of fire in the mountain, and we may know also that that fire differs from every other fire, but it is still a matter of Whats or description. However, although several kinds of relations were accepted for inference, and, although the idea of structure (*samsthāna, ākṛti*) was also known, formal logic as the science of order was not developed.

Comparison.[9b] Comparison as a means of knowledge is understood in two ways. The Naiyāyikas understand it as perception through analogy or similarity. If an American hears from a friend that a buffalo is like a bison, having the common feature x, when he actually sees the buffalo for the first time, he says, "That is a buffalo." This cognition means "That is an object characterized by the common characteristic x." But, according to Prabhākara, comparison is the cognition of similarity itself.[10] When an American sees a buffalo, whether after or without the verbal knowledge of the common characteristic, he cognizes an object with a form. This cognition is mere perception. But he says also, "That is similar to a bison." This cognition is the result of comparison, which, therefore, is a way of knowing distinct from perception and verbal knowledge.

The cognition of similarity is important for the extension of our knowledge of the world and for obtaining knowledge of universals and classes, so that we can be masters of our knowledge without losing ourselves in the forest of individuals. It is possible to compare individuals with individuals, classes with classes, and universals with universals. But class comparisons do not seem to have engaged the minds of these thinkers very much. That is why Indian logic has not developed any systematic theory of classification, although one may find some roots of the doctrine. However, Prabhākara recognizes, not only that similarity belongs to the world of objects, but also that mind has a peculiar capacity to discover similarities, and this capacity is a distinct way of knowing.

Postulation.[10a] Postulation[11] is the method by which we posit something for the completion of our understanding and meaning. If two statements p and q are opposed and yet both are true, we have to postulate a statement r that can explain both the opposition and the truth of p and q. The postulated entities may be sensible or supersensible.

An example of the sensible is:

> Devadatta is growing fat; but he claims not to eat at all, and none has observed him eating during the day.
> Then he must be eating secretly at night.

Here his having eaten is observable.

An example of the supersensible is:

> Ethical action performed in this life can produce a happy exist-
> ence in the next life.
>
> But between this life and the next there is a time interval, and
> causation is a continuous process.
>
> Then ethical action becomes and stays as an unseen potency
> during the time interval.

This potency is called the extra-ordinary (*apūrva*) and the unseen
(*adṛṣṭa*). Postulation enables us to extend our knowledge to unsee-
able realms and works mainly with the Whats. We may postulate
individual objects like the center of the earth; yet, we are still within
the realm of knowledge by description.

Non-apprehension. If the world is a world of plurality—the ethical world has to be a world of plurality—then negation in the form
of difference between any two objects and also in the form of absence of every object everywhere except where it is present has to
be accepted. But how do we know negation at all? The Mīmāṁsā
of Kumārila and some followers of Śaṁkara accept non-apprehension or non-cognition as a form of cognition itself. I cognize the
absence of the rose on the table. But this cognition is neither perception, because there can be no sense-contact with absence, nor inference,[12] because there is no syllogistic reasoning. It is a peculiar way
of cognizing, which Kumārila calls by the contradictory term non-
cognition. How can non-cognition be a form of cognition? The
Nyāya accepts the reality of negation, but rejects non-cognition as a
way of cognition. The Advaitins go along with Kumārila so far as
the empirical world is concerned.[12a] Negation enables us to distinguish individual from individual, class from class, and universal from
universal.

IV. THE VALIDITY OF KNOWLEDGE

The question of the validity of knowledge occurred to the Indian
thinkers in a peculiar way. They knew that every one of the ways
of knowing may misfire: illusions and hallucinations of perception
are false; fallacious inference cannot give truth; postulation has to
stand the test of modal negation (*tarka*); and so on. They knew
also that whatever is contradicted cannot be valid and that at our
level we can be certain only of the uncontradictable. They knew,
further, that the world is a world of action and that uncontradict-
ability cannot be attained in our knowledge of the empirical world;
so, they held that all cognition can be confirmed or disproved
through action.

But the question of validity occurred in a new form also. Knowledge is a form of consciousness which reveals objects. Its function is to reveal truth. Then should we take our cognitions as true only because they are forms of consciousness? If we cannot, then should we distrust all cognition? If we do, what else is there to trust? If the individual is to distrust every act of his consciousness, how can he know the truth about the world at all?

Hence arose the conception of the self-validity of knowledge (*svatah-prāmānya*), accepted by the Sāmkhya, the Mīmāmsā, and the Vedānta. The Buddhist Vijñānavādins and Mādhyamikas, on the other hand, maintained that all cognitions are by themselves invalid (*svatah-aprāmānya*[12b]), because cognitions present objects, but no object is real. According to the Vijñānavādins, the impersonal consciousness (*vijñāna*) that reveals itself to itself in every cognition is alone true—its content is false; according to the Mādhyamikas, even that impersonal consciousness is false—only the *śūnya* (void) is true. Then, if all cognition is by itself valid according to one group and false according to the other, why do we draw the distinction at all between validity and invalidity? The former group, except the Sāmkhya, maintains that a cognition is made invalid by something other than that cognition (*paratah-aprāmānya*), and the other group thinks that it is made valid by this other (*paratah-prāmānya*), the other being the world of action or the pragmatic world. (The Jainas accept both.) The distinction is due to the nature of the pragmatic world.

The Sāmkhya contends that the invalidity of cognition belongs to, and is cognized by, cognition itself, and cognition is therefore invalid also by itself (*svatah-aprāmānya*). This invalidity may be detected by the failure of the object of cognition to lead to the expected results (*arthakriyā*), but neither is a false cognition made false nor a true cognition made true by anything else. The Nyāya, on the other hand, maintains that cognition is neither true nor false by itself, but is made so by the proper or improper working of the means of cognition, such as the eye, the light, and the other media. Since we cannot always know whether these means are defective or not, and since the world is a world of action, the pragmatic criterion that the object of cognition must lead to the expected results can help.[13]

Thus, for the Nyāya the world is there and is pragmatic also. But the individual is deprived of his confidence in his cognitions. For the Buddhists, the world is not real—it has only pragmatic truth.[13a] The others ask the individual to trust his consciousness and yet to be careful. But, for all, the world is a pragmatic world, although they differ from one another on whether it is something more besides.

V. THE OBJECT OF ILLUSION

We generally speak of illusions in the case of perception only, but not in the case of any of the other ways of knowing. The object of illusion is always an individual. Neither is illusion mere memory, nor the object of illusion a mere impression. Memory and impressions may be factors in the perception of illusory objects, but are not themselves perception. The Sāṁkhya, the Mīmāṁsā of Prabhākara, and Rāmānuja maintain that, since all cognitions are true by themselves, the object of illusory perceptions also is real and existent, although it cannot lead to the expected results of action. The Nyāya maintains that illusion is due to the "misplacement of the universal or form (*prakāra*) in the object." If the rope is cognized as a snake, and I say, "That is a snake," then I misplace the universal snakeness in the That. Yet, the That is real, and the snakeness also is real as it exists in real snakes. There is nothing unreal in illusion; it is only a false classification. Kumārila, with the intention of upholding the self-validity of all knowledge and the reality of the objects of all cognitions, accepts the Nyāya position, with this difference, that, since the illusory snake is seen in time and space, and since the universal cannot exist in time and space but is above them, the illusory snake, which is perceived, is not a universal but some other snake seen previously. That is, the snake seen is a remembered snake, or the particular rope is seen as the particular remembered snake. Prabhākara also holds that both the rope and the snake are real objects, but adds that, since the particular snake cannot be identified with the particular rope, illusion is only the non-cognition of their difference. For the Vijñānavādins, everything except consciousness is an illusion, and all the objective forms which our consciousness takes are illusions.

The Advaitin says that "That is a rope" and "That is a snake" are both perceptions of individuals. The snake we see is neither a misplaced real universal (*sat*) nor a mere mental image or fabrication (*asat*). It is not even a remembered real snake. It is not existent, because it is contradicted by the later perception: "That is not and was not a snake." It is not non-existent, because Being shines through it through the word "is." It is, therefore, neither existent nor non-existent, i.e., it is inexplicable (*anirvacanīya*). By this interpretation, the self-validity of our knowledge is not violated, because the purpose of consciousness is to reveal Being, and Being is revealed through the "is" in "That is a snake" also. The snake does not meet the pragmatic criterion, and is, therefore, kept out of the world of action, which is the world in which we live.

VI. THE PHILOSOPHY OF LANGUAGE

We now consider the philosophy of language, particularly the theories of the word and meaning. Although we do not find in Indian thought the picture theory of language of the early Wittgenstein, we find the attempt to treat those parts of the sentence as primary which represent the main features of reality. While Cassirer[14] regards language as one of the forms of man's self-liberation from the entanglement in the world of individual objects, Bhartṛhari,[15] the Grammarian, regards the main function of language as the spiritual liberation of the individual. As Cassirer says that man is an *animal symbolicum*,[16] Bhartṛhari[17] says that man evolves out of the Word itself. Like Heidegger,[18] he says that the question of Being is deeply involved in language, not in logic. Russell[19] writes that language externalizes experience; but the Sanskrit Grammarians will add that spoken language externalizes experience, which is the internal language and which is identical with its meaning. Language is not only expression but also communication—it involves the hearer-speaker situation;[20] and, as Carnap[21] wants, it has a representative function also. But how does it have this representative power, how does it descend into the expression of the speaker, and how does it convey its meaning to the hearer? These questions also engaged the minds, not only of the Sanskrit Grammarians, but also of the other philosophers.

William von Humboldt[22] regarded the differences among languages as differences among world perspectives, and Hegel[23] called language the actuality of culture. But actual cultures and perspectives have fluid spiritual depths, which must be common to all men. What Benjamin Lee Whorf says in this connection has particular significance. He says that our ordinary languages have different patterns, but these patterns originate in a pattern *par excellence,* which is beyond time and space.[24] If this language pattern belongs to all men, what can that pattern be? The Grammarians of India were deeply interested in tracing the expressed language to this universal, inward language common to all men.

The Nairukta philosophy of language: Yāska,[25] the author of the *Nairukta,* the earliest lexicon in the world, refers to the view of Śākaṭāyana, who maintained that all nouns are derived from verbal roots. Yāska accepts this view because it agrees with his philosophy that the *Ātman* is the ultimate reality and that it is activity itself. This understanding of the *Ātman* is in accord with the etymological meaning of the word *"Brahman,"* which is derived from the verbal root *"bṛh,"* meaning "to grow," "to expand." The *Brahman* is the ever-growing, the ever-expanding. It is *sattā* (Being) itself, but *sattā,* or Being, is activity itself. "To be" is a verb and represents an act. Then the primary part of the sentence is the verb. The most basic of all verbs is the root *"as"* (to be). Every other verb is its form, i.e., every other act is a form which the primary act "to be" takes. What we have to note is that "to be" is an act, and the "is" is not a mere copula. In the Nairukta philosophy, Being is the same as becoming, and the noun is to be derived from the verb. In fact, all the other parts of the sentence are modes of the verb.[26]

The Nairukta philosophy may seem strange, but it is essentially the philosophy of language that accepts the world as activity. But activity should not be understood as unstructured and unpatterned. We can understand it in terms of play or, rather, of dance, which has a definite pattern—a beginning, an end, certain patterns, and different men and women following the patterns of the dance activity.

The Mīmāṁsā theory of language: To say that Being is only of the nature of activity and the ethical individual is nothing more than one of the modes of that activity did not satisfy the ethical realism of the Mīmāṁsakas for the individual as a free agent is responsible for his actions—they maintained that the noun and the verb, the doer and his action, are equally important and are forms of Being. This view is accepted by both Kumārila and Prabhākara, although the latter gives in his discussions greater importance to activity than Kumārila gives.

Prabhākara says that, since activity is the controller of the manifold forms of the world, the verb is more important than the noun in the sentence and holds together all the nouns and their relations and conveys the total meaning. The meaning of every word is the activity it leads us to. Prabhākara goes to the extent of saying that the being (*sattā*) of an object lies in its operational efficiency.[27] For holding such a view, he is classified with the Buddhist Vijñānavādins by Śrī Harṣa.[28] However, Prabhākara accepts the independent existence of nouns apart from verbs, but contends that, without being associated with the activities conveyed by verbs, the meaning of nouns cannot be understood. But, as the Vijñānavādins do not accept stable substantives like the *ātman,* for them, "to be" is to be a process; the world is pure process, and everything is pure process and momentary.

The Nyāya theory of language:[29] The Naiyāyikas generally accept the Mīmāṁsā theory of Kumārila. Their old school maintained that Being (*sattā*) is present in substances (*dravyas*), qualities (*guṇas*), and activities (*karmas*). However, this school tends to treat activity as a qualifying adjunct (*viśeṣaṇa*) of substance, while the Mīmāṁsā gives it an importance at least equal to that of substance. That is, the noun is more important in the Nyāya than in the Mīmāṁsā, for ethics is more concerned with the nature of actions than with that of men. Furthermore, the concept of *sattā* itself is different in the two schools. For the Mīmāṁsā, it is ontological; for the Nyāya, it is the most common feature of all beings or of everything that is. As it is understood to be the most common feature, the Neo-Nyāya rejected it altogether, for the reason that it can never be cognized. They accepted, instead, the idea of *bhāva* (positing), adding that, not only substance, quality, and activity, but also universal (*sāmānya*), inherence (*samavāya*), and the particular (*viśeṣa*) are *bhāvas*. But the word "*bhāva*" means for the Mīmāṁsā the act of being (something)—it is a verb; for the Neo-Nyāya, it is affirmation (as opposed to negation)—it is the positive as opposed to the negative.

The Vedāntic theory of language: According to the Advaita, the main purpose of language is to reveal Being (*sattā*), which is the same as *Brahman*.[30] This school accepts the view of Kumārila, so far as the empirical world goes. But Kumārila, being a pluralist and also an ethical activist, does not hold that Being belongs to *Brahman* alone, but is present in both the noun and the verb. This is what Rāmānuja also accepts, but, with this difference, that in his conception of ultimate reality, which is pluralistic in a way, he imposes monism on pluralism by accepting two ultimate categories, substance and quality, thereby reducing activity also to a quality (*viśeṣaṇa*); but in his conception of empirical reality he seems to go along with Prabhākara. Now, for the Advaitins, the same Being is revealed through all sentences. "That is a horse" is meant to reveal Being through the "is." That is why Rāmānuja[31] asks why the man who wants to purchase a horse will not be satisfied with purchasing a cow, if "That is a horse" and "That is a cow" reveal the same Being. The Advaitin would answer that the man is not interested in Being itself, but in Being in the form of the horse and not in the form of the cow. His interest is pragmatic, not ultimate.

The Grammarian theory of language: The Grammarian philosophers, e.g., the Nairuktas, are also called the wordists (*śābdikas*). Bhartṛhari[32] is the greatest among them. He accepts the Mīmāṁsā theory that Being is revealed through both the noun and the verb. But, like Śaṁkara, he is a monist. Language is meant to reveal Being, but Being is the Word itself, the Word that is God himself, the *Logos,* the Word-*Brahman*. He draws no distinction[33] between the *Logos* and the higher *Brahman*. The distinctions between the individual and the world, the subject and the object, and subject and the verb (the grammatical predicate), etc., all originate in the *Logos*. The structure of the *Logos* is the structure of the grammatical sentence. Thus, the *Logos* as the Word received a more systematic exposition in India than the *Logos* as Reason, although the *Logos* as Reason in the ontological sense was clearly enunciated in the Sāṃkhya doctrine of the *mahat* (Reason), the Upaniṣadic doctrine of the *Mahān Ātma* (the *Ātman* as Reason, so *Logos*), and the Vedāntic doctrine of the *citta* (apperception) and the *buddhi* (reason). For the wordists, including Bhartṛhari, Being is the *Mahān Ātma*[34] itself.

The word and its meaning: It is not possible in a single paper to present the doctrines of all schools in a connected form. Since the Grammarians are the philosophers of the Word, and since Bhartṛhari is the greatest among them, I shall present his views mainly and give the views of some of the other schools as differences.

The first peculiarity of Bhartṛhari's semantic theory is that there is no cognition without a corresponding verbal sentence. Thus, the cognition "That is a horse" is also the verbal expression "That is a horse." Just as the Naiyāyikas say that the object is determined by the universal "horseness," Bhartṛhari says that it is determined by the word "horse" also. For him, horseness is not a common characteristic (*sāmānya*), but is "being a horse," which is an act. Thus, "That is a horse" means: Being (*sattā*) in the form (universal) of the act (*bhāva*) of being a horse and in the form of the word "horse" has become (*vivṛtta*) that particular individual. This view is not accepted by any other school. The identity of word and meaning is called "*sphoṭa*" by Bhartṛhari. The word "*sphoṭa*" means bursting forth, and therefore what so bursts forth into the different syllables of the word, its meaning, the world, and individuals. This is like saying that the word which was with God and was God burst forth into the manifold of the World.

Every word has its *sphoṭa*. When we hear the word "ant," we do not hear the letters a, n, and t simultaneously, in that order, but successively; when one of them is heard, the others are not there. So, we say that every sound is retained in our memory, and, when the last sound is heard, it is ordered by our mind into the form a-n-t along with the first impressions, because only then can we have a meaning. But why are the sounds not ordered in the form t-a-n, as "tan" also is a meaningful word? So, it is said that a word pattern or universal called "*sphoṭa*" has to be accepted, of which, like Plato's Ideas, the hearer is reminded by the successive utterances of the sounds by the speaker. This universal sound-pattern is supersensible. Bhartṛhari would say that Plato should have acknowledged that the ideas or meanings are inseparably connected with words also.

I have already referred to the two doctrines of the universal, the universal as comprising the common characteristics of the individuals (*sāmānya*) and the universal as the act of being a particular form and called "*jāti*" (universal).[35] Bhartṛhari accepts the second view. Then, as the meaning of a word is the universal, it is the act of being a particular form, e.g., that of being a horse. According to

Bhartṛhari, the meaning of a word is never the particular individual, but the universal. That a word can mean something indicates its power (śakti), and that power is the act of being.

The Mīmāṁsakas accept the eternity of words and also the reality of the power (śakti) of words to mean, but not the doctrine of sphoṭa, as they do not accept the concept of the Logos as constituting the Being of the world. The Nyāya does not accept the eternity of words. It denies also that the word means only the concept or the universal, and says that it means the universal, the structure (ākṛti, samsthāna), and the individual. This view is accepted by many Vedāntins and some Wordists. The Mīmāṁsakas generally maintain that the word means primarily the universal, which for them is the structure,[36] and the individual is cognized through the universal, which brings in (ākṣipati) the individual, and which cannot exist without it. Here Prabhākara introduces a distinction. What is said is true in the case of cognitions due to memory (smṛti), but, in the case of actual perception, the universal connotes the intended activity (pravṛtti) and is therefore the instrument[37] of activity (pravṛtti-nimitta-para). The word, therefore, means this activity. Thus, the proposition "This is a pen" means "This is meant for writing." The Buddhists hold the same view.

As sphoṭa is not only the word but also the meaning, Bhartṛhari maintained that the sentence alone has sphoṭa,[38] but not the separate words. Words by themselves have no meaning; they have only an incomplete and derivative meaning. Prabhākara agrees with this view—we should remember that he does not, however, accept the sphoṭa doctrine—because for him also words can have meaning after, but not before, they are related, i.e., nouns can have meaning only when related to verbs meaning action, and the verbs should be imperatives, primarily for purposes of obtaining meaning. Bhartṛhari does not insist upon the verb's being in the imperative mood.

Although the Buddhists accept the operational theory of meaning, they say that words can mean particular objects, each of which is what is other than its other (apodha) and is unrelated. The Nyāya, the Mīmāṁsā of Kumārila, and most of the other schools maintain that words have their separate meanings and can later be combined into sentences.[39]

Bhartṛhari says that every word or sentence has two facets, the mere sound-pattern and the meaning-bearing sound-pattern. The former is perceived by the ear; it is not speech but noise. The latter, which is sphoṭa, is beyond time. It comes down through time to the level of the ear by passing through two stages. From the standpoint of the hearer, the sounds pass in the reverse order through the same stages. The first is called the pronounced word (vaikṛta-dhvani).[40] It has time sequence in that the sounds are pronounced one after another. It has meaning, although distinguished from itself. Having meaning is not the first facet, which is mere sound. The second stage is called the original word (*prakṛta-dhvani*), or *das Urwort*. It is, we may say, the word-universal, which appears on different lips and tongues in different ways. It is still in time on the lips and in the ears of men. The meaning has still to be distinct from it. The third stage is *sphoṭa,* which is supersensible and beyond time and in which the word and meaning are identical. It is Being itself as the Word. What the object and the pronounced word reveal is this *sphoṭa.* It is the word and its meaning, which is universal, and becomes the individual through *vivarta*[41] causality and the power of temporalization (*kāla-sakti*). *Vivarta* is the causal process in which the cause produces the effect, without itself undergoing any change. "*Vivaraṇa*" literally means articulation, explanation, etc. So, it is articulation by bursting forth. The individual is the result of the bursting forth of the universal. *Sphoṭa* as a universal, which is a formative act of Being, becomes the individuals without itself being affected by the process. Individuals may come into, and go out of, existence, but the universal remains the same.[42]

Bhartṛhari's philosophy of language is based, of course, upon the grammatical structure of Sanskrit. But his central doctrines may be of interest even for other languages. The noun and the verb are the most important parts of the sentence. Next come the suffixes and the indeclinables. The definite and the indefinite articles come under pronouns or names that can be applied to every noun (*sarvanāmāni*). Gender and number are worked out in declensions, and number alone in conjugations. Furthermore, Sanskrit has its own peculiarities, particularly the compounds. The schools differed from one another in interpreting them. Not even the Grammarians were unanimous.

It would be an oversimplification, made from a preconceived view, to think that Sanskrit cannot express the individual and that it has no articles, and so on. It is wrongly thought that "*Ayam aśvah*" is literally "It is horse"; for the original word (*prātipadika*) "*aśva,*" when declined as "*aśvah,*" means "a horse" in the nominative case. When number also has to be emphasized, the word "*eka*" is used. Further, *eka* means also "a certain"; and, when "a certain" is meant, "*eka*" has to be used. Thus, "Once upon a time there was a king" refers to a certain king, but not to any one of the past kings. Then the Sanskrit expression is "*Ekadā ekah rājā āsīt.*" Where "the" is wanted, "*tat*" is used. As Sanskrit is declensional, both *eka* and *tat* have to be declined. They have no separate meaning in the sentence, but only through the noun to which they refer. Hence, the Grammarians insist on declining them also.[43]

As the verb was taken to be important, grammar was not reduced to logic. Regarding the meaning power of the verb, the schools hold different views. If we take the example, "He is cooking food," what is the comprehension of the meaning of "is cooking"? The Wordists, including Bhartṛhari, say that it refers to the subject "he," the object or end of the process "food," and the activity (*bhāva*) of collecting the fuel, setting fire to it, and so on, which assimilates all factors into a single formative process. This agrees with Bhartṛhari's position that the meaning of a sentence is indivisible and the verb has to refer to the subject and the object. Furthermore, the verb as such refers separately to the operation of collecting fuel, etc., and the result, food, which means that the distinctions are preserved. The Neo-Nyāya maintains that the verb refers directly to the action, but indirectly to food, as action ends in the result. However, action is known as a qualification of the subject "he." The Mīmāṃsakas in general say that the verb refers to the operation only. But Maṇḍana, when he was a Mīmāṃsaka,[44] said that it refers to the result. The Advaita position is not clear, but it generally follows the Mīmāṃsā. There are several other views with varying shades of difference. What we have to note is that these differences are due, not only to the different metaphysical backgrounds and world perspectives, but also to the fact that all activity is structured, and thinkers differed in understanding which aspect of the structure is essential for activity.

VII. CONCLUSION

The attitudes of the different epistemological perspectives may now be summarized:

1. The fact that different philosophies and world perspectives can be developed in the same language shows that within the same culture there can be different world perspectives. All advanced cultures are in this sense pluralistic, their members leaning toward one or the other perspective according to circumstances.

2. The Nairukta philosophy of language shows that some thinkers of the time viewed the world, or even reality, as pure activity. It was felt correspondingly that the attitude of man toward the world had to be one of active life. The individual came in only as a mode of activity. The world consists of the modes of an infinite number of activities, which originated out of a single original Activity, the *Ātman*. It is Being itself.

3. The Mīmāṃsā attitude toward the individual and the world was different. The primary parts of the world are the individuals and their activities, which together are controlled by a supreme, unitary Activity. But this Supreme Activity is not the *Ātman*, but pure Activity as such.

4. The Grammarians, under Bhartṛhari, equated Being with the *Logos* and treated beings and their activities as articulations (*vivartas*) of the *Logos*. The individual is ultimately a formation of the *Logos* and can have no separate Being of its own. The world consists of the formations of the *Logos* and is its manifestation.

5. The Naiyāyika attitude toward the world is different from the above views. They do not treat the individual and the world as the formation or becoming of any supra-personal Being, but assign independent reality to every object.

6. For the Advaita of Śaṁkara, all knowledge is meant ultimately to reveal the primary Being itself, although in the pragmatic world we are interested in secondary beings and ignore Being. For both the Nairuktas and the Grammarian Bhartṛhari also, the ultimate purpose of knowledge is to reveal primary Being itself, however differently it is understood. Both base their philosophies on language, not merely on logic. Their methodology is etymology for the Nairuktas and analysis of grammar for Bhartṛhari, respectively.

7. Of all the Indian schools, the epistemologies of the Mīmāṁsā and of the Nyāya are the most important and elaborate, although different. The Advaita generally follows the Mīmāṁsā. But the latter's conception of the individual's intimate, ultimate, and deep involvement in the world through action is not acceptable to the former, which treats such involvement as bondage and points to Being as above becoming and therefore above action.

8. What is generally called valid knowledge (*pramā*) need not be the same as knowledge of Being (*satya*) for the Advaita, Bhartṛhari, and even the Nairuktas. So, ordinary forms of knowledge need not be knowledge of Being present in the world. Being is generally missed by them.

9. The usual epistemological forms, such as perception and inference, show how we cognize the individual and how, on the basis of perception and with the help of other forms, we construct the idea of the world.

10. The individual is regarded as cognizing himself as the particular "I," although this I-consciousness has been a problem of serious metaphysical inquiry for all the schools. The problem of the knowledge of other "I's" and of other minds does not seem to have engaged the minds of Indian epistemologists much, although it is maintained by some of them that yogic powers enable one to know other minds. It is practically taken for granted that other minds and individuals exist, although the Advaita and some schools of Buddhism deny their ultimate reality. The Vaiśeṣika uses analogy for knowing other minds.

11. All the schools, including the Advaita and Buddhism, affirm that this world satisfies *also* the pragmatic criterion of truth, although

many schools of the Vedānta and of Buddhism say that this world is only that which satisfies the pragmatic criterion. For they say that this world is only a world of action. But the others maintain that this is a world that exists in its own right also. Here we see the interpenetration of epistemology and metaphysics.

12. The individual is expressed by concrete names or nouns, not abstract nouns, and actions by verbs. The class is expressed generally by the plural, but occasionally by the singular also. It is only in the Nairukta philosophy that the noun is a mode of the verb, for, according to some Sanskrit grammarians, all nouns are derived from verbal roots. But many grammarians do not accept this view, and say that both the noun and verb are formations of Being. The rest treat the two as independent.

13. The linguistic philosophy of the Sanskrit grammarians shows that a grammatical sentence, in which the verb is important, is a fuller and better expression of reality than logical propositions, in which relation is more important than the verb. Logic cannot be an expression of life, which is a becoming (bhāva). Logical propositions can never be true substitutes for grammatical sentences. Relations are expressed by prepositions and conjunctions, but verbs are neither.

Logic expresses structure, but grammar expresses activity. The "is," "being," is a predicate in grammar, but a relation in logic. The predicate is a verb, and so an activity in grammar, but only one of the terms of the relation in logic. If logic cannot express activity as activity, it is inappropriate to ethics, the main concern of which is activity.

14. Since activity has structure—a beginning, an end, modes of operation, etc.—logic is an abstraction out of grammar but not vice versa. If we take grammar as a crude form of logic, we kill the very life of activity. The world does not consist primarily of individuals and relations, but of individuals and their activities, involving relations of course. The world itself is a structured process.

15. The verb also as activity is an object of cognition. We know, of course, that the word meaning activity is not itself activity. Yet, the word does not mean mere relation, a static constant.

16. The philosophy of the Sanskrit language points to a new doctrine of the universal, which is a good commentary and complement to Plato's theory. The doctrine has an interesting ontological significance. The universal "horseness," for instance, is not a group of common characteristics or a mere propositional function, but the formative act of being a horse. The universal is not a static form, but the formative act of being. From the logical point of view, "That is a horse" is a classificatory judgment. But from the ontological

point of view, it is the formative act of being. Ontology seems to be embedded in grammar, but not in logic.

One may express the central teaching of Indian epistemology about the individual and the world thus: The true and significant knowledge of the individual and this world is the knowledge of the individual in his field of action. But this statement is true only with regard to the empirical world.

1 General epistemology has been discussed by many authors. See my *Thought and Reality* (London: George Allen & Unwin Ltd., 1937); S. Radhakrishnan, *Indian Philosophy*, 2 vols. (London: George Allen & Unwin Ltd., 1931); S. N. Dasgupta, *A History of Indian Philosophy*, 5 vols. (Cambridge: Cambridge University Press, 1952–1957); and D. M. Datta, *Six Ways of Knowing* (Calcutta: Calcutta University Press, 1955). D. M. Datta has an article also in the Proceedings of the 1949 Conference, Charles A. Moore, ed., *Essays in East-West Philosophy* (Honolulu: University of Hawaii Press, 1951).

2 A word of explanation is necessary here. In Sanskrit, the word *"jñāna"* covers almost all forms of consciousness. Knowledge and cognition are forms of consciousness. I say, "I know the wall" and also "I am conscious of the wall." The word "conscious" has no verb form in English, and hence there may be some difficulty in understanding the Sanskrit term *"jñāna."* Yet, the English term "consciousness" comes nearest to the Sanskrit term and has to be so interpreted by adding other words to it, such as "be conscious of" or "has consciousness of." Knowledge and cognition are forms which consciousness takes.

As India's general epistemology is already known to Western students of Indian thought, I shall not discuss perception, inference, and the other ways of knowing in any detail, except insofar as they are relevant to our present topic. But the philosophy of the Sanskrit Grammarians is not so well known in the West, except to a few Orientalists. Even in India, the Orientalists have given it more attention than the philosophers have. I therefore have to give it more space than the usual epistemology—and more space to Bhartṛhari, the greatest among the Grammarian philosophers, than to the others.

3 Compare Berkeley's theory of signs.

4 Compare the interpretation of judgment given by Kant and the idealists with that of Russell and other logical analysts. Both groups accept perception and inference, but they interpret them in different ways.

5 See Rāmānuja, *Śrī-bhāṣya*, A. V. Narasimhacharya, ed. (Madras: Venkateswardud Co., 1909), Vol. I, pp. 18 fol., and 50 fol., for Rāmānuja's criticism of Śaṁkara.

5a Dialectic also is used, particularly by Buddhism and Śaṁkara's Vedānta, for establishing their conceptions of ultimate reality; and meditation also is used by almost all schools for realizing it. But neither is mentioned as one of the sources of knowledge. There is no separate name even for dialectic.

6 In fact, the number is much larger than six—perhaps as many as eighteen. As L. Śrīnivāsacārya says in his *Mānameyarahasyaślokavārtikam* (Mysore: Government Press, 1925), p. 285, God alone knows who accepts which means of valid knowledge and who rejects which. Rejection is made by denying a particular way, e.g., memory and tradition, as knowledge at all or by reducing a particular means to some accepted one. We must not forget that a means of valid knowledge does not necessarily give valid knowledge; it is only one of the possible ways of knowing truth. Then even memory is important for historical knowledge (*itihāsa*), and tradition (*aidihya*) will not be rejected by an archeologist, who begins his diggings after hearing a popular story that some gods lived in a nearby locality and went down under the earth. He could not have obtained his knowledge otherwise. One may say that his knowledge is verbal knowledge, but it is for him much more than knowledge given by the story. It has to be noted, however, that, in spite of the keen analysis of the eighteen means of knowledge in the controversies, no systematic morphology of knowledge was developed in India such as that of the idealists, e.g., B. Bosanquet, *Logic or Morphology of Knowledge* (Oxford: Clarenden Press, 1911).

7 I do not discuss which school accepts which of the six, as the information can be found in the works referred to already.

8 *Prakāratādiśūnyam hi sambandhānavagāhi tat. Kārikāvali*, Hariram Sukla, ed. (Banaras: Chowkhamba Sanskrit Series, 1951), p. 485.

9 The three types are called *sāmānyalakṣaṇa, jñānlakṣaṇa*, and *yogaja*. The last includes telepathy, clairvoyance, and direct cognition of infinitesimal entities.

9a It should be noted that Indian logicians always meant by "inference" syllogistic inference.

9b I leave out verbal knowledge now, since it will be discussed in the section of this paper on the philosophy of language.

10 Some logicians, e.g., Hobhouse, say that similarity is not an object of thought, but of perception, meaning thereby that it is directly perceived. Russell also held that similarity is perceived. Prabhākara says that it is directly cognized, but not perceived, through a peculiar way of knowing.

10a Those who do not accept postulation as a distinct way of knowing reduce it to a syllogism from a negative major premise or to a disjunctive syllogism. (See my *"Arthāpatti: Its Logical Significance,"* note 11.)

11 For a critical estimate of postulation, see the author's article, *"Arthāpatti: Its Logical Significance."* In A. S. Altekar, ed., *Proceedings of the All-India Oriental Conference* (Benares: Benares Hindu University, 1942).

12 Some Buddhists hold that negation is known through inference. See my article, "The Buddhist Conception of Negation," in G. Hanumaniha Rao, ed., *Hiriyanna Commemoration Volume* (Mysore: Mysore Printing and Publishing House, 1952).

12a The Buddhists say that non-apprehension is the same as inference. Prajñākaragupta, *Pramāṇavārtikābhāṣyam* (Patna: K. P. Jayaswal Research Institute, 1953, pp. 34–448.) The Jainas classify it under perception. Prabhāchandra, *Prameyakamalamārtaṇḍa* (Bombay: Nirnayasagar Press, 1941), p. 346.

12b Prajñākaragupta, *Pramāṇavārtikābhāṣyam*, pp. 631 ff.; pp. 230 ff.

13 The *vyāvahārika* (of pragmatics) world means the *artha-kriyākāri* (that which does or performs the purpose intended) world. I cannot discuss here the many interesting details, analyses, and implications of the *prāmāṇya* doctrines. They can be obtained from the works mentioned earlier.

13a There is every justification for using the word "pragmatic" here. For the Mahāyāna Buddhists, the objective world is produced by the *samskāras* left by practical activity and is meant for practical activity. So, the objects, not only epistemologically understood but also in their very constitution (in their *sattā*), are pragmatic by nature. For Prabhākara, also, they are so. But, for the Nyāya and the other schools, they are only epistemologically pragmatic, i.e., they are pragmatic for purposes of epistemological verification. In short, all schools that accept the doctrine of *karma* do and have to accept the pragmatic criterion, at least for confirming empirical truth. For the world, even if it has its own existence, is created according to the past actions of the souls and for the sake of their future actions and enjoyment. But we should keep in mind that the schools differ in answering the question whether to confirm truth is the same as constituting the being of the object concerned.

14 Ernst Cassirer, *An Essay on Man* (New Haven: Yale University Press, 1944), p. 228.

15 Bhartṛhari, *Vākyapadīya*, S. N. Sukla, ed. (Banaras: Chowkhamba Sanskrit Series, 1961), Part I, pp. 24, 141. Yet, Bhartṛhari's view should not be equated with that of Cassirer or Heidegger.

16 Ernst Cassirer, *An Essay on Man*, p. 121.

17 Bhartṛhari, *Vākyapadīya*, Part I, pp. 4, 72–78.

18 Martin Heidegger, *An Introduction to Metaphysics*, Ralph Manheim, trans. (Garden City, N. Y.: Doubleday and Co., 1961), p. 42.

19 Bertrand Russell, *Human Knowledge: Its Scope and Limits* (London: George Allen & Unwin Ltd., 1948), p. 72.

20 C. W. Morris, *Foundations of the Theory of Signs* (Chicago: University of Chicago Press, 1949), clarifies this situation.

21 R. Carnap, *Philosophy and Logical Syntax* (London: Kegan Paul, Trench, Trübner and Co., Ltd., 1935), p. 27.

22 Ernst Cassirer, *An Essay on Man*, p. 121.

23 Paul A. Schilpp, *The Philosophy of Ernst Cassirer* (New York: Tudor Publishing House, 1958), p. 405.

24 Benjamin Lee Whorf, *Language, Thought and Reality* (New York: John Wiley and Sons, 1958), p. 253. Whorf explains the levels in terms of the Buddhist and Yogic terms *"nāmā-rūpa"* (name-form) and *"a-rūpa"* (the formless). He does not seem to have known the philosophies of the Grammarians. J. Vendreys, in his *Language*, Paul Radin, trans., (New York: Barnes and Noble Inc., 1951), p. 234, writes: "But neither is it unreasonable, on the other hand, to claim that there is one human language which is fundamentally identical in all latitudes." This universal language must be the unexpressed, the internal language of man.

25 Yaska, *Nairukta*, L. Swarup, ed. (Bombay: Sri Venkateswar Press, 1947). He is assigned to some time between 800 and 500 B.C.

26 Thus, "That is a horse" means that "the That is a function of the universal 'horseness,' which is a function of the Is." We should remember that "horseness" is not an abstraction, but the formative act of Being (Is). Function would be the formative act, not an abstraction. We may also say that, since the formative act is the expression of power, "horseness," is a power of the Is, and that the That is a power of "horseness." We can then interpret "That is a horse" as

$$\text{That [Horseness (Is)]}$$

or as

$$\text{(That)}$$
$$\text{(Horseness)}$$
$$\text{(Is)}$$

provided we do not forget that the power here is not arithmetical power, but the ontological or the power of the act of being. One may compare this view with Plato's view of language and Cassirer's *Vieldeutigkeit* of the copula (W. M. Urban, *Language and Reality*, [New York: The Macmillan Company, 1939]), pp. 302 ff. Then "Brutus killed Caesar" will be

$$\text{Brutus→Caesar} \left\{ \begin{array}{l} \text{Past [Killing (Is)]} \\ \\ \text{(Brutus→Caesar)} \\ \text{(Past)} \\ \text{(Killing)} \\ \text{(Is)} \end{array} \right.$$

It seems that the Is cannot be avoided even when it is not used, if we want to convey the existential import. The verb itself must convey it, and the verb must be activity also. It is not a mere relation, as it is in Russell's logic. If killing is only a relation, then relations must have past, present, and future. Then they cannot be constants. If by some *tour de force* they are turned into constants, expressions become ethically lifeless.

27 Cp. F. W. Bridgman's operational theory of symbols, in Urban, *Language and Reality*, p. 532.

28 Śrī Harṣa, *Khaṇḍanakhaṇḍākhādya*, G. N. Jha, ed. (Benares: Chowkhamba Sanskrit Series, 1904), p. 1068.

29 A connected account of the Nyāya theory of language is available in Jagadīśa, *Śabda-śaktiprakāśa*, Dunderay Sastri, ed. (Benares: Chowkhamba Sanskrit Series, 1934).

29a There is a difference between the Advaita and the Mīmāṁsā at this point.

29b These meanings are not consistently adhered to.

30 Cp. *Asti bhāti priyam rūpam nāma cetyamsapañcakam, ādyam trayam brahmarūpam jagadrūpam tato dvayam:* Being, shining, pleasantness, and name and form are the five factors [of all cognition]; the first three belong to the *Brahman* and the other two to the world.

31 Rāmānuja, *Śrī-bhāṣya*, Vol. I, p. 28.

32 He is generally assigned to the second half of the sixth and first half of the seventh centuries A.D.

33 This distinction was later drawn by the Tāntric school, to which even Śaṁkara seems to have belonged in his *Prapañca-sāra-tantra*. See Śukla's commentary on the *Vākyapadīya*, Part I, *op. cit., pp.* 126–131. The Upaniṣadic view also draws the distinction. See *ibid.*, p. 19.

34 Mādhavācārya, *Sarvadarśanasaṁgraha*, Ganes Vinayakapte, ed. (Poona: Anandasrama Press, 1928), pp. 114–115. This view is attributed to one Hari and is the same as Bhart-ṛhari's.

35 This is defined by Kumārila, for instance, as *janmopādāna*, the material or substantive cause of the individual's being what it is. K. Kunjunni Raja, *Indian Theories of Meaning* (Madras: The Adyar Library, 1963), p. 237.

36 For the Jainas, also, the universal is the common structure of the individuals.

37 Cp. William James's pragmatism and John Dewey's instrumentalism.

38 The *sphoṭa* of the sentence is called *akhaṇḍa-sphoṭa*, or indivisible *sphoṭa*. There are different kinds of *sphoṭa*, that of the sentence, of the word, of the syllable, and of the letter. But that of the sentence alone is self-complete. See Śukla's commentary on the *Vākyapadīya*, Part I, *op. cit.*, p. 45. For an explanation in English, see K. Kunjunni Raja, *Indian Theories of Meaning*, pp. 100–140. Gaurinath Sastri's *The Philosophy of Word and Meaning* (Calcutta: Sanskrit College, 1959) is another pertinent book in English.

39 This doctrine is called *abhihitānvaya-vāda* (the doctrine that uttered words are related) as against Prabhākara's doctrine, which is called *anvitābhidāna-vāda* (the doctrine that related words are uttered).

40 "*Vaikṛta*" means "distorted." Since not all persons pronounce the word in the same voice, the original word is said to be distorted.

41 See Śukla's commentary on the *Vākyapadīya*, *op. cit.*, Part I, p. 146.

42 From the cosmic point of view the *Logos* (*Sphoṭa*) is said to have three stages. The first is called the *paśyantī*, the seeing or experiencing stage, in which there is no distinction between the word, meaning, and object. This is the principle of rational consciousness (*buddhi-rūpa*) itself, the *Sphoṭa* in its essence and completeness, the *Logos*. It is super-sensible; we know it only in flashes. The second is called the "*madhyama*," the intermediate stage, and corresponds to the *Urwort* (*prākṛta-dhvani*). The third is called "*vaikhari*," the gross sound, and corresponds to the pronounced word. The categorical scheme of the *Logos* is given by Bhartṛhari in terms of the grammatical structure of the sentence. The parts of speech are four: the noun (*nāma, nama-dheya, prāti-padika*); the verb (*kriyā, bhāva, dhātu, ākhyāta*); the suffixes (*upasargas*), which not only change the meaning of the root by becoming its mode, but also act as prepositions; and the indeclinables (*nipātas*), which act as adverbs also. Of these, the first two are primary, because without either there can be no meaning of the sentence. If the sentence is the unit of expressioon, then what is expressed is the unit of Being. Bhartṛhari does not give us further insight into the structure of the *Logos*. All that we know is that it is both noun and verb. It is primarily Being (*sattā*) and manifests itself as nouns and verbs, beings and activities. These can have different modes as expressed by adjectives, adverbs, etc., according to the nature of the language. Bhartṛhari seems to have avoided the discussion of the logical structure of the *Logos*, because, first, man cannot rise to the level of the *Logos* to understand it fully; second, man can have before his consciousness only single flashes of the *Logos*, but not all the possible ones together and exhaustively; third, the sentence understood by man is the appearance of the highest *sphoṭa* in time, and to grasp the whole *sphoṭa* man has to become supra-temporal; and, fourth—perhaps this is the most important reason—since the *Logos* includes activity (*bhāva*), to present it as a logical structure would be to present it as static and therefore to falsify it. Man may abstract the pure logical structure, but in so doing deprives it of Being.

Bhartṛhari's semantic analysis may be charted somewhat as follows:

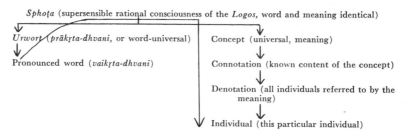

Sphoṭa (supersensible rational consciousness of the *Logos,* word and meaning identical)

Urwort (*prākṛta-dhvani,* or word-universal) | Concept (universal, meaning)

Pronounced word (*vaikṛta-dhvani*) | Connotation (known content of the concept)

Denotation (all individuals referred to by the meaning)

Individual (this particular individual)

From the standpoint of the speaker, the word starts from the *sphoṭa* and splits itself downward into the pronounced word and the individual. From the standpoint of the hearer, verbal knowledge starts with the pronounced word, goes up to *sphoṭa,* and then comes down to the individual. The concept and connotation are taken together by Bhartṛhari as meaning. I have separated them, as we do not always have the whole possible content of the universal, even when we know the universal, but get the denotation with a partial content.

[43] In fact, every idea expressed in any of the European languages can be expressed in Sanskrit or any language derived from it. See F. Max Müller, *Science of Thought* (New York: Charles Scribner's Sons, 1887), Vol. II, pp. 412–413.

[44] Tradition tells us that Maṇḍana was at first a Mīmāṁsaka and later became a follower of Śaṁkara's Advaita, assuming the name of Sureśvara. But some historical scholars believe that they are not the same person. First, whether they are the same or different is immaterial for the present paper. Second, even now scholars are attempting to prove the opposite. See *Journal of the American Oriental Society,* October–December, 1962.

NAKAMURA HAJIME[a]

Consciousness of the individual and the universal among the Japanese

Any adequate discussion of the status of the individual and of the relationship between the individual and the universal in Japanese thought and culture, in terms of methodological tendencies, requires an examination of two major aspects of the problem—the philological or linguistic and the logical,* that is, the tendency toward an absence of theoretical or systematic thinking, along with an emphasis upon an aesthetic and intuitive and concrete, rather than a strictly logical, orientation. The status of the individual tends to be determined for the Japanese mind by both of these somewhat unique tendencies of thought.

I. THE CONSCIOUSNESS OF THE INDIVIDUAL IN DAILY LIFE

The logical problem of the relationship between the universal, the particular, and the individual was not discussed with full awareness by Japanese scholars before the introduction of Western scholarship, except by some Buddhist monastic scholars who elaborated on Chinese versions of Indian Buddhist logical texts.

The concept of "the individual" can be expressed with the singular in daily usages of speech, but the singular and the plural have always been expressed in the Japanese language in terms of human relationships.

Number is not always made explicit in the grammar of Japanese sentences. A distinction is not always made between the singular and the plural. And reduplication in the Japanese language (e.g., *"yama-yama*[b]*,"* i.e., mountains; *"kami-gami*[c]*,"* i.e., gods) cannot be said strictly to indicate plurality, as reduplication requires the individuality of signification. Furthermore, not all nouns can be put into plural forms. Plurals become better indicated as we proceed higher from domestic animals to servants. Several kinds of plural suffixes are variously used to suit different occasions: *"domo*[d]*"* and *"tachi*[e]*"* are used for persons of equal or inferior status or for intimates, as, for example, *"funa-bito-domo*[f]*"* (boatmen), *"hito-tachi*[g]*"* (people),

---

* These aspects of the problem are treated at some length in my *Ways of Thinking of Eastern Peoples*, Philip P. Wiener, ed. (Honolulu: East West Center Press, 1964).

"*tomo-dachi*[h]" (friends).[1] When respect must be shown, the suffix "*kata*[i]," which originally meant place or direction, is used, as, for example, "*anata-gata*[j]" (you) and "*sensei-gata*[k]" (teachers). In short, the use of plural suffixes is determined by the relationship of social ranks and the feeling (intimacy, hate, respect, disrespect, etc.) which the speaker entertains for the persons of whom he is speaking, just as in the cases of "*tu*" and "*vous*" in French, and "*du*" and "*Sie*" in German. This clearly evidences the Japanese trait to think of things in terms of human relationships rather than as separately existing facts in the objective world. The various plural forms are therefore not strict equivalents of Western plural forms, though in modern times, owing to the influence of Western languages, number has come to be expressed in nearly the same way as in Western languages. (An affix, "*moro-morono*,"[1] can be added to any word to denote the plural.)

It sometimes happens that a plural suffix attached to a noun loses its own meaning, becoming simply a blank, meaningless component of a compound, and the compound may indicate the singular number, as in the case of the word "*wakai-shū*,"[2] which is made up of "*wakai*[n]" (young) plus "*shū*[o]" (plural suffix, people). This word may mean both youngsters and a youngster.

The Japanese do not think it necessary to represent the individual as objectively existing, but, when two people are conversing, they are clearly aware of the distinction between singular and plural. One of the most distinguishing features of the Japanese language is the lack of clear indication of number. This is not so, however, with regard to personal pronouns, particularly the first and second person. The singular and plural in the first and the second persons are clearly distinguished. This phenomenon in their language indicates that the Japanese, who are disinclined to measure the objective world with a certain established unit, are quite sensitive to the distinction between "I" and "you" in human relations. In this case, the consciousness of the individual appears conspicuously.

This does not mean that conceptualization in universals was lacking among the Japanese of the past. The move to conceptualize human affairs in terms of laws and concepts, which are universals, was effected by the Japanese to some extent. The concept of universal law came into existence very early, in the time of Prince Shōtoku[p], when he said, "Sincerely revere the Three Treasures. The Three Treasures, viz., the Buddha, the Law (*Dharma*), and the Brotherhood (*Saṅgha*), constitute the final ideal of all living beings and the ultimate foundation of all countries. Should any age or any people fail to esteem this truth? There are few men who are really vicious. They will all follow it if adequately instructed. How can the crooked ways of men be made straight unless we take refuge in the Three Treasures?"[3] Here we find the concept of a universal law, which is something beyond laws based on the inductively given status of the individual in the joint family and of the family in its respective tribe or caste. This is merely one example. The concept of natural law was most conspicuously expressed by Master Jiun[q] (1718–1804) in the modern period. But the Japanese seem not to have had the inclination to express things in an abstract way. Logic was nothing but a transplantation of Buddhist logic from India, and it did not develop from among the Japanese.

Among Japanese thinkers, a tendency to respect the natural feelings of man justifies the great importance attached in Japan to the rules of propriety based upon human relationships.

The recent trend in philosophical writings in Japan to assign individuality only to man might have come from this humanistic tendency of thinking among the Japanese. The habit of attaching importance to human relationships is manifested outwardly in their practice of the rules of propriety. Generally speaking, exchange of greetings in the West is simple. Japanese greetings are, on the contrary, highly elaborate, although they differ greatly from area to area.

Due to the stress on social proprieties in Japan another characteristic of its culture appears, viz., the tendency of human relationships to supersede or take precedence over the individual. To lay stress upon human relationships is to place heavy regard upon the relations of many individuals rather than upon the individual as an independent entity.

Personal pronouns are much more complicated in Japanese than in other languages. The choice of the proper pronoun to fit the particular situation is an ever-recurring problem in speaking Japanese. Special pronouns are required for superiors, equals, inferiors, intimates, and strangers. If one should confuse them, difficulties would ensue. A Japanese, therefore, must bear in mind such human relationships as rank and intimacy every time he uses a personal pronoun. Such restricted uses of personal pronouns are related to the use of nouns and verbs as well. A distinction is made, for example, between words used in addressing persons of superior rank and those used in addressing persons of inferior rank.

When this type of thinking is predominant, consciousness of the individual as an entity appears less explicit, i.e., always in the wider sphere of a consciousness of personal relationships, although the significance of the individual as an entity is still recognized; the recognition of the equal value of all individuals is lessened, of course, when he is placed in a class, but it means that it represents the tendency to pay more attention to each individual as the subject to which various virtues belong, not as an object like an inanimate thing.

The first person or the second person is often omitted as the subject in a Japanese sentence. Generally, in such a case the subject is implied in the whole sentence-structure, but frequently a sentence may completely lack the subject. The subject can be determined according to the context. The Japanese do not want to express explicitly the subject of an action, unless necessary. This indicates that the Japanese do not think it always necessary to mention the individual or an independent performer of actions as an objective being.

The Japanese in general did not develop a clear-cut concept of the human individual *qua* individual as an objective unit like an inanimate thing, but the individual is always found existing in a network of human relationships. It means that the Japanese always wanted to locate the individual in experience, not in the abstract. Largely because of the Japanese emphasis on concrete immediacy in experience, the individual was grasped as a living thing, and not as a bloodless, inanimate thing in the realm of the abstract. The living individual is always located in various kinds of human relationships.

II. AWARENESS OF THE RELATION BETWEEN THE INDIVIDUAL AND THE UNIVERSAL

In terms of logical thinking, the forms of expression of the Japanese language are more sensitive and emotive than directed toward logical exactness. This reflects the traditional attitude of the Japanese of laying more emphasis on the aesthetic and artistic aspect of human life.

The relation between the individual and the universal was not thought of with full awareness by the Japanese in the past. The concept of "the individual" in the logical sense was expressed by Buddhist logicians of Japan with the word *"jisōr,"* a Japanese equivalent of the Sanskrit word *"sva-lakṣaṇa,"* but it was not used by intellectuals at large.

The word *"kobutsuˢ,"* meaning the individual, was coined after the introduction of Western logic. The Japanese language does not tend to express precisely and accurately the various modes of being, but tends to be satisfied with vague, topological expressions. As for nouns, the Japanese have no clear distinction between singular and plural, nor is there a distinction between genders, and no articles are used. For verbs, also, there are no distinctions of person and number. In these respects, Japanese resembles Chinese. Genders and articles may not have anything to do with the logical character of a language. The absence of these may make it better for logical thinking. This problem needs further investigation.

The original Japanese language, as clearly revealed in Japanese classical literature, had a rich vocabulary of words denoting aesthetic and emotional states of mind. On the other hand, words denoting intellectual, inferential processes of active thought are notably lacking. In the original Japanese language, in which words were for the most part concrete and intuitive, the construction of abstract nouns was deficient. Hence, it is extremely difficult to express abstract concepts solely in words of the original Japanese. When Buddhism and Confucianism were later introduced into Japan and philosophical thinking developed, the vocabulary which was the means of expressing these philosophical thoughts was entirely Chinese, simply taken over. Although Buddhism was very widely propagated among the people, its scriptures were never translated into the Japanese language. "In our country, there is no attempt to translate [Chinese versions of Buddhist scriptures]," [4] said Kokan Shiren[t] (1287–1346), in his *Genkō shakusho*[u] (A History of Japanese Buddhism), and he cited this fact as a characteristic of Japanese Buddhism. Western philosophical ideas now prevail widely in Japan, but the linguistic means by which they are expressed are, in most cases, words coined by properly connecting two Chinese characters which are, by convention, made to correspond to the traditional Occidental concepts. The words *"gainen*[v]*"* and *"risei*[w]*,"* for instance, are the present-day Japanese terms for "concept" (*Begriff*) and "reason" (*Vernunft*), respectively. Sometimes such words are constructions of three or four characters. The pure, original Japanese had difficulty in serving as a means of expressing philosophical concepts.

The greatest obstacle in this respect seems to lie in the fact that the Japanese language does not have any fully established method of composing abstract nouns. The language does not have the infinitive form of the verb, the special character of which is to express an indefinite situation, a relation itself rather than a thing. Although the Japanese do have what is called the "nominal use" corresponding to the infinitive, this is completely identical in form with a verbal form which, in conjunction with temporal verb-endings or an adjective, forms a compound word. For example, the so-called nominal form *"warai*[x]*,"* which is completely identical in form with the form of the verb *"warau*[y]*"* (to laugh) appearing in *"warai-tari*[z]*"* (laughed), *"waraite*[aa]*"* (laughed and . . .), *"warai-goto*[ab]*"* (laughing matter), etc., signifies the act or fact of laughing. Moreover, this verb-form in time has tended to lose its special significance as an expression with a compounding function, and has also come to be used as a noun. For instance, *"warai"* has the senses both of *"warau-*

koto[ac]" (the individual act or the fact of laughing) and of *"warai-to-yū-mono*[ad]" (the universal concept of laughter); consequently, the distinction between *"die Lache"* and *"das Lachen"* is not made in terms of the forms of a word.[5]

Furthermore, the Japanese have no established method of turning adjectives into corresponding abstract nouns. As may be seen in such examples as *fukasa*[ae] (depth), or *fukami*[af] (deepness), the suffixes *-sa*[ag] and *-mi*[ah] make abstract nouns out of adjectives to some extent. But this manner of transformation or noun-building is available for only a limited range of adjectives.

Things being so, present-day Japanese intellectuals have come to add the Chinese character *"sei*[ai]" to any word to form any abstract[aj] noun. This is the Japanese substitute method for the original lack of an ending to form an abstract noun.

In short, the Japanese language, so far, has had a structure rather unfit for expressing logical conceptions. The fact that it is difficult to make derivatives representing abstract nouns means that it has not been habitual for the Japanese to be aware of the relations between the universal and the individual in terms of logical thinking. Consequently, when the Japanese adopted the already highly advanced conceptual knowledge of Buddhism and Confucianism, they made no attempt to express it in the original Japanese language, but used Chinese technical terms without modification. Again, in translating the concepts of Western learning, the Japanese used Chinese characters and did not render these concepts into pure, original Japanese directly.

When we step into the realm of syntax from that of word-construction, the Japanese language manifests its non-logical character all the more clearly. The language lacks the relative pronoun "which," standing for the antecedent, that helps develop the process of thought. We find it inconvenient, therefore, to advance closely knit thinking in a succinct form in Japanese.[6] If we repeat nouns and adjectives unsparingly, then logical exactness can be attained. In scientific works this way of expression has been carefully adopted. However, in literature it is often difficult to determine what modifies what, when several adjectives or adverbs are juxtaposed. Because of these defects, Japanese presented difficulties for logical scientific expression, which has to be exact, and, as is generally pointed out, its non-logical character naturally handicaps the development of ability in logical thinking among the Japanese people, and has actually brought about grave inconveniences in their practical lives. Indian books of Buddhistic philosophy were originally written with logical accuracy, but Chinese versions of them and Chinese commentaries upon them became remarkably non-logical. Thereafter, the Japanese continued their ambiguous and obscure interpretations of the Chinese texts without change, and, as a result, they did not attempt to analyze them logically. Although special phraseologies have been worked out in legal jargon, etc., for technical considerations, to avoid ambiguity, such a practice is by no means universal.

In the same way, Japanese frequently omits the subject, and this, too, has something to do with the non-logical character of the Japanese people. In such a case, even though the subject is omitted, we usually find it naturally suggested or can easily infer what it is by referring to linguistic context, or by looking at the situation in which the utterance is made. But it cannot be denied that at times, when the situation is not completely clear, the omission of the subject makes the meaning ambiguous and causes misunderstanding. Very often it is not clear whether the subject is an individual or a group of individuals.

In connection with the omission of the subject, we must note that anacoluthon very frequently occurs in Japanese sentences. While it is to be found also in Indo-European languages, examples there are rare,[7] whereas Japanese not only has abundant examples of it, but also even the fact that the subject has changed within a single sentence is not clearly noticed. For example, in literary works of the Heian period (794–1186), instances of anacoluthon are very frequent. And this characteristic of the Japanese way of thinking appears also in the annotations to Chinese Buddhist texts.[8] That the Japanese people can dispense with the subject in their linguistic expression is due to the fact that the intuitive understanding of the scene referred to in their discourse is usually attained beforehand by their close bonds and nexus with others. Therefore, the necessity of clearly indicating the subject occurs only in those cases in which some doubt about the intuitive understanding of the subject arises. (In other words, logically correct assertion of the "obvious" sounds harsh to the Japanese people.)

Generally speaking, logical consciousness begins with consciousness of the relation between the individual or the particular and the universal; and the Japanese on the whole have not been fully aware of this relation, or have been poor in understanding a concept apart from particular or individual instances. This exactly corresponds to the tendency, characteristic in the Japanese way of thinking, not to make a sharp contrast between subject and predicate in the expression of judgment.

Hio Keizan[aj] (1789–1859), in his two volume work, *Kunten fukko*[ak] (Restoration of Kunten), criticized the usages of *kunten*[al] (marks used in paraphrasing Chinese into Japanese) prevalent in the Tokugawa[am] period (1615–1667). According to his view, for example, scholars at that time misread the Chinese phrase *"Yen Hui che,"* which means "a man called Yen Hui (i.e., Gankai)," as

"Gankai naru mono," which is an abridged form of *"Gankai ni aru mono*[ap]*"* (strictly, "the man exemplified in Gankai"). In so doing, he argued, they committed an error in the indication of the meaning. However this may be, such a distinction is generally not recognized by the Japanese scholars, and this confusion continues to the present time. Whether or not Hio's theory is right is a question to be entrusted to experts, but in any case one can say that there was no method fully established in Japanese for expressing universals by a universal concept, in contrast to individual cases.

Therefore, the Japanese people are not inclined to present the universal concept as a predicate in a judgment, so as to make its expression concise. They are not usually content until they have presented a set of particular instances or individual cases pertaining to universal propositions.

Dōgen[aq] (1200–1253) has been called one of the greatest philosophers Japan ever had. When an Indian philosopher formulated an idea simply and definitely in a universal proposition, e.g., "The Three Worlds are but one mind,"[9] Dōgen explained the thought by enumerating various particulars. Thus:

The mind is neither one nor two. It is neither in the Three Worlds nor beyond the Three Worlds. It is infallible. It is an enlightenment through contemplation, and it is an enlightenment without contemplation. It is walls and pebbles; it is mountains, rivers, and the earth. The mind is but the skin, flesh, bones, and marrow; the mind is but the communication of enlightenment through the Buddha's smile. There is a mind, and there is no mind. There is a mind with a body; there is a mind without a body. There is a mind before a body; there is a mind after a body. A body is generated from the womb, the egg, moisture, or fermentation. The mind is generated from the womb, the egg, moisture, or fermentation. Blue, yellow, red, and white are nothing but the mind. Long, short, square, and round are nothing but the mind. Life and death are nothing but the mind. Years, months, days, and hours are nothing but the mind. Dreams, illusions, and mirages are nothing but the mind. The bubbles of water and the flames of fire are nothing but the mind. The flowers of the spring and the moon of the autumn are nothing but the mind. Confusions and dangers are nothing but the mind.[10]

A similar way of thinking may be noticed in Japanese Confucianists. Ogyū Sorai[ar] (1666–1728), for example, did not like the sort of abstract speculation found in the Sung[as] school; he made more of particular or individual "things" (*wu*[at]) than of universal "principles" (*li*[au]) :

The great sage kings of the past taught by means of "things" and not by means of "principles." Those who teach by means of "things" always have work to which they devote themselves; those who teach by means of "principles" merely expatiate with words. In "things," all "principles" are brought together; hence, all who have long devoted themselves to work come to have a genuine intuitive understanding of them. Why should they appeal to words?[11]

Words are relevant to universals. Therefore, learning consists, to Ogyū, in knowing as many particular or individual things as possible: "Learning consists in widening one's information, absorbing extensively anything and everything one comes upon." This reflects his attitude that scholarship should be based upon empirical facts. But since Ogyū ignored the science of Nature, learning, which is to amass a knowledge of particular or individual facts, culminates, for him, in the study of history—a preference which is closely related to the empiricistic character of his "learning": "Since learning is to have wide information and to have experience with realities, it culminates in history."[12] Here individual cases were emphasized.

Even the scholars of the Japanese classics, who tried to repudiate Buddhism and Confucianism, exhibited the same way of thinking. Hirata Atsutane[av] (1776–1843), for example, rejected the concept of abstract, universal "principles," and declared that we only had to know "actual things," i.e., concrete particulars or individual cases.

> In fact, that which is called the "true way" is given in actual things, whereas conventional scholars are erroneously inclined to think that the "way" cannot be found out except by reading doctrinal books. For, if we can appreciate actual things, doctrines are dispensed with; and it is only when actual things, in which the "way" is given, are lacking that doctrines arise. Therefore, doctrines are far less valuable than actual things, (i.e., individual cases). Lao Tzu[aw] fully recognized this fact when he said, "When the Way decays, the doctrines of humanity and justice arise."[13]

As is shown by the historical development of Japanese thought —although so far only a few representative thinkers have been considered—the ability to think in terms of abstract universals has not fully developed among the Japanese. They have been rather poor in ordering various phenomena on the basis of universal patterns.

Japanese expressions are for the most part abundant in aesthetic and emotional feelings. A special kind of logic may be found, but it is quite different from that generally called "logic." Japanese, rather, emphasized the aesthetic way of expression and the artistic way of life, and, with regard to scientific thinking, they tended to base their studies upon individual facts.

(There might nowadays be a question as how to reconcile this alleged Japanese preference for the particular with the commonly observed modern preference of Japanese scholarship for theoretical learning rather than the pragmatic approach. Among present-day

Japanese intellectuals there is a conspicuous tendency toward German abstract philosophy. Why the change? We would answer: This is not a real change. Such a tendency among intellectuals is due not so much to fondness for theoretical thinking as for things abstruse and productive of imaginative impressions upon them. Their alleged fondness for theoretical thinking is not always based upon the process of induction and deduction in the logical sense.)

III. WEAKNESS IN LOGICAL THINKING IN THE PAST

The non-logical character of the Japanese people naturally tended to prevent them from thinking with logical coherence or consistency.

Even in ancient times, Kakinomoto-no-Hitomaro[ax] composed a famous poem, in which he said, "In our land covered with reed and rice-ears, they have not argued since the time of the gods." Out of such a point of view, the technique of constructing universal laws reducing individuals to order is not likely to develop. Motoori Norinaga[ay] (1730–1801), a scholar who claimed to have made clear the spirit of ancient Japan, said, "In ancient times, we had no talk at all even about the Way. The classic [of Kakinomoto] declares that in our land covered with reed and rice-ears, they have not argued since the time of the gods. Not to argue means not to expatiate or have much talk, as is the custom in foreign countries."[14]

"In ancient times in our land, even the 'Way' was not talked about at all, and we had only ways directly leading to things themselves, while in foreign countries it is the custom to entertain and to talk about many different doctrines, about principles of things, this 'Way' or that 'Way.' The Emperors' land in ancient times had no such theories or doctrines whatever, but we enjoyed peace and order then, and the descendants of the Sun Goddess have consecutively succeeded to the throne."[15] "To things themselves" has been the motto of many Japanese scholars.

The way of thinking on the part of the Japanese in general could not easily be changed by the introduction and dissemination of Buddhism.

It is commonly said that Japanese Buddhism reached its maturity in the Kamakura[az] period (1186–1392). "Kamakura Buddhism," however, did not develop systematic philosophical thinking on a large scale. Such prominent figures as Hōnen[ba], Shinran[bb], and Nichiren[bc] concentrated their efforts chiefly upon demonstrating the orthodoxy or validity of their own interpretations of Buddhist sacred texts. To cite an extreme instance, Chishin[bd] (Sage Ippen[be]) (1239–1289) declared on his death bed that the people of this world should be content with the one phrase, "Pay homage to Amitābha Buddha" (*Namu Amida Butsu*[bf]), and ordered his books destroyed by fire.

On the other hand, some contemporary philosophers in Japan

have tried to see in Dōgen, who continued to write philosophical works throughout his lifetime, the pioneer of Japanese philosophy. Though it is doubtlessly true that Dōgen was a distinguished thinker, as well as a high-minded spiritual leader, he was not the sort of thinker who developed a logically coherent system of thought. In spite of the fact that he cherished deep philosophical ideas which were gem-like in character, he was not inclined to elaborate the ethical thoughts he apprehended in a purely logical system. Probably he thought that a philosophical system set forth in a systematic way was useless and unnecessary.

Dōgen opined as follows, referring to the problem of life and death: "Life and death matter little, because the Buddha exists therein. And one is not perplexed by life and death, because the Buddha does not exist therein."[16] As far as the expression is concerned, we have here two formally contradictory propositions. But the gist of what he meant by the two sentences was quite the same.

The teacher Musō[bg] (Soseki[bh]) (1275–1351) declared, very clearly, that he does not aim at fixed logical coherency:

> Clear-sighted masters of the Zen sect do not have a fixed doctrine as something to be cherished for all time. They present any doctrine as the occasion demands, and preach as their tongues happen to dictate. They do not have a fixed source to rely upon. If one asks them what Zen is, they sometimes answer in terms of the sayings of Confucius[bi], Mencius[bj], Lao Tzu, Chuang Tzu[bk], and non-Zen Buddhist teachers, and sometimes in terms of popular proverbs, and sometimes they explain what Zen[bl] teaches, point out a particular situation, or simply swing their mace in front of them or shout in a loud voice. Or they simply raise their fingers or fists. All these are means used by the masters, and called "the vivacious ways of the Zen sect."[17]

In this state, no universal proposition which is logically coherent is mentioned, but esteem of the individual situation in each case is emphasized.

Ever since the Tokugawa period (1615–1867), the schools of Chu Hsi[bm] and Wang Yang-ming[bn] have been energetically studied in Japan, but it is a question how far Japanese scholars were virtually sympathetic with them. It is likely that Japanese Confucianists did not like metaphysical speculation.

Absence of theoretical and systematic thinking is equally characteristic of former scholars of Japanese classics. Motoori, for example, did not want to express any concrete conception of method in his learning: "In final conclusion, to make strenuous efforts consecutively for long years is most essential to those who are engaged in learning, and it does not matter how they learn."[18] Motoori exhorted his disciples just to be diligent in their study, and did not develop any constructive thinking as to the learning itself.[19]

Of course, one cannot deny the possibility that one actually can express oneself as clearly in Japanese as in any other language. It is said that there is one school of thought which stresses the cultural conditioning of thought-patterns more than the limitation of a language concerned. At least, the Japanese *esprit* should not be overlooked. However, the value of ways of Japanese expression lies more in aesthetic aspects than in exactly logical ones.

Moreover, there is no intention here to advocate any sort of linguistic determinism. We admit the working influences of other factors. We just point out, with regard to logical aspects, some features of the manner of expressing thoughts by the Japanese in earlier days, for these features are quite relevant to those in contemporary times with regard to the concepts of the universal and the individual. On the other hand, Japanese expressions focus the thought and expression of the person on immediate, concrete details of life. This tendency is quite unique to the Japanese. That is why the Japanese way of thinking habitually avoids summations of separate facts into broad statements about whole categories of things, although such abstraction is necessary for logical and scientific thinking.

IV. THE DEVELOPMENT OF LOGIC IN JAPAN BEYOND INDIAN AND CHINESE BUDDHIST LOGIC

We need not despair completely, however, of the capacity of the Japanese people for logical thinking. The way of thinking of a people is simply a tendency and is capable of being reformed. There is evidence for this in the fact that modes of expression in the Japanese language have gradually been growing more and more strict and precise in recent years. Although it is true that Japanese heretofore has not tended to be fit for exact thinking, it will surely improve in this respect.

The fact that Buddhist logic did not fully develop in the past can be ascribed to the non-logical character of its immediate source, the Chinese *inmyō*[bo] (Buddhist logic). In spite of this limitation, there were Japanese scholars who tried at several points to initiate a development beyond Chinese logic in Japan. We mention an interesting, if rather trivial, example. In Chinese logic, the word *"shūhō*[bp]*"* (*tsung-fa, pakṣa-dharma*) represents the predicate of an assertive proposition (*tsung,* major term, *sādhya*) as well as the predicate of a causal proposition (*yin* , middle term, *sādhana*). Chinese technical terminology did not distinguish between the two. Even if a distinction was made at first between the two uses through pronunciation, this distinction could not be preserved for a long time in a country using the Chinese language, in which pronunciation rather frequently changed. The Japanese, distinguishing the two terms in pronunciation, read in voiceless sound *shūhō,* in one case, where it means the predicate (P) of an assertive proposition, and in voiced sound (*shūbō*), in the other case, where it means the predicate (M) of a causal proposition.[20] Moreover, before the Meiji[bs] era (1867–1911), there were several scholars who had mastered Indian formal logic and had actually applied it to the study of Buddhist ideas. As examples we can mention the names of Rinjō[bt] (1751–1810) and Kaijō[bu] (?–1805), of the Buzan school of the New Shingon sect. Surely, logic can be disseminated and developed among the Japanese people, if they endeavor seriously to study it.

There were some Japanese in the past who were willing to use terms of Buddhist logic, even with changed meanings. For example, it has been asserted that the word *"rippa[bv]"* (magnificent, splendid) is a phonetic equivalent to *"ryūha[bw]"* (assertion and refutation in a debate) and that *"mutai[bx]"* (unreasonable) also is due to Buddhist logic.[21] Although it is doubtful whether or not this assertion or conjecture is right, it is an established fact that there were some men of letters who took it that way. This means that some ideas related to logic were not alien to the common people, although they may not have been fully aware of the exact meaning of them.

It is an object of interest how far Japanese logicians developed their thought beyond the Chinese scholarship of Buddhist logic, which originated in India. Saṁkarasvāmin (at the end of the sixth century) asserted that perception (*pratyakṣa*) is caused by the individual object.[22] The traditional definition of perception in Indian and Chinese Buddhist logic was interpreted by Zenju[by], a Japanese logician (723–797), as implying individuality.[23] An ancient Japanese logician said, "That which cannot be described with any word is called the thing-in-itself (*jisō[bz]*, *sva-lakṣaṇa*), i.e., that which should be predicated (*uhō[ca]*, *dharmin*). That which should be described with a word is called 'characteristic' or 'quality' (*hō[cb]*, *dharma*)."[24]

Hōtan[cc] (1654–1738), a modern Buddhist logician, went still further. He said, "The thing-in-itself is apprehended by direct perception. Any characteristic which can be found in common throughout various things is an object of inference.[25] "The reality of things is called the thing-in-itself. It is an individual and cannot be in common with others. Genus is found throughout various things, just like a thread piercing flowers. This characteristic can be set up as an object of the mind in an ordinary situation (not in meditation). Genus in Buddhist logic is an object of inference."[26]

What characterized his concept of the individual was that he thought that the thing-in-itself is something substantial. He said, "Fire burns the body. Therefore, this fire can be regarded as an individual object. Only the fire that can burn the body is named the thing-in-itself."[27] This definition of the thing-in-itself is conspicuously empiricistic, and makes quite a contrast to the idealistic concept of the thing-in-itself held by Indian Buddhist logicians, such as Dharmakīrti, etc., who belonged to the tradition of Buddhist idealism (Vijñāna-vāda).

Dialectical thinking was not clear in Eastern countries before the introduction of Western civilization. The Tendai[cd] and Sanron[ce] philosophies of ancient China and Japan had conspicuously dialectical thinking, but it did not develop in the line of dialectics. In modern Japan there have been some individual thinkers who held some dialectical ideas. Ishida Baigan[cf] set forth the thought that negative and positive are two things and yet they cannot be separated. But, even if they seem to be one, they are the two aspects of motion and quiescence.[28]

Miura Baien[cg] expressed a theory of dialectics of his own. "The way to understand nature (or the universe) is dialectics (jōri[ch]). The secret (ketsu[ci]) of dialectics is to see synthesis (gōitsu[cj]) in antithesis (han[ck]). It is to give up one-sided preoccupation and to correct marks (chōhyō[cl])—yin[cm] and yang[cn] are antithetic to each other and constitute opposition. As they are antithetic to each other, they can be brought to synthesis."[29] Here we find the thought of dialectics in its incipient stage.

V. CONCLUSION

We have discussed the reflection on or the awareness of the concept of the individual by the Japanese in terms of the daily use of the common people and language in terms of the logical thinking by thinkers. Throughout various phenomena we may safely notice the following four features:

(1) Conflation, rather than confrontation, of different individuals was esteemed, at least in the realm of subjective reflection, reflecting the social concept in which each individual is situated.

(2) When the Japanese have discussed the significance of the individual as against the universal in terms of linguistic use, the significance of the individual has tended to be minimized, but now it is going to be emphasized as contrasted with the universal when necessary.

(3) When any proposition was made in terms of logical and philosophical thinking, individual cases relevant to the proposition were mentioned emphatically in detail.

(4) Japanese thinkers have tended to lay more emphasis upon, and have paid more attention to, empirical facts, which

should be mentioned individually. This reflects the traditional empiricistic attitude of the Japanese.

The focus of the Japanese on the facts of life did not allow for the abstraction from experience of a concept of the individual "as such," in isolation.

The above discussions lead us to an important corollary. Heretofore, it has often been said in the West as a cliché that Westerners tend to be individualistic and diremptive, whereas Easterners tend to be monistic or all-embracing. But it has been made clear that this is wrong. Insofar as Japanese thought is concerned, we can say with certainty that the Japanese have tended to be individualistic, due to the attitude of focusing on immediate experience directly.

Concerning logical thinking, we can say that, although the mass of Japanese people have been limited to a language that was rather deficient as a tool of logical exactness, philosophic thinking did develop among Japan's educated classes through the use of Chinese.

Logic can be disseminated and developed among the Japanese people, if they endeavor seriously in a right way. Logical improvement will not be impossible in the future, although it is fraught with many difficulties. This will entail a greatly increased awareness of the relation between the universal and the individual on the part of the Japanese.

It is important for the Japanese people as a nation to develop the habits and language tools of logically exact thinking. We cannot foresee the developments in the future, but industrialization, which is going on very rapidly in contemporary Japan, does not seem to change the above-mentioned features very much or easily, but to develop along the lines which have been long established and practiced among the people. It is natural that the Japanese do not want to lose their traditional aesthetic and empirical attitude.

QUESTION: There is a theory in Western philosophy that Greek concepts of reality (which still influence modern Western concepts) derived from the subject-predicate structure of the Greek language. But it is also held that it was the other way around. The Greek language-structure grew out of early Greek concepts of reality. The non-abstracting characteristics of the Japanese language might have derived from a natural temperament of concrete concerns among the Japanese people.

ANSWER: There is probably a reciprocal influence between a people's language and their way of thinking, as well as other influences bearing upon both of them, such as climate, social structure, ways of production, human relationships, and so on.

QUESTION: You mentioned the ideas of Motoori and Hirata. I understand that the so-called Kokugaku[eu] school they belonged to had been led by their teacher Kamo-no-Mabuchi[ev], who strongly insisted on the historico-linguistic approach to the Japanese classics in order to clarify the pure and real meanings of the Japanese way of thinking as well as their way of life. Motoori and Hirata and other scholars of Kokugaku also pursued their studies in strict conformity with this principle. Though their achievements and interpretations were sometimes far-fetched and might not be comparable with Indian or Western philosophy and logic of language, they were neither simple linguists nor grammarians but scholars who ardently wanted to discover the metaphysical meanings of the ancient Japanese language and words. They probably had some non-logical logic as the results of their researches.

ANSWER: The Kokugaku school had the command of a sort of logic of its own. They advocated what might be called "empiricism of language," but they did not develop a system of methodology, as did Indian and Chinese scholars. It is necessary to determine what the Kokugaku scholar had in mind concerning methodology. This calls for further study.

QUESTION: You mentioned that there were some Buddhist monastic scholars who elaborated Buddhist logic, though this school did not develop from among the Japanese. However, I understand that from the ninth to the fourteenth century the annual examination systems for the officially authorized monks as well as for the promoting of the scholarly monks' ranks in the Tendai, Hossō[ew], Kegon[ex], and Shingon[ey] sects were institutionalized. And, in these examinations, the two or three among ten to twelve questions necessarily came from the field of Buddhist logic. Therefore, many Buddhist scholarly monks necessarily had to study and learn Buddhist logic thoroughly. These currents—or training—cannot be overlooked when we observe the history of Japanese metaphysics and sciences which gradually developed from medieval to modern times.

ANSWER: It is true that Buddhist logic was enthusiastically studied by monks in the ancient and medieval periods of Japan. But few studies have been launched so far with regard to how far Japanese scholars have made progress in logical investigation beyond Indian and Chinese Buddhist logic. That is up to the scholars in the future.

QUESTION: In medieval and modern Japan we find many original and unique thinkers who have left a tremendous volume of work in which deep philosophical thinking was expressed. Do you not admit the historical significance of these thinkers?

ANSWER: I admit the historical fact that the Japan of the past produced a great number of thinkers whose speculation was very deep. But most of them wrote down their philosophical thought only in classical-style Chinese, and did not write in Japanese. I have mentioned in this paper chiefly those thinkers (except some logicians) who have expressed their thought in Japanese, and not in Chinese.

QUESTION: It occurred to me that your paper has wider implications than you claimed. It not only called attention to the Japanese preference for the "individual" over the general-categorical. It really pointed out that the present Japanese tendency is that of wishing to move toward the Western (Continental: German, French, and earlier scholastic) tendency to connect individuals, i.e., thing-words in relational-categorical-general words.

ANSWER: My paper points toward *no* structure—either universal or otherwise.

QUESTION: What I find interesting is that Japanese thought is moving in the direction of several structures, whereas the "West" is trying so to move in the opposite direction: away from the abstract, away from the general, toward the concrete, immediate perception, non-connective, "instant-by-instant" perception and experience. It could be said that the English started out with this in modern philosophy,—for example, Francis Bacon. He advocated it for scientific method (i.e., empiricism versus scholasticism). But from the nineteenth century on we got away many times from "system-building" in philosophy, mostly by way of reaction against Hegel. Existentialism had its roots in that (Kierkegaard versus Kant, too).

At present, the trend toward immediate experience and the search for a *"language"* of immediacy is especially strong in the arts—away from "general truths," from "ideas," and toward unique forms, forms that include spiritual qualities, *unique* spiritual qualities, not "general" spiritual (or emotional) qualities. The most extreme trend in this respect is the so-called "aleatoric" or "aleatory" art (alea = dice, i.e., random choice). It defies "composition" in the familiar sense of the term, and, of course, it defies "intentionality" in art. Aleatory experiments are a dead-end; but there are some good artists who take it seriously (in music, poetry, and the dance). Conclusion: The "East" (i.e., Japan) and the "West" (U.S.A. and some European cultures) are not "meeting" but are passing each other, the West turning where the East is leaving.

ANSWER: There are some evidences that the East is going in the opposite direction to the one in which it went previously, i.e., in the direction in which the West advanced in the past, and vice versa. For example, activity was exceedingly cherished in the West of the past, but now the West is going in the direction of cherishing receptivity or passivity. The East, on the other hand, is going to emphasize activity, forsaking the previous attitude of esteeming receptivity or passivity. The phenomenon which you have pointed out may belong to this same movement.

1 I mention these linguistic expressions as current in contemporary daily life. They represent the present-day usage of these words. Historically speaking, *"domo"* was used for persons of inferior status, such as *"midomo*co*"* (me). *"Tachi,"* which seems to have derived from *"doshi*cp*,"* was used for persons of superior rank in such cases as *"kindachi*cq*"* (courtiers). From around the Muromachi*cr* period (1138–1568), it came to be used for persons of equal rank also. I owe this historical information to Professor Hori Ichirō*cs*.

2 Originally it meant "a group of youngsters of the same age grade."

3 Prince Shōtoku's Seventeen Article Constitution*ct*, Article 2.

4 *Genkō shakusho*, Vol. 30.

5 Watsuji Tetsurō*cu*, *Zoku Nihon seishin shi kenkyū*cv* (Supplement to Studies in Japanese Intellectual [Spiritual] History) (Tokyo: Iwanami-shōten, 1935), p. 397.

6 Sakuma Kanae*cw*, on the other hand, maintains that the Japanese language contains words performing the function of the relative pronoun, by the suitable manipulation of which the lack of the relative pronoun may be compensated for. "Kyūchakugo no mondai*cx*," (The Problem of Agglutinative Languages), in *Kokugo kokubun*cy* (Japanese Language and Literature), VIII (October, 1938).

7 In the sentence "All beings who hear his name blissfully trust in him, and think even once—which all is the directing of their minds toward him with the sincerest effort—and who desire to be born in his country will at once be born, attaining thereby the Unretrogressive State*cz*," in the *Daimuryōjukyō*da* (The Great Sutra of the Pure Land) it is obvious that the object of the "directing of their minds*db*" is living beings*dc*, cf. *Sukhāvatī-vyūha-sūtra*, 26: *ye kecit sattvās tasya bhagavato 'mitābhasya nāmadheyam śṛṇvanti śrutvā cāntaśa ekacittotpādam apy adhyāśayena prasādasahagatena cittam utpādayanti te sarve vaivartikatāyām santy anuttarāyāḥ samyakṣam bodheḥ*, but Shinran took the subject of the phrase "the directing of their minds" for Amitābha Buddha (!); cf. his works, *Jōdo monrui jushō*dd* (Anthology of Scriptural Passages on the Pure Land), *Ichinen tanen*

158 Nakamura Hajime

shōmon[de] (Scriptural Passages on Immediate and Mediate Attainment), *Kyōgyō shinshō*[df] (The Book on the Teaching, Practice, Faith, and Attainment); see Rev. Kusaka Murin[dg], ed., *Bantō shinpon kyōgyō shinshō*[dh] (An Authentic Text of the Kyōgyō shinshō) (Kyoto: Chōjiya-shoten, 1923), p. 103.

8 Hiroike Chikurō[di], *Shina bunten*[dj] (Grammar of Chinese) (Tokyo: privately published, 1905), p. 67.

9 *"cittamātram idaṁ yad idaṁ traidhātukam"* (The universe is nothing but our presentation), *Daśabhūmika-sūtra*, J. Rahder, ed. (Paris: Paul Geunther, 1926), p. 49; *cf vijñaptimātram evedam* (The universe is nothing but our ideation), *Triṁśikā*, S. Lévi, ed., (Paris: Libraire Ancienne Honore-champion, 1932), 27, p. 42.

10 *Shōbōgenzō*[dk] (Repository of True Buddhist Teachings), chap. "Sangai yuishin[dl]" (The Universe is Nothing but Our Presentation).

11 *Tōmonsho*[dm] (Questions and Answers), Book I, in *Nihon rinri ihen*[dn] (Collected Japanese Ethical Texts), Inouye Tetsujirō[do] and Kanie Yoshimaru[dp], eds., (Tokyo: Ikuseikai, 1902), Vol. VI, p. 157.

12 *Ibid.*, p. 156.

13 *Nyūgaku mondō*[dq] (Elements of Study) in *Hirata Atsutane zenshū*[dr] (Collected Works of Hirata Atsutane), Hirata Moritane[ds] and Miki Ioe[dt], eds. (Tokyo: Hirata Atsutane Zenshū Kiseikai, 1918), Vol. 15, p. 1. (In discussion, Professor Mei expressed the idea that Atsutane's citation is a twisted interpretation).

14 *Naobi no mitama*[du] (The Honest Spirit), in *Motoori Norinaga zenshū*[dv] (Collected Works of Motoori Norinaga), Motoori Seizō[dw], ed. (Tokyo: Yoshikawa-kōbunkan, 1926), Vol. I, p. 53.

15 *Ibid.*

16 Shōji[dx] (Life and Death) in *Shōbōgenzō*, in Taishō shinshū daizōkyō[dy] (Buddhist Sacred Texts edited in Taishō period) (Tokyo: The Taishō Isaai-kyō Kankō Kwai, 1931), Vol. 82, p. 305.

17 *Muchū mondō shū*[dz] (Questions and Answers in Dreams).

18 *Uiyamabumi*[ea] (Introduction for Beginners), in *Motoori Norinaga zenshū*, Motoori Seizō, ed., Vol. IV, p. 601.

19 *Ibid.*

20 Ui Hakuju[eb], *Bukkyō ronrigaku*[ec] (Buddhist Logic) (Tokyo: Daito-shuppansha, 1944), p. 168.

21 Yamada Yoshio[ed], *Geirin*[ee] (Arts), Vol. 3 (1952), Nos. 1, 2. As for *"mutai*[ef]" (non-entity), see Chikū[eg], *Inmyō inu sanshi*[eh] (Introduction to Buddhist Logic) (1854), p. 19b. But this term seems not to have been so important in original Indian Buddhist logic.

22 *pratyakṣaṁ kalpanāpoḍhaṁ yaj jñānam arthe rūpādau nāmajātyādikalpanārahitam / tad akṣam akṣam prati vartata iti pratyakṣam // kalpanājñānam arthāntare pratyakṣābhāsam / yaj jñānaṁ ghaṭaḥ paṭa iti vā vikalpayataḥ samutpadyate tad arthasvalakṣaṇaviṣayatvāt pratyakṣābhāsam.*

The *Nyāya-praveśa*, Anandshankar B. Dhruva, ed. (Baroda: Oriental Institute, 1930), p. 7. (Gaekwad's Oriental Series, No. XXXVIII).

23 *Gengen betten shoryō shikyō*[ei] (Objects of Perception), in *Inmyō nisshō riron sho myōtōshō*[ej] (Gloss on the Commentary on the Introduction to [Buddhist] Logic) (Tradítional edition, Vol. 6b, p. 454b). See p. 461b: "It is not called 'perception' because it partakes in universals[ek]."

24 See also: "With regard to the fact that it cannot be described, it is called 'thing in itself'; if it can be described, then it is called 'universal[el],' " in *Myōhon shō*[em] (Clarification of Rules), Bussho-kankōkai[en], ed., *Dai-Nippon Bukkyō zensho*[eo] (Tokyo: Bussho-kankōkai, 1911), Vol. 4, p. 47.

25 *Inmyō zuigen ki*[ep] (Sources of Buddhist Logic), Vol. 8, published in 1711, p. 16a.

26 *Ibid.*, pp. 9b–10a.

27 *Ibid.*, p. 13a.

28 *Seiri mondō*[eq] (Questions and Answers on Nature), translated into English by Paulo Beonio-Brocchieri (Rome: Istituto per il Medio ed Estremo Oriente, 1961), pp. 19–20.

29 Saigusa Hiroto[er], *Miura Baien no tetsugaku*[es] (The Philosophy of Miura Baien) (Tokyo: Daiichi-shobō, 1941), p. 132; also his *Nihon no yuibutsu ronsha*[et] (Japanese Materialists) (Tokyo: Eihōsha, 1928), p. 93.

a 中村元
b 山々
c 神々
d ども
e 達，たち
f 舟人ども
g 人達
h 友達

i 方
j 貴方がた
k 先生がた
l 諸々の
m 若い衆
n 若い
o 衆
p 聖徳

q 慈雲尊者

r 自相

s 個物

t 虎關師鍊

u 元亨釋書

v 概念

w 理性

x 笑い

y 笑う

z 笑いたり

aa 笑いマ

ab 笑い事

ac 笑うこと

ad 笑いと言えうもの

ae 深さ

af 深み

ag さ

ah み

ai 性

aj 日尾荊山

ak 訓点復古

al 訓点

am 德川

an 顔回者

ao 顔回なる者

ap 顔回ルある者

aq 道元

ar 荻生

as 宋

at 物

au 理

av 平田

aw 老子

ax 柿本人麿

ay 本居

az 鎌倉

ba 法然

bb 親鸞

bc 日蓮

bd 源信

be 一遍上人

bf 阿彌陀佛

bg 夢窓

bh 疎石

bi 孔子

bj 孟子

bk 莊子

bl 禪

bm 朱子

bn 王陽明

bo 因明

bp 宗法

bs 明治

bt 林常

bu 戒定

bv 立派

bw 立破

bx 無體

by 禪師

bz 自相

ca 有法

cb 法

cc 鳳潭

cd 天台

ce 三論

cf 石田梅巖

cg 梅園

ch 條理

ci 訣

cj 合一

ck 反

cl 徵表

cm 陰

cn 陽

co 身ども

cp どし

cq 公達

cr 室町

cs 堀一郎

ct 聖德太子十七條憲法

cu 和辻哲郎

cv 續日本精神研究

cw 佐久間晁

cx 吸着語の問題

cy 國語國文

cz 諸有衆生 ， 聞其名號 ， 信心歡
喜，乃至一念，至心迴向，願
生彼國，即得往生，住不退轉

da 大無量壽經

db 至心迴向

dc 諸有衆生

dd 淨土文類聚鈔

de 一念多念證文

df 教行信證

dg 日下無倫

dh 坂東眞本教行信證

di 廣池千九郎

dj 支那文典

dk 正法眼藏

dl 三界唯心

dm 答問書。下

dn 日本倫理彙編

do 井上哲次郎

dp 蟹江義丸

dq 入學問答

dr 平田篤胤全集

ds 平田盛胤

dt 三木五百枝

du 直毘靈

dv 本居宣長全集

dw 本居精造

dx 生死

dy 大正新修大藏經

dz 夢中問答錄

ea うひやまぶみ

eb 宇井伯壽

ec 佛教論理學

ed 山田孝雄

ee 藝林

ef 無體

eg 癡空

eh 因明犬三支

ei 現々別轉所量之境

ej 因明入正理論明燈抄

ek 了此境與餘境分，有同相坆，不
　　明現量

el 望不加言名有自相，若加言已，
　　則名爲法。

em 明本抄

en 佛書刊行會

eo 大日本佛教全書

ep 因明瑞源記

eq 性理問答

er 三枝博音

es 三浦梅園の哲學

et 日本之唯物論者

eu 國學

ev 賀茂眞淵

ew 法相

ex 華嚴

ey 眞言

HAROLD E. McCARTHY

Knowledge, skepticism, and the individual

I

Very broadly speaking, it can be said that philosophers in the West have been concerned with a range of diverse problems bearing upon (1) the ultimate nature of the universe, multiverse, or totality of reality, in which man finds himself, whether he likes it or not, in some manner caught up and with respect to which he may regard himself a part, but perhaps a part apart from other parts; (2) the ultimate nature of man, that apparently paradoxical creature which, from one point of view exists in the sense in which a tree or a stone exists, and which, from another point of view, exists, unlike any tree or stone, or so we would suppose, in such a way as to be capable of becoming aware of itself as an existing thing; and (3) the nature of the good life and the good society for man, man being the kind of creature that he is and caught up in the kind of universe, multiverse, or totality of reality in which he is apparently caught up. Although this tripartite division is arbitrary and, therefore, not imposed by the nature of logic or by the nature of things, most of what I would call the basic philosophical questions can be brought under one or another of these three generic problems.

Epistemology, as a division of the field of philosophy, is concerned with man as a knowing or would-be knowing creature. If men did not wish to know, if men did not make cognitive claims of one kind or another, or if men were not aware of cognitive wishes or cognitive claims, then for philosophers there would be no epistemological problems. Not only do men exist, but men are capable of making cognitive claims, or so it would appear; and thus the epistemologist finds himself with a subject-matter. The epistemologist raises, with respect to this whole matter of actual or possible cognition, at least three fundamental questions: (1) Is human knowledge possible, or is what we call knowledge indistinguishable, in principle, from what we would otherwise call opinion, belief, or conviction? (2) If human knowledge is possible, what are its sources and by what marks, standards, criteria, or methods do we distinguish between what we call knowledge and what we do not or should not call knowledge? (3) If human knowledge is possible, what are its limits, if any—that is, can we say that whatever is, whatever exists, whatever is real, is knowable, at least in principle, whether it is actually known or not; or must we say, or have we any significant justification for saying, that there are things, or entities, or realities which *are* but which must be spoken of as unknowable, at least from the point of view of man and whatever faculties of knowing he may have, either by nature or by the grace of God?

At the core of epistemology there is a very basic problem, a problem which may be felt by some though probably not by all thinkers —and that problem is this: how is it possible, if it is, for an individual self to reach out beyond the individuality of itself and to relate itself cognitively to something which is not itself at all, but an *other?* There are both a paradox and a mystery here, and not a mystery to be resolved by way of a simple analogy. It is simply not enough to say that the problem of the self knowing the non-self is no more mysterious than the problem as to how it is possible for a man, who is not an apple, to eat an apple. Even if we were to grant that the process of eating goes on and that when one eats one does not necessarily eat oneself, the process of eating and the process of knowing do not have, at first glance, so much in common that we can start with both processes as indubitably going on and on all fours with one another. No doubt, an individual self may have, as modifications of itself, beliefs, opinions, persuasions, convictions, some of which may be held quite lightly, some of which may be held quite tenaciously. But having beliefs is not the same as knowing. I may believe that the moon is made of green cheese; and I may be convinced inside of myself that this is so and must be. But the cognitive question is whether my belief, however tenaciously held, reflects, in some sense, the actual constitution of what I call the moon, the moon being something other than my individual self. Seldom do we say, at least on the level of non-psychotic common sense, "I am the moon." On the other hand, we may say, or want to say, or feel like saying, *"La lune est grande ce soir,"* or something else equally pointless, idiotic, or romantic. Knowledge, it would appear, is both knowledge by and knowledge of—knowledge, that is, by or on the part of a human self or individual; and knowledge of, at least in part, something that in some manner lies beyond the so-called knowing self. The paradox, in short, is that of one part of the totality of reality being itself and yet knowing other parts.

The basic question as to whether knowledge by a finite human individual is possible or whether an individual, by his very nature, is limited to beliefs and opinions with respect to which he cannot distinguish between truth and falsity has been answered differently by different philosophers in the West. Those philosophers whom I would call epistemological skeptics do not deny the possibility, indeed the actuality (past or present) of beliefs. On the other hand, and *qua* skeptics, they are concerned with denying the possibility of knowledge by asserting that nothing can be known, objectively and with certainty, by the human individual, or, if anything can be known, the individual cannot properly distinguish between what he knows and what he does not know. Extreme, absolute, or utter skepticism, if logically possible at all, has been relatively rare in the history of Western thought. We are told that Protagoras held that "man is the measure of all things, of those that are that they are, of those that are not that they are not."[1] And, if by "man" Protagoras meant each and every individual man, then it would appear that what Protagoras was pronouncing was an epistemological doctrine of *right you are if you think you are, there is no disputing about beliefs, and what you believe to be true is true for you,* a doctrine that would automatically reduce knowledge to its opposite: diverse and shifting opinion, belief, conviction, or persuasion. In short, beliefs are many, and men may agree or disagree with respect to their beliefs. For the complete skeptic, this is the end of the story.

However, perhaps not even Protagoras can be significantly spoken of as a complete or unconditioned skeptic. Most skeptics in the West have been limited or conditioned skeptics rather than absolute or total skeptics. And here, in contrast to complete skepticism, I would like to distinguish three kinds or modes of limited skepticism: philosophical skepticism, theological skepticism, and scientific skepticism.

As for philosophical skepticism, the philosophical skeptic would hold that nothing can be known by way of any natural human faculty (be it reason, sense-perception, or intuition) concerning the ultimate nature of the universe, the ultimate nature of man, and the ultimate nature of the good life for man. In short, if philosophy is concerned with understanding things as they are in themselves, then the philosophical skeptic would hold that nothing, really, can be understood, nothing can be known, concerning things as they are in themselves. The philosophical skeptic is not without his allegedly justifying reasons, be his reasons good or bad, adequate or inadequate, relative to the support of his contention; and the reasons have sometimes been divided into the epistemological and the historical.

As for the epistemological reasons, they are, in principle, simple enough. Those, it is argued, who claim to have philosophical knowledge claim to have such knowledge by way of sense-perception, reason, and/or intuition. But sense-perception is shot through and through with relativity (what is sweet to one individual may be sour to another individual, etc.) and hence subjectivity, such that what we call sense-perceptions are subjective sensations, modifications of the self; and, since no two selves are identical, we are left with the multiple sensations of multiple selves, which sensations, *qua* sensations, give us no assured knowledge of anything that lies objectively beyond them. In short, even if it is argued that our sensations must have causes which lie beyond them, we are never in a position to say that our sensations somehow correspond (or do not correspond, for that matter) to objective realities beyond them, since, on the level of sense-perception, we are never able to compare our sensations with non-sensed realities, if any. Sensations are human sensations, sensations within the context of human beings, and their particular, individual, and finite sensory equipment. But, if sense-perception is shot through and through with subjectivity, so also are reason and intuition. It is always human, organically conditioned reason that reasons, and always finite subjects conditioned by human reason and human sense-experience that have and interpret intuitions. An intuition is always, for human beings, a human intuition; and, although the individual may be convinced that by way of intuition he transcends the subjectivity of the finite self or individual, he is, at best, transcending only the subjectivity of reason and sense-experience. Indeed, one man's intuition may be another man's psychosis, just as one man's self-evident truth may be another man's absurdity. Subjectively conditioned and operating faculties, even if called cognitive, are not necessarily reliable sources of objective and certain knowledge.

As for the historical argument for philosophical skepticism this is simple enough also. Claims to philosophical knowledge in the form of a system of philosophical, or metaphysical, interpretation have been many, diverse, and mutually incompatible. By their fruits ye shall know them. On the basis of the historical, philosophical fruits we cannot speak of philosophical knowledge, not because we have no claims to such knowledge, but because we have too many: many men, many manners, many philosophies—materialistic, idealistic, dualistic, monistic, theistic, mystical, diremptive, non-diremptive— different ways of talking, but not different ways of saying the same thing. Philosophers may communicate, perhaps, what they believe; but apparently no philosopher has been able to show that what he believes is true any more than any philosopher has been able to show that what some other philosopher believes is false. Philosophers may keep up with their patter in defense of endless chatter, but chatter, however endless, is not knowledge of man, his world, and the good life.

The position of philosophical skepticism is not, in the West, an artificial position. In general, though much qualification is necessary here, it would appear to be the position of Kant, who, for good or for bad, seems to assert, for instance, that there "exists" an objective world in itself, or a world of things in themselves, or something, but who then appears to assert that the nature of this world cannot be known by way of human reason, human sense-perception, or anything to be called a non-sensory, non-rational faculty of intuition possessed by man. What is knowable for Kant is knowable within the context of human reason and human sense-experience; what lies outside and beyond this context is not nothing but is beyond the possibility of human knowledge, individual or collective. Interestingly enough, the position that Kant appears to take with respect to the "objective world" is at least akin to the position taken by Thomas with respect to God: namely, its existence, in some sense, must be asserted or postulated, but nothing can be known about the essence or nature of this reality by way of the natural faculties—at least, Thomas would add, in this life. Readers of the *Summa Theologica* may feel that Thomas does not really stick to his guns with respect to the unknowability of God's essence, but perhaps Kant does not, either, with respect to his noumenal world. For Kant *seems* to argue that, if the phenomenal world is temporal, the noumenal world must be non-temporal, and so forth.[2] But can we know nothing about X and yet know what X is not?

As for theological skepticism, the theological skeptic by definition holds that, quite apart from the possibility or impossibility of either philosophical or scientific knowledge, nothing can be known theologically, that is—again by definition—on the grounds, alone, of divine revelation. The medieval philosopher in the West was pretty generally of the opinion that the knowing individual had at his disposal, thanks, perhaps, to the fact that he is created, maintained, and loved by God, two sources of knowledge: a natural source (reason and sense-experience) and a supernatural source (revelation as embodied in scripture and as interpreted, officially or by tradition, by the Church of Rome). Post-medieval, non-Catholic philosophers tended to be of divided opinion with respect to revelation as a source of valid and objective knowledge. David Hume was probably a theological skeptic, committing to the flames all claims to knowledge based upon divine revelation, in short, all divinity volumes, for they contain nothing but sophistry and illusion.[3] The theological skeptic is not without his reasons, one of which may well be this: that revelation, *qua* noetic, presupposes a knowing revealer, the existence of which cannot, significantly, be established by revelation (the revealer revealing his own existence and nature) or by way of anything other than revelation. Interestingly enough, Thomas, who is as sharp as a whip about most things anyway, had the wit to recognize that it is useless, if one is concerned with justifying revelation as a source of knowledge, to claim that the existence of God is known by revelation. Thus, the existence of God is, for Thomas, not an article of faith, but a preamble to the articles of faith, to be demonstrated on the basis of natural as opposed to revealed knowledge. This was both sensible and courageous, particularly when Thomas' natural arguments for the existence of God are (as Ockham sees so clearly) as open to criticism as they are. Ockham was a believer, but by and large he could not accept Thomas' arguments for the existence of God as establishing what they claimed to establish. But, quite apart from the problem of the revealer revealing his own revealing, it is quite clear to the theological skeptic that claims to revelation, from the point of view of content, are as diverse as the traditions in which the claims are made; and, even if one set of revelations could be recognized as somehow unique, the mode of revelation (as, say, embodied in scriptures) is such that it is open, as Thomas well knew, to diverse interpretations. So that, even if, somehow, one knows that what is revealed is truly revealed, one does not know *what* has been revealed until one has hit upon the true interpretation. We are left, then, with multitudinous theological beliefs and convictions (personal, individual, or collective) but not knowledge, not the truth that ought to be "common to all."

As for scientific skepticism, this is the position that what is called scientific knowledge, *qua* mediated by experimental or controlled observation, logico-mathematical analysis, and empirical verification, is not fit to be called knowledge at all in the sense of bearing the marks of objective and certain truth. Scientific skepticism is sometimes combined with either theological or philosophico-metaphysical fideism. The combination of scientific skepticism and theological fideism is beautifully exemplified in Osiander's non-commissioned preface ("To the Reader Concerning the Hypotheses of this Work") to Copernicus' *De Revolutionibus Orbium Caelestium*. Osiander's argument is simple enough. Nothing can be known by any finite creature—known absolutely, known with certainty—unless it has been revealed by God. But God has not revealed the true system of the world, astronomically speaking, and no astronomer can give us such truth. The duty, therefore, of the astronomer is

> to compose the history of the celestial motions through careful and skillful observation. Then turning to the causes of these motions or hypotheses about them, he must conceive and devise, since he cannot in any way attain to the true causes, such hypotheses as, being assumed, enable the motions to be calculated correctly from the principles of geometry, for the future as well as for the past. . . . But these hypotheses need not be true nor even probable; if they provide a calculus consistent with the observations, that alone is sufficient. . . . And if any causes are devised by the imagination, as indeed very many are, they are not put forward to convince anyone that they are true, but merely to provide a correct basis for calculation. Now when from time to time there are offered for one and the same motion different hypotheses . . . , the astronomer will accept above all others the one which is the

easiest to grasp. The philosopher will perhaps rather seek the semblance of the truth. But neither of them will understand or state anything certain, unless it has been divinely revealed to him.[4]

Osiander was speaking in the immediate context of astronomy; but, if generalized, his claim would be that what we call science, empirical science, does not give us knowledge in the sense of objective truth with respect to the inherent structure of things, but at best only a set of convenient and conventional human, conceptual instruments constructed by the imagination and functioning as instruments of systematic prediction with respect to the data of observation. Of two sets of conceptual instruments, both of which "work," the simpler is to be preferred, not because Nature loves simplicity, but because scientists do. Science, instrumentally interpreted, provides us with human tools to be used by human individuals for getting around in the flux of the data of observation. Science, in this sense, is not a substitute for metaphysics; and, whether or not metaphysics gives us truth, science, for the scientific skeptic, does not.

But, if scientific skepticism may be combined, as with Osiander, with theological fideism, it may also be combined with philosophical or metaphysical fideism. Bergson was of the opinion that what is called scientific knowledge, however useful, was at best only relative knowledge in the sense that the conceptual nets constructed by the scientist are, at best, useful tools for systematization and prediction, but, at the same time, are nets which, if they are supposed to catch absolute reality, are receipts for deceit.[5] Beyond the empirical-analytical methods of science there is, for Bergson, the method of intuition. Intuition seizes upon reality, but—it would appear—in such a way that the intuiter can say nothing at all: metaphysics, Bergson tells us, is the science (*scientia?*) which claims to dispense with symbols.[6] And, reaching outside the Western tradition into the Eastern traditions, what Bergson is saying is not too remote from what the Advaitist and Zenist are saying. For the Advaitist, if I understand him at all, if it is truth and reality that one longs to possess, then the methods of science are irrelevant, however relevant they are to getting around practically in *saṁsāra*. The method that is relevant to truth is the method of concentration and meditation, whereby, by transcending reason and sense-experience, we achieve union with *Nirguṇa Brahman,* the One without a second, with respect to which nothing can be said, strictly speaking, except *"neti, neti."* For the Advaitist, the condition of achieving such truth or reality is not that of the finite self, the finite individual, somehow gazing upon or even becoming *Nirguṇa Brahman,* but that of the true self realizing spiritually, that is, eternally, *Nirguṇa Brahman,* and that finitude belongs to the realm of relativity and illusion and must be abandoned. In the Zen tradition, science is not scorned, but scientific knowing, if I understand Suzuki at all, is not true or absolute knowing. True knowing is absolute knowing and is achieved only within the context of that mode of enlightenment called *satori* and is such that it cannot be formulated in anything even approximating denotative, or scientific, language. But when *satori* is achieved, when true knowing is had, we are no longer involved with a self knowing a non-self. The distinction between the self and the non-self evaporates and exhibits itself for what it is: one more conventional distinction which, however useful in one context, is obstructive to truth in another. Zen combines very nicely with an instrumental theory of science, but not with a realistic or metaphysical theory of science according to which the function of scientific theory is to articulate the inherent structures of nature or reality.

II

Although complete or absolute skepticism has been relatively rare in the Western tradition, more limited forms of skepticism, be they philosophical, scientific, or theological, have not been as rare as one might suppose. But the other side of limited skepticism is limited non-skepticism or fideism; and thus, historically speaking, it has been generally held in the West that, paradox or no paradox, some kind of objective knowledge is open to the individual self, knowledge which transcends the subjective opinions or beliefs of the individual. A complete historical survey at this point is impossible. I shall, therefore, limit myself to hitting a few high points with respect to knowledge and the individual.

Plato, it would appear, admitted the relativity of individual sense-experience and seems to argue that no genuine knowledge of the sensorily perceived particular is possible. Knowledge, however, of the rational or intelligible universal or form is possible by way of intellection, and the sensed particular may operate as the functional occasion of, though not the cause of, such intellection, if, indeed, we take seriously Plato's so-called doctrine of recollection. One may say that Plato did recognize a distinction between reason and sense-experience, but metaphysically he turned this distinction into a distinction between appearance and reality, the temporal and the eternal. Man, being, in part, an intellecting creature, can grasp, and thus know, eternal truths, forms, or principles. Such knowledge must be distinguished from mere sensory awareness, which is not knowledge, properly speaking, at all—such is the import of Plato's image of the divided line which has its counterpart in Spinoza's four modes of perception or knowledge as set forth in his *Improvement of the Understanding*. In either case, however, the answer to Protagoras is by way of an epistemological rationalism which finds a place for knowledge and leaves a place for belief.

As for Aristotle, he not only tells us that all men by nature desire to know, but in general is of the opinion that, the universe being what it is, and man having the faculties that he has, knowing is, in principle, as natural to man as talking or, for that matter, constructing dramas that have the power to evoke in human individuals, though not in sticks and stones, the emotions of pity and fear. Knowledge at its most certain, systematic, and refined is theoretical or speculative knowledge, to be distinguished from both dialectic and sophistry, and is itself divided into first philosophy, mathematics, and physics. Theoretical knowledge (as we are informed in the *Posterior Analytics*) begins in sense-perception ("the loss of any one of the senses entails the loss of a corresponding portion of knowledge"[7] and eventually culminates, as an acorn eventually culminates in a full-grown oak tree (if all goes well), in the form of a deductive system. There seems to be no question but that the *Posterior Analytics* was written by Aristotle with one eye on geometry in its historical development; and it may be true enough to say that Euclid constructed his *Elements* with one eye on the *Posterior Analytics* of Aristotle. Be that as it may, Aristotle recognized very clearly that in such a deductive system not all propositions could be derived without moving into an infinite regress, in one direction, or into the fallacy of circular demonstration, in the other. Thus, a closed or complete deductive system presupposes underived propositions, or first principles, which, because underived, must be known to be true (and they must be true, otherwise we fall into dialectic) other than by way of logical demonstration, that is, derivation. When Aristotle raises the question as to how the first principles of any demonstrative science are known to be true, he is raising a very crucial and a very serious question. With a slap at Plato, he contends that first principles are not innate in us; and it is clear that Aristotle is of the opinion that there are no principles which, taken in themselves alone, come stamped *true, true, true.* Aristotle remains naturalistic at this juncture, however inadequate his account. Out of sense-perception develops memory; out of memory develops experience; out of experience develops rudimentary universals; and out of rudimentary universals (within the total context of the progressive construction of a deductive system) develop the true universals, which are known, not by derivation, but by way of rational intuition. "The soul," Aristotle writes, "is so constituted as to be capable of this process."[8] There is a catch, however; for, if the soul has the power to form universals which, at a later date and in a wider context, turn out to be rudimentary as opposed to true universals (thus

Newton's principles give way, eventually, to Einstein's), one is, in principle, never in a position to know, with any kind of certainty, when one is dealing with rudimentary and when one is dealing with true first principles. And here it is fair to say that, in spite of his wealth of analysis, Aristotle deliberately strikes a skeptical note: "It is hard to be sure whether one knows or not; for it is hard to be sure whether one's knowledge is based on the basic truths appropriate to each attribute—the differentia of true knowledge. We think that we have scientific knowledge if we have reasoned from true and primary premises. But that is not so; the conclusion must be homogeneous with the basic facts of the science."[9] The best one can say is that Aristotle feels sure that he knows what demonstrative knowledge should be; but whether such knowledge can be achieved by the finite self working progressively in time in the midst of accumulating data of observation which cannot be denied is something else again. If Aristotle was of the opinion that he knew how the celestial bodies operated (via spheres within spheres), later thinkers were certainly of the opinion that Aristotle opined but did not know; and still later thinkers, such as Kepler, were apparently pretty sure that not only Aristotle, but also Ptolemy, had been led astray by a rudimentary first principle, that is, the principle of celestial motion. This principle was regarded by astronomers as absolute (with various modifications or adaptations) down to the time of Kepler; from the time of Newton on, the principle was regarded as false or inadequate. It would appear, then, that if the human soul is so constituted that it can regard true first principles as true, it is also so constituted that it can regard false principles as true also.

Turning from Aristotle to Thomas Aquinas, one can say that, while Thomas accepts completely, in his own way, the Aristotelian contention that the individual self may achieve theoretical knowledge, he also contends that in addition to such natural knowledge there is also supernatural knowledge open to man by way of divine revelation. The distinction between reason and revelation as sources of true and objective knowledge that transcends mere individual belief is, obviously, not unique to Thomas; it was common to all medieval Christian thinkers, in one way or another. But the precise form in which this distinction emerges in the opening pages of the *Summa Theologica* seems to breathe the very spirit of Thomism. Thus, Thomas' contention is that not only physics, say, is a science (*scientia*) in the Aristotelian sense of the term, but also sacred doctrine, the argument being that both are derived from first principles. However, sacred doctrine, as a science, is more certain than any natural science, since the natural sciences "derive their certitude from the natural light of human reason, which can err, whereas this derives its certitude from the light of the divine science, which cannot err."[10] One might note in passing that the suggestion that natural reason can err is, for Thomas, a rather dangerous admission, but an admission that he does not follow up. In general, it would appear that his contention is that reason is certain, so far as it goes, but is still less certain than revelation, though what anyone can make out of *degrees* of certainty is difficult to say. Be that as it may, the Thomistic position is that man, the individual man, is so constructed by God that natural knowledge is possible by way of the human faculties of reason and sense-perception; and that, in addition to natural knowledge, there is an avenue of more than natural knowledge of way of revelation. Revelation, the source of which is God and not the natural faculties of the individual, is not a substitute for natural knowledge. But, since revelation is more certain than the light of human reason, which can err, any proposition in natural science that is logically incompatible with a corresponding proposition of revelation is false—provided revelation has been properly interpreted.[11] Thus, revelation functions as a negative guide to natural knowledge. The existence of God, or at least the existence of a necessary Being, Thomas believes can be established on the basis of rational argument; but the essence of God (God not being an object of sense-perception) is unknown and unknowable to man in this life. That God, whatever his essence, is a trinity of persons we know on the basis of revelation only, and can accept, therefore, only on the grounds of faith, true faith presupposing grace, as Thomas makes quite clear. The individual, for Thomas, can know, via a twofold source of knowledge. But the individual, in this life, cannot know all things. What cannot be perceived, or significantly inferred from what is perceived, cannot be known. After all, Thomas does his best to hold to the principle: *Nihil in intellectu quod non prius in sensu fuerit.*

Descartes, undoubtedly writing with one eye on Thomas, one eye on Euclid, and one eye on Aristotle's *Posterior Analytics,* held that knowledge is, in principle, possible to the human, individual soul on the basis of natural reason, both intuitive and deductive, provided that reason itself, when properly employed, is absolutely reliable. But the reliability of reason Descartes is unable to take for granted. More explicitly than Thomas, he attempts to ground the reliability of reason in a supernatural source, a deity who is infinitely good, infinitely wise, and infinitely powerful and who, therefore, cannot be a deceiver. But, apart from a demonstration of the existence of God, there are no adequate grounds, so far as Descartes is concerned, either for asserting the validity of reason (which for Thomas could err) or even for asserting the existence of an objective and independent materio-extended world as the immediate source of our sensations. But Descartes had cut the ground out from under himself

by way of his skeptical doubts, and therefore his proof for the existence of God (even granting that he really does find within his personal self an idea of God) is specious. With one blow, so to speak,
Descartes, however inadvertently, raises questions which haunt the
rest of modern philosophy: namely, whether the existence, not only
of a transcendent deity, but also of an independent and objective
world, can be known by man, by the individual, on the basis of
natural, allegedly cognitive faculties. One might even say that, while
the traditional, medieval philosopher was quite confident that there
was a God who had created the contingent world (after all, revelation asserts that in the beginning God created the heavens and the
earth), the disappearance of God as an object of rational demonstration was all too soon followed by doubts and problems with
respect to the existence of an objective world, as if God and the
objective world were two sides of the same coin, a possibility that
Spinoza took quite seriously and all too literally from a traditional
Christian-Hebraic point of view. Descartes, with respect to knowledge, was in no sense a clear-cut rationalist. His rationalism rested
on a metaphysical theism which he attempted to justify in terms of
his rationalism. Nor did he, for that matter, consistently attempt to
challenge the reliability of revelation. Indeed, he seems to out-
Thomas Thomas when he writes in his *Principles of Philosophy*,
"Above all we should impress on our memory as an infallible rule
that what God has revealed to us is incomparably more certain than
anything else; and that we ought to submit to the Divine authority
rather than to our own judgment even though the light of reason
may seem to us to suggest, with the utmost clearness and evidence,
something opposite."[12] And yet, he seems quite capable of playing
both sides against the middle, as when he writes at the termination
of his *Principles*, "At the same time, recalling my insignificance,
I affirm nothing, but submit all these opinions to the authority of
the Catholic Church, and to the judgment of the more sage; and
I wish no one to believe anything I have written, unless he is personally persuaded by the force and evidence of reason."[13] That the
light of reason was common to all individuals Descartes did not
really doubt. The real problem for Descartes was that of tracing the
light of reason to its universal source. Since he failed in this, reason
itself is open to challenge, plus both God and the objective world.
Protagoras maintained a skepticism with respect to the gods. In the
modern world, skepticism shifts to the existence of an objective
world after centuries of more or less taking it for granted. This problem of knowing the *existence* of the objective world is a curious and
delightful one. In the middle of the twentieth century, a philosopher
who doubts or denies the existence of a transcendent deity may still

be regarded by his academic colleagues as normal, however mistaken. A philosopher who doubts or denies the existence of an objective and independent world would probably be regarded by his academic colleagues as a psychotic.

If Descartes wrote with one eye on Aristotle, one eye on Euclid, and one eye on Thomas, Newton may well have constructed his *Principia Mathematica* with one eye on Descartes and one eye on the British empirical tradition, i.e., squintingly. His goal was still the Aristotelian goal of constructing a demonstrative science (in this case, of bodies in motion) in the form of a deductive system. However, while Aristotle was of the opinion that the first principles of such a science could be known by way of rational, inductive intuition, and, while Descartes was apparently of the opinion that such first principles revealed themselves as true (granting God) by virtue of their special clarity and distinctness, Newton attempted to understand the first principles of his *Principia* as inductive generalizations. As Newton wrote, "In this philosophy particular propositions are inferred from the phenomena, and afterwards rendered general by induction. Thus it was that the impenetrability, the mobility, and the impulsive force of bodies, and the laws of motion and of gravitation, were discovered . . . and I frame no hypotheses; for whatever is not deduced from the phenomena is to be called an hypothesis; and hypotheses, whether metaphysical or physical, whether of occult qualities or mechanical, have no place in experimental philosophy."[14] And, in Rule IV of his "Rules of Reasoning in Philosophy," Newton wrote, "In experimental philosophy we are to look upon propositions inferred by general induction from phenomena as accurately or very nearly true, notwithstanding any contrary hypotheses that may be imagined, until such time as other phenomena occur, by which they may either be made more accurate, or liable to exceptions."[15] There is irony here, if it is objective and certain knowledge that Newton is seeking, and he certainly is. For, if his first principles are set up on the basis of inductive generalization, they are no more than rudimentary as opposed to true universals and therefore could be false, that is, if they also could be true. And, what is more, it is almost impossible to believe that Newton really could have regarded his laws of motion as inductive generalizations, because, if inductive generalizations, Newton must have observed what surely he never observed, say, a body remaining in uniform rectilinear motion, apparently in absolute as opposed to relative space. Whatever they may be, it would appear that Newton's laws of motion are not inductive generalizations; and, even if they were, or particularly if they were, they would not function as an adequate bridge from Newton's empirically observed phenomena to Newton's world of absolute space, absolute time, and absolute motion, a world which was most certainly never observed by Newton and which was never got at by way of simple, inductive generalization. To make matters even worse, his principle of gravitation was not only not an inductive generalization from observation, but made, as Newton recognized, practically no sense at all, that is, no physical or mechanical sense within his system, since it involved action at a distance, the whole notion of which so disturbed Newton that he was willing to complete his General Scholium by the addition of a hypothesis the statement of which violated his methodological precepts. Finally, it is well to note that Newton was not immune to theological speculation even in the midst, so to speak, of his demonstrative science of mechanics. He sets up a proof for the existence of God based upon the argument that the most beautiful system of the sun, planets, and comets could proceed only from the counsel and dominion of an intelligent and powerful Being, though part of the beauty Newton pretended to observe was somewhat cheatingly projected by Newton himself. He tells us that the six primary planets are revolved about the sun in circles concentric with the sun. He knows very well that the planets do no such thing; they move, for Newton, in ellipses. But, apparently, circles for Newton were more beautiful than ellipses and thus provided more evidence for the otherwise invisible hand of God, "to discourse of whom from the appearances of things does certainly belong to Natural Philosophy."[16] I would not say that Newton did not distinguish between theology and mechanics within *Principia*. Statements about God are not, for Newton, statements that follow from his definitions and axioms, nor do his definitions and axioms somehow presuppose (in the sense of following from) his statements about God. But, considered as a professed empiricist in matters of method who would permit only observation and inductive generalization, he certainly makes some rather odd claims, both within and outside of natural philosophy.

Hume, playing Newton's empiricism against Newton himself, but with one eye on Locke, insists that by no argument can the existence of God be established to a significant degree of probability; and, as for the so-called objective world of Locke and Newton (granted the differences), this can be established by neither reason nor sense-experience. There is, however, a crucial difference from Hume. The belief in the existence of an independent and objective world is, in its way, universal and unavoidable, at least in the long run; the belief in a single Supreme Deity is neither universal nor unavoidable. Knowledge does not extend beyond the sequences of sensations, inner and fleeting, and even here what is called scientific knowledge is supplemented by or mediated by rational, empirically non-justified hopes and expectations which belong to the realm of individual belief, however widely they may be shared by individuals. And thus Hume writes that it is "not solely in poetry and music, we must follow our taste and sentiment, but likewise in philosophy."[17]

The history of Western epistemological concern most certainly does not stop with Hume. However, one can say, very briefly indeed, that during the last 150 years there has been a growing tendency in the general area of what Thomas would call natural knowledge to distinguish, or attempt to distinguish, between science and philosophy, *qua* cognitive or would-be cognitive, disciplines. Thanks in part to the emergence of non-Euclidean geometries and the critical work of Mach, Poincare, Dewey, and Einstein, there has been a movement in the direction of an instrumentalism akin to the instrumentalism of Osiander but without Osiander's underlying theological fideism. Scientific knowledge, shot through and through with convention, is, it would now appear, less a beholding of things as they are in themselves than a complex set of rules for systematization and prediction within the sphere of the data of observation; and, it would also appear, there are as many ways of expressing what the facts are in theoretic terms as man's ingenuity allows him to devise within the context of the data of observation, on the one hand, and principles which are to be understood as Einstein has suggested, as free inventions of the human intellect or imagination, on the other: First principles, in this sense, are not imposed, but have their roots in the ingenuity, the mathematical imagination, of the individual creative scientist who, of course, always works within the context of other individual scientists, past and present, of greater or lesser scientific imagination. As for philosophy, some would allow us only critical philosophy in the form of philosophy of science (often reduced to statements about statements); some would allow us speculative philosophy, so long as speculative philosophy is understood as made up of individual visions for which consistency, scope, ingenuity, but not truth can be claimed; and some would appear to seek a way of knowing by which the instrumentalism and relativism of scientific knowledge can be transcended, such that the individual can achieve a contemplative beholding of non-conditioned truth and reality.

At the core of all of these endeavors there remains the problem as to how the individual self can transcend subjective belief and behold, or incorporate into itself, something to be called objective truth. I am not convinced that this problem has been solved or even, in the history of Western thought, adequately understood and formulated.

III

In the West, individuals, both individually and collectively, have sought knowledge—scientific, philosophical, and theological—that would reflect in the cognitive consciousness of the individual objective realities as they are apart from being known, apart from being reflected, apart from being an object to a subject. The West has produced diverse patterns of shifting and changing belief and conviction which function as mythologies, albeit abstract mythologies, that at best attempt to come to terms with, come to some kind of peace with, an unknown and mysterious order or disorder[18] (the distinction is human; a lobster couldn't make it) that we attempt to cultivate, to domesticate, by calling it *reality* in hopes that this term, together with the delineation of what we mean by "reality," will introduce a modicum of clarity into what, perhaps, could just as well be spoken of as absurdity or absolute ambiguity. History goes on, and the questions remain: "Where now? Who now? When now?" I, say I. Unbelieving. Questions, hypothesis, call them that. Keep going, going on, call that going, call that on. . . . It, say it, not knowing what . . . you must go on, I can't go on, I'll go on."[19]

QUESTION: Would you please point out what bearing your paper has upon the specific problem of this Conference, namely, the status of the individual?

ANSWER: The term "individual" is sometimes used to refer to the particular thing (and thus we may contrast an individual and the universal, though more usually the particular and the universal), and is sometimes used to refer to the individual, or particular, self or person (and thus we may contrast the individual and the society of which, in some manner, he is a member or part); and we may also contrast the finite individual and the non-finite, absolute Being, who is God, who, for the believing Catholic, is a Trinity of Persons, but certainly not finite persons.

In this paper I have been concerned, not with knowledge of the particular thing (that thing which participates, according to Plato, in a universal form or idea), but with the human individual's knowledge of anything. Western philosophers have been at least individual selves, moving, thinking, operating, believing, claiming, etc., in various modes of interaction, both direct and indirect, with other individual philosophers (selves). Thus, Lucretius wrote with one eye on Epicurus; and, although Epicurus sometimes claimed to be original in his thought, one might suggest that Epicurus, without Democritus, would have been a miracle. Western philosophers have been concerned with the achievement of objective knowledge, objective truth, that would somehow transcend individual belief or conviction. The pursuit of objective truth on the part of an array of individual philosophers has produced, historically speaking, an array of diverse philosophical claims, philosophical beliefs or contentions, epistemological, metaphysical, ethical, etc.

All in all, in the West individuality has been taken seriously, and the outcome has been philosophical diversity. Even during the me-

dieval period, when philosophical thought in the West was expected
to move within the framework of official theological doctrine, individual thinkers as diverse as Anselm, Thomas Aquinas, and William
of Ockham were produced in relative abundance, Thomas critical
of Anselm, and Ockham certainly critical of Thomas. It would appear, though perhaps I have not emphasized this adequately in my
paper, that the spirit of Western philosophy is such that, while truth,
objective truth, which transcends the individuality of the self, is
somehow hoped for, originality, that is to say, individuality of point
of view and insight, is demanded. A philosopher who can do no
more than repeat what some earlier philosopher has said would not
be regarded as a creative thinker, but, at best, only what Galileo has
somewhere called a doctor of memory. Although it may be that there
is a Truth that is, or ought to be, common to all, Western philosophers have written as if each one had a private wisdom, a private
truth, of his own. At the present time, at any rate, it is almost expected that (a) a philosopher who has anything to say of importance
has something to say that has not, really, been said before, and
(b) what he has to say will be wide open to criticism at least in the
sense that what he has to say will most certainly not go unchallenged
and, indeed, will be rejected by at least one other philosopher.

QUESTION: You seem to suggest that the dominant spirit of Western philosophy is that of epistemological skepticism. Is this not a
misrepresentation of the Western tradition?

ANSWER: I intended to make no such suggestion. Absolute skepticism, as I have defined this term, has been, at best, a minority
report. Indeed, so much so that I must look hard to find anyone
I would speak of as an absolute skeptic. Most Western philosophers
have been of the opinion that much can be known, by way of reason
and sense-experience, in the main, concerning man, his world, and
even the nature of the good life and the good society for man.
Philosophers have not universally agreed with one another with
respect to their philosophical claims (epistemological, metaphysical,
or ethical) ; but this is beside the point.

The limited skeptic has been more common in the West than the
absolute skeptic. Hume was probably of the opinion that nothing
could be known on the grounds of alleged, divine revelation alone;
and Kant was apparently of the opinion, at least some of the time,
that nothing could be known with respect to the nature of things as
they are in themselves. I find that I have some sympathy with the
view expressed by W. Somerset Maugham to the effect that "beyond
certain fundamental data which they call the given, and the existence of other minds, which they infer, men can be sure of nothing.
All the rest of their knowledge is fiction, the construction of their
minds, that they have devised for the convenience of living."[20]
Democritus, Plato, Aristotle, Augustine, Descartes, Spinoza, Leibniz,
Locke, Berkeley, and even Hume would probably not have agreed
with Maugham, nor did they agree, straight down the line, with one
another. Indeed, even I do not agree with Maugham except with
serious qualifications.

QUESTION: You say that "a lobster couldn't do it." How do you
know that a lobster couldn't do it? I have a cat who seems to have
an understanding of Kant. Animals may understand, and *do*, much
more than we usually suppose.

ANSWER: I have a great respect for animals, animals and children. God, I am sure, loves both; and if he loses his patience at all, it is only with adult human beings. A cat may well understand Kant; but whether Kant understood cats or not I would hesitate to say. Few cats wander through the pages of *The Critique of Pure Reason*. And speaking about animals, I find that I am suddenly reminded of Rilke's lines:

> Mit allen Augen sieht die Kreatur
> das Offene. Nur unsre Augen sind
> wie umgekehrt und ganz um sie gestellt
> als Fallen, rings um ihren freien Ausgang.
> Was draussen ist, wir wissens aus des Tiers
> Antlitz allein; denn schon das frühe Kind
> wenden wir um und zwingens, dass es rückwärts
> Gestaltung sehe, nicht das Offne, das
> im Tiergesicht so tief ist.[21]

[1] Sextus Empiricus, *Outlines of Pyrrhonism*, Vol. I, p. 216, quoted by Frederick Copleston, *A History of Philosophy*, Vol. I, Part I (New York: Image Books, 1962), p. 108.

[2] Kant is not always completely clear or completely consistent, and this statement can most certainly be challenged. What I have in mind is such statements as the following: "What we have meant to say is that all our intuition is nothing but the representation of appearance; that the things which we intuit are not in themselves what we intuit them as being, nor their relations so constituted in themselves as they appear to us, and that if the subject, or even only the subjective constitution of the senses in general, be removed, the whole constitution and all the relations of objects in space and time, nay, space and time themselves, would vanish." Immanuel Kant, *Critique of Pure Reason*, Norman Kemp Smith, trans. (abridged ed.; London: Macmillan and Co., 1934), p. 54.

[3] David Hume, *An Enquiry Concerning Human Understanding* (La Salle: The Open Court Publishing Company, 1949), p. 184.

[4] Copernicus, *Three Copernican Treatises*, E. Rosen, trans. and ed. (New York: Columbia University Press, 1939), p. 24 f.

[5] "Had they deceived us/Or deceived themselves, the quiet-voiced elders,/ Bequeathing us merely a receipt for deceit?" T. S. Eliot, *Four Quartets* (New York: Harcourt, Brace and World, Inc., 1943), p. 13.

[6] Henri Bergson, *An Introduction to Metaphysics* (New York and London: G. P. Putnam's Sons, 1912), p. 9.

[7] Aristotle, *Posterior Analytics*, Bk. I, chap. 18, 81^a, 38–40, G. R. G. Mure, trans., in *The Basic Works of Aristotle*, edited and with an Introduction by Richard McKeon (New York: Random House, 1941), p. 135.

[8] Aristotle, *op. cit.*, Bk. II, chap. 19, 100^a, 13–14. (*Ibid.*, p. 185.)

[9] Aristotle, *op. cit.*, Bk. I, chap. 9, 76^a, 27–31. (*Ibid.*, p. 124.)

[10] Thomas Aquinas, *The Summa Theologica*, Part I, Q. 1, Art. 5. In *Basic Writings of Saint Thomas Aquinas*, edited and annotated, with an Introduction by Anton C. Pegis, Vol. I (New York: Random House, 1945), p. 9.

[11] Thomas was completely aware of the fact that a conflict between natural knowledge and revealed knowledge could be a conflict between natural knowledge and an inadequate interpretation of a revealed statement. As he points out: "In discussing questions of this kind, two rules are to be observed, as Augustine teaches. The first is to hold the truth of Scripture without wavering. The second is that, since Holy Scripture can be explained in a multiplicity of senses, one should adhere to a particular explanation only in such measure as to be ready to abandon it, if it be proved with certainty to be false; lest Holy Scripture be exposed to the ridicule of unbelievers, and obstacles be placed to their believing." *The Summa Theologica*, Part I, Q. LXVIII, Art. 1. (*Ibid.*, pp. 637–638.)

[12] René Descartes, *Principles of Philosophy*, First Part, Principle LXXVIII, in *Descartes Selections*, Ralph M. Eaton, ed. (New York: Charles Scribner's Sons, 1927), p. 288.

[13] *Ibid.*, *Principles of Philosophy*, Second Part, Principle CCVII. (*Ibid.*, p. 311.)

[14] Sir Isaac Newton, *Mathematical Principles of Natural Philosophy* (Berkeley: University of California Press, 1947), p. 547.

[15] *Ibid.*, p. 400.

[16] *Ibid.*, p. 546.

[17] David Hume, *A Treatise of Human Nature*, Vol. I (London: J. M. Dent and Sons, 1911), p. 105.

[18] "So they build up hypotheses that collapse on top of one another, it's human, a lobster couldn't do it. Ah a nice mess we're in, the whole pack of us, is it possible we're all in the same boat, no, we're in a nice mess each one in his own peculiar way." Samuel Beckett, *The Unnamable* (New York: Grove Press, 1958), p. 119.

[19] Beckett, *op. cit.*, pp. 3, 179.

[20] *The Summing Up* (New York: New America Library, 1946), p. 161.

[21] Rainer Maria Rilke, *Duino Elegies* (London: The Hogarth Press, 1952), p. 66.

SECTION III

Religion

WING-TSIT CHAN[a]

The individual in Chinese religions

There are conflicting phenomena in Chinese religions, especially where the individual is concerned. On the one hand, in popular religions the life of the individual is strongly influenced, if not controlled, by his ancestors and other spiritual beings. In ancestor worship, his duty is to serve the deceased, and he submerges himself in group ancestral rites, in which the spirit of the ancestor is central. He believes in fate, which is beyond his control. The government used to regulate the number of temples, appoint and dismiss priests, and even promote or demote the gods he worshipped. On the philosophical level, the Confucianist aspires to be one with Heaven; the Taoist aims at identification with Nature "without differentiation"; and the Buddhist hopes to enter *nirvāṇa,* where all individual characteristics and differences disappear.

On the other hand, aside from ancestral rites, group worship has never been an institution in China, worship being largely a personal matter. Even in religious festivals, worship is individual. There has never been a central religious authority to dictate to conscience, regulate the beliefs, or control the destiny of the individual. National religious organizations were unknown until 1929, when the Chinese Buddhist Society was established. That organization was entirely for the purpose of the protection of temple properties and for social and intellectual reforms, however, and had nothing to do with personal beliefs or practices. It was not intended to be a national church. In the Taoist religion, there was not even an attempt at a national organization until 1958, when the National Taoist Society was formed in Peking[b], obviously for political control. The so-called Heavenly Teacher, presumably the head of the Taoist religion, had no more than local contact with Taoist priests and had very little influence over the faithful. His very title implies that he was custodian of a body of religious knowledge but was not an arbiter of morals or an authoritative spiritual leader. The last Heavenly Teacher merely conducted a school in the bastion of the religion, the Dragon and Tiger Mountain area in eastern China, and acted as an astrologer, and a miracle performer, believed by some to be able to "command the wind and produce the rain." The Taoist or Buddhist priest was essentially a technician and a consultant whose duty it was to advise on and to perform ceremonies, usually for a consideration. He was in no sense an agent of the worshipper before the gods or a link between them. The worshipper's approach to the gods was his own—direct, individual, and personal.

These facts clearly show that there are conflicts in the Chinese religious picture, particularly with respect to the individual. However, these conflicts are more apparent than real. When the fundamental aspects of Chinese religious life and thought are understood these conflicts will be resolved.

The best way to understand the status of the individual in Chinese religions is to see, first, what the goal in Chinese religions is; secondly, the way to achieve that goal; and, thirdly, the position of the individual in relation to ultimate reality, namely, Heaven in Confucianism, Tao^c in Taoism, and $Nirvāṇa$ or Thusness in Buddhism.

(1) *The Goal of Self-realization.* Like any other people, the Chinese aim at many things in their religious beliefs and practices, but their ultimate goal is simply the survival of the individual and the realization of his nature. Historically, the question of survival came first—and we shall consider it later.

From the very early days of Chinese history, the Chinese believed in personal survival. Records found in the oracle bones dating back to the Shang[d] Dynasty (1751–1112 B.C.) contain numerous references to sacrifices to ancestors, with offerings of food and other daily necessities and luxuries. Daily utensils and, in extreme cases, their bodyguards or even concubines were buried with them so that they could be served. These sacrifices, however barbarian, clearly indicate a definite belief in individual survival after death. Gradually the concept of the Highest God (Ti^e), or the Lord, developed. The interesting thing is that illustrious ancestors were believed to co-exist with Ti in Heaven. As *The Book of Odes* says of the founder of the Chou[f] Dynasty (1111–249 B.C.), "King Wen[g] is above/ On the left and right of the Lord./"[1]

During the Chou Dynasty, another practice became common, that of recalling the soul of the individual. After a person died, his family immediately went up to the roof and, waving some of his clothing, called, "So-and-so, please come back," and then descended to the house to offer him food.[2] The assumption was that the man's soul ascended to the sky and could return to receive the offerings. Ancient Chinese literature, especially that of the fifth and fourth centuries B.C., is fairly rich in essays and poems devoted to recalling the soul. The soul is called *"hun-p'o*[h]*."* According to ancient belief, at death a white (po) light leaves the human body and joins the moon's light. To this was later added the concept of hun, which etymologically includes the element of $yün^i$ (cloud), which is more active than light. Thus, according to the traditional theory, hun is the soul of man's vital force, which is expressed in man's intelligence and his power of breathing, whereas *p'o* is the spirit of man's physical nature expressed in his body and his physical movements. At death, *hun-p'o* survives.

This strong belief in personal survival after death certainly affirmed the importance of the individual after death, but at the same time tended to undermine his importance before death. In the Shang Dynasty no important activity was undertaken without first obtaining the approval of spiritual beings. Holes would be drilled halfway through the oracle bones. They would then be thrown into fire, and priests would interpret the message of spiritual beings by the cracks.

This practice continued into the Chou Dynasty, which succeeded the Shang, but a radical change began to take place. The new dynasty needed human talents to build a new state. When irrigation produced more water than prayer for rain, man naturally assumed an increasing importance over spiritual beings. Man came to the fore and spiritual beings were kept more and more at a distance. As *The Book of Rites* says, "The people of Yin[j] (Shang) honored spiritual beings, served them, and put them ahead of ceremonies. . . . The people of Chou honored ceremonies and valued highly the conferring of honors. They served the spiritual beings and respected them, but kept them at a distance."[3]

This trend was highly accentuated by Confucius (551–479 B.C.). He would not discuss spiritual beings.[4] He told one of his pupils that "to honor spiritual beings and keep them at a distance may be regarded as wisdom."[5] When he was asked about serving spiritual beings, he replied, "If we are not yet able to serve man, how can we serve spiritual beings," and, "If we do not yet know about life, how can we know about death?"[6] Actually, Confucius neither denied the existence of spiritual beings nor ignored ancestors. He declared, "How abundant is the display of power of spiritual beings! . . . Like the spread of overflowing water, they seem to be above and to be on the left and on the right."[7] He taught people "to serve the dead as they were served while alive, and to serve the departed as they were served while still with us." "This is the height of filial piety," he added.[8] But his way of serving was radically different from the traditional. Even during his lifetime there were two cases of human sacrifice.[9] He bitterly denounced such an inhuman practice and even the use of dummies to bury with the dead.[10] What he wanted was to replace such barbarian customs with moral principles and social decorum. He urged his pupils to serve parents according to the rules of propriety while they are alive, bury them according to the rules of propriety when they die, and sacrifice to them after death according to the rules of propriety.[11] Since his emphasis was on rules of propriety, spiritual beings came to occupy a secondary position. In this way, whether Confucius meant to or not, he weakened, if not destroyed, the belief in personal survival after death.

But the chief rivals of the ancient Confucianists, notably the Moists of the fifth and fourth centuries B.C., strongly attacked them and upheld the belief in spiritual beings. Mo Tzu[k] (fl. 479–438 B.C.) defended the belief on the grounds that people had actually heard the voices of spiritual beings, that their existence had been recorded, and that the belief in spiritual beings was helpful to personal conduct and national peace.[12] In his basic doctrine of promotion of welfare and removal of evil, he always insisted that what was beneficial to Heaven, spiritual beings, and man is good.[13] Although he never proved the existence of spiritual beings, nowhere else in ancient China was the belief in personal immortality more strongly held.

Eventually, this belief grew in two different directions, namely, in the Taoist religion and in Buddhism. The Taoists wanted immortality on earth, while the Buddhists wanted it in paradise.

The Taoist search for earthly immortality goes back to antiquity. Chuang Tzu[l] (between 399 and 295 B.C.) mentioned immortals.[14] From the first to the sixth century, Taoist priests pushed this search with great effort. They practiced alchemy, promoted exercises, developed medicine, and delved into breathing, concentration, and sex techniques, all in an attempt to achieve immortality on earth. Until recently, to become immortal remained a fervent hope for many of the faithful in the Taoist religion.

In about the same period, Buddhism began to flourish in China. One of its greatest attractions to the Chinese was its promise of eternal life in paradise, for there had been no such idea in China. The belief in paradise was especially strong in the Pure Land school founded in China in the fourth century. It has been the most popular Buddhist sect in China for the last 800 years, testifying to the strong belief in and the earnest hope on the part of millions of Chinese for rebirth in the Pure Land. So far as the masses are concerned, there is no question that the individual continues to live after death.

The story with the intellectuals, however, has been entirely different. With a few exceptions, such as the Moists, they have been consistent in rejecting belief in personal survival after death. In the first century A.D., Wang Ch'ung[m] (27–100?), one of the most rationalistic and critical philosophers in Chinese history, and one of the most influential, wrote a treatise to disprove the existence of spiritual beings. He argued that "the dead do not become spiritual beings, do not possess consciousness, and cannot harm people.[15] "When a person dies," he said, "his blood becomes exhausted. With this, his vital forces are extinct, and his body decays and becomes ashes and dust. What is there to become a spiritual being?"[16] Furthermore, "If a spiritual being is really the spirit of a dead man, then, when people see it, they ought to see the form of a nude. . . . Why? Because garments have no spirit."[17] He offered other reasons against the existence of spiritual beings. While they sound very naïve, for almost 2,000 years no one in Chinese history has successfully refuted him.

Just as Wang Ch'ung criticized the traditional belief in spiritual beings, Fan Chen[n] (b. 450) attacked the Buddhist belief. He argued that physical form and spirit were identical and that, as the physical form disappears, so does the spirit, as the sharpness of a knife disappears with the knife.[18] Later, Neo-Confucianists, from the twelfth century on, have unanimously attacked both the Taoist and the Buddhist belief in everlasting life. Wang Yang-ming[o] (1472–1529), for example, said, "The Buddhists lure people into their way of life by the promise of escape from the cycle of life and death, and the Taoists, who seek immortality, do so with the promise of everlasting life."[19] To him, as to other Neo-Confucianists, the motivation is selfish and immoral. For them, as for Chinese intellectuals from the sixth century B.C. on, immortality consists in social immortality, or immortality of influence. When the question was asked in 546 B.C. about what the ancient saying, "Dead but immortal," meant, the answer was that " the best course is to establish virtue, the next best is to establish achievement, and still the next best is to establish words. When these are not abandoned with time, this may be called immortality."[20] Confucius certainly contributed to this feeling, and it has been the feeling of the intellectuals ever since.

Does this mean that the intellectuals reject the individual? Not in the least. They, like the masses, firmly believe in the central importance of the individual, but in another way, namely, full realization of one's nature, instead of everlasting life on earth or eternal existence in paradise.

The Confucianists were the first in ancient China to propagate the doctrine of fulfillment of human nature. Mencius (371–298 B.C.?) said, "He who exerts his mind to the utmost knows his nature. He who knows his nature knows Heaven. To preserve one's mind and to nourish one's nature is the way to serve Heaven. Not to allow any double-mindedness regardless of longevity or brevity of life, but to cultivate one's person and wait for destiny (ming[p], fate, Heaven's Decree or Mandate) to take its own course is the way to fulfill one's destiny."[21] This doctrine reached its zenith in the Ch'eng brothers and Chu Hsi[q] (1130–1200) and has remained central in the Confucian tradition. Ch'eng I[r] (1033–1107) said, "The investigation of principle to the utmost, the full development of the nature, and the fulfillment of destiny are only one thing. As principle is investigated to the utmost, one's nature is fully developed, and, as one's nature is fully developed, destiny is fulfilled."[22] His brother, Ch'eng Hao[s] (1032–1085), said, "The investigation of principle to the utmost, the full development of nature, and the fulfillment of destiny—these three are to be accomplished simultaneously. There is basically no time sequence among them. The investigation of principle to the utmost should not be regarded merely as a matter of knowledge. If one really investigates principle to the utmost, even one's nature and destiny can be fulfilled."[23] Chu Hsi considered preserving the mind and nourishing the nature, and cultivating and controlling them, to be "the fundamental task," and it must be thorough.[24]

This trend of thought finds its modern expression in the contemporary Neo-Confucianism of Professor Fung Yu-lan[t] (1890–   ) and Hsiung Shih-li[u] (1885–   ). Fung said, "People in the moral sphere fulfill human relations and human duties. In doing so, they investigate human principle to the utmost and fulfill human nature. People in the transcendental sphere serve Heaven and assist in the natural transformation of things. In doing so they investigate the principle of the universe and fulfill the nature of the universe. . . . To penetrate the mysteries and to know the transformation of the universe are to complete the work of the universe. . . . And this is serving Heaven."[25] Hsiung has expressed the same idea succinctly, saying, "One's self-nature is true and real. There is no need to search for a heavenly Lord outside oneself. One can develop one's own nature to the fullest extent. One need not desire *nirvāṇa*."[26]

The word *"hsing*[v]*,"* meaning the nature of man and things, is not mentioned in the *Lao Tzu*[w], but it runs through the *Chuang Tzu*[27]. In both, the ultimate goal is to preserve the essence and vitality of man. Consequently, in the Taoist religion the aim is to realize the Three Original Principles—Essence, Vital Force, and Spirit. From the third through the seventh century, both the development of ideas and the practice of alchemy were directed to this goal. In the Southern school of the Taoist religion, the emphasis is on the cultivation of one's nature, while in the Northern school it is on the cultivation and development of one's vital power.[28] This is one reason why the Taoist religion has paid special attention to the human body. It has promoted exercises, refined Chinese cooking, and developed medicine, all dedicated to the fulfillment of human nature.

In Buddhism, the idea of the realization of one's nature was not prominent. In the quest for rebirth in paradise, the chief methods were to repeat the name of the Buddha and to express faith by making offerings, reciting scripture, etc. As the Buddhists said, "Take refuge in the Buddha." While the ultimate objective, rebirth in paradise, was centered on the individual, the method was certainly not. In the seventh century, a revolt arose and demanded the shift to self-effort, and that was the realization of one's own nature.

The movement was led, or probably started, by Hui-neng[x] (638–713), generally regarded as the founder of the Southern school of Buddhist Meditation (Ch'an[y], or Zen). In his famous *Platform Scripture,* he emphatically urged his followers to take refuge in the nature within oneself instead of taking refuge in the *buddhas* outside, for what is called the great wisdom by which to reach the Pure Land is nothing but this self-nature, and all *buddhas,* all *dharmas* (elements of existence), and all scriptures are immanent in it. Reading scriptures, building temples, doing charities, making offerings, reciting the name of the Buddha, and praying to be reborn in the Pure Land are all useless. The Pure Land is nothing but the straightforward mind. If one sees his own nature, he said, one will become a *buddha.*[29]

(2) *The Way to Self-realization.* So far we have dealt with the goal of self-realization in Chinese religions and have said something about the way to achieve that goal, but much more can be added. Each of the three religions has its own way, but in each case the way can be summed up in one word, namely, vacuity (*hsü*[z]) in Taoism, calmness (*ting*[aa]) in Buddhism, and sincerity (*ch'eng*[ab]) in Confucianism.

The term "vacuity" (sometimes translated as "emptiness") is not to be taken in the literal sense of being empty. Rather, it means absolute peacefulness and purity of mind and freedom from selfish desires and not being disturbed by incoming impressions or allowing what is already in the mind to disturb what is coming into the mind. As a feature of reality, it means a profound and deep continuum in which there is no obstruction. Lao Tzu taught people to "keep their minds vacuous," "attain complete vacuity," and "maintain steadfast quietude" in order to become enlightened and to be in accord with *Tao.*[30] Elaborating on this theme, Chuang Tzu said, "Do not be the possessor of fame. Do not be the storehouse of schemes. Do not take over the function of things. Do not be the master of knowledge [to manipulate things]. Personally realize the infinite to the highest degree and travel in the realm for which there is no sign. Exercise fully what you have received from Nature, without any subjective viewpoint. In a word, be absolutely vacuous."[31] Chuang Tzu called this state of vacuity "fast of the mind."[32] Later, in the Taoist religion, quiet sitting, which is Taoist "fasting of the mind," re-enforced by Buddhist meditation, became an institution. It was the Taoists' chief way of preserving one's nature and nourishing the spirit.

For a similar reason, the Buddhists advocated calmness. In *The Platform Scripture,* Hui-neng repeatedly asserted that one's self-nature is originally pure, and when one becomes calm he will see this pure nature and attain *buddha*hood. Calmness will be achieved when one is freed from thoughts, from the characters of things, and from attachment to them. This does not mean not to think at all or to have nothing to do with the characters of things. Rather, it means not to be carried away by thoughts in the process of thought or to be free from the characters of things while in the midst of them.[33] Thus, the conventional method of sitting in meditation, in which one attempts to eliminate thoughts, is not good. One should not sit motionless trying to look at his own mind or his own purity.[34] Imperturbability is not motionlessness but freedom from attachment to erroneous thought.[35] When no erroneous thoughts arise, there is calmness, and, when one's inner nature is unperturbed, there is true meditation.[36] If one sees his own nature, he will become enlightened, that is, achieve *buddha*hood, suddenly.

This is the new and radical doctrine of sudden enlightenment of the Ch'an school. One can easily detect the Taoist elements of naturalness and individualism in this doctrine, but the Ch'an school has pushed the individualistic element much further. One of the most famous sayings of Ch'an is, "Everyone will be self-contained, and everyone will be perfectly realized."[37]

This Ch'an saying should remind one of Mencius' well-known sayings. "All things are already complete in oneself" and "All men may be Yao[ac] and Shun[ad] [sages]."[38] In the Confucian school, the doctrine of self-realization is just as strong and was developed much earlier. There the method is neither vacuity nor calmness but sincerity. The thesis is very simple. When one's will becomes sincere, one's feelings will be correct and one's moral life will be perfect. As said in *The Great Learning*, attributed to the Confucian pupil Tseng Tzu[ae] (505–ca. 436 B.C.), "When the will is sincere, the mind is rectified; when the mind is rectified, the personal life is cultivated; when the personal life is cultivated, the family will be regulated; when the family is regulated, the state will be in order; and, when the state is in order, there will be peace throughout the world."[39]

The Doctrine of the Mean, attributed to Confucius' grandson Tzu-ssu[af] (492–431 B.C.), goes even further. It says, "Only those who are absolutely sincere can fully develop their nature. If they can fully develop their nature, they can then fully develop the nature of others. If they can fully develop the nature of others, they can then fully develop the nature of things. If they can fully develop the nature of things, they can then assist in the transforming and nourishing process of Heaven and Earth. If they can assist in the transforming and nourishing process of Heaven and Earth, they can thus form a trinity with Heaven and Earth."[40]

The reason for the all-importance of sincerity is that it makes things real. Significantly, the word *"ch'eng"* means both sincerity and realness. It contains as its basic element *ch'eng*[ag], an independent word meaning "to complete." According to *The Doctrine of the Mean,* "Sincerity means the completion of the self, and the Way is self-directing. Sincerity is the beginning and end of things. Without sincerity there would be nothing."[41] As Chu Hsi explains it, "In the moral realm, there can be the deed of filial piety only if there is first of all the mind sincerely devoted to it."[42] "If every word comes from the bottom of one's heart," he said, "what is said is true. On the other hand, if one tells a lie, what he says amounts to nothing. This is why it is said that sincerity is the completion of things."[43] Wang Yang-ming also said that, if there is sincerity in being filially pious to one's parents, filial piety will take care of itself. One of the most important passages in his *Instructions for Practical Living* says, "If it is the mind that is sincere in its filial piety to parents, then in the winter it will naturally think of the cold of parents and seek a way to provide warmth for them, and in the summer it will naturally think of the heat of parents and seek a way to provide coolness for them. These are all offshoots of the mind that is sincere in its filial piety."[44]

But sincerity is not only the way to realize one's own moral nature, but also to realize the nature of things. *The Doctrine of the Mean* says, "Sincerity is not only the completion of one's own self; it is that by which all things are completed."[45] Thus, sincerity has a metaphysical meaning. Perhaps the best illustration for it, so far as we here are concerned, is religious sacrifice.

Curiously enough, Confucius had very little to say about sincerity in *The Analects.* The word hardly occurs there. However, it is recorded there that, when he offered sacrifice to his ancestors, he felt as if the ancestral spirits were actually present. When he offered sacrifice to other spiritual beings, he felt as if they were actually present. He said, "If I do not participate in the sacrifice, it is as if I did not sacrifice at all!"[46] Commentators agree that what Confucius wanted was to be sincere. As Chu Hsi remarked, "This means that, when it is time to offer sacrifice, if one cannot do so personally because of one reason or another, but asks someone else to do it for him, it will be impossible for him to extend his sincerity to the point of feeling that the spiritual beings are actually there."[47] In the case of Confucius, the idea is that he was so sincere that, when he offered sacrifices to spiritual beings, he felt as if they were really there.

Sincerity, however, not only makes spiritual beings seem real to the person who offers the sacrifice, but also makes the spiritual beings themselves real. To explain this, we have to explain what spiritual beings are.

The Chinese words for spiritual beings are *"kuei"* and *"shen*[ab]."

Etymologically, *"kuei"* means "to return to the source," and *"shen"* means to "expand," but in ancient times, and for the masses even today, *"kuei-shen"* merely means spiritual beings. We have seen how important they were in the Shang Dynasty, how Confucius avoided discussing them, and how Chinese intellectuals have persistently denied their existence for the last 2,000 years. To them, *kuei* and *shen* are cosmic forces, more especially the activity of the negative cosmic force, *yin*[ai], and the positive cosmic force, *yang*[aj]. As the Neo-Confucianist Chang Tsai[ak] (1020–1077) put it, *"Kuei* and *shen* are but the spontaneous activity of the two material forces (*ch'i*[al])," that is, *yin* and *yang*.[48] In the Neo-Confucian view, everything is the product of the interaction of these two material forces. In the case of the human being, for example, innumerable elements of the two forces integrate, culminating in the father and the mother, and a person is born. As these elements disintegrate, he dies, and the material forces return to where they came from or expand. He has ceased to exist as a human being, and does not continue to exist as a ghost, but his forces continue to operate. This is the philosophical basis of the theory that sincerity can make the objects of religious sacrifice real.

Confucius said in *The Doctrine of the Mean,* "How abundantly do spiritual beings display the powers that belong to them! We look at them, but do not see them. We listen to them, but do not hear them. Yet, they enter all things, and there is nothing without them. They cause all the people in the kingdom to fast and purify themselves, and array themselves in their richest clothing, in order to attend their sacrifice. Then, like overflowing water, they seem to be above the heads and on the right and left of their worshippers. *The Book of Odes* says, 'The coming of spiritual beings cannot be surmised. How much less can we get tired of them.'[49] Such is the impossibility of suppressing the outgoing of sincerity."[50] To the Neo-Confucianists, this does not mean that there are ghosts that go around and possess things. Rather, it means that the forces that used to constitute ancestors pervade everything. Sincerity can cause them to interact and integrate, even to the point of being like real persons.

Chu Hsi was once asked whether, in sacrificing to Heaven, Earth, and the spirits of mountains and rivers with offerings of silk, meat, and wine, it was merely to express one's sincerity or whether some force actually comes to receive the sacrifice. He answered, "If you say that nothing comes, then why sacrifice? What is it that is so solemn above that causes people to make offerings with awe and reverence? But, if you say that some spirit comes riding in a chariot, that is just wild talk."[51] What he meant was that, while no force comes like a ghost, certain forces are affected by one's sincerity, and so they react as if spiritual beings were coming to accept the sacrifice. In other words, although the forces of ancestors have scattered, one can, through his will to practice sincerity, cause them to come together.

The reason why this is possible is that the material force of one thing is basically the same as the material force of another. The material forces of *yin* and *yang* interact, and integrate and disintegrate, in countless ways, thus producing an infinite number of things, but the material forces of these things are essentially the same. This being the case, there is a continuity between the one who offers the sacrifice and the object of his sacrifice. As Chu Hsi said, ancestors and descendants share the same material force.[52] There is not only common blood. There is also the family heritage, which is also a kind of force combining ancestors and descendants.[53] The continuity of a family is very much like the sea, to use Chu Hsi's analogy. Each generation is comparable to a wave. The wave in the front and the wave behind are different, and yet the water pervading both is one.[54] Just as the wave behind can affect the wave in front, so people offering sacrifice to ancestors can affect them.

In the act of sacrifice, then, if sincerity is extended to the utmost, the spirit of the ancestors can be collected. This means that the condition of the spirit of one's ancestors depends very much on one's sincerity. Chu Hsi said, "Wherever the human mind concentrates, there is the spirit."[55] As another Neo-Confucianist put it, "When there is sincerity, there will be the spirit. When there is no sincerity, there will not be the spirit."[56] A third Neo-Confucianist even went so far as to say, "Whenever we want spirit, there it will be. Whenever we do not want spirit, there it will not be."[57]

(3) *The Individual in Relation to Ultimate Reality.* From the foregoing, it is clear that the Chinese religion is based on the sincerity of the will, and that means the individual's own will. In this sense the individual is of great importance in Chinese religions. The question inevitably arises, however, since the goal of self-realization and its methods of vacuity, calmness, and sincerity are only for the ultimate purpose of serving Heaven in the case of Confucianists, identification with Nature, or *Tao,* in the case of Taoists, and *buddha*hood in the case of Buddhists, does this not mean that in the ultimate state, whether it is Heaven, *Tao,* or *Nirvāna,* the individual is in the end dissolved or absorbed, since in that state all distinctions and differences, and thereby all individuality, disappear? This is the question of the relationship between the undifferentiated continuum, so to speak, and the specific, individual, differentiated units. In other words, it is the question of the relationship between the one and the many, a basic question in Chinese philosophy, of which religion may be regarded as only a part. It is not within the scope of this paper to go into this question at length. Suffice it to say that in

all the three systems, Confucianism, Taoism, and Buddhism, the solution of the apparent conflict between the one and the many is essentially the same, namely, that each involves the other. In none of the three systems is the one understood as absorbing and thereby obliterating the many, or vice versa. The common conviction has been that each requires the other.

In Taoism, the question arose with the Neo-Taoists, notably Wang Pi[am] (226–249) and Kuo Hsiang[an] (d. 312). To Wang Pi, ultimate reality is original non-being (pen-wu[ao]). According to his thinking, which is developed in his commentary on the Lao Tzu, original non-being transcends all distinctions and descriptions. It is the One, pure and simple, which underlines and combines all things. To Kuo Hsiang, on the other hand, ultimate reality is Nature. According to him, things exist and transform according to principle, but each and every thing has its own principle. This doctrine is fully developed in his commentary on the Chuang Tzu. His emphasis is the many rather than the one. He and Wang Pi seem to stand at opposite poles, with no possibility of reconciliation. But the many of Kuo Hsiang all function according to principle, and, for Wang Pi, both function and substance, that is, the one and the many, are identified. The one and the many are not mutually exclusive, after all.[58]

The point is more clearly made in the Buddhist view, in which the one and the many explicitly involve and penetrate each other. In his famous treatise on the golden lion, Fa-tsang[ap] (549–623) says, "The gold and the lion are mutually compatible in their formation, the one and the many not obstructing each other. In this situation, the principle and the facts are different, but, whether the one or the many, each remains in its own position. This is called the gate of mutual compatibility and difference between the one and the many."[59] That is to say, in the case of the golden lion, the lion and every part of it involve the gold, and, at the same time, the gold involves the lion. Neither can exist without the other in the golden lion. Fa-tsang was using this simple and crude analogy to explain the one and the many, or the individual person and buddhahood. When the Ch'an school reiterates that all people have buddhahood in them or that the Buddha and the common people are not different, they are expressing the same idea.

The Buddhists had a decided influence on the Neo-Confucianists, whose solution of the seeming conflict between the one and the many follows the same pattern. The founder of Neo-Confucianism, Chou Tun-i[aq] (1017–1073), said, "The many are ultimately one, and the one is actually differentiated into the many. The one and many each has its own correct state of being. The great and the small each has its definite function."[60] This is the famous Neo-Confucian doctrine that principle is one but its manifestations are many. As Ch'eng I said, "Principle in the world is one. Although there are many roads in the world, the destination is the same, and, although there are a hundred deliberations, the result is one.[61] Although things involve many manifestations and events go through infinite variations, when they are united by the one, there cannot be any contradiction."[62] In Chu Hsi's words, "Fundamentally, there is only one Great Ultimate [the sum total of principles], yet each of the myriad things has been endowed with it and each in itself possesses the Great Ultimate in its entirety. This is similar to the fact that there is only one moon in the sky, but, when its light is scattered upon rivers and lakes, it can be seen everywhere. It cannot be said that the moon has been split."[63] Chu Hsi seems to be arguing for the oneness of principle, but it must not be forgotten that he said that each thing has in itself the Great Ultimate. One is reminded of Leibniz' monad. Chu Hsi's analogy of the moon is probably a specific, though indirect, borrowing of the famous Buddhist metaphor of the ocean. The Buddhists, especially of the Hua-yen[ar] school, were fond of saying that the ocean consists of many waves, and the many waves form the ocean, each involving the other, and one cannot be fully realized without the other's being fully realized also.

This metaphysical principle definitely lies behind the ancestral group-rites, for example. These rites involved all male descendants of an ancestor, each in his proper position according to seniority of generation and age, and performing under the direction of a master of ceremony, who was often a scholar in the clan. These rites were traditionally directed by the head of descent of the clan, but he was neither an authority nor an agent, but a symbol of the unity of the clan. It may be argued that, since the scattered forces of the ancestor required the total sincerity of the whole clan before there could be enough influence on them together, the head of descent was an authority insofar as he was a necessity. It is certainly true that he was a necessity, but the necessity was sociological rather than religious. The system of heads of descent goes back to Chou times. By the eleventh century, it had ceased to function. Neo-Confucianists, such as Ch'eng I, strongly urged its revival. He said, "In order to control the mind of the people, unify one's clan, and enrich social customs so that people will not forget their origin, it is necessary to clarify genealogy, group members of the clan together, and institute a system of heads of descent."[64] His interest was mainly sociological. While in these rites the clan acted as a group, each person had his unique place and function, and his sincerity toward his ancestor was personal and direct.

Government regulations and control of temples, priests, and even gods were not regular practices nor did they have any direct relationships with the individual's religious beliefs and behavior. The measures were mostly economic and political, treating temples, priests, and even gods as civil matters. Undoubtedly there were abuses and corruption. But, even in these matters, there is something very interesting, philosophically speaking. For instance, only a higher official could promote or demote an inferior deity. The assumption was that, just as waves can affect the ocean, so human beings can influence the spiritual world, and in this case it happens that the human force is greater than that of the spirit. From the earliest times, it was the rule that the emperor worshipped Heaven, the feudal lords worshipped the spirits of mountains and rivers, higher officials worshipped the five deities, and the common people worshipped their ancestors. Scholars are not agreed what the five deities were. Up to the end of the Manchu (Ch'ing[as]) Dynasty (1644–1912), the emperor alone could offer sacrifice to Heaven. During the Republic, President Yüan Shih-k'ai[at] (1858–1916) once tried it. It has been suggested that the system shows that the Chinese simply believed that spiritual beings lived in exactly the same manner as human beings, so that, as there is a need for an official hierarchy in this world, so there must be one among the gods. This may well have been the case. But the philosophical implication is that Heaven required the sincerity of the whole state, of which the emperor was the symbol, to be activated. In other words, in religious worship, there is a correspondence, even in rank, between the worshipper and the worshipped. Put differently, the two parties of the relations are equally important.

What can we say about the belief in fate? Here it seems the influence comes from only one side. It is certainly true that many ignorant people believe that their lives are directed by spiritual forces beyond their understanding or control. In their ignorance and ineptitude, they have failed to realize the mutual influence of the one and the many. The educated, however, understand that *ming*[au] does not mean fate in the sense of mysterious control by spiritual beings but means Heaven's Mandate, or Heaven's Decree, that is, what Heaven has given to a person, what Heaven has endowed him with. This is what *The Doctrine of the Mean* means when it says, "What Heaven imparts to (*ming*) man is called human nature."[65] This is the nature to be realized, and the way to realize it, as already brought out, is through one's own effort at moral cultivation, such as sincerity of will. This does not mean that the individual is the master of the universe, for there *are* things, such as life and death, and longevity or brevity of life, that are beyond his control. But, as we have learned from Mencius,[66] the Confucian injunction has been to cultivate one's moral life, develop one's nature, and let Nature take its course. The individual does not completely control his own destiny, but he is the master of his own ship in a sea that is not entirely devoid of uncertainties.

QUESTION: I have some slight difficulties with certain passages in your paper. At one place you emphasize strongly the fact that spiritual beings themselves are real. But in the next paragraph you say that everything is the product of the interaction of two material forces. And in the sentence before that you say that *kuei* and *shen* are but the spontaneous activity of the two material forces. I have trouble in getting the real spiritual beings together with these material forces and the spiritual beings' being but spontaneous productions of the material forces.

ANSWER: To the ignorant, spiritual beings are real, as ghosts that can appear before human beings. But, to intellectuals, what are called "spiritual beings" are but manifestations of material forces, but not as ghosts. For instance, the morning represents the force of *yang*, because it grows, while the afternoon represents the force of *yin* because it declines. Everything in the universe can be represented by these two forces. Failure is *yin*, while success is *yang*. Honesty is *yang*, while dishonesty is *yin*. Sincerity is *yang*; insincerity is *yin*.

QUESTION: Is sincerity a material substance?

ANSWER: No. The translation of "*ch'i*" as material force is most unfortunate. The word *ch'i* involves, not material substance, but some force. It is translated as "breath" or "vital force" when related to the body. But when you talk about the *ch'i* of the universe, you cannot call it "breath" or "vital force." *Ch'i* in the universe is negative or positive force, or *yin* or *yang*, conditioned by material elements.

QUESTION: You say, "The Buddhist hopes to enter *nirvāṇa*, where all individual characteristics and differences disappear." But later you say, "In none of the three systems is the one understood as absorbing and thereby annihilating the many." Perhaps there is no conflict here, but some people might think that the Buddhists say that there is a change in China. Is that what you had in mind?

ANSWER: There was a change. In an earlier stage, *nirvāṇa* meant a state in which everything is transcended. But in the Hua-yen or Kegon school, which is based on the *Avataṁsaka-sūtra*, there was a distinctly Chinese development. This school developed the idea of the correlation of the one and the many. They penetrate each other.

QUESTION: Sometimes you use the word "fate," but sometimes you use "destiny." In English the word "fate" normally implies that life is somewhat blind, but on the whole nobody speaks of destiny as being blind. Now, which of the two would you like or do you have both?

ANSWER: The word "*ming*" has not only both of these meanings but also the meaning of the verb to order, to give, to endow. To the ignorant, the uncertainty leads to superstitions. For them, the word "*ming*" should be translated as "fate." But, to the educated, the scholars, the word "*ming*" means "fate" only to the extent of covering life and death and the length and the shortness of life. It also covers success and failure, but not success and failure in the sense that we cannot do anything, but only ultimate success or failure. The general sense of *"ming"* is that, if you know what your nature is and if you do your best, you can fulfill it. The idea is that anybody trying his best can become a sage. In that sense, the word *"ming"* should be translated as "destiny."

QUESTION: What is the status of the individual woman in Chinese religious thought?

ANSWER: So far as salvation is concerned, woman is absolutely on a par with man. There has never been the idea that a woman could not become an immortal, or enter paradise.

QUESTION: Just what is the status of the individual in Chinese religion? You have spoken of individual perfection or the perfection of the capacities of human nature. Besides individual perfection, is there any such thing in Chinese religion as individual immortality? That is, if I were a sage and of perfect nature, when I die, will I completely disappear? Will I be immortal only through my influence on my society? So, religiously considered, is there any such thing in Chinese thought as individual immortality of the perfect sage?

ANSWER: For the uneducated there is belief in individual immortality, but immortality does not mean a ghost living on paradise, but social immortality, or immortality of influence.

QUESTION: The individual is eternal in the view of immortality in all the major religions, Hindu, Muslim, Christian. What about China?

ANSWER: The individual is neither eternal nor non-eternal in the absolute sense. He is a combination of many elements. The combination changes from time to time, most radically at what we call birth and death. But, even at death, certain things continue, like influence, work, children. A sage can organize the various elements in him and make himself into a perfect harmony, which can last for a long time, not in a physical sense, but in the sense of the influence of the individual.

QUESTION: How individual?

ANSWER: Confucius, for instance, is still considered to be living, not as a living person, but a living force.

You see, the idea of life among Chinese thinkers is not just one's body. We live not only as oneself but also as fathers to our children or as sons to our fathers. We live as members of society. We live in the exchange of ideas with others. At death, our bodies perish, but many other parts of our life will continue, like blood and flesh in our children, our interests, our words, and our contributions in society. Shall we say that we at death are no more or that we are still there? So, the word "immortality" as you people have been using it does not apply in the case of China.

1 Ode no. 235.

2 *I li*[av] (Book of Ceremonials), "Shih-sang li[aw]" (Ceremonies in an Official's Funeral), and *Li chi*[ax] (Book of Rites), "Li-yün[ay]" (Evolution of Rites).

3 *Li chi,* "Piao-chi[az]" (Record of Examples).

4 *Analects,* VII.20.

5 *Ibid.,* VI.20.

6 *Ibid.,* XI.11.

7 *Doctrine of the Mean,* 16.

8 *Ibid.,* 19.

9 *Tso chuan*[ba] (Tso's Commentary on), Duke Chao[bb], 13th year, and Duke Ting[bc], 2nd year.

[10] *Book of Mencius*, IA.4.

[11] *Analects*, II.5.

[12] *Mo Tzu*, III.

[13] *Ibid.*, XXXV, XLVII. See Wing-tsit Chan, *A Source Book in Chinese Philosophy* (Princeton: Princeton University Press, 1963), p. 226.

[14] *Chuang Tzu*, II, XI, etc. *Ssu-pu ts'ung-k'an*[bd] (The Four Libraries Series) edition entitled *Nan-hua chen-ching*[be] (True Classic of Nan-hua), I, pp. 12b, 40a-b; VI, pp. 36a etc.

[15] *Lun-heng*[bf] (Balanced Inquiries), *Ssu-pu pei-yao*[bg] (Essentials of the Four Libraries) edition, 62. See Chan, *op. cit.*, p. 299.

[16] *Lun-heng*, XX, pp. 92, 14a. See Chan, *op. cit.*, p. 302.

[17] *Ibid.* See Chan, p. 301.

[18] "Wu-shen lun[bh]" (An Essay on the Absence of Spiritual Beings), in the *Liang shu*[bi] (History of the Liang Dynasty), XLVIII.

[19] *Ch'uan-hsi lu*[bj] (Records of Instructions for Practical Living). See Wang Yang-ming, *Instructions for Practical Living, and Other Neo-Confucian Writings by Wang Yang-ming*, by Wing-tsit Chan, trans. (New York: Columbia University Press, 1963), sec. 49.

[20] *Tso chuan*, Duke Hs'ang[bk], 24th year.

[21] *Book of Mencius*, VIIA.1.

[22] Ch'eng I, *I-shu*[bl] (Surviving Work), Ssu-pu ts'ung-k'an edition, XVIII, p. 9a.

[23] *Ibid.*, II, pt. 1, p. 2b.

[24] *Chu Tzu ch'üan-shu*[bm] (Complete Works of Chu Hsi), I, pp. 18a-19a.

[25] *Hsin yüan-jen*[bn] (A New Treatise on the Nature of Man), p. 94.

[26] *Tu-ching shih-yao*[bo] (Essential Points in the Study of Classics), II, p. 53b.

[27] *Chuang Tzu*, VIII–XVII, XIX–XX, XXIII–XXV, XXIX, XXXI–XXXII. The word is mentioned here many times.

[28] See Wing-tsit Chan, *Religious Trends in Modern China* (New York: Columbia University Press, 1953), pp. 149–151.

[29] Hui-neng, *The Platform Scripture, the Basic Classic of Zen Buddhism*, Wing-tsit Chan, trans. (New York: St. John's University Press, 1963), 24–27, 29–31, 34.

[30] *Lao Tzu*, III, XVI.

[31] *Chuang Tzu*, chap. VII, Ssu-pu ts'ung-k'an edition, chap. III, pp. 5b-6a. See Chan, *Source Book*, p. 207.

[32] *Chuang Tzu*, IV (*Nan-hua chen-ching*, II, p. 13a).

[33] *The Platform Scripture*, 17.

[34] *Ibid.*, 18.

[35] *Ibid.*, 17.

[36] *Ibid.*, 19.

[37] A common Ch'an saying sometimes attributed to Bodhidharma[bp] (fl. 460–534), the First Patriarch of Ch'an in China, but actually its origin can no longer be traced. See Chan, trans., *Instructions for Practical Living*, p. 68, note 31.

[38] *Book of Mencius*, VIIA.4; VIB.2.

[39] *Great Learning*, the text.

[40] *Doctrine of the Mean*, XXII.

[41] *Ibid.*, XXV.

[42] *Chu Tzu yü-lei*[bq] (Classified Sayings of Chu Hsi), LXIV, p. 17a.

[43] *Ibid.*, p. 19a.

[44] *Instructions for Practical Living*, p. 8.

[45] *Doctrine of the Mean*, XXV.

[46] *Analects*, III, 12.

[47] *Lun-yü chi-chu*[br] (Collected Commentaries on *The Analects*, II, commenting on *The Analects*, III, 12).

[48] *Cheng-meng*[bs] (Correcting Youthful Ignorance), chap. I. See Chan, *Source Book*, p. 505.

[49] Ode no. 256.

[50] *Doctrine of the Mean*, XVI.

[51] *Chu Tzu ch'üan-shu*, LI, p. 50b.

[52] *Ibid.*, p. 41a.

[53] *Ibid.*, p. 41b.

[54] *Ibid.*, p. 43a.

[55] *Ibid.*, p. 52b.

[56] *Ibid.*, LI, p. 46b.

[57] *Ibid.*, LI, p. 42a.

[58] For Wang Pi and Kuo Hsiang, see Chan, *Source Book*, pp. 316–332, 326–335.

[59] *Chin shi-tzu chang*[bt] (A Treatise on the Golden Lion), sec. 7. See Chan, *Source Book*, p. 411.

[60] *T'ung-shu*[bu] (Penetrating the *Book of Changes*), XXII.

[61] Quoting *The Book of Changes*, "Appended Remarks," pt. 1, chap. 5.

[62] *I-shu*, III, p. 3b.

[63] *Chu Tzu ch'üan-shu*, XLIX, p. 11a.

[64] *I-shu*, IV, p. 6b.

[65] *Doctrine of the Mean*, I.

[66] See above, note 21.

a	陳榮捷	al	氣
b	北京	am	王弼
c	道	an	郭象
d	商	ao	本無
e	帝	ap	法藏
f	周	aq	周敦頤
g	文	ar	華嚴
h	魂魄	as	清
i	雲	at	袁世凱
j	殷	au	命
k	墨子	av	儀禮
l	莊子	aw	士喪禮
m	王充	ax	禮記
n	范縝	ay	禮運
o	王陽明	az	表記
p	命	ba	左傳
q	朱熹	bb	昭
r	程頤	bc	定
s	程顥	bd	四部叢刊
t	馮友蘭	be	南華眞經
u	熊十力	bf	論衡
v	性	bg	四部備要
w	老子	bh	無神論
x	惠能	bi	梁書
y	禪	bj	傳習錄
z	虛	bk	裏
aa	定	bl	遺書
ab	誠	bm	朱子全書
ac	堯	bn	新原人
ad	舜	bo	讀經示要
ae	曾子	bp	菩提達摩
af	子思	bq	朱子語類
ag	成	br	語論集注
ah	鬼神	bs	正蒙
ai	陰	bt	金獅子章
aj	陽	bu	通書
ak	張載		

T. R. V. MURTI

The world and the individual in Indian religious thought

INTRODUCTION

As a preliminary definition we may take the individual as a free being, exercising choice and doing actions purposefully, and as one who has attained some measure of awareness of his situation. Whether this person is ultimately free, whether his individuality or personality is real, and what is his destiny and whether it is bound up with that of other individuals are precisely the questions for which we seek an answer in this discussion. The human world may be understood as the *community* (reciprocity) of such "free" beings, or individuals. But among men there are different grades or types of spiritual temperament. Indian thought—especially the Vedānta and Mahāyāna Buddhism—expressly recognizes these empirical differences and provides for their spiritual needs.

I. THE RELIGIOUS PROBLEM

There is no religious problem for man unless, in his reflective mood, he reviews his position and is conscious of his peril. No religious problem is involved in efforts to overcome the hardships imposed by adverse Nature or in making adjustments with fellow men. Both of these could be solved without recourse to any total or transcendental effort. The religious situation emerges only when man reviews his existence as a whole. It is an awareness of the deeper aspects of life, of the root problem, and extends over his entire existence. The religious solution, like the problem, aims at a final and total solution of all problems. It is man's ultimate concern (*parama-puruṣārtha*). This statement of the religious problem would be acceptable to Buddhism and Jainism and some forms of Hinduism which do not find a place for a personal God and, therefore, cannot consider the aim of religious endeavor as the establishment of an intimate relationship with God.

We are led to this review of our existence by a deep and sustained sense of frustration. This is suffering, and it takes the form principally of disease, decay, and death. The Buddha describes suffering graphically: "Birth is ill; decay is ill; sickness is ill; death is ill; to be conjoined to things which we dislike, to be separated from things which we like—that is also sorrow."[1] If all our desires were completely and instantaneously satisfied as they arose in our mind, or, in the alternative, if our nature were completely in accord with the environment, no frustration could arise, and no suffering would result. But the very nature of the individual, or the ego, engenders suffering. As an ego, its essence consists in self-centeredness, and its pursuits and impulses are selfish. And yet, the ego has to depend on other selves and on the entire creation. A kind of implicit and inherent disharmony seems to be built into the very essence of the individual self.

Suffering, unlike enjoyment, which lulls us into a sense of security, engenders reflection. Man becomes aware of himself when he becomes aware of his deep involvement. To be conscious of suffering is to be conscious of an alternative to the present state in which we happen to find ourselves. Without the contrast between what is and what might have been, between the actual state and the possible, there could be no sense of grievance; hence no suffering. If everything that happens to us were thought to be completely inevitable and inexorable, there could be no grievance. We feel that things can be helped; they could have been otherwise; we could have done better. Thus, in all suffering, man is conscious, however implicitly, of freedom, of the non-inevitability of the present situation and of his ability to help it.

If, on the other hand, we enjoyed freedom so completely as to dominate all situations and if our will could prevail absolutely over all and always, there would be no suffering. This, then, is the inherent dialectic of suffering. Man is free, but not completely free. Suffering discloses the inherent freedom of man. And, although it is freedom in involvement, it is pregnant with possibilities. There is a demand to realize freedom fully and in final form, as *mokṣa* or *nirvāṇa*.

The germ of spirituality is implicit in suffering (*duḥkha*). Buddhism and all the systems of Indian philosophy (excluding the Cārvāka) show their keen spiritual insight in beginning with the truth of suffering (*duḥkha-satya*). To all of them, not only the actual states of painful feeling, but phenomenal existence in its entirety (*saṁsāra*) is suffering.[2] A state of unpleasant feeling is but a sample of what could befall us at all times. The awareness is not complete unless it is extended before and after this life. Its inexorability, given the causes and conditions which engender it, must be realized. Much of our pleasure is pain in the making; pleasures make us hanker after them and thus create anxiety. Frustration in this pursuit brings anger, bitterness, and conflict. Moreover, one's pleasures are by way of encroaching upon others. We seem to take for granted our right to happiness, even though it may be at the expense of others. Again, our shortsightedness and distraction in the immediate present prevent us from appraising our existence in all its comprehension and depth.[3]

Excepting the materialists (Cārvākas), every section of Indian thought without question believes and accepts the Law of *Karma* —the exercise of free will and the responsibility for its consequence and the continuous chain of birth, death, and rebirth. The doctrine of rebirth seems to be a necessary implication of the more basic doctrine of the souls (*jīvas*, individuals) as being uncreated, their existing beginninglessly and not perishing with the body. What was the mode of their existence before the actual physical birth and what will it be after the death of the body? What other more plausible explanation could we offer for the inequalities of beings than the doctrine of *karma* and rebirth, which is consistent with free will and the conservation of moral values? The Semitic religions, which assert the creation of finite souls by a personal God, not only do not seem to feel the need for the doctrine of rebirth, but are even opposed to it. The acceptance of the Law of *Karma* and rebirth means a more universal perspective. Unlike the Semitic religions, Indian religions are not necessarily committed to a theism and a personal deity. Absolute dependence on God, even for the existence of the soul, determines that the highest and perhaps the only form of spirituality is the loving personal relationship of trust of and surrender to God.

The existentialist philosophers of the present day pointedly bring out the predicament of man, his anxiety and deep distress, caused by the thought of the inevitability of passing away into nothingness. Many of their analyses and the phraseology used could be matched by passages from Buddhist and Hindu texts. What the existentialist philosophers fail to present, however, is a clear and sure way out of this anxiety and distress. Indian religious thought is most re-assuring in this respect. It definitely and most emphatically asserts that man can overcome his predicament and that he can attain freedom and the fullness of his being. It is also singularly rich in indicating some well-tried paths or types of spiritual life by which freedom can be attained.

It is common ground in Indian thought that the adoption of sec- ular means and methods do not lead to freedom or salvation. It may be held that, if we could conquer Nature and fully exploit her re- sources, we might satisfy all our wants, and as soon as they arise. The modern man in the atomic age with his immense faith in tech- nology is prone to think that the solution lies this way. But wants may still outstrip our ability to satisfy them; a leap-frog race may result. The root problem is left untouched. Technology cannot provide the wisdom and the good will necessary to make a wholesome use of our power. Control over Nature without control over oneself (self-restraint) can lead only to rivalry, domination, conflict, and suicidal warfare. The human problem is basically spiritual; it lies in self-control and self-education.

Still another ill-advised way out of the difficulty is that of succumbing to the existential situation and, in utter despair, to seek extinction and, in utter despair, to seek extinction of one's being. To succumb to instincts and to consider ourselves as sharing the destruction of the body is a species of spiritual suicide.

A third way to end suffering is what may be called purely ethical discipline by the practice of a strict regimen to control the passions calculated to stop the flow of phenomenal life. The Hīnayāna ideal of the *arhat* (Buddhist perfected man) and the self-mortification of the Jaina could be cited as instances of this. The ethical discipline in both of these is very impressive in vigor and intensity. The ego is disarmed, suppressed, and made inoperative; but it is not put to any active good use. Negatively, there is the cessation of suffering; this is not accompanied by any positive fulfillment. The *arhat* or the *kevalin* (one who has attained isolation from material adjuncts) seems to be bent only upon achieving his own salvation. There is even a lurking fear that the world would enmesh him again if he tarried here too long. Does not the very insistence on getting away smack of selfishness, and is it not therefore unspiritual? An essential mark of the spiritual is the identification of one's good with the good of all. It may well be that the egoistic tendencies are not entirely eliminated. The Mahāyāna makes pointed criticism of this.

We have, finally, the solution of suffering offered by the Vedānta and Mahāyāna Buddhism, which understand freedom as the attainment of a positive state of fullness and complete identification with all beings. It is both a negative process and a positive attainment. It is negative insofar as the "I" is dissociated from its accidental limitations by the removal of ignorance; but this results in a positive and transcendent realization of one's true nature as the Absolute.

The theistic schools of Śaivism and Vaiṣṇavism conceive the highest goal of human attainment as an intimate and inalienable relationship with God and not as complete identity.

In the kindling of spiritual life and the way to the highest attainment, the guidance of God, or revelation, is considered necessary. Otherwise, as there are several possibilities, and, if man were to rely on his unaided reason, he might go astray. It is said in the Vedānta that the *Ātman* is attained by him to whom it chooses to reveal itself; even the inclination toward the Advaita is itself the grace of God. Śaivism explicitly states, "It is through God's grace that we adore his feet," and that is a descent of grace (*śakti-pāta*). It is the deity that chooses to reveal himself to man and takes possession of him. He comes to us in the form of the *guru* (spiritual preceptor and guide).

In the context of freedom and spiritual discipline, the entire range of Indian thought can be classified under three heads:

(1) There were those who did not accept freedom or autonomy of spirit in any form. The Cārvākas denied the existence of the individual self apart from the physical body and ridiculed the very notion of salvation. As a piece of Nature and constituted by a con-glomeration of natural ingredients, consciousness or man can have no value other than gross bodily pleasures. The question of freedom does not arise. The Ājīvikas (materialists or naturalists), although they accepted the *jīvas,* conceived the world process and the entire process of the soul as an automatic and inevitable process; they advocated a most rigorous form of determinism (*niyati-vāda*). Everyone is bound to reach his destiny in the fullness of time. They advocated, according to Buddhism and Jainism, a thoroughgoing fatalism and denied the Law of *Karma.* Both the Buddha and the Jaina Mahāvīra call this doctrine a species of non-activism and condemn it as pernicious and inimical to the spiritual life.[4]

(2) There were philosophers and religious men, such as the Buddha and Mahāvīra, who accepted what we might call immanent freedom as felt and exercised in human involvement. Every man's suffering is evidence of this freedom. The Buddha took his stand, like Kant, on the moral act, the immanent freedom implicit in man's endeavor to better his condition. The emphasis is on self-effort and the right exercise of one's volition.

The fundament in Buddhism and Jainism is the autonomy of the Moral Law (*karma*)—the freedom which we feel and exercise in our actions, in our involvement, and which determines what we are and what we could be. The Moral Law is moral, i.e., it is not a natural or mechanistic operation of brute necessity. Nor is it the dictate of an inscrutable and capricious Person in God. The moral law is im-personal; it has absolute authority, no matter whether it is fulfilled frequently or seldom or not at all; its authority is innate and un-derived. The moral law is perfectly autonomous.

This was not an altogether new idea discovered by the Buddha or Mahāvīra. The Ṛg-vedic hymns speak of *Ṛta* and *Satya,* the Order and Truth of the universe; the deities Indra, Agni, and Varuṇa are invariably spoken of as upholders of the moral order (*dhṛta-vrata satya-dharma, dharmasya-goptā*). It is not as in the Semitic reli-gions, God's fiat which makes anything moral or good. There is an innate propriety (*dharma*) in things, and the deities only reveal and uphold this order; they do not create the order. The impersonality of the Law of *Karma* was first developed as a cosmic principle by the Mīmāṁsakas, who were the first to deny a personal God. Unfortunately, the *karma* or *dharma* they understood and were interested in was ritualistic *karma,* the performance of what the *Bhagavad-gītā* would term *"dravya-yajña"* (sacrifice with substance-oblations) and not duty or moral *karma.* And it was with the latter that the Buddha and Mahāvīra were concerned.

Taking his stand on the autonomy of the moral law, the Buddha was led to deny two opposed standpoints: one was naturalism or nihilism (*sva-bhāva-vāda* or *uccheda-vāda*), which totally denied, as is done by the Cārvāka and the Ājīvika, the Moral Law (free act and its result, *karma* and *karma-phala*), and reduced man to a fortuitous conglomeration of natural forces; the other opposed standpoint was that of eternalism (*śāsvata-vāda*), which stood for the transcendent freedom of God (and even of an unchanging soul or *ātman*), who is above the Moral Law (*karma*). The Buddha characterizes both *uccheda-vāda* and *śasvata-vāda* as specimens of inactivism (*akriya-vāda*).

Salvation or, rather, freedom is freedom from moral evil, from passions and their defilement (*saṁskāra*) ; spiritual discipline is the path of purification (*viśuddhi-mārga*), and this is achieved through *self-effort* and *self-regeneration.* There is no place for outside help or divine guidance. Salvation is strictly a sustained and heroic act on the part of the individual man himself. It is not an act of God or co-operation between man and God. Buddhism, at least early Buddhism, is a moral religion, a universal religion without God, a perfection of self-discipline and self-analysis. As the spiritual discipline is a catharsis or eradication of passions, the ultimate is described negatively as *nirvāṇa.*

The position of earlier Buddhism was considerably modified in the Mahāyāna. To all intents and purposes, the Buddha becomes a divine person—the free phenomenalization of the impersonal Absolute. The personality of the Buddha and the awareness of his unique position ushered in this revolution in Buddhism.

(3) The third class is represented by the Hindu (*Brāhmaṇical*) systems, which in some form or other accepted a free, transcendent being (God) besides the finite selves. It is not that this free being achieved his freedom after destroying his previous bondage. He is eternally free (*sadaiva-muktaḥ*) and transcendent (*sadaiva-Īśvaraḥ*).

If for Buddhism the fundament is the moral consciousness, and the spiritual urge is for purifying the mind of its passions, the fundament of Hinduism is God-consciousness; and the goal is exaltation or deification. The Vedas, which are the fountain source of all forms of Hinduism, are intoxicated with the idea of God, of a transcendent being, ever free and ever the Lord. The Vedic seers had an unusually quick and open sensitiveness to the transcendent being. They try to grasp him now as Agni, now as Indra, now as Varuṇa, Viṣṇu, or Rudra, and in a hundred other ways. These are predicates or characteristics of the Godhead rather than substantive entities in their own right, as has been wrongly contended. The Vedic seers had an almost overwhelming sense of the infinite impinging on man. Religion, for them, was not the labored suppression of passions, of control and regimen, as in Buddhism, but a relationship with the transcendent through prayer and devotion. This *en rapport* relationship with God is what distinguishes Hinduism from earlier Buddhism. And this consciousness has never left it at any stage of its long history. Newer deities emerge; rather, the old ones are given new names (e.g., Rudra is called Śiva; Viṣṇu is Nārāyaṇa or Vāsudeva) and are worshipped in newer forms; but the pattern remains the same. This may be theism, but it is not a theism of the Semitic type. The difference between God and man (creatures) is not absolute.

The deity is not discovered by man by his self-effort; it is the deity that freely chooses to reveal itself. Man just receives and realizes it. He is saved by this relationship, by his sense of kinship and identity with the transcendent spirit. Practice of moral virtues and concentration of mind have value as enabling one to perceive this inherent identity, just as a spotless mirror is able to entertain the image without distortion. The purity of the mirror is not, however, the source of the image; it is merely ancillary to the reflection. As realizing an already existing fact, spiritual attainment for Hinduism is symbolic, not labored and literal, as in earlier Buddhism.

It might be thought that the atheistic Mīmāṁsā and Sāṁkhya do not conform to the pattern of a transcendent pure being. But, since in both of these the Veda (the Eternal Word) is accepted as the infallible and omniscient source of truth, the conformity is essentially present.

It is interesting to note, however, that in the Hindu and the non-Hindu (Buddhist and Jaina) traditions, both the impersonal spirit and a personal God find a place. This is the basic dialectic in Indian religious thought. There is no doubt that this obtains in other religions also. This problem will engage us toward the end of the paper.

II. RELIGIOUS LIFE

Having considered the nature of the religious problem and its historical perspective, we may now proceed to consider the nature of religious life and the problems and perplexities it presents.

The religious or spiritual life in Indian thought is conceived in terms of self-control and self-regeneration. We may speak of it as a new dimension of being, much as St. Paul said, "I do not live, Christ liveth in me." This is a re-discovery or regaining of what one had lost unconsciously in ignorance.[5] It is not a new acquisition; for, if it were so, there could be no finality; the accumulation of merit could mount higher and higher, there being no conceivable limit to its amount. And, conditioned as it would be by certain specific circumstances, the state of freedom would be transitory; it might even cease to be. It would also admit of degrees. This is not how *mokṣa* is understood in the Indian religions. It is eternal, does not admit of gradation, and is unconditioned. In its attainment, there may be epistemic novelty or emergence, but ontologically nothing new is engendered. Therefore, Śaṁkara always speaks of *mokṣa* as no effect and as the nature of *Brahman.*[6] Nāgārjuna says, "*Nirvāṇa* is what is not abandoned or acquired, what is not annihilation or eternality, what is not destroyed or created."[7]

Freedom is not a conferment of something which one did not possess; it is release from delusion and suffering. God does not confer freedom; he may and does show us the way to achieve freedom. That is his grace. Freedom is therefore not exactly the same as the salvation of the Semitic religions.

The essence of self-control is the bringing about of a change in oneself, in one's mentality, and not in the environment. To control the external world, including the world of fellow human beings, is the way of worldly men. This is bound, sooner or later, to raise antagonism and strife. And this is precisely what we wish to avoid. Philosophical knowledge or wisdom (*prajñā*) does not transform the world, but only our attitude. It certainly means a radical change in our mental make-up.

The path of freedom is one of purification and disassociation from the not-self, from the false or superficial aspects of the self. Cognitively, it is a case of enlightenment or insight into the nature of things. We may call it a negative process, since it is a case of divestification of the encumbrances with which we have cluttered ourselves on life's journey. It is not negative in result. For what we are left with is not nothing, but our real being in its innate immediacy. Also, the path's being characterized in negative phraseology does not mean that we are to be inactive or that it is easy of accomplishment.

There are two fundamental presuppositions underlying this position.

One is that all our troubles are due to ignorance, primarily ignorance of oneself. This is not merely privation of right knowledge, but a positive wrong idea. I wrongly take myself as the body or the mental states or even the intellect, and, owing to this wrong identification, I gratuitously share the misfortune of the body. With its injury or death, I consider myself to be undergoing these misfortunes. This wrong identification is not a conscious, deliberate process. No one can consciously fall into illusion. One does not say, "Lo,

I am falling into illusion" or "Let me commit this error." He may get out of it consciously and also know when he gets out of it. We can consciously disassociate or disavow our connection with the body, but not vice versa. Nor is it that the self (the "I") and the body started their career as separate and independent entities and at some particular time were joined together. The Indian view is that we can begin only with their togetherness, their fusion or confusion. All accounts depicting a point of time when they were apart, etc., are merely expressions to bring out the essential purity and uniqueness of the self. It is a demand to disassociate it from the body. Although we cannot assign any conceivable beginning to this incongruous relationship, it is not inseparable. We can undo this wrong identification. We can educate and correct ourselves. Any attempt to refute this position would itself presuppose correction, i.e., the removal of my wrong views by the opponent. In fact, only wrong views are removed.

It is common ground in all the Indian systems that ignorance (*avidyā, ajñāna*) is the cause of suffering. The nature of ignorance, or wrong knowledge, differs somewhat in the various systems, depending upon their different metaphysical standpoints. In the Sāṁkhya, it is wrong identification of the self (*puruṣa*) with the object (*prakṛti*) in its various modifications beginning with the intellect; in the Advaita Vedānta, it is considering the self as finite and limited, whereas it is really the infinite *Brahman;* in Jainism, it is the intrusion of karmic matter into the soul (*jīva*); in earlier Buddhism, it is the substance-idea itself, wrongly taking things (which are really changing and perishing) as permanent and identical and clinging to them; in the Mādhyamika, it is indulging in philosophical speculation, in the setting forth of *views* of the real.

The second presupposition, which is almost a consequence of the first, is that in the make-up of the self there are several layers or aspects. To a superficial view, the individual is the "body-mind-I" complex, and in the ordinary course of life the distinction among these elements is seldom made. It is only when we become reflective and begin to raise questions about our true nature that the distinction can be made. Spiritual discipline has for its objective the progressive realization of the pure self as distinct from the body. The body itself is understood in a much wider sense, to include not only the physical body but also the sense-organs, the mental states, the intellect, the psychical dispositions, etc., which constitute the inner body, as it were. It is stripping the "I" of all its external trappings and accidental accretions. The point to be reached is a foundational consciousness that is unconditional, self-evident, and immediate (*svayaṁ-prakāśa*). It is that to which everything is presented, but is itself no presentation, that which knows all, but is itself no object.

The self should not be confused with the contents and states which it enjoys and manipulates. If we have to give an account of it, we can describe it only as what it is *not,* for any positive description of it would be possible only if it could be made an *object* of observation, which from the nature of the case it is not. We "know" it only as we withdraw ourselves from the body with which we happen to be identified, in this transition.

That such a foundational self is there and can be reached by the right kind of discipline is taught by the Vedānta. The Sāṁkhya view is not very different. Mahāyāna Buddhism implicitly affirms the existence of a deep underlying reality behind all empirical manifestations in its conception of *śūnyatā* (the indeterminate, the void), or *vijñapti-mātratā* (consciousness only), or *tathatā* (thatness), or *dharmatā* (noumenal reality). Its spiritual discipline differs considerably from that of the Vedānta or the Sāṁkhya, but the ultimate goal is remarkably similar.

We have been talking of the spirit and the spiritual; some definition of it may be attempted. In all religions, especially in the Indian religions, spirituality implies the giving up of narrow, selfish, ego-centeredness and the attainment of the universal. In its extreme form, this would take the form of complete identity with all beings, as in the case of the Advaita Vedānta and the Mahāyāna. The good of one is the good of all. The spiritual person does not divide himself from others. Nor is he divided in himself. His personality is integrated, as there is no conflict—or cross-purposes—in his inner make-up. The secular man does not react to a situation in a total way; in him, there are surface motives and deeper drives, often in disharmony. In the spiritual, the means and the end coincide. In the moral or social sphere, we do certain acts, e.g., acts of charity and kindness, for some otherworldly benefits or for social solidarity which may benefit us indirectly. Nor do moral acts carry with them their own sanctity. Their observance is commanded by external authority, fear of God, or the approval of society. The spiritual person is good, he is chaste or charitable, not because he desires to gain anything in this or the other world. It is his nature to be so; his goodness is motiveless. The spiritual act is not a means to an end; it is the end itself. It therefore carries within itself the criterion of its validity and efficacy.

Some account, or at least a general indication, of the lines of approach to the ultimate reality may be given. What strikes one in this regard is the diversity of the paths advocated, and some of them represent daring experiments with the psyche. There is an explicit recognition, not only of the obvious surface differences among individuals, but also of the diversity in their deeper psychical levels, or their spiritual temperaments. Individuality is not mere plurality, the colorless stereotyped repetition of entities, but the recognition of many distinct types. Within the basic types, there are sub-types, and these shade off into personal variations and versions. Indian religious thought is explicitly aware of the different modes of spiritual progression as depending upon basic types—*prasthāna-bheda* (differences in modes of practice) and *gotra-bheda* (differences of family relationships). Either they all lead to the same result or they meet at some penultimate point where the others are merged into one mode.

All would enjoin, as a prerequisite of the spiritual life, the practice of moral virtues and concentration of mind (*śīla* and *samādhi* in Buddhism).[8] It is customary to speak of the three paths of knowledge (*jñāna*), of action (*karma*), and of devotion (*bhakti*), as leading to *mokṣa*. In actual practice, these three are not exclusive. It is not that in the path of knowledge there is no place for an active good life or for a feeling of devotion to God. These latter would be required in the preparatory stage, to purify the intellect of its passions and prejudices and to make it one-pointed. But it is the knowledge or the insight into the real that will engender freedom, or is freedom itself. The cognitive urge to know the ultimate truth is the spearhead behind which other psychic factors work. And this spearhead gives the predominant tone to the entire discipline—that the other factors are absent. There is a psychological reason why this should be so and not otherwise. As spiritual attainment is the satisfaction of the entire man and not merely of a part of him, if the urge for active altruism or the feeling of surrender to God is repressed, there will result a split in the personality of the individual; there will be no integration of personality, which is a distinctive mark of the spiritual. It is possible, however, to organize the various factors with differing emphases. Each such organization would be a distinct and integrated unit, and not a medley of discordant notes. And this would be in conformity with the demand that the spiritual path chosen should be suited to the individual's particular spiritual temperament. One master idea or sentiment will so fully and utterly grip the mind as to bring about a catalytic reaction in the entire personality—for instance, the Advaita Vedānta knowledge, "I am *Brahman*" (*aham brahmasmi*) (i.e., I am not this body, or these mental states, or the puny creature that I have been taking myself to be) is of this nature. The thought or the conviction that I am *Brahman* makes for the individual's regeneration. This is not a mere idea or a reasoned conviction lacking metaphysical foundation, but we are not at the moment concerned with that aspect of it. When this conviction or realization sways the mind and possesses it, one no longer sorrows after the body or is drawn into the pettiness of secular life. Friendliness, charity, non-violence, and other virtues follow easily, and not labored and restricted. The picture drawn here is *mutatis mutandis* true of other modes of religious thought also.

III. INDIVIDUAL, GOD, AND ABSOLUTE

What is the state of final attainment, the goal? Is it a kind of ineffable absorption into the abyss of the Absolute (*Brahman* or *Nirvāṇa*), or is it a form of God-realization? This is bound up with the question, as to whether there is separate and individual salvation from time to time or universal salvation. The question is discussed in all seriousness and implication both in Mahāyāna Buddhism and the Advaita Vedānta, where it takes the pointed form of "freedom of one or of all" (*eka-mukti* or *sarva-mukti*).

Mahāyāna Buddhism has clearly given the answer in its doctrine of the Buddha and the *bodhi-sattva* (one whose essence is perfect wisdom). Even while entering the path of spiritual discipline for enlightenment, the *bodhisattva* makes the Great Vows. The chief one of these is that the merit and the knowledge that he would acquire would be for all beings, high and low, and not for himself.[9] "He shuns retiring into the final state of *Nirvaṇa*, though fully entitled to it, preferring, by his own free choice, to toil for even the lowest of beings for ages. He is actuated by this motiveless altruism from the very start of his career. It is not that the *bodhisattva* cannot achieve his own freedom without achieving the freedom of all. This would involve a vicious circle; he cannot free others without first freeing himself, and he cannot free himself without freeing others. No, his freedom is full and complete by itself; but he condescends to raise others to his level. This is a free phenomenalizing act of grace and compassion. A deeply religious element is introduced into Buddhism, which would have otherwise remained an exalted moral naturalism. Buddha, which the *bodhisattvas* follow and eventually become, is a Person, the Highest Person. In the Buddha, we have the conception of a person without any trace of ego. There is activity without attachment."[10] In the *Maha-vagga* of the *Vinaya-piṭaka* we have a very moving account of how Gautama the Buddha was sorely tempted, after his enlightenment, to pass away into final release, but was persuaded by Brahmā, the Great God (actually his innate religious consciousness), to accept the ministry.[11] Free, egoless personality must be accepted. It is not that as one achieves freedom one is absorbed into the Absolute wholly and at once. Though free, one has still enough of the phenomenal in oneself to feel kinship with fellow beings and to help them out of worldly life. Freedom does not repel personality; nor does all personality mean bondage. There can be a free person, and the Buddha is such a person.

In the Advaita Vedānta, too, the position is not different. It is definitely accepted that, as long as other individuals remain to be liberated, the freed self realizes his union, perhaps even his oneness, with God (Īśvara), rather than become merged in the Absolute (*Brahman*). The reason for this is that, as long as other individual souls are struggling in this world, there will continue to be the distinction between God (Īśvara) and the finite selves (*jīvas*); there is no Pure Being (*Brahman*) as such apart from its varied manifestations. God will continue to perform his function as long as there are any souls needing to realize their identity with *Brahman*. How and when will there be the state in which all the souls shall have been freed is an apocalyptic question that cannot be easily answered. The possibility of such a happy event as the total release of all souls is not ruled out. The question regarding the nature of the interim release of individual souls is fully discussed in the *Brahma-sūtra* and by Śaṁkara in his Commentary thereon.[12] It is stated with cogent arguments that identity with the Lord (*Īśvara-bhāvāpatti*) is the nature of liberation of individual souls.

In the state of union with God (Īśvara), the individual, for all practical purposes, is God; he is no longer an ego, having transcended his petty and private status. Like God, he is also an egoless personality. He freely identifies himself with others and enters into their being. Of this state it is said in the Upaniṣads, "He attains all his desires; he becomes one, two, threefold, aye, manifold." "He goes along disporting himself . . . [and so on]."[13] It is stated that even such freed souls are sent on cosmic errands (*ādhikārika-puruṣas*)[14] and actively participate in the maintenance of the cosmic order. From the nature of the case, these statements are not capable of rational explanation.

The factors which generally constitute the empirical individual and which mark him off from other individuals, e.g., the physical body, mental traits, and dispositions, aspirations and achievements, may not be present in this state. But it cannot be denied that some form of personality is present. The desire to help others and the capacity to participate actively in the cosmic good are present and may constitute the basis of personality.

It may well be asked: Why should we accept both the Absolute (*Brahman*) and God (Īśvara), impersonal and personal spirit? Could not either of them do as well? The basic dialectic in Indian religious thought, as stated earlier, is between personal God and impersonal spirit. This assertion is not made on a priori grounds but because we find it exemplified quite pointedly in the orthodox Hindu as well as in the Buddhist tradition. There is no doubt that this obtains in other religions also. Tillich speaks of the "tension between Being and God," or of "the God beyond God." Either the personal appears first, as in Hinduism, or the impersonal, as in Buddhism and Jainism. Very soon the other dialectic aspect discloses itself and has to be reckoned with. A synthesis is called for.

To explain. The personal God or gods of the Vedic hymns are the first intimations of the holy or the numinous in Hindu religious consciousness. From the personal God, there is the movement toward the unity underlying this, the Godhead behind these manifestations, *That One* (*tad ekam*) for which the gods really stand. This position is explicitly reached in the Upaniṣads and is formulated as the philosophy of the Vedānta. In Buddhism (and this is largely true of Jainism, too), the impersonal as the Moral Order (*dharma*) and the ideal of *Nirvāṇa* is the prius; the personal is even repudiated and the stand is anti-theistic. However, the inner dynamism of the spiritual life led, as explicitly admitted by the Mahāyāna, to God in the person of the Buddha. It is not that the Mahāyānists deified the human Buddha, but that the Buddha's divinity became clear to them as a new insight. In fact, the human form of the Buddha prevented his being recognized as divine. The Buddha performs the divine functions of grace and revelation, though not the cosmic functions of creation and sustenance of the world. *Dharma* or *Nirvāṇa,* being impersonal and completely transcendent, could not reveal or declare itself to man. It requires the appropriate organism, a teacher endowed with the necessary qualities; just as geometrical truths cannot reveal themselves—they require to be taught by a teacher. If *Nirvāṇa* itself could come down, as it were, and disclose itself, then we could be persuaded of its authenticity. And yet, only a person can perform this function. Paradoxically, the Buddha had therefore to be at once identical with *Nirvāṇa* (so as to enable him to have direct and intimate knowledge of *Nirvāṇa*) and also be different from it, as only a person (accepting and operating under human conditions and using human forms of communication) could reveal and declare the truth of *Nirvāṇa.* Impelled by this dialectic of religious consciousness, "The Buddhas were subjected to a six-fold process: they were multiplied, immortalised, deified, spiritualised, universalised, and unified," as Dr. Har Dayal so happily states.[15]

The problem of Absolute and God is really the problem of ultimacy and concreteness, their relation and balance. How preserve both without reducing one or the other to insignificance? God's nature is not exhausted in his relationship to man or in the performance of cosmic functions; he has a non-relational, transcendent nature of his own; he is something *in himself.* This is the Absolute. The theistic religions generally slur over this distinction. God as the "Wholly Other" has to be sharply distinguished from the creatures over whom he dominates. Here God is *one term* of the relation of difference. But God is also the being of all things, that in which they move and have their being. In the latter sense, as the foundational and only Being, God cannot be distinguished from anything, as there is no other besides him. The Advaita Vedānta rightly understands God in this aspect as the *"Great IT,"* as *Brahman,* the Great Being without a second. Even the relation of "I and Thou" is itself possible because of the Being underlying the opposites; it is the common platform on which both of them stand equally. Therefore, the Absolute cannot be denied. It stands for the principle of ultimacy, the original and inexhaustible source of being and power. It is Being without any touch or treat of non-being. As Being without any other facing it, it is the whole or universal being. Not lacking anything, as full being, it is termed bliss on that account. As the only being without divisions, without even the division of subject and object, it does not stand in need of being evidenced. Although not evidenced, it is immediate and self-evident.

There are two prevalent misconceptions regarding Being (*Brahman*). One is to take it as a particular existent, conditioned and limited. The other, which is more pernicious, is to understand Being as a conception, as a generalized idea or abstraction. Hegel is guilty of this. He created a phantom so that he could the more easily knock it down. He used what might be called the *de-ontological* argument, the ontological argument in reverse. For he reduces the Ontic Being to an idea or a descriptive character. It is less of a mistake to identify Being with any particular existent (God or man), for here at least we have a concrete experience of Being. This is why the Upaniṣads speak of it as *"neti, neti,"* and Śaṁkara understands *Brahman* as *nirguṇa* (without qualities), because it is the fullness of Being, and not a system or bundle of ideas.

If the Absolute cannot be denied, God also cannot be denied. For it is he who reveals to us the nature of *Brahman.* The truth, being impersonal, needs to be declared and proclaimed as truth by a person. *Tathatā* (the thatness of things) requires a *tathāgata* (one who has realized thatness) to reveal it to us. The two facets, then, are present in Hinduism and Buddhism, in any mature religion. They cannot be left unrelated; nor can they be related co-ordinately, as this would make for opposition. As they have to be synthesized or related in a whole, the only alternative left is to take one as higher, the other as lower—higher in the sense of providing the ground or sustenance for the other. If I may venture to coin a term for this situation, I would call it "Synthesis in Depth," to distinguish it from synthesis in comprehension, in extensity and inclusiveness. The Hegelian synthesis is of the latter kind. Depth-synthesis is the acceptance of two levels of Being, the impersonal and the personal spirit. No doubt, these are spatial metaphors, but they may help to bring out more picturesquely the relationship between the two.

Depth-synthesis also implies a mechanism or device by which the impersonal spirit can become the personal God, without loss, without being transformed or diminished. It is the logic of a one-sided relation. It may well be that all relation is one-sided. It is a connection between two terms, one and only one of which has a transcendent existence (i.e., is not exhausted in the relational context), while the other is confined to the relational context.[16] *Māyā,* or *avidyā,* is the principle of this mediation. It is a device to reconcile God's transcendence with his immanence—what he is in himself and the manner in which he chooses to reveal himself to finite beings. It is not the principle of utter rejection or negation of God or the world in the Absolute, but the insistence on the transcendence of the Godhead and the inapplicability of empirical characteristics to it. *Māyā* is not an explanation, much less a derivation of the lower from the higher (we may leave this jugglery to Hegel). The mystery remains. In fact, *"māyā"* is the most expressive term for the mystery of such so-called derivation. It affirms, however, that they are not unrelated or independent entities. The correct formula is that the lower is neither identical with nor different from the higher, the absolute (*tattvānyatvābhyām-anirvacanīya*). A sort of hierarchy is implied between *Brahman* and *Īśvara* (as between *Dharmatā* or *Śūnyatā* and the Buddha), without either of them being unreal or redundant.

In a way, *Brahman* and *Īśvara* (*Dharmatā* and the Buddha) typify the two ways in which we can understand freedom—freedom as "free *from*" and freedom as "free to do." Free Being (*Brahman* or *Śūnyatā* or *Dharmatā*) is free from empirical determination and limitations. *Īśvara* or the Buddha is a free agent, free to act; his will or act, being always in accord with the truth (*satya-kāma* and *satya-samkalpa*), is never impeded *apratihata-śaktiḥ*). In both the traditions, it is well-understood that it is only through the mediation of *Īśvara* or the Buddha that we can realize our free nature as *Brahman* or *Dharmatā,* and that the liberated individual first realizes his identity or union with *Īśvara* or the Buddha.

QUESTION: I would like to raise a question regarding your statement about the nature of relation. Toward the end of your paper you speak of the logic of one-sided relation and say, further, that "it may well be that all relation is one-sided. It is a connection between two terms, one and only one of which has a transcendent existence (i.e., not exhausted in the relational context), while the other is confined to the relational context." Would you consider this as true of all relations which common sense recognizes, such as, for instance, the two halves of this folded card or the sides of the table?

ANSWER: Relation should be distinguished from mere juxtaposition of two or more things. The latter is a static state of things and requires a third entity which steers them into that position. In relation, however, there is a higher and a lower term. The higher engenders or constitutes the other. They are not of equal status. The two terms are not reciprocally independent; for then the ground of relation would be external to them. Nor are they reciprocally dependent; for then there could be no distinction between them. The father exists before the son and generates the latter, although he would be called "father" only on the birth of the son. Cause and effect, whole and parts, substance and attribute, and other constitutive relations are to be interpreted similarly.

QUESTION: Do you think that your characterization of relation is one-sided? While it may be true of the Advaita Vedānta, would it be applicable to the Mādhyamika? Would not the Mādhyamika consider all relation as mutually implicatory?

ANSWER: Yes, it is true that for the Mādhyamika the two terms forming a relation, e.g., substance and attribute, whole and parts, cause and effect, etc., are nothing in themselves. As mutually dependent, both are inherently false. But with regard to the relation between noumenal reality (*Śūnyatā* or *Paramārtha*) and phenomena (*samvṛti*) the Mādhyamika would certainly subscribe to the one-sidedness of relation. *Samvṛti* depends on *Paramārtha* and not vice versa. The Vedānta adopts a single pattern for explaining all relation, whether between two empirical things or between *Brahman* and the World. This is the difference between the Mādhyamika and the Vedānta.

QUESTION: You observe, almost at the beginning of your paper, that "there is no religious problem unless man is conscious of his peril." I have also been saying that every religion is a kind of answer to the problem of evil. But, conceivably, religion could arise in some way other than from suffering; as, for instance, in a feeling of ecstatic wonder or sublimity with regard to the world. Perhaps, we make too much of sin-consciousness. You make the observation that "the Vedic seers had an unusually quick and open sensitiveness to the transcendent being and that religion was not the labored suppression of passions, of regimen and control, but the *en rapport* relationship with the transcendent through prayer and devotion." Would you agree that we could have religion without suffering and sin-consciousness?

ANSWER: I largely agree with you. In Buddhism and Jainism the fundament is the moral consciousness and suffering is emphasized. In the Vedic religion, the religious attitude as kinship with God is prominent. Even in this *en rapport* relation there is the consciousness of a lack of imperfection in the background. The distinction eventually turns out to be one of relative emphasis on one or the other —on exaltedness or suffering.

QUESTION: Regarding freedom, you say that in "the state of union with God, the individual for all practical purposes is God; he is no more an ego." What sort of personality does an individual have in that state?

ANSWER: Although no longer self-centered and egoistic in his pursuits and outlook, the freed individual still has a personality insofar as he unceasingly and intelligently strives for the good of others and participates in the cosmic order. He is not a mere principle. The term "ego-less personality" is not an inconsistent expression, nor is that state an incongruous one. All enlightened sages, like the Buddha, freed of their ignorance and selfishness, are concrete examples of this. They are actively free. And this freedom may be distinguished from the freedom of Pure Being (*Brahman*), which is a state of absorption and a self-completeness. Personality could significantly be attributed to one who is actively free.

1 *Samyutta-nikāya*, Part II (*Nidāna-vagga*), XV. 3 (Assu-sutta), L. Feer, ed. (London: Pali Text Society edn., 1888), pp. 179–180.

2 The Buddha gives a graphic description of this fact of suffering: "What do you think, O monks! Which may be more, the flow of tears you have shed on this long way, running again and again to new birth and new death, united to the disliked, separated from the liked, complaining and weeping, or the water of the four great oceans? . . . But how is this possible? Without beginning or end, O monks, is this round of rebirth. There cannot be discerned the first beginning of beings, who, sunk in ignorance and bound by thirst, are incessantly transmigrating and again and again run to a new birth. And thus, O monks, through a long time you have experienced suffering, pain and misery, and enlarged the burying ground; truly long enough to be disgusted with every kind of existence, long enough to turn away from every kind of existence, long enough to turn away from every kind of existence, long enough to deliver yourself from it." *Samyutta-nikāya*, II. xv. 13. (Quoted in Grimm, *The Doctrine of the Buddha*,) (Berlin: Akademie-Verlag, 1958), pp. 100–101.) Jaigīṣavya (*Yoga-sūtra-bhāṣya*, III. 18) gives expression to *duḥkha-satya* in identical terms: *daśasu mahasargeṣu bhavyatvād anabhibhūtena buddhisattvena mayā narakatiryagbhavam duḥkham sampaśyatā devamanuṣyeṣu punaḥ punar utpadyamanena yat kincid anubhūtam tat sarvam duḥkham eva pratyavaimi.*

3 *Duḥkha* is usually considered in the threefold way. *duḥkha-duḥkhatā*—the actual pain; *tāpa-duḥkhatā* (longing, desire); and the *saṁskāra-duḥkhatā*—the root causes, *kleśas* (passions), e.g., attachment, aversion, etc. In short, phenomenal existence, or all the five *upādāna-skandhas*, are pain.

4 Madhva's doctrine of predestination comes perilously close to this point of view.

5 The Christian doctrine of the Fall and Redemption may be taken in some sense as the religious counterpart of this conception.

6 Śaṁkara's *Bhāṣya* on *Brahma-sūtra*, I.i.4.

7 *Mādhyamika-kārikā*, XXV. 5–6, Louis de La Vallée-Poussin, ed. Bibliotheca Buddhica, Vol. IV. (St. Petersburg, Bibliotheca Buddhica, 1913), pp. 521, 527.

8 Śaṁkara (*Brahma-sūtra-bhāṣya*, I. i. 1), for instance, lays down four conditions as necessary prerequisites for undertaking *Brahma-jijñāsā* (*Brahma*-knowledge): discrimination between the true and the false (literally the eternal and the ephemeral), detachment from secular pursuits of this world and from heavenly pleasures; practice of the moral virtues of control and contentment, and an intense desire for freedom. The *Yoga-sūtra* enjoins the observance of restraints (*yama*)—non-violence, truthfulness, non-covetousness, continence, non-acquisition—and the practice of moral virtues (*niyama*)—contentment, purity, penance, reading of scriptures, and devotion to God—as the first steps to the higher reaches of *yoga* discipline.

9 See *Aṣṭa-sāhasrikā-prajñāpāramitā*, R. L. Mitra, ed. (Calcutta: Bibliotheca Indian edn., 1888), p. 293. See also *Śikṣā samuccaya*, Cecil Bendell, ed., Bibliotheca of Śantideva (St. Petersburg: Bibliotheca Buddhica, 1897–1902), Vol. I, p. 14.

10 Quoted from T. R. V. Murti, *The Central Philosophy of Buddhism* (London: George Allen & Unwin Ltd., 1960), pp. 263–264.

11 The *Mahā-vagga* of the *Vinaya-piṭaka*, Sec. I. Söderblom, in his *The Living God*, comments on this saying that only the Buddha or Christ could be subjected to this unique kind of temptation. (Jesus is reported to have uttered: "Let this cup pass from me, Father. Thy will be done.")

12 *Brahma-sūtra*, IV. iv. 5, 7, and the Commentary of Śaṁkara thereon; see also the *Siddhāntaleśa-saṁgraha*, (Benares: Chowkhamba edn., 1916), pp. 512–542. Consult the Symposium on *eka-mukti* and *sarva-mukti* in the *Proceedings of the Indian Philosophical Congress*, Mysore Session, 1932.

13 *Chāndogya Upaniṣad*, VII. xxvi. 2; VIII, xii, 3.

14 See *Brahma-sūtra*, IV. iv. 17–18.

15 Har Dayal, *The Bodhisattva Doctrine in Buddhist Sanskrit Literature* (London: Kegan Paul, Trench, Trübner, & Co., Ltd., 1932), p. 28.

16 For a somewhat fuller discussion of the concept of relation in the Advaita Vedānta, reference may be made to the writer's paper, "The Two Definitions of Brahman in the Advaita," in *Professor K. C. Bhattacharyya Memorial Volume* (Amalner: Indian Institute of Philosophy, 1958), pp. 136 ff.

FAZLUR RAHMAN

The status of the individual in Islam

Islam is generally believed believed to be—both by many of its modern believing exponents and a large number of non-Muslim writers—a religion emphasizing society rather than the individual.[1] It is pointed out in this connection that law, social institutions, and statecraft are the primary constituents of Islam, because this fact is demonstrated in the earliest segments of Muslim history, which the Muslims regard as an ideal. A good deal of the Qur'ān itself is also devoted to legislation and guidance of the affairs of the Community, rather than the individual. Further, the Qur'ān speaks of the Muslim Community as "The Middle Community" charged with the task of executing God's will on earth. It is then concluded that, if the Holy Book of Islam gives so much importance to society and collective existence and if the actual performance in history of the Prophet and of his immediate followers bears this out, it follows that Islam is primarily a "social religion." With this primary emphasis on collective existence and the fundamental importance of the Community, one begins to wonder what can be the status of the individual.

In the following an attempt will be made to bring out the status of the individual in Islam as a religion. Having brought out that status, we shall then attempt to put the individual in relation to society in its right perspective in the religious teachings of Islam. It will be seen at the end that, although the statements given above regarding the importance of the Community and social existence in Islam are essentially correct, nevertheless, the conclusion drawn therefrom, that Islam aims primarily or finally at society rather than at the individual, is unwarranted. It will also be seen that, when the modernist Muslim tends to emphasize society in his interpretation of Islam, he is, in fact, not so much aiming at a pure and objective statement of Islamic values *per se,* as aiming indirectly at reform of Muslim society which is his present-day business.

Now, there is no doubt that the primary locus of responsibilty in Islam is the individual. The Qur'ān says, "Today [on the Day of Judgment] you have come to us as individuals (*furādā*), just as we created you in the first place."[2] Again, "Man shall come to us alone as an individual."[3] Again, the Qur'ān tells us, "Every soul earns but for itself, and no soul shall bear the burden of another, and even thus shall you return to your Lord."[4] (This last statement is repeated in XVII: 15, XXV: 18, and XXXI: 7.) It is on these grounds that Muslim theologians reject the possibility of redemption, even though at a later stage of the development of Muslim theology, in the late second and early third centuries, the doctrine of intercession was introduced. These efforts make it abundantly clear that the ultimate repository of the divine trust is the individual person. But such a statement is not enough, unless it is made clear as to what are the ultimate objective and the real purpose behind the creation of the individual. Only when we understand the philosophy of Islam on this point shall we be able to appreciate the position of the individual and his relation to society.

In this connection, the story of the creation of man in the Qur'ān seems very revealing, indeed. We are told[5] that, when God willed to create man, the angels raised a protest, saying, "Will you create on earth a being who will work corruption and shed blood, while we sing your praises and glorify you?" God, in his reply, does not deny that man will commit errors and make mistakes, but says simply, "I know what you know not." The Qur'ān then proceeds to tell us that God taught Adam: "All the names [of things, i.e., their properties and attributes]," and this constitutes the superiority of man over angels.[6] One further fundamental statement of the Qur'ān on this point remains to be noted, viz., "We offered the Trust to the heavens and the earth and the mountains, but they refused to accept it and were frightened of it, but man accepted it."[7] These statements, taken together, show that there are certain potentialities and possibilities which can be realized only by man among all creation. In the entire range of created being, man alone is capable of real achievement and development, and, further, he is squarely charged with the responsibility for the realization of these potentialities. The proper discharge of this "Trust" is "service to God" ('ibāda), which, in Islam, does not mean the devotional side of religious life exclusively but the sum total of output of man under the moral law. The most frequently recurring term in the Qur'ān and in the Traditions of the Prophet to describe this attitude, which attunes a man to discharge his responsibilities properly and do justice to his innate capacities, is the Arabic term "taqwā." This term has been variously understood and translated both by Muslims and non-Muslims as "piety," "fear of God," and "guarding oneself."

Taqwā is an attribute of the individual and not of society, and, as we have just said, it is this principle which makes a man perform his functions as the highest creation of God properly and become man in the true sense. But, before we go any further, we must try to clarify this concept and understand it more closely. Terms like "piety" and "fear of God," although an integral part of the concept of *taqwā*, do not really convey its full meaning as they are commonly understood. Even the term "fear" is applied at various levels with regard to different types of reactions and attitudes in reference to different objects. Thus, one fears a wolf, a criminal, or a person suspected of a crime may fear the police; a child may fear his parents, or his teacher, or a bully at school. Not all these senses are identical with one another, but there is a sense which is different from all of these, and is applicable only to the human being. This is the sense in which the relative always fall short of the absolute and must tend toward it. What I am saying now in this paper, for instance, I regard as representing the truth on the subject which is being examined herein, and I am at the moment trying my best to find and speak the truth. But, despite my sincerity, effort, and whatever ability I may have, there is no certainty that a still truer and a still better picture of the subject cannot be drawn. I am charged, therefore, with the responsibility of ever trying to tend toward higher truth. In some real sense I must always be afraid that what I am saying may not be adequately true. This applies not only to one case but to all human cases. Just as with cognition, so with moral action; no matter how righteously we may try and even presume to act, there is always the scope and, what is more important, there eternally hangs the responsibility to transcend the actual. This is cognitive and moral dynamism, and a certain fearful appreciation of the inadequacy of the actual is a necessary condition of this dynamism. This is exactly the meaning of *taqwā*. *Taqwā*, therefore, is a positive and dynamic concept, and without it the *"Trust"* of man cannot be adequately discharged, according to the Qur'ān.

This dynamic movement of *taqwā* presupposes a transcendent norm of judgment, an absolute point of reference, which is God himself. It is well known that the function of God in Islam is that of a judge—indeed, one might say that the central teaching of Islam about God is that he is the sole generator of norms of judgment. Man must attempt to discover these norms within his soul and endeavor to conform to them; he cannot make or unmake these norms. Now, an individual's perception may err in locating norms which are not made for him alone but for the whole of humanity. He must therefore rely on the collective wisdom of mankind. This is the first limitation on the individual, viz., that his personal discoveries are not laws of God *simplicitor*. But it is true that the individual is the proper and primary bearer of this burden of *taqwā*. It is the individual who is responsible in the final analysis. The application of *taqwā* to societies, as we shall presently see, is genuine and, in a way, necessary, according to Islam, but it is in its secondary intention. That is why, according to Islam, it is the individual who will be answerable and not societies or nations. Certain traditions attributed to the Prophet speak of the resurrection of individuals according to their religious groups or communities, but the authenticity of these traditions is highly questionable.[8] But even the traditions do not speak of a collective soul or a transcendent being of society which will come into existence and be made answerable on the Day of Judgment.

But, although the individual, in the final analysis, is the primary reality which the Qur'ān and the teaching of the Prophet recognize, there is little doubt that Islam emphasizes the co-operative and collective functioning of human beings as a society. It is not merely the case that Islam religiously requires the organization of society and the state and directly seeks to generate the law, both of which, in the West, are looked upon as purely secular institutions, but even the specifically religious duties enjoined upon a Muslim have social overtones.

There are five well-known obligatory duties devolving upon a Muslim, which are commonly called the "Pillars of Islam." The first of these is the act of belief itself, but even the act of belief does not become valid, at least so far as society is concerned, unless it is formally and openly avowed. The second fundamental is the five prayers. The interesting point to note about these prayers is, first, that they are collective prayers and may not be said individually except in great need, and, second, part of their content refers to the individual, and part has reference to the general Muslim Community, and both are equally essential. Besides these five prayers, devotional individual prayers are encouraged and emphasized but are not considered obligatory. The third fundamental practice of Islam, namely, the obligatory fast of Ramaḍān, with its regulations, is patently and deliberately intended to produce both individual and social consequences. The fourth pillar of the Faith is the *zakāt* tax (obligatory religious charity), which is nothing more or less than the establishment of a welfare state: it is a measure of socio-economic justice through and through. Lastly, the pilgrimage to Mecca has its obvious collective functions of promoting unity and solidarity among the Muslim Community.

But even more important than the fundamental practices of Islam is the fact that, if we look at the genesis of the Islamic Movement in seventh-century Mecca and endeavor to discern its *élan,* we cannot fail to locate its collective socio-economic aspects besides the spiritual and moral aspects. If one studies the early, short, forceful, and, indeed, explosive *sūras* (sections) of the Qur'ān, which, in the standard arrangement of the Qur'ān, appear at its end, we find only two themes insistently preached there. One is the unity of God, over against the sectional and tribal godlings of the Arabs, and the other is an essential egalitarianism, along with its obvious consequences of socio-economic and spiritual justice. Indeed, so strong is this second aspect that a pre-eminent present-day scholar of Islam, Professor H. A. R. Gibb, has said that Islam is essentially a social movement pressed into religious channels.[9] There also seems to exist, on reflection, a positive link between the moral-spiritual ideal of monotheism, on the one hand, and the idea of egalitarianism and of a just society, on the other. The Qur'ān seems to say that, if there is one God, then essentially there must be one humanity. It is on similar assumptions underlying the moral equality of man that Muslims formally resist the idea of a priesthood as an intermediary between God and the individual.

But from this very idea of equality, on the one hand, and social responsibility, on the other, also arises the inner tension within Islam which affected its religious history during subsequent developments —the tension between the claims of the individual and those of the collective institutions, notably the state and its laws. A brief outline of the history of these tensions will, in turn, enable us to appreciate better the nature and the magnitude of the problem which the modernist reformers of Muslim society are facing.

Due to the early rapid expansion of Islam beyond the Arabian Peninsula and the establishment of a vast empire, the exigencies of administration required the formulation of Islamic law. Roughly during the first century and a half after the death of the Prophet, most of the legal materials had come into existence, and even much of the morphology of Islamic law had been nebulously formulated. The rapid political developments and the formulation of law created an external framework and the necessary instruments for this framework of regulating life according to Islam. Now, since law regulates the external behavior of man in a social context, one necessary consequence of this brilliant but one-sided movement had been to emphasize almost exclusively the social content of Islam. A class of men grew up known as the *'Ulama* (learned men) or the *fuqahā* (learned jurists), who expressed expert opinion about what was Islamically lawful and what was not. This movement, together with the opportunism that is more or less inherent in political life, produced a strong reaction among certain sensitive spirits, who began emphasizing individual character, purity of the spirit, and the "life of the heart." These men are the forerunners of the famous Sūfī movement in Islam. They looked askance at the social developments of Islam, particularly political and legal, as being adequately expressive of Islam. There is little doubt that their contention was genuine enough, and, as said earlier, Islam lays great emphasis and, in fact, the final emphasis, on the quality of the individual and the inclusion of the spirit of *taqwā*.

But, unfortunately, what happened was that a dichotomy occurred in Muslim society at this juncture of its development which was absent both in the life of the Prophet and in the behavior of people immediately around the Prophet whom he had trained. This organic unity of life was upset. It was as though one unicellular organism had blown up into several cells, each functioning as a separate organism. There is no scope here to portray the entire historical career of the Sūfī movement; suffice it to say that henceforth we find a permanent tension between the 'Ulama and the Sūfīs, a tension which seemed to threaten the very fabric of the Islamic Community. What further aggravated the situation was that the 'Ulama were also functionaries of the state in various capacities, notably as judges and Muftis (official expounders of Muslim law). In the eyes of the Sūfī, this made the 'Ulama appear even more "worldly" and as instruments of the often despotic Sultans and Amirs.

From the twelfth century onward, when Sūfism became the religion of the masses, the individualist trend became universal in Islam and manifested itself in a phenomenon of a more or less antinomianism of all shades. There is in evidence, not only of a general rebellion against the social ethos of official orthodoxy, but, in numerous cases, also of an assertion of strictly individual morality, often degenerating into moral nihilism. This type of phenomenon has been studied ably and sympathetically and, indeed, interpreted with fervent conviction by a notable contemporary French Orientalist, Henri Corbin, whose writings constitute a vigorous attack on what he calls "Social Religion" in defense of the value of personal experience in religion.[10] The 'Ulama, for their part, held tenaciously to the bare external, legal structure of Islam and cared little for the value of the individual and his personal experience. But the 'Ulama, against the massive onslaught of Sūfism, gradually lost ground, until, from the eighteenth century onward, new reformist movements arose, beginning with Wahhabism in the heart of Arabia. These movements tried to go back to the Qur'ān and the teaching of the Prophet and endeavored to resume the threats afresh from there.

In the meantime, another fundamental tension between the demands of change and those of permanence and stability had taken an unfortunate turn within the field of activity of the 'Ulama themselves. After three centuries of hard labor and extraordinarily creative intellectual and legal activity, the 'Ulama imposed a halt upon themselves, and, in the interests of stability, refused to allow the individual the right of creative thinking. This is popularly known as "closing of the door of ijtihād" (one original thought). The late medieval centuries of Islam were characterized by a state of general stagnation. It is these reform movements again which, under the inspiration of a few outstanding and daring souls of the medieval era, fought to restore to the individual the right of independent thinking. This process is being helped still further by modern education. But, from our point of view, perhaps the most important characteristic of all these reform movements, one of the most conspicuous of which was launched by Shāh Walīy Allāh of Delhi (1702–1762) in the eighteenth century and led by his school after him, is the restoration of the balance which had been upset due to this onesided development of Sūfism during the middle ages, with its almost exclusive emphasis on the individual to the neglect of social well-being.[11] In his writings, Shāh Walīy Allāh always emphasized the establishment of a just and balanced society and tried to formulate principles of social organization while remaining true to the Islamic spiritual ideal, viz., the creation of the good individual. He tells us that in the constitution of reality, every individual has his proper place and scope, which are irrevocable and indissoluble. The proper aim of a society, therefore, is to provide for the nourishment of each individual according to his capacities. But without adequate and effective social fabric no individual life can be really nurtured. All these reform movements also try to restrain the exclusive individualism of the medieval form of Sūfism and aim at the establishment of a solid and sure social basis. The medieval manifestations of Sūfism, therefore, have suffered a great deal at the hands of the reform movements since the eighteenth century.

When we come to the period of Muslim history since the impact of the modern West, we notice certain new factors coming into play which, at first sight, give the impression that the balance has been somewhat tilted against the individual as such in the name of the state or the nation or society. This is because all Muslim peoples have had to wage a relentless fight, first of all, to gain freedom from foreign colonial powers. This effort naturally called for a collective all-out effort wherein the totality rather than the individual was stressed. In all these freedom movements, the religion of Islam has played an important role, consciously or semiconsciously, admittedly or non-admittedly. The second phase has supervened since the gaining of independence in most of the Muslim countries. This phase, which we are witnessing currently, is also characterized by certain factors which call primarily for unity and concerted efforts by the society as a whole. The truth is that in all these countries there is a tremendous desire for a rapid development which, in turn, requires a greater concentration of attention on the collective side than on the side of the individual. In this thrust for development, where over-all planning seems extremely necessary, certain social aspects of the Islamic religious teachings are understandably invoked. This is also, however, a transient phase in the life of the Muslim peoples, and, once a certain measure of development has been reached, it is certain that the emphasis on the importance of the individual will regain its true perspective. There is no evidence that the claims of the individual as such are being impaired in these societies, which basically remain true to the fundamental faith of Islam in the individual.

QUESTION: How far is the individual really free in Islam? It is usually thought that determinism and submission are characteristic of Islam. Are they? This is the most important question for us here, I would think.

ANSWER: You are right in saying that the most important question is about the idea of determinism in Islam and how far man can be free, under the determinism of the divine will, to follow the will of God and to submit to it or to reject it. There is little doubt that the idea of an omnipotent God is not easy to reconcile with that of individual human freedom. This is a problem, however, for all religions, except a religion, like Zoroastrianism, which patently believes in dualism. But, when people talk of the allegedly deterministic and, indeed, "despotic" character of the Islamic God, they simply do not have this basic difficulty in mind. What they are worried about is, e.g., that the Qur'ān says that God guides whomsoever he wills aright and whomsoever he wills he leads astray,[12] and such frequent expressions in the Qur'ān about the evildoers and unbelievers as "God has sealed their hearts," or "God has put a curtain on their eyes,"[13] etc., etc. From such verses it is then concluded that, if he himself leads people aright and astray and puts seals on their hearts and curtains on their eyes so that they cannot see and understand, and then punishes them for doing evil and rewards them for doing good, this seems the height of caprice and arbitrariness. The basic trouble is that people do not really understand what the Qur'ān is saying when it uses such expressions as those just quoted. To begin with, the Qur'ān never says that God leads people astray unconditionally. It always says, e.g., "God has not lead the evildoers aright,"[14] or "God never guides the unjust aright,"[15] etc. Thus, to begin with, there is no unconditional interference by God in human affairs, according to the Qur'ān. But it must be asked further, what is this conditional interference? The truth seems to be that, when the Qur'ān speaks in these terms, it is, to begin with, simply describing a psychological law about good and bad conduct. What the Qur'ān is saying is that the more evil acts a person does, in normal cases, the less he becomes capable of doing good deeds, and vice versa, until a critical point is reached when a hardened evildoer or a thoroughly habituated good-doer becomes so entrenched in his habits that it becomes with him a second nature, as it were. It is at this stage that the Qur'ān says of the evildoers that God does not guide them aright and that their hearts are sealed and curtains have been put on their eyes. All the Qur'ān intends is to issue a warning that a very critical point—indeed, *almost* a point of no return—has been reached. This is the normal working of the psychological law about good and evil conduct.

The question arises, however, that, if the Qur'ān is describing simply such a scientific psychological process, why does it not use scientific language, and why does it express itself in these terms? The answer is that *actually* there is no point either on the side of good or on the side of evil which is an absolute point of no return, that there is really no point in evil from which one cannot return, or at least try to return, and, similarly, there is no point on the side of good from which no fall is ever to be feared. Such cases, in fact, have been registered in thousands of instances in history—cases of sudden conversion in which hardened evildoers who were given up by all moralists and past redemption have suddenly experienced a complete reversal in their conscience. The Qur'ān wants to keep this door open, and, in fact, it uses the language that it uses as being calculated to *influence* precisely such evil cases. This is why it uses threatening terms rather than purely scientific descriptive language. This shows that the working of the moral law is not quite like that of physical law and that God's grace is present in the former in a distinct way.

There is, therefore, no arbitrary interference on the part of God with the exercise of freedom by man. Islam is submission to God's will. But God's will, which operates both at the physical and at the moral level, has to be discovered by man and then be conformed to. This is Islam. Of course, it is possible for a man willfully to disobey the will of God, but in this very freedom consists the real greatness of man.

QUESTION: How can Sūfism be construed as being individualistic when the very ideal of Sūfism is the losing of the individual in God or the Absolute?

ANSWER: The ideal of Sūfism is not the annihilation of the individual self in God. Sūfism has developed, since the third century of the Hejira (i.e., 9th century A.C.), certain pairs of antinomical but complementary concepts which insist that the mystic experience involved two moments or a double movement of the human ego, the first toward the inner, the annihilation of the self, and the other outward, or the regaining of a richer selfhood. This doctrine has been universally accepted by the Sūfīs. The various pairs of categories used to designate this double moment are "intoxication and sobriety," "inner and outer," "annihilation and survival," "unity and plurality," etc. This should put at rest the minds of all those who think that the mystic experience of Sūfism consists in a simple annihilation of the individual self. However, what I meant in my paper by Sūfism's being individualistic was that the Sūfī sought his salvation alone and in isolation from society, and this trend, when it became general, endangered the fabric of Islam as a social texture and made Muslim society more individualistic, or, rather, tended to make Muslims into isolated individuals.

[1] H. A. R. Gibb, *Mohammedanism* (Oxford: Oxford University Press, 1961), p. 25.
[2] *Ibid.*, VI:94.
[3] *Ibid.*, XIX:81.
[4] *Ibid.*, VI:164.
[5] *Ibid.*, II:30.
[6] *Ibid.*, II:31.
[7] *Ibid.*, XXIII:72.
[8] Gibb, *op. cit.*
[9] *Ibid.*
[10] For this problem, Henri Corbin's *L'Imagination creatrice dans le Soufisme d'Ibn 'Arabi* (Paris: Ernest Flammarion, 1958) is particularly important.
[11] There is no special work comprehensively devoted to an account of these reform-movements. Wilfred Cantwell Smith's *Islam in Modern History* (Princeton: Princeton University Press, 1958), however, contains some useful material. See also my forthcoming work, *Islam*, chap. III, to be published by George Weidenfeld & Nicolson, London.
[12] Qur'ān II:26; XIV:4.
[13] *Ibid.*, XI:7.
[14] *Ibid.*, V:111.
[15] *Ibid.*, II:258.

HORI ICHIRŌ[a]

The appearance of individual self-consciousness in Japanese religions and its historical transformations

I. INTRODUCTION

I would like, on this occasion, to discuss the problem of self-consciousness and the ultimate destiny of individuals as seen in the history of Japanese religion. However, I must confine myself to pointing out only a few main historical currents, especially within the early stages of Japanese religious history, when those conceptions so pervasive to the present-day Japanese people seem to have been founded. Emphasis, therefore, will be placed primarily on the first stage or the appearance of these conceptions, and, secondarily, on the following stages of the historical transformations, which were brought about by the introduction into Japan of the Tendai sect (T'ien-t'ai[b] in Chinese), the Shingon sect (Cheng-yen[c] in Chinese), and the Amidaist movement of the Pure Land school.

II. PRIMITIVE RELIGIOUS FOUNDATION—SHINTŌ[d] IN PRE-BUDDHIST JAPAN

Primitive Shintō, or primitive religious forms, in ancient Japan, should be classified into two categories. The first category may be defined as the *ujigami*[e] type (tutelary or guardian shrine system), which was based on the particular family or clan system. Each family had its own shrine as a central symbol of its solidarity as dedicated to the ancestral spirit (*kami*[f]),[1] those who had been worshipped and enshrined successively by their descendants. This type of belief system is characterized by particularism and exclusiveness from other families, so that the main function is to integrate all the members of the family into the patriarchal hierarchy of the family system. The maintenance of the good name of a hereditary family, continuing their ancestors' glorious work from generation to generation, was the most important responsibility, not only for the patriarch, but also for all the family members.[2] Heavy emphasis on ancestor-worship and filial piety (*kō*[g]) in almost all Japanese religious groups has been connected closely with the ancient family system and the *ujigami* system founded on the cultivation of rice fields. Strictly speaking, there are

227

no means for the salvation of individuals within the *ujigami* system. Rather, the ultimate destiny of individuals was conceived in terms of their loss of identity and joining with a vague community of ancestral spirits after death,[3] although there existed distinctions according to their social, political, and also magico-religious status.

The second category may be called the *hitogami*[h] type (man-god system), which was based on the close relationship of an individual *kami* with a religious specialist such as a shaman or a medicine man. More integrative state-systems, such as village states or small-scale united kingdoms which appeared in ancient Japan, supposedly were ruled by charismatic or shamanic leaders such as Pi-mi-ko[i] of the Yamatai[j] kingdom in the third century A.D.[4] This type of belief is characterized by the strong individuality both of the individual *kami* and of its transmitter, who lived for a long time in the memory of the believers, and their functions came to influence ordinary individuals. With this type of *kami*, sincere reverence and obedience were the only conditions to gain the *kami*'s favor, regardless of the believers' origins. Charismatic personages and their descendants entered into a special relationship with their *hitogami* and created a kind of *ujigami* system independently, playing an important role in the politics of ancient theocratic ages by utilizing their divine power for blessing or curses. However, this belief in the *hitogami* seems not to have provided for any salvation or after-life for individuals, even though only the charismatic personages could be easily deified by their relationship with the *hitogami*.[5]

Under the rigidity of the ancient Japanese social structure and value system that apparently was characterized by the primacy of political values, the emphasis on *on*[k] (blessings or favors handed down, not only by invisible beings, but also by social and political superiors) and on *hōon*[l] (obligation of the recipient to return something for these blessings) had increased.[6] As Watsuji Tetsurō[m] has pointed out, the Japanese social structure and value system took the shape of a human relationship which is strictly controlled and regulated by the patriarch according to the status of each member of the family.[7] However, the patriarch, in turn, must be responsible to the higher authorities of the nation at large as well as to his ancestors. Even the emperor himself is responsible to his ancestors for his behavior and must account to them. In the Japanese way of thinking which emerged from the context of such a value system, there could be no room to develop the concept of an "Almighty God," as in the traditions of Judaism, Christianity, and Islam. On the contrary, Japanese *kami*, as well as men, are not considered as independent personalities, but as lowly figures dependent on their superior in either the divine or the social hierarchy, and in need of salvation and help. In this context, the superiors, including human beings and ancestors, were believed to be semi-*kami* (demi-gods) or even low-ranking *kami* or *buddhas*. Being linked with ancestor-worship and dependence upon superiors, the belief in spirits of the dead and also the idea of the intimate connections between men and *kami* (in other words, ease in deification of human beings) were and even today are quite widespread and important.[8] The dead are commonly called *hotokesama*[n] (*buddhas*), a fact which surprised Sir Charles Eliot. He says that this bold language is peculiar to Japan and is an imitation of Shintō teaching, according to which the dead become *kami*, superhuman beings. It could hardly be admitted that the Buddhist dead had a status inferior to *kami*, and therefore in popular speech they were termed *buddhas, buddhas* and *kami* being much the same.[9]

III. INTRODUCTION OF CONFUCIANISM AND BUDDHISM TO JAPAN AND THEIR INFLUENCE, ESPECIALLY ON PRINCE SHŌTOKU'S WAY OF THINKING

The introduction of Confucianism in the fourth century and of Buddhism in the middle of the sixth century from China via Korea to Japan greatly influenced the attitudes of the ruling-class peoples and intelligentsia from the outset. The idea of and belief in *T'ien*[o] or *Ten* (Heaven) and *T'ien-ti*[p] (Lord of Heaven), as well as social ethics and moral codes, were introduced by the Confucian teachers, and some ideas of the philosophy of Lao Tzu[q] and Chuang Tzu[r] were accepted. Several instances of Chinese influences are clearly seen in ancient historical documents.[10] On the other hand, the universalistic metaphysics and principles, such as the law of causality, the Three Seals of Law (impermanence, non-self, and *nirvāṇa*), and the equality of all human beings were introduced by the Buddhist priests. These kinds of religious and moral codes were rather contrary to the exclusiveness and discrimination of original Shintō. The aim of Shintō prayer was never individual salvation, but only group salvation or unification with the spirits of ancestors. However, Buddhist influence gradually penetrated into Shintō beliefs, introducing the element of individual salvation, so that it promoted the tendency for some Shintō *kami* to have a particular divine favor according to their own functions.

Confucian and Buddhist universalism and rationalism had a great influence on the spiritual attitude of Prince Shōtoku[s] (574–622) and his adherents. He was venerated by all Japanese Buddhist scholars and monks as the real founder of Japanese Buddhism, since he promoted Confucian ethics and Buddhist teachings in various ways. Prince Shōtoku actually declared these to be a proper basis for the state. He prepared in person the Seventeen-Article Constitution (*Jūshichi jō kempō*[t]) with the purpose of establishing an ideal harmonious state in the land. Evidently his ideas and thoughts were revolutionary and much beyond his time. The first clause pleads that harmony is to be valued and avoidance of wanton opposition to be honored, according to the spirit of the Confucian *Analects* and Buddhist teachings. In order to realize his utopian society, Prince Shōtoku recommended three major principles to his peoples: sincere reverence of Buddhism (Second Article), sincere obedience and loyalty to the Holy Sovereign (Third Article), and appropriate behavior (Chinese *li*[u]; Japanese *rei*) for their leading principle (Fourth Article).[11]

Prince Shōtoku's understanding of Buddhism and especially his viewpoint regarding individuality are to be seen in the Second Article and also the Tenth Article. He said, "Since [the Three Treasures of] Buddhism, viz., the Buddha, the Law (*Dharma*) and the Order (*Sáṃgha*), are the final refuge of all beings, and are the supreme objects of faith in all countries, what man in any age can fail to reverence this doctrine? Few men are utterly bad; they may be taught to follow the doctrine, but, if they do not betake themselves to the Three Treasures, wherewithal shall their crookedness be made straight?" Again, in the Tenth Article, he declares, "Let us cease from wrath, and refrain from angry looks. Nor let us be resentful when others differ from us. For all men have hearts, and each heart has its own leanings. Their right is our wrong, and our right is their wrong. We are not unquestionably sages, nor are they unquestionably fools. Both of us are simply ordinary men (*bom-pu*[v]). How can any one lay down a rule by which to distinguish right from wrong? For we are all, one with another, wise and foolish, like a ring which has no end. . . ."[12]

According to the *Nihongi*[w] and other documents, Prince Shōtoku usually instructed his consorts and descendants with the sayings: "This world should be empty and evanescent, while the Buddha himself alone should be real and true"[13] and "Avoid wickedness of every kind, practice good of every kind."[14] Being strongly impressed by these teachings, his eldest son, Prince Yamashiro-no-Ōye[x], refrained from military defense against his enemy's attack, saying, "For the sake of myself, I was unwilling to destroy the people; therefore, I deliver myself up to my enemy." Finally, he and all members of his family strangled themselves and died together at their family temple, Hōryūji[y]. Their tragic death marked the beginning of the Taika Reformation[z] (645–650), which put into effect their ancestors' principles.[15] Prince Shōtoku especially brought all his mind to bear upon *The Lotus Sūtra* (*Saddharma-puṇḍarīka-sūtra*),[16] which taught a social consciousness that encompassed all classes. *The Lotus*

Sūtra's promise of salvation for all mankind was in sharp contrast with pre-Buddhistic religious conceptions in Japan.

Buddhism was also conceived as a religion which gave security in this life and salvation for the individual in the afterlife. After Prince Shōtoku's death, his survivors with heartfelt prayers made two kinds of *maṇḍalas* and a life-size image of Śākyamuni Buddha for the sake of the departed Prince's spirit. The two *maṇḍalas* were called *Tenju-koku mandara*[aa] (*Maṇḍala* of the Heavenly-Life Paradise),[17] where they believed that Shōtoku's spirit must have been reborn. After this time, we find many written copies of Buddhist *Sūtras,* statues of the Buddha, paintings, and *maṇḍalas,* as well as temples, *buddha* halls, and pagodas, all of which were dedicated to the spirits of the dead with their relatives' prayers for salvation of the deceased.[18]

IV. STATE BUDDHISM AND INDIVIDUAL OR PERSONAL BUDDHISM

On the other hand, as pointed out in the previous section, the universalism and rationalism of Confucianism and Buddhism were not necessarily fully appreciated in the beginning, except by Prince Shōtoku and his followers, but were accepted on a traditionalistic level. At first, the *ujidera*[ab] system (the tutelary temple system) became institutionalized, manifesting almost the same character as the *ujigami* system.[19] For in the initial acceptance of Buddhism the Buddha had been called a *hotokegami*[ac] (a *kami* named a *buddha*) and recognized as a kind of *kami* from abroad, and the Buddhist temple was called *hotokegami no miya*[ad] (a shrine dedicated to the *kami* called *hotoke* [a *buddha*]).[20] When in A.D. 594 Empress Suiko[ae] instructed Prince Shōtoku and all of her subjects to promote the prosperity of Buddhism, the *Nihongi* says that all the princes, princesses, and subjects vied with one another in erecting Buddhist shrines for the benefit of their lords and parents (or ancestors).[21]

Also, State Buddhism flourished mainly after the Taika Reformation in A.D. 645, modeled after the state-shrine system under the Chinese influence of the unified empire system of the Sui[af] (581–618) and T'ang[ag] (618–906) dynasties. *Ninnō gokoku hannya hara-mittakyō*[ah] (*Prajñā-pāramitā-sūtra on a King Who Protects His Country*)[22] and the *Konkōmyō saishōōkyō*[ai] (*Suvarṇa-prabhāsot-tama-rāja-sūtra*)[23] were selected from the Tripiṭaka by Emperor Temmu[aj] (622–686) and distributed all over Japan to be recited and interpreted for the benefit of public security and the prosperity and the welfare of the nation.[24]

However, the harmonious connection between State Buddhism and individual Buddhism may be seen in the spirit of the erection of the Great Vairocana at Tōdaiji[ak] in Nara[al] under Emperor Shōmu[am]

(701–756) and his consort Kōmyō[an], with the explanation that this
Buddha (the Great Sun Buddha—Dainichi Nyorai[ao]) and the myth-
ical ancestress of the Imperial Family, Amaterasu Ōmikami[ap] (Sun
Goddess), are one and the same. That is to say, the emperor wanted
to make manifest his pious belief in Buddhism as well as his own
sovereignty, and, again, he eagerly desired to be reborn in the Great
Vairocana's lotus realm (*padma-garbha-loka-dhātu*)[25] following the
Avataṁsaka-sūtra's cosmological theories of the Kegon sect[aq] (Chinese, Hua-yen). This is the first historical indication of the commin-
gling of Buddhism with Shintō, which afterwards developed the
theories of the blending of Shintō *kami* and *buddhas* (or *bodhi-
sattvas*, beings whose essence is perfect wisdom; often translated
"would-be *buddha*") named *honji suijaku*[ar] (manifestation of the
prime noumenon).[26] However, Emperor Shōmu adopted the *chishikiji*[as] system when he erected the Great Sun Buddha, which had
just appeared among common believers in local communities in the
eighth century. *"Chishiki"* means a fraternity of Buddhist believers
in the same *buddha, bodhi-sattva,* or Sūtra, and *"chishikiji"* means
a Buddhist temple built with the alms and help of a *chishiki* fraternity.[27] Emperor Shōmu wanted to let all districts make contributions toward the erection of the Great Sun Buddha, even a token gift
such as a handful of soil or a spray of a tree. Having been deeply
impressed by the emperor's edict, a Buddhist saint, Gyōgi[at] (670?–
749), traveled through the country to ask the common people for
offerings so that they would be saved by the Great Sun Buddha along
with the emperor himself as the members of the *chishiki* fraternity.[28]
Here we can see the historical subsumption of individual or personal
Buddhism to State Buddhism.[29] Gyōgi also endeavored to distribute
to the common people the Buddha's teachings centering around the
law of causality, and engaged in public-welfare services based on the
way of the *bodhisattva* (*bosatsu-dō*[au]).[30]

Saichō, who aspired to develop an indigenous form of Buddhism,
favored the belief in Amida[av] (*Amitābha* or *Amitayus* in Sanskrit)
Butsu concerning ultimate destiny, as well as concerning meditation
on the mystery of existence which leads to enlightenment. He regarded the prayer and contemplation of Amida (*Nembutsu*[aw]) as
a means of clearing the mind and enabling it to concentrate on the
presence of Amida and also as a means for the spirit to be saved after
death by Amida's merciful hand.

Belief in Amida Buddha and *jōgyō zammai*[ax] practice, especially
in reference to the ultimate destiny of individuals, was strongly promoted by an eminent disciple and successor of Saichō whose name
was Ennin[ay] or Jikaku Daishi[az] (794–864).[31] Ennin studied about
nine years in T'ang (618–906) China, mainly at Mount Wu-t'ai[ba]
and in Ch'ang-an[bb]. He brought back to Japan many *maṇḍalas,*

religious paraphernalia, and *Sūtras* of both Mantrayāna and T'ien-t'ai Buddhism, as well as the belief and practice of Amida, influenced by Hui-yüan[bc] (334–416) of Mount Lu[bd] and Fa-chao[be] (about the eighth century) of Mount Wu-t'ai in the Chinese Pure Land school. After he became the third patriarch of the Tendai sect, Ennin built the *Jōgyō zammaidō*[bf] Seminary in the precincts of Enryakuji[bg] on Mount Hiei[bh]. Thereafter, the *Nembutsu* practice of the *Jōgyōdō*[bi] Seminary became, not only an important practice of meditation for Tendai monks, but also an important annual function for the salvation of the spirits of the dead.[32]

V. KŪKAI'S APPROACH TO THE CONCEPT OF SALVATION AND ENLIGHTENMENT

On the other hand, Kūkai[bj], the founder of the Shingon sect (at Mount Kōya[bk]), incorporated the insight of other sects, but his central focus was *The Great Sun Sūtra*,[33] which teaches that the phenomenal world is a manifestation of the sole ultimate reality known as the Great Sun Buddha (Dainichi Nyorai).

In contrast to Saichō[bl], Kūkai preferred, on the one hand, the belief in the Great Sun Buddha representing two aspects of *vajra-dhātu* (diamond element) and *garbha-dhātu* (womb element),[34] and, on the other hand, he entrusted his ultimate destiny to the future Buddha Maitreya (*Miroku*[bm]) in the Tuṣita Heaven (*Tosotsu ten*[bn]), who would come down to this world in order to save human beings 5,670,000,000 years after Buddha Śākyamuni's death.[35]

From the former belief, Kūkai insisted on the theory of "becoming a *buddha* in one's body" (*sokushin jōbutsu*[bo]), following the cosmological and metaphysical theories of the *Mahā-vairocana-sūtra* and the *Avataṁsaka-sūtra*. Kūkai wrote several outstanding books[36] in which he criticized and classified all the spiritual and religious stages of mankind from the lowest to the highest (or Shingon) level, proceeding through the lower stages of natural religion and ethics, Confucianism, Taoism, Theravāda, and, finally, Mahāyāna Buddhism. The highest (or Shingon) stage is not a mere system of doctrine, but the actual embodiment of the life and idea of the Great Vairocana, especially by means of the performance of mystic rites. This condition of spiritual development is called "the soul filled with the glories of mystery," which expression is explained by the analogy that the *buddhas* in the innumerable *buddha*-lands are naught but the *buddha* within our own soul; the Golden Lotus, as manifold as drops of water in the ocean, is living in our body. These words remind us of the Advaita Vedānta, but there is a difference in that Shingon theology insists that the phenomenal world is a manifestation of the only ultimate reality known as the Great Sun Buddha.

This theory of becoming a *buddha* in one's body does not mean that the individual is annihilated but that he embodies absolute reality in his body itself.[37]

These theories and beliefs, together with those of *The Lotus Sūtra* and Amida Buddha of the Tendai sect, were widely accepted, not only by all the branches of the Tendai and Shingon sects, but also by various other Buddhists. Even in the Tendai sect, the theory of *sokushin jōbutsu* was accepted by the end of the ninth century,[38] and also by Nichiren[bp], the reformer of *The Lotus Sūtra*'s school, in the thirteenth century,[39] while in the Shingon sect the belief in Amida was accepted for the purpose of securing of the afterlife of individuals.

Kūkai was believed to have become a *buddha* in his own body while still absorbed in meditation and awaiting the advent of Maitreya in the cave sanctuary at Mount Kōya. There were several mountaineering ascetics (Yamabushi[bq] or Shugenja[br]) of *shugendō*[bs][40] of the Shingon tradition who became self-mummified *buddhas* following their great master's legendary model.[41]

VI. THE AWARENESS OF THE ARRIVAL OF THE LATTER AGE OF THE BUDDHA'S LAW AND THE EMERGENCE OF THE AMIDIST MOVEMENT

Prince Shōtoku, Saichō, and Kūkai are the most remarkable personages in the early stages of Japanese religion to emphasize the dignity of individuals, as well as the ultimate destiny of individuals. However, after the two great masters' deaths, the Tendai and Shingon sects gradually declined into occult mysticism and ritualism and became secularized in conspiracy with the Imperial Family and the nobility. The high ideals and the metaphysics of the two great masters' intentions were thus degraded into superstitious performances and abused in justifying this degeneration. Consequently, if a person awakening to real religious conviction wanted to live a life of seeking after the Buddha's truth and distributing the Buddha's teachings, he had to deny the ecclesiastical organizations and escape from them anew.[42]

Having strongly resisted the extremely secularized and formalized Buddhist institutions, the new religious movement, called the *hijiri*[bt] (holy man) movement,[43] stressed the essential importance of individual faith and antisecularism. This should be described as the movement "from magico-religious and secular restrictions to the spiritual freedom of individuals." This movement suddenly appeared in the latter part of the tenth and the early part of the eleventh centuries; Kyōshin[bu],[44] Kōya[bv], Jakushin[bw],[45] Genshin[bx] (known as Eshin Sōzu[by]), and Ryōnin[bz][46] may be pointed out as *hijiri* representatives of the Amidists. Zōga[ca],[47] Shōkū[cb],[48] and others were *hijiris* from *The Lotus Sūtra*'s school, though some different attitudes should be recognized between the two groups of *hijiris*. The *hijiris* of *The Lotus Sūtra* school, for example, were characterized by strict seclusion from both the secular and the ecclesiastical worlds, while the Amidist *hijiris* were characterized by the distribution of Amida's gospel among the masses; the Lotus school *hijiris* should be defined as individualistic or self-perfectionistic, the Amidist *hijiris* as evangelistic.

Since the fear and awareness of entering the fateful Age of the Latter Law had penetrated, not only the orthodox Buddhist priests and upper class peoples, but also even the lower classes and country people, we should point out the two reactions or adjustments to this consciousness of crisis: (1) helpless despair and anxiety which largely overwhelmed orthodox Buddhist priests and the sophisticated upper class;[49] and (2) the forerunners of the new movement mentioned above endeavored to find ways of self-enlightenment to cope with this hopeless and depraved age as a given reality, as well as striving for the salvation of the common people in their everyday life. Genkū[cc] and Shinran[cd] (the followers of the Amidist group and its organizers), Eisai[ce] and Dōgen[cf] (Zen masters), and Nichiren (the successor of the Lotus school *hijiri* and the founder of the Nichiren sect) appeared in the twelfth and thirteenth centuries under the direct influence of the new movement and the consciousness of the arrival of the Latter Age.

VII. RELIGIOUS REFORMATION—FROM GENSHIN TO GENKŪ

Among the several Amidists in the tenth century, Kōya should be considered as a pioneer. Kōya hid himself among the citizens of Kyoto, strongly encouraging them in the belief of Amida and recommending the *Nembutsu* practice for the sake of their individual salvation.[50] Then Genshin (942–1017) advanced the Amidist movement in a different way. Genshin devoted himself to writing his well-known work entitled *Ō-jō yō-shū*[cg] (Birth in Amida's paradise),[51] as well as to organizing the fraternity of *Nijūgo zammai kesshū*[ch] (Assurance of Rebirth in Amida's paradise).[52] In the preface to the *Ō-jō yō-shū* written in 984, he said that the teachings and practices for rebirth in Amida's paradise were the best suited for the corrupt world of the Latter Age. Everyone, priest and layman, high and low, must be converted to faith in Amida's paradise; however, the Buddha's teachings were divided into apparent doctrines (*kengyō*[ci]) and secret doctrines (*mikkyō*[cj]) consisting of various theories and austerities. Although for the wise and diligent man it would not be difficult to understand and practice these several doctrines, the stupid and obstinate man "like Genshin" could be saved only by invoking the name of Amida Buddha.[53]

This idea expressed by Genshin struck a response in nearly every heart and gave a great incentive to simple faith in the grace of Amida, who had opened the gateway of his paradise to all without distinction of training or knowledge. The original vow taken by Amida was believed to have the mysterious power to save those unable to undergo vigorous training in spiritual exercise or disciplinary life. Emphasis was put on pious devotion to Amida's mercy and his original vow.

Genkū (known as Hōnen Shōnin[ck], 1133–1212), after having searched in the Tripiṭaka to find the best way to salvation in the Latter Age, discovered and was converted to the works of Shan-tao[cl] of the Chinese Pure Land school, as well as to the works of Genshin. Genkū abandoned and criticized the "way for the wise" (shōdō mon[cm]) through severe training, intricate ritualism, and methodic contemplation, as well as belief in "salvation by one's own power" (jiriki[cn]) and belief in the Buddhist and Shintō pantheons (in Japanese, zōgyō[co]). He taught that the way to the Pure Land is necessarily through simple faith in Amida's grace, which is called the "easy way" (igyō[cp]) of salvation. This is in contrast to the "difficult way" (nangyō[cq]) of perfection. The "easy way" is also called "salvation by another's, i.e., Amida's, power" (tariki[cr]). Genkū inevitably alienated himself from the complicated teachings and practices of the prevailing forms of Buddhism and finally came to declare his independence and to achieve thereby a religious reformation.[54]

His major work establishing the independence of his sect, named Jōdoshū[cs], is the Senjaku hongan nembutsu shū[ct] (On the Nembutsu of the Original Vow),[55] written in 1198 (or 1204). But the most intense statement of his belief and teaching is to be seen in his last handwritten essay, entitled Ichimai kishō mon[cu] (On Genkū's Final Enlightenment):[56]

> What I teach is neither a sort of meditation such as has been talked of by many priests both in China and in our own country, nor is it an invocation such as is possible only to those who have grasped by thought its real meaning. No, all that is needed to secure birth in the paradise (Pure Land) of perfect bliss is merely to repeat the words "Namu Amida Butsu"[cv] without a doubt that one will certainly arrive there. Such details as the three states of mind and the fourfold practice[57] are all included in the repetition of the expression "Namu Amida Butsu" with perfect faith. Had I any other profound doctrine besides this, I should miss the mercy of the two Holy Ones[58] and have no share in the vow of Amida. But those who believe in the power of calling on the Buddha's name, though they may have thoroughly studied all the doctrines which Shaka[cw] taught in the course of his whole life, should be-

have like a simple man of the people who cannot read a word or like an ignorant nun, and without giving themselves airs of wisdom should simply fervently call on the name of the Buddha.

Here we can clearly see Genkū's intentions: rationalization and simplification of religious theory and form; concentration of religious piety—pure and simple faith; emphasis on the rejection of over-speculation or ritualism; and emphasis on salvation of the lowest level of the people.

VIII. TRIUMPH OF RELIGIOUS SIMPLICITY AND RATIONALITY— SHINRAN AND RENNYO[cx]

Genkū's principle had strong influence on the reformative movements of Buddhism, as well as on Shintō in the Kamakura Period[cy] (1185–1333). Among them, Shinran, (1173–1262) advanced Genkū's theory several steps, though he had been a pious pupil of Genkū and intended sincerely to succeed him and to distribute his gospel. He said that as far as Shinran was concerned his sole reason for repeating the *Nembutsu* lay in the teaching of the good man (Genkū) who made him understand that the only condition of salvation is to say the *Nembutsu*.[59]

According to Shinran, human nature is originally so sinful and hopeless and the situation of the times and of society so absolutely confused that no one could attain spiritual enlightenment and peace by his own power unless he threw himself for support on the Other's mysterious power. Therefore, the original vow of Amida, expressing the desire to save without exception even the lowest and most wicked person, should be the one and only foundation for salvation of individuals in the Latter Age. His famous ironical expression that "even a good man will be received into the Buddha's Land, how much more a bad man!" played upon a saying of the regular Amidists that "even a bad man will be received into the Buddha's Land, how much more a good man!" Neither virtue nor wisdom, but faith, was his fundamental tenet, and faith itself has nothing to do with our own intention or attainment but is solely the Buddha's free gift.[60] "Calling the Buddha's name" in pious devotion and absolute trust in Amida is the way to salvation, but there is no value whatsoever in theorizing about the actual process of invocation.

Shinran carried the idea of Genkū to extreme simplicity in his doctrine of "once calling" (*ichinengi*[cz]), though Kōsai[da] and others among Genkū's disciples also advocated *ichinen'gi*.[61] Shinran was far from objecting to the repetition of the *Nembutsu*, but he held that the essential thing was to say that prayer with full faith and confidence in the Buddha; furthermore, that one such believing utterance is sufficient to secure birth in Amida's Land, and that all subsequent repetitions are to be regarded simply as expressions of joy and gratitude. Shinran strictly denied the formal temple-and-priest system of his time, following his teacher Genkū's principle, as well as the tradition of the Amidist movement in former times. He never lived in a temple but in huts or small hermitages, mainly in the East Province far from Kyoto, and preached his doctrine among the country people. He married, reared a family, and in every way lived like a normal citizen or farmer. Shinran severely criticized ritualism, magic or divination, and the worship of the old pantheon. The worship offered to Amida does not consist of prayers for health or temporal welfare or any such petitions. After a man has once obtained faith in Amida, he commits all to his power, and his worship consists of nothing but thanksgiving.[62]

The rationalizing tendencies in the Jōdo-Shin[db] sect were promoted by Rennyo (1415–1499). Rennyo was Shinran's direct descendant, and is often called the second founder of the Shin sect because of his great influence on its development and theoretical formulation. Rennyo opposed the practice of austerities and meditation, insisting on the practice of Confucian virtues in daily life and on obedience to state authorities, while, at the same time, one's inner life was to be given up wholly to Amida Buddha. Rennyo opposed any worship of Shintō deities. Until recent times, almost all Shin sect families had no shelf for the family *kami*, as well as no charms, talismans, or amulets in their house; there is merely a huge decorative Buddhist altar dedicated to Amida alone. There are no mortuary tablets in the Shin sect Buddhist altar as in those of other Buddhist families. He made an important advance with respect to the ethico-religious regulation of everyday life. He wrote his main work, entitled *Ofumi*[dc] (Collected Writings),[63] completely in colloquial Japanese (as contrasted to the formal Chinese style of writing) for the sake of the common, uneducated people's understanding. Rennyo's remark that "if we engage in business, we must realize that it is in the service of Buddhism," indicates his view of the occupational life as integrated with the religious life. He also stressed the obligation of bestowing blessings on the people, and this-worldly asceticism, as well as returning for Amida's blessings.

Here we see the most radically rationalizing Buddhist sect in Japan, together with Zen Buddhism, which was introduced from China at the time of Genkū and Shinran. Though the Shin sect gradually declined into an institutionalized religious order and became secularized in the course of its history, the principles established by Shinran and Rennyo should be recognized as a close Japanese analogy to Western Protestantism, and its ethics as quite similar to the Protestant ethics described in Max Weber's famous work.[64] This should be called the beginning of spiritual modernization in Japanese religion.

IX. CONCLUSION

By way of conclusion, I would like to point out some common tendencies manifested in the major Japanese religions as well as in the folk-beliefs which several scholars have mentioned with some validity in speaking of Japanese religion as an entity, in spite of the variety of its manifestations: (1) emphasis on filial piety (*kō*) and ancestor-worship connected with the Japanese family system and agriculture from ancient times; (2) deep-seated and common beliefs in spirits of the dead in connection with ancestor-worship, as well as with more animistic conceptions of malevolent or benevolent spirit-activities; (3) emphasis on *on* (debts or favors given by superiors, human or superhuman) and *hōon* (the return of *on*); (4) continuity between man and deity or ease in deification of human beings; (5) mutual borrowing and mixing of different religious traditions, in other words, a syncretistic character; (6) co-existence of heterogeneous religions in one family or in one person.

Because the gap between the religious élites and the masses in Japan is so broad and deep even today, consciousness of individuality among the people, in the Western sense, seems to have been undeveloped. Also, because of the supremacy of group-consciousness and the political value-system seemingly based on the ancient socio-cultural religious system, individualism and universalism did not necessarily develop completely among the common people. However, certain particularistic tendencies still survive even in modern industrial Japan.

In the first stage of the history of Japanese religion, from the earliest times to the Medieval Age, we see that, especially on the intellectual level, the vague formless conceptions of individual self-consciousness and the ultimate destiny of the individuals in the primitive Shintō age gradually became more explicit with the introduction and influences of Chinese philosophy and ethics (Confucianism and Taoism) and of Indian religion (Buddhism) as the turning points. Though there were a few exceptional intelligentsia in the pre-Buddhist age in Japan, the great role played by Prince Shōtoku at the first stage of the ethico-religious enlightenment, depending mainly upon the introduction of Confucian ethics and the Mahāyāna Buddhist spirit, was important.

The second stage was opened under the leadership of Saichō and Kūkai. Having been deeply influenced by Shōtoku's idealism, principally *The Lotus Sūtra,* Saichō insisted on and spoke out for the dignity of the individual. His idealistic theories on the equality of human nature and *buddha*hood penetrated and dominated Japanese intellectuals. Among Kūkai's doctrines, the idea and practice of becoming a *buddha* in one's *body* (*sokushin jōbutsu*) enjoyed great esteem and acceptance, not only by Buddhist priests, but also by many of the intelligentsia and common people. Even the Tendai and Nichiren sects inclined to accept this teaching. Zen Buddhists were also under the influence of this idea, though they transformed it into the idea of becoming a *buddha* in one's *mind* (*sokushin jōbutsu*). Saichō and Kūkai are presupposed to have been the theoretical pioneers of the amalgamation between Shintō and Buddhism. For the first time, they and their followers established Shintō theologies and metaphysics, respectively, and Shintō *kami* became personalized and functionalized. The prevalence of Shintō theologies based on Tendai and Shingon doctrines was considered to have had a deep influence on the common people in the development of the self-consciousness of individuals even at the popular level.

The third stage of the history of Japanese religion is in the Kamakura period (1186–1392), the twelfth and thirteenth centuries, when several religious reforms flourished simultaneously, both in Buddhist and in Shintō circles. Kamakura Buddhism might be evaluated as the establishment of a truly Japanized Buddhism for the first time, because of the following features: (1) rationalization and simplification of religious theory and form; (2) concentration of religious piety—pure and simple faith and devotion; (3) emphasis on religious practice in connection with the daily life of the believers and rejection of over-speculation as well as of complicated magico-religious ritualism—all of which were symbolized by the special term of the "easy way" of salvation.

Nevertheless, we should not overlook the factors that became the direct causes of religious reforms in the early Kamakura period: (1) the rise and prevalence of the critical consciousness of the arrival of the Age of the Latter Law, and (2) the religious movements of the *hijiri* (saintly men) groups. These emerged mainly on the basis of the self-consciousness of individuality and the ultimate destiny of individuals, and in turn stimulated that critical consciousness.

Generally speaking, Tendai, Shingon, and Zen Buddhism exerted strong influence on the religious élite and intellectuals, as is symbolized by Dōgen's famous saying that he wanted to cultivate only one disciple or even a half in his life. On the other hand, Shugendō, the Amidist sects, and the Nichiren sect have been a main basis of the formation of the self-consciousness of individuality and of the ultimate destiny of individuals among the common people. Zen Buddhism on the intellectual level and the Shin sect on the popular level have played more important roles than any other movements from the viewpoint of our present problem. Indeed, a major factor in Japanese spiritual modernization that historically prepared the basis for the Meiji Restoration (1868) and the industrialization of modern Japan was the role played by Shin and Zen believers. Their rationalistic faith and practices, together with rationalistic Confucian ethics, established the religious and moral codes of warriors (Bushidō[dd]) in the Kamakura period, and then their influence reached to the self-awareness of the way of the merchant or the tradesman's spirit (*shōnindō*[de]) as well as on the formation of the craftsman's spirit (*shokunindō*[df]) in the Tokugawa period[dg] (1615–1867).

On the other hand, the individual self-consciousness of the peasantry was enlightened and promoted by Rennyo and his followers, as witnessed, for example, in the peasant revolts in the sixteenth century waged by those who had ardent faith in Amida.

Although the Meiji Restoration[dh] and the industrialization of modern Japan were brought about directly by the new movements of Neo-Confucianism and the revival of pure or nationalistic Shintō, as well as by Western colonialism, we should not overlook the great part played in the development of individual consciousness in the history of Japanese religion and ethics especially by Shin and Zen believers from medieval to modern times.

QUESTION: You use the terms "rationalization" and "simplification" several times. I have some difficulty in seeing the meaning of "rationalization" in these connections. I wonder whether you do not have in mind "anti-supernaturalism" or some such idea. Please consider whether you really mean "rationalization" at these points.

ANSWER: By the term "rationalization" I mean the tendency of what we call "from magic to metaphysic" or "freeing the world of magic." In the primitive or "magical" religions, the concept of the divine tends to be extremely diffuse, and permeates daily life. In this way, religion undoubtedly functions toward the stereotyping of life in traditionalistic societies.

The new conception of the sacred and of religious action I mentioned which mark the emergence of universalistic religions out of primitive traditionalism are characterized by a relatively high degree of "rationalization." These original rationalizing directions had a determining effect on the subsequent development of these traditions. The concept of the divine is usually more abstract and more simple, and less diffuse, than that of the primitive religions. Concomitantly, religious action is simplified, is made less situational, and is concerned with a more direct relation with the divine. The important point of these rationalizing tendencies lies in the changes in attitudes and actions of the individuals, which lead to important effects far beyond the sphere of religion—modernization and industrialization.[65]

QUESTION: I am interested chiefly in your idea of faith. This concept has been so essential to Christianity that I am anxious to understand it in other traditions. What is the basic connotation of the term "faith" in Shinran? Does it mean committing the self to a discipline, to a belief?

I was particularly interested in why it is called "the easy way." Is that because it is opposed to self-discipline or "works"? Is it because it involves trust in a power beyond the individual self? Another way of approaching the problem is to ask what the easy way is contrasted with, i.e., what is the "difficult way"?

ANSWER: The expression "easy way" was first used by Nāgārjuna, but it was Shan-tao who elaborated this term as the most important way to attain enlightenment, because, according to Shan-tao, the essential quality of the utterance of the name of Amida is nothing but the Vow of Amida, that is, the meaning of the utterance began to change from human practice to the Buddha's practice.

The man who consummated this development of devotional piety was Genkū (Hōnen Shōnin). He said, "There may be millions of people who would practice Buddhist discipline and train themselves in the way of perfection, and yet in these Latter Days of the Law there will be none who will attain the ideal perfection. The only way available is the Gateway to the Pure Land." In this respect, Genkū represented the heritage from the culture of the preceding age, while he was a typical pioneer of the new age in his aspiration for the salvation of all. In fact, he demonstrated his zeal by abandoning all his former attainments and devoting himself exclusively to faith in the grace of the Buddha. Hōnen's religion was a simplified form of Amida Buddhism, purged of mystic elements and tempered to pious devotion.

Then Shinran carried the idea of the Buddha's grace to extreme conclusions, because no sin was an obstacle to salvation through grace. He never protested against the idea of purifying oneself from sin, yet strongly denounced it as an impediment to real faith. Any scruple about sins or depravities was, in Shinran's faith, reliance on "one's own power," and therefore a menace to absolute faith in "another's power," in the Buddha's grace. He says, "Whether sage or fool, whether good or bad, we simply have to give up the idea of estimating our own qualities or of depending upon self. . . . Our salvation is 'natural, as it is,' in the sense that it is not due to our own device or intention but provided for by the Buddha himself; everything has been arranged by the Buddha to receive us into his paradise. It is 'natural,' because his grace is intangible and invisible and yet works by 'naturalness' (*jinen hōni*[d1]) to induce us to the highest attainment. The foundation of salvation has been laid down in Amida's vows. 'Calling the Buddha's name' in pious devotion and absolute trust in him is the way thereto, but no idea whatever of invocation or supplication is to be cherished; it should be uttered as the expression of trust and gratitude toward his grace. Further, even this gratitude is a matter of reminding ourselves of the Buddha's primeval vows already completed rather than of thanking him in anticipation of the bliss to be attained."[66]

QUESTION: What is the status of the individual in Mahāyāna Buddhism, and what is the status of the individual in *nirvāṇa?*

ANSWER: As Sir Charles Eliot has remarked, Japanese Buddhism, though imported from China, has a flavor of its own. Thus, any technical definition of Japanese Buddhism as a form of Mahāyāna is inadequate. Yet, having said this, says Eliot, it may be well to point out that the singularity of Japanese Buddhism is due partly to the fact that it is the only instance of Mahāyānism now flourishing as a vital religion among the people.[67]

In this context, in Japanese Mahāyāna Buddhism the individual is not annihilated, nor does he disappear in his ultimate destiny or in *nirvāṇa*. Japanese Buddhism never uses the term *"nirvāṇa"* in its original negative meaning. The term *"nehan"* (Japanese pronunciation of *nirvāṇa*) has been used mainly to express the Buddha Śakyamuni's death. They usually use the terms *"jōbutsu"*[dj] and *"satori"*[dk] (enlightenment, becoming a *buddha*).

Only the Jōdo-Shin sect uses the term *"nehan"*[dl] as its final salvation. According to Jōdo-Shin theology, the schools of the "difficult way" and "salvation by one's own power" claim that *jōbutsu*, or *satori*, can be attained even in this world if one accumulates pure good and awakens absolute wisdom in oneself. But the Pure Land schools realize *nirvāṇa* through Amida's grace after birth in paradise. According to the explanations given by Fujiwara Ryōsetsu[dm], the Jōdo sect usually states that *nirvāṇa* can be achieved after a long period of further practice in Amida's Pure Land. However, Shinran emphasized that birth in the Pure Land is "birthless birth," which means the end of *saṁsāra,* and that birth itself is indeed the realization of *nirvāṇa*. In this case, the term *"nirvāṇa"* has a positive meaning rather than its original negative meaning, because to attain *nirvāṇa* is to achieve complete *buddha*hood, which means the perfection of absolute wisdom and compassion, both for oneself and for all others. Fujiwara says that Shinran stressed the deep significance of two kinds of merit-transference, namely, "merit-transference of going forward" (*ōsō ekō*[dn]) and "merit-transference of coming backward" (*gensō ekō*[do]). The former means that Amida transfers his own merit to enable us to attain *buddha*hood. The latter shows that it is also through his merit-transference that one who has attained *buddha*hood is given a special power to return to the defiled worlds and save all beings. According to the traditional Shin sect, theology, Fujiwara remarks, is the benefit to be given at the instance of attaining *buddha*hood. It is the crystalization of the Buddha's positive and compassionate mind to benefit all suffering beings.[68]

---

[1] The concept of Japanese *kami* is very complicated, and so it should not be translated as "god" or "deity." Motoori Norinaga[dp] explained that *"kami"* was originated from "above," "upper," or "super" in its etymology (*Kojiki den*[dq], chap. I). "Hierophany" would be completely appropriate to express the concept of *kami*. Cf. D. C. Holtom, "The Meaning of Kami," *Monumenta Nipponica*, III (1940), No. 1, 1–27; No. 2, 32–53; and IV, (1941), No. 2, 25–68.

[2] In the *Manyōshū*[dr] anthology, compiled about 770, we can find instances of the *ujigami* type of Shintō. See the *Manyōshū* (*One Thousand Poems Selected and Translated from the Japanese*) Tokyo: The Nippon Gakujitsu Shinkō kai, Iwanami-shoten, 1940), pp. 151, 179.

[3] In Japanese folk-belief, the spirit of the dead was conceived in terms of its loss of identity thirty-three years after death, when it joined with the community of ancestral spirits. The Buddhist memorial services to a personal spirit of the dead are stopped at the thirty-third anniversary service, called *tomuraiage*[ds] or *toikiri*[dt] (completion of the personal memorial service). After this, the spirit of the dead is believed to become an ancestral spirit, or *kami*. See Yanagita Kunio[du] (compiler), *Sōsō shūzoku goi*[dv] (Folk Vocabulary Concerning Funeral and Memorial Rites and Ceremonies) (Tokyo: Iwanami-shoten, 1937), pp. 206–209.

[4] Pi-mi-ko of the Yamatai kingdom was clearly documented in the Chinese *Wei chih*[dw] compiled by Ch'en Shou[dx] (233–297), this book having been published by Professors Wada Kiyoshi[dy] and Ishihara Michiharu[dz] (Tokyo: Iwanami-shoten, 1951). Other examples in old Japanese historical legends can be seen in my *Nippon shūkyō no shakaiteki yakuwari*[ea] (Social Roles of Japanese Religion) (Tokyo: Miraisha, 1962), pp. 36–70; see also my *Wagakuni minkan shinkōshi no kenkyū*[eb] (Study of the History of Japanese Folk Religion) (Tokyo: Tōkyō-Sōgensha, 1953) Vol. II.

[5] Cf. my *Wagakuni minkan shinkōshi no kenkyū*, Vol. II, especially pp. 709–766: "The Concept of *Hitogami* in the Folkbelief and the Primitive Characters and Functions of Magico-religious Wanderers," written in Japanese.

[6] Cf. Robert N. Bellah, *Tokugawa Religion, The Values of Pre-industrial Japan* (Glencoe: Free Press, 1957), pp. 70–73.

[7] Watsuji Tetsurō, *Fūdo*[ee] (Historico-climatic Characteristics of Culture) (Tokyo: Iwanami-shoten, 1935), pp. 236–257; cf. Hori Ichirō, *Minkan shinkō*[ed] (Japanese Folk-beliefs) (Tokyo: Iwanami-shoten, 1951), pp. 119–202.

[8] For example, the Meiji Shrine[ee] was erected to enshrine the spirits of the deceased Emperor Meiji[ef] (d. 1912) and his Consort, Shōken[eg]; Nogi Jinja[eh] (Shrine) for the spirit of General Nogi Maresuke[ei] and his wife (d. 1912); and Tōgō Jinja[ej] (Shrine) for the spirit of Admiral Tōgō Heihachirō[ek] (d. 1938). Yasukuni Jinja[el] (Shrine) was dedicated to the spirits of all of the unknown soldiers who had died in battle since the Meiji Restoration.

[9] Sir Charles Eliot, *Japanese Buddhism* (2nd imp., London: Routledge and Kegan Paul, 1959), p. 195.

[10] The evidences of the influence of Confucianism upon the ruling class are seen in several legends in the *Nihongi*. See especially Vol. XI, in W. G. Aston, *Nihongi, Chronicles of Japan from the Earliest Times to A.D. 697*, (London: Kegan Paul, Trench, Trübner, 1896), Vol. I, pp. 273, 278–279.

[11] *Nihongi*, Vol. XXII; Aston, *op. cit.*, Vol. II, pp. 129–130.

[12] *Ibid.*, Vol. XXII; Aston, *op. cit.*, Vol. II, p. 131.

[13] *Jōgū Shōtoku hōō teisetsu*[em] (Collections of Biography and Legends of Prince Shōtoku, a Pious Lord of the Upper Palace), which is the earliest historical document in Japan. It was published by Hanayama Shinshō[en] and Iyenaga Saburō[eo] with annotation (Tokyo: Iwanami-shoten, 1941), p. 82.

[14] *Nihongi*, Vol. XXIII; Aston, *op. cit.*, Vol. II, p. 163.

[15] *Ibid.*, Vol. XXIV; Aston, *op. cit.*, Vol. II, p. 183.

[16] *Saddharma-puṇḍarīka-sūtra, Nanjiō Catalogue*, No. 184 (Oxford: Clarendon Press, 1883) (*Hokkekyō*[ep] or *Myōhō rengekyō*[eq] in Japanese).

[17] Takurei Hirako[er] interpreted the meaning of the *Tenjukoku*[es] as being the same as Amida's Pure Land, i.e., *Muryōjukoku*[et] (Land of Everlasting Life), cited by Hanayama and Iyenaga, *op. cit.*, in their commentary of *Jōgū Shōtoku hōō teisetsu*, p. 82.

[18] See Hori Ichirō, *Nippon Bukkyō bunka shi*[en] (Historical and Cultural Materials Concerning Japanese Buddhism up to the Nara Period) (Tokyo: Daitō-shuppansha, 1941), Vol. I, pp. 228–255.

[19] For example, Katsuragidera[ev] was built as the tutelary temple for the Katsuragi Family[ew]; Kidera[ex] for the Ki Family[ey]; Kōfukuji[ez] for the Fujiwara Family[fa]; Hōryūji for the Jōgū-ō Family[fb], whose ancestor was Prince Shōtoku; the Soga Family[fc] built their tutelary temple, named Hōkōji[fd]; the Sogakura Yamada Family[fe] built their tutelary temple, named Yamadadera[ff]; the Hata Family[fg] built their temple, Kōryūji.[fh]

[20] *Gangōji engi*[fi] (Origin and History of Gangōji [Temple]), in *Dai Nippon Bukkyō zensho*[fj] (A Complete Series of the Buddhist Documents in Japan), published under the editorship of Bunyū Nanjiō[fk], Takakusu Junjirō[fl], and others (Tokyo: Bussho-kankōkai, 1911–1922), Vol. 118 (1913).

[21] *Nihongi*, Vol. XXII; Aston, *op. cit.*, Vol. II, p. 123.

[22] In Japanese, *Ninnō gokoku hannya haramittakyō* (or *haramitsukyō*); *Nanjiō Catalogue*, Nos. 17, 965.

[23] In Japanese, *Konkōmyō saishōō kyō, Nanjiō Catalogue*, No. 134.

[24] *Nihongi*, Vol. XXIX; Aston, *op. cit.*, Vol. II, pp. 346 ff. See Hori Ichirō. "Nihon shoki to Bukkyō[fm]" (The *Nihongi* and Buddhism), in his *Nippon Bukkyōshi ron*[fn] (Essays on the History of Japanese Buddhism) (Tokyo: Meguro-shoten, 1940), pp. 6–76.

[25] In Japanese, *Rengezō sekai*[fo], which was engraved on the calyx of the lotus leaves of the Mahā-vairocana Buddha.

[26] *Tōdaiji yōroku*[fp] (Historical and Legendary Documents Concerning the Tōdaiji [Temple]), supposedly completed about A.D. 1118. It was published by Tsutsui Eishun[fq] with annotations, (Osaka: Zenkoku-shobō, 1944), pp. 11–12, 15. See also Tsuji Zennosuke[fr], "Honji suijaku setsu no kigen ni tsuite[fs]" (On the Origins of the Manifestation of the Prime Noumenon), in his *Nippon Bukkyōshi no kenkyū*[ft] (Studies on the History of Japanese Buddhism) (Tokyo: Kinkōdō, 1931), 11th imp., Vol. I, pp. 49–194.

[27] *Shoku Nihongi*[fu] (Second Official Historical Document Continuing to the *Nihongi* from 698 to 794 complied by the Imperial Edict in 797), Vol. XV, Imperial Edict in 734; also Vol. XVII, Imperial edict in 749.

[28] *Ibid.*, Vol. XV, 734.

[29] Another example is also seen in the *Nihongi*, Vol. XXV. Cf. Aston, *op. cit.*, Vol. II, pp. 233–234.

[30] See *Shoku Nihongi*, Vol. XXVII. Also Hori, *Wagakuni minkan shinkōshi no kenkyū*, Vol. I (1955), pp. 256–293.

[31] Ennin, *Nittō guhō junrei kōki*[fv] (Ennin's Diary—The Record of a Pilgrimage to China in Search of the Buddha's Law); an English translation was published with annotations by Edwin O. Reischauer (New York: The Ronald Press, 1955); see also Reischauer, *Ennin's Travel in T'ang China* (New York: The Ronald Press, 1955).

[32] See Hori Ichirō, *Wagakuni minkan shinkōshi no kenkyū*, Vol. II, Part II, chaps. 1–3, "Shoji jōgyōdō no konryū to fudan nembutsu no seiko[fw]" (The Buildings of the Jōgyōdō Seminaries at the Several Buddhist Temples and the Popularizing of the Continuous Nembutsu Practices), pp. 255–256.

[33] *The Great Sun Sūtra* was formerly called "*Mahā-vairocanābhisambodhi* (*Ta-p'i-lu-che-na-cheng-fo-shen-pien-chia-ch'ih-ching* in Chinese, and *Dai-birushana jōbutsu jim-pen-*

kajikyō[fx] in Japanese). This *Sūtra* means "The Sūtra on Mahā-vairocana's Becoming the Buddha and the Supernatural Formula called *Yugandhara* (literally, "adding-holding") according to the *Nanjiō Catalogue*, No. 530, which was translated by Subhakarasiṁha in 724, and is usually called in Japanese *Dai birushanakyō* or *Dainichikyō*[fy]. (Oxford: Clarendon Press, 1883), p. 122.

34 *"Vajra-dhātu"* is translated as the "Realm of the Indestructibles," in Anesaki Masaharu[fz], *History of Japanese Religion* (Tokyo: Charles Tuttle, 1963), p. 127; or the "Diamond Element," in Eliot, *op. cit.*, p. 345; and *kongōkai*[ga] in Japanese. *"Garbhadhātu"* is translated as the "womb-store" (Anesaki) and "womb-element" (Eliot), and is *taizōkai*[gb] in Japanese.

35 Cf. *Maitreya-vyākaraṇa* (*Mi-le-hsia-sheng-ching* in Chinese, and *Miroku geshōgyō*[gc] in Japanese) (*Sūtra* Spoken by the Buddha on Maitreya's Coming Down to be Born in This World), *Nanjiō Catalogue*, Nos. 205–208.

36 For example, *Sokushin jōbutsu gi*[gd] (The Theory on Becoming a Buddha in One's Own Body), *Taishō daizōkyō*, Vol. 77, No. 2428; *Jūjū shinron*[ge] (The Ten Stages of Spiritual Development), *Taishō daizōkyō*, Vol. 77, No. 2425; and the later condensed work *Hizō hōyaku*[gf] (The Jewel Key to the Store of Mysteries), *Taishō daizōkyō*: Vol. 77, No. 2426, are Kūkai's major works. See *Kōbō Daishi zenshū*.

37 Cf. Anesaki Masaharu, *History of Japanese Religion*, pp. 131–133.

38 By Annen[gg] (841–889 or 898) in his life work entitled *Sokushin jōbutsugi-shiki*[gh] (My Understanding of the Theory on the Sokushin jōbutsu), *Dai Nippon Bukkyō zensho*, Vol. 24, "Tendai Section," No. 4; *Himitsu sokushin jōbutsugi*[gi] (Secret Theory on the Sokushin jōbutsu), *Nippon daizōkyō*, published under the editorship of Nakano Tatsue[gj] (Tokyo: Nippon daizōkyō Hensankai, 1919–1921), Vol. 43, "Tendai Section," No. 3.

39 Nichiren's theory on becoming a *buddha* in one's own body is that there are three ways of achieving this state: the original nature of mankind is *buddha*hood as it is; the completion of self-enlightenment by holding the symbolic prayer of the Nichiren sect, i.e., *Namu-myōhō rengekyō*[gk]; and, finally, the realization of perfect enlightenment after completing religious practices. The second was insisted on as the most efficacious means of actually becoming a *buddha* in one's own body. Cf. *Sōsho kōyō sakuryaku*[gl], compiled by Nichidō[gm] (1724–1789), in *Bukkyō taikei*[gn] series. (Tokyo: Bukkyō Taikei Kankō-kai, 1920).

40 *Shugen-dō* is a religious institution peculiar to Japan, which consists of a mixture of various religious elements, both indigenous and heterogeneous, including primitive beliefs and worship of mountains, Shintō magic and ritual, Mantrayāna Buddhist theories and austerities in mountains both of Tendai and Shingon, Chinese astrology and divination (*Onmyōdō*[go], or Way of *Yin Yang*), Taoistic conceptions and practices of hermit or genie (*hsien-jen*[gp] or *hsien-tao*[gq] in Chinese; *sennin* or *sendō* in Japanese), and some elements of Confucian ethics as well as Chinese philosophy and metaphysics. See Wakamori Tarō[gr], *Shugendō shi kenkyū*[gs] (A Historical Study on Shugendō), (Tokyo: Kawade-shobō, 1943; Murakami Toshio[gt], *Shugendō no hattatsu*[gu] (The Development of Shugen-dō) (Tokyo: Unebi-shobō, 1943).

41 Hori Ichirō, "Self-mummified Buddha in Japan," *History of Religions*, I, No. 2 (Winter, 1961), 222–242, especially p. 227.

42 See Hori, *Wagakuni minkan shinkōshi no kenkyū*, Vol. II, pp. 76–88.

43 Hori Ichirō, "The Concept of *Hijiri* (Holy-man)," *Numen*, V, fasc. 5 (1958), 214–215.

44 See Hori, *ibid.*, p. 205.

45 See Hori, *ibid.*, pp. 203–204. He wrote a book entitled *Nippon ō-jō gokuraku ki*[gv] (The Compiled Biographies about the Persons Who Went to Amida's Pure Land after Their Death) during 985 to 986.

46 Ryōnin (1072–1132) was the founder of the Yūzū Nembutsu[gw] school of the Tendai sect. Having integrated the Tendai and *Avataṁsaka* (*Kegon*, in Japanese) theories with the teachings of the Chinese Pure Land sects, Ryōnin systematized his own doctrine. This was that one person's merits, coming from faith and repetition of Amida's name, circulated and were added to all other persons' merits, and all other persons' merits were transferable to one's own merits, so that all human beings could gain the benefit of rebirth into Amida's paradise after death. This doctrine was based on the teachings of the Pure Land sects, the "One-and-All" idea of the *Avataṁsaka-sūtra*, and the "Salvation-for-All" idea of *The Lotus Sūtra*. See Hori, *Wagakuni minkan shinkōshi no kenkyū*, Vol. II, pp. 291–294; also Hori, "On the Concept of *Hijiri* (Holy-man)," p. 220.

47 See Hori, "On the Concept of *Hijiri* (Holy-man)," pp. 205–206.

48 He composed one poem in Chinese entitled *Kantei go*[gx] (Words About the Secluded Retreat) which really manifested his principle. See *Shoshazankyūki*[gy], Vol. II, in *Dai Nippon Bukkyō zensho*, Vol. 117, Temple-graphic Section, No. 1. See also Hori, *Wagakuni minkan shinkōshi no kenkyū*, Vol. II, pp. 19–20.

> Poor and also humble,
> Who is not ambitious after wealth and distinction;
> But love my own life.
> Though the four walls are crude,
> The eight winds cannot trespass on them;
> Though one gourd for wine is empty,
> The *samādhi* is full to the brim spontaneously,
> I do not know anyone,
> [So that] there is neither slander nor praise;
> No one knows me,
> [So that] there is neither hatred nor affection.
> When I lie down with my head resting on my arm,
> [The] delight and happiness exist in it.

For what purpose should I wish again for
[The] unstable lap of luxury like a floating cloud!

[49] For example, Jichin[gz] (1155–1225), *Gukanshō*[ha] (Outline of Japanese History), Vol. VII, in *Kokushi taikei*, Vol. 14, pp. 609–616; Kōen[hb] (–1169), *Fusō ryakki*[hc] (Collections of Japanese Historical Documents), Vol. XXIX, in *Kokushi taikei*, Vol. 6, p. 796; Fujiwara Sanesuke[hd], *Shōuki*[he] (Sanesuke's Diary), in 1023, 3 vols. *Shiryō taisei*[hf], published under the editorship of Sasagawa Taneo[hg] (Tokyo: Chugai-shoseki, 1934–1935); Fujiwara Sukefusa[hh], *Shunki*[hi] (Sukefusa's *Diary*), in 1052, in *Shiryō taisei*.

[50] Hori Ichirō, *Kōya* (Tokyo: Yoshikawa-kōbunkan, 1963), pp. 204 ff.

[51] *Ōjō yōshū* (A Selection of the Sacred Words Concerning Birth in Amida's Paradise). Edited by Hanayama Shinshō, with annotations (Tokyo: Iwanami-shoten, 1942); *Taishō daizōkyo*, Vol. 84, No. 2682. This work consists of ten chapters, the first two chapters being most famous because of the sharp contrast between the descriptions of hell and paradise which have sometimes been compared with Dante's *Divine Comedy* by contemporary Japanese Buddhist scholars.

[52] The aim of the *Nijūgo zammai kesshū*[hj] was that the members of this fraternity could be reborn without fail to Amida's paradise after death as a result of the concentrated merit of *Nembutsu* by like-minded persons. *Nijūgo zammai kishō*[hk] written by Genshin in 986 and 988 A.D. See Hori, *Wagakuni minkan shinkōshi no kenkyū*, Vol. II, pp. 284–288.

[53] *Ōjō yōshu, op. cit.*

[54] Anesaki Masaharu, *History of Japanese Religion*, pp. 170–171.

[55] *Senjaku hongan nembutsu shū* (A Selection of Passages Bearing on the Nembutsu of the Original Vow), *Taishō daizōkyō*, Vol. 83, No. 2608.

[56] *Ichimai kishō mon* (One Sheet of Paper Expressing Genkū's Final Enlightenment). *Jōdoshū zensho*[hl] (The Complete Works on the Jōdo Sect), Vol. IX (Tokyo: Jōdoshū Shūten Kankōkai, 1911–1914). Translation in Eliot, *Japanese Buddhism*, p. 267.

[57] The three states of mind are: (1) a most sincere heart, (2) a deep-believing heart, and (3) a longing heart which offers in the hope of attaining paradise any merits it may have acquired, the point being that *Ōjō*[hm], or birth in paradise, can be obtained merely by personal merit and without faith in Amida, but that any merit one may have obtained should not be devoted to any other object. The fourfold practice, as prescribed by Zendō (Shan-tao) is (1) to treat images and other sacred objects with profound reverence, (2) to practice the repetition of the *Nembutsu* only, (3) to practice it continually and, if any sin has been committed, at once to purify the heart by uttering it, and (4) to observe the above three rules continuously throughout one's life. Cf. Eliot, *op. cit.*, p. 267, note 2.

[58] The two Holy Ones are Śākyamuni and Amida Buddha.

[59] *Tannishō*[hn], written by Yui-en[ho], Shinran's disciple, Section 2, *Taishō daizōkyō*, Vol. 83, No. 2661.

[60] *Tannishō;* see Anesaki, *History of Japanese Religion*, pp. 182–183.

[61] The doctrine of "once calling" (*ichi nengi*[hp]) and the doctrine of "many calling" (*ta nen'gi*[hq]) were differentiated and disputed among Genkū's disciples. Kōsai was a representative of the "once calling" school, while Ryūkan was of the "many calling" school. The former doctrine was based on the metaphysical conception of the identity of our souls with the Buddha's, as taught in Tendai and Avataṁsaka philosophies. Being adapted to the inclination of easygoing believers, it found a number of advocates and grew in influence, joining hands with neglect of moral discipline. The other, on the other hand, imported scrupulous formalism into the religion of piety and insisted on the necessity of "many," i.e., constant, thoughts on the Buddha. This doctrine found some followers also and was identified with the prevalent method of mechanically repeating the Buddha's name, especially in company with many fellows. (*Ibid.*, pp. 179–180).

[62] Cf. Eliot, *op. cit.*, p. 381.

[63] Ofumi is also called *Gobunsho* (Honorable Writings) which was compiled by Ennyo[hr], Rennyo's grandson, in five volumes. It included 80 letters that Rennyo gave his lay disciples and Shin-sect believers, using the spoken language and Sinico-Japanese writing for the purpose of easily understanding his doctrine. *Taishō daizōkyō*, Vol. 83, No. 2668, pp. 777 ff.

[64] Max Weber, *Protestant Ethic and the Spirit of Capitalism*, English editions, by T. Parsons (3rd imp. London: George Allen & Unwin, Ltd., New York: Charles Scribner's Sons, 1950). A remarkable paper on the ethics of the Shin sect and the spirit of Ōmi merchants was written by Naitō Kanji[hs], who applied Weber's theory to this phenomenon in pre-industrial Japan: "Shūkyō to keizai rinri, Jōdo Shinshū to Ōmi shōnin[ht]" (Religion and Economic Ethics and the Jōdo-Shin Sect and the Merchants in the Ōmi [present Shiga Prefecture]), in *Shakai-gaku*, Vol. VIII (Tokyo: Iwanami-shoten, 1941). See Robert N. Bellah *op. cit.*, chap. V.

[65] Cf. R. N. Bellah, *Tokugawa Religion* (Glencoe: Free Press, 1957), pp. 7–8.

[66] Cf. Anesaki Masaharu, *History of Japanese Religion* (London: Kegan Paul, Trench, Trübner & Co., 1930), pp. 170–186.)

[67] Cf. Eliot, *Japanese Buddhism* (2nd Imp., London: Routledge & Kegan Paul, 1959), p. 179.

[68] Cf. Fujiwara Ryōsetsu, *A Standard of Shin-shū Faith*. Jōdo-Shin Sect Series, No. 22. (San Francisco: Buddhist Church of America, 1963), pp. 21–22.

a	堀一郎	at	行基
b	天台	au	菩薩道
c	眞言	av	阿彌陀佛
d	神道	aw	念佛
e	氏神	ax	常行三昧
f	神	ay	圓仁
g	孝	az	慈覺大師
h	人神	ba	五台山
i	卑彌呼	bb	長安
j	耶馬台	bc	慧遠
k	恩	bd	廬山
l	報恩	be	法照
m	和辻哲郎	bf	常行三昧堂
n	佛樣	bg	延曆寺
o	天	bh	比叡
p	天帝	bi	常行道
q	老子	bj	空海
r	莊子	bk	高野
s	聖德（太子）	bl	最澄
t	十七條憲法	bm	彌勒
u	禮	bn	兜率天
v	凡夫	bo	即身成佛
w	日本紀	bp	日蓮
x	山背大兄（王）	bq	山伏
y	法隆寺	br	修驗者
z	大化改新	bs	修驗道
aa	天壽國曼荼羅	bt	聖
ab	氏寺	bu	教信
ac	佛神	bv	空也
ad	佛神乃宮	bw	寂心
ae	推古（天皇）	bx	源信
af	隋	by	惠心僧都
ag	唐	bz	良忍
ah	仁王護國般若波羅密多經	ca	增賀
ai	金光明最勝王經	cb	性空
aj	天武（天皇）	cc	源空
ak	東大寺	cd	親鸞
al	奈良	ce	榮西
am	聖武（天皇）	cf	道元
an	光明（皇后）	cg	往生要集
ao	大日如來	ch	二十五三昧結衆
ap	天照大御神	ci	顯教
aq	華嚴宗	cj	密教
ar	本地垂迹	ck	法然上人
as	知識（寺）	cl	善導

cm 聖道門

cn 自行

co 雜行

cp 易行

cq 難行

cr 他力

cs 淨土宗

ct 選擇本願念佛集

cu 一枚起請文

cv 南無阿彌陀佛

cw 釋迦

cx 蓮如

cy 鎌倉時代

cz 一念義

da 幸西

db 淨土眞宗

dc 御文

dd 武士道

de 商人道

df 職人道

dg 德川時代

dh 明治時代

di 自然法爾

dj 成佛

dk 悟

dl 涅槃

dm 藤原凌雪

dn 往相廻向

do 還相廻向

dp 本居宣長

dq 古事記傳

dr 萬葉集

ds 弔上げ

dt 間切り

du 柳田國男

dv 葬送習俗語彙

dw 魏志

dx 陳壽

dy 和田 (淸)

dz 石原 (道博)

ea 日本宗教の社會的役割

eb 我國民間信仰史の研究

ec 風土

ed 民間信仰

ee 明治神宮

ef 明治天皇

eg 昭憲 (皇太后)

eh 乃木神社

ei 乃木希典

ej 東鄉神社

ek 東鄉平八郎

el 靖國神社

em 上宮聖德法王帝說

en 花山信勝

eo 家永三郎

ep 法華經

eq 妙法蓮華經

er 平子鐸嶺

es 天壽國

et 無量壽國

eu 日本佛教文化史

ev 葛城寺

ew 葛城氏

ex 紀寺

ey 紀氏

ez 興福寺

fa 藤原氏

fb 上宮王家

fc 蘇我氏

fd 法興寺

fe 蘇我倉山田氏

ff 山田寺

fg 秦氏

fh 廣隆寺

fi 元興寺緣起

fj 大日本佛教全書

fk 南條文雄

fl 高楠順次郎

fm 日本書記と佛教

fn 日本佛教史論

fo 蓮華藏世界

fp 東大寺要錄

fq 筒井英俊

fr **辻善之助**

fs 本地垂迹說の起原について

ft 日本佛教史之研究

fu 續日本紀

fv 入唐求法巡禮行記

fw 諸寺常行堂の建立と不斷念佛の
　　盛行

fx 大毗盧遮那成佛神變加持經

fy 大毗盧遮那經，大日經

fz 姉崎正治

ga 金剛界

gb 胎藏界

gc 彌勒下生經

gd 即身成佛義

ge 十住心論

gf 秘藏寶鑰

gg 安然

gh 即身成佛義私記

gi 秘密即身成佛義

gj 中野達慧

gk 南無妙法蓮華經

gl 祖書綱要刪畧

gm 日導

gn 佛教大系

go 陰陽道

gp 仙人

gq 仙道

gr 和歌森太郎

gs 修驗道史研究

gt 村上俊雄

gu 修驗道の發達

gv 日本往生極樂記

gw 融通念佛

gx 閑亭語

gy 書寫山舊記

gz 慈鎮

ha 愚管抄

hb 皇圓

hc 扶桑略記

hd 藤原實資

he 小右記

hf 史料大成

hg 笹川種郎（臨風）

hh 藤原資房

hi 春記

hj 二十五三昧結衆

hk 二十五三昧起請

hl 淨土宗全書

hm 往生

hn 歎異抄

ho 唯圓

hp 一念義

hq 多念義

hr 圓如

hs 內藤莞爾

ht 宗教と經齊倫理。淨土眞宗と近江商人

JOHN E. SMITH

The individual and the Judeo-Christian tradition

To present the religious outlook of "the West" concerning the nature and status of the individual is a large task indeed. Nor is it made easier by the entirely legitimate demand that clichés and stereotypes be avoided. Not only is the history of Christian thought a long and complex development, but the Hebraic religion, which formed the original background for Christianity, needs to be treated in its own right as the separate and autonomous tradition of Judaism, into which it later developed. To do full justice to the total picture is obviously out of the question. We may, however, follow the sound advice of Aristotle, who recommended that the best way to conquer a multiplicity of detail that would otherwise be endless is to encompass it with a principle. I have, in fact, two principles to suggest, and I shall state them in the form of purposes or aims. The first is to present a working summary of the basic religious ideas and doctrines in order to make critical comparison with other traditions possible. Here I shall confine myself to reporting certain well-known doctrines that form the basis of the Judeo-Christian tradition. The second principle is to interpret the current situation in such a way as to focus critical discussion, particularly regarding the status of the individual in the modern world. At that point I shall not confine myself to reporting but shall feel free to paint a small picture of my own.

I

Every treatment of concepts and themes essential to the central doctrines of the Christian religion must take into account two fundamental facts. First, Christianity, for all of its claim to uniqueness in the special person of its founder, still requires to be understood against the background of the Hebraic religion of the Old Testament, and, second, the theological elaboration of the central Christian ideas with the use of philosophical concepts that began with the Greek Fathers and continues even to the present day (despite the current strength of the position that would deny the involvement of theology in philosophy and secular knowledge generally) could have taken place only through a continuous dialogue with relevant

251

philosophical positions stemming originally from the ancient Greek and Roman traditions. To point to this background of thought is not to say that Christianity is merely a derivative religion developing out of Old Testament religion, on the one hand, and borrowing from the classical world, on the other. It is to say that, if we seek to understand the nature and status of the individual from the Christian perspective, we must attend, howsoever briefly, to the view of the individual found in the Hebraic tradition and also to the philosophical theories of the individual and the person that influenced the elaboration of Christian theology.

Before beginning with the Hebraic background, one further preliminary comment is in order. The fundamental aim of this Conference is to consider the *nature* and *status* of the individual. It has been stated that the "status" of the individual is the important topic and that we are not to become so involved in essentially theoretical speculation about the nature of the individual that we overlook the more immediate question of the value placed upon the individual and the place of importance or unimportance accorded to him in the modern world. While I would not deny validity to the distinction between nature and status, it is an error to separate the two, as is done by those who identify the "nature" of something with the "facts" and the status of that thing with "values." Apart from the fact that modern culture suffers grievously from the separation of fact from value, we cannot identify a metaphysical (and even less a religious) theory of the individual with bare fact as if it were on the same level as, for example, the findings of historical anthropology or economics. A theory of the individual stemming either from the reflective analysis of philosophy or the experience and insight of the religious consciousness purports to say what the individual *essentially* is, and the reference to the essential immediately introduces a normative element. Therefore, to say what the nature of the individual is is at the same time to indicate the status of the individual in a total scheme of things. The two go hand in hand, and they should not be separated from each other.

II

At the risk of oversimplifying the complex development of ideas in the Old Testament record, we may say that the nation and the religious community (the two units were identified to a remarkable extent at certain periods in the historical development) took priority over the individual in the formative period of the Hebraic religion, but the individual gradually emerged as a being in his own right, so that by the time in which the prophets Jeremiah and Ezekiel lived, the older idea of the relation between God and Israel was undergoing transformation so as to allow for a more individual and personal relation with God. The destruction of the temple at Jerusalem was, of course, decisive, because it raised the crucial question as to the need for the official community in mediating the relation between man and God. It was for Jeremiah to suggest that Jahweh might not be confined to his sacred abode but might visit the individual in exile. Many scholars have dated the establishment of individual or personal religion in Jeremiah's time.[1]

Two central features of the development may be cited. First, the original foundation for Old Testament religion is that of the *covenant* between Jahweh and Israel. Although we tend to think at once of the towering importance of the great individuals—the Patriarchs, and especially Moses—in the founding of Hebraic religion, the fact remains that it is originally the people or *community* with which the divine covenant is made. Even Moses has his central position as one who speaks for and in behalf of the *people* in their dealings with Jahweh. At this point in the development the individual is related to God only insofar as he is a member of the covenant community; he suffers with this community and assumes responsibility for its actions.

Second, although it is customary to interpret the Law (Torah) as defining the shape of *individual* conduct required by Jahweh, it is not until the founding of the great prophetic tradition with Amos in the eighth century that we find a thoroughgoing attack upon the inadequacies of the religious cult and an appeal to the *individual* to understand righteousness—right relations with God—primarily in terms of justice, honest dealings with others, and a regard for persons, even if they are not members of Israel. It is characteristic of the ethical orientation of the Hebraic religion that it issues in commands addressed to the individual. In the writings of Jeremiah we find the idea of a Law that is written in the "inward parts" of the individual; this New Covenant, as it is called, means a deepening of the Law. The change means more than a shift from "external" legality to "internal" morality; the development means a new emphasis on the individual as a responsible being, because only in relation to an individual person is it significant to speak of a Law written in the heart.[2]

Religion, it has been suggested, is primarily concerned with first and last things, the Alpha and Omega of all being. This is true, and we may expect to learn much about the conception of the individual in a religious tradition by inquiring into origins and endings. In the case of the Hebraic religion—and Christianity follows in the same pattern—all being, whether individual or universal, personal or social, one or many, is *created*. God originally "plants" or "founds"[3] all that exists; he does not, that is, shape it out of pre-existent material, after the fashion of an architect or artisan. The doctrine of creation has two consequences for the understanding of the individual. In being called from nothing, the individual is thoroughly dependent upon God for his continued existence; although he is a responsible being answerable to God, he never has the sense of his being entirely from himself, and, indeed, the attempt to substitute himself for the divine ground is regarded as the primary source of sin. Second, the doctrine of creation means that there is nothing in the individual, no aspect or part, that is essentially evil in itself. Since there was "nothing" over against God in creation, there is no "other" that is non-divine in nature. The individual is responsible in his freedom; he cannot trace his failures to the presence in his being of a non-divine element. On the other hand, the Hebraic tradition has not always been concerned to work out the metaphysical consequences of this doctrine and to deal with the thorny question as to how a free being can be created. But that is a speculative matter and not altogether congenial to the Hebrew mind.

So much for beginnings: With regard to endings, the picture is less clear. The Old Testament picture of the ultimate destiny of the individual remains obscure. What evidence there is has been subject to differing interpretations. It is generally acknowledged, however, that, by the time of the author of the Book of Daniel and in certain Psalms of late date, the idea of God's having a concern for the single individual and his preservation from extinction by natural death began to develop. Whatever the full truth on this topic may be, one fact is clear: the Hebraic religion generally came to understand the self as requiring *embodiment*. In keeping with their high estimation of the visible world and of natural things, Hebraic thinkers were opposed to identifying the person merely with an "immaterial" aspect of its being. The self needs a body of some sort as a medium of expression; the self is not an ethereal spirit that is without localization and definite involvement in created, visible things. This emphasis on embodiment was to be carried over into Christianity and expressed by Paul in the doctrine of the "spiritual" body or resurrected person.

III

The first point to be noticed in the presentation of the basic Christian ideas is that the later theological elaborations presuppose the Gospel as expressed in the written record of the Evangelists and in the letters of Paul. With regard to the tradition concerning the teaching of Jesus, two points are of special importance. First, in the Parables and in the Sermon on the Mount, the form of address is to the individual person. Using incidents drawn from ordinary life and experience as models, Jesus sought to dramatize the meaning of the ethical commands and divine love in the most concrete terms. In this regard, Jesus was continuing the line of the Old Testament prophetic tradition. Second, Jesus focused at the outset a dual emphasis on the individual at one pole, and the community of individuals, at the other. He spoke to the individual and addressed his commandments to him, but he also spoke, in the symbol of the Kingdom of God, of the need for a community of individuals, thus implying that the individual by himself is not complete. Jesus spoke of each individual person being known to God and as being the object of divine concern,[4] but this does not exhaust his message. He is equally insistent on the essential involvement of the individuals with each other, and his vision of humanity transformed by the power of God takes the form of a community of persons, or Kingdom, in which all individuals are united in the bond of love (*agape*). All later Christian thought has shown the results of the tension between the individual considered all by himself in relation to God and the individual as being related to God only insofar as he participates in the life of other individuals and is incorporated into a sacred community. Both aspects are present in classical Christianity.

The Pauline theology includes three ideas that are essential for any understanding of the Christian doctrine of the individual person. First, there is the insistence on the unity of the individual; each person is a living unity of mind (*psyche;* sometimes *nous*), body (*soma*), and spirit (*pneuma*). There is, that is to say, no tendency to identify the individual with but one of its aspects or functions. Second, and as a corollary of the previous point, Paul reiterates the Hebraic emphasis on the need for embodiment in the constitution of the individual self. This idea is especially evident in connection with belief about the ultimate destiny of the person. Paul does not understand the transcendence of death as the persistence of a deathless part of the individual—a soul—but, rather, as a total unified self raised to a new level of meaning and endowed with a new "body." Thus he employs the symbol of a "spiritual" as distinct from a "natural" body in order to express adequately the status of the redeemed personality within the unity of the divine life. So important is the body and so necessary for individual life that some place for it must be found even with the symbol of the ultimate fulfillment of all life in God.[5]

Third, Paul continues the dual emphasis on individual and community, claiming both that each man shall "bear his own burden" and that it is incumbent on all members of the community to "bear one another's burdens." Stern as is his condemnation of sin in the life of the individual, Paul is no less convinced of the reality of a form of corporate life, a community of many persons pervaded and unified by one spirit of love or charity that has been made possible by the work of Christ. The life of the individual, according to Paul's teaching, remains incomplete as long as it is separated from the community of love.

To avoid a fatal misunderstanding at this point a word of caution is necessary. The defect that attaches to the life of the individual as expressed in the doctrine of sin or the misuse of freedom is never, according to classical Christian doctrine, overcome by a transcendence of individuality itself. Being an individual, that is, is never the source of evil, and consequently evil is never overcome through the transcendence of that type of being. The radical misuse of freedom or rebellion against God, which means sin in Christian belief, is imputed to the individual and is viewed as a matter of individual responsibility. The imperfection that is sin, however, does not constitute the individual as such, nor does it follow from the fact of individuality. Consequently, the overcoming of sin cannot be accomplished by transcending individuality. To say that the individual is incomplete without the community is not to demand a transcendence of individuality but, rather, to point out the error of atomic existence.

IV

As Josiah Royce once remarked, Western philosophers have invariably been more adept at presupposing the reality of the individual than they have at saying clearly what being an individual means. The sense that there are individuals has frequently been stronger than the wit to explain what they are. There is a profound problem implicit in this state of affairs—the problem of relating the that and the what—but this is beyond our scope. For present purposes, it will be helpful to cite the main ideas regarding the individual that have determined the Western theologico-philosophical tradition as these are found in the works of a succession of thinkers stretching from the time of Augustine to the present day. What follows will, of course, be woefully incomplete, but that fact by itself need not be fatal. Only absolute idealists equate incompleteness with error.

Augustine. In the extensive and original writings of Augustine we find an expression of one of the perennial strains in the Western religious and philosophical tradition. The central drift of the position is summed up in the ancient motto—*In lumine tuo videbimus lumen* (In Thy light shall we see light). The individual self figures prominently in the thought of Augustine; three points may be cited. First, the starting point in the quest for God and Truth—the two are equated by Augustine—is the meditating self. The aim of the position, and at the same time the meaning of the motto just cited, is to recover, through reflection on the nature of the self and its consciousness, the presence of the Uncreated Light in the form of the timeless truths. All truths participate in Truth; in contemplating a finite truth we are in the presence of the Truth *per se*. Each individual self must carry out the meditative process for himself, and, in so doing he comes to an understanding of himself not to be gained from external observation.[6] Second, Augustine laid great stress on an idea that has persisted from his time to ours in the thought of idealist philosophers—the doctrine, namely, that the essential self, the self as it really is in its truth, is the self as it is known to God. Time and again in the *Confessions*, Augustine expressed the desire "to know even as I am known." Knowledge of each individual is secure in the depth of the divine knowledge. Third, Augustine laid great stress on the purely religious relationship between God and the individual self, even at the cost of neglecting the worlds of Nature and culture. In a famous passage in the *Soliloquia*, the person of Reason says to Augustine, "What is it that you chiefly desire to know?" Augustine answers, "God and the soul." Reason responds, "Nothing else?" and Augustine answers, "Absolutely nothing." It was equally characteristic of the entire Augustinian tradition to make the relation between the individual and God a matter of basic concern.[7]

Thomas Aquinas. In the monumental theological and metaphysical system of Aquinas we find introduced into the Christian tradition the ancient doctrine of Aristotle according to which the reality of the individual is asserted primarily as a natural fact. According to this doctrine, it belongs to the nature of reality to be segmented or differentiated; all that is real has a boundary or natural limit within which it resides. On this view, the individual is not reached as the result of a process of dialectic; the individual is, rather, the presupposition of all intelligible discourse. It is that with which we begin, and, if we cannot begin with the individual, we can never reach or derive it by specification through universals. Aquinas, it is true, spoke of the need for a principle of individuation, and this has led some to think of an individual as an instance of the principle. But such an interpretation says more than Aquinas meant. In singling out matter—*materia signata* or spatio-temporally designated matter —as essential to being an individual, he is merely going on to say what is meant by an individual once its reality has been assumed. Moreover, it is not true, as has sometimes been held, that matter is the sole condition of individuality for Aquinas. At least one further feature is specified by him when he deals with the definition of finite or created individuals, and, in the special case of the divine individuality, it is obvious that some principle other than matter must be involved. With regard to finite individuals, Aquinas refers to them as "first substances"[8] and characterizes them as subsisting (persisting) through themselves and as distinct from other things. There is an element of incommunicability in every individual that prevents it from being assimilated to another. The thorny philosophical problem attaching to this element continued to trouble Thomas' successors. Our demand for intelligibility leads us to want to conceptualize what is incommunicable, but, if we are successful in so doing, the element appears to become communicable, which is precisely what we do not want.

That special type of individual that has rationality is called by Aquinas a person, and the chief characteristic of persons is to be able to determine, at least to some extent, their actions in accordance with principles. Action is a *singular* phenomenon, and this feature is a further factor in the solidification of the individual.

In the special case of God, we can use the term "individual" only insofar as matter is not meant, but incommunicability is. Aquinas dealt with the nature of the divine individuality largely in terms of the doctrine of the Trinity and the peculiar sort of relation that subsists between the Persons and serves to individuate them. The fact is that Aquinas does not speak as openly of God as the Highest Individual, as William of Ockham was later to do. Aquinas did dismiss the ontological argument by holding that, whereas truth is evident to us, *a Primal Truth* is not, and in this way moved closer to defining God as an individual. On the other hand, Aquinas still thought within the framework of the Aristotelian moderate realism; he was not a nominalist.

There are many other important facets of Aquinas' doctrine of the individual, especially the subtle way in which he sought to preserve the connection between the soul and its body through the idea that the soul, when separated in natural death, still retains an *inclinatio* to the body of which it was the form. This *inclinatio* is what individuates the soul and keeps it from being a mere form. For our purposes, however, we must be content with emphasizing the basic point that the individual is deeply grounded in reality for Aquinas. Matter, act, and a peculiar kind of relation all serve to individuate, and individuality is an ultimate trait.

Successive thinkers found two major problems in Aquinas' doctrine: first, he had emphasized the distinctness of the individual but had somewhat neglected the problem of its uniqueness; and, second, like all positions that assert the reality of the individual as a brute or natural fact with a character of incommunicability about it, Aquinas' position leads us to inquire further into the nature of this feature. Duns Scotus was to pick up these and other issues.

Duns Scotus. Here, again, we must confine ourselves to the barest essentials. Scotus starts with the logical indivisibility of the individual; an individual is what cannot be divided into parts of which the whole can be predicated. The class of philosophers, for example, can be divided into Platonists and Aristotelians; of each sub-class the term "philosopher" can be used. Socrates, however, cannot be so divided; there is no part of Socrates which is Socrates, even if his parts do bear a special relation to the whole not found in the parts of other individuals. Scotus' first problem is to inquire into the nature of this indivisibility. In so doing, he makes a number of valuable points, first among which is the doctrine that the principle of individuality cannot be a merely negative one. Socrates, that is, is this man and not that man, but what constitutes his unity as this individual is not adequately expressed merely by saying that he is not that man. Scotus, in short, wants to find something intrinsic to Socrates that will answer the question: What makes Socrates indivisible? Putting this in another way, we may say that, for Scotus, being an individual belongs to the nature of Socrates and is not identical with the fact that he exists in some spatio-temporal framework. Scotus saw that it is just as hard to say what makes this space or this moment individual as it is to say what makes Socrates this person.

Scotus' thought represents something of a paradox at this point. On the one hand, he saw that the so-called principle of individuation specifies what is that is supposed to make an individual an individual and that the feature or features indicated, if they are to be intelligible, must already be understood by us as having individuating force. Thus, we must already know in some sense what it is to be an individual if we are to understand any principle of individuation. Yet, despite his recognition of the problem, Scotus still sought a principle of individuation. He looked, in short, for "thisness" or the essence of "this." There is a nice paradox here, but we cannot continue on this tack; it is necessary to sum up the results. For Scotus, the individual is a unitary fusion of a common nature, for example, man, and an individual nature—the positive *entitas*—that makes him this man and no other. The individual nature endows the individual, not only with distinctness, but with uniqueness; beyond this we cannot go in comprehension. The result embraces a point of great importance—the individual nature exists and is known as such to God prior to its actuality in the world, so that the uniqueness of the person is rooted in the *totality* of the divine knowledge. One who knows all the individual natures also knows that there cannot be two individual natures that are identical.[9]

From the standpoint of philosophical theory, the thinker whose work places the greatest emphasis on the ultimacy of the individual is William of Ockham at the end of the medieval period. In his interpretation of knowledge and of science, we find most clearly stated the doctrine that all existent realities are utterly particular, and that the generic structures of things expressed in universal concepts belong, not to the things themselves, but to the sign-functioning power of the human mind. "Genus is not something common to many things because of some identity in them, but because of a certain community of the sign," wrote Ockham. The problem of universals does not concern us here; the crucial point is that on this view each individual is what it is and not another thing, for universal structure is no longer in nature but in thought. No other Western thinker up to Ockham's time had presented such an unqualified assertion of the final reality of the individual.

The Reformed Traditions.[10] Here, as before, it would be folly to attempt more than the delineation of a few essential points and, perhaps, the correction of a few standard misunderstandings. The first point is that it will not do to say, as is so often said, that what the Protestant Reformers did was to substitute the individual for the Church and to put his private opinions about God in place of the traditional faith. It would be more accurate to say that, drawing inspiration from Augustine and the theology of Paul, the Reformers placed a new emphasis upon the individual's confrontation with God through the Bible rather than through an authoritative institution. Luther's concern to have the Bible translated into the vernacular —the Reformation's equivalent to the current philosopher's emphasis on ordinary language—was intended to bring the Christian message to the individual person, so that he might know exactly what he was expected to respond to. The individual comes to be understood in primarily religious and ethical terms as the bearer of responsibility for the misuse of his freedom, as the one who responds to God in faith, and as the one to whom the divine promises and commandments are addressed.

It is difficult to fit the Reformation theology into the previous patterns of philosophical theology. Luther, Calvin, and Zwingli had their theological systems, of course, and Protestantism was to develop its own Scholasticism in the succeeding century, but, on the whole, the religious and not the metaphysical interest dominated. The Reformed traditions preferred Paul to Aristotle, and the so-called rhetoric of the Bible to the logics of the Schools. Hence, we shall not find an ontology of the individual except by implication. What we find, instead, is a new practical significance for the individual and for his own experience.

We may attempt to sum up the contribution of the Reformation with regard to the individual in three points. First, the primacy given to the response of the individual in *faith* meant the location of the classic drama of salvation within the soul of man and a shift away from the previous emphasis on the cosmic setting. The stress laid by Luther upon the confession of faith in accordance with conscience focused the extent to which the individual stands alone before a God, who demands that he say what he sincerely believes; the repetition of a traditional faith inherited but not appropriated will not suffice. A large portion of the "soul-searching" ordinarily associated with the Protestant outlook stems from the demand for sincerity in the individual response to the divine Word in faith. Second, the new emphasis on individual experience gave rise to a new plurality, not only in the increase of sects and religious communities, but also in a new sense of the "varieties of religious experience" to be found within the New Testament itself. Piety became more diffused and fragmented. The mystical and the moral, the legal and the sacramental were no longer combined within the confines of a single Christendom. Different sects emphasized different aspects of Christianity, some becoming predominantly mystical in their approach, others more legalistic or moralistic. To be sure, there were excesses, as when the English poet and philosopher Samuel Taylor Coleridge said that he belonged to a denomination of which at the time he was the only member. But, on the whole, the community principle was not lost.[12] Third, the new place of importance given within Protestantism to the doctrine of election and the need to regard sanctification as a visible sign to the believer led to various forms of perfectionism and the idea that there can be churches composed of visible saints. This aspect of Protestantism had a decisive role to play in the development of religion in America, and the American Puritan divines about whom everybody has heard and few have read were instrumental in the growth of an individualistic piety that has been remarkably long lasting.

Insofar as the German philosopher Immanuel Kant has often been described as the "Protestant philosopher," no summary statement about the Protestant contribution to an understanding of the individual can afford to omit him. In a dramatic passage in *What Is Enlightenment?*, Kant set forth the motto of Enlightenment as, "Dare to use your own reason!" This motto expresses well Kant's emphasis on the individual. Freedom and the moral law, the two foci of his moral philosophy, place final responsibility for right conduct on the individual person. He alone is the one to whom the imperative of moral obligation is addressed, and from him alone can the response emanate. Worthiness to be happy, Kant's moral goal, depends entirely on the will of the individual person. The Reformers, of course, would not have accepted this complete autonomy of will, but all would have agreed with Kant that it is to the will and heart of the individual that all commands are addressed.

Before concluding with a brief consideration of certain problems
having to do with the status of the individual on the contemporary
scene in the West, a summary of the main drift of Christian thought
over the past centuries will be helpful. Despite undeniable differences
in thought and action, the following three doctrines persist: (1) The
individual person is acknowledged as a fundamental type of being
created by God, and each individual is unique. (2) The individual
person is addressed by God as a responsible being possessed of a
finite or conditioned freedom. (3) The individual person is essentially involved in other individuals in view of the fact that the
divine life is envisaged as a community of persons and the symbol of
the ultimate perfection of life is that of a divine kingdom. Though
essentially involved in each other as members of one community,
each individual remains known as such to God; there is no melting
or blending of individuals into each other. In this sense, for Christianity, individuality remains an ultimate trait.

If we now turn away from the internal expression of the Western
religious tradition to consider certain features in the culture within
which the tradition now exists, we can better understand problems
concerning the status of the individual on the contemporary scene.
Moreover, we can then see the issues raised by modern industrial
society to which the religious tradition must respond in a relevant
and constructive way in both thought and action.

Briefly stated, the plight of the individual in the modern world is
that various developments in the social fabric have led to the alienation of the individual from himself. I cite three factors contributing
to this result, fully aware of the fact that I omit the economic and
the social dimensions of the problem. These are, in any case, to be
treated later on at this Conference. From three different sides we
have witnessed the submerging of the individual in favor of what is
inherently universal. First, the tradition of modern rationalism stress-
ing impersonal, universal, objective knowledge of reality has brought
about a crisis in self-knowledge to which the philosophy of existence
and the various forms of existentialism were the inevitable response.
If modern science is to be taken as the model of all knowledge, to
many it has appeared that knowledge of the unique individual and
his own induplicable experience can neither be acquired nor communicated. Moreover, as Kierkegaard saw, the individual too easily
loses himself when he thinks only in terms of laws and universals.
Kierkegaard's favorite illustration makes the point as well as it can
be made. For centuries, he said, philosophers have been saying "All
men are mortal" without at the same time noting the singular implication, "I, too, must die." The problem is that the individual

must exist within his thought and the thought within his own experience, but this means that there must be patterns of thinking and meaning for which modern exact physical science is not the appropriate model.

Second, the development of modern technological society has brought with it the familiar phenomenon of the "mass man" and the idea of interchangeable parts. The mass man is not an individual; in fact, he is no one at all, and yet he dominates the scene alienating the individual from himself, sapping him of his moral fibre, and leading him to aspire to nothing more than anonymity. If one cannot be who one essentially is, then it is better to merge into the universal and at the least manage to escape responsibility. One need mount no campaign against either science or technology—and none is intended as such—in order to perceive the problems raised for the individual by the technologically oriented society. The unique and unduplicable in human life is sacrificed, and gradually the moral personality to whom alone an ethical command can be issued decays. It is interesting to note how often in recent years corruption in high places and low has been accompained with a total incapacity to recognize the presence of a moral issue. Again, the philosophers of existence have focused the issue for us by pointing to the decay of the moral individual; we need not agree with them in every respect, in order to see the validity of their criticism and their attempt to recover the individual as the primary reality.

Third, we have witnessed in our time the growth of the absolute state, and we have seen how it manages to deprive the individual of his individuality. It is no longer a conjecture, but a matter of plain fact that men will commit all manner of horrors and descend to the beast in the treatment of their fellow men, all with the explanation —or, better, excuse—that they were under orders from a political and military power that is absolute.

For the above and other reasons, there is a growing concern in the West at present for the recovery of the individual as a free, courageous, and responsible being, and one of the tests of the vitality of the religious tradition will be found in the extent to which it can contribute to that recovery. But there is another feature of the contemporary scene that we neglect at our peril; its existence focuses the problematic and incoherent character of modern life. On the one hand, there is the urgent need for the recovery of the individual, and yet, on the other, is the no less urgent sense of loneliness that stems from the loss of community. Here we have the underlying contradiction in Western culture at the present time; we must recover the *individual* and overcome *individualistic loneliness* at the same time. That such loneliness exists can easily be seen from the many insignificant and sordid forms of "togetherness" that many

people are prepared to accept, if only they can overcome their isolation and "belong" to some form of corporate life. How can the
two needs be met at the same time? In ideal terms the answer is that
only a true community transcends the evils of individualism and col-
lectivism at the same time. But what is the form of the true community? Can the religious tradition furnish that? This is the major
spiritual dilemma of the West at the present time.

QUESTION: How is it possible for a being that is created to be free?
Does not the dependence of the individual upon God, so much
emphasized by Christianity, mean that the individual is deprived of
the power to act freely and with responsibility?

ANSWER: The question is fundamental for Christianity and is
urged with particular force by the proponents of Buddhism and
some forms of Indian religion where the emphasis falls on the eternality of the self. I raised the question myself in the paper, except
that I formulated the problem in converse form—how can a free
being be created? The fact is that the doctrine of creation is basic to
the Judeo-Christian position. Hence, the doctrine of freedom in
Christian perspective has to be developed in conscious recognition
of the Christian belief about creation.

Two basic points can be cited: first, there is no need to interpret
creation in mechanistic fashion that completely excludes freedom;
second, Christian theologians need to develop a more subtle account
of the created being of man in order to avoid the consequence that
the entire being of the individual is "given" once and for all in
creation. With regard to the first point, the Christian belief in man's
dependence upon God for his being means primarily that no individual person brings himself into being and that his original nature
is good. The individual is finite and contingent, and this means that
he lives in and is conditioned by historical circumstances. The development of the self and the perfecting of the "real self" do not take
place in a vacuum; the self is not entirely free in the sense that it
begins its life with nothing "given" to it from outside itself. Though
dependent upon God for initial being, the self is not of the same
nature as a stone or a star. The nature of the self and the person
includes the capacity for self-consciousness, reflection, and the power
(limited, but still real) to act in accordance with ideas. The idea of
creation does not require that every creature stands only in a wholly
mechanical relation to the creator. In Christian belief, God is love,
and, as creator, God allows for the possibility of beings who can love
in return. But the capacity to love becomes meaningless without the
capacity to reject love or to hate. Hence, to create a being who can
love is to create a being who has a measure of freedom.

With regard to the second point, it is clear that the Christian
theologian cannot continue to think of the individual self as created
all at once, that is, with the total self and its destiny given entirely
at the moment of creation. We can understand how a free being or
a self can be created only if we can interpret the creation of the self
to mean the bringing forth of a creature with the capacity to develop. Two extremes are to be avoided: on the one hand, we must
not understand creation in a mechanical sense, such that the creator
becomes the only agent and the creature is reduced to a thing with-

out freedom; on the other hand, we cannot identify the total self with the "free" self that makes itself in total self-determination, for in that case the need for initial creation would disappear. We may say that the individual is created, but not entirely created, from beyond himself.

Christianity followed the line marked out in the Old Testament doctrine of God according to which the world was created or called forth by God out of nothing. Man was created a living person compounded of the clay of the earth and the "breath" or spirit of God. Though imaginatively represented and expressed in a frankly anthropomorphic way, the idea of an original creation for all things embraces two conceptual points: first, that all existing realities are contingent and dependent upon a source beyond themselves, and, second, that the original creation is essentially good, since there was no pre-existent matter to stand over against God limiting the creative act to its own potentialities or thwarting the divine plan. Now, accepting this outlook as given, the question is, How is it consistent to hold both that all finite, individual persons are created by God, and that such persons have freedom or the capacity for self-determination? If being created as an individual person is taken to mean that the person is determined completely and at once at the outset to all that this individual is and will become, there can be no meaning for freedom as self-determination. Nor can the difficulty be removed by defining freedom in such a way that it happily coincides with no more than the intellectual contemplation of a totally determined process. Some other line of answer must be found.

The key is found in the concept of the self. If being a person differs from being a stone or a star, as it obviously does, we shall have to reckon with a new factor, namely, freedom and the awareness that part of what is meant by a person is a capacity for choosing between alternatives, including alternative life-patterns of a total sort. That is, it is necessary to take seriously the possibility that a self is the sort of reality that cannot be entirely "given" or determined at once. We have to go further and consider the more radical view that the self is only what makes itself through freedom, so that it is not a question of only partial determination or "givenness" but of there being no determination from beyond the self at all. There is no question that some Christian theologians have fully accepted a deterministic thesis, claiming that all things and events are completely determined by God, so that man, though more complex in character than a star or stone, is in principle as fully circumscribed as they. The question is whether this theological determinism is a necessary consequence of the doctrine of creation. There is no reason to suppose that it is.

For a being to be created does not necessarily mean the complete determination at the outset of every future state of that being. There is no contradiction in supposing that there is a being who, though he does not bring himself into existence, is still capable of exercising a measure of choice in the direction of his existence when the stage of self-consciousness has been reached. Self-consciousness, or awareness of the self, is not identical with the coming into being of the self. A created being may be indeterminate in some respects and determinate in others. For example, it is necessary that every individual have some ideas, but not necessary that any individual have this or that idea. There is no need to assume that, on the doctrine of creation, all creatures will be of the same type. The stone or the star is not the proper model for a self-conscious being, and there is no contradiction in holding that there should be created a peculiar kind of being such that this being can realize itself through a self-conscious process, without thereby creating itself in every respect in that process. Theological determinism follows from the doctrine of creation *only* when the self is reduced to the status of an object and the peculiar nature of selfhood is forgotten. An individual self is not the sort of reality that can be created "all at once," but this is not to say that it is contradictory to say that it cannot be created in any sense at all. The individual is created as that unique set of potentialities and conditions which remain to be developed into a fully actualized person. The self plays a role in that actualization. Moreover, in not only accepting but even demanding the reality of time, change, and history, Christian thought allows for a medium through which this actualization can take place.

With regard to the second aspect of the question, namely, its consideration as a general metaphysical problem outside the Christian framework with its presupposition of creation, our experience of selfhood and of freedom leads us to acknowledge the finite and limited character of both. We can contemplate the many selves we might have been and the many selves we might become, but we contemplate as *this* self the self that we already are. Furthermore, we can consider alternative courses of action and evaluate our conduct, all of which requires freedom, but in actual fact we know that our freedom is never absolute because it requires conditions some of which stem from the individual self we already are. The conditions for freedom, plus the fact that by the time an individual becomes self-conscious and aware of its freedom as a reality the self has already been formed sufficiently so that it has an individual identity, suggest a "given" element that belongs to the self or characterizes it but which the self does not, and, indeed, cannot, attribute to its own freedom. This "given" element is the metaphysical counterpart of creation in the theological sense. Without this element there would be no individuality because every attempt to make individuality itself an achievement of freedom moves in a circle: in order to exercise freedom, a self with individuality is the only basis from which the exercise can proceed.

The Christian tradition, however, can learn something of great importance from the tradition represented by the question and it is this: the strong emphasis in Christianity upon individual will and responsibility needs to be qualified by a new sense of the importance of *being* over *doing,* and an increased awareness of what has been called the *impersonal sacred.* An exaggerated concern for the unique individual as the object of the divine providence has not been unambiguously positive in its effects. It has led to individualism and the destruction of community, and to such an increase in the moral burden of the individual that personality is often disrupted and distorted as a result. How shall we bring these insights to bear? How shall we succeed in making the point that it is not treason to their own tradition to consider the possibility that they may have something to learn from other traditions? This is a hard task, but at present no task is more important.

QUESTION: What I missed in the paper was an account of God as an individual and the influence exercised by that conception on the development of individuality in the West.

ANSWER: I did not entirely neglect the topic and touched on it in connection with Aquinas' theory of the individual, but my chief purpose was to focus on the finite individual, his status and problems, rather than on theological issues.

1 See John Skinner, *Prophecy and Religion* (Cambridge: Cambridge University Press, 1922), esp. chap. XI. Cf. Ezekiel 14:12–20; 18:1–4.

2 *Ibid.*, pp. 122 ff.; 320 ff.

3 The difference between creating, on the one hand, and shaping something out of pre-existent material, on the other, is nicely preserved in the difference between the two Greek terms, *"poiéō"* and *"ktízō."* The general sense of *poiéō* is to make or to do, where in all cases the making or doing means working on or with something that is already existent. *ktízō*, on the other hand, means to found something, as in the case of a city, or to bring something to pass for the first time. The connotation of pre-existent material with which to perform the task is lacking. Ktízō expresses more adequately than does what the Christian tradition tries to express with the idea of creation.

4 Matthew 10:29–31 expresses the utter individuality of every created reality—even the hairs of the head have their individual being—and the concern which God has for individual creatures.

5 In I Corinthians 15:44, Paul distinguishes between a "natural body" (*physikòn sōma*) and a "spiritual body" (*psychikòn sōma*), a distinction that was the source of much speculation, especially among the Greek Fathers of the Church. The distinction is cited in the present context because it shows how very strong was the need for some form of *embodiment* in the conception of the individual. Paul does not think in terms of the "natural man" as merely a "body" in contrast with a disembodied "spiritual" man, but, rather, of two types of embodiment, one of which belongs to the natural order, and the other is an imaginative (not imaginary!) expression of what a resurrected individual person would be. The point is that Christianity followed the Hebraic tradition in holding that embodiment belongs essentially to the nature of the individual person.

6 In a way reminiscent of Plato's discussion about the relative merits of the written and spoken word, Anselm opens his *Proslogium* by expressing uncertainty about whether he should commit the argument for God to paper. The point is that actual meditation by the individual forces him to confront himself and the divine presence in the process; if the argument is written and thus objectified, the individual person may be led to view the whole matter objectively and thus be distracted from moving through the meditative process himself. For Anselm, each individual person has to confront the problem for himself, and this can happen only if he goes through the meditative process in his own mind rather than looking at the record of someone else's meditation.

7 Augustine, *Soliloquia*. Detailed documentation not available at this time.

8 It is important to notice that much of what Thomas says about individual persons and their nature occurs in the context of the Trinitarian discussion. The emphasis placed on the individual depends on the doctrine of the *persons* in God, which is, among other things, a theological recognition of individuality. *Summa Theologica,* Part I, Q. 29, 30.

9 The Latin term *"haecceitas"* is usually translated as "thisness." It is not certain that Duns Scotus used this word, since it does not occur in writings that are generally accepted as authentic.

10 An emphasis on individual religious experience and concern for salvation runs throughout the works of Luther and Calvin especially, but it is also to be found in Zwingli and Melanchthon. Detailed analysis, however, reveals significant differences in outlook. Luther, for example, made the concern for justification so central that the ethical dimension was subordinated, whereas Calvin synthesized the two and the "Protestant ethic," so called, derives largely from the Calvinistic tradition. Despite particular differences, however, the stress on the importance of the individual over against the power of all institutions remains a common factor in the major theologians of the Reformation.

SECTION IV

Ethics

HSIEH YU-WEI[a]

The status of the individual in Chinese ethics

What is the status of the individual in Chinese ethics? As we all know, there are different systems of ethics in the history of Chinese thought: Confucianism, Buddhism, Taoism, Moism, and others. It is impossible to discuss all of them here. So, since Confucian ethics has always been the most influential and the most widely practiced ethics of the Chinese people, I shall answer the question from the standpoint of Confucian ethics.

Confucian ethics never downgrades the status of the individual; on the contrary, it always emphasizes the value and dignity of the individual. Confucius and his followers, in fact, recognized and asserted the equality of man's value in every individual. What the West calls "the equality of the individual," "the freedom of the individual," "the individual's relations to other individuals," and "the individual's relations to the community, i.e., to the family, the state, and to mankind," were all advocated in one form or another by Confucian ethics, too.

I. THE EQUALITY OF ALL INDIVIDUALS

The central idea of Confucian ethics is *jen*[b], "humanity." Confucian ethics could not ignore the significance of any individual; otherwise, it would be in conflict with *jen*. What is *jen*? In the *Analects* (*Lun yü*[c]), "Fan Ch'ih[d] asked about *jen*. The master said, 'It is to love all men.' "[1] Since *jen* is to love all men, the importance of the individual is necessarily emphasized. But, owing to historical accidents and to wrong interpretations by emperors for centuries, the importance of the individual in Confucian ethics was not always made explicit. Also, owing to the lack of clear discussion about the individual's equality, freedom, and rights in Confucian ethics, the suspicion naturally arose that it neglected the importance of the individual. But the implied affirmations of the importance of the individual, the individual's equality, freedom, rights, and duties, are clear.

Confucian ethics asserted the equality of the individual, but what Confucius called equality is the equality of humanity. It is the equality of man's value insofar as man is man, equality a priori, that is to say, all men are born equal. In *The Doctrine of the Mean* (*Chung yung*e), it is said, "What Heaven has conferred is called the nature,"[2] and this "nature" is human nature. Human nature is what everybody has received from Heaven. And what everybody has received from Heaven must be equal. This is the justice of Heaven. It is the equality of every man's possibility, the opportunity to be a man.

How Confucius maintained the equality of "human nature" can be seen from the Confucian conception of *jen*. *Jen* is the reality of the universe, and also the essence of man, that which makes him man. In Chinese philology, man is defined as *jen*.[3] In *The Doctrine of the Mean,* it is said, "*Jen* is man, and the greatest exercise of it is in loving relatives."[4] And in the *Mencius* it is said, "*Jen* is the distinguishing characteristic of man. As embodied in man's conduct, it is called *tao*f [the way]."[5] Thus, *jen* is clearly the distinguishing characteristic of man, according to the central idea of Confucian ethics.

But, how do we know that the distinguishing characteristic of man is *jen?* We know this by our own experience and by our own observation. As Mencius said,

> The ability possessed by men without having been acquired by learning is intuitive ability, and the knowledge possessed by them without the exercise of thought is their intuitive knowledge. Children in arms know how to love their parents, and, when they have grown a little older, they all know how to love their elder brothers. Filial affection for parents is the working of *jen*. Respect for elders is the working of righteousness. There is no other reason for those feelings—they belong to all under Heaven.[6]

That is to say, the fact that every man has intuitive ability and intuitive knowledge, or the fact that every man has "*jen*," is a fact that can be verified by children's unquestionable love for their parents.

Furthermore, the fact that every man has *jen* can be verified by the feeling of commiseration that every man possesses. As Mencius said,

> " . . . if men suddenly see a child about to fall into a well, they will without exception experience a feeling of alarm and distress. They will feel so, not as a ground on which they may gain the favor of the child's parents, nor as a ground on which they may seek the praise of their neighbors and friends, nor from a dislike of hearing such a noise. From this case we may perceive that the feeling of commiseration [etc.] is essential to man, . . . The feeling of commiseration is the beginning (or the starting point) of *jen*. . . ."[7]

This inability to bear to see the suffering of others, this feeling of commiseration, is a fact that we can see everywhere. How can we deny that men have *jen?*

But, though every man has *jen,* what a man has is merely the "beginning of *jen*," or just a seed of humanity. How, then, can we affirm the equality of all individuals? It was precisely in order to emphasize this seed of humanity that Confucius built up his ethical system. Confucius considered this seed of humanity as what is most valuable in men and what makes man man. The difference between men and animals lies in this seed of humanity. The dignity and value of man which enable him to achieve unity with Heaven also lie in this seed of humanity. If there were no such seed of humanity, ethical education would be impossible; but it is clearly possible to educate man as man, as wise man and sage.

Since every man has this seed of humanity, Confucian ethics' claim that man is born equal refers precisely to the universal equality of this seed of humanity, though not equality in other respects. When man is born, he is in possession of this seed of humanity, and what he possesses is no more and no less than any other man.

Because of this seed of humanity Confucian ethics also maintained that every man can become a sage or can become Emperor Yao[g] or Emperor Shun[h]. It is clearly declared, "What a man is Shun? And what am I? All those who try can be the same."[8] If every man can be a sage—and to be a sage is the highest ideal of man—does this not demonstrate the basic equality of all individuals?

Of course, to say that every man can be a sage is not to say that every man is a sage. Only a few can be considered sages. Hence, in fact, men are not equal. What is called equality is equality of opportunity or equality of possibility, and not equality of achievement. The highest ideal of Confucian ethics is to educate men to be sages, and, if every man has the possibility of becoming a sage, what more can we want or require?

Furthermore, the equality asserted by Confucian ethics is fundamental. All other equalities are implied by this one basic equality. Hence, the fact that other equalities, such as equality of rights, equality before the law, etc., were seldom discussed does not mean that they were denied. They were all clearly implied. At least, they are not in conflict, in principle, with this basic equality. The reason why Confucian ethics seldom talked about other equalities is that, if a man wants to become a sage, he should do his best by himself and should not depend on other men or other conditions? Even if all other conditions are unfavorable, if one does one's best, one can still become a sage. All other equalities are within this concept of *jen*. This interpretation is also asserted by most contemporary Chinese scholars. I may mention Ch'ien Mu[i] [9] and T'ang Chün-i[j] [10] as representatives.

Thus, since Confucian ethics has the spirit of "the great equality," the principle of equality in traditional Chinese ethics is undeniable.

II. THE FREEDOM OF THE INDIVIDUAL

Confucian ethics also asserted the freedom of the individual. The meaning of freedom, as we all know, is very complex. Generally speaking, freedom means political freedom, such as freedom of thought, freedom of speech, freedom of belief, etc. Such freedoms were little or seldom discussed in Confucian ethics; hence, it is often suspected that Confucian ethics denied the freedom of the individual. In fact, the freedom asserted in Confucian ethics is also fundamental and can include or at least imply all other freedoms.

The freedom advocated in Confucian ethics is the freedom to do good or the freedom to choose what is good. It is ethical freedom of choice. But such freedom of choice has its own ground and its own limits. It is a limited freedom. There is no such thing as an unlimited freedom. "Free" does not mean "free from."[11]

The truth that the freedom which is possible and which ought to obtain must have some ground or limitation is recognized in Confucian ethics. This ground or limitation is goodness. One should choose good; one should not choose evil. If we grant that every individual has the freedom to choose evil, then the freedom of everyone will be threatened by the evil. If evil prevailed, freedom might disappear. Hence, *from the point of view of ethics,* we should allow only the freedom to choose good and not the freedom to choose evil. Confucius says in *The Analects,* "When I walk alone with two others, they may serve me as my teachers. Choose what is good and follow it, but avoid what is bad."[12] Again, he says, "Hear much and select what is good and follow it."[13] Such expressions clearly indicate the idea of freedom to choose good. Later, in *The Doctrine of the Mean,* such sayings as "Choose the course of the mean"[14] and "He who attains to sincerity is he who chooses what is good and firmly holds it fast"[15] indicate the same attitude. Freedom to choose is freedom to choose, within the complex of good and evil, what is good and not what is evil. This is man's freedom, and the only freedom which is permitted in Confucian ethics.

If freedom means freedom to choose good, then what is good? What is good in the opinion of Confucius is the same as *jen. Jen* is good, and good is *jen.* All values created by men will be affirmed and protected by *jen. Jen* is most unselfish and least obstinate. What is firmly upheld by *jen* is *jen* itself, and not just *any* man's private opinion. Confucius strongly opposed such obstinacy. Confucius was not obstinate in his own opinion. It is said in *The Analects,* "There were four things from which the Master was entirely free. He had no foregone conclusions, no arbitrary predeterminations, no obstinacy, and no egotism."[16]

Confucius did not like forced uniformity of belief or opinion—

even in ethics. "The superior man is catholic and not a partisan."
He said, "The mean man is a partisan and not catholic,"[17] and
"The superior man is seeking for harmony but not sameness. The
mean man is seeking for sameness but not harmony."[18] Later, Mencius expressed the same attitude in saying, "The superior man seeks
just for *jen* and cares not for sameness."[19] This means that, if one's
words and actions are in accordance with *jen,* it is not necessary for
them to be the same as mine. To choose good is to choose the good
in accordance with *jen,* and not the good in any man's private
opinion. This is the true meaning of freedom to choose the good in
Confucian ethics.

As indicated above, the freedom to choose the good implies or
justifies the other important freedoms, *ethically.* To illustrate, Confucius traveled to different states during his lifetime. The purpose of
his travel was to choose a good prince to serve. Now, the relation
between prince and minister is a political relation. If one has the
freedom to choose which prince to serve, one is not held in bondage
by the relation between prince and minister but has political freedom. Such political freedom Confucius indicated in the following
sayings: "My doctrines make no way. I will get upon a raft, and
float about on the sea."[20] "When called to office, to undertake its
duties; when not so called, to lie retired."[21] "When right principles
of government prevail in the kingdom, he will show himself; when
they are rejected, he will keep concealed."[22] "Some men of worth
retire from the world. Some retire from particular states."[23]

Confucius also maintained, in social affairs, the freedom to choose
friends. The saying quoted above—"When I walk along with two
others, they may serve me as my teachers. Choose what is good and
follow it, but avoid what is bad"[24]—indicates his attitude clearly.

The freedom to choose a place to live was also affirmed by
Confucius. He said, "It is *jen* which constitutes the excellence of a
neighborhood. If a man in selecting a residence does not fix on one
where *jen* prevails, how can he be wise?"[25]

As to freedom of speech, Confucius affirmed this in his own deeds.
Confucius himself was free to speak as he pleased. He edited *The
Book of Odes (Shih ching*[k]) and wrote *The Book of History (Shu
ching*[l]) in accordance with his own ideas. Certainly, he would not
oppose freedom of speech. He would oppose only the speaking of
bad words or empty words, that is, words without corresponding
actions. Good words, or what should be said, one must say; otherwise, it is not ethically right. Confucius said, "When a man may be
spoken with, not to speak to him is to err toward the man."[26] He
also said, "What the superior man requires is just that in his words
there may be nothing wrong."[27] Hence, the only condition for the
freedom of speech is whether your speech is right or not. If it is

right to speak, you should speak freely even to those high above you, such as the prince or your parents. To argue with prince or parents is permitted by Confucius. He said, "In serving his parents, a son may remonstrate with them, but gently."[28] Such freedom to argue with the prince constituted one of the most important kinds of political freedom under the Chinese political system. Mencius, too, enjoyed freedom of speech. Mencius argued freely with the princes of several states, and sometimes he even scolded them. But Mencius confessed that he did not like to argue. He argued because he had to.[29] It was under the compulsion of goodness, or *jen*, that Mencius felt he had to argue. Consequently, freedom of speech has its limitation, and that limitation is goodness, or *jen*. The saying "Speak not what is contrary to propriety"[30] demonstrates this attitude of Confucian ethics.

Thus, in view of the freedom to choose the good, we have freedom to choose our prince, freedom to choose our friends, freedom to choose our residence, and freedom of speech. On condition that we choose within the limits of goodness, we can choose freely. Outside the limits of goodness, one should not be free. This is the true meaning of freedom. Freedom to choose the good is thus the same as to assert all other freedoms. No other freedoms should be allowed to violate goodness. If you act in accordance with goodness, you are free. Otherwise, you may lose your freedom. Whatever freedom you want, you should not violate this ethical principle of freedom to choose the good.

This freedom to choose the good may also be interpreted as the freedom to develop one's humanity or one's true self. Every man has *jen*, and this constitutes his true nature or true self. But this true nature needs cultivation or development. And this must be done by oneself. It is said in *The Analects*, "Yen Yüan asked about *jen*. The Master said, 'To subdue one's self and return to propriety is *jen*. If a man can for one day subdue himself and return to propriety, all under Heaven will ascribe *jen* to him. Is the practice of *jen* from a man himself, or is it from others?' "[31] This state is one of freedom. For the flowing of *jen*, or humanity, is free. It comes from one's own self, and no outside force can interfere with it. Hence, such practice of *jen*, or the development of one's humanity, must of necessity be free. In *The Doctrine of the Mean* it is said, "It is only he who is possessed of the most complete sincerity that can exist under Heaven and can give full development to his nature. Able to give full development to his own nature, he can do the same to the nature of other men. Able to give full development to the nature of other men, he can give full development to the natures of animals and things. Able to give their full development to the natures of animals and things, he can assist the transforming and nourishing powers of

Heaven and Earth. Able to assist the transforming and nourishing powers of Heaven and Earth, he may with Heaven and Earth form a ternion."[32] When a man may with Heaven and Earth form a ternion, then he is really free. But it all depends upon the full development of his own nature.[33]

III. THE DUTIES OF THE INDIVIDUAL

From the above we know that Confucian ethics called for the freedom of the individual. And freedom is one of—or expresses—the rights of the individual. Every individual has the right to be free, that is, free to choose the good. In this sense, Confucian ethics also asserted the rights of the individual. But, it was not the rights of the individual that were considered most important. Of most importance were the duties or obligations of the individual. According to Confucian ethics, in order to be a man or to be a sage, it is necessary, first, to perform one's duties, not to claim one's rights. It is the fulfillment of duties that can make a man into a man or into a sage.

The duties of the individual are the moral principles according to which one should act with regard to oneself and to others. In order to be a man or to be a sage, one must observe these moral principles in the cultivation and development of one's humanity. The equality and freedom that one enjoys are mere possibilities for becoming a man or a sage. They will not be realized unless one has done one's duties in accordance with these moral principles.

Every individual has duties, first of all, to himself. In order to fulfill one's duties to oneself, the important work one has to do is "self-inspection" (*tzu-hsing*[m]). Self-inspection is what is nowadays called self-criticism or self-examination. The belief is that the individual himself has the clearest insight into what he has done and whether it has been done in accordance with *jen*.

If one fails to carry out self-inspection, the question as to whether or not one can fulfill other duties, or the question as to whether or not other duties one performs can be considered fulfilled, cannot be answered. The reason for those acts which deceive oneself, and others, derives precisely from the failure to carry out this first duty. So, Confucius emphasized this duty of self-inspection. In *The Analects,* it is said, "The philosopher Tsang[n] said, 'I daily examine myself on three points—whether in transacting business for others, I may not have been loyal; whether in intercourse with friends, I may not have been sincere; and whether I may have mastered and practiced the instruction of my teacher.' "[34] This expression, "daily examine myself on three points" explicitly advocates self-inspection. It is also said, "When we see men of worth, we should think of equaling them; when we see men of a contrary character, we should turn inward and examine ourselves."[35] "Turn inward and examine ourselves" means "self-inspection," but also more than that.

Self-inspection is the inspection of actions that one has done. But Confucian ethics taught something more than "self-inspection," what is called "taking care of one's own will" (*shen-tu*[o]) in *The Great Learning* (*Ta hsüeh*[p]). It is said, "What is meant by making the will sincere is the allowing of no self-deception, as when we hate a bad smell and as when we love what is beautiful. This is called self-enjoyment. Therefore, the superior man must take care of his own will."[36] This "taking care of one's own will" is self-inspection before action. It is concerned with our will or intention rather than with our conduct. One's conduct can be seen by all, but one's will or intention is known to oneself alone. When action has taken place, although it is necessary to examine it by self-inspection to see whether it is in accordance with *jen* or not, it is too late to do anything when it is wrong. In order to avoid wrong action, self-inspection alone is not enough; the work of "taking care of one's own will" must be added. "Prevention is much better than cure." This taking care of one's own intention or making the will sincere constituted the outstanding characteristic of Neo-Confucianism in the Sung Dynasty (960–1279).

Self-inspection and taking care of one's own will are two important duties of the individual to himself. In regard to other men —between individual and individual—the relation should be that of "propriety" (*li*[q]). This is of first importance—to treat others with propriety.

The most obvious meaning of "propriety" is respect of man for man. Each man should pay respect to other men because such respect is respect for man as man, for the humanity (*jen*) which is possessed by every man. Though this respect is paid to others, it is in fact paid to oneself, too. It may be called the self-respect of man as man. If one does not pay respect to other men, one does not care for the humanity possessed by other men. In that case, the humanity possessed by oneself may be questioned. If one really has humanity in one's heart, one will naturally pay respect to the humanity in other men. So, Confucius considered "self-control and return to propriety as *jen*."[37] In propriety we can see the manifestation of *jen*. The importance of propriety lies here. Propriety must be based upon *jen*. If not, it can hardly be called propriety. It is said in *The Analects*, "If men are without *jen*, what use is there for propriety?"[38] It is for the sake of *jen* that one should treat others with propriety. And in such propriety, in such respectful conduct toward other men, one affirms the personality, the value, and the rights of other men. If every man has such respectfulness in regard to other men, then the relation between man and man will be in perfect harmony and without conflict.

Propriety means, then, the cultivation of harmony between man and man. "Propriety" is always connected with "concession" (*jang*[r]). If one knows propriety, one must also know concession. In case one does not know concession, and quarrels with other men, one still does not know propriety. But concession is concession of rights and not concession of duties. One should not concede one's duties, such as the duty to practice *jen*. "He may not yield the performance of *jen* even to his teacher."[39] In that case, if every man concedes rights and not duties, there would be no basis for quarrel between man and man. So, it is said in *The Analects,* "In practicing the rules of propriety, harmony is to be prized."[40] Accordingly, the aim of propriety is peace among men.

Confucian ethics maintained propriety and concession as the duties of the individual toward others. Moreover, Confucian ethics also required loyalty (*chung*[s]) and reciprocity (*shu*[t]) as principles in one's conduct toward others. It is said, "The doctrine of our master is nothing but loyalty and reciprocity."[41] But loyalty and reciprocity also come from *jen*.

For Confucian ethics, it is incorrect to interpret loyalty as loyalty to king or prince. Loyalty means self-devotion, that is, doing one's duty with all one's strength. Loyalty is loyalty to one's duty as prescribed by *jen,* or the humanity within oneself. It might be described as one's own conscience determining one's duty. And, in accordance with his conscience, or *jen,* every individual has the duty to help others. It is said in *The Analects,* "Now, the man of *jen,* wishing to be established himself, seeks to establish others; wishing to be enlarged himself, he seeks also to enlarge others."[42] For the sake of carrying out this duty, one has to do one's best, that is, one must be loyal.

The word "loyalty" first appears in *The Analects* in connection with Philosopher Tsang's saying, ". . . whether in transacting business for others, I may not have been loyal."[43] This shows clearly that loyalty is not reserved for the king only; rather, it is an attitude toward all other men. Though Confucius paid due respect to the king, his respect was paid to the position of the king, and not the king himself. The relation between the king and the minister, for Confucius, should be one of mutual respect. Hence, he said, "A prince should employ his minister according to the rules of propriety. Ministers should serve their prince with loyalty."[44] Loyalty may be paid to the prince, on condition that the prince treats his minister with propriety. Loyalty is self-devotion to the duties to other men; the prince is included, but not the prince alone.

Based upon *jen,* we have the duty of loyalty to other men. Also based upon *jen,* we have the duty of reciprocity toward other men. Loyalty and reciprocity go together in one's relationships with other men. The way to treat others is to be loyal, on the one hand, and to practice reciprocity, on the other. Reciprocity clearly comes from *jen.* It is the natural consequence of *jen,* when it is developed. A man of *jen,* in establishing himself, seeks to establish others, and, in enlarging himself, seeks to enlarge others. This is reciprocity. It consists in treating others in the same way as you treat yourself. It is the Golden Rule. It is said in *The Analects,* "Tzu-kung[n] asked, saying, 'Is there one word which may serve as a rule of practice for all one's life?' The Master said, 'Is not reciprocity such a word? What you do not want done to yourself, do not do to others.' "[45] Reciprocity is a fundamental principle for the relations between man and man. If this principle is followed by all, then peace will be established among men.

IV. THE INDIVIDUAL AND THE COMMUNITY

For the moral duties of the individual to himself, Confucian ethics maintained self-inspection and taking care of one's own will, and maintained propriety, loyalty, and reciprocity as one's moral duties to others. But what about duties of the individual to the community? The duties which the individual should perform with respect to the community were expressed clearly in *The Great Learning.* Here, it is said, "The ancients who wished to illustrate illustrious virtue throughout the world first ordered well their own states. Wishing to order well their states, they first regulated their families. Wishing to regulate their families, they first cultivated their persons."[46] This means everybody has the duty to regulate his family, to order the state, and to bring about peace in the world. Family, state, and the world (or mankind as a whole) are communities to which every individual owes a duty.

Though Confucian ethics called for duties of the individual to the community, it did not overemphasize the community and ignore the individual. In fact, Confucian ethics considered the individual even more important than the community. Confucian ethics regarded individuals as roots, and communities as leaves—or individuals as foundations and communities as roofs. The duty to cultivate oneself should come first; then come the duties of regulating the family, ordering the state, and making peace in the world. One's duties to the community depend upon one's duties to oneself. It is said, "From the Son of Heaven down to the masses of the people, all must consider the cultivation of the person the root of everything else. It cannot be that, when the root is neglected, what springs from it will be well ordered."[47] Hence, the cultivation of the person, or the individual, is fundamental. Without such cultivation of the person, or the individual, no other duties can be fulfilled by the individual.

But, before proceeding, let us see what duties of the individual to the community were prescribed by Confucian ethics. First of all, every individual has a duty to his family. Duty to the family was especially emphasized in Confucian ethics. But this emphasis on duty to the family was in fact for the good of the individual. The common mistaken view is that, since Confucian ethics emphasized the importance of the family, Chinese ethics took the family as the unit of its system, that Chinese ethics considered the family as the basis or the center to which all individuals must be subordinated, that the family is everything, and that individuals are nothing, that individuals must submit to the family and work for the family. This is not correct.

The importance of the family is specifically for the sake of realizing the individual, that is, for the fulfillment of the seed of *jen* possessed by every individual. This seed of *jen* comes directly from the family. We all get our humanity originally from the family. Since we all get our lives from our parents and grow up in the family, the cultivation and development of our humanity must begin within the family. But how do we cultivate and develop our humanity within the family? Individuals should do their duty to the family. The two important duties of the individual to the family are filial piety (*hsiao*^{v}) and brotherliness (*ti*^{w}).

Filial piety and brotherliness are moral principles which teach men to love and respect their own parents and elder brothers. These principles were based upon the little humanity inborn in all men in loving their parents, and were intended to preserve and develop it by ethical education. Confucius considered the rudimentary instinct of loving one's parents as the root of *jen*. Without cultivation, it may wither away or disappear. In order to cultivate and develop such a root of *jen*, Confucius taught the doctrine of filial piety and brotherliness in the family. So, in *The Analects* it is said, "Filial piety and brotherliness—are they not the root of *jen?*"[48] For the practice of *jen*, filial piety and brotherliness should be practiced first. The reason is obvious. If a man does not love his own parents, can he be a man of *jen*? And, if a man has the duty to love men, whom should he love first? Is it not his own parents? The doctrine of filial piety and brotherliness is intended to teach men to love and respect their own parents and brothers first, and then extend their love and respect to the parents and brothers of others. This is the way to cultivate and develop one's own humanity. It is a way to educate men in the family, in order that they can develop and realize their true selves. What is important is individuals in the family and not the family as such.

As a matter of fact, Confucian ethics considered the individual and the family equally important and mutually dependent. Individuals cannot be separated from the family. The development of an individual's humanity must begin in and with the family. Without the family, or in neglect of the family, one's *jen,* or humanity, is rootless. Can those who do not love their own parents love other men? The importance of the family lies here. On the other hand, the family can be regulated only through the development of the individual. Without the development of the individual, the family cannot be regulated. Herein lies the importance of the individual.

Just as Confucian ethics asserted the mutual dependence of the individual and the family, it also asserted the mutual dependence of the individual and the state and the whole of mankind. Confucian conceptions of the state and of mankind were not too clear, but what is clear is that, as a community, the state is larger than the family, and the whole of mankind is larger than the state. But, no matter how large the community is, the status of the individual remains unchanged for Confucian ethics: what is all-important is the cultivation of the person, or the development of *jen* in the individual. Without such cultivation or development, one cannot talk about duties to the family, to the state, and to the whole of mankind. Since every individual has his duty to the family, naturally every individual also has his duty to the state and to the whole of mankind. This is due to the development of *jen* in the individual, which will not stop short at the family, but will necessarily extend to the state and to the whole of mankind.

Although Confucian ethics asserts the duties of the individual to the community, when conflicts arise between the individual and the community, the individual must maintain his own independent decision. The individual should decide by his own conscience whether he should obey the authority of the community or obey his own conscience. There were two cases in the works of Confucius and Mencius which showed the independence of the individual in conflict with the community. One case is: if one's father has stolen a sheep, one may conceal the misconduct of one's father.[49] The other case is: if Emperor Shun's father was a murderer, Emperor Shun might abandon his empire and run away with his father.[50]

This does not mean that the individual can be independent of the community. The individual needs the community, and the community needs the individual. The relationship between the individual and the community is one of mutual dependence and equal importance.

It is not a relationship of ends and means. One cannot say that the community is an end and that individuals are means only. Nor can one say that individuals are ends and that communities are means only. In fact, for Confucian ethics, the individual and the community are both ends and are realized throughout by the development of *jen* in the individual. The key lies wholly in *jen*. If *jen* prevails, then the importance of the individual and of the community will be equally affirmed.

QUESTION: Concerning the concept of freedom, do you use the word "freedom" in a different sense than its Western origin, for "freedom to choose what is good" is not freedom in the Western sense?

ANSWER: From the ethical point of view, we should allow only freedom to do the good and not freedom to do evil. No ethics of any kind would allow freedom to do evil. This is the meaning of freedom in Confucian ethics, and it is almost the same as self-determination in the Kantian sense.

QUESTION: Concerning the conflict of values, in Confucian ethics is there room for individual conscience against one's family? For instance, if a man's father stole a sheep, to use an example you cite, should he tell the truth to the police or not?

ANSWER: For Confucian ethics, there is no abstract standard by which to resolve the conflict of values. The only solution is that every man should decide by his own conscience, or *jen*. Whatever you do, you should do in accordance with *jen*.

[1] *Analects*, XII. 22
[2] *Doctrine of the Mean*, I.1
[3] *Shih-ming*[x] (Interpretation of Names), *Ssu-tu ts'ung-k'an*[y] (Collection of Four Kinds of Classic).
[4] *Doctrine of the Mean*, XX.5
[5] *Book of Mencius*, VII.B 16
[6] *Ibid.*, VII.A 15
[7] *Ibid.*, II.A 6
[8] *Ibid.*, III.A 1
[9] *Szu-shu shih-i*[z] (Interpretations of Four Books), II. 77. (Taipei: United Publishing Center, 1953).
[10] *Jen-wen ching-shen chih ch'ung-chien*[aa] (Reconstruction of the Spirit of Humanism) (Hong Kong: New Asia College, 1956), p. 410.
[11] *Ethical Studies* (2nd ed.; Oxford: Oxford University Press, 1927), p. 56.
[12] *Analects*, VII. 21
[13] *Ibid.*, VII. 127
[14] *Doctrine of the Mean*, VII
[15] *Ibid.*, XX. 18
[16] *Analects*, IX. 4
[17] *Ibid.*, II. 14
[18] *Ibid.*, XIII. 23
[19] *Book of Mencius*, VIB. 6
[20] *Analects*, VI. 6
[21] *Ibid.*, VII. 10
[22] *Ibid.*, VIII. 13
[23] *Ibid.*, XIV. 39
[24] *Ibid.*, VII. 21
[25] *Ibid.*, IV. 1
[26] *Ibid.*, XV. 7
[27] *Ibid.*, XIII. 3
[28] *Ibid.*, IV. 18
[29] *Book of Mencius*, IIIB. 9
[30] *Analects*, XII. 1
[31] *Ibid.*, XII. 1
[32] *Doctrine of the Mean*, XXII
[33] "Reconstruction of the Spirit of Humanism," p. 410.

34 *Analects*, I. 4.
35 *Ibid.*, LV. 17
36 *Great Learning*, VI
37 *Analects*, XII. 1
38 *Ibid.*, III. 3
39 *Ibid.*, XV. 35
40 *Ibid.*, I. 12
41 *Ibid.*, IV. 15
42 *Ibid.*, VI. 28
43 *Ibid.*, I. 4
44 *Ibid.*, III. 19
45 *Ibid.*, XV. 23
46 *Great Learning*, I. 4
47 *Ibid.*, I. 6, 7
48 *Analects*, I. 2
49 *Ibid.*, XIII. 18
50 *Book of Mencius*, VIIA. 35

a 謝幼偉

b 仁

c 論語

d 樊遲

e 中庸

f 道

g 堯

h 舜

i 錢穆

j 唐君毅

k 詩經

l 書經

m 自省

n 曾子

o 愼獨

p 大學

q 禮

r 讓

s 忠

t 恕

u 子貢

v 孝

w 弟

x 釋名

y 四部叢刊本

z 四書釋義

aa 人文精神之重建

SURAMA DASGUPTA

The individual in Indian ethics

The over-all problem of the Conference is the status of the individual. One aspect of that problem is the status of the individual in ethical thought and action. For our purposes, this special problem is constituted by two major considerations, first, the individual's right of conscience as opposed to social duties and obligations, and other related problems, and, second, the relation of morality to the ultimate spiritual end that the individual strives to achieve.

In India, all such discussions have been intimately related to the consideration of the nature of man from the philosophical point of view. Since most philosophy in India became religion and had tremendous significance for practical life, ethical problems could not be dissociated from these. Yet, Hindu thinkers were not concerned with the ultimate goal alone, but drew up a practical scheme of social life and its obligations, keeping in view the final end to be achieved. Buddhism and Jainism, being monastic orders of religion, were not concerned with life in society, but, since man lives with his fellow beings, all these systems stressed the moral values of man in every sphere of life.

I

The Hindu systems, whatever differences there might be about the ultimate nature of the soul or self, all agreed that the knowledge of the self was the highest good, and that a moral life was essential for this spiritual enlightenment. Man has a dual nature: one, his spiritual and immortal essence, the other, his empirical life and character. This led to the twofold idea of the good, that of an individual's life in society, in which there is a conflict of good and evil, and the other as the complete or the wholly good, as represented by the concept of enlightenment about the nature of the self, which meant liberation from wrong perspectives and false values and passions associated with these. The latter was called the highest good (*śreyas*).[1]

The literature which discusses the legal and social duties is known as the Dharma-śāstras. They cover a wide period of Indian history, ranging from the third or fourth century B.C. to the eleventh or twelfth century A.D.—in some cases even later than that. The *Mahābhārata*, the Great Epic, is supposed to be of very ancient origin in spite of later interpolations, and so is the other epic, the *Rāmāyaṇa*. In all these texts and even in the *Caraka-saṁhitā*, a recondite book on medical science, social values in consonance with the highest good were discussed.

The Smṛtis (traditional texts) offered a plan of life according to different professions, depending on the caste system and also according to the different stages of life, such as those of the student and the householder, the stage of retirement and study, and the final stage of meditation on philosophical truths.[2] One was considered preparatory for the other, and hence life in society was to be led in consonance with the final goal to be attained. A scholar, a king, a businessman—all had to pass through all these stages, and therefore moral discipline and the observance of respective duties were emphasized.[3] In a general manner, both standards of the good, that of social duties and the other based on the spiritual nature of man, were helpful to a person in his social life. The belief that man is essentially pure and free from all impurities of passions helped him to do his duty well as a good and efficient member of society, and this in its turn contributed to his progress toward his spiritual destiny.

The *Mahābhārata* and the Smṛtis took up the practical problems of life in detail and tried to offer solutions, bearing in mind the good of society and the spiritual ideal of the individual. There cannot be any fixed or rigid standard of duties for all times, because life is complex and ever moving. What appears to be good or right in one context may not be so in another; at most, some general maxims and principles can be laid down. The *Mahābhārata* holds a realistic attitude toward life. It gives three standards of moral actions: (1) the advancement of society, maintenance of social order, and preservation of traditions and customs, (2) the realization of the self, which is the highest good, and (3) the standard of conduct to guide people in abnormal times, i.e., in times of war or political upsets or similar unusual situations.[4]

For the good of society, it was held as it is also in the *Gītā*, that, provided the heart is clean and pure and free from all passions and small self-seeking motives, whatever one does, as one's duty, has moral value. It has been repeatedly asserted in the *Gītā* by Kṛṣṇa (Krishna) that morality proceeds from the inner spirit of man. If one has achieved equanimity of mind by conquering the evil in him, he will be doing the right in doing his duty. Virtues and duties in a society have to be determined in the proper context of the situation. For instance, truthfulness and non-injury are universally valid principles of moral action,[5] but in specific situations these are modified.

For the sake of giving encouragement to a patient the physician is certainly justified in holding out hope of health and normal life. But a true statement which has a correspondence with facts but has been uttered in a spirit of malice to hurt others does not have the dignity of moral value.

A utilitarian view is expressed in the *Mahābhārata* when it says that a man can give up his own interest for the sake of his family, give up that of the family for the sake of the community, and give up that also for the good of the greater number of people; but it adds that he may give up everything for finding out the spiritual truth of the self.[6]

In the case of conflict between a general maxim and a particular, man in society should attend to the latter, since maintenance of society depends on that. For instance, it is a universally accepted principle that one should not cause hurt or injury to others; but a king or a government has to do this for the maintenance of law and order.[7]

Non-injury to others has been acclaimed in India as a great virtue but, for the protection of the weak, for the sake of a right cause, or in self-defense, one should fight the aggressor, and in times of war, the enemy.[8]

The case of Arjuna in the *Gītā* has been discussed as an instance of the way in which an individual's right of conscience was denied in a situation of emergency, that is, that of war. Taken out of context, this instance has led to oversimplification of the problem of the individual's right of judgment in conflict with social duties. The story in the *Mahābhārata* is that on the day before the war was to start Arjuna assured his eldest brother that, though their army was smaller and the enemy had reputed leaders like his great grand-uncle Bhīṣma and a teacher like Drona, he was confident that he and his brothers would be victorious because theirs was the cause of righteousness and justice, and he himself and his brothers were excellent warriors. Then, at the time when the war was about to begin, and Arjuna saw his relatives on the other side, which he knew very well would be the case, his emotions became uppermost, and he declined to fight. He was not a conscientious objector to war, as has been contended sometimes; he had loved his career as a warrior all his life and had shown exceptional talent and ability in this respect, and on the present occasion he was the leader of his army. But at the critical moment he wished to withdraw. It was not a crisis of conscience; it was a conflict of his sense of the right against his emotions such as may have been felt by many a soldier on the battlefield. Nowhere in the world when a country is at war are people in the army allowed to withdraw and desert it. In this context, Kṛṣṇa reminded Arjuna of the spiritual truth about man and of his duties as a warrior, and Arjuna declared that his confusion was removed and his understanding was clearer.

Life is full of complex situations, and, however elastic and wide the rules of guidance may be, the individual is bound occasionally to face a dilemma, a conflict of different social duties, or a conflict of these with his own good sense or conscience, whatever we may call it. In the *Manu-saṃhitā* and also in the *Mahābhārata*, a warning was repeatedly given to the individual that he should be very clear in his mind as to where his duty lies. The *Manu-saṃhitā* says there are four sources of morality (*dharma*): the Vedas (the scriptures), the Smṛti literature based on these, the conduct of good and wise persons, and the individual's own judgment.[9] In whatever he does, the individual should have the satisfaction that he is doing the right (*ātmanastuṣṭireva ca*). At all times and in all our duties we have to employ ourselves with enthusiasm and sincerity; otherwise, social life becomes insipid and dull and loses its force. That is why the awakening of intellect (*buddhi-samprajanana*) has been greatly emphasized. In the "Gāyatrī-mantra," a Vedic hymn recited in daily prayers, one prays that one's intellect may ever be alert and enlivened so that one's understanding may become clearer. In times of crisis and confusion due to an abnormal situation, it is the individual who has to decide his course of action. His own conscience is his sole guide. There is a long section in the *Mahābhārata*[10] where Yudhiṣṭhira, the eldest of the Pāṇḍu brothers, repeatedly asks Bhīṣma, the leader of the family, how one can make a proper decision in a difficult situation. Bhīṣma answers that doubts and confusions are essential[11] for a man of character—it is through such conflicts and the overcoming of them that he can grow and attain the good. Thus, Viśvāmitra, a *kṣatriya* (warrior) scholar of great repute, who had become a *brāhmaṇa*, violated the rules of conduct prescribed by society for a *brāhmaṇa* and went to a butcher and begged prohibited food for himself, because he thought this was the right thing to do. Bhīṣma said, "In times of doubt, O, son of Kuntī, one has to decide by using one's own good sense."[12] The *Caraka-saṃhitā* has mentioned that care should always be taken to avoid errors of moral judgment.[13]

Bhīṣma himself had given up his claim to the throne in favor of his step-brothers, and, in addition, took the vow of celibacy to ensure the legal rights of their descendants.[14] This was against the social practice at the time; in this action he did not follow any pattern or type of norm laid down by society, but acted according to his own values. Instances like this, in which the individual makes a special contribution of his own over and above the accepted standards followed by average men in society, are not rare.

The theory of *karma* attributes full responsibility for one's actions to the individual himself. He is also responsible for the actions of others if he induces or forces them to do a particular act. So, in spite of social injunctions, the individual has to be careful about the moral nature of his actions. Society has tried to help the average man by mapping out for him a scheme of life and duties, but it is on the individual himself that his *karma* depends, and results will accrue to him accordingly. So, from every point of view, the social good or the personal, the final responsibility for actions rests on the individual alone.

The concept of conscience has been discussed in various ways in Western thought. It is a faculty of discriminating right from wrong, good from evil. In Sanskrit, there is no one particular word to denote this, though there are expressions which would convey similar notions. Moral values are expressed by words like *"dharma"* (good) and *"adharma"* (bad), and *"puṇya"* (merit) and *"pāpa"* (demerit). The concept of intellect (*buddhi*) that helps man to distinguish these may be taken as similar to conscience.

The spiritual good (*śreyas*) is different from the social good. In social life, man is tied by obligations which may be quite customary, based on traditions or on a broader perspective of human relationships. But there is also the consideration of the individual man himself and the aspirations that he wishes to achieve. This spiritual ideal is inherent in man. We have a similar idea in Bergson when he says, ". . . the two moralities [are that of] pressure [that is, of society] and aspiration . . . they are no longer to be found in a pure state. The first has handed to the second something of its compulsive force; the second has diffused over the other something of its perfume."[15] "Immanent in the former is the representation of a society which aims only at self-preservation. . . . The morality of aspiration, on the contrary, implicitly contains the feeling of progress."[16] Similarly, it can be said from the Indian point of view that, in spite of the moral obligations laid down by society, the higher nature of man is considered to be of greater significance.

In all systems of ethics, the possibility of confusing conscience with other inclinations and impulses of man's nature has been discussed, and care has been taken to avoid this perplexity of conscience. In India, the individual has been warned over and over again about this confusion and has been asked to bear in mind this dual perspective of values, so that he can see, through the various entanglements of his social and self-seeking interests, the right course of action. That is why two sets of duties were drawn up to help the average man in society: one, virtues which have universal validity, love, charity, compassion, benevolence, forgiveness, and the like, and the other, the specific duties of man according to his profession and stages in life.

From the above discussion it is now clear that no special preference has been given to one's loyalty to personal ties like that of family or group or community. The highest loyalty is to one's moral values. Thus, in the story of two brothers, Śaṅkha and Likhita, when the latter committed a theft, the former, the elder one, sent him to the king to confess his guilt and receive punishment, because this was the right course of conduct.[17] We are reminded in this connection of Gāndhārī, the queen mother of Duryodhana (Arjuna's cousin and opponent), who pleaded with the king, her husband, to banish her own son, who was evil in character and was in the wrong. And when, in spite of her protestations, the war was started and her son came for her blessings, she said only one thing, "Wherever there is righteousness, victory will be there."[18]

Consideration of the individual's rights and duties changed the pattern and social standards in different times. In very early times, men and women were free to choose a career in quest of knowledge, in which case they could remain single and dedicate themselves to study and meditation, or they could marry and follow a normal course of life. But in the Smṛtis, marriage (householder stage) and the other stages (āśramas) in their due order were emphasized, with occasional exceptions. In later times, those who chose to renounce worldly life for knowledge could do so. Śaṁkara himself is an illustration of this. He revived Hinduism in an atmosphere dominated by Buddhist influence, but he did not accept the householder's life.

The conflict of the individual and society also expressed itself in different forms of marriage and marital rights, which underwent various changes. Though Hindu marriage was considered sacramental and, therefore, indissoluble, divorce was known to take place in the time of Kauṭilya (fourth century B.C.) and also in the days of some of the later Smṛtis. Among other grounds, mutual incompatibility was admitted for the annulment of a marriage.[19] Eight different forms of marriage were accepted for meeting the requirements of various situations.[20]

Caste duties also underwent various phases of change. In very early times, different professions and duties were assigned to people so that social structure could be maintained with efficiency. These were hereditary, and people born in a particular caste were supposed to acquire aptitude and skill for them. But this went against the individual's right of choosing his vocation, and reactions against caste set in. Viśvāmitra, a *kṣatriya* by birth, became a *brāhmaṇa* by undergoing severe penances and struggles. As individuals started choosing their own career, both because of their choice and also for economic reasons, the division of society into four principal castes and sub-castes became useless, and the system began disintegrating. Besides, since intercaste marriage was prevalent from very early

times, this had led to an intermixture of castes. In the *Mahābhārata,*
Yudhiṣṭhira said that a *brāhmaṇa* was no longer known by birth but
by the special behavior that the individual displayed.[21] In the *Chāndogya Upaniṣad,* the story of Satyakāma shows that he was accepted
as a *brāhmaṇa* because he was so truthful in that he did not hesitate
to state the fact that he was born out of wedlock and did not know
his father's lineage.[22] We may also mention that the Śaiva and
Vaiṣṇava sects did not have caste distinctions as a rule, though these
are Hindu systems of thought. Reformative sects of Hinduism, such
as the Ārya Samāj (Samāja), the Brāhmo Samāj (Samāja), and
others, as well as Buddhism and Jainism, did not have caste distinctions.

In its history of three thousand years or more, Hindu society
passed through various phases of beliefs and practices which, though
contrary to one another, were all absorbed, making a vast mosaic
structure of the co-existence of different beliefs.

Coming to Buddhism, we find that its emphasis has been on solving the problem of human misery, and, since this could be done only
by a proper perspective on things and through moral effort and great
love and compassion for fellow beings, it became a religion of love.
On the one hand, it asserted the impermanence of all things and
denied a permanent soul; on the other, it held a very noble and
lofty ideal of human character. Buddhism, being a monastic order
(though it had its followers among the householders), did not encounter complicated social problems. But, since man lives in relation
with his fellow beings, it had to deal with the moral values of human
life. Great emphasis was laid on the building up of one's character.
It carried the problem of conflict with one's environment to the
conflict within oneself. It stressed, therefore, the necessity of solving
the conflicts within a man himself. The evil proceeds, not from outside, but from within.[23] A man has to conquer the evil impulses of
his nature, hatred, animosity, and intolerance, and has to understand
others on an analogy with his own self and to extend to them the
same kindness and love that he has for himself.[24] He is responsible
for building up his own character and also for helping others.

King Aśoka (third century B.C.), who is said to have been a
Buddhist, erected Rock Edicts giving simple moral instructions to
his people. He reiterated the necessity of promoting the essentials of
all religions. He said, "One should not criticize other sects and praise
one's own, but one should try to appreciate the points of view of
other religions and realize the defects of his own."[25] The Buddhist
texts are never tired of discussing the virtues of universal friendliness
and compassion, the equality of all beings, and the ideal of peace for
all. The worst enemy of man is man himself; unless he can destroy
all passions and evil thoughts, he can never attain peace, nor can he

give it to others. Buddhism is a philosophy which, without the assumption of God or soul, has given much to the world by way of lofty ideals and thought. In the *Dhammapada* and the *Visudhimagga,* as also elsewhere, there are very detailed and inspiring discussions about moral virtues. Details as to how one can control anger and hatred and encourage good will and sympathy for others have been worked out in a well-reasoned manner.

In both Hīnayāna and Mahāyāna Buddhism, service for the good of others is emphasized. No individual, if he wishes to develop his personality, can ever exclude others. His personality becomes an all-embracing one because he expands in kindness and sympathy and becomes a part of others and makes them a part of himself. The *bodhi-sattvas* (beings whose essence is perfect wisdom) of the Mahāyana school, who held emancipation of all beings as the ultimate end, pray that their own emancipation might be postponed until and unless all beings have achieved enlightenment and peace.[26] The *bodhi-sattva* resolves that he may be able to be of any service that others may ask of him; even for those who have done him a bad turn he wishes that they may all attain enlightenment.

These principles are noble and lofty, but, still, in the task of character-building there are bound to be confusions; and the Buddha emphasized again and again the need of using one's own judgment. He said to Ānanda, ". . . be ye lamps unto yourselves. Be ye a refuge to yourselves. Betake yourselves to no external refuge. Hold fast to the Truth as a lamp. Hold fast as a refuge to the Truth. Look not for refuge to anyone beside yourselves."[27] Again, he says, "And whosoever, Ānanda, either now or after I am dead, shall be a lamp unto themselves, shall betake themselves to no external refuge, shall not look for refuge to anyone besides themselves—it is they, Ānanda, among my *bhikkhus* (monks), who shall reach the very upmost height, but they must be anxious to learn."[28] He says, again, that, of all losses, loss of character and loss of sound opinions are the worst.[29]

It is clear from the discussions brought up so far in this paper that an individual is free to challenge the socially accepted moral schemes of life, and follow his own judgment. This has been true, not only in the case of social reformers like Vidyāsāgara and Mahatma Gandhi in recent times, but also of many other less well-known personalities who have done the same thing. Hinduism and Buddhism, and Jainism too, all aim at developing man's personality in such a way that his better nature will be able to assert itself in life. A character in which various tendencies and impulses are fully integrated in the light of moral values was thought indispensably necessary for attaining any proper philosophical perspective—and ultimate emancipation.

II

I now turn to the question raised at the beginning of this paper about the relation of morality to the ultimate goal of life, which an ethical individual strives to achieve. It has been often asked, "Is morality—or the individual moral being—negated in the ultimate goal, since this has been sometimes described as a transcendental state of awareness, beyond good and evil?" It is necessary, therefore, to explain the concept of immortality, the nature of the spiritual goal, and also how this can be attained through the moral process.

The immortality of the individual man is not mere continuance of existence, but an experience of the spiritual nature of man. It is not taken as a further projection of the life in society with its values and conflicts, a repetitive existence involving moral struggle. Though the *karma* theory, or the theory of heaven and hell, implies such a continuation of human life, yet, everywhere in Indian thought this repetition of man's struggle in society and in himself as that of good against evil is supposed to end completely with the realization of the spiritual nature of man. Morality implies conflict, in human nature, of good and evil or right and wrong. There is an oscillation between the two aspects of the dual nature of man, the higher and the lower. A moral man is one in whom the right perspective and good emotions dominate and can keep the evil in check. In a spiritual man the evil has been overcome completely, and goodness has become spontaneous. This is what is meant by the concept of the saint (*sthitadhī*) in the *Gītā*—and what Kant implies as "holy will" as distinguished from a moral will. Though moral values and the spiritual nature of man are distinct from each other, they are not necessarily found in their separateness; the latter extends and transforms the former.

Throughout man's psychic history he finds that his appetitive tendency, however valuable it may appear for his self-preservation and however strongly it may be grounded throughout his biological history, subordinates itself to the superior claims of his higher social self. The history of humanity, so far as it is superior to that of beasts, is manifested by the continual assertion of the claims of the higher social self over the original strength of the primary appetitive demands and values. This social value consists in the consideration that is extended to others, but there emerges a still higher sense of values. These are in a sense anti-biological and repudiate the instruction that Nature has been giving throughout her animal history. To love my enemy as myself, to follow the advice that one should turn his left cheek to anyone who may smite on the right, is in flagrant contradiction to the formula of evolution involved in the struggle for existence and the survival of the fittest. Yet, it is by carrying out demands of this type, however imperfectly it may have been done, that the progress of humanity has been possible, and that charity, fellow-feeling, love, and forgiveness have been extended far beyond the expectations of society and have succeeded in welding humanity together as it is today. To distinguish the social ideal from the spiritual we may say that the former may have variations and sometimes be limited in its use and content, but, in the latter, human virtues such as love, compassion, and forgiveness become limitless. To do to others as you would be done by is a social or moral virtue, but to forgive your enemies when you are hurt and to pray that they may attain a correct perspective of values and attain good in the end shows an ideal of love and compassion far beyond the sense of right and wrong or fairness and justice in society.

In the Upaniṣads there is the concept of the five sheaths of the self, which are unfolded one after another, leading to the ultimate truth as the highest goal. These are: the physical (relating to matter), the biological (relating to life), the mental, the conceptual or intellectual (i.e., the higher level of knowledge), and, last, infinite knowledge and wisdom, purity and joy.[30] All these sheaths, or different levels of existence, are infinite in themselves, one leading to the other. Though all of these are contained in the self, the highest manifestation is in the infinite joy of self-realization in its purity and fullness emerging from the other levels as their continuation. It has been said that none of these levels should be thought derogatory. Each is vastly important and leads to the unfolding of the other, and in their mutual association they lead to another order of truth until they come to the highest as infinite knowledge and joy. These concepts may be compared to the emergence of different orders of value-sense that operate in each man. It can be imagined that each level will have its own values, which in their interaction make way to the superior one and eventually find their culmination in the highest.

I wish to clarify and elaborate this idea further, and will refer in places to certain passages from the book *Religion and Rational Outlook*, by the late Professor S. N. Dasgupta.

The personality of man may be briefly viewed under two aspects, the spiritual nature of man and the other, comprising his biological nature and his social self, as it were, surcharged with social beliefs, aspirations, fears, apprehensions, ideals, and the like. The individual self is a part of a larger social self. "The existence, ideally, of the entire human society and, more definitely and concretely, the family, the immediate environment and the nation within us manifests itself in directing our social self on the lines on which the society has proceeded and developed."[31] In the self that works or behaves as a person, the differences of the so-called biological and social selves are so integrated that there is usually no hostility between them. It is only when there is an inner conflict that the two selves appear to manifest their opposing characteristics, and the demands of the social self are felt as a norm which should guide the biological or the appetitive self. "We value our biological pleasure and the self-preservative instinct, but the unity that holds together the psychical elements which form the complex social self, is wider and bigger than the unity established by the appetitive self." "We thus find the rule that the more uniting, the wider and the later emergent the force of unification is, the greater is its transcendence over, and superiority to, the earlier and narrower uniting agencies."[32] We may have a series of value-senses, the economico-appetitive, the economico-social, and the spiritual or religious or supramoral. With the emergence of mind, we have found a sense of values manifested in morals and in love of truth and beauty.

The spiritual life is an awakening in which norms of our moral life are extended in a unity which, within itself, holds man and the universe together. The individual is a totality of different selves and different senses of values. The spiritual unity of all life opens up new dimensions of value, a new order of experience. This may be described as the unity of all beings and objective Nature in one Truth, as the Upaniṣads and Śaṁkara Vedānta put it; it may be the union of God and man, as theistic systems call it; it may be the awareness of man himself in his purity, as the Sāṁkhya calls it. This experience is of a different order and is, in most systems of Indian thought, associated with joy. The conflict that an individual experiences in society is dissolved with the realization of man's spiritual nature.

"The exhilaration [that comes out of this experience] of his soul, which shines as a mystic light, regulates his conduct and other experiences, his relationship with his environment, and is in intimate unity with the universe as well as his ultimate dissociation from it. At this stage the sense of joy that suffuses him does not tax him as does a moral ideal, by projecting obligatory courses and demanding submission, but it makes morality easy and spontaneous. The joy that runs through the veins and nerves deluges, as it were, all other considerations and plunges the individual into such a stream of mystical ecstasy that the complexity of the universe loses all its mystery, all doubts are resolved, and the whole personality of the individual is transformed into cheerfulness and blessedness. In its true nature there is practically no form of the intuition or immersion and we may call it by any name we please, such as the realisation of the good or of God or participation in God's love."[33] It is for this that Maitreyī said, "What shall I do with what the whole world can give me, if I do not get immortality?"[34] The Upaniṣads, in referring to this state, say, "The knots of the heart are torn asunder, and all doubts are dissolved."[35] Thus, on the spiritual level life is spontaneous, and the oscillations of moral life have vanished.[36] It is also said in the Upaniṣads that evil does not overcome him, but he overcomes all evils. Evil does not burn him, for he burns all evil. Free from evil, free from blemish, free from doubt, he becomes a true man.[37] Evil and suffering melt away in an intuitive perception which breaks open the bonds of the finite and the infinite. This is the realization of the immortal in every individual man. From this point of view, morality is not negated in the ultimate state, but has found its culmination in helping man to pass through his struggles of life, leading him to a goal which shines in its purity and fullness.

Coming to the problem of the continuation of individual personality in the ultimate stage, the answer from the theistic systems is in the affirmative. The Upaniṣads, Śaṁkara Vedānta, and the Sāṁkhya-Yoga indicate that the final awareness is in an intuitive vision of truth, in which notions of duality and of the "ego" disappear. But all these systems admit two phases of liberation: one here, on this earth, when a man attains enlightenment in this life (jīvan-mukti), and another, in its continuation beyond this (videha-mukti). In the former, the liberated man has attained a personality which is different in its nature and content from worldly experience. He lives here in this world and helps others to attain their spiritual end. His existence is illuminated through and through by the glow of his spiritual nature, in which truth is no longer an abstraction, but a reality. Faith in the highest possibilities of man has now become a conviction, and he is no longer affected by the social life, but stands over and above it. He lives to instruct others, to help them in their development toward this ultimate truth. The yogī retains his enlightened mind[38] out of compassion for others. The bodhisattvas offer their services to humanity. So do the holy men described in the Gītā and other Indian philosophical texts. The wisdom (prajñā) achieved by men in their mystical states, which defies all attempts to express it, forms the core of their existence. Yet, it does not destroy their personality, but makes it richer with kindness, love, and compassion. It may be that these mystical states (samādhi) are unrelated to worldly experience; but their effect on men is of tremendous significance, for they become freed from all impurities and struggles and live here on earth a life of immortality in the sense of purity and holiness which extends beyond death. The enlightened man thus attains an existence which is freed from the narrow, confined sense of the ego or the self in ordinary experience, and is extended to all beings and the world. This is the spiritual immortality that it is the destiny of man to attain. Since it is possible to realize this immortality in its spiritual loftiness and glory even in this life, this solves the ethical inquiry about the ultimate good, which is not a mere abstraction, but which shines in all its fullness and beauty through man's being, his character, and his aspirations.

QUESTION: Does the situation of Arjuna in the *Gītā* come under abnormal times, as stated in the paper?

ANSWER: The war is an abnormal situation. But it is normally the duty of *kṣatriyas* to take part in a war for the sake of a justified cause, as it was in this case. Arjuna himself was aware of this. The standard referred to in the *Mahābhārata* for abnormal times stands for a situation in which our normal conditions of the state, the country, or society have been disturbed owing to a political upset or this kind of unusual distress. But the war in the *Mahābhārata* took place between two well-organized governments, and there was some established code of behavior which could be followed by both parties. Arjuna's conflict in the present instance was not of different ideals of conduct. It was the conflict of his own sense of the right with his emotions which he felt for his kinsmen. Kṛṣṇa made him aware of this and reminded him of his duty as a *kṣatriya,* and of the spiritual end that an individual has to achieve through his duties and self-knowledge.

QUESTION: Can it be said that the theory of *karma* started from the time of the Upaniṣads?

ANSWER: Yes: The idea of *karma* and its consequences is mentioned in the Upaniṣads but not in a systematic and well-developed form. The Upaniṣads contain philosophical speculations but do not present them in a systematic manner. Both philosophical and ethical ideas, therefore, are collected from the Upaniṣads, and are synthesized into different streams of thought by the philosophers of later periods.

QUESTION: In the *Gītā* it is said that man is a product of Nature (*prakṛti*) and therefore is not a free individual. If man is not free to act, then he cannot be responsible for his actions.

ANSWER: The *Gītā* and the *Brahma-sūtra* are the two philosophical texts based on Upaniṣadic statements, but the former is not as systematic as the latter. The *Gītā* therefore makes statements, which sometimes appear to be contradictory but can be reconciled when we try to interpret them together. There are verses which describe the empirical nature of man, how there is an interplay of the three constituents (*guṇas*) of Nature which urges a man to act in a determinate manner. At the same time, almost immediately after this statement, there are other verses which emphasize the need of self-control in man so that he can transcend his empirical nature. Thus, the presupposition that man is essentially free in the midst of the opposite tendencies of his nature is very clearly stated and emphasized. A man is free in his spiritual nature and has to have free control over the inclinations and impulses which proceed from his psychophysical existence.

QUESTION: If the moral process leads to spiritual enlightenment, how is it that the moral struggle ends completely in the ultimate state?

ANSWER: There cannot be any sharp dichotomy between end and means, particularly with reference to a moral act and a moral means. The means by which a moral end can be achieved becomes the process of the realization of the end at each step; otherwise, the means and the end would stand completely isolated and wide apart. A moral man, through his conflicts, his success, and his failures, is getting an insight into, an intuitive touch of, the reality of the spiritual end, and that is how he can eventually overcome the conflict completely and be established in the final enlightenment, from which there is no more backsliding.

QUESTION: Does this mean that the same act may be performed by a moral man who has to make a decision in favor of his "good will" and check the evil impulses of his nature and also by a spiritual man who has attained enlightenment and that it therefore can be accomplished by him in a spontaneous and easy manner, without any conflict whatsoever?

ANSWER: Yes, the spiritual man will naturally and spontaneously do the right act, while a moral man may be doing the same act, but passing through an oscillation of his will in reaching the final decision.

QUESTION: Does an individual have the right to challenge the accepted norms of conduct laid down by society?

ANSWER: Every individual has the right to challenge any pattern or ideal of conduct presented by society. No society can ever be big enough to suppress an individual's freedom of opinion in moral life. Individuals all over the world have stood up for their own convictions, have challenged the state or society, as the case may be, have even courted death, imprisonment, and punishment, and have stood triumphant in the end, thereby correcting society and introducing reforms and new ideals.

QUESTION: Is it characteristic of Buddhism to maintain that an individual can actually overcome evil in himself through discipline? Another way of expressing this is to ask whether there is any moral process that can lead to actual perfection, or whether every moral process, just because it is to be carried through by the very self that needs the perfection that is to be the outcome, must remain incomplete and imperfect?

As a corollary of the last point, how far was it characteristic of Indian moral philosophy to hold that the "I" that is aware of the good or what ought to be done is thereby above or beyond the actual imperfections of the actual self whose conduct is being appraised and to whom commands are addressed?

ANSWER: In all systems of Indian thought (including Buddhism) it is held that an individual can achieve the spiritual end as self-realization or knowledge of the ultimate truth through the moral process. Whatever differences there may be as to the ultimately true nature of the self, it has been admitted by all the systems that a realization of this is possible through moral excellence, which helps the individual to overcome his lack of knowledge and the evil tendencies of his character. The "I" that knows is also the "I" that is above false perspective and false values; the empirical "self," whose conduct is appraised or to whom the commands are issued, has to correct and develop itself in the light of this truth and can eventually achieve enlightenment and perfection, and there is no further dichotomy between these two. In the theistic systems, the individual shares the divine nature of God in his enlightened and perfected self, which has completely overcome his imperfections and ignorance. In other systems, the ultimate state is an awareness in which this duality of the higher and lower selves, and their conflict, has ultimately been dissolved into a state of purity, and this is associated with joy.

1 *Katha Upaniṣad*, II. 1.
2 *Manu-saṁhitā*, I. 88–91.
3 *Mahābhārata*, Śāntī-parva, 60–64.
4 *Mahābhārata*, Rājadharma-parva, 15.49; also Āpaddharma-parva, 141.
5 *Yoga-darśana*, II. 31.
6 *Mahābhārata*, Udyoga-parva, 37. 17.
7 *Mahābhārata*, Rājadharma-parva, 15. 14, 20–23.
8 *Ibid.*, 14 and 15.
9 *Manu-saṁhitā*, II. 1, 6, 12.
10 *Mahābhārata*, Apaddharma-parva, 140–143.
11 *Ibid.*
12 *Ibid.*
13 *Caraka-saṁhitā*, IV.i.100.
14 *Mahābhārata*, Ādi-parva; Sambhava-parva, 101.
15 *Two Sources of Morality and Religion*. R. Ashley Audry and Cloudesley Bereton, trans., with the assistance of W. H. Carter. (New York: Henry Holt and Company, 1935), pp. 42–43.
16 *Ibid.*, p. 43
17 *Mahābhārata*, Śānti-parva, 23.
18 *Ibid.*, 76.
19 *Arthaśāstra*, R. Shamasastry, trans. (Mysore: Mysore Printing and Publishing House, 1961), Book III. p. 126.
20 *Manu-saṁhitā*, III. 21–34.
21 *Mahābhārata*, Ājagara-parva, 180.
22 *Chāndogya Upaniṣad*, IV. 4.
23 *Visuddhi-magga*, IX; *Dhammapada*, I. 1–5.
24 *Visuddhi-magga*, IX.
25 *Rock Edict of Aśoka*, Corpus Inscriptionum Indicarum, Vol. I, Girnar Rock Edict No. XII.
26 Śāntideva, *Bodhicaryāvatāra-pañjikā*, Buddhist Sanskrit Texts, No. 12 (Darbhanga: Mithila Institute, 1960), III. 5–18; *Śikṣā-samuccaya*, compiled by Śāntideva. C. Bendall, ed. (St. Petersbourg: Imperial Academy of Sciences, 1897–1902), p. 2.
27 *Dialogues of the Buddha*, T. W. and C. A. F. Rhys Davids, trans. (4th ed. London: Luzac & Company, Ltd., for the Pāli Text Society, 1959), Part II, D. ii. 100.
28 *Ibid.*, 101.
29 *Ibid.*, Part III, D. iii. 234.
30 *Taittirīya Upaniṣad*, III.
31 *Religion and Rational Outlook* (Allahabad: Allahabad Law Journal Press, 1954), p. 279.
32 *Ibid.*, p. 280.
33 *Ibid.*, p. 288.
34 *Bṛhadāraṇyaka Upaniṣad*, IV. v. 3.
35 *Muṇḍaka Upaniṣad*, II. 8.
36 *Bṛhadāraṇyaka Upaniṣad*, IV. iv. 22–25.
37 *Ibid.*
38 *Yoga-darśana* (*Vyāsa-bhāṣya* and Commentary by Nāgeśa), IV. 4; IV. 30–31.

FURUKAWA TESSHI[a]

The individual in Japanese ethics

I

The European and American conception of Japanese Bushidō is derived chiefly from the memorable work on the subject by Nitobe Inazō[b].[1] The truth is, however, that, as its subtitle, "The Soul of Japan," shows, the book is not a treatise dedicated solely to the treatment of Bushidō (way of the *samurai*) itself. It should perhaps be regarded, rather, as an attempt, under the title of Bushidō, at an introduction to Japanese morals in general. The Bushidō to be taken up here first is a little different from what Nitobe meant to describe in his book. We shall deal with Bushidō in its proper sense, or what may be called "orthodox" Bushidō, one of the most typical expressions of which is to be found in a volume entitled *Hagakure*[c] [2] (popularly known as *Nabeshima rongo*[d] or Analects of the Nabeshima Clan), written in the year 1716 or thereabouts.

In this *samurai* bible we find a famous saying: *"Bushidō to wa shinu koto to mitsuketari*[e] (Bushidō consists in dying—that is the conclusion I have reached)."[3] The correct interpretation of this saying will enable us to grasp what the Bushidō of the *Hagakure* means. The key words of the dictum *"shinu koto"* (dying) mean, first, "becoming pure and simple" in the spiritual sense. "Becoming pure and simple" in this sense means a mental attitude the *samurai* takes when he acts spontaneously from pure first motives undefiled by any secondary consideration of the possible consequences of his act. From this standpoint, the *Hagakure* strongly supports the speedy action taken in the incident of the Nagasaki Brawl in contrast to the deliberate vendetta of the noted forty-seven loyal *rōnin*[g] (masterless *samurai*) of Akaho[h] and that of the Soga[i] brothers, which it views with grave distrust.

The forty-seven loyal *rōnin* avenged the wrongs of their lord, the Feudal Baron of Akaho, an incident which was dramatized as the *Chūshingura*[j] in Kabuki[k] drama well known to and well loved by every Japanese. The Soga brothers were the heroes of a celebrated vendetta in which they avenged their father, who had been murdered by one of his relatives seventeen years before. The *Hagakure* pronounces these two famous cases in history to be far from satisfactory from the viewpoint of Bushidō, because their avenging was carried out one to seventeen years after their lord or father had been wrongly killed, during the lapse of which time the objects of their avenging might have died a natural death. The *Hagakure* claims: "The right way of avenging is to strike at the enemy without delay or hesitation, even in the danger of being killed by him. In this case, it is no disgrace at all to be killed by the object of one's vengeance. It would be disgraceful, however, not to strike at once, thus losing forever the opportunity of vengeance in the vain hope of accomplishing one's purpose satisfactorily. While one is hesitating to fight against heavy odds, time is wasted, the opportunity passes away never to return, and the project of vengeance is given up for good. One has only to cast oneself at one's enemies, no matter how heavy the odds, with an unflinching determination to exterminate them all. That determined act alone will place the glory of success in one's hands."[4]

In sharp contrast with the deliberate tardiness of the foregoing two instances of *samurai* vendetta, the Nagasaki Brawl, which took place in Nagasaki on December 20, 1700, ran its whole course with breathless speed. The origin was a very trifling matter. Two *samurai,* while walking down a street in Nagasaki, happened to pass a city official and his man-servant, who called them names for splashing the dirty half-thawed snow on the street and getting him soiled with it. Infuriated at the man's outrageous reviling, the two kicked him down into the snow and gave him a sound thrashing. Then, later that same night, the man-servant, together with some ten fellow-servants of his master, made a raid on the residence of the two *samurai,* surrounding and mauling them mercilessly. They went to the length of robbing the *samurai* of their swords and marched off in triumph. The two, overwhelmed as they were by the superior number of their enemy, found themselves reinforced by fifteen friends and relatives who, at the alarm, hurried to their rescue, only to arrive at the scene too late. They at once rushed en masse to make a sudden descent upon the enemy's house, and, after slaughtering many people, including the city official and his man-servant, they put an end to their own lives by committing *harakiri*[1], as many brave *samurai* have done.

A remarkable feature that characterizes this Brawl is to be found, as the *Hagakure* points out, in the fact that the whole affair was conducted on the impulse of the occasion with no deliberation whatsoever. Not only the *samurai,* but their servants as well, rushed pell-mell into the valley of death in a reckless attack upon the enemy, paying no attention to the peril of their own lives or to the final outcome of the whole matter. The mental attitude shown here, to act without heeding the possible consequences, described above as "pure and simple," is the one that the *Hagakure* seeks as its ideal, and to become "pure and simple" in this sense is at least one of the basic meanings of the *Hagakure* multi-significant key word "dying."

II

"Bushidō consists in dying—that is what I have found out." If this "dying" in the *Hagakure* dictum really means "becoming pure and simple," as explained above, it is self-evident that "dying" in this sense is far removed from the so-called "dog's death." This conclusion naturally follows when we read the sentence that closes the whole passage from which the above quotation was taken: "When one eternally repeats his vow to die at any moment at the call of his duty every morning and every evening, one can act freely in Bushidō at a moment's notice, thus fulfilling his duties as a feudal vassal without a flaw, even to the very last moment of his life."[5] In the same volume, we also find such passages as these: "Bushidō is a single straight way to death, practicing over and over again every day and night how to die a *samurai's* death on every possible occasion and for every possible cause."[6] "Readiness to die at the call of one's duty should be kept ever fresh and alive by repeating the vow every day and every moment."[7] From such passages it is easy to conclude that the "death" in the *Hagakure* is not death in the ordinary sense, but is such that one can die every morning and every evening ever recurrently.

Then, what does it mean to say that one dies every morning and every evening and keeps dying ever recurrently? It is clear, of course, that the "death" meant in this instance is not death in an ordinary or physiological sense. Nevertheless, it is equally indisputable that the word here means at least a kind of death which is the utmost limit of human existence. A human being essentially contains in his constitution such an utmost limit, which constantly presses upon him and makes him return to the daily possibilities of his real existence. And, in proportion to the intensity and sincerity with which a man tackles this utmost limit of his existence, its possibilities are just that much more enriched and diversified in content. It naturally follows that a man can enrich and enlarge the possibilities of his existence to their maximum by dying every morning and every evening and ever recurrently, that is to say, by keeping himself constantly face to face with the utmost limit of his existence in the world. This may be considered as a reasonable interpretation of the previously quoted sentence: "When one eternally repeats his vow to die at any moment at the call of his duty every morning and every evening, one can act freely in Bushidō at a moment's notice, thus fulfilling his duties as a feudal vassal without a flaw, even to the very last moment of his life."[8]

Instead of preaching abstract precepts, the *Hagakure* amplifies this truth with rich concreteness by relating numerous illustrative instances. Among others, here is one concerning a physician named Ikujima Sakuan[m]. He was the attendant physician who administered medicine to his lord, Baron Nabeshima Mitsushige[n] of the Saga[o] Clan who had a severe attack of smallpox. Severe or slight, any illness of the liege lord was of serious concern to all his retainers. What a shock it was when they learned that their master's illness had taken a sudden turn for the worse. The attendant nurses, greatly disheartened at the critical condition of the invalid lord, sent in hot haste for Sakuan, who came without delay, and, after examination, declared, "Oh, thank Heaven! Our lord's illness is gone! His complete recovery is near. I, Sakuan, myself will answer for it. Let every one of you rejoice!" All the attendant people, hearing this, thought to themselves in dismay, "Sakuan must have gone mad. His pronouncement is utterly groundless." Sakuan, however, paying no heed to what they thought or said, surrounded himself with a screen and set about concocting his medicine. After a while he respectfully administered a dose of his concoction to his master, whose condition turned on a sudden for the better as soon as the medicine took effect. Later on, Sakuan is said to have given his own account of the matter thus: "Since I declared that I alone would answer for the recovery of our lord, I was prepared to immolate myself in order to attend on our lord beyond the grave by disemboweling myself on the spot, if my concoction should prove of no avail."[9]

The leading motif of this episode is evidently to be found in spotlighting the absolute potency that is given only to a man who is ready at any moment to relinquish his life—in emphasizing the all-powerful virtue of concentration that a man can bring to bear upon his task when he takes the whole responsibility upon his shoulders at the peril of his own life. And it is also evident that in this episode is narrated an instance of a man's life dedicated to "fulfilling his duties as a feudal vassal without a flaw even to the very last moment." Thus, we may perhaps be permitted to say that "dying," in the sense of the *Hagakure,* means doing one's duty, ever ready to lay down one's life—concentrating upon one's task, taking all the responsibility upon oneself at the peril of one's life.

III

As seen above, the multi-significant word "dying" in the *Hagakure* means, first, "becoming pure and simple"; second, "doing one's duty, ever ready to lay down one's life—concentrating upon one's task, taking all the responsibility upon oneself at the peril of one's life"; and, thirdly, however, it may be added that the word has another—perhaps central—meaning at bottom: "Dedicating one's life unconditionally to one's master's service." That may be evidenced by a passage like this: "One can never be called a good vassal unless he dedicates himself to his lord, making it his sole object worth living and dying for to consolidate the dominion of his lord by bravely dying to all other mundane desires and making himself a ghostly being who keeps worrying over his master's affairs around the clock and who stints no labor in putting them in order."[10] This clearly shows that the dictum "Bushidō consists in dying—that is what I have found out"—can justly be paraphrased into the sentence: "Bushidō has its foundation in dedicating one's life unconditionally to one's master's service."

In the *Hagakure* this loyal devotion of a vassal to his liege lord is variously expressed in other passages: "I serve my master, not from a sense of duty, but out of a blind love of service; I hold my master dear simply because he is dear to my heart above everything else, not because he is kind to me or provides for my living."[11] "The *alpha* and *omega* of a *samurai's* life is service, service, service— nothing but service."[12] "A *samurai* has nothing else in his heart or mind but his master."[13] "To a *samurai* the pledge of loyalty is everything."[14] "A *samurai* gives himself up *in toto* at the free disposal of his master."[15]

The intensity and profundity of passion that strike us as we read these expressions in the original Japanese are past all translation and leave us in sheer wonder and admiration. What a single-hearted loyalty is expressed in the following: "Though Śākyamuni or Confucius himself were here in person to preach what we have never heard of before, we should not be a bit shaken in our conviction. Let them cast us into hell and eternal damnation: one thing needful for us is loyalty to our liege lord."[16] What an earnest faith is confessed in these words: "I am only a vassal of my lord. Let him be kind to me or cruel to me as he will; let him not know me at all; it is all the same to me. For my part, not a moment passes without my heart being filled even to overflowing with the bliss of having him for my lord whom I hold dear with my eyes swimming in tears, being penetrated with an exulting sense of thankfulness."[17] Utterances like these have to our ears some unearthly sound from beyond our world. In the same book we find an anecdote about Suzuki Shōsan[p] (1579–1655), a Buddhist priest of the Zen sect, noted in the early years of the Tokugawa Shōgunate[q] (1615–1867), for his theory of the identity between spiritual and worldly laws. According to the anecdote, he is reported to have said, "What is there in the world purer than renouncing one's own life for the sake of one's lord?", when he heard the following narrative, which is originally to be found in a book entitled, *Roankyō*[r] (Crossing the Bridge on a Donkey) :[18]

In the Province of Hizen[s] there was once a warrior who was unfortunately suffering from smallpox when a war broke out and called him to arms. All his friends and relatives tried to dissuade him from leaving home for the front, saying, "Even if you were to go to the front, your illness would prevent you from being of any service." But he would not listen to their advice, saying in reply, "If I should die on my way to the front, I should be quite happy. When I think of my lord's kindness to me, I can never stay at home with an easy mind. How do you think I can ever be satisfied but by trying my very best to prove of what little service I can be to my dear lord?" It was mid-winter, and the cold was severe. But during the whole campaign he never had an overcoat on, never resorted to any means of cure or remedy; much less did he pay attention to any sort of sanitary measures. And yet, he got well all the sooner and distinguished himself on the field, as he had wished.

On this tale of loyalty, Suzuki Shōsan commented, it is said, "What is there in the world purer than renouncing one's own life for the sake of one's lord? At the sight of a man heedless of any danger to his life in the cause of loyalty, all the gods of heaven and of earth, to say nothing of the god of smallpox, would be moved to help him."[19]

That Bushidō has for its foundation the laying down of one's own life for the sake of one's lord is rightly pointed out by Josiah Royce in his *The Philosophy of Loyalty*. According to him, Japanese Bushidō regards loyalty as the centrally significant good, and its "loyalty discounts death, for it is from the start a readiness to die for the cause."[20] Then the central meaning of "dying" in the *Hagakure* dictum ("Bushidō consists in dying—that is what I have found out") is to be found in renouncing one's own life for the sake of one's lord, in dedicating oneself unconditionally to one's master. Becoming pure and simple; doing one's duty, ever prepared to die; devoting oneself to one's task, taking all the responsibility upon oneself at the peril of one's own life—all these, in the final analysis, come to this single principle.

IV

The Bushidō of the *Hagakure* found its centrally significant good in renouncing one's own life for the sake of one's lord, in dedicating oneself unconditionally to one's master. In short, it was a moral code of self-sacrifice and self-effacement in its extreme form. Then, what

relations are there between such morals of Bushidō and the consciousness of the Japanese in general?

Professor Inatomi Eijirō[t 21] considers the Japanese to be devoid of
self-consciousness, and cites as evidence the lack of clear distinction
between the parts of speech in Japanese as contrasted with European
languages. In English, German, and French, nouns, verbs, adjectives, and other kinds of words stand by themselves, clearly independent of one another; and, when they are written in sentences,
each part of speech is written as a unit separate from the rest. Thus,
all sentences are composed of individual words, each independent
of one another. In Japanese, on the contrary, there are indeed some
words (characters) that can be clearly distinguished as forming independent "parts of speech," but there are also not a few that cannot
be strictly separated from other words. Consequently, there is great
difficulty in writing Japanese sentences with all their elements strictly
separate from one another. We experience this difficulty very keenly,
especially when we try to write Japanese in Roman letters, a proof
that Japanese is not composed of individual words distinctly independent of one another. A Japanese sentence is a composite whole,
and not an aggregate of individual words or phrases. This corresponds with the fact that in actual life a Japanese has no clear
consciousness of his individual self, but recognizes his own existence
only in the composite life of the world. So concludes Inatomi.

After examining the Japanese language from various angles, as
described above, Inatomi concludes that it is a perfect symbol of the
Japanese people in its peculiarity of lacking a definite sense of the
individual self. To quote his own words, this "perfectly corresponds
with the lack of the individual, the blank of the self, that is to be
seen in the clothing, food, and shelter of the Japanese in their daily
life." And, as one of its greatest sources, Inatomi traces this lack of
a clear sense of the individual self in Japanese character to the
feudal system that governed our country for hundreds of years.
Under the feudal system individual man could not have his own
value. Instead, he could have his *raison d'être* only in the hierar-
chical system from feudal lord down to servants. In other words, man
could have his own *raison d'être* only insofar as he had relationships
of some kind with the feudal lord. His value as a human being increased as his position got closer to the lord and decreased as it got
closer to the servants. Therefore, it was conceived that the highest
virtue of the human being consists in serving the superior, the feudal
lord, instead of regarding one's individual self as independent from
others while living faithful to one's self. All the virtues consist in self-
renunciation, self-annihilation, and unselfishness, and devotion and
service to the lord. One should not take one's own happiness or

unhappiness into consideration. In some cases it was regarded as the heroic deed to kill even one's own parents for the great cause.

After such arguments, Inatomi quotes the following passages from the *Hagakure* as the text most clearly expressing these basic virtues:

> "Whenever one is taken into service to the lord, he should serve the lord without any consideration of his own self. Even if one is dismissed or is ordered to commit *harakiri,* one should accept the action as one of the services to the lord, and should be sincerely concerned with the destiny of the lord's house wherever one may be. Such should be the fundamental spirit of the Nabeshima *samurai.* As far as I am concerned, I have never thought of attaining *buddha*hood, which would not fit me at all, but I am completely prepared to be born seven times as a Nabeshima *samurai* in order to work for the cause of the domain."[22]

If this theory of Inatomi is correct, it may be inferred that the self-sacrifice and self-effacement of Bushidō are closely connected with the lack of a clear sense of the individual self in the Japanese character.

V

In Royce's *The Philosophy of Loyalty* there is the following passage:

> Now, Bushido did indeed involve many anti-individualistic features. But it never meant to those who believed in it any sort of mere slavishness. The loyal Japanese Samurai, as he is described to us by those who know, never lacked his own sort of self-assertion. He never accepted what he took to be tyranny. He had his chiefs; but as an individual, he was proud to serve them. He often used his own highly trained judgment regarding the applications of the complex code of honor under which he was reared. He was fond of what he took to be his rights as a man of honor. He made much, even childlike, display of dignity. His costume, his sword, his bearing, displayed this sense of his importance. Yet his ideal at least, and in large part his practice, as his admirers depict him, involved a great deal of elaborate cultivation of a genuine spiritual serenity. His whole early training involved a repression of private emotions, a control over his moods, a deliberate cheer and peace of mind, all of which he conceived to be a necessary part of his knightly equipment. Chinese sages, as well as Buddhistic traditions, influenced his views of the cultivation of this interior self-possession and serenity of soul. And yet he was also a man of the world, a warrior, an avenger of insults to his honor; and above all, he was loyal. His loyalty, in fact, consisted of all these personal and social virtues together.[23]

This description naturally leads us to conclude that in the life of a Japanese *samurai* the virtues of self-sacrifice and self-effacement were not necessarily incompatible with those of self-assertion and interior self-possession. This conclusion quite agrees with the fact that representative advocates of individualism in modern Japan—

Fukuzawa Yukichi[u], Niijima Jō[v], Uchimura Kanzō[w], Nitobe Inazō, and the like—came, without exception of *samurai* stock and were ardent admirers of Bushidō. For instance, Uchimura Kanzō writes in the Epilogue to the German version of his work on Representative Japanese as follows:

> I am one of the least among the children of the *samurai* stock, and one of the least among the disciples of Jesus Christ our Lord. But one of the least as I am in both those capacities, the samurai that dwells in my present self will not suffer itself to be either overlooked or made little of. Just what befits me as a samurai's son is self-respect and independence. It becomes me as a samurai's son to be a hater of all trickery, fraud, and dishonesty. The code of Bushidō is no less than the law of Christianity that tells us: "Love of money is the root of all evil." So what is becoming to me as a samurai's son is to confront, with my countenance steeled, that other law, "Money is power," which modern Christianity is so impudent as to declare in public. . . .[23a]

The self-respect and independence which are glorified by Uchimura in this passage are the very kernel and the supreme objective of modern individualism. And Uchimura calls them "just what befits me as a samurai's son." Then it is only natural that Bushidō should have served in Japan as a hotbed upon which our modern individualism has been reared. And it is also understandable why Royce says, "This Japanese loyalty of the Samurai was trained by the ancient customs of Bushidō to such freedom and plasticity of conception and expression that, when the modern reform came, the feudal loyalties were readily transformed, almost at a stroke, into that active devotion of the individual to the whole nation and to its modern needs and demands,—that devotion, I say, which made the rapid and wonderful transformation of Japan possible."[24] It seems, then, that we should perhaps re-examine the theory that ascribes a lack of a clear sense of the individual self in the Japanese character to "feudal loyalties."

However, we cannot ignore the fact that one of the most important factors which transformed the "feudal loyalties" into "active devotion of the individual to the whole nation and to its modern needs and demands" "almost at a stroke" was Christianity. How Christianity contributed toward modernizing Japan is evidenced by the fact that monogamy became an established moral principle only after Christianity was introduced into the country.

I should like to illustrate these statements with some factual examples:

In pre-Meiji (−1868) Japanese society, the guiding principle of moral life was Confucianism, which developed in ancient Chinese society and was based primarily on the family system. The most important virtue in family-system-centered Confucianism is piety to one's parents and ancestors. To put this in more concrete terms, the highest virtue in Confucianism consists in preventing one's posterity from dying out—the effort not to break the family line. As a result, there became prevalent the idea that one might rightfully divorce a wife who did not give birth to a child within three years of married life. In line with this idea, it was regarded as only right that, in case the wife would not agree to get divorced, her husband kept a mistress and let her bring forth his child. Polygamy was a commonplace matter in pre-Meiji Japan, in accordance with the moral control of Confucianism.[25]

At present, polygamy is not recognized morally. Such a drastic change in the morals of the Japanese might not have been brought about without the influence of Christianity. The following statement of Nishikawa Joken[x][26] (1648–1724), who championed the idea of monogamy, which was extraordinary in the Tokugawa period (1615–1867), would fully support this view: "There are many people in China and Japan who keep mistresses besides their own wives. However, I am told that in the West bigamy deserves criminal punishment. We should be ashamed of polygamy before the Western people." There will be no doubt that the idea of monogamy is ascribed to the influences of Western morality, the fundamentals of which are, as Arai Hakuseki[y], who appeared a little later than Joken, also claimed, evidently based on Christianity.

As seen in the foregoing, we cannot locate the source of the idea of monogamy outside of Christianity. In this sense, we have to admit that the role Christianity played in the modernization of Japan was not insignificant. In relation to this, we are rather surprised to find that the exponents of individualism in modern Japan whom we mentioned above were ardent Christians, while they were still proud of being the sons of *samurai*. It is clear that in the minds of these exponents these two elements were harmoniously blended and produced "active devotion of the individual to the whole nation and to its modern needs and demands."

VI

But there is no denying the fact that the Japanese have certain habitual traits deeply rooted in their national character which may be called a "spirit of the governed" and "a spirit of the taught." By a "spirit of the governed" is meant that mental tendency of the Japanese which prevents them from exercising their sovereign rights and duties as autonomous people, a tendency which was fostered in their character during the long period of time when they were subjected to the iron rule of the sword. By a "spirit of the taught" is meant that moral habit of the Japanese which makes them content with the passive attitude, in which they do nothing but accept with a slavish docility that which is taught by the governing authorities. This is a habit which is devoid of positive initiative on the part of the masses to produce their own morals out of themselves and which is a result of the powerful leadership of the politically dominant, who have always been in the habit of setting themselves up as moral teachers of the populace.

The origin of these traits in the Japanese character must be traced to the deplorable fact that in Japanese society the individual has never been firmly established in his own proper rights. For instance, until her catastrophic defeat in August, 1945, Japan attached an almost almighty authority to the Imperial Edict on National Education[z] for the moral training of the people. It would not be too much to say that in prewar Japan that Edict was a virtual bible in national education. On every ceremonial occasion in every school throughout Japan, the Edict was read aloud in utmost solemnity by the principal or headmaster, with pictures of the emperor and the empress hung in the background before the boys and girls of the whole school assembled in a hall, with their heads bent low in an attitude of deepest respect and attention.

However, Inoue Kowashi[aa] (1844–1895), who drew up the original draft of the Edict, considered that, before everything else, this Edict "should not be treated as one of those ordinary edicts on political matters." Since freedom of conscience was granted to every citizen by the Imperial Constitution, the monarch was not in a position to interfere in the spiritual matters of the people. Accordingly, this Edict, intended to point out the righteous way of a citizen in nurturing the rising generation, should be regarded as "a written proclamation of the monarch on social affairs in distinction from his political ordinances." So, regarding the manner of its publication, too, Inoue thought "either of two ways should be adopted—first, that it should be given only to the Minister of Education, and not to the people at large; second, that, instead of being given to the Ministry of Education, it should be given in the form of an address to the Peers' School or to the Association of Educators at the royal visit paid by the monarch to those institutions." In short, the intention of the drafter of the Edict was far from positive for fear lest this imperial proclamation should be combined with a compulsive force to interfere with the freedom of a citizen's conscience. In the light of the actual developments of subsequent history, these fears on the part of the drafter were not in vain. The process of idolizing it and worshipping it as a document of absolute infallibility, which began shortly after its promulgation in 1890, took its ever-widening course with acceleration up to the catastrophe in 1945.

Who was responsible for such a state of affairs? Of course, those

who were at the helm of the Government were largely responsible
for that state of things, it must be admitted; but no less responsible
were the people in general, who could neither break themselves of
their "spirit of the governed" nor free themselves of their "spirit of
the taught," and remained abject followers of governmental guidance.

In the educational world of postwar Japan, which found itself
freed from the overpowering authority of the Imperial Edict, there
has again been raised a cry, though not so strong, to be sure, for
something to replace the Edict in order to clarify the moral standards
upon which the people may act. This cry, though not without plausible reasons in its favor, has its origin, after all, in the fact that in
Japan the full establishment of the individual is yet to come.

It is of great interest that Takamura Kōtarō[ab] (1883–1956) and
Saitō Mokichi[ac] (1882–1953)—two representative intellectuals modern Japan has produced—lived and died under the guidance of
their lifelong mottoes, "becoming pure and simple" and "doing
one's utmost," both of which were mentioned at the beginning of
this essay as constituting the essential meaning of the multi-significant phrase *"shinu koto"* (dying) in the *Hagakure*. Takamura, who
was a poet as well as a sculptor, considered himself a sculptor pure
and simple, declaring that he composed poems to make his sculpture
pure and simple. In a note giving the reason why he "did not give up
writing poems," he says that it was because "I composed poems for
preserving my sculpture—making it pure and simple, untarnished by
any extraneous influences, and, above all, making it independent of
literature, whose influence . . . made sculpture sick."

Saitō, a poet in the traditional Japanese style, worshipped
Kakinomoto-no-Hitomaro[ad] as the greatest of all Japanese poets, and
wrote a work of five voluminous tomes on his life and achievement.
His reasons for highly regarding the famous poet of ancient Japan
were based upon the theory that Hitomaro was a poet who put into
his poems all that was in him. In one of Mokichi's letters, written as
a confession of his passionate love for a young woman when he was
fifty-three years old, which were first published some time ago and
which attracted universal attention, we can read passages such as the
following: "There is nothing false or tricky mingled in the love of a
true lover. It is because he puts in his love all that is in him."

In this way, Kōtarō maintained his principle of "becoming pure
and simple," and Saitō maintained his principle of doing one's
utmost and putting all that is in oneself into life and artistic activities. Is it a mere coincidence that their principles were in complete
agreement with the leading tenets inculcated in the textbook of
Bushidō, which had been written two centuries and a half before
these modern intellectuals were born?

QUESTION: You emphasized Bushidō as of the essence of the Japanese ethical tradition, and, in that, you emphasized the ethics of duty and loyalty. Does this ethics of duty and loyalty violate the right of private or personal ethical convictions or conscience by requiring that the individual do whatever his duty—or the one in authority over him—requires, no matter what that is, and without any possibility of an ethical challenge if what is required seems to him to be unethical?

ANSWER: Even in Bushidō as a type of feudal morals in Japan, blind obedience was not required. A *samurai* had to remonstrate with the lord about his misconduct, at the risk of his life. In reply to the question, I refer you to the quotation from Royce in my paper. As Royce observed, "The loyal Japanese samurai never lacked his own sort of self-assertion. He never accepted what he took to be tyranny."

QUESTION: In your exposition you emphasized Shintō[am] and said little or nothing about the Buddhist aspect of Japanese ethics. Buddhism has certainly contributed to Japanese ethics, has it not? What significant aspects of Japanese ethical thought and life may be ascribed to Buddhist influence?

ANSWER: Shintō was the essence of traditional Japanese ethics, although Buddhism has also played an important part in Japanese ethics of course. For example, in Bushidō of the *Hagakure* there are four oaths.

1) We should not be inferior to others in Bushidō.
2) We should be loyal to our lord.
3) We should be obedient to our parents.
4) We should have mercy on others and do good to them.

The last oath had its origin in Tannen Oshō's[an] (Priest Tannen) teachings. Tannen Oshō was the eleventh chief Zen[ao] priest of Nabeshima's family temple, the Kōdenji[ap]. According to him, a priest must be a man of charity, but without courage he cannot be a good priest. On the other hand, a warrior must be courageous, but, if he has no charity, he cannot fulfill his duty. Therefore, the priest and the warrior must help each other.

QUESTION: What is the status of the ethics of duty and loyalty in contemporary Japanese ethics: (a) up to 1945 and (b) since 1945?

ANSWER: One of the most familiar traits in postwar Japan is the tendency to revise tradition, to reconsider the foundations of old beliefs, and sometimes mercilessly to destroy what once seemed indispensable. This disposition is especially prominent in the realm of moral education. As stated in my paper, Japan attached an almost almighty authority to the Imperial Edict on National Education for the moral training of the people until her catastrophic defeat in August, 1945. The principal virtues in this Edict were loyalty to the Imperial Family and piety to parents and ancestors. These virtues were neglected almost entirely immediately after the war had finished. The Government felt that the moral hiatus must be filled. In June, 1963, the then Minister of Education, Araki Masuo, asked his advisory agency, the Central Council on Education, to formulate such an image. The Council then appointed a subcommittee to work on the project. The other day, the subcommittee submitted what it called an "interim draft" to the Council, which disclosed it to the public. In this draft we read, "We have carried the flag and sung the anthem and loved and revered the Emperor as symbols of Japan. This was not apart from our loving Japan and paying respect to her mission. The Emperor is a symbol of Japan and of the unity of the people. We must give our deep thought to the fact that our loving and revering our fatherland, Japan, are identical with loving and revering the Emperor."

[1] Nitobe Inazō, *Bushidō* (Philadelphia: The Leeds and Biddle Company, 1899; 10th ed., New York: G. P. Putnam's Son, 1905).

[2] *Hagakure,* revised by Watsuji Tetsurō[ae] and Furukawa Tesshi. 3 vols. (Tokyo: Iwanami-shōten, 1940–1941).

[3] *Ibid.,* chap. I.

[4] *Ibid.*

[5] *Ibid.*

[6] *Ibid.*

[7] *Ibid.,* chap. XI.

[8] *Ibid.,* chap. I.

[9] *Ibid.,* chap. VIII.

[10] *Ibid.,* chap., I.

[11] *Ibid.*

[12] *Ibid.*

[13] *Ibid.*

[14] *Ibid.,* chap. II.

[15] *Ibid.*

[16] *Ibid.*

[17] *Ibid.*

[18] *Roankyo,* revised by Suzuki Daisetz Teitarō (Tokyo: Iwanami-shōten, 1948), p. 254.

[19] *Ibid.,* p. 173.

[20] Josiah Royce, *The Philosophy of Loyalty* (New York: The Macmillan Company, 1930).

[21] Inatomi Eijirō, *Nihonjin to Nihonbunka*[af] (The Japanese and Japanese Culture) (Tokyo: Risōsha, 1963).

[22] *Hagakure,* Introduction.

[23] *The Philosophy of Loyalty,* pp. 72–73.

[23a] Uchimura Kanzō, *Japanische Charakterpopfe* (Stuttgart: Gundert, 1908).

[24] *The Philosophy of Loyalty,* pp. 73–74.

[25] This fact is clearly seen in the life of Sakuma Shōzan[ag] (1811–1864), a representative scholar of Western studies in the later Tokugawa period. *Sakuma Shōzan zenshū*[ah] (The Complete Works of Sakuma Shōzan), 4 vols. (Nagano: Shinano-Kyoikukai, 1943). As the case of Sakuma Shōzan shows, it was not an unnatural thing for the Japanese people until the end of the Tokugawa period to have mistresses besides wives. It was against such a background that Ōhara Yūgaku[ai], a thinker in the later Tokugawa period, gave the following precepts: "If a man cannot get a child, first he should treat his wife more kindly; next, he should inculcate the importance of the cause of his house, keeping her mind as calm as possible; then he should make her gradually worry about having no child; and, lastly, upon her complete understanding and agreement, he should try to seek after a mistress." *Ōhara Yūgaku zenshū*[aj] (The Complete Works of Ōhara Yūgaku) (Chiba: Chiba-Kyoikukai, 1943), p. 21.

[26] *Chōnin bukuro*[ak] (Handbook for Merchants), revised by Iijima Tadao[al] (Tokyo: Iwanami-shoten, 1942).

[a] 古川哲史

[b] 新渡戸稲造

[c] 葉隠

[d] 鍋島論語

[e] 武士道とに死ぬことと見つけた
り

[f] 長崎

[g] 浪人

[h] 赤穂

[i] 曾我

[j] 忠臣藏

k 歌舞伎
l 切腹
m 生島作庵
n 鍋島光茂
o 佐賀
p 鈴木正三
q 德川將軍
r 驢鞍橋
s 肥前
t 稻富榮次郎
u 福澤諭吉
v 新島襄
w 內村鑑三
x 西川如見
y 新井白石
z 教育勅語
aa 井上毅
ab 高村光太郎
ac 齋藤茂吉
ad 柿本人麿
ae 和辻哲郎
af 日本人と日本文化
ag 佐久間象山
ah 佐久間象山全集
ai 大原幽學
aj 大原幽學全集
ak 町人囊
al 飯島忠夫
am 神道
an 湛念和尙
ao 禪
ap 高傳寺

W. H. WERKMEISTER

The status of the person in Western ethics

I

The problem of the individual and of his status as a person has been central in much of Western moral philosophy; and it is natural that this be so, for, both as the subject and as the object of action, man is engulfed in relations with his fellow men which are essentially moral. But such is the complexity of the Western philosophical tradition that the status of man in moral relations is variously interpreted—and this irrespective of his role as the subject or the object of action. I shall here refer briefly to some of the major aspects of the Western tradition, showing how man's status is revealed in ever new perspectives, and shall then focus more specifically upon the problem itself.

It will be helpful in understanding the issue if we keep in mind that two basic approaches in particular contribute to the Western tradition and to its conception of man's status in moral relations. One of these approaches centers around the polarity of "this world–other world." The other pertains to the problem of "internal" versus "external" relations. Both approaches, however, may be interrelated in the moral world-view of any Western philosopher. We may thus ask, Is the moral code imposed upon man by some outside agency —God, Nature, or society? Or does the code itself emerge out of the very nature of the individuals themselves—out of their own self-interest, their own rationality? Obviously, the status of man as a moral person will vary with our answers to these questions. Moreover, is man's moral status to be judged in the light of the results that flow from his actions—as the utilitarians maintain? Or is his moral status determined by his intentions and by his good will alone —as Kant insists?

The complexity of the Western tradition with respect to man's status as a moral person arises, in part, also from the fact that Hebrew, Christian, Greek, and scientific views are intertwined in that tradition. We thus face the commandments imposed *ab extra* by the Old Testament God: "Thou shalt not . . . ;" as well as the Christian exhortations: "Be ye perfect as your Father in heaven is perfect"; and Aristotle's argument "For man, the life of reason is

best and pleasantest, since reason more than anything else *is* man."[1]
It is evident, that in these distinct world-views the status of man is
distinctly different—he being under externally imposed law, in the
first case; being capable of molding himself by following a given
ideal, in the second case; and being able to achieve happiness by
realizing his own rational nature, in the third.

I am here concerned, however, with the essentially philosophical,
and not the religious, tradition of the West—though, admittedly, the
philosophical tradition has not escaped religious influences and, at
times, has been but a "handmaiden" of theology. Still, since I must
limit my discussion to a few pages, I shall concentrate on the obviously philosophical interpretations. Even then, however, various
perspectives of man's status as a person are clearly discernible in the
Western moral tradition. I shall briefly consider some of the major
ones.

My first reference is to the doctrine of self-realization. Its inception goes back to Aristotle. "Each thing," the Stagirite maintained,
"is defined by its end;"[2] and "reason more than anything else," as
we have seen, "*is* man." That is to say, "the function of man is an
activity of soul which follows or implies a rational principle."[3] "For
man, therefore, the life of reason is best." But a life lived according
to reason is also a life lived in pursuit of the "most pleasant," "the
best," and "the noblest" end; and this is "happiness."[4] Happiness,
in fact, is "that which is always desirable in itself and never for the
sake of something else."[5] And so it comes about that a life lived in
accordance with reason finds its completion and its fulfillment in
personal happiness.

This Aristotelian thesis found special recognition and a special
interpretation in the philosophy of Thomas Aquinas. Said Thomas,
"Since man is man through the possession of reason, his proper
good, which is happiness, must needs be in accordance with that
which is proper to reason."[6] But, again according to Thomas, there
is only one real happiness: "the last beatitude"—"to know God."[7]
To know God, therefore, is the ultimate end of "the whole man."[8]
It is in this that man finds his true and complete realization.

When Joseph Butler took up the Aristotelian theme, he gave it
still another twist: "Every man is naturally a law to himself; . . .
every one may find within himself a rule of right, and the obligation
to follow it."[9] "Reason" is now taken to mean "reasonable self-love,"
and Butler supplements it by an appeal to "conscience." It is by this
latter "faculty, natural to man, that he is a moral agent."[10] Conscience, in other words, is "our proper governor to direct and regulate all other principles, passions and motives of action."[11] In fact,
"the very constitution of our nature requires that we bring our whole
conduct before this superior faculty; wait its determination; enforce

upon ourselves its authority, and make it the business of our lives, as it is absolutely the whole business of a moral agent, to conform ourselves to it. This is the true meaning of that ancient precept, Reverence thyself."[12] Moreover, Butler maintains, "We were made [as much] for society, and to promote the happiness of it, as we were intended to take care of our own life, and health, and private good."[13] And, since "reasonable self-love and conscience are the chief or superior principles in the nature of man," it is evident that "duty and interest are perfectly coincident."[14] In living up to both, man fulfills his own true nature and realizes himself as a moral person. It is through self-realization that he attains moral status.

The rationalism of Aristotle, Thomas Aquinas, and Butler reverberates in the philosophy of Immanuel Kant; but here it again takes a new form. To begin with, we learn that "only a rational being has the faculty to act *according to the conception* of laws, that is, according to principles;" and only such a being "has a will."[15] But the crux of the matter is that "the *universal* system of laws to which [man] is subject are laws which he *imposes upon himself,* and that he is only under obligation to act in conformity to his own will."[16] The supreme principle of morality is thus "the principle of the *autonomy* of the will."[17] It follows that, for Kant, reason "relates to every maxim of the will as legislating universally," and that "it does not do this because of some other practical motive or some future advantages, but from the idea of *dignity* of a rational being who observes no law but that which he himself also gives."[18] "*Autonomy,* therefore, is the basis of the dignity of human and of every rational nature."[19] Finally, if an individual "shares in the making of the universal laws" and is himself "subject to these laws," he is a member of the "kingdom of ends." "He belongs as a sovereign to this realm if he makes the laws and is not subject to the will of any other."[20] It is in this sense that "man and every rational being anywhere exists as an end in itself, not merely as means for the arbitrary use by this or that will."[21] And it is on the basis of this understanding of the status of man as a moral person that Kant gives final formulation to his categorical imperative: "Act so that, in your own person as well as in the person of every other, you are treating mankind as an end, never merely as a means."[22]

It is not astonishing that, with this general orientation, Kant should regard motive rather than consequences as decisive in moral action. "It is impossible to conceive of anything anywhere in the world or even anywhere out of it that can without qualification be called good, except a Good Will."[23] This same idea is taken up and developed by James Martineau when he maintains that the rightness or wrongness of moral conduct is solely a matter of motive, that moral quality is found in inner springs of action alone. And, tying this fact up with the idea of self-realization, Martineau argues that "the moral law must be expressed in the form, '*Be this,*' not in the form, '*Do this.*' "[24]

A special version of this theme of self-realization we find in the philosophy of Josiah Royce. For him, full realization of the moral person is achieved only in the "loyal person"—the person loyally committed to a cause. In such a man there is "an exaltation of the self, of the inner man, who now feels glorified through his sacrifice, dignified in his self-surrender."[25] "The need of a life task is at once voluntary . . . and worthy."[26] "In [your] cause is your life, your will, your opportunity, your fulfillment."[27] Even if the cause is but a "loyalty to loyalty,"[28] "all those duties which we have learned to recognize as the fundamental duties of the civilized man, the duties that every man owes to every man, are to be rightly interpreted as special instances" of that loyalty.[29] "Have a cause; choose your cause; be decisive."[30] Therein you will find your own self-realization.

When we now turn to David Hume, the picture changes radically. "The distinction between a right and a wrong act," Hume says, "is *social opinion* . . . or *social approbation.*"[31] Such approbation "solicits one's obligation; both work toward the same end, viz., the happiness and welfare of the individual and of society."[32] We must note, however, that "approbation or blame is not an activity of rational judgment, but of the heart. . . . [It is] an active feeling or sentiment"[33]—a sentiment "shared in common with the rest of society."[34]

To be sure, Hume maintains that my own approbation of an act, "by touching my humanity, procures also the applause of all mankind."[35] But this appeal to our common humanity cannot compensate for the fact that, as the subject of action, the individual must be subordinated to the principle of social approbation; that he has dignity and status as a moral person, not in his own right and by virtue of his autonomous and law-giving will, but only as the result of "social opinion." The shift in the interpretation of man's status is both radical and frightening. It is, however, not the ultimate in the devaluation of the moral person as an autonomous agent and of his status as a subject of moral action.

Jeremy Bentham bluntly tells us that "goodness or badness cannot with any propriety be predicated of motives."[36] A man's intentions are themselves either good or bad only "with reference . . . to the consequences of the act."[37] This theme is an outright contradiction of the self-realizationist's thesis that "the moral law must be expressed in the form, '*Be this,*' not in the form '*Do this*' " (see above), and, in the end, it is a complete degrading of man as an agent in moral action.

To be sure, Bentham seems to attribute to man a new dignity by demanding that "everybody . . . count for one, nobody for more than one;"[38] but this demand loses much of its significance when we realize the abstract emptiness of the "one" who is to be counted. I shall return to this problem shortly. For the present let us note that none other than John Stuart Mill did his best to rectify Bentham's position.

To be sure, Mill seems to agree with Bentham in maintaining that "all persons . . . have a *right* to equality of treatment;"[39] but he at least recognizes the fact that "few human creatures would consent to be changed into any of the lower animals, for the allowance of the fullest measure of the beast's pleasures; no intelligent human being would consent to be a fool, no instructed person would be an ignoramus, no person of feeling and conscience would be selfish and base, even though they should be persuaded that the fool, the dunce, or the rascal is better satisfied with his lot than they are with theirs."[40] In the final analysis, so he is saying, true happiness is found only in human beings who are sensitive and intelligent—and especially intelligent. Shades of the rationalism of Aristotle!

The impact of Darwin's theory of evolution was also felt in ethics, of course. Herbert Spencer, for example, argued, in effect, that, all other things being equal, we call good every act which tends to conserve the individual and his progeny, or which contributes to a well-adjusted and complete life for self and others.[41] Adaptation and adjustment—the key concepts in biological evolution—are here taken to be the cornerstone of morality. But this thesis was at once challenged by Nietzsche. For him, the crucial fact is that "truth" is but a "life-furthering, life-preserving, species-preserving, perhaps species-rearing" condition of human existence.[42] "The false judgments" may well be "the most indispensable ones,"[43] provided they enhance or advance our existence. The ultimate question is simply whether or not "we believe in the causality of the will."[44] And it is the will which, "relative to itself," evaluates "every other thing which seeks to grow."[45] This will, however, is not simply "will to exist"; "not Will to Life, but . . . Will to Power"[46]—to an ever-growing, an ever-richer, an ever more abundant life. "Love," to be sure, "provides the highest feeling of power," for "we are godly in love."[47] But what is especially important for Nietzsche is the fact that this love, the Will to Power, is a "love of the future." We must be hard on what is at present in order to make the future the more resplendent. Only he knows "what is good and bad" who creates—"who creates man's goal and gives to the earth its meaning and its future."[48] But "we must create beyond ourselves!"[49] We must create the Man of the future, who stands above present man as high as present man himself stands above the highest animals. Man as we know him now is "something that has to be overcome." He is but a transition, "a bridge," to Superman—to that ideal of a "Caesar with the soul of Christ"[50]—"frightful in his goodness"[51] but a creator of new values.

There is, of course, a great deal of existentialist thought in Nietzsche's philosophy. But existentialist thinkers of every variety contribute a particular perspective of their own to our problem, which is the status of man in ethics. Kierkegaard's anguished outcry set the pace. The "individual" in his forsakenness is the theme of his basic position. "Had I to carve an inscription on my grave," he once wrote, "I would ask for none other than 'the individual.' "[52] And as "that individual," Kierkegaard (and every other human being) is "alone, alone in the whole world, alone—before God."[53] In his aloneness, however, the individual must make himself into an authentic self: "Not to be one's own self is despair."[54] Not to be one's own self means to be lost in anonymity, lost in "the crowd"; lost in *das man,"* as Heidegger would say. Here in Kierkegaard's philosophy and in existentialist thought in general, reason has ceased to be a guiding light; and it is this fact that drives most existentialists into despair. Moods and feelings predominate in their world-view; and one is tempted to paraphrase Hobbes and point out that he who denies the efficacy of reason to make room for anything else actually destroys all. For Kierkegaard himself there still remained the "leap" into an orthodox Calvinism. For his successors, however, that way out of despair has been barred. Theirs is that "dreadful freedom" in the face of which "man is unjustifiable."[55]

Deeply ingrained in existentialist thought is also the problem of "the Other"—of "the Self" in relation to "the Other."[56] Hegel, too, recognized this relation and its crucial importance for our human realities: *I* can only be *I* because there is an Other which is not I. And this implies that there is my "being-for-myself" and my "being-for-the-Other." The problem here encountered has at once its moral aspects, for the relation between "myself" and "the Other" is either that of love or that of conflict. Martin Buber and Ludwig Binswanger tend to give priority to the former; Jean-Paul Sartre gives it to the latter—he is obsessed by the idea that, as subject of his own experience, "the Other" reduces me constantly to a mere object;[57] and, in order to recover my individuality, I must overcome the freedom of "the Other." Because of this crucial ontological and, therefore, inescapable antagonism between "myself" and "the Other," every act between us is a conflict; and it is so unavoidably.[58] Although "human reality is a being which tries to become God,"[59] Sartre indicates no possible way toward this goal. Nor does he provide a tenable basis for moral interactions. In almost Nietzschean terms he tells us: "There is no law-maker other than [man] himself," and "man will fulfill himself as man, not in turning toward himself," but in projecting himself beyond himself, "in seeking outside himself a goal which is just this liberation [from all previously conceived standards], just this particular fulfillment" of man's personal projection.[60] And, in this sense, "existentialism is nothing else than an attempt to draw all the consequences of a coherent atheistic position."[61] But "even if God did exist, that would change nothing."[62]

II

So far I have sketched—if ever so briefly—various perspectives in the Western tradition under which the status of the individual in the moral situation must be appraised. Time does not permit a more thorough or a more complete presentation. Enough has been said, however, to enable us to attempt an evaluative interpretation of the conflicting views and, on the basis of such an evaluation, to define more specifically and more adequately man's status as a moral person in the Western tradition taken as a whole.

It is evident from the quotations given earlier that, from the beginning of articulate Western thought, moral man has been viewed either as a subject under imposed law or as an agent in pursuit of some end that was regarded as good. Throughout the centuries, however, manifold variations on these two themes have been developed, and, with them, man's status as a moral person has undergone manifold and, at times, rather subtle, changes. I shall here reduce these changes to six, leaving the subtleties for others to point up.

The first fact to be noted is that, as a rule, at least two specific aspects are discernible in each of the six interpretations here to be considered. Thus, in the case of Aristotle, for example, the two aspects are a reference to reason and one to happiness, while in the case of Kant they are a reference to reason and to law. In the case of Hume, one aspect involves the appeal to "social approbation," the other refers to "sentiment."

Closer inspection will then reveal that the two (or more) aspects are subtly interrelated in the philosophies of the various thinkers and that, in fact, their different interrelations define the different philosophical positions with respect to man's status as a moral person.

The first of the six positions to be considered is defined by its appeal to reason and the pursuit of the good. Aristotle was the first to develop it in principle. His version, however, was a form of self-realization, since, as he put it, "reason more than anything else *is* man," and, since, moreover, "the life of reason is best." In the pursuit of what is "best," therefore, man realizes his own true nature and, in realizing it, achieves "happiness."

Aquinas, retaining Aristotle's rationalism, merely redefined the end pursued: "to know God" and thus to achieve man's true fulfillment in "the last beatitude." Butler, adding an appeal to "conscience" to man's reason, saw man as fulfillng his own true nature in the pursuit of self-interest and the interest of society. But, whether we consider the particular form of self-realization of Aristotle, of Aquinas, or of Butler, the basic theme is the same: Man's status as a moral person is determined by the fact that he is endowed with reason and that he attains self-realization because of the end pursued.

When next we turn to the philosophy of Kant, the situation changes completely. To be sure, Kant retains the appeal to reason, but "reason," as Kant understands that term, no longer designates "reasonableness" in the pursuit of ends, but man's ability to act in conformity with principles, i.e., with laws. When these laws are self-imposed, that is, when a person is both, the lawgiver and the servant of the law, the autonomy of his will is preserved; and this autonomy is the basis of the dignity of human nature and, therefore, of the status of the person as a moral agent. Such an agent is entitled to respect as a person—be he considered as subject or as object of the law. And as autonomous lawgiver he is a member of that "kingdom of ends" in which Kant's moral philosophy culminates.

The third trend in the Western tradition again changes the picture radically; for it was Hume's contention that the crux in moral matters is "social approbation," and that this is "not an activity of rational judgment, but of the heart"—a matter, that is, of "sentiment." The individual, thus, has status, not in his own right, not because of his autonomy as a lawgiver, but only as a result of "social opinion." We notice here a shift from the inwardness of the person (as conceived by Aristotle and Kant) to an external appraisal; and, while the transition is not complete in Hume's own view—since he does speak of "my own approbation of mankind"—the step from here to the utilitarian position is not very great.

With Bentham—and this brings us to our fourth trend in the Western tradition—the utilitarians argue that man's intentions are neither good nor bad in themselves, but are so only with reference to the consequences of an act. It is not the motive which counts, but the result. This doctrine is a radical contradiction of the thesis of self-realization, as well as of Kant's conception of the dignity of man. And when now the utilitarians demand—as Bentham explicitly does —that "everybody [is] to count for one, nobody for more than one," one can only point out that the "one" here in question is a rather empty or shallow individual, one whose status and value are determined, not by what he is in and of himself, but by the consequences —and not necessarily the intended or foreseen consequences—of his acts. The criteria of worth and human dignity have either been forgotten or transposed entirely into a realm of happenstance and external appraisal.

The fifth trend in the Western tradition derives from the idea of evolution, but it takes two forms. There is, first, the interpretation given by Spencer, according to which adaptation and adjustment to environmental conditions and, therefore, survival of the individual and the species are the determinative criteria—a position which reduces the person to essentially nothing but an event in Nature, without intrinsic worth or dignity. The second form of the evolutionary view is represented by Nietzsche. The key ideas here are not adaptation and survival, but a drive for more abundant Life, for "Power," and the challenge to "create beyond ourselves." Man has dignity because he is a "creator of new values"; and he has status because he is "a bridge to the future"—a transition toward a Being which far transcends even the best of men. And both, his dignity and his status, are determined by his own creativity—by his rising above the circumstances of the here-and-now. Man the creator of values gives meaning even to "the Earth." That is his greatest dignity.

When, lastly, we turn to the existentialist view of man, we find, of course, a great variety of detail. The central theme, however, is reasonably clear. The individual human being is essentially alone in the world; and he must make his moral decisions in this aloneness. What is crucial, however, is that, essentially, man has nothing to guide him—neither a goal imposed upon him *ab extra*, nor an inherent human nature. Moreover, moods and feelings prevail, and reason is inadequate in dealing with the problems of existence. What others have done or are doing cannot help him, either, for, by following them, he gives up his own "authentic existence" and is submerged in the inauthentic existence of *"das man."* Actually, his relation to "others" is at least ambiguous. There is the "we of love" and there is the "we of conflict"; and, according to most of the existentialists, the "we of conflict" predominates. The individual is condemned, as it were, to make his most basic decisions in "complete freedom"—in that "dreadful freedom" of the irrationalities of the moment. What is the worth, the dignity, or the status of the individual in such a situation? There is no real answer. A person attains status (and dignity and worth) only when he achieves "authentic existence." But just what this means or how it can be achieved is not clear. The existentialists themselves have no comprehensive or clear-cut answer. Theirs is primarily the statement of a problem, not its solution.

When we now take the final step in the interpretation of the status of the individual as a moral agent in the whole of the Western tradition, we can and, indeed, we must, assume that the various trends interwoven in that tradition stress—each in its own way—discernible aspects of man's existence as a person. There is the emphasis on man's essential reasonableness and on his pursuit of ends and goals. There is also the reference to the fact that, being rational, man is capable of imposing laws upon himself, and of living by these laws. There is the recognition of the influence of man's environment upon his actions, but there is also the realization that he can rise above such influence and, in his creation of values, give meaning to the whole of his existence. And there is the realization that man's choices and decisions often reflect but a blind groping for meaning and for a value-accentuated authentic existence.

What we thus find in the Western tradition is a gradual awakening to the complexities of our human existence—an existence which involves all mankind, irrespective of race, color, or creed. While acknowledging man's interrelations with his environment and the conflicts in human situations, the basic emphasis is placed upon the inward man. His dignity and his status as a moral being are determined by what man is in his heart of hearts, not by the externalities of his actions or the circumstances of his existence. The real challenge inherent in our tradition is *"to be"* rather than *"to do."*

There is one aspect, however, which deserves special attention. It is clear from the preceding discussions that there are two basic orientations in the Western tradition. One involves the pursuit of ends or goals. It is primarily value-oriented. The other involves the recognition of laws, of duties and obligations. In the past, both orientations have been regarded as essentially moral. It may be necessary, however, to separate them and to distinguish them rather clearly. After all, the pursuit of values involves spheres of human activities other than the moral. Any evaluation and preference or choice in any field of human endeavor involves values. And a reasonable maxim reflecting this fact would be: So act as to prefer in each situation the greater rather than the lesser value. The status of the human person in the value realm would, thus, be determined by the reasonableness of his value choices.

But when it comes to obligations and duties, we are concerned with problems which are moral in a restrictive sense. And with respect to them it is evident that the status of the individual as a moral person is determined by the fact that in and through his own commitments the individual assumes obligations and duties and, thus, does become his own lawgiver. It is the autonomy of the person in an essentially Kantian sense which assures the individual's dignity and status as a person.

The pursuit of values and the self-imposition of obligations are interrelated, however, in the sense that the obligations arise analytically from our commitments, but the commitments are made in the pursuit of values.[63] And only if the individual functions in both capacities, and in autonomous freedom, does he fully achieve his status as a person and the dignity of a morally responsible individual. It is only thus that he rises above social pressures and environmental conditioning in moral responsibility and autonomy as a person. And, as far as the West is concerned, it is this fact that gives him his status as a moral agent.

QUESTION: I miss in your paper specific references to such ethicists as Max Scheler, Nicolai Hartmann, David Ross, and others. Is not their work also important?

ANSWER: Of course their work is important and deserves full recognition. I have dealt with them extensively in my book *Theories of Ethics*. But it was physically impossible to discuss all ethicists of the West and stay within the 45 minutes reading-time allotted. A selection had to be made, and selections in such circumstances are always somewhat arbitrary. That I refer to the existentialists, for example, and not to the formidable work of Nicolai Hartmann, for instance, was determined by the fact that existentialism is currently the fashion, so to speak, whereas Hartmann's work is relatively unknown. Consideration of Hartmann's work, however—or of the work of other philosophers now omitted—would not have altered the conclusions concerning the status of the individual in Western ethics.

QUESTION: Does not your reference to motives as the crucial fact in morality assume man's essential freedom to choose and to act in accordance with his choices? You did not discuss the problem of freedom in your paper.

ANSWER: All morality assumes that man has the freedom to choose and, through his choices, to determine the course of his actions. Free will in this sense is an indispensable presupposition and, therefore, a postulate of morality. The problem of free will, however, is not itself a moral problem. It is, rather, a metaphysical problem and, thus, falls outside the scope of my paper. As an indispensable presupposition of morality, however, the idea of freedom also contributes to the status of man in ethical perspective.

QUESTION: In your paper you say that "the real challenge inherent in our tradition is 'to be' rather than 'to do'." The opinion is generally held, however, that it is Eastern philosophy—notably Indian and Chinese—which places the emphasis upon "to be," whereas the West presumably stresses "to do." Would you comment on this?

ANSWER: As I have indicated in my paper, in Western ethics stress is laid on the motive of our actions. Motives, however, pertain to the inner orientation of the person acting, not to the actual consequences of an act. In Western ethics that inner orientation reflects either man's striving for self-realization or his status as an autonomous lawgiver who imposes laws of conduct upon himself. Whichever is the case in a particular instance, man's moral choices and actions are, thus, but manifestations of what he himself is in his heart of hearts. The emphasis, therefore, rightly rests upon the "to be" rather than the "to do," although *being* culminates in *doing*.

QUESTION: I am especially interested in the concluding statement of your paper. But let me make a slight substitution. Let me read it this way: "Only if the individual functions . . . in autonomous freedom does he fully achieve his status as a person and the dignity of a morally responsible individual. . . . And, as far as China is concerned, it is this fact that gives him his status as a moral agent." In other words, in your paper, representing the West, you have forcefully stated the Chinese point of view. Would you care to comment upon this?

ANSWER: I am delighted that Chinese and Western ethicists are in such close agreement on so crucial an issue. As a matter of fact, as I have listened for the last few weeks to the various papers on metaphysics, epistemology, religion, and ethics—both East and West —I have become convinced that it is in the field of ethics more than in any other field of philosophy that a profound mutual understanding can be achieved. Human beings in human situations acting from motives that reflect either ideals of self-realization or man's position as autonomous lawgiver by and large find the dignity and intrinsic worth of man, his status as an individual in ethics, in very much the same way. I suggest that this fact be further explored in co-operative studies, East and West.

[1] Aristotle, *Ethica Nichomachea,* W. D. Ross, trans., *The Works of Aristotle,* Vol. II (Oxford: The Clarendon Press, 1925), 1178a7–8.

[2] *Ibid.,* 1115b24.

[3] *Ibid.,* 1098a8–9.

[4] *Ibid.,* 1099a24, 30.

[5] *Ibid.,* 1097a28–38.

[6] Thomas Aquinas, *The Summa Contra Gentiles,* Laurence Shapcote, trans.; edited and annotated by Anton C. Pegis. (New York: Random House, 1945), Book III, chap. 34.

[7] *Ibid.,* chap. 25.

[8] *Ibid.*

[9] Joseph Butler, *Fifteen Sermons,* W. R. Matthiews, ed. (London: G. Bell & Sons, Ltd., 1953), pp. 51, 63.

[10] *Ibid.,* p. 54.

[11] *Ibid.,* p. 57.

[12] William Sahakian, *Systems of Ethics and Value Theory* (New York: Philosophical Library, 1963), p. 81.

[13] Butler, *op. cit.,* p. 40.

[14] *Ibid.,* p. 68.

[15] Immanuel Kant, *The Fundamental Principles of the Metaphysics of Ethics,* Otto Manthey-Zorn, trans. (New York: Appleton-Century-Crofts, 1938), p. 29.

[16] Immanuel Kant, *Groundwork of the Metaphysic of Morals,* translated by H. J. Paton as *The Moral Law* (New York: Barnes & Noble, 1950), pp. 101–103, 106–107, 112, 114, etc.

[17] *Ibid.,* p. 100.

[18] Kant, *Fundamental Principles,* pp. 52–53.

[19] *Ibid.,* p. 54.

[20] *Ibid.,* p. 52.

[21] *Ibid.,* p. 45.

[22] *Ibid.,* p. 47.

[23] *Ibid.,* p. 8.

[24] James Martineau, *Types of Ethical Theory,* 2 vols. (2nd ed.; Oxford: The Clarendon Press, 1886.), Vol. II, p. 24.

[25] Josiah Royce, *The Philosophy of Loyalty* (New York: The Macmillan Company, 1908), p. 40.

[26] *Ibid.,* p. 59.

[27] *Ibid.,* p. 42.

[28] *Ibid.,* p. 121.

[29] *Ibid.,* p. 139.

[30] *Ibid.,* p. 187.

[31] David Hume, *An Enquiry Concerning the Principles of Morals,* in *Enquiries,* L. A. Selby-Bigge, ed. (Oxford: The Clarendon Press, 1902), pp. 219, 230–31, 271, etc.

[32] *Ibid.,* p. 278.

[33] *Ibid.,* pp. 290, etc. See also David Hume, *A Treatise of Human Nature* (London: John Noon, 1739), Book III, chap. I.

[34] *Enquiry, op. cit.*

[35] *Ibid.,* p. 274.

[36] Jeremy Bentham, *An Introduction to the Principles of Morals and Legislation* (London: The Clarendon Press, 1876), p. 102.

[37] *Ibid.,* p. 93.

[38] Henry Sidgwick, *The Methods of Ethics* (Chicago: University of Chicago Press, 1962), p. 417.

[39] John Stuart Mill, *Utilitarianism* (London: Parker, Son, and Bourn, 1863), p. 93.

40 *Ibid.*, p. 12.

41 Herbert Spencer, *The Data of Ethics* (Chicago, New York: Rand, McNally & Company, 1879), chap. III.

42 Friedrich Nietzsche, *Beyond Good and Evil,* Helen Zimmern, trans. (Edinburgh, London: T. N. Foulis, 1911), pp. 8–9. For my interpretation of Nietzsche, see W. H. Werkmeister, *Theories of Ethics* (Lincoln, Nebraska: Johnson Publishing Company, 1961), chap. VI.

43 Friedrich Nietzsche, *The Will to Power,* Anthony M. Ludovici, trans. (Edinburgh, London: T. N. Foulis, 1910), Vol. II, p. 20.

44 *Beyond Good and Evil,* p. 52.

45 *The Will to Power,* p. 124. See also Friedrich Nietzsche, *The Genealogy of Morals,* Horace B. Samuel, trans. (Edinburgh, London: T. N. Foulis, 1913), p. 89.

46 Friedrich Nietzsche, *Thus Spake Zarathustra,* Thomas Common, trans. (Edinburgh, London: T. N. Foulis, 1911), p. 137.

47 Nietzsche, *Will to Power,* Vol. I, p. 147.

48 Nietzsche, *Zarathustra,* p. 88.

49 Friedrich Nietzsche, *The Twilight of the Idols,* Anthony M. Ludovici, trans. (Edinburgh, London: T. N. Foulis, 1911), p. 269.

50 Nietzsche, *Will to Power,* Vol. II, p. 380.

51 Nietzsche, *Zarathustra,* p. 174.

52 Søren Kierkegaard, *Journals,* Alexander Dru, trans. (Oxford: Oxford University Press, 1939). An 1847 entry.

53 *Ibid.*

54 Søren Kierkegaard, *The Sickness Unto Death,* Walter Lowrie, trans. (Princeton: Princeton University Press, 1941), p. 44.

55 Marjorie Greene, *Dreadful Freedom, A Critique of Existentialism* (Chicago: University of Chicago Press, 1948), p. 149. See also Wilfrid Desan, *The Tragic Finale* (Cambridge: Harvard University Press, 1954).

56 Martin Buber, *I and Thou,* Ronald Gregor Smith, trans. (Edinburgh: T. & T. Clark, 1937). Ludwig Binswanger, *Grundformen und Erkenntnis Menschlichen Daseins* (Zürich: Max Niehaus, 1942). See also John MacMurray, *Persons in Relations* (New York: Harper & Brothers, 1961).

57 Jean-Paul Sartre, *L'Être et le Néant* (Paris: Librairie Gallimard, 1943), pp. 312, 329, 429, 431, etc.

58 *Ibid.*, p. 502.

59 *Ibid.*, p. 653.

60 Jean-Paul Sartre, *Existentialism* (New York: Philosophical Library, 1947), p. 60.

61 *Ibid.*

62 *Ibid.*, p. 61.

63 Werkmeister, *Theories of Ethics,* chap. X.

SECTION V   **Social Thought and Practices**

Y. P. MEI[a]

The status of the individual in Chinese social thought and practice

The predominant molding force of traditional Chinese society is Confucianism. Confucianism places dual emphasis on the importance of the proper development of the individual for the well-being of society, and, at the same time, on the importance of social responsibility for the perfection of the individual. While this double-barreled Chinese outlook on the status of the individual in society has been cultivated mostly by the teachings of Confucianism, its roots to a considerable extent go back to social thought and practices antedating Confucius. We shall take up some samples of pre-Confucian Chinese social thought and practice in the first section of the paper.

I. EARLY CHINESE SOCIAL THOUGHT AND PRACTICE

Valuable glimpses of the status of the individual in Chinese social thought and practice in its prototypal forms can be gained by consulting Chinese mythology and Chinese classical literature. Mythology is employed here, not for its religious significance, but as an expression of time-honored, deep-rooted, and widespread attitudes on the part of the Chinese people. We have in mind specifically the status of man in the concept of a cosmic triad as manifested in the legend of the Three Sovereign Groups. The Three Sovereign Groups, the earliest rulers China had, are said to have consisted of the Celestial Sovereign Group of twelve brothers, each reigning 18,000 years; the Terrestrial Sovereign Group of eleven brothers, each reigning 18,000 years; and, interestingly, the Human Sovereign Group of nine brothers, reigning for a total of 45,600 years in 150 generations. Of course, nobody believes in such tall tales, not even the Chinese. The thing that is notable in this legend is the Chinese insistence on the importance of the generic man. Man is so important that he is matched from the beginning of time with Heaven and Earth to make a cosmic triad. In Chinese, the term for the triad of Heaven-Earth-man is *san ts'ai*[b], meaning three powers, three forces, three origins, etc. Throughout the long history of Chinese thought, in the popular mind as well as in classical literature,[1] there has been persistent emphasis on the importance of man. Man is often spoken of in the same breath with Heaven and Earth. It is doubtful whether any other major world-civilization has laid an emphasis to a comparable degree on the cosmic importance of man. The emphasis on the importance of the generic man in relation to Heaven and Earth has provided the undergirding, in Chinese thought and practice, for the collateral emphases on the importance of the common man in relation to his ruler, as well as the importance of the individual in relation to society.

The social significance of man and his life in the early Chinese tradition manifests itself further in the Chinese attitude toward immortality. Until the introduction of Buddhism and related ideas from India, the Chinese had only the vaguest notions about heaven and hell and about future life in general. Insofar as they had any sense of or interest in immortality, it was mainly some form of social immortality. In the *Tso chuan*[c] is kept the following record of a conversation on immortality:

> When Muh-shuh[d] (P'aou[e]) went to Tsin[f], Fan Seuen-tsze[g] met him, and asked the meaning of the saying of the ancients, "They died but suffered no decay," . . . Muh-shuh said . . . "I have heard that the highest meaning of it is when there is established [an example of] virtue; the second, when there is established [an example of] successful service; and the third, when there is established [an example of wise] speech. When these examples are not forgotten with length of time, this is what is meant by the saying —'They do not decay.' "[2]

This conversation on immortality, which took place in 549 B.C., is instructive in itself and significant for the tremendous influence it has exercised. While the masses may be thinking about their future life in terms of heavens and hells, to this day educated Chinese are much more interested in "leaving behind a fragrance lasting for millenniums[h]." And the way to attain this distinction lies in one's achievement during one's lifetime, in virtue, in public service, and in teaching,[3] as stipulated in the conversation just quoted.

Among the pre-Confucian social practices in China, probably the most noteworthy for us is the trend of the gradual rise of the worth of the individual. In the dim, distant past, China had her share of inhumane social practices, including human sacrifice. When a great lord died, his harem of women and his household of servants were buried alive with his corpse. Eventually, clay figurines were used as substitutes for real people at these burials, and this type of human sacrifice became extinct. Prisoners of war at first were killed as a matter of course, but later they were enslaved rather than killed. At one stage there was the practice of what might be called "fixture slavery." Under this practice, the slaves were treated as part and parcel of the land that they worked. When (and only when) the land

changed hands so did the slaves change hands. The eventual appearance of slave trade and the slave market was in fact, a significant
step in social and humanitarian reform. The scattered records of
slave trade in ancient China showed a definite upward trend in the
value of the slave. One bronze vessel of the reign of King Hsiao[l] of
Chou[j] (909–894 B.C.) bears an inscription recording the exchange
of five human beings for one horse plus one skein of silk. Some four
hundred years later, Yen Ying[k] (died 493 B.C.), the Prime Minister
of Ch'i[l], offered one of his superb horses for a slave whose appearance impressed him.[4] The worth of the individual increased about
five times over the period of four hundred years. These accounts are
isolated instances, to be sure, but the trend of the rising worth of the
individual in ancient China, as signified by his market price, is
unmistakable.

By the time of Confucius, China was dominated by a number of
powerful feudal states. The imperial house became more and more
a figurehead as the rivalry among the leading feudal states became
more fierce and militant. The condition of chaos and disunity in the
empire, however, notably enhanced the increasing worth of the
individual. The contending feudal lords were contending for power,
and power consisted of troops and food, both of which depended in
turn on the size of the population. Although the ambitious feudal
lords uniformly regarded the views of Confucius about government
and the other idealistic teachers as counsels of perfection and im-
practicable, they could well appreciate, from their own selfish interest, Confucius' yardstick of good government: "Good government
obtains when those who are near are made happy and those who are
far off are attracted."[5] The practice of a measure of benevolence in
their despotic rule evidently became the best policy under the circumstances. Whatever the motivation, be it self-interest or human
compassion on the part of the rulers, there was a decided trend of
the rising worth of the common man in ancient China.

II. STATUS OF THE INDIVIDUAL IN CONFUCIAN SOCIAL THOUGHT

Confucius[m] (551–479 B.C.) lived in an age of growing confusion and
chaos. Dedicating himself to the task of bringing order out of chaos,
the sage became firmly convinced that a society could be only as
good as its members. Even if it should be too much to expect every
member of a community to be a superior man, at least the leaders
and rulers must be exemplary individuals before the community
could expect to achieve its well-being. The relation of the individual
to society is here envisaged, not in terms of a collection of disparate
atomistic units to form an aggregate, but in terms of a continuing
permeation of the quality of the character of the individual through-

out the ever-broadening circles of society. This qualitative relation of the individual to society is categorically stated in the celebrated passage of the *Ta hsüeh*ⁿ (*The Great Learning*), as follows:

> The ancients who wished clearly to exemplify illustrious virtue throughout the world would first set up good government in their states. Wishing to govern their states well, they would first regulate their families. Wishing to regulate their families, they would first cultivate their persons. Wishing to cultivate their persons, they would first rectify their minds. Wishing to rectify their minds, they would first seek sincerity in their thoughts. Wishing for sincerity in their thoughts, they would first extend their knowledge. The extension of knowledge lay in the investigation of things. For only when things are investigated is knowledge extended; only when knowledge is extended are thoughts sincere; only when thoughts are sincere are minds rectified; only when minds are rectified are our persons cultivated; only when our persons are cultivated are our families regulated; only when families are regulated are states well governed; and only when states are well governed is there peace in the world.
>
> From the emperor down to the common people, all, without exception, must consider cultivation of the individual character as the root. If the root is in disorder, it is impossible for the branches to be in order. To treat the important as unimportant and to treat the unimportant as important—this should never be. This is called knowing the root; this is called the perfection of knowledge.⁶

This passage is important in several respects. Particularly noteworthy is the conclusion that everyone, whether he is in high place or low, must consider cultivation of the individual character as "the root" of social well-being and harmony. One of the outstanding characteristics in Chinese social thought is the emphasis on obligations rather than rights and prerogatives of the individual in relation to society. Do not ask what society can do for you; ask what you can do for society—exhortations such as this fall right in line with the Chinese spirit. And what can the individual do for society? Of course, the specific answers will vary with each individual. But there is a basic answer common to all men, and this is what the Chinese sages have been insisting upon, namely, the cultivation of one's character. The cultivation of the character of the individual, according to the *Ta hsüeh,* as quoted above, includes five inward steps of self-perfection and three outward steps of social extension spreading to the family, the state, and the whole world. This eight-step scheme has served in China as a master plan of moral and educational development as well as a blueprint for social and political administration.

While the individual in China does not ask what society can do for him, he cannot do without society for his achievement of the good life. The Chinese ideal for the individual is sometimes described as "sageliness within and kingliness without,"⁷ a kind of double-barreled ideal. An individual is expected to be a man of enlightenment and a man of affairs. He is to be a citizen of the universe and at the same time a member of society. His is a life that is in the world and yet not of the world. It is in society that the individual lives, moves, and has his being, and, furthermore, grows into the fullness of his manhood, even sagehood. According to Confucian teaching, there is in some sense an identification of the sage with the universe, but the identification is here achieved by way of society and not in spite of it. Social well-being depends on the proper cultivation of the individual, to be sure, but the individual can achieve the full realization of his destiny only through public service and social participation. Social obligations and responsibilities of an individual are not chains and burdens to be escaped from, or to be borne and suffered. To the contrary, it is in the fulfillment of these social responsibilities that the individual realizes his complete personal fulfillment. In a very fundamental sense, the individual and society in Confucian social thought are mutually dependent.

While social service and participation are indispensable to the perfection of the individual, his status in society is defined, according to Confucianism, not by social esteem or other external circumstances, sometimes in spite of them, but by one's inner sense of personal integrity and dignity. "Man is born for uprightness,"[8] said Confucius. It is well known that the key concept in Confucianism is jen[o], human-heartedness, or love, or, according to James Legge's translation, virtue. I presented a summary statement on this central concept of Confucianism at an earlier Conference,[9] and repetition will be avoided. Here attention is directed specifically to the intuitive and spontaneous quality of jen. The following are some of the sayings of Confucius from *The Analects* (*Lun yü*[p]):

> Is virtue (*jen*) a thing remote? I wish to be virtuous, and lo! virtue is at hand.[10]
> Is anyone able for one day to apply his strength to virtue (*jen*)? I have not seen the case in which his strength would be insufficient.[11]

Thus it is evident that *jen* is not the special endowment of some privileged class, but the "spark of divinity" planted in every man without exception. For the seed of *jen* to grow into the full-blown virtue of *jen,* it takes, of course, cultivation and education. Confucius declared in feudalistic China, some two thousand five hundred years ago, "In teaching there should be no distinction of classes."[12] No one could have said such a thing under the circumstances of Confucius' day, if he did not have an unswering conviction in the native integrity and dignity of the individual. Both Mencius[q] and Hsün Tzu[r], the great followers of Confucius, maintained that every man on the street could become a Sage-King like Yao and Shun[s] according to Mencius and like the Great Yü according to Hsün Tzu.

Chinese thinkers have not interested themselves in human rights as such. But the conviction in the inviolable worth of the individual lies at the heart of Confucian teaching and accounts for a good measure of the democratic spirit in Chinese life.

The character of integrity and dignity of the individual gives him a sense of confidence and serenity. He is not easily swayed, or ruffled, or affected by the fortunes of the day. He has an inner frame of reference and scale of values, and his life is ordered through self-control. In one passage in *The Analects* of Confucius several of Confucius' sayings on this point are recorded, and we quote some of them as follows:

> "The Master said, 'The commander of the forces of a large State may be carried off, but the will of even a common man cannot be taken from him' " (Chapter XXV).
> "The Master said, 'Dressed himself in a tattered robe quilted with hemp, yet standing by the side of men dressed in furs, and not ashamed—ah! it is Yu who is equal to this!' " (Chapter XXVI).
> "The Master said, 'When the year becomes cold, then we know how the pine and the cypress are the last to lose their leaves' " (Chapter XXVII).
> "The Master said, 'The wise are free from perplexities; the virtuous from anxiety; and the bold from fear' " (Chapter XXVIII).[13]

This ancient list of three freedoms of Confucius should be heeded, we submit, as much as the contemporary list of "Four Freedoms." Similarly, both Mencius and Hsün Tzu left a description of the great man, and what they considered as the great man was the man of integrity. In spite of the radical disagreements between these two great Confucian teachers on several basic subjects, the two descriptions are almost identical. We quote first Mencius and then Hsün Tzu as follows:

> He who dwells in the broad house of the universe, stands firm on the true base of the universe, walks in the great way of the universe, if successful, walks in the way for the good of the people, if unsuccessful, walks in the way all alone; he whom riches and honor cannot corrupt, poverty and obscurity cannot move, threats and violence cannot make bend—he it is that may be called a great man.[14]
> Therefore, power and gain cannot influence him; mobs and multitudes cannot sway him; the whole empire cannot move him. By this [perfect character] he will live and by it he will die, and this is what is meant by moral integrity. With moral integrity one could achieve firmness, and with firmness one could achieve flexibility. Possessing firmness as well as flexibility, he may be said to be a perfect man. Heaven is prized for its brilliance; the earth is prized for its vastness; the superior man is prized for his perfection.[15]

III. STATUS OF THE INDIVIDUAL IN NON-CONFUCIAN SOCIAL THOUGHT

Chinese social thought is not limited, of course, to Confucian thought. Mo Tzu[t] (470–391 B.C.?), for instance, taught the doctrine of universal love. On appearance, this teaching might be expected to uphold egalitarianism of all individuals. But, in social and political thought, Mo Tzu actually advocated "identification with the superior," i.e., submission of one's individual will in conformity with that of one's superior.

The Taoists had little use for society, and were completely indifferent about the social status of an individual. Organization of any kind was regarded by the Taoists as anathema, and social participation as an impediment to the life of freedom and spontaneity.

The Legalists placed the state above the individual, and the status of the individual would be determined solely according to his usefulness to the state, that is, the sovereign.

Buddhism, with its monastic order, introduced what might be called extra-societal egalitarianism of the individual. In the eyes of the Buddha, all men are blinded by their passion and ignorance and are equally in need of compassion and enlightenment. The status of the individual in ordinary society is immaterial, except as an indicator of the desert of his accumulated past deeds according to the Law of *Karma.*

While these various systems have exercised their influence in various degrees, the main current of Chinese social thought has been Confucian social thought since the second century B.C., when in the early Han[u] Dynasty (206 B.C.–A.D. 26) Confucianism began to assume supremacy over rival indigenous systems.

IV. STATUS OF THE INDIVIDUAL IN CHINESE SOCIAL PRACTICE

The phenomenon of the status of the individual in Chinese society extends over a broad spectrum. Topics like slavery, prostitution, women, children, the aged, etc., would all make interesting material for discussion, but such discussions belong more naturally elsewhere. Concerning the more relevant considerations regarding the status of the individual in social practice, this paper will confine itself to the two outstanding Chinese characteristics of social cohesion and social fluidity. Generally speaking, it is the family system and the civil service examination system that, over the centuries, have fostered, respectively, these qualities of Chinese society, and cast a unique light over the status of the individual in society. We shall proceed to consider these two institutions briefly.

The central position of the family in Chinese society is well known. The family in China is not only the primary social group, as it is everywhere, but it is also the prototype of all social organization. The term for emperor in Chinese is "Son-of-Heaven," the local magistrate is addressed by his charges as "parent-official," and good friends become sworn brothers.[15a] Social organizations and social relations in China are patterned after the family. A system of five social relations—those between father and son, sovereign and subject,[16] husband and wife, brother and brother, and, finally, friend and friend—together with the respective obligations pertaining to each relation, has been developed. The individual achieves his inner stature as well as his social status through his participation in the social process and his contribution to society, and the family is the point at which to begin. Take, for instance, the basic virtue of *jen,* or human-heartedness, of Confucius. While the seed of *jen* is inborn in all men, its flowering and flourishing depend on proper cultivation. The family situation provides the first and most favorable opportunity for the exercise and development of this virtue, a sort of nursery for nurturing the seed of *jen.* If battle was to Homer the furnace for the forging and testing of heroes, then the family must be to Confucius the gymnasium for the developing and the perfecting of men of *jen.* Looked at in this light, filial piety is but an expression of *jen* in the specific context of the child-parent interrelationship. The cultivated individual is prepared for regulating the family, and thereby governing the state, and then, in turn, bringing peace to the world, according to *The Great Learning,* as we have learned. Chinese society might be said to be a system of "familiocracy," and the basis for familiocracy lies in the Heaven-endowed feeling of *jen.*

For ordinary purposes, an individual is a member of a family, i.e., a father, a son, a brother, etc. An individual is an individual only rarely and by abstraction, as it were. A wedding in China, for instance, is as much an exciting affair for the young man's family (clan) as for the two individuals involved. But, since it means an addition of a permanent member to a close-knit intimate group, which only death can alter, all members of the group might well take a personal interest in the occasion. Divorce is provided for only on the strictest conditions, and is resorted to very rarely indeed. The family shares in the successes of its members and is held responsible for their failures. Hence the widespread practice of nepotism and the feature of family-group responsibility in the administration of law and social justice in China.

Such a family system has naturally generated a high degree of cohesion and stability. An individual thinks twice in making a decision—once about the consequences to himself and once about the consequences to the family. The quality of social cohesion in traditional Chinese social practice makes itself conspicuous in Chinese communities located in a contrasting cultural setting, such as the

Chinatowns of New York and San Francisco. During the year 1955, for instance, the phenomenon of the absence of juvenile delinquency among the Chinatown teenagers in the United States was discussed in three popular American magazines, namely, *Saturday Evening Post, America,* and *Coronet.*[17] In these articles, the point is repeatedly made that the Chinese children keep off the streets and keep out of trouble because they feel that the home, no matter how humble, is the place for them to live in and because consideration for their folks and family is in their minds whenever they have to decide what to do and what not to do. Lately, however, we begin to hear of isolated cases of "Chinese American J. Ds." Perhaps some Chinese youths are beginning to "progress" away from the traditional "social stagnancy," terms not infrequently used by modern Western observers in discussing Chinese society.

The force of modernization has, of course, already affected the family system in China considerably, and it will influence it much more in the years ahead. Modernization, however, is a universal phenomenon affecting for better or for worse everyone without exception, with a stronger impact on the older societies, to be sure, than on the newer ones. The problem everywhere is one of devising a structure of family organization that will permit a large degree of initiative and freedom of thought and action on the part of the individual and yet assure a proper measure of family cohesion. Individuals crave not only for freedom, but also belongingness, togetherness. Robinson Crusoe, until the appearance of Friday, was completely free and completely miserable. Human rights should indeed be emphasized and fought for where necessary, but human rights are only the minimal conditions for man. Human obligations should be at least equally emphasized because they are essential for the fulfillment of the supreme mission of man, for man to break out of his individual shell and become completely social, human, and therefore divine—a point that Confucius realized clearly two thousand five hundred years ago, and a point that the Chinese have learned to insist upon ever since.

Finally, a few remarks on social mobility in China and the operation of the Chinese civil service examination system. Chinese society is said to consist of four classes, namely, the scholar, the farmer, the artisan, and the merchant. It is to be noted that this fourfold classification is nothing more than an indicator of the profession of the individual at the moment. It is entirely possible for people to change their profession and classification, and this is done all the time. There are the natural factors of inertia, tradition, and material advantage for the son to follow the profession of the father, but there is little in the form of arbitrary barrier preventing anyone from making a change. The degree of social mobility in China is remarkable. The American cliché "from shirt sleeves to shirt sleeves in three generations" is not inapplicable to the Chinese social scene.

Probably the most potent factor contributing to social fluidity and mobility in China is the politico-educational institution of civil service examinations.[18] According to Confucianism, some men, because of their talent and virtue, are fit to lead and some to follow. That the leaders should be given the responsibility of government is a matter of natural law as well as one of noblesse oblige. But how are such men to be discovered and identified? This was a perplexing problem even in Confucius' day.[19] The Confucian doctrine of government gave rise to the institution of the civil service examination system in China. The first attempts at discovering men of virtue and talent and appointing them to public office go back to 165 B.C. The full-fledged system of examinations had operated in China for well over a thousand years before it was abolished in 1905 in favor of the modern Western-styled school system. While the examination system was in operation, it occupied the center of attention of all young men of ambition in the land. The competition was keen, but the reward, in honor, glory, riches, and beautiful wives, was high. Over the centuries the system brought about a unity of culture for the nation, and produced a class of government leaders and an intellectual élite who stood at the top of the list of the four social classes.

The remarkable feature about the civil service examination system for our purpose is the fact that, by and large, it operated as an open system. With minor exceptions varying from dynasty to dynasty, the examinations were open to all men who had properly prepared themselves. Youths of well-to-do families and children of degree-holders had an advantage over the boys from poorer families, to be sure, but Chinese folklore is filled with success stories of self-made men. The Chinese self-made men were the successful candidates, who, coming from destitute families, had prepared themselves by studying under moonlight and even by the light of fireflies kept in a bag of gauze. The civil service examination system served as a social equalizer, and contributed to social mobility in China through the ages. This means there has been a considerable degree of fluidity in the status of the individual in Chinese society.

Certain modern investigators have questioned such assumptions by enlarging upon the differences of opportunities between children of the high-born and of the low-born, and the tendency of the degree-holders to attempt the perpetuation of special privileges within their own families and class. Such phenomena are present in every land. They are not completely absent in China. The important point is, however, that these open examinations in China served to an appreciable degree as a corrective to such tendencies and as an agent for social equalization. The signal significance of the examination system in itself and in relation to the social history of China is evidenced by the recent publication of several English-language studies on this problem within a period of two years.[20] The most thoroughgoing work is the one by Professor Ping-ti Ho[v], from which we quote one of the author's noteworthy conclusions as follows:

> So common was the fact that trade and other productive occupations either alternated or were synchronized with studies that many Ming-Ch'ing[w] [1368–1911] social observers were of the impression that the status distinction among the four major occupational categories (scholars, farmers, artisans, and merchants) was blurred. What is more, all types of literature agree that the most striking characteristic of the post-T'ang[x] [*ca.* 900–   ] society was that, on the one hand, social success depended more on individual merit than on family status, and that, on the other hand, high-status families had little means of perpetuating their success if their descendants were inept.[21]

The phenomena of social cohesion and fluidity are outstanding features of Chinese life, and they are factors that should not be lost sight of in any consideration of the individual and society in China. The status of the individual in Chinese social thought and practice admittedly leaves room for improvement, particularly in the context of modern life. However, while we stress the importance of independence for the individual, we should not overlook the importance of interdependence for his happiness and perfection. In this respect, the relation between the individual and society rather resembles that between the individual nation and the "family of nations," a term and a notion with a noticeable Chinese flavor and a note on which it would not be inappropriate to conclude a paper on Chinese social thought and practice.

QUESTION: Do you want to comment on alleged authoritarianism in Confucian social thought?

ANSWER: One might speak of a degree of authoritarianism in Confucius in the same way, and only in the same way, as one might speak of a degree of authoritarianism in Immanuel Kant. The authority lies within the individual with Confucius as it does with Kant. The Categorical Imperative indeed carries authority with it, but this authority is self-realized and is in no way externally imposed.

QUESTION: Since there is the conviction of the inviolable worth of the individual at the heart of Confucian teaching, why is it that Chinese thinkers have not interested themselves in human rights as such?

ANSWER: The difference between Western thinkers, who have placed a great deal of emphasis on human rights, and the Chinese thinkers, who have been interested in the inviolable worth of the individual, is mainly a difference of idiom. The idiom of thought and expression is, of course, a growth out of a whole cultural background. It would not be very rewarding to expect every culture to be employing the same idiom, even when these cultures are directing their attention to the same human experience. It is possible, for instance, to conceive of formulating a set of philosophical concepts and issues in the idiom of, say, Indian philosophy and require Western writers to discuss Western thought in terms of that idiom. There would then be a good deal of embarrassment and perhaps not much enlightenment. My plea here is for a readiness on the part of participants in a discussion of East-West philosophy to appreciate and, insofar as possible, translate the other man's philosophical idiom into his own.

QUESTION: What has been the status of freedom of thought in your tradition? Or, expressed otherwise, has there ever been any serious curtailment of freedom of thought—either in theory or in practice—in the Chinese tradition?

ANSWER: The problem of freedom of thought has many facets. Religious and political freedom ranks perhaps ahead of social freedom in importance. Within the sphere of social thought and practice there is a remarkable measure of freedom of thought in traditional China. The classical period of Chinese philosophy, from the time of Confucius to the unification of the empire in the late third century B.C., is referred to among the Chinese as the "Period of Hundred Philosophers." (Curiously, the 1957–1959 period of communist rule in China is now known as the "Bloom-Contend Period." This is because Mao Tse-tung[y], in urging the nation to speak out their criticisms of the communist administration, used two of the popular sayings among the Chinese: "Hundred flowers bloom together" and "Hundred philosophers contend together.") Historically, the "hundred philosophers" did contend together, and taught a great variety of doctrines. The worst punishment that could happen to a thinker was to be considered a queer fellow and to have few listeners. If a teacher, like Confucius, did not get the proper kind of attention and respect from one feudal lord, he proceeded to the next feudal state and tried his luck with the next ruler. Confucius did not emerge supreme among the "hundred philosophers" until several centuries after his death. Eventually there developed, an orthodoxy, i.e., Confucianism, as the ruling ideology of the nation, and the civil service examinations were tailored very closely along orthodox Confucian lines. But, then, not everyone needed to take up civil service, and no one was subjected to these examinations just to be tested on the point of orthodoxy. Actually, dissidents existed in China in large or small numbers in every age.

In the course of Chinese history, there have been religious persecutions and literary proscriptions. The actual causes for these limitations of freedom have usually consisted of political threats to or economic encroachment upon the authority of the throne. Such discussions, however, would more properly belong to the Sections of this Conference dealing with religious and political thought concerning the status of the individual.

QUESTION: In the American social tradition, the concept of "equality of opportunity" plays a very prominent role. Is this concept equally prominent in Chinese social thought, and equally emphasized in Chinese social practice?

ANSWER: Yes, I would say so. In my paper I have quoted the saying of Confucius, "In education there should be no discrimination."

(The wording I actually used was the standard translation by James Legge, which says, "In teaching there should be no distinction of classes.") This saying should be read together with another by the Master, "By nature all men are pretty much alike; it is by custom and habit that they are set apart."[22] (Significantly this quotation is used, and is the only one used, in UNESCO's pamphlet, *The Race Question*,[23] published in 1950.) In a popular rhymed primer, which for centuries countless Chinese school boys have been made to commit to memory in traditional China, there are these lines: "Generals and high ministers do not come from designated stocks; /Every man should exert himself to the utmost" (*Rhymed Primer for the Training of Beginners*)[z]. There is a deep-rooted and widespread conviction among the Chinese, since Confucius' day, that, with the necessary effort on the part of the individual himself, any man should and could have the opportunity to "make good." The most effective and influential Chinese institution giving expression to the conviction of the potentiality and educability of the individual is, of course, the wide-open civil service examination system.

One has to admit that traditional China did not develop the idea or institution of universal education, i.e., the requirement by law that all boys and girls must attend school for so many years. But, then, universal education is a very recent phenomenon everywhere in the world and is operating in contemporary China, but our purpose here is to discuss characteristics of traditional cultures.

[1] See, for instance, James Legge, trans., The *Yi King*[aa] (*The Classic of Changes*), X. 63. Sacred Books of the East, Vol. XVI (Oxford: The Clarendon Press, 1899), p. 402.

[2] The *Tso chuan*, the 24th Year of Duke Hsiang[ab] (549 B.C.), James Legge, trans., in The Chinese Classics, Vol. V., the *Tso Chuen* (London: Henry Frowde [China, 1939]), p. 507.

[3] Hu Shih[ac] used "worth, work, and word" as English equivalents for the three items, and called the idea the Chinese three-W theory of immortality. See Hu Shih, "Concept of Immortality in Chinese Thought," in *The Harvard Divinity School Bulletin*, 1945–1946, pp. 40–41.

[4] This incident is recorded in the biographical essay on Yen Ying[ad] in the *Shih chi*[ae] (*Historical Records*) by Ssu-ma Ch'ien[af]. Both of the incidents referred to in this paragraph are cited in Kuo Mo-jo[ag], *Collection of Ten Critical Essays*[ah], (rev. ed., Peking: Hsian Hua Book Shop, 1954), p. 41.

[5] James Legge, trans., *Confucian Analects*, XIII. 16. The Chinese Classics, Vol. I (Oxford: Clarendon Press, 1893), p. 269.

[6] The *Ta hsüeh* (*The Great Learning*), Y. P. Mei, trans., in William T. de Bary, ed., *Sources of Chinese Tradition* (New York: Columbia University Press, 1960), p. 129.

[7] The first appearance of this ideal in Chinese literature is to be found in Chapter 33, the last chapter of the *Chuang Tzu*[ai]. For a recent discussion of this ideal in relation to Taoism and Confucianism, see Y. P. Mei, "Ancient Chinese Philosophy According to the *Chuang Tzu*, Chapter 33," in *The World of Thought*, with an English Translation of the Chapter, with the Chinese text (*Tsing* [Ch'ing] *Hua Journal of Chinese Studies*[aj], New Series, IV, No. 2, February, 1964), pp. 186–211.

[8] James Legge, trans., *Confucian Analects*, VI.17; Legge, Vol. I, p. 190.

[9] Y. P. Mei, "The Basis of Social, Ethical, and Spiritual Values in Chinese Philosophy," in Charles A. Moore, ed., *Essays in East-West Philosophy* (Honolulu: University of Hawaii Press, 1951), pp. 304–305.

[10] James Legge, trans., *Confucian Analects*, VII. 29; Legge, Vol. I, p. 204.

[11] *Ibid.*, IV. 6; Legge, Vol. I, p. 167.

[12] *Ibid.*, XV. 38; Legge, Vol. I, p. 305.

[13] *Ibid.*, IX. 25–28; Legge, Vol. I, pp. 224–225.

[14] *Mencius*[ak], IIIB. Translation by Y. P. Mei, *Tsing* [Ch'ing] *Hua Journal of Chinese Studies*, New Series, II, No. 2 (June, 1961), 367. James Legge's translation is to be found in The Chinese Classics, Vol. II, *The Works of Mencius* (Hong Kong: Lane, Crawford & Co., 1861), p. 141.

[15] *Hsün Tzu*, I, "An Exhortation to Learning." Translation by Y. P. Mei in *Tsing Hua Journal of Chinese Studies*, New Series, II, No. 2 (June 1961), 375–376. H. H. Dubs's translation is to be found in *The Works of Hsüntze* (London: Arthur Probsthain, 1928), p. 41.

[15a] The *China News Analysis*, a weekly report on all significant developments in Communist China, published in Hong Kong, contained in no. 416, April 13, 1962, pp. 6–7, a brief article on "Filial Piety." It is mostly a summary of an article on the same topic published

in the *Chinese Youth Daily*[al]. One of the key sentences, perhaps the concluding sentence, runs as follows: "Indeed, our Socialist Fatherland is a great happy family of the people!"

16 The relation between sovereign and subject has, since the overthrow of the imperial dynasty of the Manchus in 1911, been replaced by that between the state and the citizen.

17 "No Chinese American J. Ds.," *America*, 93 (July 23, 1955); James C. G. Coniff, "Our Amazing Chinese Kids," *Coronet*, 39 (December, 1955), 31–39; "Why No Chinese-American Delinquents?" *Saturday Evening Post*, 227 (April 30, 1955), 12. Two other magazine articles might be mentioned: William A. McIntyre, "Chinatown Offers No Lesson," *New York Times Magazine*, October 6, 1957, pp. 49 ff.; Chandler Brossard, "Americans without a Delinquency Problem," *Look*, 22 (April 29, 1958.), 75 ff.

18 For a compact description of the Chinese civil service examination system, see Ssu-yü Teng[am], "China's Examination System and the West," in H. F. MacNair, ed., *China* (Berkeley: University of California Press, 1946), pp. 441–451.

19 See James Legge, trans., *Confucian Analects*, XIII. 2, The Chinese Classics, Vol. I, pp. 262–263.

20 We cite here three items as follows: Robert M. Marsh, *The Mandarins, The Circulation of Elites in China, 1600–1900* (New York: Free Press of Glencoe, 1961); Wolfram Eberhard, *Social Mobility in Traditional China* (Leiden: E. J. Brill, 1962); Ping-ti Ho, *The Ladder of Success in Imperial China, Aspects of Social Mobility, 1368–1911* (New York: Columbia University Press, 1962).

21 Ping-ti Ho, *ibid.*, p. 257.

22 *Analects*, XVII. 2.

23 UNESCO and Its Programme III, UNESCO Publication 791.

a 梅貽寶		u 漢
b 三才		v 何炳棣
c 左傳		w 明清
d 穆叔		x 唐
e 豹		y 毛澤東
f 晉		z 將相本無種，男兒當自強
g 范宣子		訓蒙幼學詩
h 留芳千古		aa 易經
i 孝王		ab 襄公
j 周		ac 胡適
k 晏嬰		ad 晏嬰
l 齊		ae 史記
m 孔夫子		af 司馬遷
n 大學		ag 郭沫若
o 仁		ah 十批判書
p 論語		ai 莊子
q 孟子		aj 清華學報
r 荀子		ak 孟子
s 堯舜		al 中國青年報
t 墨子		am 鄧嗣禹

S. K. SAKSENA

The individual in social thought and practice in India

When an individual is given the same freedom which any other individual may claim for himself, he is treated as an individual and is given the rights of individuality. Another way to stress the same point is by the use of the concept of ends and means. If an individual is treated as an end in himself—in terms of equality of freedom and status—and never as a means to another individual's purposes, he is then considered a genuine individual.

But this kind of individualism is a purely abstract and atomistic individualism, on which alone no society can be based, and practically all social philosophies recognize this fact, in India as elsewhere. Expressions of pure individuality are always suspect in all societies. All sane societies put a limit to individualism in the interests of social welfare and other values which alone make individualism respectable. About India through the ages one fact stands out prominently. It is this highest regard for such over-individual ends through which alone an individual is supposed to live his life in society and be a significant individual. But this does not mean that the rights of an individual are thereby disregarded.

It has been superficially assumed by some observers that the Indian[1] social set-up itself is anti-individualistic, that in Indian social thought and structure there is too much authoritarianism, that not all men are regarded as individuals having equal rights in themselves, that the right of underprivileged persons to improve their individual social status is denied to them. In spite of the fact that such anti-individualistic practices have existed at times in India, the whole spirit of Indian social thought and structure originating from the most ancient times of the Vedas up to the present time has accorded due regard to individuals as individuals. All efforts of social theorists have been directed in India, not only toward the betterment of the individual, but also toward the opportunity of every individual ultimately and finally to attain his social destination. Society exists for the sake of the individual, and the social heroes in India have always revolted against discriminating practices. India has always tried to accord social equality to all individuals, though with little success during its dark ages.

Indian tradition has always been tied in intellectual and emotional admiration only to individuals who created and molded the society. The heroes in the Indian social mind are all individuals—sages and saints—and not schools or "isms" or ideologies. The Indian mind traditionally does not bother about ideologies or "isms" as such. It allows them all to co-exist and has a genuine tolerance toward all ideological diversities. Rāma, Kṛṣṇa, the Buddha, hundreds of medieval saints, and such reformers in recent times as Tagore, Gandhi, Ram Mohan Roy, Ramakrishna, Aurobindo Ghosh, and Nehru are all prized as individuals. What is adored in social Hinduism or in any social period is not a historical social process as such, but a particular individual who has brought about social betterment. Not the adoring of the age of Gandhi, but Gandhi himself.

It may be worth noting also that the recent linguistic wrangle among the different zones of India and even the traditional style of personal names are other interesting signs of individualism.

EARLY PERIOD

The history of the early Indian period reads like that of a perfectly modern and individualistic society wherein the standards of equality and of the freedom of the individual as an individual irrespective of any kind of discrimination are firmly established in theory and in practice. No differential treatment existed. Women had the same freedom and equality as men; there was absolutely no seclusion. Women sometimes had more education than men and had a prominent position in religious and social gatherings. Monogamy was the rule of life. Neither prohibition on remarriage of widows nor the evil of *sati* (the practice in which the wife immolates herself of her husband) was known. This was a time in India when, according to Davies, "There was no woman question at Athens because all women were as mere vegetables, and there was no woman question at Sparta because both men and women there were little better than animals. Whereas in India, boys and girls underwent a ceremony of *upanayana,* or initiation, into education together."[1a] Even much later we have the names of great women participating with men in religious and philosophical debates. It is well known that women were among the great Upaniṣadic philosophers. Men and women performed sacrifices together. There is no doubt in the minds of scholars and historians about the extreme liberality of attitudes toward all, including even fallen women and women captured in war. To die in defense of women was regarded as the surest way to heaven. Megasthenes, the great Greek historian, who was in India in about 300 B.C., has left a life-like picture of the Indian people. The Greek ambassador observed with admiration "the absence of slavery in

India."[2] This is perhaps an exaggeration, because there was slavery of a kind in India during that period, although it was of an altogether different kind from that prevalent in other parts of the world during the same period.

There is positive evidence of equality among the different races that came to India from the outside in early times. The characteristics of the early Indians to absorb different social elements into a unity has been so predominant as to become one of the chief points of Indian culture. That there were marital relationships between these outsiders and Indians is also well known. All this on the basis of recognition of the equality of all as individuals.

The Indian theory of *varna,* or classification of society into four classes, was in perfect conformity with contemporary ideas of freedom and the status of the individual and social justice, and was and remains democratic with regard to the individual's status and his relation to society. It is supposed to be of divine origin, but this is not to be taken literally. It has purely ideological and functional bases and is universal inasmuch as society must have classes of individuals according to their qualifications, interests, and abilities to engage themselves toward the progress of society and toward their own fulfillment, religious or secular. This does not mean that the classification was static or immobile or that an individual, if he was endowed with ability and knowledge, could not attain to whatever classification he aspired to.

In India they recognized the learned as the highest class, because only the wise can lead or lay down and perpetuate the faith for the people. They were called *brāhmaṇas,* who are supposed to give us the ideals and faith to live by. The *kṣatriyas* were second—they were the political and military leaders, who were supposed to defend the policies and ends of the social order. Third was the class of the wealth producers and distributors, called *vaiśyas.* The last class was that of the manual workers, craftsmen, and artisans, the *śūdras.* This classification was not based on heredity; birth had nothing to do with it. In their ideological functions there is to be found no fifth class, according to the *Mahābhārata* and the much-maligned Manu also.[3] One's *varna* is determined completely by one's actions, pursuits, and ideals. By man's own nature he falls into these four types, the *varnas.*

While the first three classes are said to be twice-born, the fourth is said to be once-born, and therefore inferior. This means only that the members of the fourth class have not had the education and do not have the skill of the other three classes. There are persons who are only biologically born, but not born a second time by the training of education and culture. The qualities which are predominant in each one of the four classes are not exclusive of one another. The

Gītā says that the four classes were established on the basis of *"guṇa,"* which means ability, and *"karma,"* which means actions or vocations.[4] The most sacred *Bhāgavata-purāṇa,* which is well known even by the illiterate, says, "I consider *śvapaca* (literally, a dog), that is to say, the lowest class, whose mind, speech, activity, purpose, and life are fixed on the lotus feet of Viṣṇu (God), to be better than a learned *brāhmaṇa."*[5] "A person should be identified by the class whose characteristics he possesses even though that class is not his own by birth."[6] We read further, "By devotion a *śūdra* may attain the highest status."[7]

It is interesting to note that not only was Suta, the narrator of the *Bhāgavata-purāṇa,* himself born of the lowest class, but so were numerous spiritual and moral personalities who are regarded as teachers of the highest truths, such as Nārada, Prahlāda, etc. They were all men of low-class origin, a fact not very often stressed. Numerous lower-class men and women, such as hunters and even *caṇḍālas* (lowest in the social scale), have attained the abode of Viṣṇu. The *Bhāgavata,* which is the most representative of all the Purāṇas, does not at all depict the viewpoint of the later-established orthodox social or economic group. According to the *Bhāgavata,* the devotees of Viṣṇu should be free from all pride in their birth and should recognize no distinction between themselves and others. The main point of the teaching of the *Bhāgavata-purāṇa* is the absence of qualifications based on birth, etc.

The primary objective in the whole of India's extensive devotional literature is to refute the idea that a person's social status or class membership is of any significance at all. It is well known that the *gopīs,* the cowherd girls of the Kṛṣṇa *līlā* (play), are the primary examples of true devotion, despite their low-class status. The most singularly condemned in the *Bhāgavata-purāṇa* are the twice-born members of the three upper classes. In the Rāmāyaṇa, Rāma, the divine incarnation, ate berries previously tasted by Śabri, a woman of the lowest class (*bhīlinī*).[8] What is central is that the *Bhāgavata* does not acknowledge the superiority of even *brāhmaṇas* on the basis of their birth alone. The famous story of Satyakāma Jābāla in the *Chāndogya Upaniṣad* is refreshingly pertinent in this connection.[9] In the *Mahābhārata,* great warriors like Droṇa and Aśvatthāmā, etc., were all *brāhmaṇas.* In Vedic times, the *brāhmaṇas* were all agriculturalists. As a social practice, old persons—men and women —and the blind had precedence over kings and *brāhmaṇas.*

Dakṣa says, "One who desires happiness should look on another just as he looks upon himself."[10] Devala says that "the quintessence of *dharma* is that one should not do to others what would be disliked by oneself."[11] The same is repeated in the *Āpastamba-smṛti,* and in other *Smṛtis,* too. Mitākṣara remarks that *ahiṁsā,* or non-hurting, and other qualities are the *dharmas* (duties) common to all, even the *caṇḍālas*.[12] The *Mahābhārata* says that "for protecting a family, one individual may be abandoned; for protecting a town, the family may be abandoned; for protecting the society, the town may be abandoned; and for protecting the true self, even the world may be abandoned."[13] The great empire-builders of India, the Nandas, the Mauryas, and the Guptas, were all low-born. The Gupta emperors married *licchavis* (lower-class dynasty).

Young girls had a decisive voice in the selection of their husbands. On festive occasions and at tournaments girls appeared in all their gaiety. In the Vedic period, women did not suffer from any special disabilities. In the *Mahābhārata*, Śvetaketu's father says, "The women of all classes on earth are free."[14] A single standard for both men and women prevailed. Women were so sacred in India that even the common soldiery left them unmolested in the midst of slaughter and devastation. Wrote Dubois, "A Hindu woman can go anywhere alone, even in the most crowded places, and she need never fear the impertinent looks and jokes of idle loungers. . . . A house inhabited solely by women is a sanctuary which the most shameless libertine would not dream of violating."[15]

The refrain of the prayer in the *Mahābhārata* is not for the *brāhmaṇas* or for any special class of individuals. We read, "May all beings be happy, may all attain bliss. . . ."[16] This emphasis on "*sarva*," meaning "all," without distinction of caste, class, or creed, is typical of the Vedic and the Epic literature or periods. The *Āpastamba* declares that "there is nothing higher than the soul" and the *Śatapatha-brāhmaṇa* says, "None among souls is, on the whole, greater than any other soul."[17] Numerous quotations from other sacred literature can be adduced in support of similar social sentiments. When Nārada, a household name in Hindu society, lists the thirty features of the *sāmānya-dharma* (the duties of all the people), he specifically states that these are for all men. That is to say, they are not the *dharmas* of any particular group or class or caste of people, but are *sarva-dharma*, i.e., for all men. The *Manu-smṛti*, the Śānti-parva of the *Mahābhārata*, and the *Bhāgavata-purāṇa* abound in similar sentiments.[18]

Socially, in the Indian spirit all people have been regarded as different and separate individuals living their lives as different entities, responsible for their thoughts and practices, and expected to rely on their own efforts toward their betterment and ultimate liberation from bondage. The Indian doctrine of *karma* has had tremendous social effects on the Indian mind. Because of this law, an Indian regards himself as completely responsible for all his deeds. In fact, the Law of *Karma* is the greatest contribution of the Indian mind in having formulated a truly individualistic attitude *vis-à-vis* society.

It is the most powerful social element of individualism in Hinduism and also in Buddhism. Everyone is exclusively and completely responsible for his or her actions and their consequences. No individual is saved or condemned by any force outside himself—in some schools, not even by God. The Law of *Karma* is an affirmation, in the strongest terms, of the principle of personal individuality and responsibility.

But, in spite of all this, the existence of slavery of some kind admits of no doubt. Emperor Aśoka (third century B.C.), when proclaiming his law of piety, enjoined that the law of piety consist in kind treatment of slaves and hired servants.[19] In the *Artha-śāstra*, Kauṭilya gives important kindly provisions about slaves.[20] Manu speaks of different kinds of slaves.[21] Malcolm writes that male slaves were "generally treated more like adopted children than menials."[22]

MEDIEVAL PERIOD

Such is the story of the status and dignity of the individual in India in relation to society for about two thousand years of its early history —in the basic and classical texts and in the life of the times. Then came a long period of what is known as India's Medieval Period. India lost its political status and unity. There was no one central authority to legislate for the Indian population as a whole. The country stood divided and separated into hundreds of local or regional kingdoms, all competing and vying with each other to keep their own powers intact. India lost its original spirit of freedom and free enterprise, its earlier outlook; it felt oppressed and driven to mere existence. All efforts centered on preserving its identity, allying all social customs and behavior completely to its religions, which remained the only common bond among the Indians.

Then the caste (as distinct from the *varṇa*) system of India became rigid. Enslaved Hindus, with no education or freedom of the spirit, found it easier to take up and grow in the profession of their fathers and forefathers. To try to do anything new, or to seek new careers, would have been not only too hazardous but practically impossible. All those professions which continued as hereditary became *jātis*, castes, and each caste took to social relationships between its own group in inter-dining and inter-marrying. There came to exist some 3,000 castes based on occupation for livelihood.

Along with this, it was natural that ideas of hierarchy were introduced. The *brāhmaṇas*, being responsible for religious ceremonies and the reciting of the sacred *mantras* (hymns) and being the only literate men, were still at the top, and at the bottom came the practitioners of the dirty work of cleaning the latrines or dealing with the skins of dead animals, etc. Since personal cleanliness was a surviving heritage, it gave rise to ideas of pollution and untouchability. The learned kept reading and studying ancient texts and copying manuscripts even in this age, but the people at large were practically living animals under their own religious beliefs, devoid of all spirit of dignity and of free inquiry and criticism.

The caste system, all sorts of discrimination, restrictions on widow marriage, forced *satī*, slavery, early marriage, etc., spread on grounds of sheer survival. These are not the social thoughts and practices of civilized India in its period of glory; they are the survivals of a dead India in itself unfree and slave.

CONTEMPORARY INDIA

The new India wants to eradicate these evils as quickly as possible. They do not represent the living India, which has come to breathe its own air again only recently, though India had always been looking backward to its earlier period, the *"Sat-Yuga,"* the period of truth, justice, and freedom. As India became a political unity and free once more after centuries of political slavery, her freedom of spirit revived. The evils of India are not her representative or characteristic theories of the status of the individual in society, but abominations attempted in its own defense at a critical period for its own preservation. They have to be rooted out from Indian society in spite of the place they found in the Hindu Dharma-sāśtras, which give only the record of a time and do not prescribe eternal truths or facts. Even orthodox Smṛti writers like Manu recognized that a time may come when their rules might become obsolete, and therefore declared that, if any rules framed by them are found to be not conducive to the welfare of society or against the spirit of the age, they should be unhesitatingly abrogated or modified.[23] As the famous Indian poet Kālidāsa says, "Nothing is good simply because it is ancient, and nothing is faulty merely because it is new."[24] The same sentiment is expressed in the Śānti-parva of the *Mahābhārata* also. The modern challenge to caste is by no means the first challenge caste has encountered. The evils of caste have dogged India for centuries, to be sure, but they and the entire institution itself have been under repeated challenge and criticism. Over the centuries, long before the arrival of the British, new reform movements within India repeatedly attacked the caste system.

A religion on the defensive has to be reactionary, and consequently the growth of Hindu feeling at the time did not create conditions suitable for a reorganization of social life. The situation is different today. The Hindu feeling which has developed now is primarily secular and not religious. Today, there is no danger to Hinduism, and the urge for reorganization of society for the individual is there. It is an uprising of the lower classes and the unprivileged groups. The transfer of political power has provided the masses with the power to destroy social institutions based on privilege and on heredity. Social problems are being tackled from the point of view of a reawakened social conscience. The desire of the Indians to take their place with the progressive nations of the world, which is one of the major motivating forces in India today, has an urgency. It may be asked, if the variety of anti-individual customs which until now constituted the social structure of Hinduism have been destroyed or replaced, what will be left that will be characteristically or traditionally Hindu? The answer is that, except for the *varṇas* and the *āśramas* (stages of life), other social institutions of Hinduism are in no way integrally connected with the inner spirit of Hindu religion. No Hindu would argue that, if the joint family ceases to exist in the very near future or castes cease to operate as an institution, Hindu religious thought would be affected. (Incidentally, only 14 per cent of families in India are of the joint type, and so the view that the joint family greatly lessens or denies the significance of the individual does not apply seriously to India as it apparently does to the Chinese and Japanese traditions and cultures.)

For a proper appreciation of Hinduism, with its basic principles of equality of opportunity and for *"loka-saṁgraha,"* or the common good, and for the perfection of man, it is necessary that it should not be confused with or infused by the social order of medieval times. The challenge of "modernism" that Indian society faces today is something which it never had to face before. It is the authority of the national state armed with legislative powers and motivated by a desire to bring Indian institutions in step with new ideas that is new today. Once this movement starts, it cannot stop. During the present transitional period, many Indians seem to live simultaneously in two worlds, the traditional, static, caste-bound, family-centered, and the new, Westernized, modernized, rationalistic world of dynamic individualism and social progress. This is probably inevitable, and it is not altogether bad, so long as the quite visible changes toward individualism inherent in industrialism and modernism hasten to destroy all remnants of social injustice.

To some, the economic planning of contemporary India indicates or implies an anti-individualistic program which is often interpreted as socialism. This is not an accurate picture even of contemporary India and surely not true to the Indian tradition in its economic life. Economic freedom in the sense of free and equal opportunity for all has been the essence of the Indian way of life throughout history, except during the Medieval Period. No one has been prevented from making his or her livelihood or seeking economic welfare and even accumulating money—almost in any way one pleases, provided, the books say, this is achieved without violating the rules of morality (*dharma*). There were no anti-individualistic curbs on the economic activities of the householder except *dharma*. As a matter of fact, the householder was praised as most important by Manu as being the supporter of society as a whole.[25] True, what did not exist in the earlier centuries—and to a certain extent recently—were the actual opportunities for attainment of financial security and economic accumulation. But the freedom for such opportunities was always recognized.

After the coming of freedom, India introduced a number of agricultural and land reforms for the betterment of the people as a whole. Landlordism, in which the great mass of individuals had practically no economic status, was abolished. Also, a new movement for the consolidation of scattered and small holdings of individual farmers has been established. Also, the Government has aided in providing mechanical tools, irrigation projects, and improved techniques. But little of this is actual socialism—the economic system of India is only partly socialistic—but, rather, development in the direction of social welfare for all the people. The so-called socialistic program of India's economic life does not deny individual opportunity, individual wealth, or individualistic economic justice, and is not in any way connected with any political ideology of an anti-individualistic nature.

The reforms that have been made have been directed against those who were without any sense of social welfare or social responsibility, and do not have any destructive effect whatsoever upon the opportunity, the freedom of choice, or the right of economic pursuit by individuals. There has been some socialization or nationalization of industries which are vital to the country as a whole, but this has been indispensable in view of the unscrupulous attitudes and practices of many of the big industrialists and manufacturers and in the interest of social and economic justice for all.

These reforms have been based largely upon practical concerns. Neither these economic nor any other alleged social monistic tendencies really find their bases in any alleged philosophical monism, such as the Advaita Vedānta, which is, after all, only one philosophical point of view, the most extreme of all, and not typical even of Indian metaphysics, or any other Indian philosophical schools, as some are inclined to think.

CONCLUSION

We have given, in the foregoing pages, a brief survey of the social ideas and practices of the Indians spreading over a three-age period of about three thousand years. Our conclusions are three:

First, India has a glorious tradition of respect, freedom, and dignity of the individual, and the individual in relation to society—as glorious as any country has today. This ancient tradition of India was, of course, never purely individualistic. This was because of the religious and moral teachings of the Hindus and Buddhists, that the highest destiny of the individual lies in the perfection of his individuality in a way which inevitably takes him outside his narrow egoism and brings him fulfillment in relation to the society in which he lives. That is one reason why Hindu social structure provided for deep sanctity of social institutions such as the family, the school, the four *varṇas,* and the four stages of life.

Second, in Indian society the main concepts which governed the individual were those of his duties and obligations toward other individuals or something extra-individual. This is the reason they did not give a prominent place to the *rights* of the individual. Rights are there, but rights always carry obligations, and, if the concept of one's obligation is kept in the forefront of one's mind, society should be deemed (other things being equal) as giving a praiseworthy place to the individual and his relation to society. In terms of Indian thinking, no individual can be completely perfected if the core of his being lies merely in his insistence on his own rights. The rights of an individual are the minimum he should have and should not be deprived of. But no individual should be content with merely the minimum. He should rise above his rights and perfect himself by concentrating on his duties and obligations. The Indian emphasizes his qualifications or abilities rather than his rights. After all, it is one's qualifications (*adhikāras*) that determine his rights. Without qualifications there are no rights. If an individual fails to perform his duties, he is deprived of his qualifications and rights.

Third, ever since India obtained the authority of legislating for itself as a nation, it has, in keeping with its past tradition, passed legislation against the practice of all obsolete and anti-individualistic practices between individuals and between society and the individual. Thus it has once again shown its ancient tradition of respect, dignity, and equality of all men. There are numerous working factors, such as the spread of education of both sexes, increasing industrial and economic opportunities, equality of the sexes, the example of socially advanced countries, and the urge of individuals and groups which been discriminated against to catch up with the lapses of centuries—it is these factors that make the Indian people hopeful that medieval undemocratic social practices will become a relic of history much sooner than has been achieved in any country in the past.

There are some modern writers who emphasize the inevitable cultural lag, the distance between the democratic laws enacted in present-day India and the actual social practices, and the fact that in practice India is still tied to its traditional discrimination. Such a cultural lag is probably inevitable, but this feeling only shows our impatience and does not take into account the reality of the situation, the centuries for which the individual has been neglected. In fact, nobody can foresee or foretell how long it will take India to become factually and in social practice completely democratic, giving every individual perfect equality and opportunity to make himself into whatever kind of individual he wants to be under the law. But the writing on the walls of the time can be easily read. The modern Indian democratic ideal in society is no gift obtained from Western people alone, whose own ideas of democracy and freedom and universal individuality are quite new. India's contact with the West is certainly one of the main causes of the acceleration of the speed of reform. But the reforms are in the spirit and tradition of Indian society itself.

It is only now, quite late in her long history, that India has come to have an idea of the whole Indian community as such, the nationhood of the Indian people, secular and humanitarian, and, as such, divorced from religion, and has come to think of the status of the individual and the whole community in a secular fashion. Today, even the poor, the illiterate, and the low-caste have all become conscious of their human rights, as well as duties. And so, now—at long last—the original Indian spirit of the dignity and freedom of the individual shows signs of significant revival.

QUESTION: Do we have enough historical factual data to justify the explanations you have given?

ANSWER: I do not know how to answer the question for the simple reason that it does not indicate any specific instance of factual or historical inaccuracy in the paper. After all, everything said in the paper has been supported by quotations from either authoritative texts or authoritative historians. Of course, quantitatively, many more references in support of all that I have said or maintained could have been given, but there was neither space nor time for such elaboration. I feel that the information in the paper is quite adequate under the circumstances.

QUESTION: The Buddha was critical of the caste system and therefore did it not exist essentially in its later objectionable form prior to the Middle Ages?

ANSWER: This may be true, but the question does not challenge the statement made in the paper that the Vedic and earlier periods in Indian history were much more liberal and individualistic than its later degeneration in the medieval period, in which caste distinctions came to be based entirely on birth rather than on qualifications or profession. Distinctions of some kinds are bound to exist in all societies and at all times, and the Buddha, looking at the society of his time, must have criticized all distinctions from an exclusively moral standpoint. My point was and is simply that caste distinctions as they existed in the medieval period, or even in the British period, never existed in earlier India, a statement for which numerous references have already been given from the *Gītā*, the Epics, and even the Purāṇas and the Dharma-śāstras.

QUESTION: Do you not confuse the social philosophy and the religious philosophy of India—for example, do not the Dharma-śāstras essentially ignore the spiritual goal of man, whereas you relate it intimately to social philosophy?

ANSWER: Such terms as *"mokṣa," "mukti,"* and *"niḥśreyas-siddhi"* (the attainment of the highest) are to be found in almost all basic texts. And, although it would be correct to say that the social goals in India had nothing to do with the individual's spiritual goal, almost all individuals in India are conscious of the idea of their own *mokṣa,* at least in the later stages of lives. The religious goal of life had a primacy even in the secular spheres of life. The separation of life into autonomous compartments of the political, legal, economic, and social spheres is a purely contemporary phenomenon in India.

QUESTION: Your justification of duties as prior to the rights of the individual seem to be open to question. Would you elaborate a bit?

ANSWER: The point is simple enough. A society in which all individuals are conscious only of their individual rights and do their duties exclusively for fear of losing their rights would not be a strictly ethical society, nor would the behavior of the individual be strictly ethical. We can still imagine a society wherein all individuals are prompted and motivated in action solely by regard for their ethical duties in all circumstances. The Indians thus based their social structure on duties and obligations rather than on rights. The social end in both cases may be the same, but the difference lies in the Indian emphasis on the ethical motivation.

---

[1] What has been said here pertains primarily to Hindu society. The Buddhist in India, from the time of the Buddha himself, protested against all kinds of class or birth distinctions and gave full dignity and status to all individuals, but, later, Buddhism almost disappeared from the country of its origin. When the Muslims came to India in about the twelfth century A.D., though they adopted in practice the Hindu social evils of caste hierarchies in daily life, they were by their religion not supposed to have any social distinctions between man and man. Thus, what pertains socially to Hindu society is true of the entire Indian social structure, in thought and practice.

[1a] J. L. Davies, *A Short History of Women* (New York: Viking Press, 1927), p. 172. Quoted in A. S. Altekar, *The Position of Women in Hindu Society* (Benares: The Cultural Publishing House, 1938), p. 407.

[2] J. W. McCrindle, *Ancient India as Described by Megasthenes and Arrian* (Calcutta: Thacker, Spink & Co., 1877), p. 71. Quoted in P. V. Kane, *History of Dharmaśāstras,* 4 vols. (Poona: Bhandarkar Oriental Research Institute, 1941), Vol. II, Pt. 1, p. 183.

[3] *Manu-smṛti,* X. 4.

[4] *Bhagavad-gītā,* IX. 13.

[5] *Bhāgavata-purāṇa,* VII. 9–10.

[6] *Ibid.,* VII. 11–35.

[7] *Ibid.,* VII. 23–32.

[8] The *Rāmāyaṇa,* Āraṇyaka-kāṇḍa, 31–33.

[9] *Chāndogya Upaniṣad,* IV. iv. 1–5. Jābāla went to learn *Brahma-vidyā* (knowledge of *Brahman*) from a *guru* who asked him the name of his father. He said he did not know but would ask his mother. His mother told him that she herself did not know because in her youth she slept with many young men. He told this to the *ṛṣi,* whereupon the latter said that he was fully entitled to the highest wisdom because few men and women dare tell the full truth.

[10] Dakṣa, *Dakṣa-śāstra,* III. 22: *"Yathaivātmā 'parastadvad draṣṭavyah sukhamicchatā sukhdukhāni tulyāni, yathātmani tathā pare."* Quoted in Kane, *op. cit.,* pp. 5n, 7n.

[11] Devala: *"Ātmanah pratikūlāni pareśām na samācharet."* Quoted in Kane, *op. cit.,* p. 7n.

[12] Mitākṣara on *Yajur-veda,* I. 1.

13 *Mahābhārata,* I. 115. 36: *"Tyajet ekam Kulasyārthe, Kulam tyajet grāmam janapadā-syārthe, Ātmārthe prithīvim tyajet."*

14 *Mahābhārata,* I. 122. 44.

15 Abbé Dubois, *Hindu Manners, Customs and Ceremonies* (Oxford: Clarendon Press, 1877), p. 340.

16 Mahābhārata: *"Sarve ca sukhinah santu, sarve santu nirāmayah sarve bhadrāṇi paśyantu mā kaścit dukhabhāg bhavet."* Quoted in S. Radhakrishnan, *Religion and Society* (London: George Allen & Unwin Ltd., 1947), p. 91n.

17 Āpastamba, *Dharma-sūtra,* I. vii. 2: "Āpastamba declares that there is nothing higher than the possession of the soul." Quoted in S. Radhakrishnan, *Religion and Society,* p. 62.

18 *Manu-smṛti,* X. 63: *"Ahiṁsā satyam asteyam, sauchamindriya nigrahaetam sāmāsikam dharmamcāturvaiṇeya abravin manuḥ."* Also, *Mahābhārata,* Śānti-parva, 72. 8–12.

19 Aśoka, 9th Edict Rock, in the *Corpus Inscriptionum Indicarum,* Vol. I.

20 Kauṭilya, *Artha-śāstra,* III. 13.

21 *Manu-smṛti,* VIII. 415, and Kane, *op. cit.,* pp. 183–185.

22 Sir John Malcolm, *Memoir of Central India* (London: Printed by Kingsbury, Parbury, & Allen, 1923), Vol. II, p. 202.

23 *Manu-smṛti,* IV. 176. Also, *Mahābhārata,* Śānti-parva, 160–161.

24 Kālidāsa, *Mālvikāgnimitram,* I. 2.

25 *Manu-smṛti,* VI. 89–90; III. 77–78.

KŌSAKA MASAAKI[a]

The status and role of the individual in Japanese society

I. INTRODUCTION

Before I begin to treat the problem, I would like to clarify my procedure.

First, I am not going to consider the problem of the status of the individual in Japan from a sociological point of view, but from a historical point of view, or, to be more exact, from a topographical point of view.

Second, I would like to describe the frame of reference of my study of the status of the individual. Detailed examination is impossible in the time available, but can be included in the discussion.

Third, I will treat the history of Japanese culture and society by dividing it into four periods. The characteristic which runs topographically through all the periods is aestheticism. This aestheticism should not be neglected when we consider the relations between individuals and the group, for here lie both the strong point and the weak point of the Japanese attitude.

II. THE AGE OF AESTHETIC CULTURE (700–1200)

The aestheticism which constitutes the core of the Japanese mind took definite form in the first period. Therefore, I would call it the age of aesthetic culture. But what was this age really like? I would like to characterize it, first, through the legendary stories of the Court, and, secondly, through the activities of the authoresses.

This first period, which covered nearly five hundred years, began with the era of Empress Suiko[b], to which great splendor was added by her Prince Regent, Shōtoku Taishi[c] (574–622). Many of the records which relate the achievements of Prince Shōtoku belong almost to legend. But these records, though legendary, or because they are legendary, show the kind of ruler the Japanese from olden times have regarded as ideal. Conversely, expectations on the part of the people prescribed the characteristics of the emperor.

One of the most famous stories was that he could listen to appeals from several persons at the same time. He was sagacious and fair, too. It may well be noted that the fundamental principle of his politics was the spirit of harmony. "Most prized is harmony" was the fundamental principle of the famous Seventeen-Article Constitution[d] (*Jūshichijō kempō*) (A.D. 604), which is ascribed to the prince. His ideal was not in power politics, but in moral politics (on this point he is influenced by Confucianism).

One of the articles of the Constitution states: "Highly respect the Three Treasures[e] (*tokukei sambō*)."[1] The Three Treasures are the Buddha, the Law (*Dharma*), and the Assemblage (*Saṅgha*). The same spirit asserted itself in the words of Emperor Shōmu[f], who ordered the construction of Tōdaiji[g] (temple) (A.D. *ca*. 750). He said, "We are the servants of the three treasures."[2]

Even the most destructive historian, who doubts all the historical facts about Prince Shōtoku, accepts as his own statement the inscription which reads, "The world is fiction; only the Buddha is truth." It is considered to have been written by him in honor of his wife, Tachibana-no-iratsume[h]. This phrase expressed his outlook on life.

Prince Shōtoku said, "Highly respect the Three Treasures." And Emperor Shōmu declared, "We are the servants of the Three Treasures." They devoted themselves to the supreme existence, to which they were only servants.

Reviewing Japanese history, we find many emperors noted as master calligraphers or masters of *tanka*[i] (short poem) poetry. They were patrons of culture and at the same time were required to be well cultivated themselves. Even today, the New Year Poetry Party and the New Year Lectures are held. The former is the ceremony at which *tankas* of emperor, empress, and princes and princesses are presented to the public, with those of the general public chosen from among the poems appropriate to the occasion. The New Year Lectures, which cover a wide range of subjects, from history, politics, and literature to natural science of the latest development, are given by prominent scholars and are attended by the royal families.[3]

Historically, the actual power of politics was not in the hands of the emperor, but was for some time in the hands of the nobles and later for a longer period of time in the hands of the *samurai*[j] class. When the emperor tried to regain political power, unfortunate incidents sometimes ensued. The role of the emperor was originally to venerate the gods. In other words, he was more symbolic than political. It is clear from this that the emperor was not an absolute monarch who oppressed the people. The Japanese emperor was more humane. Note that the duties of the emperor were basically ceremonial, while the nobles of the court and the *shōguns*[k] served as actual rulers.

Parenthetically, there was no slave system in the full meaning of the word. The Japanese did not know how to conquer other races to make them slaves.

So far I have talked about the Imperial Household in the period which I call the age of aesthetic culture. Now, I will touch on the literary activities of women in this era.

There are two very old books which are popular among the Japanese even today. One is the *Manyōshū*[l] (A Collection of Myriad Leaves), the other the *Genji monogatari*[m] (*Tale of Genji*). The former is an anthology containing verses and *tanka* poems numbering more than forty-five hundred. This twenty-volume anthology is a collection of works of many years, perhaps over three hundred years, the main period being the seventh and eighth centuries. The latest one of the poems which was dated was composed in A.D. 759. It contains some very old poems whose dates cannot be precisely determined.

Now, from the sociological point of view, what are the characteristics of this anthology? The first feature is that the social background of the writers is highly heterogeneous. There are, of course, poems by emperors, empresses, and nobles of the Court. But there are also those of *sakimori*[n], those soldiers who were called up for defense of the Kyushu[o] district, and those of their wives expressing their sorrow at parting from their husbands. There are poems of professional poets such as Kakinomoto-no-Hitomaro[p] (7th century) and Yamabe-no-Akahito[q] (8th century), who are respected as representative poets even today. There are also poems of nameless people. *Azumauta*[r], poems of people in the Kantō[s] district, which had not been civilized in those days, and other folk-songs are also included in the anthology. The variety of poets was the product of a highly democratic editing principle, and it also means that the society of Japan in those days was not stratified into strictly segregated classes.

The second feature is the status of women. Many poems by women are in this anthology. They must number one fourth or one fifth of the total. This is rare and has no parallel in the world. The form of marriage in those days was that wherein the intended husband visited the house of his intended wife to meet her. This type of marriage contributed to the production of love poems (*sōmon no uta*[t]), and the status of women was not inferior to that of men in these poems.

Among these poets was a beautiful and talented woman, Nukada-no-Ōkimi[u], who was loved by two emperors successively. Some delicate, some passionate poems of such women rank highest in the anthology. Japanese culture in the Manyō era[v] (7th and 8th centuries) was supported by women to a considerable extent. They were not slaves of the other sex.

But it was in the age of the *Genji monogatari* (10th and 11th centuries) that the activities of women in the cultural field reached their apex. Women, rather than men, played a leading part. And it goes without saying that the woman who represented this tendency was Murasaki Shikibu[w] (10th and 11th centuries), and that the masterpiece of the period was her *Genji monogatari*. Other women writers were Nagon Seishō[x] (11th century), author of the *Pillow Books*[y], Aka-some-mon[z] (11th century), Michitsuna-no-haha[aa], mother of Michitsuna[ab] (10th century), and so on. Women writers appeared in great number and formed a new genre of literature, namely, diary literature. The literature of this age was made colorful and rich by their works. Many of them were women of the Court. We must remember therefore that there once existed in Japan a type of culture which may be called woman-culture.

III. THE AGE OF RELIGIOUS CULTURE (1200–1600)

As pointed out above, in the age of aesthetic culture the emperor was never a sort of tyrant with absolute power, but was at the center of cultural activities, and women were not slaves of men but were educated persons with brilliant personalities.

These facts are very much at variance with the patterns of Japanese culture which Ruth Benedict described.[4] Moreover, she said that Japanese culture was a shame-culture and not a guilt-culture, and that the Japanese had neither conscience nor guilt-consciousness. But is this true? I think not. Good evidence against her interpretation is given in the second period, the age of religious culture.

This second period began when Minamoto Yoritomo[ac] opened the *bakufu*[ad] (A.D. 1192) (the federal government) at Kamakura[ae] in the twelfth century, and continued until the seventeenth century, when the Tokugawa[af] Government (1603–1867) was firmly established at Edo[ag] (now Tokyo). The characteristics of this period can be best described by examining prominent priests and the *samurai*[ah] class, who were the *Kulturträger* of the age.

The sect of Buddhism which holds the greatest number of devotees in Japan is the Jōdo-Shin sect[ai], which was founded by Shinran[aj] (1173–1262). It is safe to say that Shinran was the greatest of those who made Buddhism the religion of the common people in Japan. It was at the time of Prince Shōtoku that Buddhism was introduced into Japan. Five hundred years passed from the days of Prince Shōtoku to those of Shinran, and there were changes in the Japanese view of Buddhism and its functions after Shinran, as Professor Hori has reported in his paper.

Buddhism of the first period was characterized by three features. First, it played the role of vehicle of continental culture. Perhaps it was more cultural than religious. It was not so different from the way the Japanese in the Meiji era[ak] accepted Christianity. In the case of Prince Shōtoku, the Buddhist and Confucian elements were mixed together. As beautiful Buddhist images and Buddhist temples in Nara[al] show, admiration for Buddhism was inseparable from the longing for beauty. It was, so to speak, an aesthetic religion. And the legends of Kōbō's[am] spanning bridges, digging ponds, and curing diseases show that he was respected as an excellent engineer and doctor. In short, Buddhism was more cultural and aesthetic than simply religious.

Second, it was the religion of the aristocracy, the main believers being the courtiers and the nobles. Emperor Shōmu was said to have had temples and convents constructed all over the country, which should be considered as an enlightenment movement from the aristocracy. Priests played a very important part in it. And temples gradually became the privileged owners of vast lands and even had military power. Buddhism was not the religion of the people.

Third, it was a religion of mundane interests. Or, it would be better described as an incantatory religion. For individuals, the purpose was to cure disease and to avoid misfortune. For the nation, the purpose was to pacify and defend it. It was believed that floods, droughts, earthquakes, and epidemics could be avoided by the power of prayer.

However, this aesthetic, aristocratic, and incantatory religion was to be greatly changed by Shinran and others. Incantation gave place to genuine faith, and the purpose was no longer mundane interests but the relief of the souls of the individuals suffering from the consciousness of guilt. In this way, aristocratic religion became the religion of the common people. Its characteristics are as follows:

First, the types of priests were different. There were many excellent priests in the aesthetic and incantatory religion, and they sought relief in research on the philosophical principles in the scriptures, or by strict observance of moral commandments. But Shinran, who called himself "a silly man," realized that even the highest wisdom of man was haunted with errors and was nothing but an illusion, and that man was an incarnation of avarice and guilt or sin who would not keep any commandments perfectly. So, he concluded that there was no way of relief except through genuine faith. This was his view of Buddhist invocation.

Man could not be saved by knowledge or morality, but only by believing in the Buddha's love. Shinran called himself "a person who falls short of any austerities," and said, "Hell is the fixed dwelling."[5] Man is a lump of guilt. All men are essentially wicked. It is not the power of any man but the love of the Buddha, who pitied such a wicked man, that would save him. His famous words—"Even a good person can attain *nirvāṇa*. Then, how much more so a wicked man!"[6]—originated from these ideas.

Second, this consciousness of guilt is deeply connected with the self-consciousness of the individual. Shinran said that it was not for his father and mother, and not for his country and society, that he prayed to Amida[an] Buddha, but only for himself. So, he said, it was "solely for Shinran" that the Buddha pledged to save man. And he said, "Shinran will have no disciples."[7]

Third, accused of heresy, Shinran was driven from Kyoto and exiled to a rural district, where he married. This may remind us of Martin Luther. His new Buddhism (with the principle that man was not saved by the study of difficult traditional scriptures or by the observance of the minutely regulated commandments but only by praying to Amida Buddha) was spread among peasants and the common people.

My direct purpose here has been to show how mistaken Ruth Benedict is in saying that Japanese culture is a shame-culture and not a guilt-culture. The Japanese do have a consciousness of guilt. It is the nucleus of Shinran's religion, and Shinran's sect, Jōdo-Shin sect, is the largest of all the Japanese sects of Buddhism.

I shall deal now with the *samurai* class to explain the kind of outlook they had on life and death. But I cannot treat details. The *samurai* society was a defensive community, but it was based on two different principles. On the one hand, there existed a kind of affectionate relation like that between parents and children, as is shown by the phrase " '*Ie*' *no ko*"[ao] (the children of the family), which was used to signify the rank and file of the *samurai* group. But, on the other hand, the relation was a contractual one like that of lord and vassal, employer and employee.

Accordingly, there appeared an interesting mixed relation in a *samurai* group, a mixture of a natural relation like that between parents and children and an obligatory relation like that between lord and vassal, employer and employee. The lord put his vassals under an obligation and had an obligation to compensate for it. There was a kind of implied contract composed of a presentation and a counterpresentation. This compound relation supported "an extended '*ie*'[ap]" (family or household) which formed the core of the *samurai* group. A lord does his vassals a favor, and they are loyal to him. The morality of devotion observable in this relation became Bushidō[aq], or chivalry, in the course of time.

What was the status of the individual in *samurai* society? Was an individual like an atom buried in an extended or a small family? Not in the least. Even in the *samurai* group as an extended family, those who excelled in bravery were especially respected, for it was a fighting community, and there arose a rivalry for leadership. On the other hand, a *samurai* was required to be affectionate. Therefore, it can be said that a good *samurai* was one who was both brave and affectionate.

In the case of family succession, the eldest son was not always the heir. Sometimes the successor was he who was the ablest and most talented in the eyes of the parent. Similarly, in the field of the arts, the supreme secret of the family school was handed down, not only to the kindred of the family, but also to the eminent pupil.

However, it should be remembered that the status of women underwent a fundamental change as *samurai* families were gradually formed. The former type of marriage, in which the intended husband visited the house of his intended wife, was replaced by a new procedure in which the intended wife came to the house of her intended husband to live. With this change, men came to be more respected than women. Men are more important than women in an age of war.

Also, the primogeniture system replaced the old parcenary system, in order to keep the fortune of a family intact. This change, together with the change of the status of women in the family, strengthened the power of the father. This new system continued through the Tokugawa period (1615–1867) up to the Meiji era (1868–1911) and even to the end of World War II. It is not true, however, to say that the rights of women were completely neglected. The Jōei Code[ar] (A.D. 1232) (Collection of Maxims and Rules for Administrators) decreed that the rights of the wife be protected.

Also, it should not be forgotten that the people of those days attached great importance to the family and the family line. They were proud of their good lineage. However, there was a brief interlude in the growth of the authority of the family. At about the time of the civil war of Ōnin[as] (1467–1477), there appeared the trend of the lower overpowering the upper. The former wrested the position of superiority from the latter. The *shugo daimyō*[at] (Protector Feudal-Lords) were replaced by the *sengoku daimyō*[au] (Fighting Feudal-Lords). For the *shugo daimyō* had been restricted to the " '*Ie'-no-ko*" of the Genji family, but they had lost real power, so that they could not resist the onslaught of the *sengoku daimyō*, who gained power not by their status but by their ability. Some Japanese historians even assert that the social structure was completely changed during the time of the civil war ("Sengoku era" 1467–1560).

Toyotomi Hideyoshi[av], who conquered the whole country and unified it, was of peasant origin. Also, there was the example of Sakai City[aw] (later Osaka[ax]), the citizens of which gained power by wealth acquired in foreign trade. In those days, the abilities of individuals were freely developed, as is evident in pictures and other works of fine art of the Azuchi-Momoyama era[ay] (1568–1615). But these free activities of individuals were to be restricted by the feudal system and by the national isolation policy of the Tokugawa Government.

IV. THE AGE OF POLITICS (1600–1850)

The Japanese mind was thus formed in the first and second periods. As Watsuji Tetsurō[az] rightly pointed out, Japanese culture has a multi-strata structure. The old element is not lost when a new one is introduced, but the new is added onto the old.[8] When the third period began, at the beginning of the seventeenth century, the same pattern appeared, but with a slight difference. The Tokugawa era provided another stratum added to the Japanese culture already developed.

But it did more than that. It gave a framework to it, thereby giving it a certain character and modifying the preceding culture. Consequently, some contradiction appeared between the framework, namely, of the feudal system, and the substance, namely, the emotional life, religion, and the arts. The contradiction, the symbol of which Ruth Benedict saw in her *The Chrysanthemum and the Sword,* was thus originated. Let us look at the several traits of this period.

First, this period was the age of politics, for political unity and control were effected for the first time in Japanese history. And the political mechanism rigidly regulated the arts, religion, morals, and thought.

Second, the *Kulturträger* of this period was the *samurai* and the *chōnin*[ba] (townspeople). The former had been the *Kulturträger* since the Kamakura era (1185–1335), but had undergone a very significant change. The *samurai* class in the Tokugawa era was not engaged in war, but was busy with administration. The *samurai* were bureaucrats of a kind. Two hundred and fifty years of the Tokugawa era constituted a period of undisturbed peace unparalleled in world history. It was natural that the *samurai* should become bureaucrats, since they had to rule in peace.

While the center of this *samurai* bureaucracy was in Edo, the center of the merchant activities was in Osaka. In the feudal system of Tokugawa, there was a rigid hierarchy of *shi-nō-kō-shō*[bb]: the *samurai* coming first, the peasant, the craftsmen, and the merchant, in that order. The merchants were put at the bottom, since they were considered to produce nothing, but to gain huge benefits by simply trading the products of others. It is the same with the *samurai*, who also produce nothing. Then, wherein consists the prestige of the *samurai? Samurai* should act like gentlemen. This is the source of their prestige.

But, as the economy flourished in the peace of the Tokugawa era, the merchants gained real economic power. Even the *daimyō* refrained from offending the merchants of Osaka, for they were their debtors. As the culture of the Tokugawa era was that of merchants, Osaka became its center. Consequently, Osaka could compete with Edo, the latter being the center of politics and the former being the center of economics. In this sense, Japan was in a bipolar situation.

Third, *"ie"* stood above the individual as the ethical reality. The individual was the secondary existence within the structure of the *"ie"* to which he belonged. The wife and children were under the authoritarian rule of the father, who represented the ethical reality called *"ie."* Everyone should serve the *"ie"* under the guidance of the father, and it was held a sacred duty of the family member to respect the name of *"ie."*

The picture might give one a somber impression, but it does not follow from this structure of the *"ie"* that the individual was neglected. It is true that the *daimyō* succeeded as head of the house even if he was not competent. But the real power was not in his hands but in the hands of his retainers, whose duty it was to take good care of the *daimyō's* household. Naturally, real power passed into the hands of able retainers. The same thing happened in the households of big merchants, and the *bantō*[bc], or head clerks, held real power. They served their master's house, of course. But, if it was necessary to keep the *"ie"* intact, they often remonstrated with the *daimyō,* their masters.

It can be said, therefore, that the power of the *daimyō* and the master was nominal rather than substantial. Knowledge and originality, ability and talent, were highly regarded among the merchants of Osaka. Successful merchants were entrepreneurs who gained through their originality and knowledge.

Fourth, the thought of Nakae Tōju[bd], who was called the saint of Ōmi[be], had one aspect which has been unfortunately neglected, but throws clear light on the life and ethics of the Tokugawa era. He thought that *kō*[bf], filial duty or piety toward parents, was the highest virtue of all. But he made a meaningful distinction between *daikō*[bg], the great filial duty, and *shōkō*[bh], the small filial duty. The latter was ordinary filial duty, that is to say, duty to serve the parents well.

But, according to him, the right filial duty was to admonish and make the parents amend their wrong attitude when the parents were in the wrong. This he called *daikō* (the great filial duty).[9] Parents give birth to us, but there are more basic, greater fathers and mothers, who give birth to the world. He called these greater parents *Tenkun*[bi] (the Lord of Heaven), and considered it our duty to serve him. Consequently, to remedy the error of our physical parents is to fulfill the duty of serving the greater parents through our conscience. Also, he deemed the human being a small cosmos microcosm, in contrast to the great cosmos macrocosm, which words remind us of Leibniz' doctrine that the individual is the living mirror that reflects the great cosmos.

V.   THE AGE OF ENLIGHTENMENT

The hundred years since the fall of the Tokugawa Government—to the present—is the age of *bunmei kaika*[bj] (the age of enlightenment). Tokyo, which name took the place of Edo, became the new capital, and the center of Westernization, modernization, industrialization, and urbanization. Tokyo became the symbol of the age. In this sense, this age might be called the age of Tokyo.

Several interpretations of the Meiji Ishin[bk] (Meiji Restoration) have been proposed, but it was a reform rather than a revolution. The reform began in the domain of politics and gradually expanded into social reform, economic reform, and, finally, spiritual reform. The general trend has been the industrialization and Westernization of the country. Seen from a different viewpoint, it has been the clash of what is Japanese and Oriental, on the one hand, and what is Western, on the other, the amalgam of the two being the result. Nevertheless, it has been predominately an age of modernization (*bunmei kaika*). I will briefly treat of the characteristics of the age, especially the status and role of the individual, as follows:

First, the transition of the ideal person for the Japanese is very significant. In the first twenty years of the Meiji era, statesmen and soldiers were respected above all, the most prominent being Peter the Great, Napoleon, Bismarck, Washington, and Lincoln. But, in the second twenties, the Japanese discovered the names of Shakespeare, Goethe, Heine, Byron, Hugo, Tolstoi, Descartes, Kant, Newton, and Darwin as ideal persons. The interests of the people were now expanded to include scholars, men of letters, and artists. It is interesting that Rousseau was known as the author of *The Social Contract* in the first twenty years of the Meiji era, but as the author of *Confessions* in the second twenties. Chief interest was now centered in man himself.

Second, individualism appeared in the twenties, which decade was called by Uchimura Kanzō[bl] the decade of spiritual revolution. Also, statism, nationalism, and socialism appeared. Socialism passed through three phases, that is, the phases of Christian socialism, French socialism, and Marxist socialism. It was also in the twenties that *heimin shugi*[bm] (presumably a translation of democracy) was introduced. After World War I, in the Taishō era[bn] (1912–1925), the translation was changed to *minshū shugi*[bo] and this became very popular. But this democratic movement was unfortunately over-whelmed by the tide of chauvinism. The problem that the Japanese have faced since the Meiji Restoration has been to find a suitable place for Japan and Japanese culture in the world, and a place for the individual in society.

Third, the emancipation of women was first advocated also in the twenties of the Meiji era, and in the thirties the Japanese "Blue Stockings" appeared. To them, the predominant problem was the relation between the family and the individual, on which the decisive change took place after the end of World War II. The reform by the Occupation Forces weakened the authority of the father and legally established the dignity of the individual. But it also effected the disintegration of the family ethic.

Fourth, Japan is now enjoying a considerably high social mobility. This is proved by the fact that the leaders since the Meiji Restoration came from the middle and lower classes. The Japanese are most enthusiastic about sending their children to the universities. For ability, instead of status, assures the child success in life.

Fifth, the problems to be solved are the relation between the individual and the state and that between the individual and the various social groups. As the Japanese has deemed strong self-asser-tion ugly, he seldom expresses his opinion in the presence of others. To eliminate what was bad is relatively easy, but to eliminate or alter what was good but is no longer deemed highly appropriate is very difficult. Here lies one of the fundamental problems for the Japa-nese. For the virtue non-self-assertiveness that was once respected is now either inappropriate or insufficient for modern society.

Note: Shintō[bp], the traditional Japanese religion, is a religion which detests impurity and tries to drive it out. It is more funda-mental to the Japanese not to stain one's name than not to shame it. Strongly influenced by Shintō, the culture of ancient Japan was not a shame culture but a culture of impunity. Nietzsche said, *"Jenseits von Gut und Böse."* The Japanese in ancient times had no category of good and evil in the Christian sense of the words. It is, as men-tioned above, under the influence of Confucianism and Buddhism, and especially since the middle age of Japan, that the Japanese have had the categories of good and evil. The most important categories for the Japanese were those of beauty and ugliness. The Japanese in ancient times esteemed health, life, and beauty more than anything else. In sharp contrast to this, it was disease, death, and ugliness that the Japanese disliked. Today we use such expressions as "Have a 'clean mind'!" or "Don't do a 'dirty' act!" It is clear from these expressions that the things explained under the categories of good and evil in later years fell under the categories of beauty and ugliness. Morality in ancient times was aesthetic, just as the culture of those times on the whole was aesthetic.

SUPPLEMENTARY COMMENTS

The definition of the term "aestheticism." There are many kinds of values, for example, utility, pleasure, happiness, freedom, truth, and so on. If there is a culture or society wherein beauty stands at the top of the value system, such a culture is aesthetic. This is what I mean by the term "aestheticism." But what I mean by beauty is not limited to physical beauty, i.e., beautiful flowers, beautiful women, but involves spiritual beauty also. Therefore, Japanese ethics demands purity of mind, refinement of tastes, harmony of individuals, mutual love.

Morality based upon sympathy and love. It has been said that there are two basic orientations in the Western tradition. One involves the pursuit of ends or goals. It is primarily value-oriented. The other involves the recognition of laws, of duties and obligations. This may be called duty-oriented.

But there is still another, a third orientation. This involves love, mercy, kindness, and so on. This morality may be called love-oriented, and its basic principle is sympathy. We can very easily find such morality in Christian, Buddhist, Hindu, Chinese, and Japanese ethics. But there are slight differences among them; however, sympathy is basic to them all.

Now, when we sympathize with each other, so far we become one. But this does not mean that we lose our individualities. We are not melted into simple oneness. I am I, you are you. In this sense, individuals do exist in the East. "One in manyness, many in oneness" is the fundamental principle of Japanese ethics and metaphysics.

Concerning the alleged emphasis upon rights in the West and duties in the East. Before the introduction of European political thought into Japan, the Japanese did not use such terms as "rights" and "duties." Instead of such terms, we used the term "righteousness." Righteousness, or justice, is required from those at the top and those below at the same time. They are equal from the point of view of justice and righteousness. From the Western standpoint, this equality is limited to morality but not extended to law. This is true indeed, but I wonder whether it is very desirable to make such a strict distinction between morality and law.

CHRONOLOGY

I. The Age of Aesthetic Culture (*ca.* 700–*ca.* 1200)

552	Introduction of Buddhism to Japan
592–628	Reign of Suiko Tennō[bq]. Shōtoku Taishi, regent
604	*Seventeen-Article Constitution*
645	Taika Reform[br]
710	Establishment of the first permanent capital, Nara
712	*Records of Ancient Matters* (*Kojiki*[bs])
720	*Chronicles of Japan* (*Nihongi*[bt])
752	Dedication of the Great Buddha at the Tōdaiji in Nara
ca. 770	*Manyōshū* (A Collection of Myriad Leaves, an Anthology)
794	Heian-kyō[bu] (Kyoto) becomes the capital
ca. 990–1020	*Tale of Genji* (*Genji monogatari*) and Pillow Book *Makura sōshi*[bv]

II. The Age of Religious Culture (*ca.* 1200–*ca.* 1600)

1192	Founding of Kamakura Shōgunate
1232	The Jōei Code (Collection of Maxims and Rules for Administrators)
1262	Shinran (1173–1262), founder of the True Pure Land sect (Jōdo-shin)
1274	First Mongol invasion
1281	Second Mongol invasion
1338	Ashikaga Takauji[bw] becomes Shōgun
1467	Ōnin War[bx]. Commencement of endemic civil wars throughout Japan
1568	Oda Nobunaga[by] controls the capital
1571	Nobunaga destroys the Enryakuji[bz] on Mt. Hiei[ca]

III. The Age of Politics (*ca.* 1600–1860)

1582	Toyotomi Hideyoshi succeeds to power (Death of Hideyoshi, 1598)
1603	Establishment of Tokugawa Shōgunate
1637–38	Shimabara[cb] Revolt
1640	Europeans excluded
1648	Nakae Tōju (1608–1648)
1685	Yamaga Sokō[cc] (1622–1685)
1688–1704	Genroku Period[cd] (Saikaku[ce], Chikamatsu[cf], Bashō[cg], and Ukiyo[ch] prints)
1705	Itō Jinsai[ci] (1627–1705)
1801	Motoori Norinaga[cj] (1730–1801)
1858	United States–Japanese commercial treaty

IV. The Age of Enlightenment (*ca.* 1860)

1868	Meiji Restoration
1912	Death of Emperor Meiji

1920   Prewar liberalism (Taishō Democracy)
1925   Universal male suffrage
1931   Manchurian "Incident"
1941–
1945   Pacific War
1952   End of military occupation by Allied Forces

QUESTION: You have emphasized the aesthetic point of view as specifically characteristic of the Japanese mind. What significance does this have for the status of the individual?

ANSWER: The aesthetic point of view, which I emphasize as specifically characteristic of the Japanese mind, causes people to recognize the value of personality. The value of the individual is not dissolved into that of the group, as one can see in the literature of ancient Japan.

QUESTION: How do you make your interpretation accord with the almost universal—of Japanese and outsiders—interpretation to the effect that in Japanese social thought and practice or culture the individual does not have significant status, but only group status, chiefly family, even labor or employee group, and ordinary political unity?

ANSWER: The aim of my paper is to refute the interpretation which you consider almost universal and to provide a different point of view.

QUESTION: The point has been made that guilt is individual, whereas shame is social. Do you have any comment to make on this?

ANSWER: It has been the basic principle in Japan, as well as in China, that one should feel shame in one's conscience. Therefore the dictum "Control yourself" has been emphasized. The same philosophy is found in the expression, "Even if others do not know, Heaven knows, Earth knows, and I myself know."

QUESTION: Aren't you, near the end of your paper, confirming Ruth Benedict's point of view?

ANSWER: I think Ruth Benedict's error lies in her generalizing those points which are true about the Tokugawa period or part of it. She has taken these points as characteristic of the whole history and the entire society of Japan. If Ruth Benedict had limited her assertion to the Tokugawa period or to a part of Japan during the Second World War, I would not deny that there is truth in what she said.

[1] *Nihonshoki*[ck] (Chronicles of Japan), section on Emperor Suiko, April, 12th year.
[2] *Zoku Nihonki*[cl] (Records of Japan, Continued) section on Emperor Shōmu, April, 1st year.
[3] *Tenju koku shikuchō*[cm] (Works on the Felicitous Land).
[4] Ruth Benedict, *The Chrysanthemum and the Sword* (Boston: Houghton Mifflin Co., 1946).
[5] *Tannisho*[cn], sec. 3.
[6] *Ibid.*, sec. 2.
[7] *Ibid.*, secs. 5, 6.
[8] *Watsuji Tetsurō zenshū*[co] (Collected Works of Watsuji Tetsurō), Vol. IV. i. *Zoku Nihon seishinshi kenkyu*[cp] (Supplement to Studies on the Spiritual [Intellectual] History of Japan), chapter entitled "Nihon bunka no jūsōsei[cq]" (Multiple Characterization of Japanese Culture) (Tokyo: Iwanami-shōten, 1962).
[9] *Tozu Sensei zenshū*[cr] (Collected Works of Tozu Sensei), Vol. I, p. 192. Also, Vol. III, pp. 84–85.

a	高坂正顕	at	守護大名
b	推古天皇	au	戰國大名
c	聖德太子	av	豊臣秀吉
d	十七條憲法	aw	堺市
e	篤敬三寶	ax	大阪
f	聖武天皇	ay	安土桃山時代
g	東大寺	az	和辻哲郎
h	橘郎女	ba	町人
i	短歌	bb	士農工商
j	侍	bc	番頭
k	將軍	bd	中江藤樹
l	萬葉集	be	近江
m	源氏物語	bf	孝
n	防人	bg	大孝
o	九州	bh	小孝
p	柿本人麻呂	bi	天君
q	山部赤人	bj	文明開化
r	東歌	bk	明治維新
s	關東	bl	內村鑑三
t	相聞歌	bm	民本主義
u	額田王	bn	大正時代
v	萬葉時代	bo	民主主義
w	紫式部	bp	神道
x	清少納言	bq	推古天皇
y	赤染衛門	br	大化改新
z	枕草紙	bs	古事記
aa	道綱の毋	ht	日本紀
ab	道綱	bu	平安京
ac	源賴朝	bv	枕草紙
ad	幕府	bw	足利尊氏
ae	鎌倉	bx	應仁の亂
af	德川幕府	by	織田信長
ag	江戸	bz	延曆寺
ah	東京	ca	比叡山
ai	淨土眞宗	cb	島原の亂
aj	親鸞	cc	山鹿素行
ak	明治時代	cd	元綠時代
al	奈良	ce	西鶴
am	弘法大師	cf	近松
an	阿彌陀佛	cg	芭蕉
ao	家の子	ch	浮世繪
ap	家	ci	伊藤仁齋
aq	武士道	cj	本居宣長
ar	貞永式目	ck	日本書記
as	應仁	cl	續日本記

cm 天壽國繡帳
cn 歎異鈔
co 和辻哲郎全集
cp 續日本精神史研究
cq 日本文化の重層性
cr 藤樹先生全集

E. W. STRONG

Searches for agreement by persuasion

Suffering, or any other experiencing, occurs only in an individual, for only individuals are equipped with nervous systems. Each of us recognizes this focalization in his minding of it. However we name the recognition—whether we call it self-consciousness or the inner life—each of us knows it to be a source of autobiography as he remembers and recounts his feelings, his motives and purposes, his frustrations and fulfillments. Yet, none of us could make confessions had not human association provided a language of communication and interpretation. Only individuals apprehend, comprehend, and intend when they seek to tell each other what each feels, thinks, and values; yet, each draws necessarily on some communality established, or establishable, through association with others to speak and to be understood.

When we concern ourselves with social thought and practices, our attention is directed to associations of individuals and to character-istic ways in which these associations elicit and engage the interests of their members. Each of us exhibits in his thought and valuations an array of traits acquired within the society in which he has lived through his modes of association and participation within that society. Ortega y Gasset had this socially conditioned individual in mind when he said, "What a man has is not a nature; what he has is history." Or, put another way, we can say that the nature an individual has at birth is his biological endowment; the roles he plays in human history are shaped by, within, and from his cultural acquisitions. In acquiring ability to analyze and judge, and in exer-cising choice among alternative courses of action, individuals become self-determining and are held to be morally responsible for what they do.

We have in common an initial capacity to enjoy and suffer, to hope and fear, to love and hate; but, as we acquire preferences and loyalties, conflicts of interest arise within and between societies. Familiar questions about ends and means then follow. Are the parties engaged in dispute at odds about ends or goals being sought? If so, on what grounds can priorities be assigned in deciding which ends deserve precedence over others? Given agreement on a desirable end but dispute about conditions and means of realization, how is such dispute to be brought to settlement? Parties of conflicting interest cannot be expected to settle their differences by reasoning them out if they cannot first agree on the grounds on which decisions are to be reached. It is the concern of this inquiry into inquiries to examine the obtainability of initial agreement. Where such agreement is lacking, each side can be expected to advance its own preferences and valuations, upholding these in jealous self-advocacy. In such a situation, coercion by physical force establishes only who is the stronger and not, in outcome, who is in the right, save for those who maintain that might makes right.

I

If, with the Sophists and Plato, we begin with conflicting opinions (and the interests they manifest), two courses of inquiry may be taken. The first institutes a search for universal principles designated as natural or pertaining to Nature in contrast to the conventional, that is, to the customs and institutions of society, historically circumstanced. We are directed to go beneath or beyond the welter of the many and changing conventions of societies to discover a firm natural ground for our commitments and decisions. Those philosophers who have announced discovery of the universals sought have assumed, hoped, or claimed that these universals would command the acknowledgment of all rational individuals. They have never done so. Both in the locating of the ultimate principles and in the authority assigned to them, the discoverers have not been in agreement. There was no way by which further reasoning could yield a reconciliation of conflicting claims respecting location and authority, given the initial opposition of Nature to convention.

Starting from this opposition, the subsequent inquiry attempts to discover first principles separable from, and independent of, historical circumstances and conditions. Each professed discovery of a principle claimed to be naturally basic or original sets forth a thesis accompanied by a prescription. There is thus the thesis that conventional morality and laws by convention are subordinate to a natural moral law and should be brought into conformity with it. There is the thesis that in each individual there resides innately a moral faculty, conscience, light of reason, moral sense, or moral will which ought to be heeded as showing him the right way—a way all others will acknowledge in universalized form. There is the thesis of an original innocence or rectitude which, before corrupted in individuals by social artifice, issued in a mutually supportive, other-regarding community, which should be restored. There is the thesis of an unalterably egoistic human nature which, for its restraint in keeping the peace among men, requires a strong, centralized authority vested in the state. There is the thesis of the natural rights of men to which all other rights are subsequent and subordinate such that, when their exercise is withheld by any government, men have just cause for opposition and civil disobedience. There is the thesis of an original community free from class oppression and exploitation to be again attained by abolition of the conditions to which class divisions and conflicts are attributed. There is the thesis that every individual is capable of self-government and would so govern himself as to live amicably with others if the power vested in some men to rule others were eliminated.

I shall comment on just the first two of these several theses. Who has proof against the skeptic who doubts the existence of a natural moral law that is universal, timeless, and applicable to all men and every society? But let us assume that there is such a law of known requirement. We are not helped at all unless obedience to it can be secured, after a tribunal has determined that a social practice is not in compliance with the higher authority. The decision having been rendered, enforcement becomes necessary when the decision is not followed by compliance with it. Unless the enforcement is not in human hands, the intervention of the enforcers can readily be viewed and rationalized internally as an aggression against local interests by a party of opposed interests. This predicament might have been averted had evidence been amassed to show that compliance would best serve the compliers, not because punishment would be escaped, but because disobedience would be self-defeating.

Let us note, however, that persuasion effected by an appeal to consequences evidentially advanced, while it may be aided by belief in a natural moral law, needs in no way to be predicated on the truth of that belief. Those who assert an absolute authority vested in a natural moral law or in an innate moral will or sense look for reinforcement of belief by pejorative evidence as concerns conventional morality. In opposing Nature to convention, the evidence to be sought is that which calls our attention to the relativity and instability of conventions. So long as we remain within the historical morass, we cannot hope to reach firm ground—the ground of universal and certain principles. Once convinced of this, the first step of our liberation is completed. We are still in the swamp, but we know it to be a quagmire of insecurity.

Further historical study will only discover more of the same to us. Philosophy must thus come to our rescue, lifting us by reason out of the phenomenal world of the many and changing customs to discover within ourselves and beyond ourselves—and independent of all human institutions—a rock of certainty on which to rest our judgments and decisions. Time and again, philosophers have announced revelation of sure guides to the perplexed. Wisdom has been imparted, but no concordance of guides issues from the testimonies.

We know that, were we stripped of all cultural acquisitions, our species would inhabit an animal world with everything to make and learn which differentiates human histories from animal existence. Yet, acknowledging this, we may also believe that the cultures produced by human effort could not have had merely an animal origin. We may argue that some higher power, nature, principle, or essence must have been implanted to thrust up and draw forth the achievements of creative individuals. The attempt, however, to intuit an identity of soul, spirit, or active intellect at work as a prime mover —an attempt each can make for himself and none can make for another—yields conflicting testimony. Some are sure that they have found this nucleus, and some are equally sure that they have found only a bundle of sensations, impressions, and ideas in flux. Apart from the conflicting testimony, the attempt itself is consequent upon acculturation and impossible without it. Although one may attribute the aspirations and strivings characteristic of human but not of animal histories to a spiritual nature peculiar to man alone or, at some level of purification and refinement, to a more universal life coming to spiritual expression in man, the attempt to be at one with this nature by stripping away sophistication is itself sophisticated.

Our inner lives are culturally invested and endowed. Yet, whenever and wherever it appears to us that a mode of human association withholds from any individual a betterment of his life within that individual's capabilities and obtainable by a feasible change of the mode, would we think it morally defensible to advocate that nothing be done to effect a change? Are we perplexed, then, in seeking for reforms, by radical disagreements about the constituents of a good life, individually considered? Is this the heart of our problem? Or does the heart of our problem lie rather in a claim to knowledge, for example, the claim that an individual's race renders him incapable of certain developments and fulfillments and thus precludes the feasibility of a change of mode? If the latter, then the requisite task of inquiry is the submission of the claim to the test of evidence. When tests show the claim to be false, those who still insist that they are justified in opposing a reform have final recourse to contentions about desirabilities. Such contentions about desirability, as these pertain to social practices, call for policy decisions. These decisions, responsibly taken, rest on knowledgeable assessments of feasibility in means-to-ends relationships.

Plato, in *The Republic*, ordered his inquiry into justice by asking, first, what was desirable and, on the supposition of agreement about the nature of justice ideally defined, proceeded to the second question, how can justice be made to prevail in actual societies? In seeking for grounds of initial agreement, I will start where Plato started, with conventions, but will pursue a different course. Staying with conventions, I shall inquire how we may lay hold of them in knowledge and employ this knowledge in seeking for settlements of societary disputes.

II

By definition, an institution, practice, standard, criterion, or sanction is conventional if originated by human artifice. All characteristics of human conduct attributable to invention—to circumstances, situations, and conditions originating within cultures in their historical emergence and persistence—are subsumed under this definition. The diversity of these culturally acquired traits and their variabilities over time are made known to us by historians and social scientists.

Inventories and descriptions of acquired kinds of behaviors inform us about states of affairs in times and places. If the factual correctness of a description is in question, doubts raised have their settlement in further empirical investigations and findings. The extent of illiteracy, the amounts and kinds of employment, the kinds of institutions and their practices, educational opportunities afforded, and a host of similar matters are factually determinable. Resources needed to carry out a program or project are also determinable. As accurate descriptions are forthcoming, these may, of course, be rejected, distorted, suppressed, or willfully ignored by a group in defense of interests it believes would be adversely affected by acceptance of the descriptions or by their dissemination. In situations of this kind, all those who have respect for publicly examinable evidence have common cause to call either for admission of a well-supported description or for submission of counterevidence, if such be claimed to exist. Propositions or proposals submitted for acceptance on a cognitive basis as pertains to matters of fact must be compatible with well-substantiated descriptions to be rationally defensible.

The internationality of science has its foundation in respect for evidence. No line is drawn between descriptions in the natural sciences and descriptions in the social sciences. In all sciences and in the same way, although with differences of content, evidence is arrayed in confirmation of an hypothesis, and phenomena are correlated in conditions-consequence relations affording causal explanations. In coming to know the consequences that follow regularly from sets of conditions, we are made more capable of exercising controls of processes to yield desired results. Whether these processes be natural or cultural, our endeavor to exercise controls engages us in deliberations on policy. Policies prescribe what is to be done on behalf of consequences deemed to be desirable. Both workability and desirability come under assessment.

Causal explanations tell us how a society functions in its economy, in its institutional practices, and in career opportunities and incentives in effect for individuals in relation to sex, age groups, financial circumstances, class membership, traditions, status, and the like. When we proceed from explanations to the formulation of policies, normative interpretations centering in and around human desires and interests engage our attention. Philosophers, historians, biographers, poets, dramatists, and novelists are interpreters. So, too, are those social scientists who not only describe human activities but also concern themselves with the utilization of knowledge on behalf of human well-being.

Attention to qualities uniquely focalized in an individual's career is not incompatible with attention to common traits collectively exhibited. Classification and generalized characterization are not enemies of individuality. It is a serious mistake to oppose individuality or individuating features to common traits, typical features, statistical averages, and common conjunctions, as though attention to the individualized demanded repudiation of the generalized, and as though attention to collective characteristics had to be prejudicial to the appreciation of singularities. Each human career is the history of a person, a history he is conscious of enacting in his interactions with other persons; and each human career is caught up in kinds of association. The individualized and the generalized constitute polar extremities of a field of understanding. If knowledge by kinds and sorts is totally rejected, only an ineffable mysticism is left. If perception or intuition of individuality is thrust aside and at no point admitted, the accounts rendered will be depersonalized and dehumanized. There are collective behaviors and there is each person's will and range of choice. There are institutional patterns and there is the individually counted cost of conformity or non-conformity with them. In seeking for grounds of agreement upon which to formulate policies, neglect of either pole of attention will cripple our interpretations.

The social sciences provide us with our most reliable generalizations about individuals in associations and about their collective behavior. It is no reproach to these sciences, but, rather, it is their proper task to proceed by abstracting and correlating. Through comparative studies, with attention to case histories, similarities and differences are sorted out and brought under attention. In being furnished with empirical knowledge of conditions and situations, this knowledge, or more of the same, provides a positive basis of agreement concerning matters of fact. More than that, it provides a basis for assessing whether policies and programs under consideration are workable.

By knowing what it takes to increase agricultural production, to improve public health, or to expand educational opportunity, we put ourselves in a position to analyze and assess obstacles and difficulties standing in the way of attaining our goals. To feed the hungry, to protect health, and to banish illiteracy are social tasks. Men will work willingly for that which they want, value, and have hope of securing. Presumably, they seek to work effectively. As they acquire knowledge about how to get what they want, they come to the test of their earnest within a society or toward another society. Either they seek and support ways to recast the conventions that thwart desired fulfillments, or they remain trapped within them as they are.

The fabric of a culture consists of conventions historically accreted. As there are many histories, so there are many cultures. Individuals living in associations shape and are shaped by fabrics of conventions—vestments for which we have no universal moral authentication from Nature or by Nature generally agreed upon. These vestments we need to know to have self-knowledge and, for controls, we need scientific knowledge. To recut and reshape a fabric intelligently and effectively, we have to know what needs to be changed, what the difficulties are, and how, practicably, the difficulties may be overcome. One incentive to effort evident today in many countries seeking to develop their resources and competencies is found in their conviction that benefits gained and enjoyed by others, whether accruing from self-government, industrialization, public health measures, increased educational opportunity, or other sources, can also be obtained by them. Achievement of political independence does not, in and of itself, provide capabilities requisite for fulfillment of hopes attached to freedom. Liberation from those who ruled previously shifts a burden of responsibility to new shoulders. What a country in its people comes to be free *for* depends on what they are enabled to be and do.

The vision of a life worthy to be lived—a vision impelling individuals and commanding their allegiance—may be cruelly deceptive. As a people have their history interpreted to them, as poets, prophets, and philosophers sway their emotion and thought, so aspirations and hopes are kindled. Individuals, hungering now for the better life depicted, cry out and reach out for sustenance. A kindness has been done them if those who incited and encouraged their hopes did so out of knowledge that the means requisite to their fulfillment were procurable. They have been cruelly deceived if they have been brought to hunger in vain, or if that which is promised to many is had, or can be had, only by a few. One could argue, to the contrary, that a greater cruelty would be inflicted if men were robbed of courage, kindled in them by the vision of a bright future, by informing them that the vision was hopelessly Utopian. But men are in a sorry state indeed if, to make their condition bearable to them, they must be told noble lies and promissory myths.

To be competent to judge and interpret modes and patterns of association—their ingredients, their traditions and functionings, their constraints, their value preferences, their ideologies, their persistent or recurrent problems—philosophers need to be knowledgeable. Had philosophic search for a natural moral law or like universal natural principle independent of conventions yielded a discovery commanding the assent of all reasonable individuals, such inquiry would have enabled us to transcend the pluralism of cultural assents. From a calm height of philosophy, we could proceed to adjudicate the differences and conflicts of these cultural assents. Failing in this search for an essential nature of man separable from cultural textures woven historically into the lives of individuals, we must turn our inquiry to these very textures and weavings. Insofar as reliable knowledge of conventions is forthcoming, agreement about matters of fact and about practicable ways of exercising controls is within reach. When we know what, in fact, some human group desires and know also the means or conditions of realization, we are in a position to make judgments about the feasibility of proposed courses of action.

What is desired in fact and attainable by action is still subject to judgments of desirability. When we find ourselves, as philosophers, in dispute about desirabilities, we must, if responsibly concerned, inquire into relative feasibilities. That which any one of us esteems as eminently desirable, not just for himself but for and in human associations and the focalizations they engender in individual lives, he esteems responsibly insofar as the means to realization are knowledgeably assessed. It is easy enough to voice preferences, to extol what we prize, to contrast the ideal with the actual, to proclaim the dignity of the individual, to call for remedy of defects in a society. It is an exacting task to formulate a policy fit to be carried out.

Faced with a social practice judged by some to be undesirable, how can those who dislike the practice persuade those who do not to relinquish or change it? Assuming that the individuals to be persuaded actually desire the practice, persuasion is feasible if it can be pointed out that the practice is incompatible with an obligation which the practitioners, in common with those who object to the practice, acknowledge as desirable of fulfillment. Given such acknowledgment, the removal of the incompatibility calls for conforming practice.

We have a different and more difficult situation when the practice is not only desired in fact but is also regarded by the practitioners as desirable in principle, for example, racial segregation in South Africa or in Mississippi. Here the practitioners contend that what they want and do is what they ought to want and do, or are justified in desiring and practicing. The attempt at persuasion here shifts to an examination of interest represented in desire and act. As a first step, an investigation could determine with whom the interest is shared and the opposition which this shared interest engenders. If an agreement on facts is reached, a next step would undertake an appraisal of what it now costs, or of what the costs can be expected to be, of pursuing the practice against the opposition to it. The hope of those attempting persuasion is the hope that, when costs are counted, the gain sought will be judged not worth the expense or risk entailed in continuing the practice.

Combined with, or alternative to, the examination of interest is an appeal to a moral principle which, if embraced, overrides a conflicting principle by which the practice has hitherto been justified. Unless or until there is reason to suppose that the individuals to whom the appeal is made are in some way socially motivated, conditioned, or disposed to respond to it favorably, reliance upon exhortation is misplaced. Those who seek to educate others in order to persuade them have first to inquire how these others can be reached.

If one man's peace is another man's poison, there will be no peace between them. Desire for freedom and for world peace is strong among the peoples of the world—a world caught up in a time of troubles, dissensions, deprivations, and recriminations. To realize hopes for desired freedoms and securities which can be enjoyed only by individuals, many changes need to be made out of knowledge of how to proceed. Confronted with societary dissensions and disputes, we can keep the peace only if agreements can be reached through persuasion with respect to practices to be changed and on means to be utilized. Human history is of human making. The history men have is the history we need to know to make for a better world. The difficulties in the making are many and formidable, the tasks arduous and reaching far into the future, the accomplishable progress in doubt. If, now, knowledge of our man-made institutions, their practices, and our own social behaviors and their consequences is not grasped to produce agreements on policies and programs feasible of execution for the alleviation of needless misery and woe, the blame is our own. If we lay waste our powers in the world of our own making, then indeed the world will have been too much with us.

QUESTION: My two questions pertain to preferences and values as socially acquired by an individual and as culturally conditioned in an individual: (1) Are all goals thereby relative, or may some goals be absolute? (2) What freedom does an individual have in society?

ANSWER: (1) A goal, for example the goal of individual self-realization, has been declared by many philosophers to be a universal, highest value-principle. Abstractly, an absolute ultimacy of this goal is asserted; but, when such goal is fleshed out concretely by an individual, its content will be found to be relative to that individual's acculturation. This is not to say, however, that an individual or the community of which he is a member will regard this goal and seek for its attainment in a shifting and contingent way. The value assigned may be firm, imperative, and ultimate for the individual or for the group.

(2) Individual freedom of action is always limited. Coercions and compulsions opposed by an individual subjected to them constrain and restrain an individual's freedom. Furthermore, an individual is limited in what he is free to be and do by external circumstances and by the kind and extent of his own capabilities. The fact that preferences are culturally conditioned and acquired does not compel an individual to choose one rather than another course of action, but the courses open to him for effective choice are, within limits, both external and internal.

QUESTION: You state that, by definition, the term "conventional" signifies practices originated by human artifice and designates all characteristics of human conduct attributable to invention. This definition may be taken to assert that every trait of a culture is conventional as having been instituted by some artifice or invention. Is it not true, however, that there are traits characteristic of human conduct which emerge and develop "naturally" and not by invention?

ANSWER: The definition of "conventional" was set forth to differentiate between what is acquired culturally by an individual and his biological endowment. I quite agree, however, that *mores* and folkways emerge and persist, not by deliberate attempts to institute them, but simply by accretions that become habitual and customary. I would agree, too, that there appears to be no radical break or division separating the most primitive human groups from the anthropoids. Nonetheless, immense differences have been created within human groups over an immense journey from primitive beginnings—differences made possible by the tool-making capabilities of the human hand and the symbolizing capabilities of the human brain. My definition of the term "conventional" intended no denial of the continuity of human history with natural history, no neglect of the biological conditions of human productivity and striving, and no ignoring of any traits that are "natural" as biologically common to all individuals. To survive we must eat, and to have successors we must reproduce our kind. Values in common can be rested on recognitions of whatever is common to our human condition.

COMMENT 1. I recognize in the Western humanistic philosophy in your paper much that is in accord with the thought of Confucius.

COMMENT 2. I agree with that comment, but is there not a basic difference? In his philosophy of humanity (*jen*), Confucius bases his teachings on the innate natural goodness of man.

ANSWER: I, too, have recognized in the thought of Confucius, as explicated by several Chinese members of this Conference, many affinities and correspondences with Western humanistic thought.

The agreements of the latter (and later in time) with the former do not include a premise of the innate natural goodness of man. As born into the world, the human infant is not yet, in my philosophy, either good or evil. He has the potentiality of doing good and being good in relation to others and, no less, the potentiality of inflicting suffering ruthlessly on others and of becoming a bad man. If it be said that a child is born lacking the saving graces which alone commend him morally or spiritually, I take no exception to this, provided such lack is not interpreted to signify an originally sinful nature. The initial potentiality for good and evil in an infant is a malleable capacity. The influences and teachings to which the learning youngster is exposed eventuate in the kind of man he will become in his motivations, valuations, and actions. Concern for the goodness or the perfecting of an individual, viewed developmentally, cannot reasonably and practicably be isolated from concern for the goodness or the perfecting of communities in which he is a participating member. I believe that I am here in agreement with Confucius.

Legal and Political Thought and Institutions

JOHN C. H. WU[a]

The status of the individual
in the political and legal traditions
of old and new China[1]

I. THE INDIVIDUAL AND THE STATE: A DIVERSITY OF VIEWS

How does the individual in China stand *vis-à-vis* the state? Here we meet with a refreshing diversity of views.

The Taoists set the highest value on individual freedom. For them, that government is the best which meddles and taxes the least. The ancient "Song of Mud Balls[b]"[2] was evidently of Taoist inspiration:

> As the sun rises I get up.
> As the sun sets I go to rest.
> I dig a well for my drink.
> I till the fields for my food.
> What has the power of the emperor to do with me?

This love of personal freedom is well exemplified in the life of Chuang Tzu[c],[3] the greatest Taoist after Lao Tzu[d].[4] Once a certain king sent some emissaries to invite him to be his prime minister. He declined because he wanted to "wag his tail in the mud" like the tortoise.[5] On a similar occasion he said that he would rather be a free bird seeking its food in the hills than be domesticated and petted to death.[6]

To the Taoists, then, everybody is free to lead the quiet tenor of his life, and no government has the right to interfere with his freedom, much less to compel him to take office. They chose to be recluses.

Confucius (551–479 B.C.) was of a different mind. When some recluses[7] warned him against his vain attempts to turn the current of the age, he said with a sigh, "It is not in the nature of man to find his social life among the beasts and birds. If we do not remain in the society of men, with whom else can we associate ourselves? Moreover, if the world were in good order, I should not be trying to change it."[8]

However, to remain in human society is one thing, but to join a government is another thing. Confucius would serve only a prince whom he considered worthy of his service. He traveled from one state to another for many years in search of a princely prince who would go along with his principles and ideals.[9] As he found none, he returned a disappointed man to his native state, where he continued to teach his pupils and compile his books.

In this connection, two points are worthy of note. First, both Confucius and the rulers seem to have taken for granted that an individual was free to choose the prince he would like to serve, and that he was even free to leave his office if he was displeased with the prince's ways.[10] Second, in all his travels from state to state, there is no record to show that there was any need of a passport and a visa. This shows that in those days there was complete freedom of movement among the states.

In *The Book of Changes*[e] we find this significant saying: "Absorbed in the high and noble interests of his own, he refuses to serve the prince and duke."[11] This book was a common source of inspiration for Taoists and Confucians alike, although in this particular instance the Taoists followed its teaching more unconditionally than the Confucians. Later, when Buddhism came to China, it re-enforced the Taoist stand. The Buddhists went to the extent of declaring that "monks owe no veneration to the king."[12]

Thus, the three main traditions of Chinese thought and religion have, each in its way, upheld the freedom of the individual *vis-à-vis* the state, because all of them recognized a sort of Natural Law which derives its authority from a higher source than the state. For the Confucians, this higher source is found in Heaven and Heaven-ordained human nature.[13] For the Taoists, it lies in *Tao*[f], the Law of Nature. For the Buddhists, *Buddha-dharma* is the Supreme Law transcending the laws of this world. Taoists are *in* the world, but not *of* it. Buddhists consider themselves as neither *of* nor *in* the world, but *out* of the world, the world being, in their view, an impermanent phenomenon.[14] As to the Confucians, they are both *in* and *of* the world. They are resolutely involved in human relationships and wholeheartedly committed to the fulfillment of all the duties entailed. Still, they are not without a transcendental dimension in their total involvement, for the Law which ordains those duties is not made by man but by Heaven. The Buddha and Lao Tzu soared into the heights and dived into the deeps, but Confucius walked on the solid ground, coping with all situations of life according to the dictates of his conscience. He did not withdraw from the world, but played the part of a "wooden bell," i.e., a teacher and a conscientious objector.[15]

Mo Tzu[g] (470–391? B.C.)[16] was even more positive in spirit than the Confucians. He was willing to sacrifice himself for the welfare of others, and worked most strenuously to stop the states from going to war. Like Confucius, he found the Higher Law in the will of Heaven, and he preached the noble doctrine of universal love. But it is regrettable that he seems to have by-passed human nature and the family.[17] With vigorous logic he stressed uniformity at the expense of diversity.

If the Taoists tended to ignore the state, the Legalists[18] tended to ignore the individual. To them, the state is all-important. The state is the end, while the people are merely means to the end. They rejected all private standards of right and wrong. They recognized no authority above the state, nor any law higher than the positive laws of the state. Theirs was a radical positivism. To them, "right" meant what the rulers want, and "wrong" what the rulers do not want.[19] Under their Rule of Law, all individuals are indeed equal; only, they are equal in being slaves of the state. They denounced and outlawed all the traditional moral virtues as subversive of the public order of the state. Nor did they tolerate the traditional emphasis on family relationships. In their ideology, the individual does not belong to the family or even to himself. He belongs exclusively to the state. They wanted the people to work, fight, and die for the state. In the words of Lord Shang[h] (d. 338 B.C.), "A people that looks to warfare as a ravening wolf looks at a piece of meat is a people that can be used. In general, fighting is a thing that people detest. A ruler who can make the people delight in war will become the king of kings."[20] It was by means of the Rule of Law, with its system of penalties and rewards working as inexorably as fate, that they succeeded in expanding the state of Ch'in[i] (255–207 B.C.) into an empire. But, by isolating the Rule of Law from the fundamental humanity of men, they foredoomed it to a catastrophic collapse.

It is a pity that the Rule of Law should in the hands of the Legalists be wedded to a totalitarian, materialistic, and militarist ideology, so that, instead of securing the rights and freedom of the individual, as it normally should, it became actually a ruthless instrument for dehumanizing the people and turning them into tigers and wolves. So far as China was concerned, this unhappy wedding spoiled the chance of a genuine balanced Rule of Law for over two millenniums.

Of all these lines of thinking, the way of Confucius would seem to be the most balanced. It excels Moism by its catholicity, and excels Buddhism by its sense of reality. It steers between the anarchistic tendencies of Taoism and the totalitarianism of the Legalists. It recognizes the need of unity, but at the same time it sees the desirability of diversity. As Confucius himself put it, "Men of superior quality aim at harmony, not uniformity; while the small-minded aim at uniformity, not harmony."[21] This is in the best tradition of political wisdom, and is still a living ideal.

At this point I wish to enter a caveat. In this paper I will speak rather critically of the "legalization of Confucianism," or, what amounts to the same thing, the "Confucianization of the law."[22] This must not be taken to indicate criticism against Confucius and his teachings. He would be the last person to approve of the legalization of Confucianism. He was a great teacher and respected the personal ideals of each of his pupils.[23] He often asked them to tell him their aspirations, and never tried to impose upon them his own ideals, still less to reduce the diversity of their wishes into a dead monotony. He saw clearly that each individual had his unique qualities and peculiar faults, which were but the defects of his qualities.[24] He was a pioneer of individualization in pedagogy. Extremely many-sided in his interests, he was appreciative of different types of excellence in others.[25] He had an almost religious respect for the free choice of each and every individual.[26] Even in inculcating moral principles in the minds of his pupils, he would use only the method of dialogue and persuasion.[27] Compulsive morality would be inconceivable to him.[28]

It is true that Confucius laid great stress on the rites and rules of propriety, but his attention was focused on the underlying spirit rather than on the formalities and the letter of specific rules.[29] Confucius knew that the basic principles of morality, e.g., the Golden Rule, are immutable and of universal validity. But he also knew that their applications and expressions must vary according to the changing conditions and circumstances of life.[30] It was for this that Mencius called him the "Sage of Timeliness."[31] Solid like a mountain, he was yet as flexible and adaptable as water.[32] He was too broadly human to be a mere familist, too pure to be puritanical, too moral to be moralistic, too reasonable to be rationalistic, too thoroughgoingly moderate to be immoderate even in the virtue of moderation, and, finally, too genuine and well-integrated an individual person to be an individualist.[33] It is most regrettable that his moral teachings have been distorted beyond recognition and rigidified into an official system since the period of Han[j] (206 B.C.–A.D. 220), when Confucianism was wedded to the cosmic philosophy of the Yin-Yang[k] school and lost its original rationality, purity, and flexibility.[34]

II. THE STATUS OF THE INDIVIDUAL UNDER THE OLD LEGAL SYSTEM

The old legal system of China began to take form in the (former) Han period[l] (206–23 B.C.), came to its maturity under the T'ang Dynasty[m] (618–905 A.D.),[35] and remained stagnant through the succeeding dynasties until the end of the nineteenth century, when the legal-reform movement was set on foot. This defective system of law was formed under the influence of "Yin-Yang Confucianism," which polarized morality and law as the positive and negative aspects of government.[36] Morality sets up the norm of conduct; law sanctions it by penalizing its violation. When morality and law are thus wedded, the result is a system of compulsory morality, under which individual freedoms and rights can hardly be developed. What the Yin-Yang Confucianists brought about was the enforcement of Confucian social ethics, as they interpreted or, rather, misinterpreted it, by the machinery set up by the Legalists. Confucius himself would have condemned such a queer combination. Not that there was nothing good in it, but it could have been much better.

Let us look at some of its characteristic features insofar as they bear upon the status of the individual.

1. *All law was penal in nature.* There was no civil law. Even breaches of contract and injuries by negligence were penalized. The underlying philosophy was that law is the handmaid of ethics, and that any acts which are morally wrong constitute crimes, which it is the function of the law to inhibit and punish. In all the codes from T'ang (618–906) to Ch'ing[n] (1644–1911), there is a general provision to the effect that *whoever does what ought not to be done shall be punished.*[37] Although in practice this article was rarely invoked, in theory at least it must have been like the sword of Damocles hanging over the head of everybody.

2. *The problem of equality.* Were all persons equal before the law under the old system? Yes and no. Yes, in the sense that all persons, including the emperor himself, were required to respect and observe the law as it was. In an early case, Chang Shih-chih[o],[38] the Commandant of Justice under the reign of Emperor Wen[p] of Han (reigned 179–156 B.C.), maintained the sovereignty of law against the Emperor's wish to impose a heavier penalty than was prescribed by the law, and uttered these unforgettable words: "The law must be upheld by the Son of Heaven as by everyone in the whole empire. Seeing that the penalty that I have imposed in the present case is what the law prescribes, to impose a higher penalty would be to discredit the law in the eyes of the people. . . . It is the duty of the Commandant of Justice to hold the scales of justice even and equal for the whole empire. If once the scales were overturned, the entire legal system of the empire would fall into confusion, and the people would not know where to put their hands and feet. May I ask Your Majesty to give serious consideration to this?" After a long silence, the Emperor said, "I believe you are right."[39] Chang Shih-chih established the principle of judicial independence, which became a sacred tradition for the judges of succeeding generations; and the good example set by Emperor Wen was seldom if ever departed from by later sovereigns.

Although there was no written constitution like the Magna

Charta, the powers of the emperor were severely restricted by immemorial constitutional customs and by the unquestioned authority of the Confucian classics, effectively sanctioned by the fear of being called a "wicked monarch" in the ages to come.[40] From the Hans to the Manchus[q], there were some mediocre and weak monarchs, but there have been no despots and tyrants who placed themselves above the law. In this sense it can be truthfully asserted, that under the old system all persons were equal before the law.

Yet, in another sense, not all persons were equal before the law. For, although no one was above the law, yet the law itself created categories of people for special treatment. Prominent in all the codes were the eight categories of persons who were entitled to special consideration when guilty of crimes not of a treasonable nature. They were: (1) relatives of the sovereign, (2) old friends of the sovereign, (3) persons of great virtue, (4) persons of great ability, (5) persons who had achieved great merit, (6) high-ranking officials, (7) persons who had served the government with exceptional zeal and diligence, and (8) the guests of the dynasty, that is, the descendants of the superseded dynasty.[41] Now, what were the privileges they were entitled to? For one thing, they could not be arrested or investigated before special permission was granted by the emperor. In some dynasties, they could not be fettered.[43] In other words, they were not privileged to commit crimes, but only to have their cases reported to the emperor for his final decision, and be immune to certain procedures and methods of trial. Taken all in all, these privileges did not amount to much.

3. *The legal status of the individual in the family.* Traditionally, a Chinese seldom thought of himself as an isolated entity. He was his father's son, his son's father, his elder brother's junior—in other words, an integral member of his family. He was a concrete individual person who moved, lived, and had his being in the natural milieu of the family. The ties of blood and, to some extent, of marriage created for him a network of human relationships in which he had his proper place. Each family had a head, to whom his wife, his children, his daughters-in-law, his grandchildren, and the domestics owed unquestioning obedience. I know of no other system of law which is so meticulous in enforcing the duties of filial piety. So long as the parents were living, it was a crime for the sons, including those who were married, to set up a separate household.[44] Children were betrothed by the mutual agreement of the heads of the families involved, and the parties themselves had no voice in the choice.[45] Nor were the young man and girl supposed to see each other before their wedding. Marriage within the period of mourning for one's parents entailed heavy penalties and was null and void.[46] It was a crime for a married son to beget a child within the mourning pe-

riod.[47] This rule was in force for many centuries, until it was abolished at the instance of Emperor T'ai-tsu[r] of Ming[s] (reigned 1368–1399), who held that it was against human nature and therefore could not be the teaching of Confucius.[48] Confucius himself would have seen eye-to-eye with Emperor T'ai-tsu. Confucius was indeed insistent on the three-year mourning for parents, but his epigones have out-Confucianized him in this, as in so many other respects. When we speak of the "Confucianization of law," we must take care not to think that Confucius would have been happy to see some of the extremities to which his teachings were made to go at the hands of his later followers. For instance, Confucius did say that it was all right for father and son to conceal each other's crimes.[49] If the father had committed a crime, the son had no duty to testify against him. This privilege not to testify against one's parent was extended after the T'ang Dynasty to all members of the family living under the same roof, and the prosecutor was forbidden to ask anyone who was thus allowed to conceal the crime to bear witness.[50] So far, this seems to be reasonable, and it has its counterparts in other systems of law. But what was peculiar to Chinese law was the rule that anyone who accused his parents should be put to death, even if the accusation proved to be true.[51]

In all crimes of one member of the family against another, the degrees of relationship between the offender and the victim were used as an index to the degrees of punishment. Generally speaking, in crimes against the person, such as killing and wounding and slandering, the closer the relationship the higher the punishment; while in crimes against property, such as stealing and embezzlement, the closer the relationship the lighter the punishment.[52]

Chinese law was so geared to the idea of the family that it treated even religious communities as families. The relationship of master and novice was assimilated to that of uncle and nephew. The objects of worship were probably regarded as ancestors, as may be inferred from the following provision of the Code of T'ang: "Whoever steals or destroys an image of the Lord of Heaven (the supreme deity in Taoism) or the image of the Buddha shall receive three years' imprisonment. If a Taoist priest or nun should steal or destroy an image of the Lord of Heaven, or if a Buddhist monk or nun should steal or destroy an image of the Buddha, the penalty shall be banishment with penal labor. If the image in question is that of a True Man[t], or a *bodhi-sattva,* the penalty shall in each case be reduced by one degree."[53]

From the above examples, it is easy to see the legal status of the individual in the family. Each family was a little kingdom, which may be called a "familiadom," in which each member occupied a unique status different from all the others.[54] He might be superior to some and inferior to others, but never altogether equal to anyone, for the simple reason that even brothers were classified into elder and younger with important legal differences. But this does not mean that their status was static; for, if the sons survived their parents, they could set up their separate households and thus become family heads themselves.

4. *Inequality between sexes.* Under the old legal system, the status of woman left much to be desired. In the eye of the law, a woman was under a perpetual coverture. According to an old saying, a woman was subject to threefold dependence. Before her marriage, she was dependent on her father; after marriage, on her husband; when widowed, on her sons. But nowhere is the inequality more glaring than in the law of divorce. The wife could under no circumstance divorce her husband, but the husband could divorce his wife on no fewer than seven grounds, namely, childlessness, adultery, negligence in serving her husband's parents, loquacity, stealing, jealousy, and loathsome disease.[55] Some of these grounds, as you will see, are simply ridiculous. Especially negligence in serving the parents-in-law as a ground of divorce became a prolific source of heart-rending tragedies in family life. In some cases, the husband and wife were in perfect harmony with each other, but they were forced to be divorced because her mother-in-law did not like her. A story of this kind is told in the well-known poem, "The Peacock Flies to the Southwest."[56] And Lu Yu[u], a great poet of the Sung[v] period (960–1279), divorced from his beloved wife at the instance of his mother, continued to exchange love poems even after she was remarried into another family.[57]

However, the law enumerated three conditions under which the wife could not be divorced on any of the seven grounds, except adultery. The conditions were (1) that she had no close relatives to whom she could return, (2) that she had worn three years' mourning for her husband's parents, or (3) that her husband's family was poor at the time of their marriage but had grown prosperous afterwards.[58] The third condition is particularly significant, for it indicates that the law was not blind to the fact that the building up of a home usually depended upon the co-operation of the wife.

In actual life, the Chinese woman's role was as important as her legal status was low. There is no telling how many monarchs and statesmen and scholars have attained greatness with the silent help of their wives and their mothers.[59] There was a popular proverb on the lips of everybody: "The mother is as lovable as the sun in winter; the father is as severe as the sun in summer." Poor man, what he had gained in legal authority was more than offset by his loss in spontaneous affection and devotion on the part of his children.

5. *Equality as the rule.* From the above, one may have been led

to conclude that there are no general principles of law and justice underlying the legal system of Old China which are applicable *equally* to all persons. This would be an erroneous impression. Although family relationships did modify the general principles to a notable extent, they did not exclude them altogether. It would not be far from the truth to observe that particular relationships and general principles formed the warp and woof of the law. Then, too, we must realize that most cases that came before the magistrate were between parties not in any way familially related to each other, and they were governed by the general rules of the law. In all such cases, there was perfect equality of all persons before the law.

As the magistrates were drawn from the ranks of Confucian scholars, they were, as a rule, steeped in the spirit of classical teachings. Two passages in the ancient classics seem to have had the greatest influence on their minds. One is a saying of Tseng Ts'an[w] as recorded in *The Analects*. A friend of his, newly appointed to a judicial office, came to call on Tseng Ts'an and asked for some words of advice. Tseng Ts'an said, "The rulers have departed from the right Way, and the people have been demoralized for a long time. In trying a case, if you should get at the truth of the charge, cherish a sense of sorrow and compassion for the culprit and by no means feel elated."[60] It seems as though Heaven itself were speaking through the mouth of honest Tseng Ts'an.

But the *locus classicus* of the fundamental principles of criminal justice is to be found in a dialogue between Emperor Shun[x] and Kao Yao[y], as recorded in *The Book of Documents*[z].[61] This remarkable dialogue between a sage-emperor and a sage-minister presents in a nutshell all the essentials of the Chinese philosophy of penal justice. It teaches that penal law is a subsidiary means of education, that the ultimate end of punishment is to bring about the cessation of all punishment, that intention is an essential element in a crime, and that, although an act may fall within the letter of the law, one should sacrifice formal regularity rather than run the risk of punishing an innocent person. All these ideas would seem to belong to the perennial philosophy of justice, springing directly from the natural reason of man. They constitute the living fountain from which Confucian magistrates through the ages have drawn their inspiration and their guidance. Even Su Tung-p'o[aa], who used to declare airily that he had never in his life set his eyes upon the statutes, wrote a beautiful eulogy of Kao Yao's ideas of justice.[62]

6. *A touch of humanity in the judges.* Although Confucian scholars did nothing to develop the law, they had the merit of not forgetting that the law was made for man and not man for the law, and that punishment was but a means of education. That is why, in hearing litigations between family members on property rights, for

example, the first impulse of a magistrate would be to try to reconcile the parties. Let me relate a typical case. Two brothers were disputing for farms. Su Ch'iung[ab], the magistrate, said to both of them, "The most precious thing in the world is brotherly affection, and the least precious is a piece of land. Why should you quarrel over the least precious at the expense of the most precious?" Moved by this sagacious admonition, the brothers embraced each other and after ten years of estrangement,[63] were reconciled. In this kind of atmosphere it was impossible to develop a rigid law of property. Instead of trying to solve the case by threshing out the rights and wrongs involved in the dispute, the magistrate simply disposed of it by dissolving the dispute itself. Nevertheless, this typical way of settling a case of this nature has an irresistible charm which will cast such a spell upon one's mind that one would sooner have a judgment like that than read a dozen learned treatises on the law of property.

Another case is even more interesting. When Chen Shih[ac] was a magistrate in a certain district, a thief entered his house one evening and hid himself on the top beam. Chen Shih espied him but pretended not to notice him. He called the members of his family together and began to preach a moral lesson to them. "Each of you," he said, "must diligently attend to his duties. You should know that robbers and thieves are not bad by nature. They become such only through the habit of laziness. For example, the gentleman on the top beam is a case in point." The burglar was so frightened that he fell to the ground. Chen Shih spoke gently to him, "Judging by your appearance, you are not a bad man. I only hope you will correct your mistakes and do good. Probably your wrong-doing is due to your poverty; I here give you two pieces of silk to help you start anew." The gentleman was profoundly moved, and after that became a reformed man. When this was known to the public, all the people were converted by the report of Chen Shih's kindness and magnanimity.[64] There was neither thief nor robber in his district after that. The Chinese have a euphemism for thief: "The gentleman on the top beam." After all, Old China had its unique qualities, and the lack of legal experts was but a defect of its qualities.

III. THE STATUS OF THE INDIVIDUAL UNDER THE NEW SYSTEM

1. *The Influence of the West*. Communications between China and the West began long before the last century, but China did not feel the real impact of the West until the latter part of the century, the heyday of Western individualism. The good Emperor Kuang-hsü[ad] (reigned 1875–1908) saw the urgent need of a thoroughgoing overhauling of the old institutions. He wanted to introduce a constitu-

tional monarchy after the pattern of England and Japan. Unfortunately, this was frustrated by the infamous Empress Dowager. But the Emperor's initiative in the reform of the criminal law proved fruitful. In 1902, he issued an edict appointing a commission to revise the laws "on the basis of a comparative study of the laws of all nations, to the end that our new laws may be applicable both to our own people and to foreigners, and that our administration of justice may be improved."[65]

In the end, the penal system was considerably modernized. The new penal code was promulgated in 1910, which the Emperor did not live to see. Although it has been superseded by later codes, it marked the beginning of the new legal system.

There was also some attempt to produce a code of civil law, though it did not pass beyond the drafting stage. But the very fact that the law was now divided into penal and civil was a tremendous gain for the rights of the individual. Moreover, the legal profession was for the first time recognized by the law, and law schools began to appear.

2. *The "San-min chu-i*[ae]*" as the Foundation of the Present System.* As we have seen, the old legal system was based upon the Yin-Yang philosophy. It was not until this all-embracing cosmology was replaced by the *San-min chu-i*,[66] the philosophy of the threefold well-being of the people—the people's nationhood, the people's political powers and legal rights, and the people's livelihood—that a truly Chinese system of law could be established. The *San-min chu-i*, which Sun Yat-sen[af] formulated, was based, on the one hand, upon Lincoln's idea of government "of the people, by the people, for the people,"[67] and, on the other hand, upon the best political, legal, and economic traditions of China from the earliest times to the present day. Horizontally, it draws from the collective experience of Western democracies. Perpendicularly, it makes itself heir to the inexhaustible legacy of Old China. Consequently, it is broad and cosmopolitan in spirit; and, at the same time, is deeply rooted in the native soil. It represents a magnificent harmony between the one and the many, doing justice at once to the urgent claims of unity and universality and to the vital urges of diversity and uniqueness.

In the present Constitution, a whole chapter is given to the formulation of the basic rights and duties of the people. It begins with a declaration of the equality of all citizens before the law, "irrespective of sex, religion, race, or party affiliation."[68] Time does not permit me to enumerate here all the freedoms and rights guaranteed by the Constitution. The author of the first draft made it a special point to incorporate the institution of *habeas corpus* in his draft; and it has been preserved in the permanent Constitution.[69] Only two duties are mentioned, namely, paying taxes and performing military service in accordance with law. Another noteworthy point is that the constitutionally guaranteed rights cannot be restricted by law "except by such as may be necessary to prevent infringement upon the freedoms of other persons, to avert imminent crisis, to maintain social order, or to advance public welfare."[70] This is similar to the "Due Process Clause" of the American Constitution.

All these provisions, inspired by the spirit of the *San-min chu-i,* would seem to furnish a firm legal foundation for the development of a vibrant and full-blooded individual person and a working democracy.

3. *The Civil Law*. Although the civil law as an independent branch of the law had emerged in the early years of this century, it was not until 1930 that the civil code was promulgated. This code is a major accomplishment in the history of modern Chinese law. With the *San-min chu-i* for its guiding spirit, it embodies general principles drawn from comparative law, and at the same time it gives specific articulation to many of the prevailing customs and attitudes of the people.[71] Thus, both the universal and the unique have found a hospitable abode in its spacious premises, in which every individual in China may feel at home.

a) *The Place of Good Morals in the Civil Law*. To turn a moral wrong as such into a crime would constitute a great threat to individual integrity; but to turn a moral wrong into a civil wrong or a tort would involve, at most, a question of compensation. This is why the civil law can afford to be more hospitable to moral considerations in the determination of liability. There is a plethora of provisions in which "good morals" is made a decisive criterion of civil liability or of the validity of a transaction. Let two samples suffice: "A juristic act which is contrary to public order or good morals is void."[72] "A person, who, intentionally or by negligence, unlawfully infringes upon the rights of another is bound to compensate him for any damage arising therefrom. The same applies when the injury is done intentionally in a manner contrary to good morals."[73]

It is true that many such provisions are adopted from modern European codes. But the Chinese legislators have not done so blindly but selectively. They have selected precisely those new principles of Western law which are most congenial to the spirit of Chinese tradition. By a fortunate coincidence, the Chinese civil code was produced at a time when Western juristic thought had for several decades been turning away from the extreme individualism of the nineteenth century and heading steadily toward a humanistic and sociological position strikingly similar, in spirit, to the Chinese philosophy of the human-minded and well-integrated individual, who thinks of his duties more than his rights.

b) *The Equality of the Sexes Before the Law.* The most revolutionary feature of the civil code is the complete legal equality
between men and women. In the first place, all provisions of the
code applied to both sexes alike. In the second place, for the first
time in the history of China, women were entitled to inherit in equal
shares with men in the law of intestate succession.[74] In this, the
principle of *agnatia*, which had prevailed for at least three millenniums, was replaced by the principle of *cognatia*.

Marriage is no longer a matter arranged between two families,
but is based strictly upon the mutual consent of the parties themselves.[75] Only when a minor makes an agreement to marry or concludes his marriage is parental consent required.[76] The only material
difference that the law makes between the sexes is with regard to
the marriageable age, which for man is eighteen and for woman
sixteen.[77] In all other respects, they are equal before the law.

4. *The Penal Law.*

a) The present criminal code starts out with a recognition of the
democratic principle of *Nulla poena sine lege:* "An act is punishable
only if expressly so provided by the law at the time of its commission."[78] This means that, however evil the act may be from a moral
point of view, it is not subject to punishment as long as there is no
explicit prohibition by the law. The object of this law is not to
encourage people to do evil, but to secure their freedom from the
possibility of arbitrary judgment of the court.

b) While all the old codes highlighted the eight classes of persons
entitled to special consideration, the new code puts all offenders on
an equal basis. The law has equal respect for all persons, special
respect for none. If there is special respect at all, it is for certain
persons against whom a crime has been committed, as may be seen
from Article 116, which provides that any crime against the person
or reputation of the chief executive of a friendly state or its duly
accredited representative is subject to a higher punishment than that
which is provided for a crime of the same nature committed against
other persons.[79]

c) It is interesting to note that family relationships still play an
important part in the measurement of punishments in certain situations. This serves as a link between the old system and the new.

The accusing of one's family relations is no longer prohibited as in
the old law; but in a number of situations the existence of family
relationships controls the degree of punishment. In offenses such as
false testimony, malicious prosecution, profaning the dead, homicide,
causing bodily injury, and abandonment, the presence of a family
relationship between the offender and the victim raises the degree of
punishment.[80] On the other hand, in offenses such as fraud, breach

of confidence, theft, and embezzlement, the presence of a family relationship reduces the punishment. In some cases the judge is authorized even to remit the punishment.[81]

In all such cases, the law is doing nothing more than being responsive to the realities of human relationship and family solidarity so deep-rooted in the Chinese tradition.

d) The last but not the least significant feature of the criminal code is the large scope of discretionary powers that it gives to the judges in meting out punishment. In almost all cases, the law prescribes a maximum punishment and a minimum; between these limits there is often a large leeway, thus making possible the individualization of punishments.[82] Besides, the code permits suspension of punishment in cases where the sentence is no more than two years' imprisonment.[83] It has also adopted a system of parole.[84]

But the most typical example of individualization of punishment is to be found in Article 16: "Criminal responsibility may not be avoided on the ground of ignorance of the law, but punishment may be reduced according to the circumstances. If a person believed with good reason that his act was permitted by law, punishment may be remitted." In this, the Confucian empathic principle of consideration toward every individual finds a happy expression.[85]

While the whole movement of the individualization of punishment is one of the most advanced developments in Western jurisprudence, it accords surprisingly well with the old Chinese tradition of fitting the punishment to the concrete individual person rather than to the abstract nature of his crime. This is but an instance of the intriguing paradox that the East in seeking to be Westernized has often encountered its dormant self, just as in some other spheres, especially in philosophy of life and spiritual cultivation, the West is beginning to discover its aboriginal self in exploring the profundities of the Eastern mind.[86] In each case, the excursion is really a homecoming.

The East and the West so closely interpenetrate each other that one is often tempted to say that East is West and West is East. Perhaps it is more accurate to say that, while East is East and West is West, there is East in the West and West in the East! Each instinctively seeks the other for its own completion and fulfillment. Let us therefore treasure their differences; for, without differences, they would not be able to enrich each other. And let us also treasure their essential oneness, without which their existential differences would not be able to evolve into a harmony. But, thanks to their real unity and real diversity, there is great reason to hope that all the bewildering multiplicity of cultural processes can be an inexhaustible source of counterpoints to feed an ever expanding and ever deepening symphony of humanity, in which unity becomes infinitely vital and rich and diversity acquires eternal meaning and significance.

QUESTION: In the last part of your paper, where you speak of the features of the present criminal code of China, you cite Article 16 as an example in which the Confucian principle of consideration finds a happy expression. Now, the legal principle underlying this provision is familiar to all students of modern criminology. My question is: Is this Article an original Chinese invention or is it adopted from the West?

ANSWER: It is not a Chinese invention, but an adoption from the West. But, although it is not original with the Chinese, the choice is conditioned by Chinese preferences, which are definitely Confucian.

QUESTION: Your description of the legal system of modern China is particularly interesting to me as a student of Japanese law. You point out that, even in the modern modifications of the old legal tradition, the Chinese law-makers have managed to preserve a certain continuity with the spirit of the past. What strikes me is that these modifications coincide on so many points with the Japanese modifications. This must be because there is a fundamental similarity in the social structures of the two countries which condition their choice of exactly the same elements from the legal systems of the West. Or, is it because there have been mutual influences between China and Japan?

ANSWER: My own impression is that the similarity of social structures of the two countries can be traced to a great extent to the fact that in her formative days Japan absorbed Confucianism quite thoroughly. Of the contemporary Chinese law-makers, not a few received their juristic training in Japan, although a greater number have studied in the West. Anyway, the mutual influences between China and Japan have been inevitable. However, the greatness of a nation does not depend so much on its originality as on its capacity to assimilate congenial ideas from others.

QUESTION: You mention the eight categories of privileged persons, giving the impression that under the old Chinese legal system not all persons were really equal before the law. Were there no counterbalancing responsibilities against those privileges? For instance, there was a well-known maxim prevailing in olden times: "When those who should know the law transgress it, the punishment should be doubly severe." That is to say, the greater your knowledge, the greater your responsibility. Now, the privileged classes are usually more educated than the unprivileged ones. So, in fact, the inequality was as great as your presentation would make it seem to be.

ANSWER: There is a point in your question. But there is a distinction between "de jure" and "de facto." I have pointed this out in connection with the legal inequality of the sexes. "In actual life, the Chinese woman's role was as important as her legal status was low." Similarly, on this question of privileged classes, there were certainly some counterbalancing responsibilities. Politically and constitutionally, for instance, the supreme privilege of the emperor was coupled with his supreme responsibility, to such an extent that in case of grave breaches of the trust imposed upon him by the Mandate of Heaven, the leaders of the people had not only the right but the sacred duty of revolution. But there is one thing I have to bring out in connection with your question, and that is that, although many persons belonging to the privileged classes were educated, not all educated persons belonged to the privileged classes.

In this connection, let me introduce a pet theory of mine—the *principle of neutralization*. Where, for instance, the starting point is equality, inequalities creep into the system in practice, thus neutralizing the official theory. On the other hand, where the starting point is inequality, equalities creep into the system in practice, thus toning down the harsh consequences of the theory. Truly, as Justice Holmes once remarked, the life of the law has not been logic; it has been experience.

The same is true of women's "right of inheritance." Legally, it is absolutely correct to say that a woman had no right of inheritance. Yet, this does not mean that therefore all women were in danger of starvation. In fact, rich families as a rule provided fine dowries for their daughters on their marriage; and, as a learned member of this Conference has pointed out, although a girl did not inherit from her father, she "inherited," together with her husband, from *his* father. Of course, in a legal sense, she could not be said to "inherit," but, if the husband became rich, she could not remain poor in fact, at least in normal cases.

[1] This paper is strictly confined to the question of individual freedom and equality. For a general background of legal and political thought and institutions, the reader is referred to my article on "Chinese Legal and Political Philosophy," in Charles A. Moore, ed., *Philosophy and Culture—East and West* (Honolulu: University of Hawaii Press, 1962), pp. 611–630.

[2] See Shen Te-ch'ien[ag], *Ku-shih yüan*[ah] (*Origins of Ancient Poetry*, An Anthology of Old Poems). This anthology was first published in 1719, but has been reprinted innumerable times. The song quoted in the text is the first poem in the anthology. It is purported to date from the third millennium B.C. This is of more than doubtful authenticity. The first two lines of the poem are found in the *Chuang Tzu* (28) without reference to any such song. It is likely that the song was produced after the time of Chuang Tzu. But, whatever the date, it was certainly of Taoist inspiration.

[3] Chuang Tzu (between 399 and 295 B.C.)

[4] Lao Tzu, author of *Tao-te ching*[ai], was, traditionally, an elder contemporary of Confucius. His dates have been perhaps the most controversial question in the history of Chinese philosophy. Some scholars have put him even later than Chuang Tzu. But the latest tendency among Chinese scholars is toward a confirmation of the traditional date.

[5] *Chuang Tzu*, XVII.

[6] See, for instance, the *Chuang Tzu*, XVIII, containing the following story: "Formerly a sea-bird alighted in the suburbs of Lu. The marquis went out to meet it and brought it to the ancestral temple, where he treated it with a banquet. Exquisite ancient music was played for it; an ox, a sheep, and a pig were killed to feed it. The bird, however, looked at everything with dim eyes, and was very sad. It did not venture to take a single bit of meat, nor drink a single cupful; and in three days it died."

[7] Several such encounters are recorded in *The Analects*[aj]. See, for instance, *Analects*, XIV. 34, 41, 42; and XVIII. 5, 6, 7.

[8] *Analects*, XVIII. 6.

[9] Confucius had great confidence in his statesmanship. "Were any prince to employ me, in a twelvemonth something could be done, and in three years there could be some worthwhile result" (*Analects*, XIII. 10). This does not mean that he would accept any kind of employment. When he was in the state of Wei[ak], Duke Ling[al] asked him about military tactics. He replied curtly, "With sacrificial rites I have indeed an acquaintance, but as to military matters I have never studied them" (*Analects*, XV. 1). The next day he left the state. (*Ibid.*)

[10] When he was the Minister of Crime in Lu[am], as the Prime Minister, the neighboring state Ch'i[an] was afraid that Lu would grow so strong as to constitute a menace to its safety. So, Ch'i presented a company of eighty beautiful dancing girls as a token of homage to the ruler of Lu, with the result that the latter neglected to attend to the business of government. Eventually, Confucius went abroad. (See Ssu-ma Ch'ien, *Shih chi*[ao], Bk. XLVII: "Confucius: His Life and His Family[ap]").

[11] *I ching*[aq], under the *Ku* (eighteenth) Hexagram[ar]. The quoted words constitute the oracle attached to the sixth and topmost line.

[12] See *Hung-ming chi*[as] (An Anthology of Essays in Defense of Buddhism, Compiled by Seng-yu[at] of the Liang[au] Dynasty [502–556]), Bk. 5, contains a thoroughgoing exposition, by *Hui-yüan*, 344–416[av], of the reasons why Buddhist monks do not venerate the king[aw].

[13] *Chung yung* opens with a clear-cut statement: "What is ordained of Heaven is called 'Nature.' The following of this 'Nature' is called 'Tao,' or 'Moral Law.' The refinement of the *Tao* is called 'Culture.'"

[14] This does not mean that Buddhists believe this world to be nothing. It is a conglomeration of elements, which is only temporary. Because of its intrinsic impermanence, human existence is not real in the same sense as *nirvāṇa* is.

15 "Wooden bell[ay]" is really a metal bell with a wooden tongue. Its function was to awaken people and call them together, especially in times of danger at night. *Analects*, III. 24.

16 Mo Tzu, 470–391 B.C.? See *The Ethical and Political Works of Motse*, Mei Yi-pao, trans.[az], (London: Arthur Probsthain, 1929). Refer also to *A Source Book in Chinese Philosophy*, translated compiled, and edited by Wing-tsit Chan[ba]. (Princeton: Princeton University Press, 1963), pp. 211 ff.

17 His doctrines suffered from an excessive asceticism. For instance, his wholesale condemnation of music ignored the fact that music is a necessity of life and can be turned into a potent factor of education. His exaltation of uniformity of thought at the expense of salutary diversity unwittingly paved the way for the Legalists' unification of thought by the force of the state.

18 See *The Book of Lord Shang*[bb], J. J. L. Duyvendak, trans. (London: Probsthain, 1928), and *The Complete Works of Han Fei Tzu*[bc], Liao W. K.[bd] (London: Probsthain, 1939).

19 See Arthur Waley, *Three Ways of Thought in Ancient China* (London: George Allen & Unwin Ltd., 1939), p. 200.

20 *Ibid.*, p. 221.

21 *Analects*, XIII. 23. In this, as in so many other aphorisms, Confucius' merit did not lie in originality but in his unsurpassed gift of expressing a whole tradition into a living epigram. Yen Tzu[be], an elder contemporary of his, had eloquently said same thing to Marquis Chin of Ch'i[bf] by means of some interesting illustrations, such as the preparation of a soup and the composition of music. "If water is flavored with water, who can enjoy its taste? If the lute and the harp had but one note, who could enjoy their music? Such is the undesirability of uniformity!" See *Ch'un ch'iu, Tso chuan*[bg], under year XX of Duke Chao[bh] (522 B.C.).

22 See T'ung-Tsu Ch'u[bi], *Law and Society in Traditional China* (Paris: Mouton & Co., 1961), pp. 267 ff.

23 *Analects*, XI. 25, where Confucius was asking his disciples to state their ideals of life. When one of them hesitated to speak, because his ideal of life was so different from those of the others, Confucius urged him on, saying, "What does it matter? After all, each of us may speak of his own ideals."

24 For instance, *Analects*, XVII. 16, where he pointed out that, even though the ancients, too, had their defects, those were the defects of their qualities, while the moderns have the same defects without any corresponding qualities to counterbalance them. Also in *Analects*, XVIII. 10, Confucius quoted the advice that the Duke of Chou[bj] gave to his son that he must not seek perfection and all-aroundness in any one man.

25 See, for instance, *Analects*, XVIII. 8, where he praised the different types of excellence among ancient worthies, while admitting that he himself was different from all of them, since he refused to be pinned down to any definite pattern. The important thing is to be true to oneself: in the choice of styles, there is "no *must* and no *must-not*."

26 *Analects*, IX. 25: "You can take away the commander from the forces of a large state, but you cannot take away the free will from a person, however humble he may be."

27 Cf. *Analects*, III. 7; I. 15.

28 It is well known that Confucius laid emphasis on the transforming influence of virtuous example; he would be the last person to try to reform popular morals by resorting to legal measures and punishments.

29 *Analects*, III. 3: "If a man is not human, what has he to do with rites? If a man is not human, what has he to do with music?"

30 According to Confucius, one must, first of all, have a sincere desire to learn; then he must be able to stand on the principles he has learned; finally, in applying the principles, he must be able to *weigh*[bk] the exigencies of the times and circumstances. See *Analects*, IX. 29.

31 *Book of Mencius*[bl], VB. 1

32 According to Confucius, the good take delight in the mountains, while the wise take delight in the waters. (*Analects*, VI. 21). Confucius himself seems to combine the two.

33 Just as true virtue is not self-righteous, so a truly integrated person cannot be deliberately individualistic.

34 Confucius' conception of Heaven (*Tien*)[bm], like those of Mo Tzu and Mencius, was fundamentally theistic. When, in the Western Han period (206 B.C.–A.D. 25), Confucianism was wedded to the Yin-Ying philosophy, Heaven-and-Earth began to take the place of Heaven, and there emerged what may be called a cosmic pantheism. In the hands of Confucius and Mencius, "*T'ien-ming*[bo]" was Divine Providence. With the Han scholars, it became equated with fate.

35 The *T'ang-lü su-i*[bp] (*The Code of T'ang with Annotations*), which was drafted by a committee consisting of eight high-ranking ministers and ten Doctors of Law under the chairmanship of Chang-sun Wu-ch'i[aq] was submitted to the Throne in 653. It contains 502 articles divided into twelve parts. Each article is followed by annotations, which were considered an integral part of the Code. The Code summed up the best elements handed down from the previous dynasties after the Han, and served as the model for codes which came later.

36 In the introductory commentaries to Book I of the Code, we find the polarity of law and morality formulated in these words: "Virtue and morals are the foundation of government and education, while laws and punishments are the operative agencies of government and education. The former and the latter are necessary complements to each other, just as it takes morning and evening to form a whole day, or spring and autumn to form a whole year." However excellent the Code of T'ang was, it was limited by the cosmological frame-

work of Yin-Yang Confucianism, which was by that time deeply intrenched in the Chinese mind.

37 See Article no. 450 of *The Code of T'ang*. All the later codes contain a similar provision. See, for instance, *Ta T'sing Leu Lee*br, Sir George Thomas Staunton, trans. (London: T. Cadell & Davies, 1810), p. 419: "Whoever is guilty of improper conduct, and such as is contrary to the spirit of the laws, though not a breach of any specific article, shall be punished, at the least, with 40 blows; and when the impropriety is of a serious nature, with 80 blows."

38 Ssu-ma Ch'ien's biography of Chang Shih-chih has been translated by Burton Watson in his *Records of the Grand Historian* (New York: Columbia University Press, 1961), Vol. I, pp. 533–539.

39 Cf. *ibid.*, pp. 536–537.

40 An important branch of Chinese literature consists of memorialsbs to the Throne. This forms an inexhaustible source of history and wisdom which is still little explored.

41 For a detailed treatment, see T'ung-tsu Ch'u, *op. cit.*, note 22, pp. 177 ff.

42 Deleted in proof.

43 *Ibid.*, p. 178.

44 See *The Code of T'ang*, Article no. 155.

45 Under the old law, to disobey the will of one's parents would be an act of filial impiety, which was listed as one of the ten gravest crimes. Marriage was primarily the concern of the family, meant to continue the family lineage and traditions. To the Western reader, this system must seem incredibly cruel; he is apt to think that every marriage must have been a mockery of marital happiness. But, in fact, unhappy marriages were the exception rather than the rule. On the whole, parents were very careful in choosing spouses for their children. Their children had implicit confidence in their judgment, and would feel too bashful to comment even if they were consulted.

In Confucius' day, marriage was not primarily a matter for the family. The parties knew each other before the wedding. This can be inferred from the considerable number of poems on courtship and marital happiness in *The Book of Songs*bt, which Confucius loved so much that he set every one of the three-hundred-odd odes to music, and never wearied of encouraging his pupils and even his own son to read them. Confucius was certainly much more modern than his later epigones. In this paradox lies the key to a proper understanding of the cultural history of China.

46 See *The Code of T'ang*, Article no. 179.

47 *Ibid.*, Article no. 156.

48 *Ming T'ai-tsu hsiao-tz'u lu hsü*bu (Emperor T'ai-tsu of Ming, Preface to *Models of Filial Piety and Paternal Affection*), quoted in Yang Hung-lieh, *Chung-kuo fa-lü ssu-hsiang shih*bv (*History of Chinese Legal Thought*), (Shanghai: Commercial Press, 1936), Vol. II, p. 290.

49 The *Analects*, XIII. 18.

50 See T'ung-Tsu Ch'u, *op. cit.* note 22, pp. 70–71.

51 *Ibid.* p. 72.

52 This is a beautiful expression of humanism in the law, laying greater emphasis on the integrity of the person than on material interests.

53 The *Code of T'ang*, Article no. 276.

54 This unique status is not fixed once and for all in its content. It may vary from day to day, from year to year. Let us suppose a family of seven members, consisting of the parents and five grown-up sons. The father is the head of the family. If the father dies, the sons cannot yet establish their separate families, because the mother is still living. The eldest son becomes the legal head of the family, possessing an authority over his younger brothers similar to that of the father. So far as the eldest son is concerned, his status has undergone a radical change following the death of his father. If the eldest son dies, the second son takes his place as the head of the family. If the mother dies, all the sons are free to establish their separate households. Thus, at any moment the status of each member is determined by the law; but, at the happening of an external event, he may be transposed from one status to another.

55 See the *Code of T'ang*, Article no. 189 *et seq.*

56 *K'ung-chüeh tung-nan fei*bw. For an English translation, see Robert Payne, ed., *The White Pony: An Anthology of Chinese Poetry*, (New York: Mentor Books, 1960), pp. 117–125.

57 For an English translation of Lu Yu'sbx poem and his former wife's response, see Teresa Li's (Li Te-luan)by "Fifty Poems from the Chinese," *T'ien Hsia Monthly*, IX (1939), 286, 304–306.

58 The *Code of T'ang*, Article no. 189.

59 For some of the illustrious examples, see Albert O'Hara, S.J., *The Position of Woman in Early China: Including Translation of Lieh Nü Chuan* (Hongkong: Orient Publishing Co., 1955).

60 The *Analects*, XIX. 19.

61 See "Ta-Yü mobz" (Counsels of the Great Yü), in *Shu ching*.

62 See his famous essay, *Hsing-shang chung-hou chih chih lun*ca (The Acme of Clemency in Punishment and Reward), in which he expounded the principle laid down by Kao Yao that in doubtful cases the sovereign should err on the side of leniency and generosity rather than try to follow the strict letter of the law. This essay is included in many popular anthologies.

63 See *Pei-Ch'i shu*cb, Bk. 46. (*History of the Northern Ch'i Dynasty*).

64 See *Hou-Han shu*cc (*History of the Later Han Dynasty*), Bk. 92.

65 See Yang Hung-lieh, *Chung-kuo fa-lü ssu-hsiang shih* (*History of Chinese Legal Thought*), Vol. II, p. 305.

66 Commonly translated as "Three Principles of the People."

67 See "Wu-ch'uan hsien-fa[cd]," in *Kuo-fu ch'uan-chi*[ce], Chang Ch'i-yün[cf], ed. (Taipei: United Publication Center, 1960), p. 165.

68 *Constitution of the Republic of China*, Article 7. On the spirit of the present Constitution, see Sun Fo[eg], *China Looks Forward* (New York: John Day, 1945).

69 *Ibid.*, Article 8.

70 *Ibid.*, Article 23.

71 For a more detailed account, see my article, "Chinese Legal Philosophy: A Brief Historical Survey," *Chinese Culture Quarterly*, I, No. 4 (April, 1958), 7, 39 ff. The Constitution of the Republic of China, The Criminal Code, and the Civil Code are available in English translation in *Laws of the Republic of China: First Series—Major Laws*, published by the Government in Taipei, 1961.

72 Civil Code, Article 72.

73 *Ibid.*, Article 184.

74 *Ibid.* The expression "lineal descendants" (Article 1138) denotes both males and females without distinction. Even in the case of a will, the testator has no power to deprive any heir of his or her "compulsory portion," which is one half of what he or she would have received in the absence of a will.

75 *Ibid.*, Article 972.

76 *Ibid.*, Article 974.

77 *Ibid.*, Article 980.

78 Criminal Code, Article 1.

79 This, of course, is motivated by the national solicitude to keep peace with other nations.

80 The *Code of T'ang*, Articles 170, 251, 272, 280, 295, etc.

81 *Ibid.*, Articles 162. v, 324, 343, etc.

82 *Ibid.* Some general standards are laid down for the guidance of the judge in meting out punishment; but these standards are flexible in their application. See Article 57.

83 *Ibid.*, Article 74.

84 *Ibid.*, chap. X, on "Conditional Release"; also see Articles 77–79.

85 The Confucian doctrine of *shu*[ch] (which has been translated as "mutual consideration" or "reciprocity") finds its expression, negatively, in the formula: *Not to do to another what you would not like to have done to you* (*Analects*, XV. 23). On the positive side, it finds its expression in the formula: *Try to extend to others what you desire for yourself* (*ibid.*, VI. 28). These are the substantial principles of *shu*, which merges in its farthest reaches into *jen*[ci]. In its strict sense, *shu* is the *functional* aspect of *jen*; it is the "art of *jen*," which consists in the ability *"from one's own self to draw a parallel for the treatment of others"* (*ibid.*). This means that one must step into the shoes of another in order to understand him by seeing things from his standpoint. The ideal judge should be able to do so with the parties before him. Only thus can he avoid rash judgment and render a truly impartial and fair decision.

86 I have adopted the term "aboriginal Self" from Emerson's essay on "Self-Reliance," where he says, "What is the aboriginal Self, on which a universal reliance may be grounded? What is the nature and power of that science-baffling star, without parallax, without calculable elements, which shoots a ray of beauty even into trivial and impure actions, if the least mark of independence appear? The inquiry leads us to that source, at once the essence of genius, of virtue, and of life, which we call Spontaneity or Instinct. We denote this primary wisdom intuition, whilst all later teachings are tuitions. In that deep force, the last fact behind which analysis cannot go, all things find their common origin." In this he anticipated the upsurge of interest, in the contemporary West, in Far Eastern traditions, especially in Zen and the philosophical Taoism of Lao Tzu and Chuang Tzu.

a	吳經熊	l	漢代
b	擊壤歌	m	唐
c	莊子	n	清
d	老子	o	張釋之
e	易經	p	漢文帝
f	道	q	滿清
g	墨子	r	太祖
h	商鞅	s	明
i	秦	t	眞人
j	漢	u	陸游
k	陰陽	v	宋

w 曾參

x 舜

y 皐陶

z 書經

aa 蘇東坡

ab 蘇瓊

ac 陳寔

ad 光緒

ae 三民主義

af 孫逸仙（即孫中山）

ag 沈德潛

ah 古詩源

ai 道德經

aj 論語

ak 衛

al 靈公

am 魯

an 齊

ao 司馬遷，史記

ap 孔子世家

aq 易經

ar 蠱卦

as 弘明集

at 僧祐

au 梁

av 慧遠

aw 沙門不敬王者

ay 木鐸

az 梅貽寶

ba 陳榮捷

bb 商君書

bc 韓非子

bd 廖文魁

be 晏子

bf 齊景公

bg 春秋左傳

bh 昭公

bi 瞿同祖

bj 周公

bk 權

bl 孟子

bm 天

bn 天地

bo 天命

bp 唐律疏義

bq 長孫無忌

br 大清律例

bs 奏議

bt 詩經

bu 明太祖孝慈錄序

bv 楊鴻烈，中國法律思想史

bw 孔雀東南飛

bx 陸游

by 李德蘭

bz 大禹漠

ca 刑賞忠厚之至論

cb 北齊書

cc 後漢書

cd 五權憲法

ce 國父全集

cf 張其昀

cg 孫科

ch 恕

ci 仁

TARA CHAND

The individual in the legal and political thought and institutions of India

I propose to deal in this paper with the thought and institutions of India during the three stages of the development of her history—ancient, medieval, and modern. The span of time covered by the paper is long. But it has to be remembered that Indian thought and institutions emerged thousands of years ago and possess an unbroken continuity. The situation of today is indissolubly linked with that of yesterday and the day before. No understanding of contemporary India is possible, therefore, without a knowledge of the past.

Let me begin with the broad features of Indian life as they manifested themselves in the first stage of development in ancient India.

How did the Indian thinker define the individual and visualize the relation between man and society? The individual (*jīvātma*), according to Indian philosophy, is a union of nature and spirit. *Jīva,* literally "that which breathes," or the biological organism, in some mysterious inexplicable (*anir-vacanīya*) way becomes associated with *Ātman* (the spirit). The first represents the element of finiteness, the second infinitude, and their coming together produces the ensouled body, the individuation of the infinite. Dialectically, body and spirit —non-being and being—become synthesized in the individual.

The spirit is in essence self-conscious, self-illuminating, the knowing subject, the organizer of experience, and therefore the principle of order. The body, on the other hand, becomes conscious by the light of the spirit; it is the object, the chaos of experience, which seeks to be organized and rendered meaningful. Spirit is knowledge (*vidyā*); body is nescience (*avidyā*). One is the real, unchangeable, not bound by the categories of time, space, and causation—the unmoved mover. The other is relative, ever changing, ever becoming, ever moving, conditioned.

The life of the individual is a confluence of two different principles that make it a continuum of inner conflicts, and man's natural endeavor is to resolve and transcend them. This may be achieved through the perfection (*samsiddhi*) of the individual and the welfare of the world (*loka-samgraha*). The two together contribute to the realization of the individual's freedom. They are the values whose pursuit is most worthwhile, for in them is enshrined the supreme good of man. The search for other goods is secondary. The identity of perfection with world welfare is important. Equally important is the view that the pilgrimage of man's life is divided into four stages (*āśrama*)—studentship and celibacy, marriage and householding, seclusion and withdrawal, and renunciation and world welfare. Kālidāsa bears witness that the *āśrama* principle was followed by the kingly descendants of Raghu (the ancestor of Rāma).[1]

The individual's perfection is a continuous, life-long process in which all stages are of equal value. The *āśrama-dharma* (duty) reinforces the teaching of the *Bhagavad-gītā* and places action and renunciation on the same level. The same truth is indicated in the doctrine of the *puruṣārthas*—the four objects of life's striving. They are *dharma* (performance of the duties of the social order), *artha* (gaining of wealth), *kāma* (gratification of biological impulses and enjoyment of pleasures not opposed to *dharma*), and *mokṣa* (liberation or beatitude). Life is a devotion to all its fundamental urges, but beatitude is supreme, although attainable only by the select few. Among the other three, the *Mahābhārata*[2] regards *dharma* as the best, *artha* as middling, and *kāma* as the lowest, and subordinate to the other two.

Laws and institutions make full provision for the functioning of the individual so conceived. Society is a whole of interdependent parts, with certain necessary vocations which answer to the needs of the individual—of the spirit and of the body.

Indian legal and political theory takes society for granted, co-existent with man, natural. It does not, therefore, speculate about its origins. Man's needs are primordial, and so is his society. Nor is theory concerned with the question whether society exists for the individual or the individual for society. As both are oriented toward the same end—the realization of the great objects of human endeavor—there can be no incongruity in their claims. Society, however, is a structure which has parts and functions. Society is a community of communities, and not a mere conglomeration of isolated individuals. The parts of society are the factors which perform the necessary functions of social life; namely, knowledge, security, wealth, and service. They are the four *varṇas* (classes), viz., *brāhmaṇa, kṣatriya, vaiśya,* and *śūdra.* The communities which constitute society are family, caste (*jāti*), and sub-castes. They determine the status and occupation of the individual, and his relationships with others.

Society's organization and functioning are so devised as to enable the individual to fulfill his function as an individual—a free spirit associated with the whole apparatus of mental, biological, and ra-

tional substructures. This plan contemplates the maximum autom-
atization of the activities of the inferior part so that the maximum
opportunity may be available for the consummation of the free self.

Let us examine the Hindu social organization in order to see how
far it fulfills this purpose. In the hierarchy of groups which form the
social pyramid, the family comes first. The constitution and principles of the family are described in the Smṛtis, or law books.[3] The
joint and undivided family was the normal unit of Hindu society.
It consisted of the male members descended lineally from a common
male ancestor, together with their mothers, wives, and unmarried
daughters, down to the seventh generation. The joint family for the
purposes of holding property shrank into the coparcenary, which
consisted of the persons who by birth were entitled to an interest in
the property of the holder for the time being. The coparcenary
commenced with a common ancestor and included the holder of the
property and the male descendants down to the third generation.
Thus, the family of coparceners was a legal entity, a corporate body,
in which ownership, possession, and enjoyment of property were in
common, but the share of each fluctuated with births and deaths in
the family. The father (great-grandfather or grandfather) was the
manager (kartā) of the property, empowered to dispose of it by
mortgage, sale, or gift in times of distress, in the education of children, in marriage, and in performance of religious rites of the members of the family, who had the right of maintenance, but no right
of disposal.

The individual was thus merged in a group which was founded
upon birth and which was perpetual but purely legal. The family
was the basic association of the social system established by Nature
and recognized by law. It rested upon two fundamental instincts—
preservation of man and propagation of species. It relieved the individual from any anxiety regarding his livelihood. It dispensed with
the need for orphanages, poor houses, old-age pensions, and life insurance. To this association may be appropriately applied the phrase
of Burke, "partnership of the past, the present and the future."

The second group in the social hierarchy was the caste and the
sub-caste. In the social philosophies of Aristotle and his follower
Hegel, an intermediate association is recognized between the family
and the state. This, according to Aristotle, was the union of families
for discharging the function corresponding to the animal part of the
individual.[4] Broadly, it is responsible for the economic activities of
society. Hegel gives the name "Civil Society" to it. It is comprised of
the agricultural, industrial, commercial, and ruling classes.

The intermediate association of the Hindu system occupies a
position which is somewhat similar. It mediates between family and
society. According to Hindu law, the social system (samājā) is made

up of four classes (*varṇas*). Each class consists of a multiplicity of castes and sub-castes (*jātis*). Each caste (*jāti*) comprises a number of families, and a number of castes are grouped together under one or the other class. Some castes, however, are regarded as outside the four classes. They are the untouchables.

The confluence of castes constitutes society.

In the Vedic age, the system of class and caste was fluid. But, in later times, caste regulations became inflexible and their guiding principle was heredity. The functional inflexibility of caste was somewhat modified, however, in practice; for example, not all *brāhmaṇas* were devoted to learning, and many took to other occupations, including agriculture, which was frowned upon by the Smṛti writers; many *kṣatriyas* also followed professions other than the military. Some of these deviations were sanctioned by the law books.

By and large, the caste was an inward-looking institution which defined the duties of its own members. But apart from determining the status of the individual, it prescribed few obligations of the castes *inter se* and toward society as a whole. It is true that co-operation between *brāhmaṇa* and *kṣatriya* was considered necessary for success, and *kṣatriyas* were enjoined to protect the *brāhmaṇas* and *dharma,* but the fact remains that the *vaiśyas* were required to live apart from the two higher classes and to render obedience to them, and the *śūdras* had mostly obligations and few rights.

This was the result of the specialization of functions which the system enforced. Thus, a *brāhmaṇa* was required to study and teach, but the teaching was confined to *brāhmaṇas* principally and to *kṣatriyas* secondarily. The *vaiśyas* were legally entitled to education, but a large majority of them were deprived of it in practice. The *śūdras* were even legally excluded. Then, again, the *kṣatriyas* alone were expected to bear arms and to fight. The others were exempted from this duty.

As probably more than 80 per cent of Hindu society consisted of *vaiśyas* and *śūdras*—these castes which were regarded culturally and socially inferior and were debarred from participation in defense—it lacked the inner cohesive strength needed to resist aggression, as was demonstrated again and again in history.

Caste placed strict limitations upon the liberty of the individual, and constrained him to unalterable conformity with what is called *jāti-dharma,* the rule of the caste. As caste was autonomous in enforcing this rule, and as it possessed judicial authority, including punishment of breaches of its regulations, a large part of a man's life was taken out of the sphere of the individual as well as of the state.

Family and caste covered a large sector of the life of the individual and provided strong and unyielding bonds of social solidarity. Beyond the ground occupied by them, the larger association, the social organism, had little more to offer. But there remained one basic need of society and the individual which was so urgent and so vital as to require the creation of an institution possessed of capability equal to the demand. It was the state (*rājya*).

The state in India was unique in both function and structure. It was not the *Polis* of Greece, nor the *Imperium* of Rome. It had some resemblance to the *Regnum* of medieval Europe, but nothing in common with the modern sovereign state, autocratic or democratic. It was not an independent institution endowed with absolute power.

The state, in the abstract, was not discussed by Hindu writers on polity, for they were concerned with social order and concrete government (*rājya* or *rājan*). Not *Staatrecht* but *Sittlichkeit* was the subject of their study.

The *rājan,* or prince, was an instrument of society, an upholder and protector of social law (*dharma*). But he had no authority either to make or to modify law, for *dharma* was divine, ancient, revealed in words heard from God (Śruti) and preserved in memory (Smṛti). After *dharma,* custom, usage, or the tradition of the people, or the wisdom of ancestors, was binding upon king and society. Conscience was the guide in judging. Thus, the function of legislation was wholly denied to the state.

The second important division of the powers of the state is the organization of the judiciary and the dispensation of justice. This power, too, was hedged in by many limitations. The *Artha-śāstra* of Kauṭilya (fourth century B.C.) speaks of a court presided over by the king and assisted by learned *brāhmaṇas*. This court was, in all likelihood, the highest judicial authority for the administration of criminal laws. This may be inferred from the fact that the king was the bearer of *daṇḍa,* the power to punish. But whether there were other subordinate criminal courts similarly constituted or not is difficult to say. The probability is that officers entrusted with executive and military functions were charged with apprehending and punishing crime, and, therefore, there was no regular hierarchy of courts and criminal justice.

In the villages, the caste *pañcāyats* (committees of representatives) dealt with petty offenses.

It is difficult to say whether the government established any civil courts. The inscriptions on copper plates of the twelfth century give titles of state dignitaries. We find among them mention of such officers as *Dharmādhikaraṇika* (judicial officer), and *Mahā-dharmā-dhyakṣa* (supreme judicial officer), who were obviously concerned with *dharma*, or the law. But it is impossible to say exactly what their duties were. The probability is that civil laws and customary laws were administered by arbiters chosen by the parties, or by *pañcāyats,* or by learned *brāhmaṇas,* who possessed the reputation of knowing the Dharma-śāstras.

This leaves to the ruler real and unlimited authority only in the executive branch of government. In a society in which legislation was virtually non-existent and justice largely private, where the concept of man-made law was inconceivable and crime was considered more a sin than a violation of social order, the whole emphasis of political theory was on the aspect of the force of the state. It is not surprising, therefore, that the wielder of the force—the *rājan,* or prince, should have been endowed with superlative authority. High-sounding titles were conferred upon him, e.g., *Mahārāja* (great king), *Samrāt* (emperor), *Mahārājadhirāja* (overlord of kings), *Parambhattāraka* (the Supreme Lord or Master), *Parameśvara* (the Supreme Lord), etc.

The origin of his authority was curiously both divine and contractual—in its nature divine and in its form contractual. Says Manu: "The Lord created a king for the protection of the whole creation, taking [for that purpose] eternal particles of Indra, of the wind, of Yama, of the sun, of fire, of Varuṇa, of the moon, and of the Lord of Wealth."[5]

Manu also holds that kingship was set up for the protection of the people and their laws in exchange for a sixth part of their produce. Kālidāsa[6] echoed this sentiment when he wrote, "In order to advance the welfare of the subjects, he [the king] took from them the tax of one sixth; in the same way as the sun takes up water in order to give it them back a thousand fold."

Āryadeva, a Buddhist monk, chided a king in these words: "What is thy pride worth, O king, who art a [mere] servant in the *gana* [multitude, i.e., body politic] and receiveth the sixth part as wages?"[7]

This account of the origin of Lordship suggests what ought to be the duties of the king. They are all instrumental and not originating functions and are comprehended in the word "protection"—(1) protection of *dharma,* i.e., maintenance of the *varṇāśrama* (division of classes and stages) system; (2) protection of people from natural and man-made calamities; (3) protection of culture, education, literature, art, music, painting, dance, etc.; (4) protection of economic activities, e.g., control of commerce, banking, professions, occupations, and labor, the promotion of state trading and agriculture, famine relief, provision of roads, inns, etc. Thus there was hardly any aspect of the people's life which was considered beyond state protection and control.

What about the relation of the state and the individual? Considering how almost every aspect of life, almost all potentialities, capabilities, and needs were provided for in minute detail by the various branches of *dharma, kula-dharma* (family law), *varṇa-* and *jāti-dharma* (class and caste law), and *rāja-dharma* (law of the state), precious little seems to have been left for the exercise of the freedom of the individual.

Against this conclusion, however, a caveat must be entered. The state of Hindu theory is not at all a replica of its Hegelian counterpart. It is not to be regarded as the end but as the means, the instrument. The purposes and objectives of life were formulated, not by the state, but by society and its God-made law. The state's function is to see that they are fulfilled, that the necessary conditions are maintained and fostered. Therefore, the individual obeys the state because it is a necessary aid to the realization of the supreme end of life, that is, self-realization.

The Hindu state is not Hegel's objective mind which comprehends all of man's capacities for feeling, willing, and knowing. It is simply an important and essential part of society and has to function as such. But there are other limitations upon the state. Not only does society transcend the state; the *brāhmaṇa* is only partially within the ambit of the state; he, too, stands somewhat above it, for the state is identified with the *kṣatriya* class.

But there was a more serious delimitation which was inherent in its very structure. The state was composed of units, viz., the villages. Now, each village (*grāma*) was an almost autonomous republic. The village was a self-sufficient, isolated economic unit, and at the same time a political unit. It not only controlled the agricultural and industrial activities of the villager; it also made arrangements for peace and order, for which it had its own police and judiciary. It looked after education, culture, entertainment, fairs, and festivals. Each village had its own deities (*grāma-devatā*). The village *pancāyat* was the instrument of village administration. When invaders came, the state toppled, but the village continued almost unconcerned. It paid to the state its share of the produce, but it scarcely minded as to who wielded the lordship or held the state scepter.

In another way the relationship of the state to the individual was circumscribed. The individual as such, as a separate atomic unit, had few dealings with the state, for he was a member of one group or the other—family, caste, guild, village—and it was through them only that the state impinged upon him.

Obviously, such a state is neither sovereign nor autocratic. The description "Oriental despotism" does not apply to it. The individual is hardly a citizen, for he is primarily a member of a hierarchy of associations, socially of a family, caste, *samāja*, politically of a village, economically of a sub-caste and a guild.

But there is one capacity of the individual which is not exhausted in these associations and institutions. The individual is the bearer of a precious principle. He is essentially a sharer in and is identical with what is timeless, extentless, uncaused. His involvement in society provides for his temporal existence in order that he may be released from the pressures of the world and find opportunity to attend to the needs of his real self.

The family, caste, village look after his creature needs and comforts, but the individual alone and by himself traverses the path which leads to true freedom. Neither the ties of the family, nor the restrictions of caste, nor the regulations of village and state can obstruct him in following this path. This flight of the alone to the alone takes place in an empyrean where there are no clouds.

The legal and political theories and institutions of the Hindus followed logically from the metaphysics which defined the concepts of man, Nature, and reality. It may be said that this metaphysics made too sharp a distinction between the two aspects of man, spiritual and temporal, and tended to attach too mean a value to the temporal, with the result that the Hindus had to pay dearly for the shortcomings of their philosophy and the defects of their institutions which embodied it. Nevertheless, it must be admitted that the truths that these theories and institutions contain have a value for humanity, and this is becoming recognized more and more by both the East and the West, as the convening of this Conference shows.

Hindu polity and its legal system failed to meet fully the challenge of history. When, in the eleventh century, the Central Asian Turks, who had received Islamic religion and culture through Iran, penetrated into India, they met with little resistance and were able to overthrow many Hindu principalities easily. By the fourteenth century, their dominion had spread over a greater part of the country as far south as the Kaveri river. But in another hundred years the impulse to conquest was exhausted, and the fifteenth century saw India divided again into numerous kingdoms, many under Muslim rulers but some still under the sway of the Hindus, particularly in the south. Then the Mughals, who were Turks by race, invaded India under the command of Babur, a descendant of the two great conquerors of Central Asia, Timur and Chengiz. His successors built up an empire whose wealth and magnificence Shakespeare and Milton extolled. Their decline in the eighteenth century opened the gates for the influx of Western adventurers—Portuguese, British, Dutch, and French.

For six hundred years, Muslims and Hindus lived together, or, rather, the Muslimized tribes from Central Asia and Afghanistan settled down in India, made it their home, and lived among the peoples whose religion and culture were indigenous. The rulers brought with them their own legal, social, and political systems. These systems bore the deep impress of Islamic canonical laws and principles evolved by the early Muslim theologians. But they retained some features of their original culture and acquired some as a result of their residence in India. The Muslim divines, however, who were the custodians of their conscience, were strict traditionalists, and they sought to approximate their practice to Islamic theory. But India was far from the centers of Islamic civilization, and the milieu in which the Indian Musalmans lived was so different from that of the Muslims of the homeland that deviations were inevitable.

The *shari'at* (law) of Islam, like the *dharma* of the Hindu, was all-embracing, seeking to regulate the life of the individual and the community in every aspect—religious, social, economic, and political. But encounter with the realities of India obliged the Muslims to effect compromises. While the majority of the *Sunnis* (sects of Muslims who constitute the majority of Muslims in India) followed one of the codes compiled by the four Imāms (religious leaders), and the *Shiahs* (a minor sect of Muslims in India) had their own jurisprudence, many converts from the Hindu fold either retained their personal laws or adapted their customary laws to the requirements of their adopted religion.

The Muslims, in turn, adopted many elements of Indian culture. Among the most important was language. While the educated among them continued to study Arabic and Persian, the spoken language of both the educated and the uneducated became the language of the region of their residence.

So far as religion was concerned, they continued to profess the dogmas and doctrines of Islam and to perform the rites and ceremonies prescribed, but the mysticism of the Hindus deeply affected their religious attitudes. Muslim *Sūfis* and Hindu *yogīs* came very near one another, with the result that many Muslims became latitudinarians. On the other hand, the Hindus developed *bhakti,* devotional movements, which bore the impress of Muslim thought and practice. Among the uneducated Muslims many followed Hindu rites and ceremonies and shared Hindu modes of worship and superstitions. The uneducated Hindus reciprocated.

In social life, the exchanges were striking. The division into hereditary castes, which was the mark of the Hindu social system, affected the Muslim society and the distinction of high (*ashrāf*) and low (*ajlāf*), and the specialization of occupations based on birth became established among them. Although the divisions among the Muslims never became as rigid as they were among the Hindus, yet, surprisingly, the Muslims recognized the four-class system of the Hindus.

But the greatest departure from the *sharī'at* appeared in the Muslim polity. From the time of the early Turkish sultans until the complete eclipse of Muslim rule in India in the nineteenth century, there was almost continuous complaint and protest by Muslim jurists against the non-conformity of the sultans and emperors with the political principles of Islamic law.[8] In the circumstances of India, it could not have been otherwise. The laws of Islam were developed in lands where the religion of the overwhelming majority of inhabitants was Islam. In India, the conditions were just the reverse, and, naturally, practice could hardly follow the law.

Now, the *sharī'at* in Islam had the same position as *dharma* in Hinduism. It provided the standards of morality and right. It was for the divinely instituted community of the Muslims the divinely given law. Although the state was expected to enforce it through the courts, the learned jurists (*'ulamā*) were its real custodians. It was their self-imposed responsibility to guide the community on all matters comprised in the *sharī'at,* both those that concerned the spiritual (*'ibādat*) duties and also those that affected social or human (*mu'āmalāt*) welfare. The supreme object of both the *sharī'at* and *dharma* was to establish conditions in which the individual could live as enjoined by God for the salvation of his soul.

As the *brāhmaṇa* scholar (*pandit*) was expected to lead a dedicated life independent of the favors of the ruler, so was it expected of the Muslim scholar that he would remain aloof from the patronage of the powerful and the wealthy. Exceptions were provided by self-seeking individuals who were ready to play to the whims and fancies of princes.

Yet, as the *sharī'at* differed from state-made law in its origin, substance, and sanctions, the rulers found it irksome, if not actually politically dangerous, to give effect to it. There was always some tension, therefore, between the wielders of temporal and spiritual authority.

But, in spite of deviations, whether dictated by political expediency or necessitated by sociological situations, that is, whether deliberate or unintended, the *sharī'at* constituted an unalterable standard to which all Muslims were expected to conform. Thus, the *sharī'at* was instrumental in holding the whole world of Islam together in loyalty to one divine law. The modern conflict in the Muslim world between the concepts of Pan-Islamic society and Muslim nationality finds its battleground in the *sharī'at*.

From the point of view of the individual, the grasp of the *sharī'at* is as close and its scope as comprehensive as that of *dharma*. No aspect of human life and no detail of conduct, however insignificant, is beyond its purview. Yet, the *sharī'at* leaves more room for the play of the individual's personality than does *dharma*. For instance, in Islamic law, the family is not so well knit, and property is not so collectivized, as in Hinduism. Again, the individual in Muslim society is master of his conduct—although only to a limited degree —and possesses a certain measure of freedom (*ikhtiyār*). He is not irrevocably bound to the wheel of *karma,* nor destined to an unlimited series of births and deaths until he has earned his release by exhausting his action through devotion or through vision of the ineffable.

Again, although Islam believes in the equality of men, commands mutual deliberation and consultation in determining the community's affairs, in actual practice, until recent times the individual was almost completely excluded from politics. Legislation, as in the Hindu system, remained altogether beyond the authority of the state and became completely stereotyped. During the early days, the principle of consensus (*ijmā'*) had allowed some scope for innovation (*ijtihād*), but since the ninth century the door has remained closed, and *taqlīd* (tradition) has so dominated the *sharī'at* as to leave no room for any departure from the rigid code. In the domain of justice, though crime was under the jurisdiction of the state, the state-appointed judicial officers functioned almost exclusively in the towns, leaving the great majority living in the villages largely to their own devices. Much of the civil adjudication was in the hands of the people themselves or with the learned jurists selected by the parties to the dispute. In this manner the state was mainly the instrument of executive authority. Notwithstanding law, the executive authority was exalted to dizzy heights, and epithets similar to those used by the Hindus were conferred upon it. The monarch was the shadow of God (*Zill-i-Allāh*).

In India, the *sharī'at,* or Islamic law, was applicable, however, to Muslims alone, with the result that non-Muslims were left to be governed by their own laws. Thus it happened that throughout the period of the rule of Muslim monarchs the Hindus continued to live under the regime of ancient Hindu law (*dharma-śāstra*) as propounded by lawgivers like Manu and interpreted by later commentators. But in different parts of India, different interpretations of the Smṛtis were accepted. These differences, however, did not radically affect the general character of the law.

In the middle ages, therefore, two legal systems existed side by side, the *sharī'at* and the *dharma-śāstra.* Both were upheld or recognized by the state. Both were equally sacred in the eyes of their respective followers. But their assimilation was rendered impossible, because they were both regarded as divine, and this fact has been responsible for the sharp division in India between the Hindu and the Muslim communities. This division retarded also the growth of national consciousness and the unity of India. For, so long as the sanctity of the two systems remained intact, even the fusion of the other elements of the two cultures—art, music, language, and litera- ture—could not bring about the merger of the two.

In spite of this legal dichotomy, however, there was a substantial unity of outlook between the two systems concerning the position of the individual. Under both cultures the individual was divested of freedom in temporal matters in order to safeguard freedom in mat- ters which were considered of supreme value, i.e., in spiritualities. So long as nothing obstructed the realization of the highest aims of life, it did not matter if the individual allowed society to direct and control his entire earthly conduct. To gain spiritual freedom, the individual could afford to sacrifice temporal freedom.

This situation was completely changed when the West, with a different philosophy of life, with different social and political norms, and a different conception of the individual, intruded upon the East and brought to bear upon its society the full weight of modern civi- lization. During the first stages of the conflict between the East and the West the verdict of history seemed to condemn the East lock, stock, and barrel. So much so that some Western observers began to hear the tocsin of its death and the rumbling of the tumbrels for the removal of its cadaver. But the doomed patient refused to oblige.

For the last two hundred years a strange drama has been played on the Indian stage. The drama is unique, and its issue is still in doubt. Two forces are contending to possess the soul of the people. Which will gain the victory? It is hard to tell. Maybe the two will be reconciled in a synthesis which transcends both.

Meanwhile, the battle is on, and the ground is strewn with *membra disjecta*—the moribund bodies of Indian polities, the wrecked organs of Indian economy, and the headless trunk of In- dian society. During the battle a fierce attack was launched upon the whole of Indian culture—its laws, its social institutions, its reli- gion and philosophy, its way of life, its art, and its literature. The Christian missionary, the British schoolmaster, and the government official joined forces to demolish the edifice of heathendom, to civi- lize the barbarian, and to raise a new structure of civilization *à la Occident*.

But, out of the general devastation and as a result of the new economy, the new administrative system, and Western education there sprang up a new social class—the middle class—which assumed the lead of Indian society. This class was composed of several groups, of which the more important were three: (1) the agrarian group consisting of big and small renters, landholders, and village moneylenders, (2) the urban business groups, which included merchants, bankers, contractors, etc., and (3) the professionals, some of whom followed independent professions such as law, medicine, teaching, engineering, etc., and others who provided personnel for governmental, semi-governmental, and private services. These groups were not rigid or self-contained; ingress into and egress from them were easy. They were eager to acquire modern education without which admission into professions was impossible.

But the middle class was not large in numbers; in fact, it was like an island in the ocean—the ocean of ancient tradition, blind conformity, custom and status, which supplied it with sustenance and the sap of life.

The middle class faced the challenge of the West. The ingredients of this challenge were a critical and rational approach to the problems of thought and life, an objective scientific attitude toward Nature and the universe, a self-authorized morality, a legal system of human origin and of earthly sanctions, and a political order deriving its authority from the will of the people, a society bound together with ties of secular interests—above all, an individual who is free to think, to act, and to associate, who owns attachment to his territorial group and loyalty to his territorial state, and who identifies his supreme end with the rational good and disregards the good which transcends reason.

The operative conditions in which the middle class lived and the ideas which it imbibed from Western education and from direct contact with Western people and their culture inevitably affected its intellectual make-up, attitude of mind, and system of values.

The British-devised legal and political set-up fostered and stabilized these changes. Under this system, the status of the individual has been transformed. In the first place, property has become individualized. In pre-British days, no one possessed absolute and exclusive rights in land. The peasant had a hereditary right to cultivate, but he shared the produce with some middleman—landholder—and the state, and his rights of alienation by sale, mortgage, or gift were strictly limited. The landholder was similarly bound. He could not evict the tenant so long as he did not default in payment. He was only a mediatory between the cultivator and the state, which could deprive him of his share and transfer it to others. But the state, too, was not the owner.

The British abolished the old system and created three classes of owners of land: (1) in Bengal and some other territories, landlords who possessed absolute rights, (2) in Bombay and Madras, peasants who cultivated the land, and (3) in the Panjab village, joint-holders who were made responsible for collection and payment of government revenue. This was a vast and far-reaching revolution. Land became a marketable commodity and the landowner the holder of a commodity which he could sell. Property had acquired movement, and the village community as a collective unit was broken up.

Under British rule, an entirely new economy had thus come to be established. The old Indian economy dominated by a self-subsistent agrarian system was replaced by an economy in which production was geared to foreign demand, to the world market, in which barter was giving way to exchange through the medium of money; and in which the dominance of agriculture was modified by the growth of trade. Population was multiplying; urbanization was increasing. Communal property in land had become individual property. Thus, the sea of humanity became agitated by the fresh winds that blew.

The new administrative order reinforced the economic change. The system of direct taxation, the introduction of election and representative institutions—municipal and district boards, legislative councils, etc.—the establishment of direct relationships between the government and the individual and the disregard of all intermediary groups such as the *pañcāyats*, the recognition of individual rights and obligations, converted society from a community of communities to an amorphic congeries of isolated and atomic individuals. Status gave place to contract. Natural and traditional fellowship yielded to artificial law-based partnerships and associations.

The family system began to disintegrate under the new laws of marriage and inheritance. In 1856, the Hindu Widows Remarriage Act legalized the marriage of Hindu widows. In 1872, the Special Marriage Act with its amendment of 1923, permitted the solemnization of purely civil marriages without the accompaniment of religious rites. In 1954, the Special Marriages Act provided a special form of civil marriage and gave recognition to marriages of persons belonging to different faiths. The Hindu Marriage Act XXV, passed in 1955, insists upon monogamous marriages, lays down the minimum ages for the bride and bridegroom, and provides for the dissolution of marriages.

The Act has effected fundamental changes in the sacramental laws of the Hindus. "The religious character of the institution has been blurred in the modern notions of matrimony based upon the Western culture and social outlook."[9] It has also done away with all the restrictions against intercaste and intercommunal marriages and has abolished once and for all the polygamous connections sanctioned by the Śāstras.

The Hindu Marriages Disabilities Removal Act of 1946 made marriages between subdivisions of a caste valid, and the Acts of 1954 and 1955 opened the door for intercaste and interreligious marriages.

The Indian Succession Act of 1865,[10] as amended by the Act of

1925, the Hindu Inheritance (Removal of Disabilities) Act of 1928, and the Hindu Succession Act of 1956 have made deep inroads into the ancient Śāstric laws and the old ideas relating to family relations and women's status in society.

The first official attack on the caste system was made in 1850, when the Caste Disabilities Removal Act secured to the convert the right of inheritance on change of religion, setting aside the provision of Hindu law which penalized the renunciation of religion or exclusion from caste.

Marriages between castes, prohibited by Hindu lawgivers, had been held legally valid by the Bombay High Court, even before the Acts of 1954 and 1955.[11] Thus, the rigors of caste in the vital matter of matrimony were mitigated.

The Constitution of India has struck further blows. It declares, in Section 17, that untouchability is abolished, and its practice in any form is forbidden. The enforcement of any disability arising out of untouchability is an offense punishable in accordance with law. Section 19 of the Constitution gives to everyone the right to practice any profession, or to carry on any occupation, trade, or business, and Section 16 guarantees equality of opportunity for all citizens in matters relating to employment or appointment to any office under the state, and abolishes all discrimination based on religion, race, or caste in the matter of state employment.

All these new laws and constitutional provisions have had the effect of legally dissolving all caste barriers which had divided individual from individual and group from group. The trends of social evolution under a modern system of government have been wholly contrary to the traditional order. A new social system is gradually supplanting the old, and a new individual is emerging in succession to the traditional one. In the new world he finds his temporal and natural potentialities released from old bonds, and material and worldly interests besiege his mind to the progressive exclusion of traditional interests which appear remote, unreal, and mystical.

The direct, intuitive vision of reality which gave him certainty, stability, and finality is receding and becoming dim, and the second-hand, indirect knowledge based upon senses and subject to change both in its formal and empirical content is invading and possessing his intellect.

The Indian seems embarked upon fulfilling Macaulay's prophetic description made over a century and a quarter ago. He foresaw "a class of persons Indian in blood and color, but English in tastes, in opinions, in morals and in intellect"[12] replace the generation living in his times.

But this surely cannot be. The past will not be wiped out so easily. The values cherished in India through the ages are too precious to be denied, especially now that the world—even the Western world —is beginning to recognize their relevance to man's life and destiny. Carlyle, a hundred years ago, drew attention to these values. He wrote, "This earthly life and its riches and possessions, and good and evil hap, are not intrinsically a reality at all, but are a shadow of realities eternal, infinite; that this Time world as an image, fearfully emblematic, plays and flickers in the ground still mirror of Eternity; and man's little life has Duties that are great, that are alone great, and go up to Heaven and down to Hell."[13]

Jacques Maritain says: "We know well enough how emphatic the East is about its calling to the contemplative life and how proud of it; while the West with no less pride—a pride which is beginning to suffer much—boasts that it has chosen action . . . we see . . . that activism and pragmatism, the rejection of contemplative values, the dethronement of Wisdom, are the West's greatest woe. It seems as if to-day the West sought a remedy in the frantic exaggeration of this evil. . . . The West has here much to learn from the East and from its fidelity to the primacy of contemplative values."[14]

Northrop writes, ". . . for the first time in history, not merely in war but also in the issues of peace, the East and the West are in a single world movement, as much Oriental as Occidental in character. The East and West are meeting and merging. The epoch which Kipling so aptly described but about which he so falsely prophesied is over. The time is here when we must understand the Orient if we would understand ourselves and when we must learn how to combine Oriental and Occidental values if further tragedy, bitterness, and bloodshed are not to ensue."[15]

How is India responding to this need of East-West understanding? It is doing so, through the concepts of the new individual and the new society. They are taking concrete shape in India's new institutions, laws, and politics. The new individual has taken to his bosom the freedoms of the West. He has discovered through experience that an exclusive devotion to the transcendant values of the self and relative evasion of the claims of the other is a boomerang which jeopardizes the realization of both. The two builders of this New India joined together to raise the edifice of the new society, in which the elements of the two cultures are mingled. Gandhi told the individual to discipline himself through the exercise of the old five yogic virtues—non-violence (*ahiṁsā*), truth (*satya*), honesty (*asteya*), abstinence (*brahmacarya*), and non-covetousness (*apari-graha*). He prescribed for him, for the disciplined individual, the aim of life to be the service of mankind, or, more concretely, of God, who lives among the poor and humble (*Daridra Nārāyaṇa*). Thus, ancient discipline finds fulfillment in modern aims.

Nehru, the radical rationalist who had discarded much of past dogma and tradition, declares, "I do not wish to cut myself off from the past completely. I am proud of that great inheritance that has been, and is, ours, and I am conscious that I too, like all of us, am a link in that unbroken chain which goes back to the dawn of history in the immemorial past of India. That chain I would not break, for I treasure it and seek inspiration from it."[16]

Nehru gave form to the Gandhian ideal and worked for the establishment of a society free from want, hunger, disease, and ignorance, a society based on equality and liberty, a society which offers security for the needs of the body, but a society which provides at the same time opportunities for the realization of the highest capacity of the individual. Thus, Indian laws and Indian institutions, in Independent India, are seeking to translate the dream of Gandhi and Nehru into the life and conduct of New India, and in them the old teaching of the *Bhagavad-gītā* comes to life again: "But a man of disciplined mind, who moves among the objects of sense, with the senses under control and free from attachment and aversion, attains purity of spirit. And in the purity of spirit, there is produced for him an end of all sorrows; the intelligence of such a man of pure spirit is soon established in the peace of the self."[17]

[1] Kālidāsa, *Raghuvaṃśa*, Canto I.

[2] *Mahābhārata*, Śānti-parva, 167, 8–9.

[3] P. V. Kane, *History of Dharmaśāstra*, 4 vols. (Poona: Bhandarkar Oriental Research Institute, 1930), Vol. III, chap. XXVIII. N. R. Raghavachariar, *Hindu Law: Precedents and Principles* (Madras: Law Journal Office, 1960), chap. VIII; Sir Henry Mayne, *Treatise on Hindu Law and Usage*, N. C. Aiyar, ed. (11th ed., Madras: Higgenbotham's Ltd., 1953), chap. VIII.

[4] Vide Aristotle's *Politics*, Book I.

[5] *History and Culture of the Indian People*, R. C. Majumdar, ed. (Bombay: Bharatiya Vidya Bhava, 1953), Vol. II, p. 305.

[6] Kālidāsa, *op. cit.*, Canto I, verse 18.

[7] R. C. Majumdar, ed., *op. cit.*, Vol. II, p. 305.

[8] For earlier differences between the Caliphs and the jurists see the lives of Abu Hanifa and Ibn i Hanbal.

[9] Raghavachariar, *op. cit.*, pp. 878 ff.

[10] Mayne, *op. cit.*, p. 73.

[11] Bai Julab v. Jivanlal (1922). 46 Bombay, 871, Natha V. Mehta Chhotal (1931) 55 Bombay 1. Mayne, *op. cit.*, p. 163. See D. F. Mulla, *Principles of Hindu Law* (12th ed., Bombay: N. M. Tripathi, Private Ltd., 1959), p. 610, notes b, c.

[12] T. B. MaCaulay, *Minute on Education*, February 2, 1835.

[13] Thomas Carlyle, *Sartor Resartos*.

[14] Jacques Maritain, *Scholasticism and Politics*, translation edited by Mortimer Adler (New York: The Macmillan Company, 1941), pp. 170, 190.

[15] F. S. C. Northrop, *The Meeting of East and West* (New York: The Macmillan Company, 1947), p. 4.

[16] Extracts from the Will and Testament of Jawaharlal Nehru.

[17] *Bhagavad-gītā*, II. 64, 65.

KAWASHIMA TAKEYOSHI[a]

The status of the individual in the notion of law, right, and social order in Japan

I. INTRODUCTION

At a previous meeting of this Conference, Professor F. S. C. Northrop pointed in his paper to a very important correlation between non-normative assumptions, or epistemology, and legal and ethical theory, and in connection with this he emphasized the contrast between the epistemology of naïve realism and that of logical realism. The former accepts images of men and society, with their immense variety of attributes, as they are perceived by the senses naïvely and with radical empirical immediacy. The latter construes the images of men and society through abstractions with concepts by postulation. Each of these assumptions finds its respective counterparts in legal and ethical philosophy.[1]

When we look at the traditional notions of the Japanese people about Nature as well as society, what impresses us most in contrast with the prevailing view of contemporary Western society is the fact that, in the traditional culture of the Japanese, Nature and society are accepted as they appear to the senses in their empirical immediacy. The indeterminateness of Nature and society with immense variety and subtle nuances is therefore their everlasting attribute, and, hence, it is to be valued because it is in its very nature unlimited and contains infinite possibilities for development and expansion.[1a]

The basic assumption of empirical immediacy and the evaluation based on it permeate traditional Japanese culture. Probably this is evidenced by the peculiar nature of the Japanese language habit, since language is a vehicle for conveying ideas. The language habit of the Japanese people is not suitable for detailed and determinate expression or communication, for, as the novelist Tanizaki Junichirō[b] pointed out, the *Tale of Genji* (*Genji monogatari*[c]) had to be translated into English with longer sentences containing numerous detailed expressions so as to make it understandable to Western readers. He says:

> In the English manner of writing, the meaning becomes clear, but at the same time it becomes limited and shallow. . . . We do not

make such useless effort, but use those words which allow sufficient leeway to suggest various things, and supplement the rest [that which is not expressed with words] with sensible elements such as tones, appearance of letters, rhythms, etc., . . . of the sentence . . . [whereas] the sentence of the Westerners tries to restrict its meaning as narrowly and detailedly as possible and does not allow the smallest shadow, so that there is no room at all for the imagination of the reader.[2]

Viewed from this cognitive and evaluative perspective of naïve realism, men and society appear with immense variety in their subtle nuances and do not fit the abstractions with concepts by postulation. Each individual appears as a discrete entity with its own status and value. There is in this viewpoint no room for the existence of the image of an individual who is "equal" to every other on the ground that he is "independent" of every other. In a society with such assumptions, law and ethics aim at maintaining the social order consisting in the statuses of men with immense variety as they actually exist and not at imposing a social order which is postulated by intellect or ideal. The basic philosophy of law commonly held by the Japanese is in this respect in striking contrast with that of Western society at large.[3]

II. ON THE LEVEL OF SOCIAL LIFE

The Japanese traditionally expect that in principle social obligations will be fulfilled by a voluntary act on the part of the person under obligation, usually with particular friendliness or benevolence. They consider it improper for the other party[4] (beneficiary) of an obligation to demand or claim that the obligated person fulfill his obligation. An obligation is considered valueless, if, although it is fulfilled by the obligated person, he does not fulfill it in addition with a special friendliness or favor toward the other party. In other words, the actual value of social obligations depends upon the good will and favor of the obligated person, and there is no place for the existence of the notion of "right";[5] in the Japanese vocabulary there was no equivalent word for "right" or "*Recht,*" "*droit,*" and so on in Western languages,[6] until the Dutch word "*Regt*" was translated into Japanese as "*kenri*[d]." Social obligations in the traditional culture are, in their very nature, indeterminate. "When a Japanese makes a promise with another, not the promise as such, but the kindness and friendship with which the promise is made is crucial for him, and, as long as he holds such *magokoro*[e] (an ambiguous term meaning something like true-heartedness), it is all right even if he does not fulfill the promise exactly as the verbal expressions of the promise require."[7]

The indeterminateness of social obligations is idealized in the concept of *"wa^f"* (harmony, concord). The classical statement of this notion is the well-known, frequently quoted, phrase of Article I of the "Seventeen-Article Constitution^g" of Prince Shōtoku^h: *"Wa* is to be esteemed."[8] But with particular reference to law and the status of individuals, as well as in contrast with law and social order in Western society, the following statements are to be noted.

> In individualism there can exist co-operation, compromise, self-sacrifice, and so on, in order to adjust and reduce contradictions and oppositions, but in the final analysis there exists no real harmony *(wa)*. . . . The *wa* of our country is not mechanical co-operation, starting from reason, of *equal individuals independent* of each other, but the grand harmony *(taiwa^i)* which maintains its integrity by proper statuses of individuals within the collectivity and by acts in accordance with these statuses. . . . After all, oppositions of opinions, as well as differences of interests deriving from [various] standpoints, are integrated into a unity of grand harmony proper to Japan and originating from a common source. Not conflicts, but harmony is final.[9]

"Harmony consists in *not making distinctions;* if a distinction between good and bad can be made, then there *wa* (harmony) does not exist."[10]

In a concept of social obligation which does not have the counterbalancing notion of "right," the interest of the individual is not made distinct and fixed. Here, an individual is *not considered to be an independent entity*. Rather, his interest is *absorbed in the interest of the collectivity* to which he belongs, and the interest of the collectivity is recognized as having primary importance, while the interest of the individual has merely a secondary importance.

Under this notion of the individual, there has been no place for the concept of "human rights." This does not mean, however, that a sense of respect for the honor, life, and feelings of other persons did not exist in traditional Japan. Buddhism taught the virtue of *"jihi^j"* (mercy),[11] and Confucianism taught the virtue of *jin^k* (Chinese *jen*; human-heartedness).[12] The doctrine of "the spirit of *wa,"* which has been taught as the traditional spirit of Japan, also contains some notion of human love. But what makes these notions differ from the idea of "human rights" in Western society is that the essential element of the concept of "human right" is the emphasis on the notion of "right" in the sense that every individual is endowed as a human being *per se* with human "rights" by which he can *demand* that other people, particularly his own government, respect, or refrain from infringement upon, the interests which are vital for his existence as a human being. This very nature of a human right never occurred in the traditional culture of the Japanese until the early years of the Meiji period^l (1868–1912). (See below.)

Nevertheless, the above should not be construed as contending that there has never been a notion of "right" in Japan. With respect to some kinds of interests (e.g., land, forests, personal effects, etc.), the Japanese have for centuries had a notion of "entitledness."[13] What is to be emphasized, however, is that there has been *no clear and definite notion of "right"* to the effect that the person who has the right is entitled to demand other persons to act in conformity with his interest invested in "right." Expressions such as "a right which is not a right,"[14] which looks like a verbal absurdity, actually convey the idea of what the traditional Japanese has conceived to be his entitled interest.

The fact that the traditional notion of social obligation has not had, in principle, the notion of "right" as its counterpart means that in the traditional culture of Japan a law, in the sense of the *Recht* or *droit,* etc., of the continental European countries, was not differentiated from morality,[15] whereas the differentiation of law from morality has been characteristic of the culture of Western society since Roman law. Related to this may also be the fact that the history of Japan lacks an equivalent for the notion of the "law of Nature" or "philosophical law," which has been recognized as an independent system of its own, which provided determinate positive standards for criticizing a positive legal law, and in which the belief that people had the right to criticize the positive law was incorporated.[16]

Moreover, illustrative of these beliefs and this value of social obligations and rights are the following facts:

In the world of business, people in Japan traditionally avoid defining the contractual obligations and rights in the process of negotiations prior to the conclusion of a contract. Even to think of a possible dispute in the future between contractual parties, not to mention actual negotiations on the terms for eventual resolution of disputes, would indicate a mistrust of the other party to the contract and would damage the relationship of *wa,* the most valid reason, in the minds of the contractual parties, for compliance with the obligations assumed under the contract. Therefore, contracts were rarely documentated.[17] Whenever a dispute arises out of a contract, both parties expect to reach an *ad hoc* agreement through negotiations to settle the dispute, because the parties combined in the contract are not merely "persons who pass one another by on the street,"[18] but are instances of the proverb: "When people touch each other at the sleeves, it is by the '*en*[m]' (tie) in their past lives."[19] Contractual parties are supposed to participate in the relationship of *wa* as expounded by Prince Shōtoku in his "Seventeen-Article Constitution" about 1360 years ago,[20] so that the only, if any, contract clause foreseeing the possibility of future disputes may reasonably be that which provides that they have to negotiate in case of a dispute.[21] Western people would surely feel insecure with such a contract clause, but the

Japanese feel insecure with any contractual clause which provides for contractual obligations in specific and determinate terms, because under such a clause there is no place at all for them to make adjustments for the specific contingencies which may arise in the case.[22]

The concept of social obligations in traditional Japanese culture, as described above, has been closely related with patterns of the social life out of which social obligations arose. In the past, social obligations arose in most cases out of close, face-to-face social relationships of a high degree of particularism and more or less long duration,[23] such as the family, kinship groups, landlord and tenant relationships, employer and employee relationships (particularly domestic servants, master-apprentice, etc.).[24] Even employee-employer relationships in modern business firms or factories[25] and merchant-customer relationships were in principle of the same nature in the past.[26] The social tie in these relationships was considered, so to speak, to be predestined by the *"en"* in the past lives of the individuals concerned. The term *"giri"* indicates obligations arising out of these relationships.[27]

In social obligations of this sort there has been no place for a settlement based upon a judgment determined by fixed, objective standards, namely, the administration of justice.[28] In other words, social obligations of this sort do not fit the lawsuit, which will inevitably bring about a breach of the close personal relationships based on the spirit of *wa*. "With the Code of Civil Procedure," once argued a member of the House of Representatives in the Diet, "the bureaucrats of the Meiji government destroyed the peaceful society of Japan."[29]

III. ON THE LEVEL OF LAW

In Western society, it is taken for granted that in principle there exist tensions between legal rules and the social world, and that the latter is evaluated and controlled by the former.[30] The most striking, or exaggerated, expression of this idea is *"Fiat iustitia pereat mundus."* Japan, however, does not have the idea of this determinate dualism. What has existed in Japan is not a tension between these two antitheses, but a continuum from one to the other, or, rather, a compromise between these two antitheses. As Northrop points out, what the people of the West approve as "sticking up for one's rights" would be regarded in Japan as "trouble making," and lawsuits which the people of the West would approve as "law enforcement" would be viewed by the Japanese as unjustified resort to political power, which would not help to settle disputes.[31]

In Western society, particularly in America, it is expected that statutes, once promulgated, will function like a machine. A typical example of this idea was the Volstead Act (the Prohibition Amendment) of 1919 in the United States, which, from the Japanese point of view, seemed to be an extremely unrealistic legislative attempt in view of the strong and widespread alcoholic habits of the nation, but the U.S. Government persistently made an effort to enforce the law in spite of the hopelessness of the actual effectiveness of the law.[32]

In Japan, however, a statute is considered, according to the prevailing view, to be nothing but a *"denka no hōtō°"* (a sword handed down from ancestors as a family treasure), which means that it is not for actual use, but for symbolic manifestation of the prestige of the family. In fact, the government has usually been reserved in enforcing statutes: (The first case of prosecution in compliance with the Prostitution Surveillance Law [Law no. 118 of 1956] was in 1958.[33]) Even during the *"Totalkrieg"* of World War II the enforcement of the Food Control Law (Law no. 40 of 1942), which prohibited the sale of staple food outside of the legally sanctioned channels, was fairly liberal. The enforcement of the Road Traffic Law (Law no. 105 of 1960; prior to this Law, Road Traffic Surveillance Law no. 130 of 1933), which has no actual effect unless it is enforced like a machine, has been almost as liberal as the enforcement of the Food Control Law; from time to time, a "Traffic Safety Week" was declared by the police, during which violations of traffic regulations were watched strictly, but the rest of the time violations were only occasionally noticed and prosecuted. Apparently the police have hesitated to enforce the Traffic Regulation Law in a machine-like manner.

The lack of the concept of "right" was particularly evident on the level of court practices with respect to infringement by the government upon the interests of private persons or their associations. When the translation of the French civil code, in which the expression *"droit civil"* was translated into Japanese for the first time as *"minken^p"* (right of a subject or citizen), was under debate in a conference of the Ministry of Justice in 1870, some of the members of the conference were not familiar with the concept that citizens have any rights whatsoever, and raised the question: "What on earth does it mean to say that a citizen has a right?"[34] This point is expressed in exaggerated form in *Kokutai no hongi^r* (Grand Principles of National Polity) as an authoritative statement by the government:

> "To conceive of relationships of dominance and obedience as rights and duties is a rationalistic view which, based on an individualistic viewpoint, considers everything to be relationships between equal persons. Our relationship between the emperor and his subjects is not a shallow flat one at all in which the emperor and his subjects confront each other, but a relationship of identification through self-denial which, starting from this very base

(*konpon*[r]), never loses this base (*konpon*). It can never be apprehended by the individualistic way of thinking."[35]

Until the new constitution became effective in 1947, it had been taken for granted that the government by its very nature transcended the law insofar as the exercise of administrative powers was concerned, and that neither the government nor its functionary was responsible for any act of the functionary performed in the capacity of an administrator, regardless of whether the functionary did it intentionally or by negligence.[36]

This basic attitude to law is illustrated by various actual practices of the administration of justice.

First, the Penal Code allows the court wide discretionary powers in meting out punishment in specific cases. The most striking example is article 199, which provides for capital punishment, life imprisonment, or imprisonment for over three years for all kinds of murder without making a distinction between first-degree murder and any other kind of murder or assault (i.e., indeterminateness with respect to both the definition of crime and the nature of its punishment). The court can reduce the period of imprisonment or the amount of fine up to half of the legal minimum, in case it recognizes the existence of mitigating circumstances, without making a distinction in the nature of the crimes. Furthermore, the court is allowed such a wide discretion in suspending executions of the punishment that ultimately the effect is to cancel the sentence itself (article 25, Penal Code). Therefore, in case the court recognizes the existence of mitigating circumstances, it is legally possible for the court to render a sentence with suspended execution even for cases of first-degree murder.

The important point, however, is not that there are such provisions, but that the enactment of these provisions was possible from the first with no opposition worth mentioning. On the contrary, the legislation of a law which introduced the institution of suspended execution as early as in 1905 and the amendment of the Penal Code for liberalizing the punishment of murder in 1947 were both welcomed by legal specialists.[37]

Second, court practices in criminal cases are apparently illustrative of the Japanese high regard for the indeterminate, as is also found in the expressions of the provisions of the Penal Code. The wide discretionary power which is allowed the court is actually exercised to a high degree, and the actual sentenced punishments are frequently very light. Particularly, sentences with suspended execution are quite frequent. (See Table 1.)

Those who cause the death of, or bodily injury to, other persons in automobile accidents, e.g., are rarely prosecuted for murder but almost always for negligent bodily injury or negligent homicide, and

TABLE 1

Crime	1951			1952			1953			1954			1955		
	A	B	%	A	B	%	A	B	%	A	B	%	A	B	%
a	917	617	67.3	773	452	58.5	729	432	59.3	643	405	63.0	648	405	62.5
b	1,327	903	68.0	1,197	1,507	42.4	1,155	389	33.7	1,277	462	36.2	842	350	41.6
c	1,157	427	36.9	958	351	36.6	1,011	385	38.0	1,160	390	33.6	1,403	459	32.7
d	27,774	2,211	8.0	32,775	2,071	6.3	38,419	2,103	5.5	44,092	2,432	5.5	55,227	2,791	5.0
e	6,651	234	3.5	9,588	266	2.8	15,795	308	1.9	22,373	366	1.6	30,077	507	1.7
f	61,859	24,754	40.0	56,726	22,263	39.2	47,415	17,860	36.7	46,173	18,576	40.2	52,692	21,301	40.4
g	3,525	698	19.8	2,615	438	16.7	2,144	345	16.1	2,032	353	17.4	2,546	383	15.0
h	11,595	5,318	45.9	11,530	4,670	40.5	11,272	4,566	40.5	11,249	4,750	42.2	11,764	5,017	42.6
i	2,724	1,362	50.0	2,699	1,129	41.8	2,428	994	40.9	2,846	1,249	43.9	3,505	1,573	44.9
j	7,150	4,328	59.3	6,743	4,005	59.4	6,633	3,492	52.6	5,829	3,291	56.5	5,355	3,130	58.5
k	6,001	4,177	69.6	5,770	3,647	63.2	4,631	3,030	65.4	3,383	2,212	65.4	3,632	2,343	64.5

Crime	1956			1957			1958			1959			1960		
	A	B	%	A	B	%	A	B	%	A	B	%	A	B	%
a	808	485	60.0	801	504	62.9	717	461	64.3	702	465	66.2	762	516	67.7
b	921	441	47.9	835	354	42.4	659	307	46.6	740	366	49.5	802	353	44.0
c	1,295	449	34.7	1,261	410	32.5	1,474	462	31.3	1,581	447	28.3	1,404	426	30.3
d	62,885	2,972	4.7	68,025	3,031	4.5	71,825	3,298	4.6	71,441	3,355	4.7	69,628	3,613	5.2
e	41,527	630	1.5	51,468	761	1.5	59,031	866	1.5	73,343	1,027	1.4	84,771	1,482	1.7
f	55,126	24,080	43.7	51,474	22,872	44.4	45,896	19,422	42.3	43,987	18,902	43.0	40,350	17,949	44.5
g	2,473	378	15.3	2,208	347	15.7	2,486	380	15.3	2,330	305	13.1	1,901	327	17.2
h	10,532	4,726	44.9	9,753	4,339	44.5	8,867	4,357	44.2	9,227	3,957	42.9	8,467	3,806	45.0
i	4,096	1,925	47.0	4,097	2,060	50.3	4,966	2,520	50.7	5,420	2,759	50.9	5,407	2,777	51.4
j	4,908	2,954	60.2	4,424	2,739	61.9	3,864	2,287	59.2	3,694	2,100	56.8	3,590	2,098	58.4
k	4,078	2,797	68.6	3,643	2,534	70.0	2,987	1,848	61.9	2,962	1,899	64.1	3,203	2,135	66.7

a = documentary forgery
b = official corruption
c = homicide
d = bodily injury
e = bodily injury through negligence
f = larceny
g = robbery
h = fraud
i = extortion
j = embezzlement
k = crime regarding stolen property

A = number of persons sentenced guilty
B = number of persons sentenced guilty without suspended execution
% = 100B/A

From Saikō Saibansho Jimusōkyoku cr (General Secretariat, Supreme Court): Shihō tōkei nenpō cs (Annual Rept., Judicial Statistics), 1951–1960.

prosecutions on the ground of *dolus eventualis* are extremely rare, though it is admitted in theory. Most of the cases of bodily injury caused by intoxicated drivers are prosecuted as crimes of negligence, and the punishment provided in the Penal Code for negligent bodily injury is a fine under 1,000 *yen* (approximately three dollars), and for negligent homicide imprisonment from two up to fifteen years (articles 210 and 205, Penal Code), and consequently the sentences of the courts result in relatively light sentences.[38,39]

Third, in civil affairs, the parties in dispute are reluctant to sue in the court, and not simply because lawsuits are expensive and time-consuming.[40] They expect, and are ready, to settle disputes by compromise (either judicial or extra-judicial),[41] and the courts also usually try to effect a compromise.[42] In Western society, people also seem to be inclined to avoid lawsuits if possible and tend to prefer compromise ("A lean compromise is better than a fat lawsuit"). But, when we look at the percentage of compromises in civil cases in Japan, we have to take into consideration the fact that people usually try to reach a compromise by any means, and that they sue in court only in case they feel a solution by compromise is hopeless and only if they do not care if their opponents become bitter enemies.

It is probable that every society generally endeavors to make the meaning of its statutes clear and determinate in order that the latitude of the court to interpret the meaning of the statutes be limited. In Japan, however, the indeterminateness of the meaning of the statutes is taken for granted, and so scope for widening or narrowing the meaning of the statutes has been almost limitless. In Japan, it has been extremely rare for a court to explain the reason for a decision on grounds which cannot be derived by interpretation of the statutes. In connection with this, it is to be noted that the movement for "free interpretation of statutes" (*Freirechtsbewegung*) in Germany after World War I was readily accepted by Japanese jurists.

IV. HISTORICAL CHANGE

The above description of the characteristics of the Japanes notion of social obligation and right should not be taken as meaning that these characteristics are, so to speak, inborn or racially predestined in the Japanese.[43] By the late nineteenth century there had emerged some changes in attitudes in the direction of some patterns of Western thought. The French ideology of "human rights" based on the Law of Nature was introduced by philosophers and political scientists and readily accepted by political leaders of the strong nation-wide political movement for democracy (Jiyū Minken Undō[t], Movement for Freedom and People's Rights).[44]

Though the government almost succeeded in oppressing this movement by about 1890, a new wave for democracy and human rights emerged toward the end of World War I, when the traditional social system became disorganized to some extent as a result of the industrialization brought about by the war. Labor unions, farm-tenants' associations, house-tenants' associations, land-lessees' associations, etc., were organized against the oppression by the government and claimed the recognition and confirmation of their "rights" on the level of actual interpersonal relationships, as well as on the level of law, particularly statutes.[45] Facing this situation, the government tried to suppress this historical change by reorganizing and intensifying the education of the ideology of filial "piety" in primary and secondary schools, as well as by introducing the procedure of *chōtei*[u] (mediation) by legislation for disputes of farm tenancy, house tenancy, land tenancy, and labor, by which the claim on "rights" was expected to be absorbed into the "harmonious" relationship reorganized through the compromise reached by mediation on the principle of indeterminate social obligations.[46] In the period of more extensive disorganization of the traditional social system as a result of the industrialization after the Manchurian Incident, the government moved further in intensifying the inculcation of the ideology of filial "piety," and denounced self-assertion and individualism by issuing official textbooks on authorized totalitarian ideology, such as *Kokutai no hongi* (Grand Principles of National Polity), *Shinmin no michi*[v] (The Way of Subjects), and *Senji katei kyōiku shidō yōryō*[w] (Basic Principles of Wartime Home Education).[47] The spirit of *wa* was proclaimed as a supreme value,[48] and the argument (*kotoage*[x]) for private interest was condemned as a vice.[49]

Nevertheless, these attempts did not succeed in suppressing the growth of the notion of "right." This is evidenced by the fact that the notion of "human rights" was accepted universally when the political power which had suppressed its growth collapsed with the defeat in 1945.[50]

The notion of "right" developed also with respect to relationships between private persons. A very interesting study on this point was made by Professor Sasaki Yoshio[y],[51] who made a survey of the attitudes of rural and urban areas toward lawsuit and mediation. Its result shows that, of the total samples, 25 per cent (urban) were reluctant to resort to court on the grounds that "to make a distinction between black and white with respect to a dispute is not proper" or "both parties of a dispute have their reasons," and that a large portion of the samples were ready to resort to court only if a lawsuit would have been less expensive and time-consuming than they were.[52]

The change in this respect is illustrated more evidently in the official statistics of the Supreme Court: filings of mediation cases have decreased, whereas those of lawsuits have increased in recent years. (See Table 2.)

TABLE 2

Year	A	B
1948	54.2	45.8
1949	61.5	38.5
1950	70.5	29.5
1951	71.6	28.4
1952	73.4	26.6
1953	74.9	25.1
1954	78.5	21.5
1955	79.2	20.8
1956	79.6	20.4
1957	80.7	19.3
1958	81.8	18.1
1959	82.9	17.1
1960	83.1	16.9
1961	83.9	16.1
1962	84.4	15.6

A = Filings of lawsuits and other court cases
B = Filings of mediation cases
The above figures show the percentage of filings of respective categories within the year.
From Hōsō jihō[ct] (Lawyers Association Journal), 15, No. 12, 1963, 60.

Another indication of this change will be found in the revision, 1962, of Standard Stipulated Terms for Contracts for Work in Construction Projects, which was effected by the proposal of the representatives of the construction industry, whereas in former years amendments in the same direction had been rejected by the representatives of the construction industry itself. The Central Construction Industry Council of the Ministry of Construction passed a resolution to change the clause which had provided that the amount of the damage or change of the remuneration be contingent upon conferral between the parties into a more determinate clause according to which the right for change of the remuneration and the right for damages be recognized *ipso iure* (without conferral between the parties) under specific circumstances provided in the clause and the amount of damages be fixed by specific standards in the clause.[53]

Furthermore, indicative of this change is the frequency of reports of judicial cases in an ordinary newspaper and the degree of interest the editor feels in reporting judicial cases (as the index of which I use the size of headlines), which, I presume, will indicate the extent to which society at large is interested in judicial decisions. In the period 1962–1963, the frequency of news reports on judicial cases was 59 and 61, respectively, whereas the frequency in 1930 was 29, and in 1935 was 43. The average size of headlines and standard deviation of news reports on judicial cases was 3.34 ± 4.11 in 1962, and 3.44 ± 5.66 in 1963, whereas it was 2.37 ± 1.56 in 1930, and 1.98 ± 2.41 in 1935.[54]

In view of these changes, it is clear that the Japanese attitude toward law, right, and social order will continue to undergo changes in the direction of the patterns of Western society, and probably other nations of Asia also will not be able to avoid changes in more or less the same direction, though probably to a different degree from Western societies, when the traditional social structure becomes disorganized as the process of industrialization proceeds.

V. CONCLUSION

In traditional Japanese culture, the individual is conceived as an existence which appears to the senses in its empirical immediacy —hence with an immense variety of attributes and subtle nuances. Consequently, there is no place for the concept of the individual as an independent entity equal to other individuals. In such a culture, the social order consists of social obligations, which are defined, not in specific, determinate terms, but in diffuse, indeterminate terms, and the indeterminateness of social obligations of this nature contains the possibility of flexible adjustment to contingent circumstances. The indeterminateness of social obligations—hence the lack of concepts of equality and independence of individuals—does not allow the existence of the concept of "right" as the counterpart of social obligations.

In view of such an image of the individual, there is lacking the antithesis between the actual social world and legal rules which is characteristic of Western society. Given such an image, law is not expected to function with the precision of a machine. A lawsuit, which in its nature makes distinctions between right and wrong, is, in contradiction to the social order, based on diffusely defined indeterminate social obligations; hence, it is undesirable; and mediation is the means which fits the indeterminate social order.

Japanese society, however, continues to move in the direction of Western society with respect to these notions, presumably as a result of industrialization and disintegration of traditional social structure. This would lead to the assumption that other nations of Asia also will not be able to avoid the same or similar changes of thought, once they expose themselves to the influence of industrialization.

Furthermore, the case of Japan suggests that the image of the individual which a society holds is the key with which it is possible to understand the basic characteristics of legal thought and the structure of the law of the society.

QUESTION: You have associated the emergence of the individual in Japan with the loss of community, citing industrialization as the cause. I feel a kind of anguish about this, because I would judge that you have had community in a more significant sense than we in the West in recent years, but you are losing it, as we have lost it. If one can achieve the individual only by losing the community, that is a very high price to pay. Furthermore, there is a kind of dialectic in this, for, having lost significant community, you will lose the individual, too; there will be a loss of depth in the kind of individual then possible.

Earlier in the discussion, you cited some new types of community relationship appearing in Japan. I recognize all of these types, because we have them in America. The meeting of the housewives; this is the morning coffee hour, the *kaffeeklatsch*. They meet in one or another of their almost identical houses to discuss one or another of their almost identical problems. And business men have weekly meetings of the Lions and the Elks, etc.

But the point is that these are forms of nominal community, casual, uninspired, and almost rootless. What we need, of course, is significant individuality and profound community. But we do not have it, and you do not have it. This is a deep problem for this Conference, and for every nation represented here. I do not know the answer; but, if you have insight on this problem, I would like to have that insight.

ANSWER: In this connection, those "communities," or *Gemein-schaften* which were disorganized as a result of the development of free, independent individuals have maintained their existence by exercising various kinds of group pressures which were in contradiction to the independence and freedom of individuals who were members of the groups.

COMMENT: I think that this problem is one of the basic problems, not only of this Conference, but of our time. For the dialectic referred to has reached, today, an especially ominous stage.

Individuality initially tends to affirm itself against what it considers to be the heteronomy of the group. In the West, the modern humanistic awakening to the autonomy of the individual actually occurred far in advance of industrialization. It is true that the rising middle class turned this into an ideology as they promoted first the commercial and then the industrial revolution.

In this development, the great and powerful individuals who emerged, for example, the captains of industry, often turned into robber barons who trampled roughshod over the smaller, less powerful individuals. This drove many of the latter into the formation of a new kind of collective, the labor union. Today, however, even the erstwhile industrial titan-tycoon is rapidly giving way to the managerial executive, the "organization man" in the "gray flannel suit" living in a stereotyped community in suburbia or ex-urbia. Thus, at present, whether at the top, in the middle, or at the bottom, there is neither the sense of rootage or security which obtained in the old organic social group nor too much evidence of a real individuality with a viable autonomy of freedom. And then, further, cutting across all levels are the dehumanizing, patternizing pressures of the hidden and the not-so-hidden persuaders of the mass media.

I would suggest that the best way to break this dialectic is not simply, as has been suggested by some, to seek for a new rooting or sense of solidarity by going back to the positive values of one's particular social or historical tradition, but, rather, by going down into the depth dimension of human existence toward the root-fulfillment of one's true self. For in the awakening to one's true self the dialectic or duality of the individual and the other, of individuality and community, is broken through. It has become quite clear at this Conference that there can be no true individuality without true community, and no true community without true individuality. It is precisely in realizing the non-duality one's real self that there is realized that true individuality which is true community, that true community which is true individuality. Once attained, this non-dualistic fulfillment must then work to express itself in all the dimensions of human existence, not only the personal but also the social, economic, political, and historical; and not only for some particular group but for all mankind. This is the present task of both the East and the West.

ANSWER: I agree with every point of your analysis.

QUESTION: It seems to me that even in "communities" or *Gemeinschaften* in which the principle of *wa* prevails it is possible to make a distinction between right and wrong. Why do people in these social groups not want to maintain their social order by way of deciding right or wrong?

ANSWER: Of course, in many cases it is possible to make a judgment of right or wrong on behavior within the group. But, at the same time, such a decision is more or less difficult in such a group, because the standard according to which a decision of right or wrong is to be made depends in its nature on the contingent circumstances of the case, particularly the subtle nuances of the temperament, mood, feeling, etc., of the parties involved.

QUESTION: The politics of Japan was not taken up in your paper. I have been wondering if the democracy in Japan is merely a veneer without sufficient background. The prevailing view in the West rather tends to consider that Japan is lacking sufficient foundation or background for genuine and lasting democracy.

ANSWER: I am afraid that my paper might have given the impression that I support the view which you mention. But I cannot agree with that view.

Japan is now in the process of transition from pre-modern to modern society, and there co-exist in social and political life in Japan pre-democratic elements along with democratic elements. The existence of pre-democratic elements which are the remnants from the feudal period does not mean that democracy in Japan has a merely superficial or temporary existence. We should not overlook the fact that Japan experienced, in the past, three major democratic movements. The first was the Jiyū Minken Undō (Movement for Freedom and People's Rights) in the 1870s and 1880s, a large-scale movement which arose and spread all over Japan, and its outcome, and, in a sense, a peace treaty of the government with it, was the Constitution of 1889. The second was the Democratic Movement (Minpon Shugi, and, later on, the Socialist Movement) since around 1914, the main outcome of which were the Jury Law (*Baishin hō*[z]) of 1923 and the Universal Suffrage Law (*Futsū senkyo hō*[aa]) of

1925. The third was the democratic movement after World War II, which was released by the Occupation Forces from suppression by the government after General Tōjō Hideki's[ab] regime, in which a large variety of people were involved, i.e., not only intellectuals and workers, but also women and rural people. In other words, the desire for democracy and civil rights has existed ever since the Meiji Reform[ac] on a national scale, though we might get an opposite impression when we look at the official ideology disseminated and imposed upon the nation, which was nothing but a means of the government to overcome the democratic ideas persisting within the nation, which constituted the evidence of the existence of democratic ideas. Democracy in Japan is now firmly grounded in the minds of the people, and any political attempt to infringe upon democracy and civil rights would encounter the strong opposition and the resistance of the people in the future.

1 See F. S. C. Northrop, "Comparative Philosophy and Science in the Light of Comparative Law," in Charles A. Moore, ed., *Philosophy and Culture—East and West* (Honolulu: University of Hawaii Press, 1962), pp. 251 *et seq.*

1a Northrop points out in his pioneering work that this is characteristic of Oriental culture in general. See F. S. C. Northrop, *The Meeting of East and West* (New York: The Macmillan Co., 1953), pp. 381 *et seq.*, particularly p. 386: "The good which is identified with the indeterminate, all-embracing factor is the only good which is absolute in the sense that it holds for all people under all circumstances. It has this absolute character because in fact it is not transitory or different in one person or thing from what it is in another. The good which is identified with the determinate, limited, differentiated factor is relative, not varying merely from person to person or from thing to thing but also, for a given person, from circumstance to circumstance and from time to time."

2 Tanizaki Junichirō, *Bunshō tokuhon*[ad] (*Reader of Composition*), in *Tanizaki Junichirō zenshū*[ae] (*Collected Works of Tanizaki Junichirō*) Vol. 21 (Tokyo: Chūōkōronsha, 1958), pp. 34 *et seq.*, particularly p. 44.

3 In this paper I use the term "West" or "Western" as meaning the modern West-European and American society in its ideal type in the sense of Max Weber.

4 This became most evident when Mediation Laws were under debate in the Diet in the period immediately after World War I. The Director of Civil Affairs Bureau, Ministry of Justice urged: "By endeavoring to be sympathetic and by expressing harmony, we amicably reap rights which are not actually rights in themselves." (*Dai 45 kai teikokugikai shūgiin iinkai sokkiroku*[af], Stenographic Record of House of Representatives' Committee in the 45th Session of the Imperial Diet, Category 5, no. 5, 2nd session, at p. 4, 1922.) He also urged: "Handling this matter as merely a determination of the problem of the rights of a lessee of land or a tenant of a house so that the owner may assert his own rights even to the point of rapacity, in a period such as that of today when a shift in society in the harmony of supply and demand brings only shortages, with anyone being able to assert his own rights exclusively, makes it quite difficult, in the final analysis, to obtain true stability of rights. Therefore, the establishment of the Mediation Law is not so that someone by sticking to the law can determine the relationship of rights among the parties. That is, the relationship between a tenant and a houseowner, a land lessee and a landowner differs from that between people passing by on the street [complete strangers]. Therein is the personal expression of sympathy; therein is morality. And in the sense that it attempts to base settlement on these things exists the *raison d'être* of mediation." (*Ibid.*, 3rd session, at p. 1, 1922.) Another member argued: "Shōtoku Taishi, who drafted the 'Seventeen-Article Constitution,' wrote [in Article 1] that harmony is to be honored. Japan, unlike other countries where rights and duties prevail, must strive to solve interpersonal cases by harmony and compromise. Since Japan does not settle everything by law as in the West but rather must determine matters, for the most part, in accordance with morality and human sentiment (*ninjō*[ag]), the doctrine of mediation is indigenous to Japan. . . . The great three-hundred-year peace of the Tokugawa (1615–1867) was preserved because disputes between citizens were resolved harmoniously through their own autonomous administration, avoiding, so far as possible, resort to court procedure. . . . However, later the judicial bureaucrats, assuming upon the appearance of the Code of Civil Procedure that the bureaucracy should attempt to settle all problems in dispute, extremely perverted the thought of the People." (*Dai 51 teikokugikai shūgiin iinkai sokkiroku*, Stenographic Record of House of Representatives' Committee in the 51st Session of the Imperial Diet, Category 5, no. 18, 3rd session, at p. 2, 1926.)

5 "In recent publications, original as well as translated works, we encounter words such as '*kenri*[d]' (power and interest; right), '*kengen*[ah]' (competence or authorized rights), '*kenryoku*[ai]' (power), '*kenri*[aj]' (power and reason; right), '*kokken*[ak]' (state power), '*minken*' (civil right), etc., which are intelligible to those who understand foreign languages or to scholars who have studied translated books extensively, but which are not easy for laymen to understand, because in China as well as in Japan these Chinese characters were very rarely used in the meanings they have now." Fukuzawa Yukichi[al], *Tsūzoku minken ron*[am]

(Treatise on Civil Rights), originally published in 1878, in *Fukuzawa Yukichi senshū*[an] (Selected Works of Fukuzawa Yukichi) (Tokyo: Iwanami-shoten, 1952), Vol. IV, p. 30. "But perhaps the most interesting feature of the new Japanese code [civil code] is not the similarity of some of its provisions to those of one foreign code or another, but, rather, its adoption of one characteristic principle of modern European law which introduces an entirely new concept into Japanese legislation. This is the concept of rights as contrasted to obligations. Here we have a distinct and undoubted case of the exertion of direct Western influence upon Japanese culture, for the notion of rights is foreign to the jurisprudence that Japan borrowed from China in the seventh century and on which all her subsequent legislation was based. Instead, not only in its laws but in its customs the social system of Japan was penetrated by the idea of duties to the exclusion of the idea of rights. So unfamiliar was the concept of the rights of the individual subject that in purely Japanese legal writings there is no term that closely corresponds to the word "rights" as expressing something that is due a person and that he can claim; nor indeed did familiar speech include such a word in its vocabulary." Sir George Sansom, *The Western World and Japan* (New York: Alfred A. Knopf, 1950), p. 446.

6 When the Dutch word *"Regt"* (right) was introduced into Japan in the late nineteenth century, there was no equivalent for this word in the vocabulary of the Japanese language, and a scholar had to create a new word, *"kenri,"* by a combination of two Chinese characters, *"ken*[ao]*"* (power) and *"ri*[ap]*"* (reason, logic). Later on, the latter character, *"ri,"* was changed to another *"ri,"* which means interest, thereby maintaining the pronunciation (*kenri*) of the word as it had been originally.

7 Hattori Shirō[aq] (Professor of Linguistics at the University of Tokyo), "Hōritsu to Yakusoku ni tsuite[ar]" (On Law and Promise), in *Asahi Shinbun*[as] (Newspaper Asahi), December 20, 1952, 12th ed., p. 6.

8 On the authoritative statement by Buddhist Prince Shōtoku Taishi, see Nakamura Hajime[at], "Basic Features of the Legal, Political, and Economic Thought of Japan" (cited hereafter as "Basic Features"), in Charles A. Moore, ed., *Philosophy and Culture—East and West*, p. 633.

9 Monbushō[au] (Ministry of Education), *Kokutai no hongi* (Grand Principles of National Polity) (Tokyo: Naikaku-insatsukyoku [The Cabinet's Printing Office], 1937), pp. 50, 51, 57.

10 Ono Seiichirō[av], *Nihon hōri no jikaku teki tenkai*[aw] (Self-conscious Development of Japanese Philosophy of Law) (Tokyo: Yuhikaku, 1942), p. 300.

11 On the virtue of *jihi* (mercy), see Nakamura Hajime, "Basic Features," p. 632; Nakamura Hajime, *Jihi* (Mercy) (Tokyo: Heirakuji-shoten, 1955), pp. 124 *et seq.*

12 On teachings on *"jin" ("jen"* in Chinese) by Japanese Confucian scholars, see Robert N. Bellah, *Tokugawa Religion: The Values of Pre-industrial Japan* (Tokyo: The Free Press, 1957), pp. 94, 141, 156. See also Clarence Burton Day, *The Philosophers of China* (New York: Philosophical Library, 1962), pp. 304-305.

13 The lack of a word which is the equivalent of "right," however, does not necessarily mean that words which signify "right" to any limited extent did not exist at all. In any society there exists some kind of property, and the notion of right existed in that sense and to that extent. In Japan, also, prior to the introduction of Western legal systems, there were in usage words such as *"nauke*[ax]*," "mochiji*[ay]*," "mochigiri*[az]*,"* etc. *"Nauke"* means registration in the *Kenchichō*[ba] (tax register, equivalent of *Domesday Book* in medieval England) of the name of a farmer who was obliged to pay rent or tribute to the *daimyō*[bb] (territorial lord), which at the same time functioned as recognition of the property of the farmer whose name was registered. *"Mochiji"* meant the actually owned land. *"Mochigiri"* meant common land in use by the village community as a collectivity. The fact that, besides these words which signify each specific kind of property, there did not emerge a general term which corresponds to the word "right" draws our attention. Probably this was because in each of these interests there were contained at the same time restrictions or obligations which were so inherently combined with these interests that the concept of right could not emerge as such. See also F. S. C. Northrop, "Linguistic Symbols and Legal Norms," in L. Finkelstein, H. Hoagland, and R. M. MacIver, eds., *Symbols and Society, Fourteenth Symposium of the Conference on Science, Philosophy and Religion*, L. Bryson (New York: The Conference on Science, Philosophy and Religion in their Relation to the Democratic Way of Life, Inc., 1955), pp. 55 *et seq.*

14 See note 4. The expression "a right which is not a right" sounds very strange, of course, not only to Westerners, but also to present-day Japanese. This expression was probably intended to point to an interest which is defined by indeterminate social obligations, and so it can hardly be called a right in the proper sense, but still contains some elements of a right, or resembles a right.

15 See, for example, Ono Seiichirō, *Nihon hōri no jikaku teki tenkai*, p. 64. On the undifferentiated state of law and morality in contemporary China, see Jean Escarra, *Le droit chinois* (Paris: Sirey, 1936), Part I, chap. 4; John C. H. Wu, "Chinese Legal and Political Philosophy," in Charles A. Moore, ed., *Philosophy and Culture—East and West*, pp. 616 *et seq.*

16 See Reinhardt Bendix, *Max Weber, An Intellectual Portrait* (New York: Doubleday & Co., 1962), pp. 398-399. For a comparison with Japanese tradition, the following statement by Paul Vinogradoff about the emergence of the Law of Nature in ancient Greece is particularly interesting: "It is at a later stage—with the advent of Stoicism, especially in its Roman form—that the law of nature began to be considered as a source of law in the practical sense of the term. The explanation of this fact may be found, I think, in the powerful development of equity in the jurisdiction of the democratic courts of the classical period, which left to the popular juries great latitude in the interpretation and application

of positive law." Sir Paul Vinogradoff, *Outlines of Historical Jurisprudence* (Oxford: Oxford University Press, 1922), Vol. II, p. 42.

[17] Kawashima, "Hōken teki keiyaku to sono kaitai[bc]" (Feudal Contracts and Their Disorganization) (cited hereafter as "Hōken teki keiyaku"), in Kawashima, *Hōshakaigaku ni okeru hō no sonzai kōzō[bd]* (The Structure of Law in Sociology of Law) (Tokyo: Nihonhyōrōn-shinsha, 1950), pp. 201–202.

[18] See note 4.

[19] Undoubtedly, this remark originates from the Buddhist belief.

[20] See notes 4 and 8.

[21] Examples of a contract clause of this kind are as follows: "In the case of the prior paragraph, if B has sustained damage, A shall compensate him for this damage, the amount of compensation to be determined by *conferral* between A and B." *Kensetsu kōji hyōjun ukeoi keiyaku yakkan[be]* (Standard Stipulated Terms for Contracts for Work in Construction Projects). Feb. 21, 1950, Ruling of the Third Meeting of the Central Construction Industry Council, as amended through the Oct. 3, 1956. Ruling of the Twenty-first Meeting, Second Session of the Central Construction Industry Council, Art. 16. (Italics mine.) The same expression is also found in Article 22 of the same Standard Stipulated Terms. On details, see Kawashima Takeyoshi and Watanabe Yōzō[bf], *Dōken ukeoi keiyakuron[bg]* (Treatise on Construction Contracts) (Tokyo: Nihonhyorōn-shinsha, 1950), note 13 at pp. 57–70, also 140–143; Kawashima, "Dispute Resolution in Contemporary Japan" (cited hereafter as "Dispute Resolution"), in Arthur von Mehren, ed., *Law in Japan* (Cambridge: Harvard University Press, 1963), pp. 46–47.

[22] See Kawashima, "Dispute Resolution," p. 47.

[23] Most of these relationships or groups can be characterized (a) as "familistic" or "patriarchal" in the sense that the superior (landlord, employer, etc.) has a power of indeterminate scope and intensity contingent on *ad hoc* circumstances, and (b) as "feudal" in the sense that the power of the superior over the inferior is founded on and legitimized by "*on*[bh]" (special favor or benevolence which corresponds to "*beneficium*" in the feudal society given by a lord to a vassal, to which the vassal in turn is indebted by a limitless obligation to reciprocate). See Kawashima, "Hōken teki keiyaku," pp. 190 *et seq.;* pp. 208 *et seq.*

[24] See Kawashima, "Hōken teki keiyaku," pp. 185 *et seq.*, on the patriarchal or familistic nature of farm tenancy; Ishino Iwao and John W. Bennett, *The Japanese Labor Boss System: A Description and a Preliminary Sociological Analysis* (mimeogr.) (Columbus: Department of Sociology, Ohio State University, 1952); and John W. Bennett, *Social Aspects of Japanese Forestry Economy: Two Case Studies* (mimeogr.), Department of Sociology, Ohio State University, 1953, pp. 26 *et seq.*, on the same nature of forestry labor.

[25] James C. Abegglen, *The Japanese Factory* (Glencoe, Illinois: The Free Press, 1958), pp. 17, 66, 94; Kawashima, "Hōken teki keiyaku," pp. 205–206.

[26] Kawashima, "Hōken teki keiyaku," p. 206.

[27] See Ruth Benedict, *The Chrysanthemum and the Sword* (New York: Houghton Mifflin Co., 1946), chaps. 7, 9; Kawashima, "*Giri*," *Shisō[bi]* (Thought), No. 327 (September, 1951), 21 *et seq.*

[28] See Kawashima, "Dispute Resolution," pp. 44 *et seq.*

[29] See note 4.

[30] Reinhard Bendix, *Max Weber, An Intellectual Portrait*, pp. 115 *et seq.*

[31] F. S. C. Northrop, *The Taming of the Nations* (New York: The Macmillan Co., 1954), chaps. 2, 3, 7, 10; Gray L. Dorsey, "Influence of Philosophy on Law and Politics," in Charles A. Moore, ed., *Philosophy and Culture—East and West*, pp. 538 *et seq.*

[32] Comparing the situation with that in America, Professor Hattori Shirō writes: "The Americans observe law, regulation and promise, whereas the Japanese do not have a clear notion of these things; instead, they value and rely on *jōjō[bj]* (situational circumstances), *giri, ninjō* (friendship) *magokoro.* . . . It seems to us very strange that Americans are sensitive to law and make thorough precautions to prevent crimes committed by outmanoeuvring the law. . . . The American society is mechanical, not only materially but also socially; for those Japanese who are not used to this the interpersonal relationships [in America] might seem too mechanical and *mizukusai[bk]* [officious, austere]. . . . The Americans make a promise for promise's sake; hence the promise has to be fulfilled faithfully." Hattori Shirō, "Hōritsu to yakusoku ni tsuite" (On Law and Promise), in *Asahi Shinbun* (Newspaper Asahi), Dec. 20, 1952, 12th ed. p. 6. ("*Magokoro*" is hard to translate. "True sincerity" or "true-heartedness" is close to the implied meaning.)

[33] According to unpublished statistics of the Tokyo District Prosecutor's Office.

[34] Hozumi Nobushige[bl], *Hōso yawa[bm]* (Night Stories from a Study of a Law Professor) (Tokyo: Yuhikaku, 1916), pp. 212–213.

[35] Monbushō (Ministry of Education), *Kokutai no hongi* (Grand Principles of National Policy), pp. 35–36.

[36] Murakami Setsuko[bn] vs. State (Osaka City), Great Court of Judicature, IV Civil Department, August 31, 1953, *Hōritsu Shinbun[bo]*, no. 3886, p. 7; Takeuchi Yoshi[bp] vs. Takahashi Katsuchika[bq] (judge), Great Court of Judicature, Civil Department, May 14, 1906, 12 *Daishinin minji hanketsuroku[br]* (Collection of Civil Great Court of Judicature Cases) 817; Naitō Tsunejirō[bs] vs. Itō Junzō[bt] (President of Kyoto Medical College Hospital), Osaka Court of Appeal, I Civil Department, Dec. 19, 1905, *Hōritsu Shinbun*, no. 338, p. 7; Awaya Kumatsuchi[bu] vs. Tsurumi Moriyoshi[bv], *et al.*, Tokyo District Court, III Civil Department, Jan. 10, 1916, *Hōritsu Shinbun*, no. 1064, p. 27. For detail see Kawashima, *Nihon no shakai to seikatsu ishiki[bw]* (Japanese Society and Mentality) (Tokyo: Gakuseisha, 1955), pp. 30 *et seq.*

37 Professor Miyauchi Hiroshi[bx] points out that the enactment of Law Regarding Suspended Execution, 1905, was not an outcome of the growth of democracy or individualism as was the case in Europe and America, but, rather, an attempt by political leaders to liberalize or enlarge the discretionary power of the court and to correct the provisions of the so-called old penal code of 1882 based on individualism and democracy, drafted under the strong influence of the French philosophy of a Law of Nature. See Miyauchi Hiroshi, *Shikkō yūyo no jittai*[by] (Actualities of Suspended Execution) (Tokyo: Nihonhyōron-shinsha, 1957), p. 90; Takikawa Haruo[bz], Nakatake Yasuo[ca], Hiraba Yasuji[cb], and Miyauchi Hiroshi, "Nihon keihō no ayumi[cc]" (Historical Changes in Japanese Criminal Law), in *Hōritsu jihō*[cd] (Law Journal), XXIV, no. 11 (1952), 35–36. The law of 1905 was kept valid even after the new penal code of 1907 was promulgated. Miyauchi raises the question that the institution of suspended execution and its liberalization in later years are to be studied from the viewpoint of the liberalization of the discretionary power of the court—in other words, as an illustration of the ideology of law which is specifically Japanese. (*Ibid.*, p. 90.)

38 Some examples: the Yokohama District Court sentenced to imprisonment for terms of two years and one and a half years, respectively, two criminal defendants who had left their intoxicated friend on the track of an electric railway to be run over and killed by a train. The prosecution had demanded a two-year sentence. *Asahi Shinbun*, Nov. 28, 1961, 12th ed., p. 15, emphasized the fact that these defendants were sentenced to imprisonment without suspended execution by a three-column headline, "Sentence without suspended execution to two criminal defendants of a joint crime." At the end of this report, the paper referred to another decision by the Nagoya District Court which sentenced to one-year imprisonment (presumably without suspended execution) a *sewayaki*[ce] (a foreman who controlled his workers' room and board) who had left an intoxicated worker under his care outside of the barracks during the winter and the worker thereupon froze to death; the Tokyo District Court sentenced to two-year imprisonment a criminal defendant who had run over a young man and dragged him some distance with his truck while driving at 50 kilometers an hour, though the young man repeatedly cried, "Stop the car." *Asahi Shinbun* commented in its report on this decision that this was the first decision ever rendered by the Tokyo District Court which recognized the intention of bodily injury resulting in death—n.b., not the intention of homicide—in an automobile accident and which sentenced the defendant to imprisonment (Dec. 11, 1962, 3rd ed., p. 7); a bus driver, pulling up to a bus stop, hit a 72-year-old man, thereby seriously injuring his head and other parts of his body, while he was crossing the road and signaling the driver by raising his left hand. The driver, sentenced to a fine of 5,000 *yen* by summary procedure, appealed for regular trial and was acquitted on the ground that the victim was also at fault (this reminds us of the adage "*kenka ryōseibai*[cf]" (both parties of a dispute are to be punished). The Court of Appeals sentenced him to a fine of 3,000 *yen*. *Mainichi Shinbun*[cg] (Newspaper Mainichi) commented in its report on this decision: "In traffic-regulation cases drivers tend to attribute the responsibility of the accident to the fault of the victim." In view of this fact, this decision draws our attention as it imposes 'strict' liability on the drivers from the standpoint of the victim (Dec. 6, 1961, 13th ed., p. 13). In this connection, an epoch-making decision was rendered by the Niigata District Court, which was upheld by Tokyo Court of Appeals on June 28, 1963. A criminal, driving a truck without a license, struck and killed a young woman carrying her baby on her back at an intersection in the city of Nagaoka and drove on about 300 meters, dragging her husband, who had jumped on the truck and asked the driver to stop. The Niigata District Court sentenced him to five years imprisonment for homicide with *dolus eventualis* (eventual intent), and the Appellate Court upheld this decision. This was the first case in which a hit-and-run driver was prosecuted for intentional homicide "after careful deliberation" in the prosecutor's office (see *Mainichi Shinbun*, Dec. 6, 1961, 13th ed., p. 13). *Asahi Shinbun*, June 28, 1963, 12th ed., p. 15, commented on this case in its report on the decision of the Appellate Court that this was the fourth decision ever rendered by the court which, in a hit-and-run automobile accident case, imposed punishment for homicide, and noted that this "severe attitude of the court was noteworthy."

39 "It is (*jihi*) (the mercy) of the East to embrace criminals of every kind of crime and not to cast them away. . . . It is the philosophy of law of the East, and Japan as well, to abstain from inflicting punishment." Ono Seiichrō, *Nihon hōri no jikaku teki tenkai* (Self-conscious Development of Japanese Philosophy of Law), pp. 108, 110. "When [Vice President] Nixon apologized, 'It was the fault of U.S. by mistake,' we are moved all at once and think 'we have to save his face.' Even a raped girl or her parents, if the criminal visits them early in the morning and apologizes with tears, are easily moved and inclined to forgive him. . . ." (Anonymous comment in *Asahi Shinbun*, Nov. 23, 1953, 12th ed., p. 3.)

40 Sasaki Yoshio, "Minji chōtei ni okeru 'gōi' no kentō[ch]" (Analysis of "Agreement" in Civil Mediation), in *Kanagawa hōgaku*[ci] (Kanagawa University Study of Law), IX, No. 1-2 (1963), 6. *et seq.*

41 See Kawashima, "Dispute Resolution," pp. 50 *et seq.*

42 See *ibid.*, p. 55. For statistics, see Kawashima, "Dispute Resolution," table 12, II at p. 69.

43 Sometimes the racial or inborn nature of these characteristics has been emphasized by nationalist writers. See particularly Monbushō (Ministry of Education), *Kokutai no hongi* (Grand Principles of National Polity), p. 97; Toda Teizo[cj], *Ie no michi*[ck] (The Way of the House) (Tokyo: Shakai-kyoiku-kyokai [Social Education Association], 1942), p. 43.

44 See Sir George Sansom, *The Western World and Japan*, pp. 343 *et seq.*

45 See Kawashima, "Kenri no taikei[cl]" (Systems of Rights), in Kawashima, *Kindai shakai to hō*[cm] (Modern Society and Law) (Tokyo: Iwanami-shōten, 1959), p. 163, n. 17.

46 Leased Land and Leased House Mediation Law, Law No. 41 of 1922; Tenant Farming

Law, Law No. 18 of 1924; subsequently, Monetary Obligation Temporary Mediation Law, Law No. 26 of 1932; Personal Affairs Mediation Law, Law No. 11 of 1939.

47 Monbushō, *Kokutai no hongi* (Grand Principles of National Polity); Monbushō, *Shinmin no michi* (The Way of the Emperor's Subjects) (Tokyo: Shakai-kyōiku-kyōkai [Social Education Association], 1941); Monbushō, *Senji katei kyōiku shidō yōryo* (Basic Principles of Wartime Home Education) (Tokyo: Monbushō, 1942).

48 "Tracing the development of our country since its foundation, we always find the spirit of *wa*," (Monbushō, *Kokutai no hongi*, p. 50).

49 "Even a cup of rice or a kimono is not my own property; even during play or sleep there is no self apart from the country; everything exists in its bond with the country." (Monbushō, *Shinmin no michi*, p. 63).

50 See Kawashima, "Dispute Resolution," pp. 58 *et seq.*, on some of the findings in the survey of the social attitude by the Ministry of Labor. *Hōkensei ni tsuite no chōsa*[cn] (A Survey Regarding Feudal Characteristics), No. 7 of *Fujin kankei shiryō shīrizu*[co] (Materials Relating to Women Series, 1951) and the survey of Kokuritsu Yoron Chōsajo[cp] (National Public Opinion Research Institute). *Shakai kyōiku ni tsuiteno yoron chōsa*[cq] (A Public Opinion Survey Regarding Social Education) 1953.

51 Sasaki Yoshio, "Minji chōtei ni okeru 'gōi' no kentō" (Analysis of "Agreement" in Civil Mediation), in *Kanazawa hōgaku* (Study of Law of Kanazawa University), (9), No. 1–2, 1963, pp. 1 *et seq.*

52 In sampling of an urban area (Osaka City), 31.6 o/o gave as the reason for avoiding lawsuit that it is time-consuming, and 44.9 o/o that it is too expensive; and in a sampling of a rural area (13 districts of Shimane Prefecture) 28 o/o alleged that lawsuit is time-consuming and 40.5 o/o that it is too expensive. See Sasaki Yoshio, *op. cit.*, p. 14.

53 Article 19 (B) and Article 23 of the Standard Stipulated Terms for Contracts for Work in Construction Projects as amended by the Central Construction Industry Council on September 15, 1962.

54 The frequency shows the number of news reports of *Asahi Shinbun* on judicial cases for civil, labor, and administrative cases (excluding criminal cases, which were often reported in the newspaper with particular interest in the scandalous nature of the case). The size of headlines shows the length of headlines in terms of the number of columns covered by the headlines. In counting the frequency, news reports on the same case in the same issue of the newspaper are counted as 1, and, in counting the size of headlines, the length of headlines regarding the same case in the same issue of the newspaper is regarded as a headline of a single report as stated above and totaled. The distribution of the size of headlines is shown in the chart below.

Size of headlines	1930	1935	1962	1963
1	3	13	11	16
2	18	20	8	12
3	5	8	22	17
4	2	2	7	6
5	0	0	5	1
6	0	0	0	4
7	1	0	3	0
8	0	0	1	0
9	0	0	1	1
10	0	0	0	1
11	0	0	0	1
13	0	0	1	0
15	0	0	0	1
21	0	0	0	1
Total	29	43	59	61
Mean	2.37	1.98	3.34	3.44
Standard deviation	1.56	2.41	4.11	5.66

a 川島武宣
b 谷崎潤一郎
c 源氏物語
d 權利

e 眞心
f 和
g 十七條憲法
h 聖德

ⁱ 大和

^j 慈悲

^k 仁

^l 明治期

^m 縁

ⁿ 義理

^o 傳家の寶刀

^p 民權

^q 國體の本義

^r 根本

^s 円

^t 自由民權運動

^u 調停

^v 臣民の道

^w 戰時家庭教育指導要領

^x 言あげ

^y 佐々木吉男

^z 陪審法

^{aa} 普通選舉法

^{ab} 東條英機

^{ac} 明治の改革

^{ad} 文章讀本

^{ae} 谷崎潤一郎全集

^{af} 衆議院委員會速記録

^{ag} 人情

^{ah} 權限

^{ai} 權力

^{aj} 權理

^{ak} 國權

^{al} 福澤諭吉

^{am} 通俗民權論

^{an} 福澤諭吉全集

^{ao} 權

^{ap} 利

^{aq} 服部四郎

^{ar} 法律と約束について

^{as} 朝日新聞

^{at} 中村元

^{au} 文部省

^{av} 小野淸一郎

^{aw} 日本法理の自黨的展開

^{ax} 名受

^{ay} 持地

^{az} 持切

^{ba} 檢地帳

^{bb} 大名

^{bc} 封建的契約とその解體

^{bd} 法社會學におりる法の存在構造

^{be} 建設工事標準請員契約約款

^{bf} 渡邊

^{bg} 土建請員契約論

^{bh} 恩

^{bi} 思想

^{bj} 情狀

^{bk} 水臭い

^{bl} 穗積陳重

^{bm} 法窓夜話

^{bn} 村上節子

^{bo} 法律新聞

^{bp} 竹內芳

^{bq} 高橋克親

^{br} 大審院民事判決録

^{bs} 內藤常二郎

^{bt} 伊藤準三

^{bu} 粟屋熊槌

^{bv} 鶴見守義

^{bw} 日本の社會と生活意識

^{bx} 宮內裕

^{by} 執行猶豫の實態

^{bz} 瀧川春雄

^{ca} 中武靖夫

^{cb} 平場安治

^{cc} 日本刑法の歩み

^{cd} 法律時報

^{ce} 世話燒

^{cf} 喧嘩両成敗

^{cg} 毎日新聞

^{ch} 民事調停における合意の檢討

^{ci} 神奈川法學

^{cj} 戶田貞三

^{ck} 家の道

^{cl} 權利の體系

^{cm} 近代社會と法

^{cn} 封建制についての調査

^{co} 婦人關係資料シリーズ

^{cp} 國立世論調査所

^{cq} 社會教育についての世論調査

MIGUEL REALE

Legal status of individuals

Professor Miguel Reale, Professor of The Philosophy of Law at the University of São Paulo, in Brazil, was invited to the Conference to present a paper on the status of the individual in the legal tradition of the West. At that time he was serving as Secretary of Justice in the State of São Paulo, and therefore could not attend the Conference. Also, at about that same time, his country experienced a revolution in which he was involved, a revolution which, as he said, relieved Brazil from the perils of communism. In view of this complex situation, Dr. Reale found it impossible to attend or prepare a special paper for the Conference. He therefore translated and adapted—very co-operatively—the paper which he had already written,[1] and submitted it for use at the Conference. This paper was read at the Conference and was discussed extensively.

However, in view of the fact that the paper has already been published, it cannot be republished in this volume. This is regrettable, but unavoidable.

In view of this situation, Professor Richard P. McKeon, of the University of Chicago, was asked late in the Conference to prepare a paper on the status of the individual in the legal philosophy and institutions in the West. He generously consented to do so. Dr. McKeon's paper constitutes the next one in this volume.

However, before Dr. McKeon had been requested to write his paper, the Conference Director, under the impression that, because of Dr. Reale's absence, there would be no opportunity for adequate discussion of the question of the status of the individual in Western law, proposed to him some questions which could be submitted to the Conference along with his answers. These important answers are presented herewith. The questions, it will be noted, are related both to Professor Reale's paper itself and also to interpretations expressed at previous Conferences and in published works by Professor F. S. C. Northrop. They clearly provide valuable supplementation to the other work of the Conference in this area.

QUESTION: Northrop says: "The law of contract expresses the conceptually different mentality [of the West] by its dictum that the law is no respecter of persons."

ANSWER: The idea of "contract" is so essential to the Western legal mentality that, from the rise of the Modern Age to the French Revolution, many authors assumed this idea was the genesis of, or the reason for, society and the state (contractualistic theories). Even though we know now that the contract is a historical development, corresponding to an advanced phase of civilization, not even then has the concept of the contract lost its relevant signification for Western culture, which cannot be understood without the recognition that *every man has the right freely to bind himself.*

The law of contract in the West—as one of the component elements of the legal *status* of the individual—is based on the principle that the only limit for the liberty of each is the liberty of others. As George H. Sabine says, "The crux of any general theory of the State has always lain in the relations to be assigned to fact and value." In the West, the limited authority of the state lies in the prevalent conception of the individual as of intrinsic value, the sufficient condition for his power to enforce legal rights and obligations either for himself or for others.

This is why the more we multiply the ways of state interference on the grounds of "contractual life," there always remains an untouchable center, that is, the *capacity of autonomous choice by individuals as an ethical requirement;* without this requisite man *would not have a status* but *would be a status,* scattered in the web of collective interests. Between democracy and contract there is, therefore, an essential connection, although it has been realized that Spencer's prediction about the progressive "contractualization" of society, i.e., the social evolution from "status" to "contract," was mistaken.

QUESTION: What is the accuracy and significance of the following statement from Northrop: "The history of Western law from the Scaevalas to Justianian is the story of the increasing triumph of the universalism of the *ius gentium* over the pluralism and the normative incompatibilities of the diverse examples of the *ius civile*"?

ANSWER: The particularism of the various *"iura civilia"* was gradually superseded by rules of law valid for all men and consequently considered as *ius gentium.* Greek philosophy, Roman jurisprudence, and Christianity contributed to this universalization, which is still progressing. The cause of Western democracy is inseparable from this sense of *iuris* universalization.

It is necessary to add from this process of universalization of law results, as a consequence, the ideal of one juridical *status,* more and more extensive to all men, but in such a way that it does not force anybody to be *this* or *that,* but allows every man—using his legal status—to be what normally corresponds to his personality.

QUESTION: "On the basis of your paper, are we to assume or conclude that the legal spirit of the West has been that of democracy —at least in theory, if not in fact?"

ANSWER: Surely. My paper aims to prove that the history of the West is substantially the history of democracy. This is, from my point of view, a "historical conquest" that Western man has been living through in phases whose "decisive moments" I tried to establish in my paper.

The Western juridical sense is democratic. The reciprocal thesis is also true: there is no democracy without juridical spirit, that is, without the acknowledgement of the autonomous value of individuals as members of the State. Without men's juridical *status* there is no democratic *State*. Both concepts demand each other; without one, the other could not exist. The Western juridical spirit is based upon the conviction that every man has the *capacity of being different* from other men and of acting in accordance with this diversity.

QUESTION: What, actually, is the validity and implication of Northrop's interpretation of Western law in terms of Greek science and Stoic legal philosophy, that all individuals are equal under the law, as examples of a universal?

ANSWER: Equality of all individuals under the law cannot be understood only in terms of Greek science and Stoic philosophy, because it is the result of Western history as a whole. It is impossible to find the conscience of the democratic legal status of individuals in the Greek world, whose conception of freedom is very different from ours, as I have pointed in my book *Horizontes do Direito e da História*[2] (Horizons of Law and History).

On the other hand, equality of all individuals, nowadays, may not be understood as a *formal equality* under the law; it is, rather, a claim for *concrete equality* in life. The law must not only guarantee, but must assure the possibility for each one to have—as Dewey says—a "kind of work" which can also be the "kind of life" that he is capable of living.

QUESTION: Is it true, as was strongly contended at our past Conferences, that in the West we have rule by law, whereas, in the East there is no such rule by law but rule by men—such that the status of the individual is determined by law in the West but by status of various kinds in the East?

ANSWER: In the West the *status* of the individual is more *recognized* than established by law.

The *status* of the individual is not a legislator's creation or a mere result of the fact of technological progress or the effect of the amendment of usages and customs abstractly considered: all these factors have to be considered in connection with the intersubjective relations that constitute the social *corpus*.

It is important, indeed, that no differences among individuals result from other reasons except their own capacities and abilities, not being conditioned by birth or external assignment. But it is important also to assume that *objective* situation as the necessary corrective of the "status" of conscience of the citizens. Without the polarity of these subjective and objective elements, the law cannot determine the legal status of individuals, according to democracy.

It is the legal conscience of one's own social *status* that characterizes the individual in Western democracy. It is the conscience of the intrinsic value of his "own being" in society that implies the recognition of his legal *status*.

The legal *status* of the individual, in the West, is the result of the *concomitant* recognition of what every man has *of his own* and *in common* with other men.

QUESTION: Is there any single comprehensive or constant or universal theory—and practice—of the law in the West as related to the status of the individual? If not, do the variations in the legal attitudes involve differing status for the individual at different times and in different areas of the West?

ANSWER: The variations which have occurred in the *status* of individuals throughout history, as well as the differences found in different areas, do not exclude the existence of some values that Western culture considers as *definitively acquired,* at least up to the limits of the present democratic process: all these values are based, however, on the recognition that the human being is an intrinsic value, whose various virtualities are renewed and revealed in social and historical experience.

---

[1] "Os Valôres Fundantes da Democracia," (The Universal Values of Democracy), in Miguel Reale, *Pluralismo e Liberdade* (Pluralism and Liberty) (São Paulo: Edição Saraiva, 1963), pp. 285–296.
[2] São Paulo: Edição Saraiva, 1956.

RICHARD McKEON

The individual in law
and in legal philosophy in the West

INTRODUCTION: LAW, NATURE, AND COMMUNITY

The history of law in the West is a history of the development of
the individual and of the concept of the individual. The actions and
therefore the character of man as an individual are determined,
positively and negatively, by the prescriptions and prohibitions of
law. The nature and the definition of man as an individual, that is,
as a responsible agent in a natural environment and a human community, are consequences of the operation of law and of conceptions
of what law is.

The history of the individual has been a progressive evolution in
which the powers of the individual to act have been increased and
the exercise of those increased powers has been spread more and
more widely to form more highly individuated and more numerous
individuals. This progress has been influenced by ideas and discussion, and even by philosophical inquiry and controversy, as well as
by facts of nature* and of human nature. Portions of the history
have frequently been recounted, as rhetoric, propaganda, or power-
maneuver, as if the character of a society depended on the influence of a single philosophy (as if the "closed society" "follows" from
Plato's philosophy, Roman law from the Stoic philosophy, or the
American constitution from Locke's philosophy) and as if the stages
of the development of man and society were periods of ideological
dominance of successive philosophies. A plurality of philosophies
contributed to the progress of law and of the individual, and the
transitions from stage to stage of that progress resulted from the
interplay of many philosophies.

The contribution of law to the formation of the individual cannot
be understood by appealing to what everybody knows about the laws
of nature and the laws of communities. It is a mark of philosophic
problems that the meanings of *all* the terms used in philosophical
explanation are influenced by the principles posited in the explanation. Different philosophic conceptions of the "individual" may be

* "Nature," usually capitalized in this volume, is not capitalized in this paper, in accordance with the author's wishes.—Ed. note.

453

set forth in terms of different philosophic conceptions of "law," provided one takes into account different philosophic conceptions of "nature" and "community."

We have long attached a number of adjectives to "law" which have elaborated and modified the ancient distinction between natural law and political or civil law. We have from the first introduced "natural law" into the promulgation and operation of civil law, and we have discussed, at each stage of the advance of science and of society, whether the laws of physical and biological motions and the laws of political, economic, and social processes are both "natural," and, if "natural law" is to be restricted to one portion of these laws, whether the laws of nature are prior to the laws of the history of society, or whether the laws of society determine the formulation of the laws of nature.

We have long differentiated within the broad concept of law between prescriptions and rights. We tend to use two words to express the distinction—*nómos* and *díkaion, lex* and *ius, loi* and *droit, Gesetz* and *Recht, law* and *right*—but the distinction does not provide the definition of the two words. From the first and at each step of the advance of human associations and of human individuality we have discussed whether law and right are synonymous and mutually re-enforcing, or independent and mutually exclusive, and, if they are distinct, whether one is prior and more fundamental than the other—whether rights are consequences of the enactment and enforcement of laws, or laws are formulated and put into effect by the exercise of rights.

The individual is affected and defined by laws of nature and laws of communities. But what is the relation between "nature" and "community"? The universe has been considered a community of gods and men, itself an organic whole which is not only intelligible and the source of intelligibility but intelligent and rational. The communities of men have also been considered different in kind from the congeries of things and the herds and flocks of animals which form the environment and conditioning circumstances of human communities. The regularities of nature which are expressed in natural laws have been considered different in kind from the contingent laws men imposed on themselves and other men. The laws of probability have also been considered the sufficient, and only possible, guides for the life of man and human communities, and the sufficient, and only possible, predictions of the motions of particles and galaxies.

To consider the influence of legal philosophy on the individual as well as on the conception of the individual is to treat problems of the nature of philosophy as well as problems of the nature of the individual. Some of these problems of the nature and function of philosophy are at the center of the problems of the individual in the present. (1) The conscious life of the individual is an exploration of how thought may influence action. The treatment of philosophic problems may be thought to have a direct relevance to practical problems, or philosophic problems may be thought to be distinct from the problems in other fields and their treatment to be relevant only indirectly to life, like the application of other technical formulations. (2) The life of the individual is a response to a vast number of pressures, associations, attractions, claims, continuities, changes. The agreements he comes to with others, practical or philosophical, may be thought to depend on acceptance of common principles and the institution of a common philosophy, or genuine agreement may be thought to depend, unlike coercion or persuasion, on the interplay of different principles for the investigation of truth and the enrichment of values. (3) The problems which the individual faces are presented simultaneously or successively as dilemmas to be solved only by refuting one of the alternatives and, in extreme cases, silencing or exterminating its proponent, and as problems to be solved by advancing beyond the oppositions in which they arose to the consideration of new common problems which open up new values. The relations among philosophies—the relations between schools and within schools—may be thought to be an operation of controversial opposition and successive refutation, or it may be thought to be an exploration of inquiries based on different fundamental hypotheses which are adjusted to new data made available by the solution of earlier problems worked out by application of one of the hypotheses. (4) The courses of action and the modes of thought among which the individual must choose are presented to him as tested by long experience and by tradition, or as certified by recent discoveries and by innovations which go beyond old misconceptions and partial knowledge. Philosophy may be thought to be a continuing process in which one learns truths and refutes errors of past and living philosophers, or it may be thought to undergo revolutions which purge it of meaningless questions and uncover absurdities in the odd things most philosophers, particularly the great masters and one's own master, have said.

It is improbable that the problems of the individual today will be solved either by returning to good old positions long neglected and newly interpreted or by inventing useful new positions based on new facts certified by a new science. The circumstances and powers of the individual today make him a different individual and face him with different problems than those found in the actions of individuals in the past or in past conceptions of the individual. If a plurality of philosophies has contributed to the development of the individual, a consideration of the philosophic significance of a plurality of philosophies, in its turn, may contribute further to the formation of the individual and also to the clarification of the concept of the individual.

I. LAW AND THE NATURE OF THE POLITICAL INDIVIDUAL

Ancient epics and dramas, early histories and records of ancient laws and constitutions depict the problems of individuals as they are determined by the communities of men and gods and by the nature of the universe and of things. Philosophers, including poets, historians, and lawgivers in their philosophic pronouncements, have given various interpretations to these accounts of the nature and problems of individuals. From the earliest explicit philosophic discussions, the influence of law on the individual has presented two central problems: (1) Is law, by which men are associated in communities, nature or convention? (2) Is law based on justice or is justice based on law? In the ancient formulation of these problems a choice was necessary between the alternatives: law is either natural or conventional; law is either prior or posterior to justice. One of the marks of the modern formulation of the problem, since the seventeenth century, is that both answers are given without ambiguity: law is both natural and conventional; law is both prior and posterior to justice. The philosophies of Plato and Aristotle are detailed analyses of conceptions of the individual and the state based on nature and justice; the philosophies of the Atomists and the Sophists base the state and law on contract and agreement and derive justice from the resulting conception of law.

To seek a natural basis for the state and justice is to seek to determine the ends of the lives of individuals and communities by reason and therefore to base them on reality, against theories which hold that ends are determined by emotions and therefore that values are based on the preferences of men, not on the nature of things. Plato and Aristotle set forth two theories of the relation of reason to action. Plato argued that virtue is knowledge, that the ends of men and of states are discerned by wisdom or, in its absence, by right opinion, and that the grounds of justice and law are transcendental. Aristotle argued that virtue is habit, that the ends of men and states are discerned by prudence or, in its absence, by judgment of one's interests, and that the grounds of justice and law are laid in character and institutions. If the associations of men have a natural basis, they both argued, justice is prior to law, because the natural relations of men influence the prescriptions enforced to regulate those relations. Plato defined justice as the performance by every man of his proper functions as determined by his nature and by the division of labor in the community. Aristotle defined justice as the influence of the customs and *mores* of the community in determining the ends of the individual and the distribution of offices in constitutions and the operation of institutions in providing redress of injuries, civil and criminal, suffered from the action of others.

Plato's examination, in the *Republic,* of the development of the individual in a perfect state, which Socrates specifies never did and never will exist but does serve as a model to guide actual states, is a treatise on *justice.* The virtues of the individual and the community are determined by wisdom. The only laws in the perfect states are the laws governing education; there are no other laws, civil or criminal, public or private. Plato's examination of actual states, which are second-best, is called the *Laws.* As substitutes for reason, laws depend on persuasion and force, and all laws are divided into those two parts. A perfect state would be ruled by philosophy; actual states are ruled by opinion, sometimes by *right* opinion, which has a source similar to that of the insights of prophecy, poetry, love, and drink.

Aristotle's single science, politics, has two parts, ethics, which is concerned with the virtues of individuals, and politics, which, in the strict sense, is concerned with the institutions of states. As an individual, the good man is distinct from the good citizen; the two coincide sometimes in the good state. But in all states the character of the individual depends on the influence of the state, and the constitution of the state depends on the character of its citizens. The connecting link is justice, which is a virtue in the individual and an equality in the state. Justice forms the character and virtues of the individuals relative to others, and it determines the distribution of powers and offices in the state. There are as many kinds of justice as there are kinds of states, for each state has its characteristic form of equality. Laws are determined by the constitution and by the particular form of justice of the state. The rule of law is preferable to the rule of men because law is free from human passion, but, since laws provide general regulations, justice must be supplemented by equity to take into account particular circumstances. The method by which legislation is carried out in assemblies and by which differences are adjudicated in courts of law is rhetoric, not logic, for rhetoric is adapted to the consideration of questions and cases encountered by the individual in his particular circumstances and conditions.

To seek a basis for the state and justice in agreement or contract is to seek to determine the ends of individual and common life by the impulses and wishes of men and therefore to base them in the purposes men form, against theories which reduce human nature to understanding or reason and neglect spontaneity and impulsion. The Atomists and the Sophists developed two forms of the contract theory of the state based on two forms of hedonism. Democritus argued that men, as bodies, take on individuality from the actions induced by their impulsions to act and from the passions they undergo as a result of actions. They seek pleasures in action and art, and form states by agreements concerning ends desired. The Sophists viewed knowledge and action both from the perspective of the individual conceived as measure and maker. Nature as well as the state is a product of agreements among men. Justice is the product of law in both forms of contract theory, but in the one there are laws of nature distinct from the laws of states, while in the other the laws of nature and the laws of the state are both determined operationally.

Democritus distinguished sharply between science, which consists of cognitive judgments concerning the motions of the atoms, and ethics and aesthetics, which consist of emotive judgments determined by impulse, pleasure, and pain. Later atomists held that the state is a contract to institute and advance what members to the contract seek. The nature of the individual is manifested in his passions, including passions which are at variance with his true nature and which can be treated therapeutically by recourse to knowledge of the nature of things.

The Sophists played an important role in the development of Greek democracy by their teaching of rhetoric and of the virtues which enable individuals to state and defend positions, win cases of law, and participate in the enactment of laws. They applied operationalism to knowledge and to practice. Justice is a consequence of agreements instituted or of power used. There is no antecedent nature to impose criteria to distinguish right and wrong desires.

The transition from the Hellenic city-states to the Hellenistic kingdoms was mediated by the empire of Alexander. The size of the communities of men had expanded; men were equal within larger groups, but their liberties tended to become uniformities or eccentricities. It was the period of the development of Rhodian maritime and commercial law and of the advance of scholarly learning and empirical science at Alexandria and Pergamon. The philosophy of the Cynics had prepared for the period by removing the individual from the oppositions among city-states and between Greeks and barbarians to make him a citizen of the world and a brother of other men. The orations of Demosthenes and Isocrates had prepared for this by opposing the ideal of rights and laws preserved by fidelity to the Athenian constitution to the ideal of rights and laws to be achieved in the larger Panhellenic community. The basic oppositions of nature and contract, right and law, were continued in the Hellenistic philosophies, but all the terms in which the oppositions were expressed had taken on new meanings.

The Stoics developed the idea of the law of nature, in which the individual uses reason to adjust himself to the reason of nature in a universe which is through and through rational. In the cosmopolitan city of the universe, in which men and gods are citizens, the rule of reason prevails; the cities of men are diversified and opposed to each other by the passions. The Epicureans developed the idea of the social contract which establishes a common good on individual interests and provides the context for the individual pursuit of private goods. Reason is used by the individual in the pursuit of pleasure, and reason induces the individual to participate in politics to avoid the pains that might be consequent on the rule of others.

The city of Rome became a vast empire. Its institutions and their functions were set up and limited by laws as those of no previous state had been, and Roman laws made provisions for rights in a sense never discussed by the Greeks. Modern conceptions of law and of the individual derive from Roman innovations, and the history of Rome is an early instance of a problem which has recurred repeatedly in the development of communities and individuals: the formation of Roman law was the constitution of a republic; the codification of Roman laws was the work of jurisconsults pronouncing on real and imaginary cases and compiling *Digests* and *Institutes* in an empire which preserved the external forms of the republican constitution as a mechanism for the operation of absolute power.

Two philosophies of the individual developed on the basis of opposed conceptions of community and nature. Cato and Censor opposed the introduction of Greek culture into Rome because it would endanger the native Roman virtues, which he sought to strengthen by study of the "origins" or history of Rome. The circle of Scipio the Younger, which Cicero, the last defender of the constitution against Julius Caesar, presents in conversation in his dialogue *De Re Publica* found the foundations of Roman law in reason and nature; and Cicero argued that education consists in the study of the great artists and thinkers to which he gave the name *humanitas,* for those works show the nature of man in his supreme accomplishments.

The titles of Cicero's works *De Re Publica* and *De Legibus* suggest that he had the example of Plato in mind, yet his departure from Plato's ideas is noted by one of the interlocutors in the *De Re Publica* who observes that Scipio has been using a new method of discussion, unknown to the Greeks, who either presented a theoretic state invented by one mind and little adapted to men's actual lives and habits or discussed different types and structures of states without analyzing any clear model or form.[1] The perfect state which Scipio presents is drawn from the history of Rome, and Scipio expressed his agreement with Cato that the Roman republic was based upon the genius, not of one man, but of many, and was established, not in the life of one man, but in several centuries and ages.[2] But

Scipio also argued that to engage in such inquiry one should go beyond history to eternity and to the universe and should consider not merely civil law but the common law of nature. One should therefore esteem wisdom and recognize that, although others may be called men, only they are men who are perfected in the arts proper to humanity.[3] The constitution which Rome evolved was a mixed constitution, which is the best constitution.

Since the *De Re Publica* described a perfect state which was an actual state, the *De Legibus* does not go on, like Plato's *Laws,* to describe actual states distinct from the perfect state, but examines the laws and rights of the perfect state. Law (*lex*) is the highest reason implanted in nature (*ratio summa insita in natura*), which commands what ought to be done and prohibits the contrary; that reason is firmly fixed and developed in the mind of man.

> Therefore, since there is nothing better than reason, and since it exists both in man and in god, the first community of man and god is a society of reason (*rationis societas*). But those who have reason in common must also have right reason in common, and since right reason is law (*lex*), we must believe that men are associated (*consociati*) also with the gods in law. Further, those who have a communion of law (*communio legis*) also have a communion of right (*communio iuris*), and those who share these must be considered members of the same commonwealth. If indeed they obey the same authorities and powers (*imperium et potestas*), this is even more true; but as a matter of fact they do obey this celestial system, the divine mind, and the god of transcendent power. Hence we must now conceive this whole universe as one commonwealth (*una civitas communis*) of gods and men.[4]

Cicero conceived law as the bond of civil society (*civilis societatis vinculum*), and, since right (*ius*) based on law (*lex*) is equal, a state cannot be held together without equality among its citizens. More than five hundred years later the phrase *iuris vinculum* is used in Justinian's *Institutes.* Law is prior to right, and right means equality. The state, finally, is only one form of association or society: there are other societies of men within the society of the universe, which is nature and reason.

The means by which laws are enacted in legislatures and applied in courts is rhetoric. The problems which rhetoric treats are different from the problems of philosophy or science, because they concern definite individuals (*certae personae*). The controversies of orators are called "causes" or "hypotheses," that is, special cases; the controversies of philosophers are called "questions" or "theses," that is, general problems. Cicero notes that some rhetoricians, like Hermagoras, extend rhetoric to the treatment of both kinds of problems;[5] repeatedly since the time of Cicero, in the past and at present, philosophic problems have been restated by rhetorical methods to take account of individuals and facts. One of the consequences of inverting Plato's position that justice is prior to law is apparent in the definition of justice. Plato had refuted Polemarchus' definition of justice, rendering every man his due, and had made justice a positive virtue defined by the state of the agent, not of the recipient, every man performing his proper function. Polemarchus' definition, not Plato's, has been accepted by Roman law and later legal philosophers. Cicero relates that definition operationally to civil law and natural law.

> Justice is a habit of mind which renders every man his due (*dignitas*) while preserving the common advantage (*utilitas*). It has its source or principle in nature; thence certain things came into custom by reason of utility; afterwards these things which proceeded from nature and were approved by custom were sanctioned by fear and reverence for laws (*leges*). The right of nature (*ius naturae*) is that which is not born of opinion but is implanted in nature by a kind of power: it includes religion, piety, gratitude, revenge, reverence, and truth.[6]

Law and morals are both concerned with duties, and, in both, distinctions must be made between perfect duties, whose objectives are good in themselves (*honesta*), and imperfect duties, whose objectives are utilities (*utilia*).

The handbooks of law in the Roman Empire make use of Cicero's language, but reverse Cicero's order of law and right, and come to make right prior to law. The mark of the law of nature is still that it is discerned by reason, but the operation of reason is sought, not in civil law, since that is the enactment of one people, but in the law of nations, since that is common to all men. The distinction is difficult to express in English, since *ius* and *lex* are both translated frequently by *law,* yet the distinction between *ius* and *lex* is clearly marked. Gaius writes in the second century A.D.

> Whatever any people has established as law (*ius*) for itself, this is proper to it alone and is called civil law (*ius civile*), as a kind of law peculiar to the state; whatever, on the other hand, natural reason has established among all men, this is observed uniformly among all peoples and is called law of nations (*ius gentium*), as a kind of law which all races employ. And so the Roman people employ a law partly peculiar to themselves and partly common to all men.[7]

Laws (*leges*) are classified on the basis of their authority. What the *people* command is law; what the *plebs* and what the *senate* command have been given the position of law; what the *emperor* ordains holds the place of law because he had received his *imperium* by a law. According to the *Rules* of Ulpian, in the third century, the precepts of law are to live uprightly, to injure no one, and to render to each his right. Public law is concerned with the gods or the state; private law, which pertains to the interests of private individuals, is threefold, deduced from rules of nature (*ius naturale*) or of nations (*ius gentium*), or of a particular nation (*ius civile*). Right, or *ius,* had come to mean, like *dikaion,* the substance and criterion of law, the just; law, or *lex,* had come to mean, first, the specific rule of application, like *thesmos,* or customary law, and then the general rule, like *nómos,* or written law.

With the coming of Christianity the law of the Old Testament and the law of the New Testament were added to civil law and natural law, and the ends of the law were extended from welfare and security to salvation. Nature was the creation of God and mirrored him in the marks of his workmanship, and individual men were created by him in his image and likeness. St. Ambrose adapted the Stoic concept of duty from Cicero's *De Officiis* in his *De Officiis Ministrorum,* and St. Augustine borrowed from Plato and the Stoics to demonstrate that the misfortunes suffered by Rome were not a consequence of the new religion and to distinguish the City of God from the terrestrial cities by the differences in the loves that determined their ends and, ultimately, by the difference between charity and concupiscence. Scripture contained the revelation of divine law, but scripture, like other statements of law, requires interpretation, and the community of the faithful must take form and operation in a context of other communities. Augustine used rhetoric as the art of interpreting scripture in the *De Doctrina Christiana;* and, as rhetoric is concerned with things and word, *res et verba,* three books of that work expound the nature of things, and one book the verbal forms, necessary for Christian learning. Augustine's defense of the community took form in his numerous refutations of pagans, heretics, and schismatics, as well as in his examinations of himself and his meditations on God.

The development of canon law and the revival of civil law, with which the names of Irnerius and Lanfranc are associated, together with the development of medicine in the eleventh century, prepared for the renaissance of the twelfth century. Gratian's *Decreta* were early known as the *Concordance of Discordant Canons.* The method of interpreting apparent conflicts in authoritative pronouncements was a continuation of the uses of rhetoric in the interpretation of texts, and the relevance of that method to the individual is apparent in the divisions of Gratian's work: the first part consists of "distinctions" relevant to the sources of canon law and to ecclesiastical persons and offices, the second consists of *"causae,"* or cases of conflict for resolution, and the third with the regulation of ritual and sacraments for salvation.

Canon law contributed to the scholastic method, by which arguments for opposed solutions of "questions" were judged, and scholastic philosophy placed canon law in the context of the basic laws which provide principles for the resolution of conflicts. The basic question of the relation of ecclesiastical law to civil law, of church to state, was treated increasingly by elaborating the consequences of opposed principles (justified by interpretation of the Bible and Aristotle) by which either might be subordinated to the other or the two might be distinguished. St. Thomas Aquinas' philosophy of law, thus, separated the functions of revealed law from those of natural law without setting them in opposition. Law is a rule or measure of acts by which man is induced to act or is restrained from acting; it is a precept of practical reason. Eternal law (*lex aeterna*) is a dictate of reason emanating from God, who is the ruler of the whole community of the universe.[8] Since all things are ruled by eternal law, the participation of things in divine providence gives them their respective inclinations to their proper acts and ends, and this participation of the rational creature in eternal law is called natural law (*lex naturalis*).[9] Human laws (*leges humanae*) are particular determinations by human reason from the precepts of natural law used as common and undemonstrable principles.[10] Divine law (*lex divina*) provides directions concerning actions to the end of eternal happiness.[11]

II. LAW AND THE RIGHTS OF THE ECONOMIC AND SOCIAL INDIVIDUAL

Laws as legislation rather than law as established custom and rights as liberties rather than the right as absolute or delegated power over others are modern and Western innovations. The medieval equivalent of legislation was finding precepts whose binding force comes from their conformity to universal reason or to immemorial custom. The highest royal power, according to legal writers of the Middle Ages, is "judgment." The mark of sovereignty, acccording to Bodin,[12] is to be able to give law to citizens collectively and individually. The new sovereignty was legislative sovereignty, and its exercise was possible in the new "nation," which had developed legislative organs competent to exercise it. This transition of "law" from declared custom to enacted rule was affected by the development of "rights." The medieval king was a feudal lord, *dominus* as well as *rex*. He bargained with his subjects, and, at propitious junctures of bargaining, subjects were sometimes able to impose checks on his arbitrary acts and to exclude him from interference with their private rights. In this process, the British, American, and French bills of rights of the seventeenth and eighteenth centuries marked culminations of changes that gave a new status to the individual. Doubtless the concepts and principles they employed had all been used and elaborated in previous philosophical speculation. But the bills of rights had legal status in the context of constitutions which were fundamental law. Law-making is a consequence of the exercise of rights; rights are instituted and protected by laws.

The basic antitheses that divided philosophers of law were transformed in the light of these changes. The philosophers of the seventeenth century were not faced by a choice between law as nature or as contract. Hobbes, Pufendorf, Spinoza, Locke, and most of their contemporaries based the Social Compact on Natural Law. As a result, they speculated concerning a state of nature prior to the civil state, but they were not faced by a problem of the priority of right or law, for there are rights and laws of nature as well as rights and laws in the civil state. Two other basic questions took the place of these ancient antitheses as a result of the new conceptions of law-making and of rights. Laws are made either as commands of a sovereign power or as prescriptions of a sovereign will; adjudication according to law is either by examining the consequences of actions for which the individual is accountable or by examining the intentions imputed to him for his actions. The distinction between command and will re-expresses the earlier opposition of arbitrary and natural in the law; and the distinction between accountability and imputation re-expresses the earlier opposition of lawful and right. From the Renaissance to the nineteenth century the main lines of Continental legal philosophy evolved by will and imputation, while British legal philosophy explored the structure of command and accountability.

Pufendorf wrote *The Elements of Universal Jurisprudence* to remedy the inadequate state of the science of law and equity, which is not comprehended in the laws of any single state but which governs the duties of all men to each other, by laying down the definitions and axioms and by deriving the propositions of that science. The first definition is of human actions: "By human actions are meant the voluntary actions of a man in a commonwealth considered with the imputation of their effects."[13] It is followed by a definition of moral objects, suppositious (status) and positive (persons and things). Status is made the basis of moral affairs in the third definition: "Status is a suppositious moral entity in which positive moral objects and, above all, persons, are said to be."[14] The moral person is then defined as "a person considered under that status which he has in communal life."[15] In his *On the Duty of Man and Citizen according to Natural Law*, Pufendorf bases his definition of law on human actions and the wills of individuals.

> Because human actions depend upon the will, but the wills of individuals are not always consistent, therefore, in order to establish order and seemliness among the human race, it was necessary that some norm should come into being, to which actions might

be conformed. . . . That norm is called law (*lex*), that is, a decree by which a superior obliges a subject.[16]

Christian Wolff, in *The Law of Nations Treated According to Scientific Method,* holds that nations may be regarded as individual free persons in a state of nature, subject to the same duties and possessed of the same rights by the law of nature. Rights and duties are derived from that unchangeable law (*lex*) based on the nature of man. The law of nations (*ius gentium*) is therefore part of the law of nature and may be called the *natural* law of nations, from its source, or the *necessary* law of nations, from its power to bind.

> Since nations are moral persons and therefore are subject only to certain rights and duties, which by virtue of the law of nature arise from the social contract, their nature and essence undoubtedly differ very much from the nature and essence of individual men as physical persons. When therefore the duties, which the law of nature prescribes to individuals, and when the rights, which are given to individuals to perform the duties, are applied to nations, since they can be such only as are allowed by their subjects, they must be suitably changed by them, that they may take on a certain new form. And thus the law of nations does not remain the same in all respects as the law of nature in so far as it controls the acts of individuals.[17]

Kant continued the tradition of will and imputation (*Zurechnung*) with modifications required to adjust it to the critical philosophy.

Nature is the art by which God made and governs the world, according to Hobbes, and the study of the commonwealth, which is an artificial man, follows in sequence of the sciences of body and of man. The *De Corpore Politico: or the Elements of Law, Moral and Political* begins with men who are equal in the state of nature and differentiates the covenant by which the state is formed from the law by which the distinction between right and wrong is established.

> . . . law implieth a command; covenant is but a promise. And not every command is law, but only when the command is the reason we have for doing the action commanded. And then only is the reason of our action on the command, when the omitting is therefore hurtful, not because it was hurtful of itself; and doing contrary to a command, were not at all hurtful, if there were not a right in him that commandeth to punish him that so doth.[18]

The absence of obligation is the difference also between a counsel and a law.[19] Right, or *ius*, which is liberty, is the contrary of law, or *lex*, which is obligation,[20] and sin and crime are transgressions of the law, by word or deed, or contempt of the legislator.[21]

John Locke begins *The Second Treatise of Government*[22] with the state of nature in which all men are free and equal and have the right to execute the law of nature. Moral good and evil result from conformity to law.

Good and evil, as hath been shown, are nothing but pleasure or pain, or that which occasions or procures pleasure or pain to us. Moral good and evil, then, is only the conformity of our voluntary actions to some law, whereby good or evil is drawn on us, from the will and power of the law-maker; which good and evil, pleasure or pain, attending our observance or breach of the law by the decree of the law-maker, is that we call reward and punishment.[23]

There are three sorts of moral laws: the divine law, or rule of God, by which men judge whether their actions are sins or duties; the civil law, or rule set by the commonwealth, by which they judge whether they are crimes or innocent; and the philosophical law of opinion or reputation, by which they judge whether they are virtues or vices. Civil law is the result of the establishment by social compact of a body politic under one supreme government, in which each member authorizes the society to make law for him, and the first and fundamental law of all commonwealths is the establishing of the legislative power, which is the supreme power.[24] Bentham, Austin, and John Stuart Mill continued the tradition of command and accountability. Bentham was the first philosopher to use the term "responsibility." Mill defines "responsibility" as punishment, and he uses "accountability" to distinguish the individual from society in two maxims: "first, that the individual is not accountable to society for his actions, in so far as these concern the interests of no person but himself," and "secondly, that for such actions as are prejudicial to the interests of others, the individual is accountable, and may be subjected either to social or legal punishment, if society is of opinion that the one or the other is requisite for its protection."[25]

The conceptions of the community and of the individual were altered by these changes in the conceptions of laws and of rights. Hamilton was convinced that advances in political science made a large republic possible for the first time in the eighteenth century,[26] and Madison argued that popular government depends on the interaction within the republic of many "factions."[27] The French Revolution was an opposition of classes, and it was thought by many besides Babeuf that a second revolution to secure economic equality was needed to reinforce political equality. Economic and civil rights were recognized and increased in the United States under the operation of political rights by decisions of the Supreme Court and by Federal and State legislation. The problems presented by economic and social relations in France and in Europe led to distinctions in the theories of Saint-Simon, Comte, Prudhomme, Marx, and others, in which economic equality is sometimes sought as a prerequisite to political equality, and freedom is achieved with the disappearance of coercive power and the withering away of the state and law. The philosophy of law sought new foundations in further study of forms of imputation (in pure theories of law based on will) or of accountability (in analytical theories of law based on command) developed in historical, economic, anthropological, and sociological philosophies. By the end of the nineteenth century, the concepts of "accountability" and "imputation" were merged in the reflexive concept of "responsibility." The distinction between legislation and judgment ceased to operate as a principle when the realists in jurisprudence turned attention from precedents cited to actions performed in judge-made law and in judicial functions of administrative agencies, and when analysts of legal language examined the possible significances of what was said. Changes in the status of the individual and in the processes of law have made consideration of concrete facts of existence and experience more relevant than speculation on the antecedents and consequences of intentions and commands in the philosophy of law.

III. LAW AND THE RESPONSIBILITIES OF THE CULTURAL INDIVIDUALS

Rights proclaimed to be natural and inborn in general must be specified in particular rights acquired by individual men in the evolution of society. The number of rights and the number of individuals able to exercise them have increased vastly since the first declarations of rights. Laws enacted by a sovereign power must be interpreted, and sanctions must be applied to violations. The number of legislative functions exercised by judiciary and administrative bodies has vastly increased since law-making became a function of society. These changes have been changes in the community and the individual. The universe and the law of nations have been called communities since antiquity, but a new world community has grown up by the extension of the political and civil rights of the bills of rights to new nations. Human rights are natural rights of all men, but the great increase of self-governing nations in the world community since 1945 was the result of the development and growth of other rights: economic rights, due to new knowledge and technology; social rights, due to new self-awareness of peoples, classes, and races; and cultural rights, due to improved communication among parts of the world and traditions. A new nationalism has developed with each stage of the new internationalism. The constituent communities of the world community and of the new communities have also increased. Political imperialism has declined, but international political parties and information services continue to extend and protect political empires. Military imperialism has developed new forms of aggression, and economic imperialism has adapted its operations to new transactions and new agents. Cultural imperialism has transformed and in part appropriated the older forms of imperialism. These changes in the world community and its member communities are reflected in the smaller associations within states and in the lives of individuals, who belong to an increasing number of communities which may restrict their liberties by enforcing conformity or increase them by providing additional opportunities for individual deviance.

The kinds of rights as they developed historically are characterized by the conditions under which they are possible as freedoms. Civil and political rights are freedoms exercised by the individual, and infringements on his freedom of speech or his right to vote may be remedied by removing the obstacles that impede him. Economic and social rights are freedoms which depend upon the circumstances of the individual, and infringements on his freedom from want and from fear can be remedied by putting him in different circumstances or by changes in the community or, ultimately, in the world community. Cultural rights are freedoms which depend on values which the individual finds in communities and which he creates to modify communities, and the exercise of cultural rights guides and transforms the exercise of political, civil, economic, and social rights. The new prominence of cultural rights transforms the concepts of law and right, *lex* and *ius,* in the influence they have in determining the status of the individual. This change is clear if one examines the treatment of recent problems of rights.

The Civil Rights Law passed recently in the United States is a law (*lex*) to enforce rights (*ius*). The rights in question were already guaranteed by amendments to the Constitution. The way to the legislation had been prepared by decisions of the Supreme Court and by actions of administrative agencies of the Federal Government. Appeals to law and actions to arouse public opinion were employments of rights. The use of those rights depended, in turn, on prior exercise of rights by Negroes to improve their economic conditions and to acquire education.

The right to education was esteemed in the United States, in the nineteenth century, because it opened up better careers and access to higher classes in society. The discussion of the right to education is more complex in the twentieth century. It raises questions of changes of standards (and the criticism that departures are debasements), questions of providing facilities and teachers for a vast horde of new students (and the criticism that provisions cannot be adequate), and questions of motivation and occupation of students (and the criticism that the enforced education of all contributes to juvenile delinquency and leisured conformism). The discussion becomes involved in old antitheses of church and state, of local and national supervision for education, and of provision of funds and control of practice. Yet, the increase in the right to education should provide opportunities to reconsider the ends, the contents, the devices, and the continuing operation of education in the life of man.

The formation of the new self-governing states of the last two decades depends on more than the acquisition of the right to self-rule. The problems presented by need of experience in self-government and of trained personnel are not novel difficulties in the exercise of the new right, for the right to self-rule has often in the past led to misrule and massive corruption. There are also economic problems of providing a minimum standard of living and health which have inspired economic and technical assistance and co-operation programs, which are innovations of the twentieth century. There are problems of rights in the aspiration of peoples to progress and to achieve values esteemed. There are problems raised by the rights of the peoples to make their own ultimate decisions. Programs of co-operation to improve material conditions and economic rights may easily run into questions of political interference and political rights, and co-operation for common ends may easily run into questions of disagreement concerning values and order among values and problems of social and cultural rights.

The individual in his relations with others and the individual in his freedoms to act is affected by these changes in lawmaking and in rights. The changes in the conceptions of law and rights present new problems in legal philosophy which are particular instances of changes in the problems presented to philosophy by conceptions and facts encountered in the communities of men and in the nature of things.

Lawmaking in a society has ceased to be a question of identifying the proper authority or power, and has become instead a question of how to secure agreement by discussion as opposed to coercion or subterfuge. The exercise of the political rights of the individual is defined by the conditions of discussion, whether he casts an enforced vote for a single party with no issue or a free vote for one of two or more parties on unclear issues. Philosophy has a function in clarifying issues, and the clarification of issues in laws might be part of the clarification of questions in philosophic discussion by coming to agreement concerning the issues under consideration and concerning the requirements for their resolution. Self-realization is a right exercised in philosophy as well as in lawmaking.

The right to come to agreement by discussion is balanced and influenced by the right to achieve values and to make progress for oneself and those with whom one is associated. What seems to be agreement and consensus is sometimes based on misconception by the other or on self-deception by oneself. Honor, praise, and esteem are signs of what others conceive to be good; material goods are payments or rewards for the good; pleasures are accompaniments of the good. The relation between virtue and honor, pleasure, and property, and the difficulty of determining whether a given act, even one's own, has been performed for duty or for profit are continuing philosophic problems. Parties, schools, traditions, and cultures are placed, where issues are considered, in controversial opposition which can be ended only when controversy is abandoned and discussion is begun by breaking off description of doctrinal differences and by beginning consideration of common problems for which common solutions might be found based on different presuppositions and reasons. Self-perfection is a right which is sometimes a rectification and sometimes an instrumentality of the right of self-realization.

Rights in a society have ceased to be a question of absence of restraining law or deleterious effects on the interests of others, and have become, instead, a question of how to benefit by the advances of knowledge to satisfy one's need and how to participate in the advances of culture to stimulate one's spontaneity. Philosophers have long recognized that the satisfaction of minimal needs is a fundamental good indispensable to other goods, but they have also recognized that wants are susceptible to infinite expansion and that the pursuit of material goods leaves time for no other pursuit. The natural connection formerly seen between work and virtue is involved in the modern paradoxes of increased productivity of the individual and of the machine, and of increased difficulty of distributing products where they are needed and of using time which is not needed for production. Philosophers have suggested that charity alone can place a limit on cupidity and concupiscence. The philosophic consideration of the relation of what is desired to what is desirable might serve as an introduction and model for the philosophic consideration of problems in other fields of thought and action. Self-determination is a right that is sometimes based on nature and sometimes on frustrations and suppressions contrary to nature.

Rights are powers and consist in the exercise of spontaneity. The right to determine one's own ends is no less fundamental than the right to agree on means to recognized ends, or the right to pursue an acknowledged transcendent good, or the right to satisfy one's wants and needs. Like those other rights, it, too, has been advanced as the controlling objective in establishing the rights of the individual and the laws of the societies he forms. If there are self-realizations, self-perfections, and self-determinations, the institutions, the goods, and the natures on which they depend are conceived and formulated ultimately by individuals. Recognition of the right of spontaneity introduces flexibility into the philosophic consideration by which conceptions and purposes are grounded in reality and provides the possibility of growth in the knowledge of truth, of advance in the values pursued, and of coherence in the satisfactions achieved. Spontaneity is a right which permits the testing of opposed ideas, the exploration of divergent insights, and the judgment of diversified pleasures.

1 *De Re Publica*, ii. 21–22.
2 *Ibid.*, ii. 2.
3 *Ibid.*, i. 26–28.
4 *De Legibus*, i. 23.
5 *De Inventione*, i. 8.
6 *Ibid.*, ii. 160–161.
7 *Institutiones*, i. 1.
8 *Summa Theologica*, Ia IIae, q. 91.a.1.
9 *Ibid.*, a.2.
10 *Ibid.*, a.3.
11 *Ibid.*, a.4.
12 Jean Bodin, *The Six Bookes of a Commonweale*, K. D. McRae, ed., Bk. I, chap. 10 (Cambridge: Harvard University Press, 1962), p. 159.
13 Samuel Pufendorf, *Elementorum Jurisprudentiae Universalis*, Liber I, Definitio 1 (Cambridge: Hayes, 1672), p. 1.
14 *Ibid.*, Definitio 3, p. 7.
15 *Ibid.*, Definitio 4, p. 19.
16 Samuel Pufendorf, *De Officio Hominis et Civis*, Bk. I, chap. 2, par. 1–2 (Cambridge: Hayes, 1682), p. 12.
17 Christian Wolff, *Jus Gentium Methodo Scientifica Pertractatum, Praefatio.* (Frankfort, 1764). English translation J. H. Drake. (Oxford: Clarendon Press, 1934), p. 5.
18 Thomas Hobbes, *De Corpore Politico: or the Elements of Law, Moral and Political*, Part II, chap. 8, par. 6. Sir William Molesworth, ed. *The English Works of Thomas Hobbes* (London: Bohn, 1860), Vol. IV, p. 205.
19 *Leviathan: or the Matter, Form, and Power of a Commonwealth, Ecclesiastical and Civil*, Part II, chap. 25. Molesworth edition, Vol. III, p. 241.
20 *Ibid.*, chap. 26, p. 276.
21 *Ibid.*, chap. 27, p. 277.
22 John Locke, *The Second Treatise of Civil Government*, chap. 2, J. W. Gough, ed. (Oxford: Blackwell, 1946), pp. 4–10.
23 *Essay Concerning Human Understanding*, Bk. II, chap. 28, par. 5. A. C. Fraser, ed. (Oxford: Clarendon Press, 1894), Vol. I, p. 474.
24 *The Second Treatise of Civil Government*, chap. 7, par. 89; chap. 11, par. 134; chap. 13, par. 149.
25 John Stuart Mill, *On Liberty*, chap. 5, "Applications." Everyman's Library ed., pp. 149–150.
26 *The Federalist*, No. 9. The Modern Library Edition. pp. 48–49.
27 *Ibid.*, No. 10, pp. 59–62.

RAYMOND POLIN

About the political status
of the contemporary individual in the West

The determination of the political status of the individual in Western civilization is confused today by the reference to the myth of the absolute individual dear to Rousseau. One often used to present the individual, to defend or to condemn him, as if he were a being radically distinct and separable from the others and from the group. But, in reality, the word individual designates expressly an indivisible being.

Whether man is a political animal by nature or by artifice, we must always return to Aristotle's formula: *Anthrōpos, zōon, polītikon* (Man, a political animal).

Certainly, the character, or, at least, the minimum pretension of the individual is to assert himself as a reasonable government of himself: the human individual—otherwise, he would not exist—recognizes himself as a being capable of intelligence and liberty. He exists as soon as he asserts himself, even if he is wrong, as a reasonable existence of a self-contemplating and self-controlling liberty.

But that free individuality has meaning only in relation with social and political structures, in the midst of which it manifests itself and which it confirms in manifesting through them its liberty. The general characteristics of this historical dialectic define the status of the individual in the state where he lives, the sum of the influences which he undergoes, the sum of the influences which he exercises, either by spontaneous reaction or in deliberate fashion. We shall not study this dialectic in general; we shall limit ourselves to the choice of its essential political features for Western Europe in our time.

There is no need, indeed, to emphasize the social conditions of any individual existence, the conditions which make of any individual a social being historically situated, definable at first sight by his participation in a given political community. We are in touch only with civilized individuals, with "moral individuals," according to Rousseau's formula, and not at all with natural individuals, radically isolated and independent.

But, in a social framework, the individual is bound and opposed

473

to everything which is not himself, because he is free in his principle. When opposition arises in a struggle between one individual and another, it bothers and denies one, only to strengthen and to affirm better the other: spontaneous individualism, which was not then in question, was not conscious of itself. On the contrary, it is the individual in himself which is menaced and reduced, submitted, enslaved, when he finds himself opposed to the Sovereign state, capable of deciding on individual rights and capable of allowing or of preventing their exercise. The struggle is concentrated at the still abstract level of the definition and defense of rights: the philosophies of the individual progressively begin.

This is, in fact, the traditional problem: it is a question of defending the individual and his power to govern his life freely and reasonably against the Sovereign, possessor of a power incommensurably larger and capable of coercing, under penalty of death, those who are under his domination, arbitrarily at his pleasure. This is the problem of the time of Locke and Montesquieu. The principles of its solution had been then established, once and for all, even if their application has not stopped being the object of a constantly renewed effort. On one hand, Locke imposed the conviction that the existence of a constitution alone could both assure the good functioning of the Sovereign Power and impose on it respect for necessary rules and limits to safeguard the autonomy of the citizens in the framework of laws. On the other hand, he provoked the acknowledgment of the existence of every human individual as implying natural rights, certain of which were inalienable; these rights were to be acknowledged in the state, in the form of civil rights, guaranteed by it against any attack.

In order that these two principles have a chance of being applied efficiently, there must exist in the state an independent judiciary power to which the individuals can appeal, and a legislative power, the Sovereign Power, in fact, which draws its good will from the fact that it emanates from the people, whereas the people draw their own good will from the fact that it constitutes the origin of the Sovereign Power. Still we must not forget that the rights of individuals thus safeguarded are abstract and formal rights which protect the individuals only in negative fashion by interdictions against exterior attacks; but it is left up to the individuals to use their capacities in order to give these rights a real and concrete content.

The contemporary political problem is entirely different. Certainly, Western democracies give individuals the civil rights which guarantee negatively their lawful protection. But the individuals find themselves from then on, although remaining under the protection of laws and rights, in the presence of a political power become gigantic, and characterized by its narrow centralization, its omnipotence, its ubiquity, its omnipresent administrative organization. The individuals must be gifted with a very exceptional personality; they must be particularly energetic and persevering, or particularly intelligent, or, better, all of that at the same time, and the circumstances must favor them largely, so that they may, by themselves alone, and by their own action, use effectively their rights, give them a concrete existence and develop their capacities in the highest and most harmonious way, in the form of original and coherent individualities. Without these gifts, without this chance, what can average individuals do, what can any individual do, in the presence of a political power which is so transcendent and so immense.

In the face of the omnipotence of the state, the differences between the citizens are erased: they are as if they do not exist. The contemporary democratic feeling consists largely in the consciousness of this de facto equality, in the form of the will of equality, of the wish for homogeneity, which is the principal emotional content of the theory of equality of rights. We feel, indeed, especially in the collective situations of scarcity and misery, a particular comfort in knowing that all of us share an identical destiny. A misery that all undergo is a more easily suffered misery. The more we undergo this equality in misery, the more we feel the solidarity, very often passive and specious, of the weak.

But, opposite this omnipotent state, the individuals are equal in weakness and all the more so, in their situation of independence one from the other, in which they too readily see the testimony and the guarantee of their individuality, when they find themselves isolated and abandoned each to himself. They enjoy all the civil rights of the individuals, but that is what isolates them and makes them equal in weakness, equal in insufficiency. Alienated from their concrete existence, they merely enjoy a specious and abstract kind of autonomy, unconscious as they are of being moved by the whole society they live in. They are weakened by their very individualism.

By a sort of ricochet, Rousseau's type of will to depend on the state rather than to depend on other indviduals, reinforces the state, pushes it toward totalitarianism, or, at least, encourages it to fulfill all sorts of functions which depend, not on the state as a sovereign public person, but on the state as Providence. It is no longer a question of assuring the safety of each person against the menaces of others, but a question of substituting progressively the state for the individuals in the accomplishment of tasks which were their own by nature, and which they have become incapable of assuming, to the state's satisfaction or even to their own satisfaction, so isolated and lost are they in a too-vast and complex mass.

It is, then, the state which, depriving or delivering the parents from their natural attributes, tends to replace the adults in the education of the young. It is the state which replaces the individuals and assumes the functions of prudence and assurance, of which the individual most often proves himself incapable. It is, again, the state which assumes public services which dispersed and isolated individuals prove themselves incapable of organizing and assuming. And, finally, the state, no longer content to define the common good and to pursue its realization, pretends to become judge of individual good. The obligations and the sacrifices, the limits to rights of property which it imposes on the individual no longer concern only the good of all; they prepare what the state considers the private good of individuals.

Being financier, businessman, and consumer, the state, either directly or indirectly, by the weight of its decisions and its orders on the market, has become the principal economic power of the nation. Whether the planning established is rigid or supple, even if it leaves a large field to private initiative, the state is ready to condition closely the economic life of its citizens, to control their activity, to make this activity more or less perilous or profitable. Close or far, the modern state has more or less submitted groups and individuals to its economic guardianship.

Everything happens as if the state, considering itself more and more responsible for the individual destiny of each of its members, decided to take upon itself the controlling and the accomplishment of it. One used to see, very long ago, princes who pretended to assure the eternal salvation of their subjects, with their consent or in spite of it. They were told—by Locke, for example—that they confused the temporal domain, which was entirely theirs, with the spiritual domain, which escaped them. Today, it is biological and social salvation of its citizens which the state pretends to assure. It is within the temporal domain that the state wants to add to the negative efficiency of its power to make laws and to proclaim rights the positive efficiency of the power to administer and to organize. The state not only strives to guarantee the rights; it tries also to impose manners, concrete and effective ways of life.

Besides, from the moment that the state gives itself the right to decide on the particular good of each person and the method of acquiring this good, and then attributes to itself the means to accomplish it, its empire has no more boundaries. The liberal state finds itself caught up in the gears of the totalitarian state. It not only acts for the individual; it also thinks for him: it chooses for the individual his duties toward himself, his personal good, and even his preferences. It pretends even to make him "happy" and "free," with him and even in spite of him, if necessary. So great is the power of the state that it esteems itself as in the end capable of forging a new nature for each man.

From this moment on, is not the state able to assure the happiness of individuals, in fashioning for each person a custom-made nature and in giving to each person his liberty, as well as his duty, to exercise this nature?

Naturally, insinuating itself to such a point into the private life of individuals, political power can take into account only what is common to the personal interest of individuals, in other words, that which concerns personal preservation, peace, order and safety, life and health, safe succession of generations, which are, at best, occasions and conditions for material well-being. True personal life, in whatever it has of uniqueness and originality in each person, finds itself then expelled toward the spiritual and emotional, toward intellectual reflection, adventures of affectivity, personal whims, as much as there remains room for non-illusive autonomy, in a domain so narrow, so de-socialized, so disincarnate. Each individual would be reduced to the circumstances of his human relations, of his career, to his *curriculum vitae,* to his social security number.

Reciprocally, the initiative and the weight of decisions on which the general homogeneity of equals is modeled belong to a limited number of individuals whose individual personality is exalted to the highest point. These are able to deploy fully developed and affirmed individualities. But the eminence of their position makes them exceptional characters, hard to separate from the immediate legend with which excessive use of mechanical means of mass information envelops them. They find themselves placed so far above simple citizens that their situation has hardly any common measure with the situation of the man on the street, and that they can in no case serve as a standard model for the simple citizen, who is, in principle, equal to all the others.

Their action manifests itself through the bonds of personal fidelity woven between them and the members of the team which they have formed and used during their ascension; it happens then that a sort of fidelity is organized around them in the heat of action; it can be made of instantaneous convergence of efforts, sacrifices, interests, or ambitions, rather than of the experienced community of a fundamental human attitude toward the world. But human and direct contacts of leaders with their followers, once power has been achieved, are soon limited in breadth and in intensity. The repercussion of their action develops throughout the state by the intermediary of an administration more and more complicated, more and more bureaucratic, more and more impersonal, which manifests, as opposed to scattered individuals, tentacular and obsessive ubiquity of the state, in a systematically mechanical and irresponsible form.

The selection of men of Government follows strange procedures: how could talents of state leaders be formed, in a natural way, in the midst of a mass of individuals deprived of essential responsibilities, and worried especially about assuring their equality, even if in weakness? The basic equalitarianism of democratic society hates rational organization of the selection and formation of ruling élites. The pressure of mass education and of education en masse, the permanent evocation of an equalitarian justice, hinders, in fact, the research and the education of those who could appear as privileged beings. In nations where aristocratic structures do not subsist, there, where intermediary bodies propitious to the formation of their own élites do not develop, Statesmen are sometimes recruited, at least the more important ones, under the trial or the emergency of events, the others among administrators broken in by the manipulation of groups or among technicians; the latter impose themselves on the mass by their dexterity of technocrats and their intelligence of executors, the former by their force of character and by the courage of their passions. But it is chance, circumstances, good fortune, which, in fact, play the essential role in the selection. Democratic processes of choice, founded on voting, produce political technicians especially, men skillful without greatness, politicians and not political men.

In periods without history, the repercussion of equalitarian tendencies felt through the manners and the employees of the state; the same tendencies encourage the formation of balanced forces which are reciprocally neutralized and mutually rendered inefficient. The instruments of an omnipotent power are assembled, but the state, entangled in its machinery, oriented in contradictory directions by contradictory exigencies, becomes slowly paralyzed and hardly good for the traditional administration of current affairs: the Government disappears behind the Administration. If new problems or exceptional perils should arise, there would be all the more reason for the development of the conditions of existence and the temptations of an authoritarian regime, soon perhaps despotic. Should a team of resolute men appear, the omnipotence of the state could soon recover all its efficiency over the homogeneous mass of individuals blended together in a common equality and similar powerlessness.

When the event arises, can one still have many illusions about the efficiency of the democratic character of the state when, at long intervals of time, the people, by its vote, designates the representatives who legislate and govern in its name? One knows that there are many ways to falsify a popular election or to make the results specious, even when this procedure keeps its meaning and still allows one to say that the people are sovereign; what can one say of the individuals and of the infinitesimal and spasmodic authority which each person gets, every four years, to be a member of the Sovereign?

Can one see, in a general way, a satisfactory affirmation of the individual in such a juridical abstract framework, when customs, a certain form of civilization, are alone able to permit each person to play a real role conforming to his personality? Democracies of this type, are they not predisposed to the appearance of tyrannies? Montesquieu, de Tocqueville, Elie Halévy, each, in his turn, has feared or observed this downfall.

Until now, liberal democracies have not come in general to this point. Precisely because there always reigns among them a spirit of liberty relatively respectful of individuals, because one cares to give a real exstence to the rights of each person, and because there exist enough individuals to manifest their individuality and to defend the individuality of others against encroaching power, against the oppressing solicitude of Administration, and against absorption in the homogeneity of the masses.

Constitutions, or the practice of constitutional habits, still appear there as the keystone of the life of the people. The consultation of the sovereign people is there considered, not only as a symbol, but as a technical necessity and as a political requirement. The impartial practice of a system of free elections or of free referendum appears as the only means in a representative state to restore, at least by intervals, to each individual an authority permitting him, first, to choose men to represent him in the exercise of sovereignty, then, to try to orient a policy in a certain direction, and, finally, to control, or at least to interrupt its execution. However imperfect this practice may be, the effort which arbitrary regimes make to push it aside proves very well, in the long run, its efficiency in the defense and exercise of individual liberties.

In the liberal state, the tribunals have still kept their independence in respect to political power; they maintain, above this power, laws and right; one even sees them resist the invocation of Reason of state when they judge it gratuitous and ill-timed. It remains possible for the individual to defend himself against the arbitrary, and even against the dissimulated, grasp of the state, by the practice of all the forms of liberty to which the state recognizes the individual's right of appeal even if it is against itself.

And, last but not least, in this liberal state, customs and manners are really liberal in the relationships between one individual and another, and the traditions of personal autonomy and of respect for others are profound, as well at the level of opinions as at the level of personal conduct. I want as proof only the universal will to organize, in one way or another, a really democratic education, more and more open to the masses, where selection tends to be made especially according to merit, and where social promotion is the object of growing care and worry. No doubt, one must not see in these tendencies manifestations of virtue and generosity, but the expression of this diffused taste becomes a tradition in favor of equality and liberty, which makes Western democracies living democracies. Democrats according to this fashion would gladly call justice the effort to proportion the situations obtained to individual merits, every time that this effort was inspired by the recognition of free activity for each person and by the will to assure the equality of conditions, the quality of opportunity, in which this activity is exercised. They would have the greatest scruples not to share at least in principle, this will of Justice.

This liberalism of manners has been vigorous and open enough, moreover, to prevent each individual from enclosing himself in a selfish isolation and to provoke collective reactions of defense among individuals: the latter, taking advantage of the liberties of association, of which the respect has been progressively imposed, have, little by little, reconstituted those intermediary bodies whose disappearance had been often deplored by the liberal philosophers, from Montesquieu to de Tocqueville. To the vestiges of the subsisting constituted bodies have been added, little by little, groups of all sorts: to the churches and the universities have been added economic societies, political parties, professional groups, syndicates, unions, in the midst of all of which individuals have been able to develop an action which becomes more efficient in a framework more restrained, and to form in this action their own social abilities. The education of personalities has there found a more appropriate framework, better adapted to their forces, and, at the same time, their defense has been better assured against the pressures of the state and against their being reduced to a homogeneous mass.

Above the inorganic network of incoherent reactions to which individuals quite vainly abandon themselves opposite the state is constituted, little by little, a game (inco-ordinated moreover) of pressure groups capable of obtaining, in the state considerable advantages for themselves, acting as interest groups, or for their members. By a sort of reciprocal action, the state, placed in the presence of solid forces, is brought back to the role of umpire or of trustee of the general interest. Forced to bring about compromises between divergent interests and to control their execution, it is encouraged to use its power, not to reinforce its own strength, but to arbitrate the division of national revenue and to enlarge common prosperity from which all citizens can hope to benefit individually.

These observations on the vitality of individuals, on their persistent capacity to assert their autonomy, their initiative, are not simple hypotheses. A very new phenomenon in modern states, the appearance, on many occasions, of movements of profound and efficient resistance, often impossible to destroy, could furnish a valid proof of these observations.

Certainly, the right to resist and to revolt poses a traditional problem which philosophers have discussed and which written constitutions have rarely admitted. One cannot imagine that a modern state makes such dispositions legal.

But, in the disorder provoked first by foreign wars and then under the pressure of minority passions, one sees, in a modern state, acts of systematic disobedience to the law, before the production, not of organized attempts at revolution, but of terrorist acts or efforts to bring about disorder in state organizations, or even to reduce it to powerlessness. Techniques of clandestine struggle are little by little perfected. Guerilla warfare is established and reveals itself, when animated by resolute men, very efficient in its enterprises and most often irreducible, even in the long run, by the heavy and massive means which are the only means the modern state knows how to put into effect.

Most often, resistance movements of this type receive the help of some foreign power in the course of a hot or cold war. They tend to organize themselves in coherent groups. But, at the origin and even in the course of action, because of the systematically dispersed character of their interventions, it is the individuals who play the decisive role. One sees small teams maneuver, and each of them is animated by some particularly vigorous personality; one expects almost everything from the initiative and bravery of the individuals. Most often, it is exceptional personalities who start the movement; in the beginning, they are almost alone. Never has the affirmation of the individual, entering into revolt against the state, been more manifest. And, on the warp of favorable circumstances, the network of dissidence is woven from one individual to another: only person-to-person relationships can, in the shadow of secrecy form clandestine and strong enough bonds.

Especially in countries accustomed to the exercise of individual rights, this practice of resistance, always possible, is the best proof that, whatever the omnipotence of the state may be, the liberty of the individual remains, not only imprescriptible, but also, in spite of the worst lethargy and the longest silence, impossible to discourage and to reduce. Totalitarian regimes are precarious because they are totalitarian: the enslavement of individual liberties is never definitive because nothing human lasts without the help of the force of the labor of the individuals and without the force of their active freedom.

In other words, if the best guarantee of individual liberties resides, even in liberal states, in the existence of a veritable liberalism in manners and in customs, this guarantee finds its source, its inexhaustible source, in the nature of man and of human groups.

One must not forget that, within the necessary dialectic of the individual and the state, the very source of this political dialectic is found in the existence of the political individual, individual and social being at the same time, who is finally a moral existence. Whatever may be the political structures and the circumstances of his existence, in the last resort, the individual must, in his liberty, defend himself, free himself, save himself. To be or not to be oneself, that is the moral problem, and the principle of the political problems of the individual.

Even in totalitarian democracies, the pre-eminence of the personified Whole in the total state provides only one of the moments of the dialectic; it implies necessarily, if one does not recognize that history has been terminated, the affirmation of the other moment, the individual, the living principle of liberty, negation, active transcendence, creation. Whatever one does and however one appreciates him, the individual always remains the individual, in his prison of flesh, with or without his conquests, his rights, his possessions, and his works, with his power to desire and to judge, with his power to refuse and to transcend, and who is never satisfied, and who is never happy, and who can always risk his life for his values.

Western democracies are from then on social democracies, even when they pretend not to be socialist. They all require and assure in fact the narrow participation of the state with the life of its individuals. But they hardly accept the recognition *de jure* of the primacy of the Whole; they refuse to admit that the individual is nothing if not a member of the political community and that his own existence is only the product of a common work which surpasses him on all sides. For, even if he were then the essential mediator, he would be neither principle nor end. The principle and the end would be, actually, the state in its totality and, finally, humanity and man as such. Liberal democracies maintain that, if nothing is accomplished except in the state and through its institutions, everything comes from the individual and must be accomplished, in the last analysis, for him. Each individual, no doubt, finds his task his most exacting duty in the collaboration with this work which surpasses him. But this entire work is destined to make possible, now and in the future, the highest development, the most complete and the most personal one, of each person, so far as it is compatible with that of the others.

At the border of that democratic conception, and perhaps not without relation to certain of its latent intentions, some people, in a perspective one should call more aristocratic, in the best sense of the word, would envisage, willingly no doubt, once average well-being corresponding with national prosperity is assured for all, that the most gifted in each generation could develop their individualities and accomplish their personal work in a privileged fashion.

In the last analysis, in a modern state—in France, for example —what do we call an individual? It is, first, a human being in which as such one recognizes an incomparable dignity, because he is capable of freedom; it is in this sense that the individual is given, but only in its principle. It is, next, the same human being, on the one hand, because he is fundamentally identical with all others in his principles of existence, and, on the other hand, because he is fundamentally different from all others in his very existence, in his very original being. And that definition would suffice if it were merely a question of an individual *de jure*.

But, considered only in his rights, the individual still remains an abstract and partial being; he has now just to exist. The concrete individual, the individual par excellence, is the individual existing because of an internal obligation, he who animates the efficient works of his freedom with reasonable meaning; in his works, reason and freedom are identified for himself and for others, in spite of, by virtue of, their strict individuality. That individual is never entirely an individual, in solitude and for hmself alone. He has a chance to become that complete individual only with others and by relationships helps with them, through the understanding and the acknowledgment which they are lead, by his works, to accord to him. This is a meaningful individual, a meaningful man.

Thus, if the individual is sufficiently given as such in his principles, if he is made possible by his rights, he arrives at concrete existence only as long as he succeeds in fulfilling his obligations in respect to himself and to others. But the requirements of practical reason, which are the requirements of freedom, stay always open. The individual remains imperfect and dissatisfied, and because he fulfills himself freely, and as long as he remains capable of accomplishing this obligation, and because he depends always on other liberties: does not liberty maintain a distance between what one is and what one should be or what one wants to be.

How can one be surprised, then, if individual existence is always a challenge, if it appears always fragile and threatened, if one must always defend it from within and from without, purify and protect it, fight for it?

But nothing is ever lost, since the permanent source of human existence springs from individuals alone. For them, it is always a matter of education of oneself and of others. Through the pressures one undergoes, in whatever situation one exists, to make of oneself a concrete individual represents an obligation, and one can proclaim that this achievement depends always, in the long run, on oneself. To be recognized as an individual, to exist as an individual among other individuals, that is always the human existence, the human risk, the human adventure, because, if that effort is always up to oneself, it is also up to others and to fortune or, as one used to say, to history.

Appendix

Public Lectures

STERLING M. McMURRIN

The individual in American philosophy

If we cast about in the variegated field of American thought that now abounds with so many species of the better known Western *isms* —real, ideal, pragmatic, positive, phenomenal, and existential—in search of a general characteristic, common quality, or basic ingredient that provides some unity in the diversity and describes American philosophy in terms of some distinctive feature by which it can be at least roughly identified, the search is soon rewarded. For nothing is more immediately evident in all these isms than what might be called an almost preoccupying concern for the individual, the unique, the particular. If this is not an original, it is at least an indigenous property that infects every school of American thought, every major philosophical construction. It is a property that informs the character of both metaphysics and ethics and transforms whatever else it may touch, a radical individualism that insists that reality resides in the individual as such, the individual thing, event, or person, and that value, however else it may be described, is in the end definable only with reference to the individual. It is perhaps not too much to say that this concern for the individual, which is the common ingredient of American thought whether the issue is social, metaphysical, religious, or moral, must be built securely into any future philosophic endeavor that hopes to capture a responsible segment of the American mind, inspire viable responses in the attitude and practice of the American people, or importantly affect the character of their institutions.

This is not a matter that pertains simply to technical or academic philosophy. It is true of philosophy considered in the broadest possible sense, to include also the body of half-articulate ideas and attitudes that compose what might be called the general disposition of the culture, a kind of sub-philosophy that resides even in the folkways and deeply affects the colloquial language, and that on occasion reaches expression in national oratory, poetry, fiction, and eventually in religion, theology, and academic metaphysics. For in the various and subtle ways by which practice and theory influence and determine one another, philosophic doctrines summarize and express both the form and substance of a culture and at the same time are among its major determinants. If individualism is a common and dependable ingredient of the technical philosophy, it is also a large factor in the ordinary assumptions, practical attitudes, and social action of the people.

This philosophical individualism, which is so much a part of the American mind and temper, which discloses so much of the nation's character, and is the foundation of its democratic institutions, is clearly rooted historically in old-world origins, communicated to the American people largely as a British inheritance. The broad outlines of at least three major agents of this legacy are readily distinguished —Puritanism, the Common Law, and the empirical method and nominalistic metaphysics of traditional British philosophy.

Puritanism, without question the most powerful single cultural force in the shaping of American society, shared with the whole of the Judeo-Christian religion its overwhelming commitment to both the reality and intrinsic worth of the individual person. The soul is created by a free act of God. By the divine fiat it now exists where nothing existed—not a part, or facet, or aspect, or phrase, or element of the divine being—not an emanation, effusion, radiation, or other issue of that being—but a substance, simple and not composed, freely created, that might not have been created, something genuinely real with the realest of reality, added to the world, that might not have been added. The Calvinist theology, which was the foundation of the whole structure of Puritanism, in greatly accentuating the Biblical conception of God's transcendence, setting him ontologically over against his creation, thereby insured the distinctive reality of human souls by pointing up their contingency and finiteness. Man lives and moves and has his being in God, by the grace of his creative act. But man's being is not the being of God. The Christian Church had always shunned pantheism as at best a kind of sentimental and at worst a deceitful atheism, and even its mystics were often under suspicion because of their monistic and somewhat anarchistic proclivities. And in Calvinism, with its overarching concern for the divine sovereignty, there was a willingness even to court the dangers of deism rather than risk the seductions of pantheism that are incipient in every theistic dogma that fails to celebrate the transcendence of God and to remind us thereby of his ontological distance from his creatures.

But more than that, the Puritan theology, which provided the chief context of intellectual life and thought for the American people in their early years, and by whose backwash we are still profoundly affected, raised the individual to a plane of high dignity, notwithstanding its excessive doctrines of sin and guilt and election. For it magnified the importance of the moral will of the individual person, placed the autonomous moral conscience at the center of individual being, and ennobled the vocation of man as the finite person engaged in the creation of the kingdom of God. There was always the tension of the individual with the Church and the community, but there was no question about the direction of the word of God. It aimed straight for the conscience of the individual. No doctrine of divine election or theory of physical or social determinism, however subtle or sophisticated or closely reasoned, has relieved the individual of his awful responsibility for moral decision. More than anywhere else, it is here that he encounters his own being, for it is here that he stands over against his fellow men, God, and the world.

If theology and religion came to America with the English Bible, the Common Law was transported simply by the English language. It was taken for granted like the air and the sunshine, as one of the elements that provided and sustained life. Until quite recently, Blackstone's interpretation of the Common Law dominated American legal thought and practice, the ultimate supremacy of the law conceived as a compound of natural rights assured by an eternal reason and the will of the supreme power in the state. For Americans, this was the will of the people.

The law was the guardian of the liberties of the individual. It secured his rights, established him in the courts and in the political life of the community and nation, and protected his person and his property from seizure by thieves or tyrants. When eventually the utilitarian and pragmatic disposition of American thought uprooted the law from its cosmic ground and made it more responsive to changing social circumstance, the individual's liberties and rights were already secured, ideally though not always in fact, by constitutional and statute guarantees.

That American philosophy in its more creative decades has been on the whole remarkably relevant to the facts of experience and to the problems of human existence, a practical quest for the proximate good rather than a speculation on ultimate reality, is due in part to its inheritance of the British preference for empirical as against rationalistic method and analysis as against speculation, a kind of common-sense worldliness and a willingness to deal with parts rather than wholes and to settle for something less than total and certain knowledge. It is not that American thought has not gained much from its commerce with other cultures, especially French and German, and more recently Oriental. But any listing of philosophical ancestors who have contributed fundamentally to the making of the American mind must include the two Bacons, Ockham, Locke, Berkeley, Hume, Adam Smith, Bentham, John Stuart Mill, and Darwin, those very names which suggest a primary interest in individual things and events, a dependence on sensory experience, the virtues of inductive procedures, the priority of the individual over the universal, and a hearty dislike for the Absolute.

It was Locke, of course, among America's intellectual forebears, who left the deepest imprint on this country's individualism. For, not only did his empirical method and nominalism have a lasting effect upon the character of America's metaphysics, his social philosophy helped to shape both its political thought and institutions of government, in which the state is conceived as an instrument in the service of the individual, the protection of his person and his property. From Jefferson, in whom the psychology, metaphysics, and social theory of Locke joined the even more radical individualism of Rousseau, issued the classical American political theory that the state is a non-organic contractual entity composed of individuals whose freedom is protected by it but not derived from it or achieved through it, and that government is with the consent of the governed, a theory that has sunk deep into the political consciousness and moral conscience of the American people. Such a philosophy is not without theoretic and practical difficulties, for it treats society as a mechanical conjunction of otherwise disconnected individuals, and it fails to regard fully their living organic relationship to one another and to the social whole. But it has worked remarkably well as a ground for democratic political and social action, and in recent decades, with the increasing complexities of society, its negativism has yielded to a more positive conception of the constructive function of government. And, most importantly, it has been the chief guardian of American individualism against the absolute or totalitarian state.

Whitman and Emerson may be taken as representative of the literary expression of American individualism—not because they are typical, but because they so eloquently voiced the deep-rooted sentiments of a culture old in its inheritance and young in its hopes and aspiration. They belonged to the romantic era between the flourish of political thought in the American Age of Reason and the rise of academic philosophy. It was an era when American philosophy was borne largely by poets and men of letters, a time of pioneer exuberance, of increase and expansion, but a time marked as well by the tragedies of slavery and civil war.

Whitman was a poet-prophet, alive with enthusiasm and energy, with passion, optimism, sympathy, and expectation. His subject is the meaning and destiny of America, but the primary object of his interest is the individual person—the common person, each man equal to every other, not the great and the heroic, unless every man and every woman can be great and heroic.

"Under neath all, individuals!," he said.
"I swear nothing is good to me now that ignores individuals,
   The American compact is altogether with individuals,

> The only government is that which makes minute of
>   individuals,
> The whole theory of the universe is directed to one
>   single individual—namely to You."

Emerson, too, was a poet and prophet, but also a reformer. In him the moral fires of Puritanism were still ablaze albeit amidst somewhat unfamiliar surroundings. He was a champion of difference, independence, and non-conformity. The individual's virtue is in his own individuality. "What I must do," he said, "is all that concerns me, not what the people think. . . . This rule may serve for the whole distinction between greatness and meanness . . . . the great man is he who in the midst of the crowd keeps with perfect sweetness the independence of solitude." The individual is found in his own creativeness, in his own freedom, in the self-reliance that is an "aversion" to conformity.

It is not that Whitman and Emerson were wanting in synoptic vision, that they failed to judge the moral solidarity of mankind or had no real sense of totalities or grasp of unity, integrity, and wholeness. Far from it. Whitman had his moments of pantheism and the great weight of Emerson's thought, especially in his later years, was thrown solidly behind a spiritualistic monistic conception of reality. Nature, he held, is a revelation of the divine spirit, and every person a configuration of it. Emerson was opposed to the sensory-knowledge claims of the empirics and was indifferent to science and its methods. He was intuitive, mystical, and oracular, and in his pantheistic inclination bore a strong resemblance to Schelling, who had greatly influenced him. Indeed, Emerson's monism places such a large strain upon the pluralistic thesis of this paper that I am sorely tempted to accuse him of being at times downright un-American. As when he says, for instance, "Of the universal mind each individual man is one more incarnation," or "I am part and parcel of God," or "I wish to speak with all respect of persons," but "they melt so fast into each other . . . . it needs an effort to treat them as individuals."

But elsewhere he is at least partially redeemed, as when he speaks of Nature, that all-enveloping Divine, "rushing into persons," persons who have the freedom to live or break the moral law.

> For he that ruleth high and wise,
>   Nor pauseth in His plan,
> Will take the sun out of the skies,
>   Ere freedom out of man.

All of which supports an important corollary of my thesis, that even a quite determined absolutist finds his own absolutism difficult to live with on American intellectual soil.

It would be a gross error, of course, to suppose that because absolutistic metaphysics is not indigenous to America it has made no serious impact here. On the contrary, the impact of the German-born idealistic absolutism has been great and has had a lasting effect even on the character of American individualism. When Hegel died in 1831 he was already established as the center of European philosophical interest and the chief philosophical influence of his era. The Hegelian system of absolute idealism, though it was something of an anomaly in a scientific age, expressed the large literary, historical, religious, social, and political interests and attitudes of the time, a luxuriant speculation that wrapped up the total universe in a single package that accounted for everything from the motion of atoms to the movement of human history and described reality ultimately in good nineteenth-century style as dynamic growth, process, and progress. The influence of Hegelianism, first in Germany, and then throughout the world, extending into virtually every area of thought, was without precedent since the impact of Plato and Aristotle on Hellenistic and Christian civilization. To contend seriously and with sophistication in matters pertaining to religion, history, society, or politics meant at least to come to grips with the dictates of the Hegelian absolutism, to accept, reject, revise, or at least to vilify that theory, but not to ignore it.

Now, the point of mentioning Hegelianism here is simply that in its several versions it was the chief source of American idealism, and where it reached the United States, as it did in a variety of forms, perversions, and connections, it was the chief threat to the native philosophical individualism. The strength of that individualism, therefore, can be measured by its performance in the ensuing battle.

The basic question here, in the discussion of individualism and absolutism, is the question of where the crux of reality lies. Does reality reside primarily and essentially in concrete particular individuals, whether things, events, or persons, so that when taken in their totality, as, for instance, the totality of society, that totality is really a totality, that is, a total of individuals or particulars, where ontological priority belongs to the particulars and not to the total? Or does reality reside essentially in the whole, and not in any constituent parts or elements of the whole, and, therefore, the whole is not simply a totality in the sense of being a total, or sum of something, but is rather an entity which has genuine being, indeed is being as such, so that whatever else may be real enjoys its reality by being a part or facet or aspect of this single whole? For there can be only one whole, which is the Absolute, unconditioned and unrelated, whose reality, as in Hegel, may not be transcendent to the particulars of experience, and may even have no life or experience apart from those particulars, but which is, nevertheless, the concretely real by virtue of the total internal relatedness of all things. Or, finally, are particulars ontologically definable only in terms of the whole, and the whole only in terms of the particulars, a kind of metaphysical reciprocity?

Though in the United States absolutism in its various forms has had strong advocates and partisans, at their hands it has been radically transformed, for invariably it has received the kiss of death, the kiss of American individualism. This was true in the case of the St. Louis Hegelianism, and it was also true in the philosophy of Josiah Royce, the foremost American idealist, who, though not by any means a Hegelian, imbibed idealism directly from the German fount and tried heroically all his years to be a good conscientious absolutist.

Royce's philosophy was far more original and American than many suppose. He was deeply affected by James's voluntarism, and in logic he drew more from Peirce than from the Hegelians. His absolutism followed from his logic and his social and religious interest. Royce's primary concern is exhibited in the very title of his Gifford Lectures, *The World and the Individual,* the classic instance of American metaphysics. Here the Absolute was declared and defended, but, by means of shrewd and subtle logic involving the principle that unity and diversity are mutually dependent, the genuine reality of individual minds was insisted upon. ". . . our primary question in regard to the finite human individual," he said, "in his relation to the divine life, is merely the question. In what sense does the finite Being retain, despite the unity of the whole divine life, any individual significance of his own, and what is the relation of this finite significance to the meaning and plan of the whole?"

In opposition to the British idealist Bradley, who in his monumental work *Appearance and Reality* had advanced an essentially impersonal absolutism that admitted the individual self as a fact but denied that it had genuine reality, Royce argued that Reality's "unity in its wholeness, and its infinite variety in expression, are both of an individual character. The constituent individuals are not 'absorbed' or 'transmuted' in the whole. The whole is One Self; but therefore is all its own constitution equally necessary to its Selfhood. Hence it is an Individual of Individuals." That the Absolute to be genuinely absolute must be a Self and that it must be in some sense an embodiment of genuinely individual selves whose individuality is not thereby destroyed was argued almost endlessly by Royce.

Royce was obsessed with the idea and ideal of community. Not a simple collection of individuals, but an organic whole in which is ultimately realized the Christian blessedness. It is the Spirit of Community that is the Absolute. But, because it is a genuine community, the Absolute does not destroy the individual. Here is the conjunction of the one and the many where it is the very involvement with a total unity that gives a fullness of meaning and value to the individual. Each has his own worth and his own destiny. It is in his will, purpose, and action, which relates to the life of the whole, that the person finds his genuine individuality. In decision and action the individual stands alone with his responsibility.

Royce's idealism for a time enjoyed a large influence in American thought, religion, and morals. But today, like all idealisms, it is in decline, eclipsed, at least for a time, by analytic, existential, and positivistic thought. It cannot be said that he fully succeeded in reconciling the principle of unity with the fact of multiplicity, the world with the individual. But it can be said with some assurance that no philosopher at any time or place has brought to that large problem a greater dialectical skill, more impressive intellectual equipment, or a more sensitive and dedicated purpose.

A second exhibit of the clash of the Absolute with American individualism is the personalistic idealist Borden Parker Bowne, a contemporary of Royce, whose influence has produced disciples to the third generation and, like that of Royce, has had a large impact not only upon academic philosophy but as well upon the character of much Protestant thought in this country. Bowne's Hegelianism came especially through the German philosopher Hermann Lotze, and his main concern was in fashioning a philosophical justification for Christian theism and Christian piety by establishing personalistic foundations for reality in opposition to the prevailing mechanism of his time. He was not a genuine full-fledged absolutist, therefore, even by profession, because absolutism is in principle antithetical to Christian theism.

The World Ground itself, to use Bowne's language, the ground of all being, must be conceived as personal, as Divine Personality, for only in the fact of personality can be found the key that unlocks the paradoxical metaphysical mysteries; only personality as the ultimate reality can overcome the contradictions of unity and multiplicity, of static being and the process of becoming, of transcendence and immanence. God as a Divine Person is both the creator and ground of the world, including finite individual personality. The individual human person is not in any absolute sense independent and self-sufficient, for his existence is contingent upon the creating and sustaining power of God, the only complete and perfect personality, the Infinite Being and ground of all reality. But the human self is, nevertheless, genuinely real, a center of reality and a center of value, with authentic freedom and self-determination. It is not lost in the totality of being, either in its ontological station or its ultimate intrinsic worth. The defense of such a personalism by the employment of idealistic arguments drawn especially from the

Kantian-Hegelian metaphysics has not been a simple task for the successors of Bowne, but today theirs is among the most vigorous schools of American philosophy.

One more example of American idealism exhibiting the Hegelian influence without the conventional absolutism, this time a radical revolt against the Absolute rather than a calculated compromise with it—the pluralistic personalism of George Holmes Howison, who established academic philosophy on the Pacific Coast. Reality, he argued, in his now famous but rarely read lectures, consists essentially of individual selves, or minds, or souls—uncreated, underived, and indestructible. These constitute a great community, a communion of minds that is the foundation of all reality. There is no absolute God who is the ground of the being of all other selves, for God is one of them and together they move the world. Howison was opposed to every form of absolutism, whether materialistic or pantheistic, and in his doctrine that the souls of men are not different in character from the personality of God he expressed at one and the same time the case for Christian theism and the radical pluralism and individualism of American life and of the American social and political ideal.

Now, I have presented three major instances of American idealism as exhibits of individualism, because idealism has been responsible for much of the world's absolutism, not only in the Occident and in modern times, but in the ancient world and in the Orient as well. But the case for philosophical individualism has much support from other quarters in indigenous American philosophy, from the realists, whose work in both logic and psychology has been original and creative, and especially from the pragmatists. Now, a few words on the individualism of pragmatism, because here is the philosophy that is at one and the same time most native to American intellectual soil, most original as an American product, and the most consistently pluralistic and anti-absolutistic of the American schools.

In his youth, Dewey was a Hegelian, and in an inverted sort of way his Hegelianism affected, and I believe for good, the general character of his individualism. No one, certainly, could fail to recognize that John Dewey was one of the strongest, most persuasive, and most intelligent advocates of a genuine individualism. Although his moral philosophy was opposed in principle to absolutisms of every kind, it is probably fair to say of Dewey that he made an absolute value of the freedom of the individual. More than any other person, he symbolizes the ideal of liberal American culture—the full commitment to the worth of the individual, to reason, and to the democratic process, faith in the capacity of intelligent men of good will to achieve the good society through the instrumentality of scientific knowledge.

Dewey was an empiricist, of course, and a nominalist, and his ethics was grounded in social and psychological considerations rather than in abstract metaphysics or dogmatic theology. His moral philosophy clearly shows his Calvinist heritage in spite of his humanistic heresy and his contempt for most of what Calvinism represents in both religion and morals. Dewey's Hegelian education made a lasting impact upon his philosophy, especially at the point of his concept of the individual, for he refused to consider society as an atomistic collection of discrete individuals in the typical empirical tradition of Locke and his successors. He argued, rather, for a conception of the individual person that described him essentially within an organic social context. There is no individual person in total abstraction from society, insisted Dewey, and this principle, profound in its meaning and far-reaching in its consequences for psychology, religion, social theory, and social and political practice, became the watchword of the later pragmatic philosophers, who, with Dewey, believed that moral philosophy carries a burden of responsibility for the moral improvement of the individual and his society.

My final exhibit of American individualism is, of course, William James, a philosopher less orderly in his thought than Dewey and the instrumentalists, less given to the niceties of reason and logic than Royce and the idealists, and less sophisticated than both in his grasp of the structure of society and the social nature of the individual. But no one will ever be a more committed champion of the individual. No one will ever blast the Absolute with a stronger blast or attack more ruthlessly its intellectual foundations. James suffered an intellectual allergy to Hegelianism in all its forms—its rationalism, its intellectualism, its pantheism, its eternalism, its aestheticism, its absolutism. Perhaps at times he grossly overstated the case of what he called the "block universe," but his purposes were clear and commendable. He had contempt for whatever rode roughshod over the authentic life of the individual, over the fact, the "aweful" fact, of moral freedom—contempt for whatever denied the reality of personal hope and joy, of suffering, failure, loss and despair. In short, James did not like the Absolute. He opposed the concept of the metaphysical Absolute because he believed that it robbed man of the moral seriousness of life, that it destroyed the meaning of originality and heroism, of moral spontaneity and freedom, that it made a mockery of every discrimination of good and evil. Though James was a genuine cosmopolitan with a European education, though being born to wealth and refinement he knew nothing of the struggle for existence that was a chief root of his country's individualism, and, though his metaphysics showed a decided influence from the French personalists and the British utilitarians, he was the epitome of the genius of American philosophy. Here was the chief celebrant of the individual in the whole history of Occidental philosophy—the most ruthless enemy of the Absolute.

Now, to make a long story short, James said that the universe is not really a universe; it is a multiverse. All one has to do to see this, he said, is to look around. The world is a collection of things that are individually real—objects, events, and persons. Reality resides in *them,* not in some kind of grand unity from which they derive their being. The world in principle is temporal and additive. Things could conceivably be added to it, or subtracted from it, because they are real in their individuality. Everything, including the human individual, is related to every other thing by relations that are external to it, that stand between the things and events that are related and prevent them from being swallowed up by another and eventually by some monstrous Absolute. The world is what it appears to us to be before we are corrupted by the subtle machinations of rationalistic philosophy. We should refuse to permit logical prostitutions of the mind to deny the most obvious facts of experience.

And what, for James, is the importance of all of this? Simply that even God must come to terms with the fact of the individual person and his moral freedom. Though he was a defender of the mystics and even had a confessed longing for unity with the divine, James insisted that God is not some timeless, motionless Absolute containing the world in his being, or a sovereign Creator creating it from nothing. Not is he an absentee deity whose world deteriorates by neglect and default, or a Divine All in whom all evil is transmuted into good, for whose total perspective moral distinctions have no meaning, or for whom evil is simply the privation of the good. For James, good and evil are genuinely real, because the individual and his moral freedom and moral responsibility are genuinely real. And his God is not in some far-off heaven where all is well. In times like these, he seems to say, God has no business hanging around heaven. He is, to use James's own language, down in all the muck and dirt of the universe struggling to clean it up—struggling to achieve a moral victory in an unfinished world where dangers are real and failures as well as successes are real, and where there are no guarantees because human freedom is real. God is struggling in a struggle in which the moral decisions of finite human beings make a difference, not only in human history, but perhaps the difference between death and life for the world. This is genuine individualism. It is individualism with a kind of melodramatic recklessness, and certainly with a vengeance. But it eloquently expresses the genius and spirit of American thought and culture.

Now, the American people have a deep and firm conviction that in some way the good of the individual is coincident with the good of society and with the good of the culture, and that, therefore, to pursue ends that are defined by the well-being of the individual person is not only to serve his proper interests and enhance the quality of his life, but also to build into the social order whatever virtues of cohesion, integrity, and rectitude are required for its health and security, and to bring to the culture those qualities of excellence that must adorn the life of a free people, and to bring to it also that spirit and strength and purpose without which no civilization can look confidently to the future. Indeed, it can be said that this faith in the implications of an authentic individualism lies right at the heart of the meaning of democracy and of what might be called the democratic consciousness. For it justifies a free society in concentrating its energies upon the individual, regarding first his intrinsic worth and effecting those social arrangements necessary, not only for the security of his person and property, but also for the realization of those intellectual, moral, aesthetic, and spiritual qualities that are the distinguishing properties of a cultivated personal life.

Yet, if in the past it seemed obvious that everything was moving nicely onward and upward in an inevitable progress, with all things taking care of themselves as long as the individual had his way, this now does not seem obvious at all. We have suffered a profound disenchantment of our world, and now the evils that men can do both individually and collectively and the moral failures of our society, as indeed of all societies, are more clearly seen by us, and we are more conscious of the almost demonic impersonal social forces that partially shape our world, frustrate our best efforts, and distort even our highest ideals. But, if our optimism on human history has faded into disillusionment, we are now at least more perceptive, more sophisticated, and more ready to come to grips with the harsh mean facts of an imperfect world, and to face more realistically the grim realities of the human predicament.

In our concern for the individual, nothing deserves our continuing attention and thoughtful consideration more than the task of achieving and preserving freedom, for only in his freedom is the individual genuinely a person. But freedom is difficult to define. The difficulty arises especially from the fact of its being a quality of experience rather than a particular thing, action, or event, and because as a quality it belongs to the life of the mind or the spirit and has about it that ambiguity and elusiveness that so commonly characterize whatever is both profound in meaning and ultimate in value. Since freedom is essential to the meaning of the individual person, there is nothing to which it can be compared or by which it can be judged, measured, or explained. And in a sense it is impossible, therefore, even to form an adequate conception of it. But, if it cannot be fully comprehended, freedom, nevertheless, can be grasped within the context of living experience, and there it is known intimately as the very ground of personal life. It is not some kind of abstract absolute that controls our thought and determines our ideals and is known through reason and meditation. We know it, rather, by possessing it, by living with it, or living without it, indeed, by being it, and in some degree we have cultivated the sensitivities and practical wisdom by which we can perceive it and appreciate its various and subtle forms and values.

But, however much we may think of freedom as a simple, single quality of our personal or social experience, it is in fact multiple and complex. There are many freedoms, as many freedoms as there are varieties of basic experience. Some of them are real when others are simply ideal. Some seem always to be just coming into being, or about to be born. And some are fully secured, while others endure precariously or diminish and are lost. We commonly speak of freedom as if it were something that we either possess in its wholeness or not at all. But the achievement of freedom is an arduous and never-ending task. Freedom is something that must be continually won in the struggle of men and institutions and nations, created out of the clash of attitudes, ideas, and social forces, and nourished and shaped by the conflict of moral ideals and of human reason and passion.

So, when we ask the question, what is a free man, we must be prepared for a compound reply. We seem justified in believing in the reality of free will, though both its definition and justification are far from simple tasks. And there is clearly a profound meaning in the Stoic conception of freedom that refers especially to the rationality of man, where the free man is one who in a sense overcomes the world and establishes in himself a moral autonomy through understanding the world and understanding his own involvements with it. But, in addition to the natural freedom of the will and the freedom that comes from virtue and wisdom, there are the freedoms from constraint and restriction and the freedoms of positive action. We rightly speak of many freedoms—intellectual, moral, political, social, and religious. Though we refer to them as general and abstract, there are no abstract freedoms. There are only the specific concrete freedoms that belong to the individual as properties of his mind and will and soul, because they have been written into the law of his society, or into its habits and customs, or are in countless ways incorporated into its institutional life. They are the products of centuries of struggle in the arena of force, oppression, and aspiration. They are the freedom to come and go and the freedom to vote—freedom to worship or not to worship—freedom to speak and to read and to write—freedom to receive judgment by one's peers.

There are other freedoms that are not guaranteed by law or even nourished by custom, and they exist therefore most precariously.

But they are not for this reason unworthy of achievement or less precious to the person who has them or is deprived of them. They are such freedoms as the freedom to work and freedom from want, from pain, and from fear—freedom from ignorance, custom, conformity, superstition, triviality, and boredom—freedom from oppression by both minorities and majorities—freedom from the mean discriminations that in countless ways violate the sanctity and dignity of the person—freedom to think unfettered by subtle patronage and by vicious instruments of propaganda—freedom from the tyranny of the past and from every form of tyranny that can oppress the mind and heart and soul of man—freedom to be genuinely and authentically an individual, in whom difference and uniqueness are encouraged and independence and autonomy are real.

Our freedoms have not been achieved easily, and some of them not at all. Always they are in danger of loss by neglect and indifference and in danger of destruction by the encroachments of powerful political or commercial tyrannies and in danger of suppression by prejudice, bigotry, fanaticism, or racial hatred. Those who genuinely value the individual must be committed to the protection of his freedom. Not with a fanatic vigilance that is dishonest, irresponsible, and unconscionable, that generates suspicion and distrust and eventually must destroy what it professes to protect. Rather, with a concern for freedom that has a fine sensitivity to its full nature, that understands its foundations and grasps its subtle and sometimes delicate meanings, a concern that is motivated by neither selfish nor class interest and that places its confidence not in the harangue of demagogues but in the guarantees of reason, deliberate judgment, reliable knowledge, and the law.

Clearly, it is now the great task of the American people, as of all free societies, to move toward the fulfillment of the democratic ideal —to justify the faith that a society of strength and a culture of high achievement and lasting power can be built on a foundation of genuine individualism, where the intrinsic worth of the person is the acknowledged ground of all value, where the integrity of the individual is not dissipated in the totality of society, and where his freedoms are not defined in terms of totalitarian purpose and collectivist action. This is a task that steadily becomes more difficult and that in the future may confront overwhelming odds, for our world becomes daily more complex and more confusing, and the relation of the individual to the total society and to the state becomes more difficult to define and to negotiate. Added to the usual problems of complex social relationships and social organization we face the serious dislocations in our economy that arise from the necessities of military production, from the difficult social and moral issues related to the growth of our great centers of population, our patterns of urbanization and suburbanization, our severe racial strains and conflicts, the expansion of industry, the increase in mechanization and automation, chronic unemployment and poverty, and from the nation's assumption of a vast responsibility in international affairs. And always we have with us the problem of government, whether local or national—the question of its regulative and constructive functions in personal and social affairs, the proper employment of its powers, and the setting of limits upon them.

American individualism is now beset with severe dangers. On the one hand, the individual is under the threat imposed by those social and psychological forces, large and small, that in various ways impair the achievement of full and genuine personality. On the other hand, there is the tendency of the American people, despite their sincere concern for the individual, to confine their conception of individualism to essentially political and economic terms, neglecting the intellectual, moral, and spiritual facets of a genuine individualism. There is grave danger to the individual in the increasing mechanization of society, if it is permitted to regiment the life of a man to the last detail and rob him thereby of his sense of freedom in his own affairs and of a free and creative involvement with the life around him. There is danger in the growing complexities of society that may produce so many intrusions upon his space and time that they will destroy the solitude and privacy upon which human dignity so much depends. There is danger in our gross and sometimes vulgar commercialism that so often violates the dignity of the person, or in the bigness and rudeness of our corporate organizations, both public and private, that so commonly abuse the individual, who so often becomes a number and not a name, a statistic and not a person. There is danger in the bigness of our cities, in the immense power of the state, and in every impersonal, dehumanizing, and depersonalizing force that can organize, constrain, and regiment the life of the individual, destroying his initiative and creativity, reducing him to mediocrity, eroding and subverting his freedoms, and corroding and callousing his personality.

To confront this ominous threat and prevent the destruction of the distinctive personal quality of life is now our sovereign task—to save the individual, and not simply as an individual but as a free and autonomous person, whose personality is not crushed by the great weight of his society and whose values are not destroyed by the processes of mechanization and automation.

But a plea for a more authentic individualism is not to argue for some kind of social anarchy or laissez-faire morality, or to advocate the virtues of past and simpler societies, or to hope for a world in which the individual would be free of concrete involvement. And certainly it is not to argue against an even more rapid scientific, technological, and industrial advancement, or against either the regulative or constructive functions of government. Nor is it to deny the increasing necessity of large scale collective decision and action. Rather, it is to recognize that the integrity and freedom of the individual must be preserved and enlivened within the framework of new and more difficult circumstances, and to urge a more intelligent effort to come to grips with the problems of the individual person caught within the vice of subtle and massive social forces that, though sometimes creative, are often destructive.

We face a crisis of the spiritual life, a decline of faith and commitment, a threatened loss of the sense of purpose in existence, the anguish of estrangement and meaninglessness. We have encountered powerful forces that could well destroy the very meaning of personality, its uniqueness, its diversity, its creativeness—crushing from it its spontaneity and vitality and its very enthusiasm of life. Yet, here on the edge of destruction, threatened by the despair of annihilation, we must continue to construct and reconstruct the edifice of our ideals and protect and nourish the sources of our intellectual, moral, and spiritual strength—amidst the hard mean facts of impersonal demonic power, to keep alive the hope of peace and an eventual human felicity.

CONSTANTIN REGAMEY

The individual and the universal in East and West

I must begin my lecture with apologies: its contents will not correspond to what you may expect from its title. To tell the truth, I do not know what you can expect. The longer I examine this title the more I feel that there are only three words which have a definite and non-ambiguous meaning: "the," "and," and "in." All the others need commentaries. The terms "East" and "West" are not conceived as a confrontation of well-defined and clearly distinct concepts. After so many conferences and discussions concerned with this confrontation, we can notice that on many essential issues the disagreements arise between the representatives of different Asian cultures or among Western philosophers, rather than between the two sides of the problematic boundary supposed to separate East and West. On both sides we find a profusion of inner divergencies, and, since we now know each other much better, it is very difficult to sum up in a few words the respective general outlooks. Whatever you can affirm about Eastern or Western thought, it is always possible to quote a doctrine which says exactly the opposite. If you try to summarise the prevailing trends in a concise formula, you surely will meet the reproach that your selection is highly subjective or that it is an over-simplified cliché.

Besides, it is easy to find on both sides of this imaginary boundary very similar if not identical philosophical systems—I will quote later some striking examples—and yet, in discussing them we often seem to go astray. The source of this frequent misunderstanding—not exactly between East and West, but between Indians and Chinese and Japanese and Muslims as much—is to be sought, not in irreducible divergencies of systems, not even in the contrasts of the ways of thinking, but, rather, in different almost instinctive approaches to the simplest and yet fundamental concepts and words, in particular emotional reactions to them, and in the incommensurate ranges of unconscious associations pertaining to these basic concepts. In a word: *we do not have the same self-evidences.*

One of such crucial self-evidences is the concept of the *individual,* which we are now discussing. Here, again, I must add the remark that when speaking of the individual and the universal I will surely not analyze the endless problems of the relation "particular-general," but that my purpose is to examine the concept of the human individual as confronted with some universal entities or norms which constitute links between the individuals or provide a common reference to them. But, I am afraid, I will not so much speak about the status of the individual (which is the main topic of our Conference) as about the nature of the individual. Most misunderstandings in our discussions of the status are conditioned by the fact that we have rather divergent and unclarified ideas of the nature of the individual.

I will surely not propose my own concept of the individual, nor will I add a new speculation to hundreds of existing explanations. Since the concept of the individual is a self-evidence, it is very hard to analyze it. The more we try to explain it from the metaphysical, ontological, psychological, or logical point of view, the more complicated the explanations grow. I will attempt, rather, the reconstruction of the stage of human evolution in which the intuition of the individual has not yet been blurred by philosophical precisions, and I will try to circumscribe the pre-philosophical self-evidence of this concept which can be, and actually is, that of an average man in both East and West. The reconstruction of this primitive basis will perhaps enable us to understand that some peculiar conceptions of the individual which we can find in the East (and also in the West) are not so eccentric as they appear at first glance to be, that they are not products of abstract speculations but are deeply rooted in the intuitions of the pre-philosophical man. And a similar reconstruction will perhaps afford some new contexts to the history of the concept of the universal.

I will try to do this as unphilosophically as possible (my ignorance of philosophy will be for me a tremendous help in this respect), and I invite you to get rid, for a moment, of all our preconceived ideas, of inherited points of view, and of deeply rooted concepts which are unconsciously molding the reactions even of those who do not know and do not understand anything in philosophy. But, as I will surely not invent an artificially primitive way of thinking, and, as I attempt a reconstruction based on evidences we possess, it will not be possible to avoid all philosophical reference, since most of our self-evident and apparently naïve convictions reflect unconsciously and in a simplified way some philosophical concepts, and, on the other hand, some peculiarities of the primitive way of thinking can be reconstructed only through the speculative systems conditioned by this outlook.

You may ask: since we deliberately ignore philosophical intricacies, why so much talk about so simple a thing? If we leave aside the idealistic, monistic, illusionistic speculations, what is simpler than to know that I am not you and you are not me. Yet, for a primitive man this is not at all evident. I (I am now a pre-philosophical man) am I; and you—I do not yet know what you are. I am surely my body, but I am also my perceptions and memories, thoughts and feelings, sensations, intentions, and actions—in a word, all that I can call my states. And you—you are the content of my perceptions, thus also my states. I probably do not distinguish my states from my body. Even my thoughts and my perceptions are in a way produced in my body. Non-distinction of mind and body is well attested for the primitive mentality; it is, besides, not very different in some modern materialistic theories, although the latter, when speaking of our mental states, use more scientific terms, such as epiphenomenon, conditioned or inhibited reflexes, etc.

That which seems to prevail in the individual consciousness at this first stage is not so much the feeling of distinctness (distinctness from what? from the contents of my states?) as the sense of unity. Although my body and my states are a set of many divergent elements, I feel that this collection is an indivisible whole. Let us recall that etymologically the word "*individuum*," as much as its Greek prototype "*atomos*," does not mean "particular," "separate," "distinct," but "*indivisible*," and, as such, is not a correct antithesis of concepts such as "general," "collective," "universal." Thus, in the individual consciousness the feeling of being a unity is prior to the feeling of being a unit among others.

But soon, even as a primitive man, I discover that my states and my body are somewhat irreducible to the same pattern, that they are of different kinds. I can see and touch my legs or my head; with some reflection, I can locate my visual perceptions in my eyes, sound perceptions in the ears, etc., but where do my feelings, my desires, my thoughts function? Of course, we still speak of the brain as the organ of thinking, of the heart as the seat of feelings. These localizations, however, are not based on direct experience; they derive from associations which are not the same in different cultures. For ancient India, the heart is the seat of intuition and thought; for the Greeks, the midriff was the organ of almost all our psychic states; for the Romans, the site of feelings was the liver. Besides, we can discover that, while the parts of our body as a rule live in harmony, there exist conflicts between our desires, intentions, and thoughts and our body, and that the "states" try to be the "rulers." Thus we gradually come to the distinction of "mind" and "body." But we still consider this mind-body set as indivisible, without being sure, however, where the unifying center of this complex organism is to be located.

Now, among the multifarious contents of my perceptual world I find a great number of peculiar entities which have bodies fairly similar to my body, but which seem to be remarkably independent of my will, by which I feel myself strangely attracted or with which I can enter into conflicts. And each of these entities claims to be, like me, the center of a world, strikingly similar to my world. Here, for the first time, I am confronted with the very embarrassing problem of the *other*. The fact that these entities are independent of my will does not yet mean that they are not parts of my world; hunger pangs are also independent of my will, and yet they are definitely mine. That the bodies of these strange beings are distinct from my body I can easily verify: they do not feel my toothache, their eyes have not the same field of vision as my eyes have, etc. But how does it happen that their world is so strangely similar to my own and yet somewhat different? The simplest answer, that this world exists outside of us and independently of any individual that beholds it, is not at all the most immediate evidence; in order to come to this conclusion we must resort to indirect inference and tacitly accept the idea that the simplest explanation is the true one. Such a "Copernican" solution of the problem will come much later. The instinctive solution of the primitive man is that, however distinct our bodies are, we have a common consciousness. Small differences of our "private world visions" are but those of degree. This solution has nothing to do with the highly speculative doctrines of epistemological idealism: our common world is not the product of our mind, is no illusion—it exists really as contents of our collective perception.

This solution is not so absurd as it appears at first glance. Logically, there is no necessity of ascribing states of consciousness to anyone. You will say that this is a highly speculative hypothesis and that it is unlikely that it may arise in the mind of a primitive man; yet, we do not hesitate to assume such a collective consciousness in animals. And my statement is not a hypothesis. Studies of primitive tribes have brought many confirmations of collective consciousness. As an illustration, I can quote a fact reported some forty years ago by a noted French sociologist and philosopher, Lucien Lévy-Bruhl. In one of the French African colonies two girls of a very primitive tribe were accused by the local sorcerer of having eaten a child. During the investigation of this case by French authorities, the girls confessed that they had actually eaten the child; but the corpse of the child was discovered undamaged, and it was obvious that the child had died because of a disease. Yet, the girls insisted that they had eaten the child. The authorities were completely puzzled by this contradiction. The explanation given by Lévy-Bruhl and supported by other evidence was that this tribe had a collective consciousness and that the sorcerer was the interpreter of this consciousness. As long as he had ascertained that the girls had eaten the child, this was the only acceptable truth, against which the girls' own perceptions and memories were not valid, even for themselves.

Of course, we have here to do with a very primitive stage of human consciousness. It would be interesting, however, to add that precisely this story was recalled some fifteen years ago by a prominent communist writer who chose freedom in the West as a parallel to the "spontaneous confessions" at the trials during the Stalin period. The author, who spoke of his own experience, insisted upon the fact that these obviously false confessions had been forced on indicted communists neither by terror nor by brainwashing, but simply by the fact that for a truly orthodox communist the objective truth does not depend on his individual conviction but is defined and established beyond any doubt by the Party. And, if the Party had decided that he had committed a crime, his not recalling having done this was absolutely irrelevant.

I have quoted these two rather extreme examples only to show that both the consciousness of being an individual and the individual consciousness are neither self-evident nor inborn qualities of a human being. They have to be acquired through a gradual development of self-consciousness, and they can also be lost, and their loss can be accepted even in modern times by intellectually trained men. We can observe similar phenomena, in a weaker degree, in our world, with its clan or group commitments, blind sectarian beliefs, political passions, and mass psychoses. We may consider the fact that in China and in Japan groups based on family relationship or social hierarchy are of greater importance than individuals as reminiscences of this very ancient stage of collective consciousness. But, of course, members of such groups and classes, in spite of their complying with the behavior and the demands of the group, are yet perfectly conscious of their distinctness, and do not confound their bodies and their mental states with those of other members of the group. And we can take it for granted that even at the low stages of human evolution this attitude was prevalent.

Coming back to our pre-philosophical man, this attitude means that he ascribes mental states to corresponding bodies and by the same token fully accepts the existence of the "other." The source of this acceptance is, I suppose, again the feeling of an indivisible unity of my body and my "states," a feeling that by analogy I transfer to other bodies. These now become individual in the full meaning of this word: indivisible and separate. Much evidence proves that the acceptance of other individuals is primary to the recognition of a world existing independently of my experience of it. As evident as this latter recognition seems to be, it is a result of a set of reasonings, whereas the acceptance of the "other" is rather non-intellectual, more immediate. In spite of the fact that other individuals are contents of my perceptions, there is in them something which escapes me. Being so strangely similar, they remain others in spite of my efforts to assimiliate them. And, unlike the other contents of my perceptional experience, they arouse in me the need to establish a relation with them, be it that of attraction or repulsion. Thus we discover the *thou* and by the same token the intuition of the *I*. (*He* is an intellectual abstraction.)

The discovery of the I-thou relation is a decisive step toward self-knowledge and self-assertion of an individual. It appeals no longer to perceptions or instinctive drives alone, but awakens the richness and variety of our emotional life and intentional forces; it gives them a direction and differentiates their functions. It reveals the immense field of contact and communication. And, through the differentiation and functional implementation of one's passive states, it transforms them into active faculties. The vague conglomerate of psychophysical drives and reactions kept together by a half-conscious feeling of unity begins to be an organized unit, an individual.

But what happens with the world of non-individuals? Since we no longer have a collective consciousness, this "outside world" becomes a collective entity, a thing or things that we share in common. Thus, parallel to the self-discovery of the individual, the intuition of a universal or of universals emerges in our consciousness. Since we live and perceive the same world, there must be entities which are at the same time mine and yours and also belong to all others. This world is not yet completely independent, remaining outside us: it is, rather, a collection of universals which permeate the individual beings. Things that we perceive are not individuals—they are only particular manifestations, signals of a universal. This conception, which is well attested for every civilization in its beginnings, is far both from the scientific world-view and from logical distinctions of general and particular. Universals are not abstractions from particulars: they are primary, the true reality—particular things are but their reflections or parts of them.

We can study this pre-scientific, magical world-view not only in the conceptions of primitive tribes, but also in those cultures which have reached a relatively high level. The Brāhmaṇas of ancient India provide one of the best elaborate systems of this type. In this doctrine, the world is a plurality of universal "things" or "forces" (the terms "substances" and "world-stuff" suggest too precise philosophical associations to be used here) which are both physical constituents of the world and psychophysical processes of an individual, but are also "states" such as health or disease, fecundity or sterility, wealth or poverty, happiness or misfortune. Since these "universals" are in us and in the world, we can handle them; we can by magical manipulations draw good luck to us or send disease to our enemy. The task of all magic is to be able to influence things which are not within one's reach by means of things or acts at one's disposal and in a way linked with the former. These purely "pragmatic" needs have developed conceptions of great importance for further philosophical studies. Everywhere in the world, magic operates by means of "equivalences." The Brāhmaṇas developed a detailed system of such equivalences between the macrocosm (universal in the world), the microcosm (the same universals appearing within the individuals), and ritual (magical manipulations equivalent to these universals). The equivalences between things depend on some common features: similar names for these apparently different things, the fact that these things appear in groups counting the same number of elements (four castes, four seasons, four verses of a spell), comparable appearance (eyes correspond to sun, wind to breath, hair to plants), etc. The magical functioning of the "equivalence method" is explained by the fact that the principles of equivalences are themselves universals of a higher order: names, numbers, forms, etc. These universals of universals are not abstractions, but the very essence of single objects or individuals.

The next step in the evolution of magical methods is the attempt to find out the highest instrumental universal allowing the magician to dominate other universals through it. The Brāhmaṇas discovered such all-embracing universals for each of the three sets: *brahman,* the universal magic force contained in the recitation of Vedic hymns —for the ritual: *sat,* Being, as fundamental entity of the macrocosmos; and *ātman,* breath, as the essential part of every individual). The search for an all-embracing single principle will be achieved by the identification, in the Upaniṣads, of *ātman* with *sat* and *brahman.* In this period, however, the goal was no longer world domination through magic but the religious ideal of immortality—the identification of the three principles was no longer the result of more or less arbitrary speculations but the achievement of the mystic experience and the newly discovered highest universal was no longer a magical instrumental force but the metaphysical ultimate.

The importance of the pre-philosophical magical outlook lies in the fact of having molded the intuition of the universal, which exists in itself underlying concrete particular things and which at the same time permeates all the individuals. The magical world-view will gradually disappear, giving way, on the one hand, to scientific investigation guided by experimental methods, but pursuing the same goal of domination of world forces through the knowledge of their interrelations, and, on the other hand, to religious revelation or philosophical system which, however, will be centered around the same concept of universal. As such will be conceived the basic elements of the physical world, namely, earth, water, fire, air, and ether, which we find in ancient Iran, in the Indian Brāhmaṇas, and in most later systems, in the Chinese *Book of Changes* (which grew out of the magical practice of divination and developed a macrocosmic doctrine of equivalences: thunder-activity, fire-brightness, etc.), and in Greek pre-Socratic philosophy. In all these traditions, the further development will strive for reducing the many universals to a few fundamental ones: *yin-yang* and later *Tao* in China, the One (*ekam*) in India and in Parmenides, etc.

And when religious and philosophical evolution will lead man to the discovery of aspirations which cannot be reduced to merely sensorial processes or physiological needs of food, shelter, procreation, and pleasure, when he becomes aware of demands for order, freedom, justice, love, immortality, of intuitions of beauty or truth, demands which often induce him to act against his instincts and physical needs —these principles will also be conceived as universals common to every human being, but existing also in themselves.

This "existing in itself" was identified with existing as a "thing," a substance. In that respect, the heritage of the magic way of thinking has lasted much longer than we generally believe. So is conceived the ultimate of the Upaniṣads and even of the Advaita Vedānta; such is the *Tao* and, at least in the beginning, the Confucian principles of *jen* (humanity), righteousness, etc.; such were to be the Ideas of Plato, the universals of Western medieval realists, and even the fundamental concepts of Descartes and Spinoza.

The liberation of the magical inheritance appears with the new concept of universal as a norm, a law, a form—no longer a thing, but a relation. It is universal, since it is the same for every individual and does not depend upon their particular features and desires, but, on the other hand, it can be realized only in and through individuals. This new conception, which marks the beginning of abstract thinking, appeared earliest in Greece and in China. In India, its first evidence can be found in the doctrines of Hīnayāna Buddhism (the universal law of causality working without any substantial support, as pure relation), but the Mahāyāna, in spite of its negative definition of reality, resumes the older concept of universal-thing. Most of the Hindu systems never departed from this concept.

There is, and there have been since much earlier times, the third concept, that of "individualized universal" or of the individual as the source of all universals—God. But this depends on religious revelation, and the very notion of a personal God presupposes the concept of a fully developed individual.

We left our pre-philosophical man when he discovered the I-thou relation and was obliged to admit the existence of universals in order to explain the common experience of the world. The opposition "individual-universal" arouses the question of the *limits* of the individual and entails new oppositions: "inner-outer" and "subjective-objective." They are not synonymous with the opposition "I-thou." The relation "inner-outer" corresponds to the consciousness of the limits of our body and derives from the analysis of our sense perceptions, our actions, and our desires. But, on account of the impossibility of settling the limits of our emotional and mental states, the distinction "inner-outer" does not necessarily correspond to the distinction of I and non-I. Nor does the distinction "subject-object," although the concept of subject represents the unifying principle of my individual being. As such, it is my faculty of apprehending, of knowing, and object is that which is apprehended and known. Other individuals are objects for my subject, but my body and my states are also objects of my apprehension. Consequently, the subject cannot be identified with my psychophysical organism. It is, rather, a "point" in my individual being. Which one?—in this respect the philosophical interpretations differ to such an extent that, according to the answers they give to this question, there arise radically divergent doctrines of human behavior. There is also the problem of universals. Even when I assume that they penetrate my individual being, some of them appear to be objects for me, in the same way as my body does. But the highest universals, those which command all my behavior and induce me to act against my biological or even emotional drives —they seem to play in my life as important and incomparable a rôle as the subject. And, in fact, the majority of philosophical systems identify them with the subject, which appears to be the fundamental universal constituent of an individual. And they agree on another point, too. The progressive discovery of the nature of the individual proves that individualization is a *process,* a *becoming.* A human being is not given as an individual from the beginning; it has to determine itself as such, and this self-determination goes on. For most of the doctrines, both in the East and in the West, the ideal of self-realization is the maximal development of universals in an individual. But the ways of conceiving this "universalization" differ considerably in each great philosophical tradition.

Before we examine some of the most striking divergencies concerned with this problem, let us come back to the opposition I-non-I. Although we are no longer in the pre-philosophical stage, but in the period of conscious, speculative self-analysis of the individual (it is now that the disagreements begin), we still do not know what are the limits of the "I." And this is easy to explain. We have, on one side, the opposition "inner-outer," which coincides with the limits of

our body. On the other side, we have the consciousness of our
"subject," which is a point within our individual being. But the "I"
we identify with the whole compound unity, which also includes
our "states," which cannot be located. And the contents of my states?
Some of them are within my body, some are certainly outside it. But
does this mean that they are not "mine"? They are objects for me,
but the "inner contents" of my states (e.g., the toothache) are also
objects for my subjective "point." As long as I do not identify myself
with my body, the limits of my "I" cannot be established. For Western habits, this reasoning appears a little surprising, but it is perfectly
logical. And a few evidences will prove that it was not at all surprising outside the Western tradition. In the choice of these evidences
I deliberately exclude idealistic and illusionistic doctrines, which
are concerned wtih a somewhat different problem.

Probably the most ancient systematic doctrine of India, the
Sāṁkhya, assumes two fundamental, eternal, non-created categories
of reality: an infinite number of spirits, pure subjects (*puruṣa*), and
one potential object (*prakṛti*). The union of these two principles
gives birth to empirical reality, presented in the Sāṁkhya as a
hierarchy of layers of concreteness. It is this hierarchy which may
puzzle our Western habits. *Puruṣa* is not individual, because the
direct products of his union with *prakṛti* are universal, as e.g., *buddhi*,
"reason." It is only in the next lower layer that the consciousness of
being "I" (*ahaṁkāra*) appears. The individual mind is the result
of this consciousness, and at the bottom of the hierarchy, we find
senses of perception and action and, as "outer counterparts," their
objects. Thus, the contents of the states of an individual, his "outer
world," a really existing and not imaginary world, are, nevertheless,
parts or products of the individual.

The only speculative difficulty of this conception was the problem
of the interference of this world with the worlds of other individuals.
And I would like to quote an attempt to avoid this difficulty which
we find in another old realistic and radically rationalist system of
India, in the Vaibhāṣika school of Hīnayāna Buddhism. In conformity with the general trends of the Hīnayāna, this school admits
no central, permanent subject in an individual. The individual is
conceived as a stream of constantly changing psychophysical factors,
and in empirical reality there exists nothing else save the infinite
plurality of these individual streams. Among the psychophysical
factors there are "inner" ones (faculties of perception) and "outer"
elements (objects of perception). Thus, when, for example, I see the
sun, this means for the Vaibhāṣika school that in this moment in
my individual stream there appear factors of seeing, "objective"
factors of the perceived sun and the factor of contact between the
two. But there exists no sun ouside me. As in the Sāṁkhya, the

Vaibhāṣika school locates the "world" within the limits of an individual. But the difficulty of interference is here avoided through the denial of any possible contact between individual streams. They are presented as absolutely isolated entities, each having its private world. There are as many suns as individuals beholding them.

This is a typically rationalist way of thinking which, in order to achieve logical coherence, does not hesitate to violate common sense. And the Vaibhāṣika doctrine is an archaic one which can be accused, and actually was, of rigidity and awkwardness. Yet, we find in the West, almost two thousand years later, a strikingly similar rationalist conception in Leibniz' doctrine of windowless monads, each constituting its private and totally isolated world. Still more striking is that the two completely independent systems present a very similar explanation of the main difficulty implied by their doctrine: how does it happen that these "private worlds" are so similar and include also the experiences of contact with other individuals? The Vaibhāṣika answer is: the continuity of an individual stream is secured by causal interdependence of its factors and regulated by the universal Law of *Karma*. The similarity of world experiences, the fact that many individuals see at the same time the same sun, means that for this special point they all have the same *karma* determining the same configurations of factors. The analogy with the Leibnizian doctrine of pre-established harmony cannot be overlooked. It affords a fine proof of the universality of reason which both in the East and in the West and at a distance of so many centuries gives similar solutions to similar, and even very unusual, problems.

The systems examined above show that the question of the limits of the "I" present real difficulties. There exist other solutions of this difficulty. The whole problem of limits can be left open. This seems to be the Japanese instinctive conception of the *overt individual* viewed independently of the "I-non-I" opposition. One can go further and suppress even the subject, as Buddhism does theoretically and Zen achieves practically. Or, on the contrary, one can stress the subject. Before we examine this last, by far the most frequent solution, we have to examine some of the fundamental divergencies in the interpretation of the subject in the East and the West. It is impossible to survey here all the conceptions concerned with this problem. Instead, I will quote two characteristic texts presenting the fundamental difference between Indian and Western conceptions, a difference which to a large extent determines the divergent attitudes toward the problem of the individual.

It is said in the *Bṛhadāraṇyaka Upaniṣad* (III. iv.) : "One cannot see the seer of the seeing, one cannot hear the hearer of the hearing, one cannot think the thinker of the thinking, one cannot know the knower of the knowing. This is thy innermost self." And St.

Augustine says, "When we perceive a color, we do not in like manner perceive, by the sense itself, ourselves perceiving; nor, when we hear a sound, do we also hear our own hearing; nor, when we smell a rose, does our very smelling also emit some odor to us; nor, when we taste something, does taste itself savor in our mouth; nor, when we touch something, are we able also to touch the sense of touch itself. . . . But reason—does it comprehend itself by some other thing than itself, that is, by reason? Or would you know that you have reason otherwise than by perceiving it by reason?"[1]

And, St. Augustine adds that there is nothing higher than reason save God. This conception of reason as of our only faculty capable of knowing itself (and of all the rest in our individual) and consequently needing no higher "knower" is, of course, much older than the quoted text; it was already Greek. But I have deliberately chosen this passage, so closely parallel to the Upaniṣadic formula, in order to show that this conception was predominant both in Greece and in Christianity, the main roots of Western thought.

Indian thought, or, rather, inward experience, in search of the true center of an individual, discovers it in the self, in the pure subject, which is above reason and inaccessible to any lower psychic faculty. We cannot know it unless we identify ourselves with it through the mystical experience of immediacy. And, consequently, we cannot identify ourselves with the rest of the components of our individual. The mystical experience being radically incommensurable with any other of our states, there appears an existential gap between this highest component of our nature and the rest; hence the analysis of the individual into three main and distinct layers: body, mind, and self or spirit, with a sharp limit between body and mind, on one side, and spirit, on the other. Since the latter alone is the true center, it is no longer necessary to establish the limits of the "I."

The decisive mystical discovery of the Upaniṣads was also the identification of this self (ātman) with Brahman, the essence of the whole reality, the ultimate. Thus, the self is the highest universal. Since it is inaccessible to intellectual grasp, it can be no norm, no law, no relation; it is the universal of the "older type"—a "thing," the pure Being (and when Mahāyāna Buddhism gets rid even of this last positive definition of the ultimate, it does not do it in order to transform it into a pure relation, but conceives of it as an absolutely undefinable Vacuity, which, besides, is synonymous with the infinite, ineffable, and unanalyzable Plenitude).

In conformity with these ontologial conceptions, the development of an individual is conceived of in India as the cultivation of this self through gradual elimination of, or detachment from, body and mind. But this way is a way of disindividualization, if we conceive individuals as distinct and unique entities. In the Kevala Advaita school of

Hinduism, the final goal is the absorption of individual selves into the universal undifferentiated *Brahman*. But, even in doctrines like the Sāṁkhya, which admit the infinite plurality of pure spirits, the spiritual realization leads to the loss of individuality. The liberated spirits are "egoless." Egolessness does not mean simply "non-selfish"; it is a complete detachment from all the lower layers of the Sāṁkhya hierarchy which we have already spoken about. In this hierarchy, the consciousness of being a distinct individual (*ahaṁkāra*) is even lower than reason. It is one of the obstacles to self-realization and has to be discarded, as much as reason. Thus, all the features which make individual distinctions between the liberated spirits disappear; the *puruṣas* are just a plurality of ultimates, identical in their nature, passive, and non-involved onlookers of world events. With the exception of some religiously important doctrines which stress the notion of individuality, for most Indian philosophies the development of the individual is not self-realization but the realization of the universal Self.

The Western trend that has been characterized by the quotation from St. Augustine entails a quite different view of the individual. The capability of reason to apprehend itself dispenses with implying a higher subject. It can be identified with the subject, and, at the same time, it can govern lower psychic faculties. There is no gap between it and the other components of an individual. And even when Christianity introduces a scheme of the individual person similar to the Indian distinction of spirit-mind-body, the limit between the spiritual and the temporal (because non-immortal) will separate spirit-mind from body, and not, as in India, spirit from mind-body. This limit, however, is not very sharp: both Greek philosophical and Hebraic religious traditions postulate the necessity of body for the constitution of an individual, and this necessity was later emphasized by Christian theology with its doctrine of embodiment and even the need of a spiritual body after the resurrection. In all these traditions, the individual is identified with all three constituents.

Reason is also universal, as it is accepted by all philosophical traditions. But this universal is not necessarily a "thing"; it can be, and actually will be, conceived as a norm, a universal law, a relation (it is, besides, the only universal present in an individual human being which can be so conceived). Such a universal does not eliminate individual distinctness: individual reasons are universal by the fact of complying with the same norms of thinking; they can achieve unity without merging in oneness. Reason can also apprehend things without the necessity to identify itself with them; it is no longer necessary to consider the contents of my perceptions, feelings, and actions as being mine. This conception, jointly with the reduction of the individual to the spirit-mind-body scheme, allows us to restrict the limits of our "I" and compels us to admit the existence of an external world. But this emphasis on the essential separateness of individuals does not eliminate universality: this is achieved through *communication*. It is a striking *paradoxon* that the Indian search for universality attains it through negation of individual distinctions, and yet realizes this oneness in an exclusively personal incommunicable mystical intuition; the West discovers the totality which maintains individual separateness, and yet secures universal union through the communicability of the truth and the generalizing power of reason.

Reason is, besides, not the only instrument of communication. All our psychic faculties are means of communication. Communication is love, which requires the distinctness of the "other." We communicate also through desire, volition, and action. We can communicate even the immediacy of our inner "unity in diversity" by means of art. But, since communication implies distinctness between the "partners," the originality and uniqueness of the inner harmony is, in the creative work of art, as important as its cohesion. Since truly aesthetic values are inaccessible either to reason or to feelings, but can be grasped only in the way of immediacy, they might be as incommunicable as the contents of mystic experience. But this is precisely the reason artistic creation needs the medium of an external object, of the work of art appealing to our senses and impelling each of the "partners" to reconstruct in himself, without aid of reason an analogous (but not identical) specific "unity in diversity."[2]

Thus, the predominant Western ideal of the self-determination of an individual is conceived as a gradual development of all its constituents and the transformation of its inner complexity into a perfectly harmonized individuality rich in its creative originality but conforming itself to universally valid norms (not the realization of the self, but simply self-realization). Its subject is a kind of central point, both unifying its inner variety and, outside, creating a harmony of relation with other individuals.

Western thought recognizes, however, the existence in every individual of an absolutely incommunicable principle which, since Aristotle or Thomas Aquinas, is identified with pure Being. At first glance, there is identity of view with Indian philosophy. But in Indian systems Being is universal and undifferentiated, and all individualization results from rational distinctions, whereas in the West this incommunicable Being is precisely that which prevents one individual from being confounded with another, which, from the very beginning, decides that it is *this* concrete individual. For most Western thinkers, with very few exceptions, e.g., Duns Scotus, Being is the principle of individualization, and the generalizing reason is universal. This radically individual conception of Being is not abandoned even in the schools which deprive reason of its dominating position—for instance, in the philosophy of the existentialists.

In Chinese philosophy, the standpoint of Taoism seems to be near the Indian conception: *Tao* is a universal "thing," not very different from the Indian ultimate. This leads to an interpretation of individual development along similar lines. But in Confucianism, especially in its later development, we find conceptions rather resembling Western ones: universals such as humanity, righteousness, sincerity, and principle (*li*) are norms which do not exist concretely, but are realized through and in the individual. The climax of this doctrine of universals appears in the "new tradition" of Fung Yu-lan.[3] And the ideal of the self-edification of the individual is the cultivation of the universal, so that in its highest achievement, in the sage, the individual becomes a harmonized collection of universals. As such, he practically ceases to be an individual. He becomes immortal, not as an individual being, but as an eternal model of perfection, as an ideal and an abstract norm. The concept of Being does not play such a decisive role as in India or in the West. But there is another more important difference from the Western outlook: the self-determination of a Confucianist individual is the cultivation of static ideal universals which, to be sure, are concretized through it and by it, but which are, so to speak, given a priori, and which already exist as norms and ideals in themselves. In the Western conception, the individuals *create* universals which are neither given nor static, but expanding and continually renewed norms. Reason, by the collective effort of individuals, constantly transcends itself and reaches higher regions. And a similar ascending renewal appears in other fields of human activity, in social, affective, and artistic life.

The limits of time do not allow me to examine all these problems in both religious and aesthetic perspectives. I can merely quote the conception of this dynamic development of the individual as it is conceived by the modern school of personalists. "As being, he [man] is individual; as spirit, he strives for participation in the universal. As such, he is more than an individual: he is or, rather, has to be a person. And person is not an achieved thing; it is a goal, a steady aspiration for self-transcendence. The spirit realizes himself through reason—in science and philosophy; through will—in moral conduct and practical life; through sensibility—in art. In all these fields he enters in contact with the world, but he reveals himself. Reason allows him to introduce through abstract conceptual constructions his own unity in the multifarious and in themselves unorganized data of existence; in art, he reveals to himself the same unity of multiplicity by means of concrete constructions of the sensuous, the unique domain where he can be fully free and creative. In his moral, juridical, social, and political activity, he strives for the same universality and is guided neither by sensibility (by what he merely likes) nor by reason (the intelligent utility of conduct) but by a direct and irreducible-to-other-psychical-approaches intuition of *value*."[4]

---

[1] *De libero arbitrio*, 3. See Richard McKeon, trans., "On the Free Will," *Selections from Medieval Philosophers* (New York: Charles Scribner's Sons), Vol. I, pp. 11–69.

[2] The conception of art in which the creative artist expresses his own unique and original inner harmony is a typically Western doctrine which looks for universal values in the highest achievement of individual originality. Almost all Oriental aesthetic theories consider art a way of evoking and suggesting, through the sensuous medium, a supra-individual universal.

[3] See, e.g., *The Spirit of Chinese Philosophy*, E. R. Hughes, trans. (Boston: Beacon Press, 1962), chap. X. In this volume he defines this new tradition as a "new system."

[4] C. Regamey, "The Meaning and Significance of Spirituality in Europe and in India," in Charles A. Moore, ed., *Philosophy and Culture—East and West* (Honolulu: University of Hawaii Press, 1962), p. 339.

DAISETZ T. SUZUKI[a]

The individual person in Zen*

I

At the outset, I wish to say a few words regarding the terms "philosophy" and "religion." In Japan, perhaps in China, too, there were no words corresponding to these two terms before the people came into contact with Western culture. They had to coin new words expressive of the ideas. "Philosophy" is *"tetsu-gaku*[b]*"* (*che-hsüeh* in Chinese), whereas "religion" is *"shū-kyō*[c]*"* (*tsung-hsiao*). These words, therefore, have been in use for not more than eighty years.

In the Far East, philosophy was not a special branch of study apart from telling us how to live this life as we human beings find ourselves in these surroundings, social and natural. So it was with religion—it was not something extra to our daily way of living.

This being the case, what corresponds to "philosophy" in the East was always closely related to life itself. Whatever we got from the study of philosophy was not just knowledge conceptually abstracted—it was something concrete, directly applied to our daily life. Knowledge was not something to know and stop there; it was something individually related to the significance of life in our daily contact with Nature, as well as with our fellow beings. This meant that the study was to be applied immediately to each individual's way of living. A philosopher in the old sense was a better human being: his ideals of life were higher, his behavior was nobler, he had no self-assertive motives, he was free from greed and sloth and from attachments of all kinds. He was really the "superior man."

In the East, philosophy was not, again, so distinctively separated from religion; they were both intimately related to one's actual life. The "philosopher" was also a highly "religious" man; he was perhaps more deeply intellectually disposed and interested in giving a metaphysical interpretation of life and Nature generally.

I think it was Kierkegaard who said of Hegel that the philosopher is like an architect who builds a fine house for others to live in, while he himself is satisfied with a hovel for his residence. The

* Most unfortunately, since the public lectures were televised, a time limit was set on all the lectures, and Dr. Suzuki did not finish the technical part of his lecture. Those who attended his lecture and those who are reading it here are not getting the advantage of the superb supplementary lecture he gave the next day to members of the conference.—Editor's note.

intellectual or dialectical system the philosopher would construct may be magnificent to all appearances, but it has no practical use for him because he does not live it. The house has no personal use. All that the builder does for it is merely conceptual and has no direct concrete contact with life itself. Philosophy separated from life has no personal moral value whatever.

Kierkegaard evidently thinks that mere reflection or intellection has no significance unless it takes part in the transformation of the author's personality—which is the Oriental understanding of philosophy. If it does not help in building a noble-minded personality, it does not deserve the name.

In this respect religion is not to be distinguished from philosophy. They are both of no value unless they help develop one's spirituality.

To understand Zen one must have in mind its close relationship with life itself. It has nothing corresponding to what Western thinkers refer to as "knowledge for knowledge's sake" or "art for art's sake," disregarding intimacy with life and its activities. Knowledge, of course, is one of such activities. But, when it goes off its track and tries to check their natural creative course, it ends in killing itself. Zen keeps its feet always on the ground, that is, on reality itself.

II

It is considered difficult to enter into the meaning of Zen[d]. Yes, it is, as long as one tries to grasp it by means of *words*. You may then say, "If not for words, how is communication possible?" Zen's answer is: Words are indeed needed; but, when they are used, they are to be used in a way altogether contradictory to the ways they are ordinarily used. The reason is that words always tend to become conceptual, removed from realities. When we say "a tree," the word is not the tree itself; it merely indicates it. It is by human ingenuity and creativity that we invented words in order that we can conceptualize, but at the same time we are tempted to take words for realities, since words are convenient to manipulate in place of the things themselves. They are like coins or bills; you can carry the whole universe in your pocket and sell it or buy it, but, as far as the actual use of the bills is concerned, as such they cannot protect you from cold or heat. In a similar way, words are useful and significant in the world of finites, where time and space rule. But, when we try to apply them in a realm beyond spatial and temporal limitations, they are absolutely of no use. On the contrary, they are damaging. They keep us from getting into close contact with realities, and thus with reality itself. The following *mondō*[e] (question and answer) illustrates what I mean:

Chimon Kōso[f], a Zen master of the early Sung[g] (960–1279), was asked, "What is the lotus flower before it comes out of the water?"

The master answered, "The lotus flower."

"What is it after it comes out of the water?"

"The lotus leaf."

The master's answers do not at all conform to the common-sense view of things. The lotus flower is a lotus flower when it is out of the water, and then the leaf is no flower. How could men of ordinary sense come to an understanding of Zen if it so outrageously contradicts human intelligence? It might help to know that Zen people are not talking of the lotus of "this-world." Their lotus belongs to an altogether different order of things, where our notion of time and space does not avail.

Questions and answers of a similar character are frequently exchanged among Zen people, who can never rest until they reach ultimate reality, from which they all derive their existence in this world of time and space:

"What was there before the Buddha came into the world?"

"What do we have before light divides itself from darkness?"

If the idea involved here were translated into Christian terms, the questions would probably run something like this:

"What does Christ mean when he says, 'I am before Abraham was'?"

Or, "Where is God himself before he uttered 'Let there be light,' after which fiat the whole universe of Light and Darkness is said to have started?"

Let me quote another Zen master's answer to the question:

"What about [it] before the Buddha made his appearance in the world?" The master raised his *hossu*[h] [a sort of mosquito flapper often carried by the masters as a sign of office]. The questioner went on, "What about after the Buddha's appearance?" The master again raised his *hossu*.

If a Christian father were asked about Christ's isness even before his historical appearance among his fellow beings nineteen hundred sixty-four years ago, what answer would the questioner get? Should the father give him thirty blows of a stick as was often done by a Zen master?

The meaning of Zen is thus seen not to be lying in words or gestures themselves, which appeal only to our ordinary logical appreciation. Words are significant only in the realm of the senses and intellect. Zen masters generally apply no abstract verbalism of any kind to ultimate reality. When any verbal application takes place, they have for it such simple expressions as "Just this," "This little," or simply "It."

The term *"dharma"* is used very much in Buddhist literature. It corresponds to "reality" when it appears in philosophical treatises. Ordinarily, it means an object of any kind, material or psychological, objective or subjective, physical or metaphysical. It also means "norm," "law," "standard," and all their cognates. Zen has also adopted it, mostly in the sense of reality or teaching, as in the following *mondō* between Nansen Fugwan[i] and Hyakujō Ekai[j] of the T'ang[k] (618–960). The *mondō* is illuminating especially in connection with what has been discussed so far.

> Hyakujō asked, "Is there any *dharma* which has never been expounded to people generally by the wise men of the past?"
> Nansen said, "Yes, there is."
> Hyakujō pursued, "What is that which has never been expounded by them?"
> Nansen replied, "Not mind, not the Buddha, not reality."
> Hyakujō exclaimed, "Expounded!"
> Nansen, quietly, "This is as much as I can. How about you?"
> Hyakujō said, "I am not one of those wise men, and how can I know what is expounded and what is not?"
> Nansen responded, "I fail to understand."
> Hyakujō concluded, "After all, I've done a great deal of expounding for you!"

III

With these preliminary remarks, we may start to see what views Zen entertains regarding the significance of the individual. In presenting the Zen position, I wish to resort to as much Christian terminology as I think desirable for this occasion.

In short, the Zen view of the individual is: As far as our limited experiences are concerned, there is no justification for the individual to claim an independent ontological position. Its existence is in every sense relative and conditioned and illusory. It has no right to claim that "I am," as if "I" were an absolute authentic reality and in permanent existence.

Are we, then, all living in delusion, one might wonder? Zen answers, "No." This existence is in truth real. It is phantasmagorical only when each one of us does not come to the realization of his identity with "It" or "The *Dharma*," which is "not mind, not the Buddha, not an object," or with the Godhead, with him who says, "I am that I am," or with the Buddha, who pronounced upon leaving his mother's body, "In Heavens above and on earth below, I alone am the most honored one." As soon as one becomes aware of this identity, he gains his original individuality and creativity as an agent co-operating with "the creator," who is at once transcendent and immanent. The awareness here experienced thus constitutes the mystery known as divinity in humanity and humanity in divinity. The "I am" of Yahveh on Mt. Sinai meets here with the "I am" of Jesus Christ, when he said, "I am before Abraham was." The latter symbolizes humanity, for what he did stands for all mankind, not only in historical time, but throughout the entire course of time.

The communion of divinity and humanity, which means the individual's opportunity of regaining its original creativity and rising above its dependence upon earthly finite conditions, takes place when God comes out of his inner sanctum and becomes the creator. For this is when Light separates itself from Darkness and God's image is seen reflected in the mirror of his children, who thereby become aware of the absolute meaning of "I am." Here Eckhart pronounces, "God's isness is my isness, and my isness is God's isness," or "I and my father are one."

We live in a created world of time and space and divide this time into the three periods of past, present, and future, and talk about historical events as if they would never happen again. In this we are greatly mistaken. "I am" is an event that is taking place every moment, which means that creation is continually going on and that God's "only begotten Son" comes among us even at this moment and in this place where I am speaking.

Let me quote Eckhart more fully:

> . . . to say that God created the world yesterday or tomorrow would be foolishness, for God created the world, and everything in it is the one present Now. Indeed, time that has been past for a thousand years is as present and near to God as the time that now is. The soul that lives in the present Now-moment is the soul in which the Father begets his only begotten Son and in that birth the soul is born again [into God].[1] It is still one birth, however often the soul is reborn in God, as the Father begets his only begotten Son.[2]

Eckhart's idea of the soul's living in the present now-moment and of its one simultaneous birth in the Father and the Son is illuminating. Buddhists talk in terms of enlightenment, not of birth, but the underlying idea is identical, and they are mutually supporting. The truth is universal. To get into it, something more than knowledge, analytic or otherwise, is needed. One must live through it once and taste it personally. It is not transmittable by mere words or gestures and cannot be placed on the market for sale. But anyone who has once tasted it by his own body can readily recognize it wherever and whenever he encounters it. He fails, however, to teach or describe it to you.

St. Augustine says, "If no one asks me, I know, but, if I try to explain to one who may ask, I know not." When Bodhidharma warned his disciple Eka[1] not to take "it" for an utter negation, Eka answered, "No, Master, I know it uninterruptedly with nothing mediating, yet, when told to express it in words, I fail." St. Augus-

tine and Eka are referring to the same form of realization of which
both are perfectly conscious within themselves in their inwardness,
but to which they cannot, when asked, give any verbal expression
in the manner words are generally used in this world of relativity.

Zen people generally prefer concrete terms to abstract concepts,
and acts to words, for concrete terms and acts are more direct and
expressive of real experiences. Says Kant, "Concepts without intuition are empty, and intuition without concepts is blind." Zen people
are well aware of this and also of the truth that negation implies
affirmation and vice versa. It is principally for this reason that
ordinary people find Zen difficult to understand.

In Evans's translation of Eckhart, she has, "The vilest thing
present in God as being is better than angelic knowledge."[3] This is
superficially misleading, for nothing vile can be present in God.
What Eckhart means is: When what cannot be explained in words
in ordinary logical or experientially decent manner, the master often
resorts to an altogether violent way of verbalism. For example:
"What is the Buddha?" One master answers, "Three pounds of
flax;" another gives this, "Your name is Echō[m];" a third one, "the
Buddha." When too impatient for words, the masters will appeal to
direct actions and will give the questioner "thirty blows of a stick."
Sometimes they may add, "O you, a specimen of stupidity!"
"Knowledge" may be angelic, logical, consistent, plausible in every
way, but it is of no value before the Zen master, indeed before those
who really have the awareness or constant knowledge of "I am."
To know, or, better, to be aware of, "I am" is to know God. Here
humanity merges itself into divinity.

In the following quotation from Evans's translation of Eckhart,
replace "Being" by "I am," and the meaning of the whole passage
will become clearer. The Biblical "I am that I am" is Christ's "I
am before Abraham was," and these "I am"s are the Buddha's
"In Heaven and on earth 'I am' the most honored one," and also
the birth cry "I am" as described by Sandburg in *The Family of
Man* (my interpretation), and Scriabin's joyous cry, "I am," "resounding all through the universe" (also from *The Family of Man*
in reference to the newborn infant's cry).[4] Eckhart states:

> God's idiosyncrasy is being. The philosopher says one creature
> is able to give another life. For in being, mere being, lies all that
> is at all. Being is the first name. Defect means lack of being. Our
> whole life ought to be being. So far as our life is being, so far it
> is in God. So far as our life is akin thereto, so far it is akin to God.
> There is no life so feeble but taking it as being it excels anything
> life can ever boast. I have no doubt of this, that if the soul had the
> remotest notion of what being means she would never waver from
> it for an instant. The most trivial thing perceived in God, a flower
> for example as espied in God, would be a thing more perfect than
> the universe.[5]

IV

Let us see for a while what right this little baby has to cry out "I am!" when its coming into this world is due to the biological laws of birth and death, to the chain of karmic causation, which cannot be controlled by anybody's free will. It is here at this moment in this family like any other animals or even like plants thriving on this earth. In spite of this consummation of all these inevitabilities, the baby claims "I am!" As if it were its own free master, it bursts out in "Ogyā^n!"[6] which Scriabin, the Russian composer, describes as a "joyous cry" and as "resounding all through the universe." How could this be possible?

When, however, we look more inwardly, instead of objectively, into the matter, we find that there is something in the baby's "Ogyā!" which reminds us of God's first fiat, "Let there be Light!" With this fiat God, who was "in the Void," came for the first time out of himself and became God the Creator and got the name "I am that I am." The Buddha's first cry, "In Heavens above and on earth below I alone am the most honored one!" corresponds to it in every way. The cry is the Word in Christian terminology. This, however, cannot be comprehended in the realm of the senses and intellect. It is beyond the sphere of logic and sciences, which are concerned only with so-called objective facts. There is really in the baby's first cry something extraordinarily revealing, for in its "I am" there lies deeply hidden something beyond human understanding. And an individual that is no other than a mere mechanically necessary unit in a system beyond his control gains for the first time the real value of individuality. This is the time when he dives deeply into the inmost recesses of his soul and interviews God in his act of giving the fiat, or the Buddha, when he walks seven steps in the four directions of the universe, and, pointing to Heaven with one hand and to earth with the other, cries out, "In Heaven and on earth 'I am' the most honored one!" The individual in no other sense can be an "I am!"

"The Family of Man" was an exhibition of photographs shown in New York a few years ago depicting the various phases of human lives.[7] It later appeared in book form and was prologued by the noted writer Carl Sandburg, who wrote: "The first cry of a new-born baby in Chicago or Zamboango, in Amsterdam or Rangoon, has the same pitch and key, each saying, 'I am! I have come through! I belong! I am a member of the Family!' " Quite naturally Sandburg concentrates here on the theme of the exhibition, the family. But what strikes me as most interesting is the baby's opening exclamation, "I am!" How is such an exclamation possible? As I said before, the baby has no right to claim its absolute existence for itself when it is not here on its own independent account. It owes its being in every way to causes over which it has no will of its own, and therefore no responsibility whatever. It is highly presumptuous for it to burst out, "I am!" In truth, it is not logical at all—it is altogether unreasonable and impermissible—and then why is it that we accept the baby's first claim as an individual as an irresistible assertion, as if it were a most plausible statement? It is possible that Sandburg did not attach much importance to it, as we generally do not. We may say that he was not metaphysically or spiritually deep-minded at the time. But, when we inwardly reflect on the statement "I am!" we cannot help wishing to unravel all the deep, secret significance which we unconsciously attach to it.

The Buddha's baby cry, as well as the Biblical God's fiat, is mythological and has no historical foundation. But both are deeply rooted in our religious yearnings. I do not like the odium tradition-ally attached to the word "religious," but there does not seem to be any other suitable English word for expressing what moves in the inmost recesses of human beings and is identical with the essence of humanity in its deepest and most significant sense. Any-thing that comes out of it or comes in touch with it is commonly given the value of sense-reality, though, in fact, overcoming every-thing that belongs to the world of the senses and intellect. Nobody ever actually heard the infant Buddha's cry, nor God's exclamation, but we are ready, when driven to "man's extremity," to accept them as "gospel truth." We then say with Eckhart, "God's isness is my isness, and my isness is God's isness," and also realize that upon hearing the Buddha's "Ogyā!" we turn, each of us, into the master of himself and individually pronounce "I am!"

Let me supplement this with a few more pertinent Zen *mondō*. When Bodhidharma wished to return to his native country, he had his disciples come together and made each present his understand-ing of Zen. When Eka's turn came, he just came out of the gather-ing; he was not at all vociferous. He simply stood with his hands folded before his chest. The master said, "You have my marrow. I now hand all the innermost treasure over to you. Take good care of it!"

When Hyakujō was asked, "What is the most wonderful fact?," he answered, "Here I sit on top of Mount Daiyū°!" Sitting or standing or crying does not make any difference; if, only, one has an inner understanding, one may express it in any way he pleases at the moment, and all will be equally pointing at the moon. Sand-burg probably did not realize what a profound spiritual truth he was asserting by having all babies cry, "I am!" How many souls, modern and ancient, have staked their whole existence to find the meaning of all this! Kierkegaard's pronouncement that "Truth is

Subjectivity" points also to the same truth from another angle. When "I am" is comprehended in its genuine form, divinity meets humanity, and it is here that the individual attains its real significance.

The following two *mondō* demonstrate the "I am" idea in a somewhat different style, perhaps more dynamically. Especially the second is characteristic of Zen *mondō*, and it may be difficult for the "outsider" who has no Zen training of some years to understand.

When Seppō[p] was residing in a hermitage, a monk visited him and made bows to him in the desire to be instructed in Zen. Seeing this, Seppō came to the opened door and, thrusting himself out, said, "What is this?" The monk responded, "What is this?" Seppō then lowered his head and withdrew.

Ummon[q], who founded the Ummon school of Zen, asked a monk, "Where do you come from?" (In Zen, this question of the whence of one's being is no idle one.) The monk indifferently answered, "From Seizen[r]." Ummon went on, "What is Seizen teaching now?" The monk extended both his arms without a word. Ummon gave him a slap. The monk protested, "I do have something to say." This time Ummon extended his arms. The monk was unable to say anything, and Ummon struck him.

v

As far as Zen is concerned, it asks us to go even beyond this "I am," that is, even before God uttered his fiat. Zen states that it is already too late if we wait for any sign or token to make its appearance. If you wish to know what reality really is, it must be grasped where there is yet nothing graspable, Zen would say. But the Godhead cannot remain transcendent all by itself, as it were. He is to be immanent in his "I am" and all other things. He is to be merged into humanity, and humanity into divinity. They cannot be separated; each finds itself in the other. The "I am" is to be identified in that which "is" even before the "I am" came to be. *The Gospel According to Thomas*[8] gives us a certain glimpse into the situation in which we find ourselves now. Thomas starts with something which transcends the senses and intellect. We read, "I will give you what eye has not seen and what ear has not heard and what hand has not touched and what has not arisen in the heart of man."[9] Of this, the disciples ask: "Tell me how our end will be." This is a natural question following Jesus' description of something beyond the senses. What will be the end (or meaning) of such a strange object, if it is an object at all? Jesus answers: "Have you then discovered the beginning, so that you inquire about the end? For where the beginning is, there shall be the end. Blessed is he who shall stand at the beginning, and he shall know the end, and he shall not taste death." Jesus goes on, "Blessed is he who was before he came into being." This last sentence is important as indicating the presence of something which is before the "I am."

In Buddhism, this is called the *Dharma*-body, corresponding to the Christian Godhead. Zen treats the subject in its characteristic way. When it was asked, "What is the *Dharma*-body?" a master nonchalantly answered, "The six cannot take it in." In this case, "the six" may refer to the six senses.[10] One of the comments on this has:

> One, two, three, four, five, and six;
> Even the Patriarch fails to count it all to the end.

Does the commentator mean that the *Dharma*-body belongs to the realm of the infinite and hence is beyond the limits of the human way of counting? Does it, then, stand transcending our world and looking down upon us? Adds the commentator mysteriously, "No, last night it was seen passing the night facing Mount Nyū[s]!"

VI

Divinity standing aloof over humanity is no divinity; humanity divorced from divinity has no use for it. Divinity is seen as incarnated in humanity, and yet God is God, man is man, and they are not to be confused. This is the mystery of being.

Let us see how Pär Lagerkvist of Sweden as a modern thinker treats this mystery. In this connection, I find it very provocative to introduce his thought to this audience, if you have not yet heard of or read him. He is one of our contemporaries, a Swedish poet or thinker or just a wise man—I do not know, it does not matter. He is an enlightened man, and I am sure he will not object to my Zen interpretation of his wisdom.

The Eternal Smile[11] is the title of a short book in which Lagerkvist tells us how God is found working as an old man sawing wood and saying that he has done his best in shaping the world as we have it before us today. The book is a most illuminating one and acquaints us with the deep insight the poet has into the working of reality and life, though the problem itself may remain incomprehensible.

All the dead people, who were, while in this world, statesmen, scholars, businessmen, laborers, and so forth, gathered in the world of darkness, which prevails there, and talked about their former lives. This may sound strange, but we generally like to believe in an afterlife as if there were no such event as death or an ending in life; we feel as if we are going to live forever. We seem to believe

somehow in a state of continued existence, and there is a great deal
of truth in this feeling which must not be brushed aside as of no
worth, as fiction or illusion. Then, finally, the question was raised:
Who is God, after all, who made this kind of world for human
beings, a world with all kinds of sufferings and enjoyments, happiness one moment and then an unbearable situation the next? Now
let us all go out and look for God to complain to him about this
state of things. So, they walked and walked. The book does not say
where they walked, in which direction they walked—they just
walked. Years after years, not a few but millions of years, ages
after ages, they walked. And then they came to see a certain faint
light in the distance. Strange, but even in the afterworld they have
distance, too, but we have to speak of all these things to make
things more realistic, this-worldly.

When they approached this flickering light, there was an old
man sawing wood in a manner that inspired the feeling of eternity.
They approached him and asked, "Are you God?" The old man
said nothing and looked confused. When pressed again for a reply,
he seemed to make a small nod. They asked him why he had made
such a horrible world, in which beings were made to live. The old
man said nothing and went on and on with the sawing of the wood.
Again, they demanded a reply, and he said, "I have done the best
I could, I have done the best I could." This was all the answer they
could get.

Then, an interesting thing happens. The children, a few at a
time, then many, were captivated by the old man. They appeared
somewhat shy at first but soon grew familiar with him and played
with his face and climbed all over him. The old man looked very
happy, and said, "I didn't mean it for them." When the mothers
saw this sight, they were moved to tears.

The vast crowd, after they were somehow satisfied with the inter-
view, left the old man and returned to the place where they originally started. There a great discussion ensued. Each seemed to have
his own interpretation or understanding in regard to the intention
of the old man. Lagerkvist writes:

> Silent and thoughtful they advanced. What they had experi-
> enced with God was gathered together and fell into place for
> them. The secret was mingled with the manifest; then the secret
> sank down to the depths of their soul while what was manifest
> was spread transparent above it. Each thought of what was his;
> each one was alone with himself. While they were thinking they
> felt their oneness with all the others; while they were by them-
> selves they felt they were all among the others. Slowly and im-
> perceptively as they advanced together there collected within
> them, as if in different vessels, something that was the same for
> all.[12]

This passage strikingly resembles the Kegon[t] (Hua-yen) school of Buddhism, in which the doctrine of the four aspects of the *Dharma-loka-dhatu* (reality or realm of principle) (*hokkai*[u] in Japanese; *fa-chieh* in Chinese) is given:

(1) Reality viewed as individual particulars;
(2) Reality viewed as reason;
(3) Reality viewed as a world in which (1) and (2) are interfused;
(4) Reality viewed as a network of infinitely complicated interfusion of particularized objects.

Reality here is considered from an ontological point of view, while Lagerkvist's is psychologically sociological. Something of the mystery of divine transcendence-immanence may be read here, too. God as an old man sawing wood is an example of divine humanity. At the same time, it is to be noticed that Lagerkvist represents God, not as an august imperialistic figure commanding reverence and subservience, but as a common laborer whom we might meet in a country village.

The author of *The Eternal Smile* goes on:

> Then they began to speak, each of what was his, but turning to the others that they might hear and believe. They spoke to each other as brothers, simply and quietly, one by one as something ripened and came to certainty within him. They spoke to each other as before, only more quietly than before. They no longer spoke so many words nor so great; they didn't give the whole of their inner selves, they gave only their faith, that which belonged to all. This they offered each other with opened hands.[13]

Among many other inspiring things they discuss, the author introduces us to another old man:

> There walked an old man. His head was aged, but he looked straight ahead, as if a long way still remained for him. He said, "I acknowledge you, dear life, as the one thing conceivable among all that is inconceivable."[14]

This old man is not the one who was seen under a feeble light sawing wood, but one of those who traveled the distance to seek God and who came away inspired with a new outlook on life, for he evidently had a profound insight into life itself. For this old man appears again toward the end of the book[15] repeating the same idea as given expression here about the "conceivability" of life, of "dear life."

It is indeed at this moment when the "conceivability of life" is born in a man that he is a real individual, an individual in every sense of the term, in whom what I may call "pure, primary creativity" prevails, inspiring God to utter his fiat and keeping the inhabitants of Eden in a state of "innocence," free from the defiled "knowledge" which breeds all forms of false individuality.

In conclusion, I wish to quote more Zen stories each of which gives expression to the Zen master's understanding in accordance with his individuality, where resides his real creative and authentic person.

Gutei[v], a noted figure in the annals of T'ang (618–906) Zen, kept a small temple in the country. One late afternoon he was visited by a nun-pilgrim. As she entered, she neither took off her headgear nor set aside her traveling stick, as was customary, but went directly into the temple, and found Gutei seated in his chair absorbed in meditation. She circled his chair thrice, then stood before him and said, "If you can say something, I will take off my hat." ("Saying something" here means saying something in evidence of his understanding of reality, to speak out of his own authentic individuality.)

Thrice she demanded a response from Gutei, but he would say nothing, whereupon the nun, whose name was Jissai[w], turned to take leave. Gutei, remembering his duty as a temple keeper, called to the nun-pilgrim to offer the night's lodging. But Jissai said, "If you have something to say, I will." Gutei again failed to give a response, and the nun gave him a blow with her stick and left.

Gutei sighed, "I am a man, but I have no manly stamina. What am I?" He then made up his mind to leave the temple in search for a master to instruct him in Zen. That night, however, he had a dream in which the mountain god told him, "You need not go away from here. Tomorrow you will have another visitor who is a *bodhisattva* incarnate, who will help you to attain enlightenment."

As was predicted in his dream, Gutei had another pilgrim-caller in the person of Tenryū[x]. Pleased and eager, Gutei lost no time in relating the happenings of the previous day, and beseeched Tenryū to enlighten him on the incident.

Master Tenryū did not say anything. He simply lifted a finger before him, which suddenly opened Gutei's mind to an altogether new experience, as if the bottom of the cask had broken through. (A word of caution. This account describing the events leading to Gutei's inner experience is handed down to us in its most abridged version. It does not furnish for us the years—in some cases, decades —of inward and outward struggle that must have attended the seeker. Behind this "sudden" opening of Gutei's mind lies the full history of man's attempt to reach his extremity that God may have his opportunity. The nun Jissai and Master Tenryū were but providing Gutei "that moment.")

After this, Gutei used to raise his finger to whatever question came his way. When he was about to die, he gathered his followers about him and said, "As regards my understanding of Tenryū's one-finger Zen, I have not been able to exhaust its use all my life. Do you wish to know what it is?" At which he lifted a finger and quietly passed away. (Again, caution. The finger itself has nothing to do with Zen or its understanding of life. The one-finger here is like "pointing at the moon," the moon which is in the inmost recesses of one's subjectivity.)

Kwasan[y], another T'ang master, said, "When you cut yourself off altogether from learning, you are approaching." One of his disciples came and asked, "What is the real passing-over, then?" Kwasan said, "I know how to play the drum, *don doko don*[z]*!*" "What is the truth?" "I know how to play the drum, *don doko don!*" "What is meant by 'It is neither Buddha nor Mind'?" "I know how to play the drum, *don doko don!*"

From the common-sense point of view, this sounds nonsensical, absolutely devoid of sensibility. But, as in the case of the finger, the drum-beating itself has nothing to do with the point at issue. If you ask me, "What made you come all the way here crossing the great Pacific Ocean? Did you come just to tell us about this nonsense?" I might then beat the drum like Kwasan, *don doko don,* but, remember, in my own original way.

Here is the Zen world of "innocent creativity" or "creative innocence," where we are all what Lagerkvist makes one of his people say: "We are not happy in the way that the poor and miserable ask to be. We are happy in the way that man is happy *when he is occupied with living his life.*"[16] And this man, thus occupied, is the individual person in Zen.

1 Cf. Franz Pfeiffer, *Meister Eckhart* (Leipzig, 1857). Translation with some omissions and additions by C. de B. Evans (London: John M. Watkins, 1947), p. 209.
2 Raymond B. Blakney, trans., *Meister Eckhart: A Modern Translation* (New York: Harper & Brothers, 1941), p. 214.
3 See Evans, trans., *op. cit.,* p. 206.
4 What "The Family of Man" is will be told in the following section.
5 Evans, trans., *op. cit.,* p. 206.
6 The Japanese description of a baby's first cry.
7 Edward Steichen, *The Family of Man.* (New York: Published for Museum of Modern Art by Maco Magazine Corporation, 1955), p. 12.
8 *The Gospel According to Thomas,* Coptic Text Established and Translated by A. Guillaumont, H.-Ch. Puech, G. Quispel, W. Till, and Yassah 'Abd Al Masīḥ (London: Collins, 1959).
9 *Ibid.,* p. 13.
10 Buddhism has five senses plus another for "mentality" in general.
11 Pär Lagerkvist, *The Eternal Smile and Other Stories* (New York: Random House, 1954).
12 *Ibid.,* p. 60.
13 *Ibid.,* p. 61.
14 *Ibid.*
15 *Ibid.,* p. 65.
16 *Ibid.,* p. 63 (italics mine).

a 鈴木大拙（貞太郎）
b 哲學
c 宗教
d 禪
e 問答
f 智門光祚
g 宋
h 拂子
i 南泉普願
j 百丈慧海
k 唐
l 慧可
m 慧超
n オギヤー
o 大雄山
p 雪峰
q 雲門
r 西禪
s 乳峰
t 華嚴
u 法界
v 俱胝
w 實際
x 天龍
y 禾山
z ドンドコドン（解打鼓）

Summary and Concluding Remarks

RICHARD McKEON

The individual in East and West: review and synthesis

A little more than a hundred years ago, in 1859, John Stuart Mill used the distinction between individual and society as the basis of his argument on liberty. The first stage of the struggle between liberty and authority was an opposition between individuals, between ruler and ruled. A second stage was initiated, Mill argued, when, with the spread of self-government, the ruled became ruler, and the new tyrannies of the majority and of common opinion required analysis of the relation of the individual and society. We still use Mill's distinction although we have become aware that we have entered a third stage in the evolution of liberty and authority with the growing recognition of the many ways in which individual men are influenced by the societies which they form, and of the many ways in which individual societies influence each other in forming the society of mankind. Endless books have set forth reasons why the individual cannot survive this growth of collectivities, but it is no less apparent that the increase of associations and contacts among individuals presents new opportunities for individual realization and individual freedom. The problem of the individual in the modern world is a new problem for a new kind of individual.

The first three East-West Philosophers' conferences, in 1939, 1949, and 1959, undertook the task of establishing communication among philosophic traditions which had frequently influenced each other in the past, but which tend to be labeled by the differences in the principles they posit, the methods they use, the problems they consider, and the perspectives in which they orient their respective cultures. Once a beginning had been made in mutual understanding among philosophical traditions, the test of that understanding, philosophical and empirical, was consideration of a common problem. The Fourth East-West Philosophers' Conference made that step by discussing a concept central to intellectual and practical co-operation. Since the problem was new, it was important to set up the issues to be discussed in a neutral frame, unbiased by leaning to any one philosophy or culture. The questions were therefore stated on a gridiron formed by the divisions of philosophy and the divisions of cultures: in six weeks the individual was considered in (1) metaphysics, (2) methodology, (3) religion, (4) ethics, (5) social thought and practices, and (6) legal and political thought and institutions. Each week, the basic positions on each of these sets of problems were examined in (1) Chinese, (2) Indian, (3) Japanese, and (4) Western thought and practice. In the process, we have learned a great deal about the parts of philosophy which we would not have noticed if we had remained within a single cultural tradition, and we have learned a great deal about the nature and varieties of culture which we might not have understood if we had not concentrated on the concept of the "individual" and the actions of individuals. Recurrently we have discovered that neither the parts of philosophy nor the differences of cultures are rigidly fixed: part of the problem of the individual is due to the ways in which the "individual" determines them and is determined by them.

I. THE METAPHYSICAL QUESTION

Since our concern was with "the world and the individual" and with "the status of the individual in reality, thought, and culture," it was natural to begin with reality. Metaphysical first principles are needed to give clarity to a concept, even in its specific applications and practical uses; but the metaphysical examination of the "individual" involves that concept at once in all the well-known metaphysical problems and in all the well-known oppositions of metaphysical schools. During the week in which we explored the basic status of the individual we treated problems of universal and particular, of whole and part, of one and many, of real and phenomenal. We found that all these pairs of terms (and many others) were used in most of the philosophical and cultural traditions, and that the individual may be defined by either of the opposites or even by both.

The individual is a kind of "unity." The basic unity may be sought in a "one" that is "real" or "experienced;" in one cosmic whole or one perfected part; in a transcendent one or an immanent one; in one kind—generic, particular, or singular; in the unity of indivisible atoms or of composite structures. The characteristics of the individual may be determined internally or externally. Relative to himself he must be free and active; relative to others he must be plural and related. His definition may depend on a transcendental assimilative force or on an individual distinctive force; and the quest for the individual may extend to all forms of "individuation" or may be limited to entities capable of life, of cognition, and of self-cognition. Self-cognition is held by some philosophers to be the reflexive mark of the individual, since it marks the identity between the knowing subject and the subject known, between subject and object. We dealt with the problems of distinguishing true unities from fictive unities, "entities of reason," and we found that true unities are sought in either of the two opposed directions which are marked by the search for an all-comprehensive unity and by the quest for many dispersed unities such as are sought in the diremptive tendencies prominent, it was argued, in the West.

If anyone had hoped that the contacts of the metaphysical inquiries and systems, of different cultures or within a single culture, would lead to a consensus concerning the principles that determine the status of the individual, his expectation must have been frustrated by the discussion of the first week. Those who sought an exploration of the basic distinctions that must be used and of the basic issues that must be faced, however, came from it equipped with ordered hypotheses and assumptions that were to reappear again and again in the discussions of the next five weeks. The problems of metaphysics are not meaningless or unanswerable, because they are the problems raised by the meaning of any question and their answers can be detected and tested in any answer.

II. THE METHODOLOGICAL QUESTION

In the examination of the being or the existence of the individual it soon becomes apparent that what is in question is a *known* individual, and that differences in what is conceived as the individual raise problems of criteria and forms of knowledge. Even while we were considering the nature of the individual, we became involved in problems concerning whether anything can be known about the ultimate nature of the individual or, at the other extreme, whether any assertion can be thought to express knowledge if it is not verifiable by reference to individuals in their concrete specificity.

Methodology, epistemology, or critical philosophy may be necessary as a propaedeutic to metaphysics, but the ways of knowing the individual follow routes and encounter problems similar to those that are familiar landmarks along the ways of being. Thinking about the individual may depend on identifying him as an objective existence, as a self-conscious moral subject, as vacuous and receptive in the presence of the transcendent, and as immanent and transcendent. Moreover, problems of the expression of knowledge may be integral parts of problems of knowledge; or semantic problems may be distinct from and additional to epistemological problems; or semantic problems may take the place wholly of epistemological problems, and thought may be made to consist of problems of symbols and things without need of additional entities called "ideas." In treating the adjustment of languages to thought and to things in the various traditions, we were frequently faced with the possibility that some languages are better adapted to concrete facts than to logical abstractions, and the further possibility that statements of truth may be tested alignments of things, and thoughts, and signs, or that reference to things, or to thoughts, or to words, as independent factors, may constitute an obstacle to the formulation of truth or the testing of such formulations.

The individual is known differently in a dialectic of assimilation, in a logic of categories, in a logistic of atomic facts, in a canonic of laws of thought, and in an operationalism of linguistic rules. In the confrontation of this multiplicity of divergent methods, the individual seeking knowledge of the individual finds the method of skepticism a beginning point and a critical instrument—even to the ultimate point of doubt about the possibility of doubting the truth—which is exercised by refuting erroneous alternatives as a means of establishing the truth.

III. THE INDIVIDUAL AND RELIGION

The nature and status of the individual are not determined wholly by the findings of reason and understanding. The circumstances and functions of an "individual" in society and in the universe cannot be established in fact or be known in experience by processes of action and reaction, of demonstration and refutation. Religion provides the individual a new place and status, both as misguided and ignorant and as saint and sage. It discovers in him a spiritual status related to an empirical status. It provides a supplement, or base, for knowledge in faith. It provides a new freedom in deliverance from suffering and sin; different ways of life appropriate to different aspects of an individual or to different kinds of individuals; a security and happiness transformed into salvation and beatitude; a relation to God as creator of the individual and guide of his self-realization; an exercise for his love, hope, and faith, as well as for his contemplation, wisdom, and knowledge.

With the transformation of the individual, the communities of men are transformed by religion. The relations of men are set forth in the Golden Rule, which has been promulgated in some form by all the religions of the world: the Golden Rule is a statement of the dignity of the individual man expressed in a precept, and that precept is easily expanded into a set of precepts or laws to constitute the moral code of the individual and the community structure of the ecclesia. Religious precepts sanctify the family in filial piety and in ancestor worship; they form communities and polities; they prepare for the City of God.

But, although religions have contributed to the formation of the individual and to the development of the idea of the individual, they have also impeded both. The choice among religions which seek to be universal is divisive; religions foster superstition and depravity as well as enlightenment and morality; they lead to controversy and strife as well as to faith and peace, to doubt and frustration as well as to assurance and self-realization, and to intolerance as well as to love. Individuals in the modern world still find their fulfillment in religion, but the problems of the individual in the modern world have a complexity which will not be solved by religion alone, because, as prophets have preached in the past, precepts become abstract and commandments ineffective in the face of new problems. The religions of the world face new problems which have never been faced before and which depend for their solution on a new consideration of the nature and status of the individual in a world transformed in potentialities and values, in communications and associations.

IV. ETHICS

What the individual and the world he finds about him are, what they are thought to be, and what is believed to be their origin and destination are inextricably interconnected. The being of the individual, knowledge of him, and belief about his genesis and fate are not unambiguously distinguishable. In a somewhat less ambiguous sense the individual manifests himself in his actions and is known by what he does. Moreover, his powers or his virtues determine what he becomes, what he thinks, and what he believes. The problems of the individual in the ethical context rediscover in questions concerning what he ought to do a need to relate the individual to the cosmos, to his empirical circumstances, to his associations and communities, and to his impulses and emotions. The course of moral action can be explored by going back to judge the character, wishes, and intentions in which the action originated or by going forward to calculate the growth, satisfactions, and consequences to which the action leads. In many cultures a conception of "humanity" embodies both a notion of equality of individuals in opportunity and a freedom of individuals in ethical choice. The conception of humanity brings with it a conception of duty and a corresponding conception of rights—duties to oneself and to others, relations between the individual, the family, neighbors, society, and the state, relations which range from utility to love, from prudence to wisdom. The awareness of humanity brings with it the notion of maximizing the goods accessible to the individual and of maximizing the number of individuals who are able to achieve the increased goods available.

Philosophies all over the world and from the beginnings of recorded speculation have elaborated the implications of these distinctions. To do this, moral problems have been considered in the context of other problems—the potentialities of the material and biological bases of human action and the actualities of human spiritual and ideal fulfillments; the inculcation of conformity to accepted moral schemes and the critical challenge of those schemes; the morality of circumstantial and cultural adjustment and the morality of radical and ultimate aspiration; loyalty, righteousness, and innovation. From the interplay of these needs and aspirations, these commitments and conceptions, there have arisen many ethics which have set forth rival conceptions of the meritorious, the right, and the good, and have co-operated in the development of a world in which the individual has more opportunities for further developments of individuality and more dangers of unnoticed and unexpected suppressions—ethics of self-realization, of self-perfection, of conformity to law, of submission to social approbation, of calculation of consequences, of adaptation to environment, of creative spontaneity, of response to desperate freedoms or creative perplexities. The moralist in the modern world tends to turn prophet again to portray the moral individual destroyed by the fixed rigidities in the massive structures of his environment or enriched by new opportunities in the diverse possibilities of his environment.

V. SOCIAL THOUGHT AND PRACTICE

When the discussion turned to social thought and practices in the fifth week of the Conference the effort was to turn to the external conditioning forces which molded or impeded the internal tendencies and the awarenesses of ideals and perfections which had previously been considered as defining factors of the individual. The facts of conditioning circumstances and environing influences, however, are never neutral or impartial observations of objective data, for institutions and records are permeated with social values, and the facts of epochs and peoples are colored by the interpretations in which they are stated. What is the case in a time and a place influences what people then and there think, believe, and wish, but the examination of what is the case makes its own commitments to principles, conceptions, beliefs, and wishes.

The facts of social thought and practices receive their early expression in myths which set forth the aspirations and frustrations of godlike men and gods, and exemplify the obligations recognized and praised by men of that culture and the ideals of personal integrity, dignity, spontaneity, and humanity sought by them. They are restated later in a structure of religious and speculative thought, when conditions in the society provide leisure for the reflection and reform of saints and sages. Obligations are reformulated in the insights and prescriptions of religion, and meanings are developed in the analyses of interpreters and the systems of philosophers. The combination of belief and reason in early social thought provides an authoritative orthodoxy and a pluralism of interpretations expressive of the same cultural values but often opposed in their concrete applications and practical objectives. As the individual emerges in the exercise of his obligations and his rights, the associations of men take on an importance which prepares for the differentiation of secular from religious aspects of authority and for the separation of political from religious and cultural functions. Finally, there emerges a conception of *human* rights in social thought and a search for *social* means of achieving the ends common to mankind while preserving essential freedoms and fruitful diversities of thought, expression, and aspiration.

As a result of these broad similarities in the development of social thought and practices, it is possible to trace in some cultures, or to locate in the interpretation of all cultures, a sequence of aesthetic culture, religious culture, political responsiveness, and cultural enlightenment. For the same reason, it is possible to interpret the adaptation of new forms and the acquisitions of new rights in any society as a return to ancient ideals. The same evolution, finally, provides materials for arguing that the only alternative to violence in conflicts of interest at any stage of evolution is agreement arrived at by discussion. Despite the variety of ways in which the facts of social thought are stated, however, several structures of facts recur in the formulations. All accounts of the development of societies must take into account both social cohesion and social fluidity. The interplay of unity and pluralism as one mounts from smaller to more inclusive forms of association has brought to attention from the beginnings of social thought both the analogies and the differences of forms of association. The attractions and the dangers of the analogy of other communities to the family has been the subject of controversy since antiquity—"fraternity" is a democratic ideal by which all men are seen as brothers; "paternalism" is a despotic ideal by which divine rights are accorded to a father image. The division of labor in all societies tends to the formation of classes, and the stratification of classes may prevent the state from achieving its end, the common good, and the individual from achieving his objective, self-realization. Even education is both an instrumentality of social fluidity and a mechanism for the stratification of classes.

VI. LEGAL AND POLITICAL THOUGHT AND INSTITUTIONS

It is difficult to detect the emergence of the state and political thought in any culture. The difficulty is aggravated by the tendency to analogize the state to the family, by the fact that some early states were conceived to be theocratic, even to the extent of acknowledging a covenant with God, and by the difficulty of drawing sharp lines between religious laws, moral laws, and political laws. Some of the monuments of the history of the emergence of the state in the West are based on the denial of the analogy of family and state. The opening chapter of Aristotle's *Politics* is a refutation of Plato's assumption that the qualifications of a statesman, a king, a householder, and a master are the same in kind and that they differ only with respect to the number of subjects to which the authority applies. Locke's first treatise *On Government* is a detailed refutation in which the "false principles and foundation" of Filmer's *Patriarcha* "are detected and overthrown," and the opening chapter of the second treatise reiterates the distinctions between paternal power and the power of a magistrate. Spinoza wrote his *Tractatus Theologico-Politicus* to separate sharply the functions of religion, politics, and ethics.

In the West, the history of political thought and institutions has been a history of the merged institutions and a history of the progressive separation of political institutions from the family, the household, the village, and the religious community. It has been a history marked by the recognition of immunities or rights and by the establishment of constitutional checks. In the course of this evolution, the ideal of a "mixed constitution" was conceived in antiquity and was developed in two related forms—a mixture of monarchical, aristocratic, and democratic institutions, and a mixture effected by a separation of powers, administrative, legislative, and judicial. The first variety of mixture was operative in the drafting of Western constitutions and in the continuing effort to secure a popular basis for democratic decisions, an effective use of *aristoi*, of experts and men of moral integrity, and executive power for quick and definitive decision in crises. It is at the basis of present problems of reapportionment in the United States, where the democratic ideal of one vote for one man meets various forms of aristocratic arguments for forms of proportional weightings for a large variety of reasons. The second variety of mixture was introduced into modern constitutions by the establishment of checks and balances, and it has been operative in recent efforts to advance civil rights in the United States in the decisions of the Supreme Court, the legislation of Congress, and the administrative actions of the Department of Justice.

The history of political thought and institutions in the West provides crucial distinctions which are applicable to the political histories of other cultures at the point at which questions of self-government and human rights become important. In the political histories of other cultures, as in the early history of the West, there were *lawgivers* rather than *lawmakers*. The source of the law was transcendental, either god-given or discerned by reason or sanctified by immemorial custom. Under such systems, law tended to be largely or wholly penal. The individual enjoyed many equalities. Indeed, justice or right was defined as equality. The administration of the law was the recognition and application of such equalities. The individual was characterized and recognized in the equalities of justice and in the adjustments of equity. Rights were the content of laws, and laws were the formulations of rights. In a strict sense, however, there was no *lawmaking,* nor were there *human rights,* in the West before the modern period; the effective histories of both begin in the seventeenth century. In the continuity of development, the terms and institutions of earlier political and legal systems were modified and adjusted to the new forms and laws.

If it is difficult to detect the state in the early period, except by analogy and by application of modern distinctions to processes that had been conceived in other terms, the history of modern states is one of rapid and proliferated growth which seems to some to threaten the existence of the individual, and to others to provide for the first time the conditions for his existence and action. Paradoxically, the individual can be defined least ambiguously by the *external* determinations of law and rights. Human rights in a strict sense have existed only three hundred years. They are no older than the bills of rights which provided means for the realization and protection of specified rights. The problem of the individual, internally or externally determined, is whether he can make the present relations of men to their communities and to mankind a stage toward the further development of the freedom of the individual or whether the oppositions of communities and individuals will make it impossible for him to take the further step to world order and universal rights.

I have not tried in this summary discussion of the six weeks of the Conference to give a résumé of the contents of papers or the interchange of discussions, but I have tried to trace the sequence of some lines in a continuing inquiry and dialogue. I have been faithful to the views expressed, in the sense of indicating a place for all of them, and I have borrowed phrases and expressions from the individual papers in stating the positions. I have used this manner of summary because it seemed to me to be particularly well adapted to the accomplishments of the Conference. We did not try to come to a doctrinal consensus; therefore, I did not try to enumerate our agreements. We did not arraign ourselves in controversial oppositions; therefore, I did not enumerate our oppositions. We did try to bring a plurality of philosophies and a plurality of cultures to bear on one set of problems, the problems which we found in the status of the individual as conceived in our philosophies and as established in our cultures.

We found in the course of our discussions many respects in which the philosophies are the same and many respects in which they are different. Our descriptions of the cultures showed them to be the same in some respects and different in others. Sometimes the differences in cultures were correlated with differences in philosophy; sometimes the cultural differences were not presented as expressions of the different philosophies. At times we argued as if there were Eastern philosophic positions and Western philosophic positions, and that the one set of positions tended to be unintelligible to, or at least to be systematically misinterpreted by, philosophers of the other tradition. At other times we were struck by identities of a basic philosophic kind which gave meaning to the argument that when philosophic foundations are reached East is West and West is East. What was even more striking, however, was the frequency of discussions in which the multiplicity of interpretations was applied by the representatives of a single culture to their own culture and philosophy, and like differences of interpretation were thereafter acknowledged as operative in other cultures. Far from being a mark of the separation of cultures, the pluralism of interpretations found within different cultures was a mark of likeness and a foundation for the extension to a world dimension of problems and hypotheses that have already been countered in the smaller cultural communities that are now brought into relation and communication.

Since the pluralism was encountered in this diversified cultural manifestation there was little temptation to transform pluralism into relativism. The differences were discussed, not with the tolerance of orientation, which concedes "what you say may be true for you," or the indifference of fixity, which assumes "what you are talking about has nothing to do with the problem under consideration," but with the adjustment of inquiry, which discovers "what you say indicates an additional problem which ought to be explored more fully and related to the problem I have expounded." At worst, I detected a tendency to underrate some positions as doomed to error—the hedonists and the materialists were repeatedly and summarily assumed to be excluded from access to higher values, or to truth, or to moral law; it was repeatedly asserted that "atomic" or "absolute" individuals could never be united in a true community or be in possession of rights and freedoms; we were so concerned, much of the time, with the perfect individual and his spiritual realization that we neglected the actual individuals who are all imperfect; we said almost nothing about "property" as a means to the realization of individuals, in spite of the fact that it sometimes takes the place of the "pursuit of happiness," with "life," and "liberty," in summary enumeration of inborn rights of man.

We explored the influence of philosophic interpretations and cultural formations on the individual and the idea of the individual. A third element was therefore prominent in our discussions—facts about the status of the individual have a history independent of the history of their philosophic interpretations or their cultural evaluations. We found that it is possible to trace comparable histories of the individual despite philosophic and cultural differences. The comparable stages of the evolution of the individual in the development of his duties and the acquisition of his rights reinforced and diversified our approach to the new problems of the individual faced by all philosophies and all cultures in the inclusive community of mankind today.

How does one face a common problem for the viewpoints of different philosophies? The problem is at the center of the revolutions in philosophy and the revolution in the communications of peoples and of cultures today. Our experience suggests the interrelation of those two sets of problems—that the co-operation and mutual understanding of peoples depend on insight into basic principles and fundamental values which are philosophic, and that the philosophical problems we consider and their formulation and treatment depend on experience and evaluation of data accessible to all but judged in various modes. This interaction of philosophy and culture is one of the emerging themes of these East-West Philosophers' conferences.

The nature of philosophic questions and the universality of cultures may be illustrated by what happened to the six questions which we treated in six weeks. We began with metaphysical questions concerning the individual. Metaphysics has been called an "architectonic" science, in the sense of an examination of the first principles employed in *all* knowledge and *all* action. We ended with political and legal questions concerning the individual. Politics has also been called an "architectonic" science, in a totally different sense from that of metaphysics, because the inclusive structure and power of the state set the chief forms of activities and pursuits in the state and determine both what will be encouraged as private activity or undertaken as official policy and what will be indifferent, unesteemed, or prohibited. The discussion of each of the four weeks between these extremes of architectonic determination became similarly architectonic: methodology in the recognition that all contacts with reality, facts, data, and values, are forms of experience and knowledge; religion in including all human actions in the adjustments of piety to the sources of our being to spirituality in the fulfillment of our potentialities; ethics in the discovery of the sources and values of all action in the character of individuals, their virtues, duties, and responsibilities; social thought in the converse discovery that individuals and their assumptions and preferences are formed by societies.

The mark of a philosophic question is that all questions can be and have been made architectonic, and that all questions can be and have been subordinated to the consideration of other questions. We are coming to recognize that a new form of philosophizing must emerge, and is beginning to emerge, in a world community. It is a philosophy which begins to be formed when different philosophies are brought into relation, not to engage in controversial opposition nor to exhibt themselves to each other, but to undertake common work on common problems without laborious preliminary investigation of credentials or invidious imputations of dubious assumptions, methods, or conclusions. It is possible, in philosophy as in other undertakings, to come to agreement concerning a problem, concerning the issues it involves, and concerning the requirements of an acceptable solution of the problem, without ideological consensus on principles and methods. Each of the parties to the philosophic dialogue continues to apply his own philosophy and to speak his own intellectual and affective language. Each has the opportunity, without need of apostasy or conversion, to adjust to new insights, repair newly recognized deficiencies, and consider new problems previously out of the purview of his philosophy. Philosophic discussion may then be directed to the solution of problems rather than to the projection and advertisement of optimistic or pessimistic anticipations. The exploration of the status of the individual has been a clarifying experience concerning which we shall all want to think more. It is a stage in a new philosophic enterprise; we should be guided by it and we should build on it.

We have had a full six weeks. The Conference has opened up new perspectives of philosophical methods and new conceptions of philosophical problems. I have attended many other meetings in which the characteristics of cultures and philosophies have been set forth and many meetings in which concepts like "individual" have been examined. The present Conference, by relating different cultural and philosophical traditions to a concept central to intellectual and practical co-operation, has made an important contribution to my understanding of basic problems in the use of reason in action, in the relation of plural philosophies to agreement and consensus, and in the interplay of continuity and innovation in a world transformed by increasing basic knowledge and increasing phenomenal change. For this and for like experiences I express my gratitude and that of my colleagues and fellow workers to the organizers and patrons of the Fourth East-West Philosophers' Conference and to the University of Hawaii, the sponsor of the Conference.

CHARLES A. MOORE

Concluding remarks[1]

I

I have no intention of making a speech. All I intend to do is to retreat from the scene as gracefully as I can—after 25 years and four Conferences—and make a few remarks concerning these Conferences of ours, particularly this one of 1964.

Naturally, I bow out with mixed feelings. It is with some qualms and regret that I realize the end has come.

However, I am quite happy and proud of what these Conferences have accomplished, and I am confident that in saying this I am speaking for all who have been closely connected with the Conferences. I am sure we are all happy about the contribution which these Conferences have made to the cause of world understanding, or at least to East-West understanding, and also to the expansion of the philosophical and intellectual horizons of philosophers in East and West. We have helped to create a "New Frontier" in philosophy. These Conferences have also contributed greatly to mutual intellectual respect among the philosophers of East and West, surely of those who have participated in these meetings.

Permit me to make a few remarks about this particular Conference.

For one thing, it has been the best of our four Conferences, philosophically speaking. This has come about because we have had the opportunity to discuss widely, penetratingly, and in depth most of the all-important detailed aspects of our problem.

At our opening meeting, you will recall, I said we should not expect any "miracles" as a result of our deliberations; but I now feel that we have done very well, indeed. I have never seemed to lose—and I know this applies to all of you—the sense of being thrilled at the discovery of a new idea, a new explanation, a new interpretation, a new experience in understanding. We have had many such experiences during this Conference. A partial list of these will constitute a Supplement to these "Concluding Remarks."

This has been an exciting Conference and a rewarding one—even inspiring at times. It has certainly been intellectually stimulating and challenging. Also, the frankness, the degree of objectivity, and the

547

willingness which has been shown in coming to grips with most of the basic issues have been a virtue of our work.

We have decidedly advanced the fundamental purposes behind all these Conferences. We have greatly improved mutual understanding between those of us who are from the West and those from the East. We have successfully challenged many mutual misunderstandings. We have "melted ice caps" and "bridged chasms."

Also—and here our work is more strictly of philosophical significance—we have decidedly furthered the second major purpose of these Conferences, that of developing total perspective in philosophy, what E. A. Burtt once called "world philosophizing"—thinking in terms of the knowledge and wisdom and experience of all philosophers, East and West, the stretching of the intellectual horizons of philosophers from both East and West. In this, we have looked far beyond the provincialism and parochialism and intellectual isolationism—and narrow nationalism—which so widely prevail and which are so deadly for philosophy. Philosophy must be characterized by total perspective or it is not philosophy—as John Wild pointed out so forcefully in 1949.

We have also accomplished very much indeed with respect to the specific problem with which we have been concerned throughout these past six weeks, namely, the status of the individual—and sometimes the nature of the individual—in the several major traditions with which we have been concerned. Certainly we are all much more knowledgeable about the problem of the individual in its many East-West ramifications. Surely, too, after this Conference, nobody here will ever be guilty of the oversimplification and facile generalization that the East ignores or gives little status to the individual while the West is uniquely and exclusively individualistic. The key to much of our work—if not most of it—has been the realization of the complexity, diversity, and historical changes in points of view in all traditions. We have had our confusions and our disagreements, but also our clarifications and explanations. We all now realize that, even on this ticklish problem, we are much more of one mind than we thought actual or even possible when this Conference began. This does not mean, of course, that we reached complete agreement or identity of perspective. This we would not want. But, certainly, most clichés concerning the status of the individual in East and West are now recognized as out of order, and so are the mutual misunderstandings and mutual criticisms that have been produced by these clichés—many of these are often due to social or linguistic idiom.

II

I am grateful as Conference Director—and I know I speak for all of you in this—to the many, many people who have made these

Conferences, and this particular one, possible and who have contributed so generously and effectively of their time, effort, and ability to make them the successes which I hope you will let me call them. A great number of people have contributed to these Conferences. It is the happy part of my remarks tonight to thank these people. However, it is literally impossible to do justice to this opportunity—there are simply too many people who have contributed significantly. It is impossible to single them all out for individual praise.

In this, I am thinking, not only of this particular Conference, but of all the Conferences—in 1939, 1949, 1959, and 1964. And, if I may go back for a moment, I must pay a very special and enthusiastic tribute to the two gentlemen in whose minds these Conferences were originally conceived, namely, President Emeritus Gregg M. Sinclair, then Director of the Oriental Institute at the University of Hawaii, who proposed the idea of bringing scholars from Asia and the West to the University of Hawaii so that they might think and work together, and Dr. Wing-tsit Chan, who proposed that we start with an East-West Philosophers' Conference. That is how the whole thing began. Dr. Sinclair gladly accepted Dr. Chan's suggestion. We all owe tremendous gratitude to these two gentlemen and scholars. From the beginning I have been merely the implementer—though Dr. Chan objected when he read this manuscript that I am being overly modest.

Looking back for one more moment, I must pay respect, for myself and for all of us, to all the members of all the Steering Committees who have done so very much in organizing and planning these Conferences. Their advice and help have been invaluable and indispensable—and continuous, as our files of correspondence make crystal clear.

And now to this Conference. I simply do not know where to begin or where to end in expressing appreciation—to President Thomas H. Hamilton, who took such a cordial personal and official interest in the Conference and in our work; to Dr. Willard Wilson, our liaison member of the Administration, who was always ready, cordially willing, and able to provide official guidance; to Professor Winfield E. Nagley, Chairman of the Department of Philosophy and of the Local Committee, who did such an outstanding job in taking care of the many arrangements for the Conference; to my associates in the University of Hawaii Department of Philosophy, of course— Dr. Winfield E. Nagley, Dr. Harold E. McCarthy, Dr. S. K. Saksena, Dr. Kenneth K. Inada, Dr. Michael D. Resnik, Dr. Chung-ying Cheng, and Dr. Richard P. Haynes; to each and every member of the 1964 Steering Committee—Dr. Wing-tsit Chan, Dartmouth College; Dr. Cornelius Krusé, Wesleyan University; Dr. Sterling M. McMurrin, University of Utah; Dr. Hajime Nakamura, University of Tokyo; Dr. S. K. Saksena, University of Hawaii; and Dr. W. H. Werkmeister, University of Southern California; to Dr. Shunzo Sakamaki, Dean of the Summer Session, for his unqualified co-operation in connection with our special courses in the Summer program; to those members of the press, TV, and radio who supported our work so generously and so well, and so importantly; to the remarkable public of Hawaii for their great and very welcome interest in our activities; to Dr. Hung Wo Ching and the 100 citizens of Hawaii who by their generosity made this Conference possible;[2] to the Rama Watumull Fund for a grant to enable the Conference Director to visit Asia to discuss the Conference and their papers, in advance, with our Asian representatives; to the Asia Foundation and the Edward W. Hazen Foundation for financial assistance to enable us to bring to the Conference some younger philosophers from Asia; to Dean Hubert V. Everly of the College of Education; to the officials of the East-West Center for many courtesies and particularly for invaluable help in preparing the formal papers for distribution at the Conference and for scholarship aid to attending graduate students—and to Dr. Alexander Spoehr, then Chancellor, for his assurance of significant help from the Center; to the Drama Department for their assistance with the John F. Kennedy Theatre for our Public Lectures; to Mrs. Elsie Boatman, of the University Food Service, who helped to make our valuable Coffee Hours possible and enjoyable; to all the members of the Local Committee; to the Chairmen—and all members—of the Special Sub-committees of the Local Committee that served our needs and wishes so well (Mrs. G. J. Watumull, Dr. Beatrice Yamasaki, Dr. Walter Wittich, Mr. Frederick Y. Smith, and Dr. Kenneth K. Inada); to those in the community who co-operated with these committees in their important activities; to Mr. George K. Tanabe, who as fiscal officer kept our financial matters on an even keel; to the graduate students who so willingly performed the innumerable chores and odd jobs they were called upon to handle; to those who so generously sponsored very enjoyable receptions (President and Mrs. Hamilton; China's Consul General and Mrs. Raymond S. H. Hoo and their associates, Mr. and Mrs. Hung Wai Ching and Mr. and Mrs. Wah Lee Young; Japan's Consul General and Mrs. Jiro Inagawa, and the Honolulu Academy of Arts)—and to the *many* others who I hope will forgive me for not mentioning them by name.

A very special vote of thanks must go to you distinguished scholars from Asia and the West who, as Panel Members, made this Conference so significant (and I would like to include those of previous Conferences here, too). We are all extremely grateful to you for accepting our invitation to participate, for the great dedication you have shown throughout our activity, and for contributing of your tremendous ability and your energies to the cause to which these Conferences are devoted. If—or since—I can speak for all who are responsible for this Conference, I hereby give you a "standing ovation" of appreciation. Our thanks also go, most heartily, to all of you philosophers from East and West who came to participate in the Conference—some of you at serious personal cost in time and money.

I also want to express regret on the part of all of us who were charged with responsibility for the planning and conduct of the Conference to those members—very few, I trust—who found the Conference "less than perfect." No Conference can meet such an absolute ideal. There are always aspects of any meeting of this kind which do not meet with unanimous approval. All I can say is that we planned the over-all program very seriously and after thoroughgoing consideration of all aspects of the situation and in the light of our combined best judgment.

I would like to request that those of you who found things not to your complete liking might think, in more positive terms, of the values and merits rather than in terms of the difficulties. There were many values: philosophical, intellectual, personal, social, cultural, and even hedonistic. I trust that the difficulties will evaporate with time but that the values of what we have done here and of our personal experiences here will long endure.

If you will permit me, I would like to make one further suggestion: Let us not let this Conference end with this meeting here tonight. What we have said and thought during these six weeks is and can be of great significance in our future thinking, if we will let it. The Bible suggests: "Think on these things." The Upaniṣads suggest: Hear it from a teacher, think about it and examine it by reason, and then mediate upon it so as to make it genuinely significant. May I humbly commend these thoughts, so that the work of this Conference will be of great and lasting importance to all of us—and, through our future thinking, teaching, and writing, of importance to thinkers and educated people everywhere.

III

Finally, in the interest of complete honesty concerning the significance of the Conferences, let us abandon undue modesty and humility, and look frankly at this Conference and its predecessors in terms of accomplishments.[3]

This Conference and those which preceded it constituted a highly significant adventure of the minds of men in open and cordial study of the philosophies and cultures of other peoples with profoundly different attitudes toward life and seemingly irreconcilable theories of man and reality. These Conferences have been truly unique. At no other time in history and perhaps nowhere else in the world, past or present, have such open-minded, profound, and frank—yet, cordial—confrontations among the great *philosophical* traditions of the world been undertaken. These have been daring adventures of the minds of men of vastly different cultures, seeking understanding and an avowed stretching of philosophical horizons—their own!

In a rather remarkable circumstance, outstanding and committed representatives of the great philosophical traditions of Asia and the West have come together with a genuine desire to learn about and to learn from peoples of other convictions and other traditions— traditions which throughout historical time have maintained and defended their philosophical superiority (and implicitly or explicitly denounced all other claims to wisdom and truth).

The minds of great men—outstanding thinkers—of both East and West have at these conferences been opened to and enriched by the wisdom of other great areas of mankind. Clearly all have learned very much indeed.

Dogmatism and traditional bias have not been destroyed, perhaps, but they have been significantly challenged. It is fairly safe to hope that they have been somewhat shattered. It is next to impossible to destroy one's cultural conditioning—and in this sense these Conferences have tried the impossible. However, it is fairly safe to say that at these Conferences the rigidity of the cultural and philosophical conditioning of every one of us has been lessened markedly.

Because of what might be called intrinsic difficulties in this area of thought, we have undoubtedly learned less from each other than we have about each other. Perhaps we have gained in understanding far beyond what we have gained in richness of philosophical perspective. However, no individual will leave this Conference—or could read the record of our past Conferences—without having gained in philosophical knowledge, in philosophical wisdom, and certainly in philosophical perspective, without having enriched the "magazine" of his philosophical mind, as Professor Hocking once called it. Surely no one can have failed to encounter new ideas and to be challenged by them; and no one can have missed new and enriching interpretations of man, his values, and his world.

We have proved at these Conferences that through frank philosophical discussion in depth and in terms of basic issues understanding can be achieved. It is doubtful that genuine understanding can be achieved through any other avenue of approach. Through philosophy, the comprehensive perspective of philosophy, and because of its concern with essentials, and in terms of reason in the sense of unrestricted and critical and thoroughgoing examination, we have come together at these conferences with a rather remarkable open-mindedness and cordiality to strange or alien ideas. We have reasoned with each other. We have argued. We have challenged. We have asked questions, but we have not always accepted the answers and explanations in reply. This is healthy, of course. We have experienced remarkable admissions on the part of outstanding thinkers from both East and West that theirs had been a narrow perspective, that their bias had blinded them to different points of view, and that, in some cases, it had not been realized that basic assumptions could be so significantly and seriously challenged. One senior member of one Conference openly admitted that he left "deeply chastened" in this respect.

We have explored *together* the depths of philosophical truth, of human values, of the ways of thinking—in depth—in the joint search for truths which will stand up under the scrutiny of critical examination. We have demonstrated that genuine philosophers from significantly diverse backgrounds and traditions can talk together openly and frankly and intelligibly in the name of philosophy and through the medium of universal reason. Some of us have even challenged reason, but we have reasoned together; and nobody, no representative of any tradition, has been unintelligible to the others—one of the marks of a *philosophical* attempt to achieve a meeting of the minds.

These Conferences have been Conferences in philosophy. Our minds have always been fixed upon fundamentals, a mark of philosophy. True, we have studied the cultures of the peoples represented here, but we have studied them in depth, in terms of the philosophical principles and concepts and values upon which those cultures are built and in which they find their justification. We have recognized the necessity of mutual understanding of cultural values and cultural practices, and we have called to our Conference table social scientists, political scientists, lawyers, religionists to provide "the facts of life" and to lend factual substance to our deliberations. But we have always—uniquely—kept our eyes and our minds in focus—in the direction of the fundamental convictions of peoples and their justifications for their convictions. From this procedure we have—again, uniquely—gained genuine mutual understanding.

But we have also gained something else. We have at long last achieved the universality, the totality of view, thought in terms of all-time and all-existence, which has been called "total perspective," without which philosophy is not philosophy. It may not be true, but it should be, that no one with these conferences as a part of his intellectual background can ever again approach any problem of philosophy from the sole perspective of his own provincial tradition. We are far from comprehensive knowledge of all the traditions to which we have been exposed at these conferences, but we surely realize now that every one of these great traditions has significant contributions to make—positive or negative—to every philosophical problem that the mind of man has faced or will face. Partial perspective is anathema to philosophy. Total perspective is indispensable. We now have no excuse to evade the responsibility of seeking and using such total perspective.

In modesty or immodesty, we have no reason to blind ourselves to these accomplishments of these Conferences or to the significance of what we have done together over these last 25 years. Undoubtedly— or should we say "hopefully"?—our work together will live with all of us from now on.

It is to be hoped, also, that something like the same profound effects upon the minds of those of us who have participated in these Conferences will also reach deeply into the minds of those who, though not present at any of the Conferences, will give their full and open-minded—and *concentrated*—attention to the abundant knowledge and wisdom between the covers of this volume and of those which have preceded it as the products of earlier conferences. There are exciting and profound new ideas in abundance in these genuinely significant volumes. We can all learn much from them— but only if we come to them dedicated to the spirit of philosophy in its determined search for truth and the avoidance of prejudice, and with a determination to understand and to consider with deep seriousness those new ideas which demand acceptance.

IV

Speaking for myself, for all of us at the University, and also for the community, I trust that all of you visiting scholars have enjoyed the lighter side of life as well as the work of the Conference—and also the personal associations which have been a major part of our experience. We hope, too, on the somewhat serious side, that you have seen with your very eyes the practical feasibility of understanding and harmony among different ethnic groups as evidenced in the Hawaiian community. We in Hawaii are proud of this achievement. We feel that it provides a most appropriate background or milieu for these Conferences. We trust you agree with us. It was good to have all of you here. We only trust we did our part in making you glad you came.

And now, in retiring, I hand over the responsibility for the work I have been doing at these Conferences to those who will carry this significant work forward in the years to come. I most sincerely wish them the greatest of success in maintaining the high quality of the work of our past Conferences and in carrying the Conferences forward to new heights of significance—toward, if I may repeat, our two important goals: first, greater mutual understanding of Asia and the West, and, second, the expansion of the horizons of philosophers in both East and West toward the total perspective which is demanded of philosophy and philosophers everywhere.

V. SUPPLEMENT[4]

We encountered a wealth of ideas, suggestions, interpretations, and pointed statements in the formal papers, in the formal discussions at the regular meetings, in the informal but concentrated discussions at the Coffee Hours, and in the personal give-and-take discussions that took place throughout the Conference.

It might not be inappropriate, as a Supplement to these "Concluding Remarks," to bring together a number of these especially interesting and sometimes truly exciting ideas, both as reminders to those who attended the Conference and to those who have now read the volume, and also to point up the tremendously significant intellectual interchange that took place at the Conference—and the intellectual excitement that was involved rather constantly in the work of our six weeks together. As a matter of fact, the following, which are not my contribution to the Conference, are only relatively few of the interesting, exciting, valuable, enlightening, provocative, corrective, sometimes dramatic, sometimes paradoxical, sometimes enigmatic, sometimes even confusing, at times possibly irritating, and always potentially fruitful ideas that stood out—at least, in my mind—and call for special mention.

The list is not intended as anything like a comprehensive summary or review of the work of the Conference.

Nor is there any implication here that the members of the Conference or the readers of this volume need to have these points called to their attention. It is simply a case of my having been somewhat overwhelmed—at the end of the Conference and in thinking back upon our work—by the realization that so very much had transpired. I therefore felt impelled to share with you the realization of just how much we actually accomplished in the direction of greater mutual understanding, in the direction of broadening our philosophical perspectives, and, in some cases, in the direction of realizing, perhaps more than at any previous Conference, some of the difficulties (especially in terminology, idiom, presuppositions, and general perspectives) that tend to make genuine understanding more difficult of achievement than we might wish.

And now simply to list these items[5] (Section by Section and, at the end, in summary fashion):

SECTION 1—METAPHYSICS

Dr. Raju's emphasis upon activism as of the essence of Indian philosophy, with its necessary implication of individualism.

Dr. Mei's astonishment—in view of what the West has been told repeatedly by Indian scholars—at Dr. Bhattacharyya's downgrading of the Advaita Vedānta—absolutism and monism—as merely one of many systems and theories in the Indian philosophical complex.

The inevitable conclusion that Buddhism, in its various major and minor subdivisions, accepts, respectively, practically every fundamental interpretation of the status of the individual—from what might be called pure individualism to pure monism, including also the typical Chinese interpretation of the one in the many and the many in the one (of the Fa-yen school), and, further, the near impossibility of stating any of these doctrines clearly and to a Westerner's satisfaction.

The apparently great division within Buddhism pertaining to Hīnayāna and Mahāyāna on the status of the individual—as expressed in the papers of Dr. Malalasekera and Dr. Ueda, respectively.

The surprising concluding part of Dr. Malalasekera's paper, where he seemed to be emphasizing an over-all oneness despite an earlier overwhelming emphasis upon the individual self as the essence of the Theravāda point of view.

The constant emphasis by Asians upon the qualitative nature and status of the individual as contrasted with what was called the "actual" status, as emphasized in the West. The Eastern emphasis seemed to be on what man should be to be a genuine or ideal individual, whereas the Western point was that the individual is an individual regardless of enlightenment, character, etc. (This seemed to be a major conflict in points of view.)

The aforementioned emphasis by Asian representatives on the qualitative criterion of the individual as not exclusively Asian, but also present in the West, as indicated in some Western papers.

The statement: "Throughout the history of Chinese philosophy, Yang Chu was the only one who spoke audaciously for the actual individual. But all other thinkers have looked askance at him."

The remark, repeated two or three times, ascribing illusionism or the view that the world—and, therefore, the individual—is unreal in Buddhism, and the strong Buddhist reaction against this interpretation.

Dr. Hsieh's exposition of the Confucian view of the equality of all human beings (in view of the possession by all men of the seed of humanity—*jen*)—which would seem to be in some conflict with the qualitative interpretation differentiating among individuals as individuals exclusively on a qualitative basis.

Dr. Findlay's complete rejection of any significant monism in the Western metaphysical tradition—thus confirming the usual interpretation that the West emphasizes the individual as contrasted with the "monistic East"—and his categorical rejection of a challenge to this pluralistic interpretation as exclusively and comprehensively characteristic of the West.

The rather continuous—but not universally accepted—point that it is impossible to discuss the status of the individual without discussing, first, the nature of the individual.

The at least apparent irrelevance of the Chinese emphasis upon humanism as an over-all basic characteristic of the Chinese mind—possibly irrelevant because this does not determine or indicate the status of the individual human being.

Dr. Mei's contention that only in Chinese philosophy is there the view of the basic cosmic importance of man.

The point that inequalities, aristocracies, hierarchies, social and legal inequalities, etc., have been significantly present in all the traditions under discussion, Eastern and Western.

The individual can become a *buddha* in Buddhism, a Sage in Confucianism, and identical with *Brahman* in the Vedānta, all indicative of the at least potential ultimate significance in the East of every individual without distinction.

The Western difficulty in understanding the Chinese concept of the mind as "vacuous and receptive," as characteristic of the mind of the genuine individual.

The rather surprising interpretation that "transcendental metaphysics" is a characteristic Chinese doctrine of reality, with significant implications for the status of the individual.

What is the actual status of the individual in "the foremost unity of all things" as cited from Taoism, which elsewhere is called wholly individualistic?

It seems to have been left up in the air just what the ultimate status of the individual is in Śaṁkara's Advaita Vedānta. There was an apparent unwillingness to uphold complete absorption into an Absolute with the loss of all individuality, along with an attempt to indicate that such identity with *Brahman* is genuine individuality— a point difficult for Westerners to comprehend.

With reference to the status of the individual in the Advaita Vedānta, just what is the full meaning for the individual of the doctrine, "I am *Brahman?*"

The statement: ". . . a Chinese . . . takes no pride in a type of individual in estrangement from the world he lives in or from the other fellows he associates with." (Would any other tradition?)

The challenge that in the Advaita Vedānta the empirical life and body are ultimately unreal and the individual should therefore not be genuinely significant.

The problem of the empirical status versus the ultimate status of the individual, especially in Hinduism, but also in Buddhism, was never really and adequately examined and explained.

The apparent tendency among Chinese representatives to emphasize Confucianism to the relative neglect of other basic schools of Chinese philosophy.

". . . . the Chinese contemplative minds have been fascinated with the world and the human individual, which are taken, however, not so much in natural as in dramatic regard." (Fang)

"In their [Confucius, Taoist, and Buddhist] eyes, any other way of affirming the status of the individual [except in terms of the ideal individual in a transfigured world] would be a premature mode of thought in an essential lack of wisdom." (Fang)

". . . I regard all wholly unifying philosophies as distorted and self-destroying just as I regard all diremptive philosophies as equally so." (Findlay)

"Sheer monisms and splintered atomisms represent the two opposed poles of the philosophically unacceptable. . . ."

SECTION 2—METHODOLOGY

"At the core of all these [epistemological] endeavors there remains the problem as to how the individual self can transcend subjective belief and behold, or incorporate into itself, something to be called objective truth."

The contention that it is impossible to understand Buddhist philosophy and to accept its explanations if one is restricted to typical

Western Aristotelian logic—and the *question* as to whether or not Buddhist philosophy does actually violate the principle of contradiction.

Dr. Nakamura's emphasis, from the point of view of the Japanese language, upon the lack of abstract thinking and generalization— thus emphasizing the immediate, the particular, and the individual.

The repeated emphasis by at least three Japanese representatives upon the language aspect of Japanese thought and culture—always in the direction of emphasizing the particular and the individual.

Dr. Nakamura's comment concerning "the Japanese trait to think of things in terms of human relationships rather than as separately existing facts in the objective world." And his related comment: "To lay stress upon human relationships is to place heavy regard upon the relations of many individuals rather than upon the individual as an independent entity."

Also, his point that special language-forms are needed or used as determined by "the relationship of social ranks" and as "required for superiors, equals, inferiors, [as well as] intimates and strangers."

The extremely important point that language difficulties seriously prevent actual mutual understanding—for example, Dr. Chan's comment that the Chinese think in terms of analogies, Dr. Mei's comment that the different idioms involved are vitally important, and Dr. Nakamura's point that even the word "individual" is not an Oriental or Asian word—and there were other comments to the same point.

The point, too, that the very word "individual" is taken "in the East" to stand for egotism and selfishness and therefore has a negative and derogatory connotation—intrinsically.

The rebuttal to all this—by an Asian—that the words used do not seize the basic meanings but that similar meanings can be clear despite differences of terminology.

The feeling—at least my own—that the nuances and idiosyncracies of speech, of language, and of interpretation, especially in some of the Chinese papers, and also in some of the Japanese, made it doubtful that others were fully appreciating or even understanding of the points being made or the interpretations being offered.

The seemingly greater degree of difficulty in understanding the points of view of the Chinese and the Japanese as compared with those of Indians, whose points of view seem to be more literal, more factual, more, shall we say, logical, and therefore more clearly intelligible to the Westerners.

The Chinese tendency to be superbly literary in expression—but therefore sometimes difficult to understand fully and clearly . . . in a manner that may be of basic significance to communication and reciprocal understanding.

Dr. Fang's remark that his presentation—to be true to the Chinese point of view—was and had to be "dramatic" rather than literal in its interpretation of the status of the individual.

The repetition of a point made frequently at the 1959 Conference, namely, the emphasis in Japanese thought, in all its aspects, upon empirical immediacy of experience, with obvious implications in the direction of the particular and the individual.

The point that, in a sense, the East as a whole is more conscious of the specific individual than the West, if we go along with the almost innumerable citations in the Asian papers, perhaps especially those by Chinese and Japanese, but also by some Indians, who refer exclusively to the aforementioned "empirical immediacy of experience" and other purely individual facets of culture, life, society, even literature. Compare this with the scientifically dictated conceptual perspective of the West, in which the individual is merely an example of a universal or a concept—as well illustrated, it would seem, in Western law and even in Western ethics. (This point was not faced directly enough or discussed adequately, in spite of its extreme significance, especially for the Far East versus the West and India.)

Emphasis upon the purely individualistic character of intuition.

Emphasis upon the individualistic character of mysticism, specifically at least in Islam.

SECTION 3—RELIGION

The contention that the individual comes into his own only in religion.

The contention—against a wide interpretation to the contrary—that there is no absolute individualism in Christianity, that the emphasis is equally on "community."

Dr. Smith's point that there is no either-or in Christianity concerning the status of the individual, but, rather, complexity, variety, and change of point of view and interpretation.

The explanation that Japanese Confucianism and Buddhism—and

even pluralistic Shinto—brought about a general development of the sense of individuality in Japanese religion.

In religion, there was not one case—even the religious aspect of the Advaita Vedānta—of complete denial of the ultimate status or significance of the individual. In fact, the exception seemed to come, not in the allegedly monistic Asian religions, but in the emphasis upon "community" and the denial of absolute individualism in Christianity.

Dr. Smith's contention that the contemporary world faces "the paradox of loneliness and togetherness," and that religion must "do something about" this contemporary predicament of the individual.

In religion, representatives of all traditions contended that the individual has freedom of belief and freedom to do or to reject the will of God—even in Islam, which is widely thought to be deterministic.

One member cited as the most important specific idea of the Conference Dr. Wu's comment in his paper: "The excursion [of the West to the East for spiritual wisdom] is really a homecoming." (Dr. Wu's statement goes on to speak of the "intriguing paradox" that the East in seeking to be Westernized has often encountered its dormant self, just as in some spheres, especially in philosophy of life and spiritual cultivation, the West is beginning to discover its original self by way of exploring the profundities of the Eastern mind.")

Dr. Smith's citing of *inclinatio* in Christianity—with possible interpretations comparable to the urge to rebirth in Hinduism and Buddhism.

At times one got the impression that many Asian representatives thought not only that the West advocated the doctrine of atomistic individuals, but also interpreted any defense of significant status for the individual as a plea for egotism, selfishness, etc., the essence of evil. Many feel that Westerners might reject both of these interpretations.

A Westerner: "Being an individual, that is, is never the source of evil, and consequently evil is never overcome through the transcendence of that type of being. . . . The imperfection that is sin . . . does not constitute the individual as such, nor does it follow from the fact of individuality." (Smith, p. 256)

[In the Hebraic religion] "the self needs a body of some sort as a medium of expression; the self is not an ethereal spirit that is without localization and definite involvement in created, visible things.

This emphasis on embodiment was to be carried over into Christianity and expressed by Paul in the doctrine of the 'spiritual' body or resurrected person."

"For them [Neo-Confucianists], as for Chinese intellectuals from the sixth century B.C. on, immortality consists in social immortality, or immortality of influence. . . . They, like the masses, finally believe in the central importance of the individual, but in another way, namely, full realization of one's nature instead of everlasting life on earth or eternal existence in Paradise." [See also Dr. Chan's Answers to Questions in discussion.]

". . . The individual is of the utmost importance in Chinese religions. . . . In none of the three systems is the One understood as absorbing and thereby obliterating the many. The common conviction has been that each requires the other."

". . . there is no doubt that the primary locus of responsibility in Islam is the individual."

"To say that the individual is incomplete without the community is not to demand a transcendence of individuality, but, rather, to point out the error of atomic existence. Though essentially involved in each other as members of one community, each individual remains known to God as such; there is no melting or blending of the individuals into each other. In this sense, his Christian individuality remains an ultimate trait."

SECTION 4—ETHICS

Mrs. Dasgupta's interesting and revealing interpretation of the problem of Arjuna in the *Gītā*—to the effect that his case was not an instance of freedom of conscience, and her contention that the Indian ethical situation provides for complete freedom of individual conscience.

The point—made by an Indian—that no civilization has ever been able to deny the individual the right of conscience.

Dr. Furukawa's emphasis upon duty and obligation as the essence of Japanese ethics—along with his uniquely Japanese interpretation of the concept of *"wa"* (harmony), which denies the interpretation of mere submission or unwilling conformity to duty or that the individual is ethically required to do *anything* his duty demands, regardless of conscience.

The emphasis upon the concept of *"wa"* by several Japanese members—all of whom emphasized the harmony and cordiality of the relationships involved—all contrasted the spirit of *"wa"* with Western perspectives.

Dr. Werkmeister's contention that a meeting of the minds of East and West can best be achieved in ethics—not in such areas as metaphysics.

The point that India's perspective is ethical and that in such a perspective duties are necessarily prior to rights, the latter being actually interpreted as selfish and therefore unethical.

The heated debate on the status of individual conscience in the form of individual conscience versus individual conformity with external, social, or religious ethical judgment—as exemplified in the virtue of honesty, especially as related to the apparently superior significance of the family—versus the Western point of view, generally speaking —and the denial of all Chinese representatives that Confucian ethics condoned such dishonesty. (This seemed to remain a controversial point.)

Dr. Werkmeister's point that the individual's motive or inner attitude is of the essence of morality in the West—in spite of the emphasis upon self-realization throughout the history of the Western ethical tradition—*and* the immediate response of Asians, either challenging this point of view as representative of the West or welcoming it as actually expressing the Oriental interpretation. (Dr. Werkmeister's distinction between "to be" and "to do" brought such immediate response from Asian members.)

The point cited by representatives of all the Asian traditions that loyalty, which Westerners tended to interpret as anti-individualistic does not mean that, but means loyalty to character, loyalty to *jen,* loyalty to one's moral values, and loyalty to one's superior in a voluntary and welcome way.

In ethics, all representatives seemed to say, quite positively, that the individual has the right of individual moral conviction and does not have to submit to any external authority.

The point that freedom in Confucian ethics is restricted to freedom to do good . . . . the point being challenged by some Westerners, but also to a degree defended by one Westerner on the ground that a similar view is not lacking in the West.

The not-too-surprising interpretation that *karma* is in its very essence individualistic, in ascribing complete responsibility for one's life to oneself as an individual. No Easterner espoused the view that *karma* is deterministic and deprives the individual of freedom.

The observation by a Japanese that Shintō and Bushidō are, even now, fundamental to the Japanese way of life and to the ethics of the Japanese.

The apparent unanimity of Indian representatives on the point that morality is exclusively, and certainly primarily, simply an aid to an ultimate spiritual experience which more or less transcends the ethical—and the accompanying idea that in this respect the East is distinct from the West, the latter emphasizing morality as a personal and social phenomenon, not necessarily related intrinsically to one's spiritual destiny.

In ethics, one major interpretation was to the effect that individual self-realization—although this always called for more than merely isolated individuals—is the ideal or the goal of ethics in all traditions.

The confusion that came out concerning the status and "power" of filial piety as a basic ethical doctrine—in view of several comments to the effect that the individual is not dominated or overly subordinated by this theory and practice, as compared with Dr. Wu's statement that "filial piety *by law* is unique to China" and that in the Chinese tradition the law carries grave penalties for disobedience. (Dr. Hsieh, in the course in Comparative Ethics, contended that all ethics begins with filial piety because this is the first and best-established of all ethical attitudes.)

One Western member said, "The interpretation of Bushidō by Dr. Furukawa as 'becoming pure and simple'—together with his citation of Royce on loyalty—seemed to me to be important."

"This cry [for something to replace the Education Edict], though not without plausible reasons to plead in its favor, has its origin. after all, in the fact that . . . in *Japan the full establishment of the individual is yet to come.*"

SECTION 5—SOCIAL THOUGHT AND PRACTICES

The strong emphasis on duties rather than rights in the East—with rather numerous interesting explanations of the status of rights in this connection (some of which are cited elsewhere among these items).

Dr. Hsieh's point that the many freedoms provided by Confucianism for the individual actually constitute significant rights of the individual in spite of the many duties involved.

Dr. Mei's comment, puzzling to some Western members, "The Chinese thinkers have not interested themselves in human rights as such. But the conviction in the inviolable worth of the individual lies at the heart of Confucian teaching and accounts for a good measure of the democratic spirit in Chinese life."

The impressive set of circumstances and instances cited by Dr. Nakamura in his paper and by Dr. Kōsaka in his which reflect an almost dominant emphasis upon the individual and the particular—in contrast with the widespread conviction of the anti-individualism of Japanese tradition.

The point made repeatedly by Asian representatives that emphasis on the group, in every Asian tradition, does not mean or imply no status for the individual—the individual finding fulfillment, security, "belongingness" in the group.

The thought that the East and the West are not so far apart on the idea that the individual can achieve fulfillment only in and through the group. No representative, Eastern or Western, advocated absolute individualism.

Dr. Hsieh's strong emphasis upon the significance of the individual in relation to both the family and society.

The repeated contention of Chinese representatives that the Western interpretation of the overpowering dominance of the individual by the family is not of the essence of Chinese thought and culture.

Dr. Hsieh's citing of the right of the individual to challenge—or at least to remonstrate with—his parents, his prince, his teachers, and his society, in conformity with his individual conscience (and *jen*). (See also Dr. Kōsaka: ". . . the right filial duty was to admonish and make the parents amend their wrong attitude when the parents were in the wrong.")

The related point that even in China the individual is more important than the family or society or the community—that the family is *for* the welfare and development of the individual.

On the matter of the relative status of the individual and the family, it would seem that the question was not "solved" or the relation clearly explained or established—a confusion which persisted at the end of the Conference.

The Chinese emphasis upon synthesis of conflicting or extremely opposite points of view—although the actual essence of the doctrines seemed somewhat difficult for the Westerners to understand.

Speaking of rights (as related to duties), one Indian and one Chinese insisted that rights are only minimal in their respective traditions.

The seeming implication of metaphysical qualitative individualism in the direction of hierarchy or aristocracy, even though it implies moral or qualitative aristocracy.

The point—by an Indian—that contemporary democracy in India has not come from the West, but is a revival of the great tradition of the real India before its perversion in the dark Middle Ages and before its domination by outside powers.

One Japanese representative's emphasis upon the Education Edict, which dominated the thought-life of students and required complete compliance with governmental edicts.

In this connection, Dr. Furukawa's explanation of the "spirit of the governed" and the "spirit of the taught" as indications of Japanese psychology and culture.

Even Japan's (allegedly) anti-individualistic social structure and political order were explained in qualified terms as not nearly so anti-individual as is the common opinion.

No representative of any tradition admitted that the society of his tradition dominates the individual or denies him distinct individual status—and freedom.

The confusion and lack of agreement concerning the actual status, connotations, and significance for the status of the individual of the caste system in India. There seemed to be general agreement in defense of the system as properly interpreted, but not even this was universal, for example, in one Indian's contention "the caste system prevented genuine individuality."

Freedom of thought was claimed for all traditions—except, again, for Japan, where there still seemed to be some doubt—as, for example, in the point made by Dr. Nakamura in 1959: "Just as religion was the basis of the ethical thinking of the Indians, family the basis of the practical morals of the Chinese, so the State was the basis of all thought in Japan."

A quotation from Confucius: "A superior man is seeking for harmony but not sameness. A mean man is seeking for sameness but not harmony."

In answer to a Discussion question, the appropriate representative of all the Asian traditions defended the status of equality of opportunity as basic to his tradition, even if there was not actual social equality.

The description of Chinese society as characterized by "social cohesion and fluidity"—a description that seemed to apply to all the cultures under consideration.

A Japanese, speaking about postwar Japan said: ". . . to eliminate or alter what was good but is no longer deemed highly appropriate is very difficult. Here lies one of the fundamental problems for the Japanese. For the virtue non-self-assertiveness that was once respected is now either inappropriate or insufficient for modern society."

". . . the difference between Western thinkers, who have placed a great deal of emphasis on human rights and Chinese thinkers who have been interested in the inviolable worth of the individual is mainly a matter of idiom."

One Indian: "Caste placed strict limitations upon the liberty of the individual, and constrained him to unalterable conformity with the rule of the caste."

Another Indian: The new India wants to eradicate these evils [caste system and other discriminative restrictions] as quickly as possible. They do not represent the living India."

"The Master said, 'The commander of the forces of a large state may be carried off, but the will of even a common man cannot be taken from him.' " (Cited by at least three Chinese Members.)

"In a concept of social obligation which does not have the counterbalancing notion of "right," the interest of the individual is not made distinct and fixed. Here, an individual is not considered to be an independent entity. Rather, his interest is absorbed *in the interest of the collectivity* to which he belongs, and the interest of the collectivity is recognized as having primary importance, while the interest of the individual has merely a secondary importance."

Another Indian: ". . . no individual can be completely perfected if the core of his being lies merely in his insistence on his rights."

SECTION 6—LEGAL AND POLITICAL THOUGHT AND INSTITUTIONS

One Indian's admission, in response to a question, that in his opinion the new democracies of Asia are probably a veneer, without substantial foundation in tradition.

The point expressed by several Asians about the recentness of democracy and genuine respect for the individual in the West—and that it is not genuine or universal even now.

A Westerner's admission, in response to a question, that genuine democracy did not exist in Greece—and even in the West generally in its historical tradition—until, perhaps, very late.

The point made in different ways by several Westerners that the contemporary West, especially in its political aspect, is not genuinely respectful of the individual—in terms of the state's domination of the individual and the "depersonalization" of the individual.

The point that the West, at the present time at least, is confused in its views concerning the status of the individual as related to the state.

The point made by a Westerner in a Coffee-Hour discussion with some Chinese members that in the West the individual is taken so seriously that his freedom must be defended even at the expense of the security of society—a point which the Chinese in that discussion found utterly unacceptable.

The contention that there was equality under the law in traditional China, *along with*—to the surprise and confusion of some Westerners—a list of eight groups of people who were exempted from such equality and who received favored treatment before or under the law.

Dr. Kawashima's point that Japanese law—in its treatment of individual offenders—has never been literal, machine-like, etc., as contrasted with Western law. (In this connection, Dr. Kawashima defended Dr. Northrop's interpretation of Eastern law as contrasted with Western—the East being on the side of conciliation, etc., and the West on precision by conceptual application.)

One recalls Dr. Dorsey's point at the 1959 Conference that the West insists that the individual has a right to stand up for his rights—a point which would seem to have been rejected by many Asian representatives at this Conference.

The point that—*before 1945*—there had been repeated movements in the direction of democracy in Japan—politically and legally—but that they had all been denounced by the government and thus prevented from succeeding.

The point, contrary to some opinion, that, even under the law, and in all traditions, there is no genuine equality of all individuals—let alone in social thought and practices, where inequality was admitted to be inevitable.

The point that, even if there is formal legal equality under the law, the inevitable cultural lag prevents such equality in practice—as, e.g., in the caste system in India and the Negro situation in the U.S.

The categorical denial of the applicability of the frequently heard expression "Oriental despotism" to the Asian world—perhaps to the "Near East," but not "Asia."

The continuing uncertainty concerning the status of the individual in Japanese thought and culture—most of the papers denying dominance over the individual, whereas there seemed to be evidence, in sociological studies and in political history, for the traditional anti-individualistic spirit of Japan.

It is in this connection that a comment by Dr. Kōsaka is pertinent: "The reform by the Occupation Forces weakened the authority of the father and legally established the dignity of the individual. But it also effected the disintegration of the family ethic."

The comment that in matters of law Japan will probably continue to develop toward Western points of view, and the other comment, by a Japanese, to the effect that Japan is at the crossroads and must now decide what values are important.

In political philosophy—and perhaps legal philosophy, too—there was the remaining serious question as to whether all contemporary democratic movements in Asia are grounded in tradition, are compatible or incompatible with tradition, or are what was called a "mere veneer," without a basic foundation in tradition and resulting from somewhat artificial, if not forced, influences of the day.

The comment that, in traditional Chinese law there was "a touch of humanity in the judges" and that this typically Chinese way of settling a case has "an irresistible charm which will cast such a spell upon one's mind [that] one would rather have a judgment like that than read a dozen learned treatises on the law of property"—an interpretation that some Westerners had difficulty with.

The charge—and largely unanswered question—that Asian legal (and political) systems, because of personal, family, and other exemptions, do not have a place for the kind of justice which does not qualify the application of law by personal or family considerations.

Many Asians indicated the influence of Western legal theory and practice upon Eastern systems, all in the direction of greater respect for the individual, but all Asian representatives in this connection also indicated that duties rather than rights remained primary in the Asian systems.

Democracy means many things to the many traditions we studied. (Recall UNESCO's study of the meanings of democracy throughout the world.)

GENERAL COMMENTS AND OBSERVATIONS

The often-mentioned complexity and variety and diversity of views in every one of the traditions under consideration, such that any single characteristic doctrine is clearly an unsound over-simplification

—and such, therefore, that all the clichés with which our general concern at these Conferences and our specific concern with the problem of the status of the individual have been beset are to be condemned and rejected.

The thought—or feeling—that every basic theory or interpretation is to be found significant in every major tradition—such that, in fact, even the theory of a single characteristic *emphasis* is open to serious question.

The feeling that all anti-individualistic clichés about Asia—and/or individualistic clichés about the West—are false (except probably for a lingering doubt about Japanese thought and culture because of conflicting aspects and interpretations of that particular tradition).

The feeling that there must exist a great conflict in Japanese thought and culture on the status of the individual—the feeling of lack of clarity and an unwillingness to give equal or adequate attention to the seemingly well-founded historical sociological and political and educational control of the individual and his mandatory group-status—along with obvious elements of individuality.

The statements in many papers by Asian representatives which seemed to defend the non-significant status of the individual—while at the same time expressing the view that the Asian tradition or traditions do respect the dignity, the conscience, the freedom, and the relative independence of the individual. (This was one of the confusions that remained to the end.)

The confusion that existed almost throughout the Conference in terms of the several approaches to the basic problem, some of them seemingly not directly pertinent, such as, in addition to the status of the individual, the nature of the individual, individualism, individuality, the qualitative criterion of the individual, etc.—indicating the difficulty of studying any one problem in the Asian or East-West orientation in isolation or in exclusiveness.

The difficulty found by the Asian members in the sixfold departmentalization of our work. Such distinctive classification constituted a significant conflict of perspectives between the Eastern traditions and the West.

In no tradition did we find either absolute monism or absolute pluralism as basic and characteristic. In *all* traditions there seemed to be fundamental recognition of the validity of *both* sides of the monism-pluralism "dichotomy" and both a theoretical and a practical synthesis of the two views. A few pertinent statements—in addition to those cited in the particular Section in which they occurred —are the following:

"Society is . . . not a mere conglomeration of isolated individuals."

"Expressions of pure individuality are always suspect in all societies. All sane societies with a limit on individualism in the interests of social welfare and other values which alone make the individual respected."

"Individual freedom of action is always limited."

"It has become quite clear at this Conference that there can be no true individuality without true community, and no true community without true individuality."

"Whatever you can affirm about Eastern or Western thought, it is always possible to quote a doctrine which says exactly the opposite. If you try to summarize the prevailing trends in a concise formula, you surely will meet the reproach that your selection is highly subjective or that it is an over-simplified cliché."

The status of the individual is not a problem to be simply posed once and for all; its answer is not to be found ready-made once and for all. The question about it has to be continually asked. In different epochs of time and in various contexts of thought, the answers to it would be radically different.

The often-repeated statement that the individual is important, possibly most or all-important, even ultimate in status, in spite of equally often-cited explanations concerning the subordinate or secondary status and occasionally, though very rarely, the ultimate unreality of the individual. All this is evidence of the falsity of any single-theory interpretation.

The interesting situation wherein representatives from the various traditions differed among themselves as to the correct interpretation of their own tradition's basic point of view. This applied to practically all the traditions, though sometimes there was hesitancy in expressing such differences of opinion. Here is another compelling reason for rejecting *any* single interpretation or doctrine as characteristic.

There seemed to be frequent instances of a failure to achieve a meeting of minds. Often, Asian ideals—or explanations of them—seemed questionable or confusing or even self-contradictory to some Westerners, whereas to the Easterners in question no such difficulties were felt.

Dr. Smith's pungent remark: "It must no longer be considered treason to consider other traditions seriously."

One Westerner said, "I was struck with the fact that almost every Western position could be matched by some Eastern and vice versa, albeit with different languages and also different emphasis."

This same Westerner said, "I was struck, too, with the fact . . . that Indian, Japanese, and Chinese participants . . . not to speak of Westerners, *differed among themselves.*"

This same writer said, "Also, of course, the *bewildering complexity* was striking. . . ."

The insistence by Orientals that the East was not so much being Westernized as modernized, industrialized, urbanized—with reference to the status of the individual as in all other respects.

An observation by one member: "There are possibly more differences between the old and the new in all traditions than between the East and the West."

The net result of our work seems to be that there is little justification, ever again, for anyone to speak of the "individualistic West," or the "anti-individualistic" or the "monistic" East.

Someone said that the "winner" in the Conference as a whole was the significance and dignity of and respect for the individual human being—but the observation comes to mind that this, though generally true in what was emphasized, must be modified by the many qualifications expressed in some of the papers, Eastern and Western. It may well be that the essence of our "Conclusion" would be that the individual enjoys a qualified status in all the traditions, characterized by complexity and variety as they all are, and marked by significant changes in the course of time . . . with greater emphasis on the significance of the individual at the present time, especially in the East, than ever before, but possibly, paradoxically, with less emphasis upon the individual in the West in the light of the growing power and dominance of the state.

The "winner" at the Conference, to be sure, *was* the significance and dignity of the individual human being in all the traditions under consideration—regardless of and in apparently serious opposition to the usual clichés and pre-Conference notions about the East. The enthusiastic and sometimes almost belligerent defense of the status of the individual by the Asians was especially interesting and significant and sometimes quite surprising.

Basically, it does not matter whether this attitude was a response to Western emphasis upon the individual or to contemporary psychology, or whether the Asian representatives really found adequate justification in their traditional systems, or even whether they were possibly somewhat idealizing (?) traditional views. The fact is that the individual was recognized as of genuine and significant status by practically all representatives of all traditions. Paradoxically, the alleged complete "individualism" of the West was frequently questioned—by Smith, McMurrin, Polin, and McKeon. Thus the pre-Conference cliché was *essentially* undetermined.

A *vital point* that seemed to be ignored by more than a few members is the fact that practically all papers, starting with traditional points of view, applied those points of view to the present situation in each of the traditions, and even pointed to the future in the light of the past and the present. This was, in fact, one of the outstanding and especially important aspects of the entire Conference, and yet, most surprisingly, it was the most frequently and most strongly expressed criticism of the Conference.

To quote Dr. Tara Chand in this connection: "The situation of today is indissolubly linked with that of yesterday and the day before. No understanding of contemporary India is possible, therefore, without a knowledge of the past." This, I take it, was the approach undertaken by the Conference in general and in most of the papers—and it would seem to be the only sound approach to all basic issues, as well as to the specific problem of the status of the individual.

And representatives of all traditions explained that their thought-and-cultural traditions are in a state of significant transition combining the old or classical and the new—in varying (and not always welcomed) degrees of synthesis. To bring together some of the pointed comments made by different people at different times, we "melted ice peaks," "bridged chasms," "annihilated clichés"—*and,* positively, enlarged the perspective of all traditions and all members . . . and enhanced understanding in depth and breadth, both with reference to the status of the individual and also with reference to the respective and different perspectives of the several major traditions under consideration.

For everyone, surely one of the most thrilling features of the Conference—as in all our previous conferences—was the sheer fact that so many unquestionably outstanding intellectual leaders of the major traditions of East and West were sitting at our Conference table and describing and discussing, as only such outstanding scholars and representatives of their traditions could, the basic ideas and ideals of their peoples in open-minded, objective, and frank comparison with equally great thinkers and spokesmen for the other major philosophical traditions represented.

Patrons

Takashi Anbe & Associates, Inc.

In Memory of J. Ballard Atherton,
Hawaiian Trust Company, Ltd.

Henry P. Baldwin, Ltd.
J. Walter Cameron, President

Bank of Hawaii
Edward A. Schneider, President

Edwin L. Bauer

William Blackfield Associates
William Blackfield, President

Samuel N. and Mary Castle
    Foundation

Castle & Cooke, Inc.
Malcolm MacNaughton, President

Central Pacific Bank
Kazuo Ishii, President

Hung Wai Ching

Hung Wo and Elizabeth Ching
    Foundation

Harry Y. K. Chock
A. C. Chock, Ltd.

Chock-Pang Clinic
Dr. H. Q. Pang

Makiki Nursery
Wilbert H. S. Choi

John P. Chong

Paradise Sportswear, Ltd.
Calvin C. S. Chun, President

C. Q. Yee Hop Co., Ltd.
Kwai Dick Chun, President

Chun-Hoon Properties, Ltd.
Henry Chun-Hoon, President

Harry C. C. Chung
Twentieth Century Furniture, Inc.

C. Robert Clarke, President
Pacific Cement & Aggregate, Inc.

Charles M. and Anna C. Cooke Trust
T. A. Cooke, Chairman

Dole Corporation
Malcolm MacNaughton, President

The Evergreen, Ltd.
Harry S. Uehara, President

First National Bank of Hawaii
N. F. Banfield, Executive
    Vice-President

Mr. and Mrs. Robert L. Fong

George E. Freitas

Honolulu Sash & Door Co., Ltd.
Richard H. Gray

Hauoli Sales Company, Ltd.
James K. C. Doo, President

Hawaii State Steel Company, Ltd.
Kenneth Imamura, President

Hawaiian Electric Company, Inc.
Ralph B. Johnson, President

Herbert T. Hayashi, Owner
Pagoda Hotel & Floating Restaurant

Canada Western Steel, Ltd.
Gerald H. B. Hobbs, President

Honolulu Construction & Draying
    Co., Ltd.
Robert L. Muller, President

Honolulu Sporting Goods Co., Ltd.
Harrison R. Cooke, President

George K. Houghtailing

International Travel Service
Loui Leong Hop

Johnston & Buscher, Inc.
Henry W. Buscher, President

Occidental Underwriters of Hawaii,
    Ltd.
Lawrence T. Kagawa, President

Dr. Abraham Kamsat
In Memoriam Helen N. Kamsat

Keiji Kawakami
Iolani Sportswear, Ltd.

Robert M. Kaya

State Senator and Mrs. Mitsuyuki
   Kido

Gilbert D. Kobatake

Lawrence B. C. Lau, President
American Security Bank

Yau On Leong
Oahu Furniture Company

Liberty Bank of Honolulu
C. T. Wong, Executive
   Vice-President

Donald T. Lo

Q. C. Lum

Lum Yip Kee, Ltd.
Y. T. Lum, President

Jack H. Magoon, Jr., President
Hawaiian Airlines, Ltd.

Harold H. Manago
H. Manago Hotel

Matson Navigation Company
W. R. Starr, Vice-President

McInerny Foundation

Medical Specialty Clinic
Dr. Richard K. C. Chang

Melim Tire & Rubber Co., Ltd.
T. C. Melim, Jr.

Mid-Pac Lumber Co., Ltd.
Wallace J. D. Lai, President

Mid-Pacific Insurance Agency, Ltd.
Walter Takiguchi, President

James H. Miyake

Mrs. Diana T. Moncado
Moncado Foundation of America,
   Ltd.

Nakakura Construction Co., Ltd.
Lincoln S. Nakakura, President

Orchids of Hawaii
Kei Yamato, President

Dr. David Lee Pang

Park Associates, Inc.
K. D. Park, President

Mrs. William P. Roth

William M. Roth

Dr. Richard Y. Sakimoto

Sealy Mattress & Furniture Company
Leonard Fong, President

Sears, Roebuck & Company
Morley L. Theaker, Manager

Francis F. Sen, President
Oahu Plumbing & Sheet Metal, Ltd.

Shell Oil Company
D. Campbell Ross, District Manager

Chuck G. Shima

Smith, Wild, Beebe & Cades

Philip E. Spalding

Philip E. Spalding, Jr.

Jack K. Taniyama

Times Super Market, Ltd.
Albert T. Teruya, President

Dr. K. S. Tom

Watumull Foundation

C. S. Wo & Sons
Robert C. Wo, President

B. Y. Wong Estate
Willard Wong

Harry C. and N. C. Wong

Dr. Haw Tung Wong

Hei Wai Wong

Kwai Lum Wong & Sons

Mun Charn Wong, C.L.U.

U. Yamane Properties, Ltd.
Kazuo Yamane, President

Clyde and Frank Yamamoto

Hirotoshi Yamamoto

Hiroshi Yamane

Mr. and Mrs. Masami Yamauchi

Dr. Raymond C. Yap

Dr. Mung Yee

Oahu Construction Company, Ltd.
W. T. Yoshimoto, President

Dr. Richard You

Kee Fook Zane

[1] This is a considerably revised and enlarged version of a talk made at the banquet held as the concluding event of the Conference.

[2] Complete list of patrons is given on pages 574–576.

[3] And we are not even considering here such tangible results or accomplishments as books, articles, courses, visiting or exchange professorships (and studentships), or even the new status of Oriental philosophy which these Conferences have helped create and develop in the West.

[4] This Supplement is in its entirety an addition to the original presentation as given at the banquet at the end of the Conference. Since these are for the most part, ideas of others —not my own—I plead not guilty to any possible charge of having exceeded the limits of length applied to papers personally presented at the Conference.

[5] In most cases names of members will be omitted for fear of possible distortion of their statements. In some instances, names are cited, especially where quotations are given.

Who's Who

Director, Centre of Advanced Study in Philosophy; Professor and Head of the Department of Philosophy, Visva-Bharati University. B.A., 1932, M.A., 1934, Ph.D., 1945, Calcutta University.

Lecturer in Philosophy, Vidyasagar College, Calcutta, 1936–1944; Lecturer in Philosophy, Calcutta University, 1944–1951; Associate Professor of Indian Philosophy, Department of Post Graduate Training and Research, Government Sanskrit College, Calcutta, 1951–1954, Professor of Indian Philosophy, 1954–1956; Principal, Vidya-Bhavana (College of Post-Graduate Teaching and Research), Visva-Bharati University, 1961–1964.

Honorary Professor, World Academy of Sanskrit, Bharatiya Vidya-Bhavan, Bombay, 1954–1956; Khudiram Basu Lecturer in Philosophy, University of Calcutta, 1962; Buddha Jayanti Lecturer, Indian Philosophical Congress, Waltair, 1960.

President, Section of Logic and Metaphysics, Poona Session of the Indian Philosophical Congress, 1951; Delegate, Entriens, International Institute of Philosophy, Paris; Member, Board of Studies in Philosophy in the Universities of Calcutta, Gorakhpur, Mysore, Banaras, Saugar, Andhra; Member, Council of Cultural Relations, New Delhi, 1961; Member, Philosophy Review Committee, University Grants Commission, India, 1961; General Secretary, Indian Philosophical Congress, 1961–1964; Honorary Fellow, Indian Academy of Philosophy, Calcutta; Member, American Philosophical Association, Eastern Division; Member, Rabindra Bharati University, Calcutta.

Author of *Alternative Standpoints in Philosophy; Object, Content and Relation; The Concept of Cause in India and the West; The Indian Concepts of Knowledge and Self; Language, Logic and Philosophy;* and many articles in professional journals. Editor of *Recent Indian Philosophy* (Selected Papers from the Proceedings of the Indian Philosophical Congress, 1925–1934) and *Rabindranath Tagore Birth Centenary Celebrations,* Vol. III (Proceedings of the Indian Philosophical Congress, 36th Session). Editor or member of the editorial boards of *Indian Philosophical Quarterly; Journal of the Academy of Philosophy; Bharat Kosa; Rabindra Centenary Publication,* Vol. III; *K. C. Bhattacharrya Memorial Volume; Viśva-Bharati Quarterly; Viśva-Bharati Journal of Philosophy.*

WING-TSIT CHAN

Professor of Chinese Culture and Philosophy, Dartmouth College. A.B., Lingnan University, Canton, 1924; M.A., 1927, and Ph.D., 1929, Harvard University; A.M. (Honorary), Dartmouth College, 1943.

Dean of Faculty and Professor of Philosophy, Lingnan University,

1929–1936; Professor of Chinese Philosophy, University of Hawaii, 1936–1942; Chairman, Division of The Humanities, Dartmouth College, 1951–1955.

Guggenheim Fellow, 1948–1949; Rockefeller Foundation Research Grantee, 1955–1956; American Council of Learned Societies and Social Science Research Council Grant, 1959; American Philosophical Society Grant, Social Science Research Council Grant and Rockefeller Foundation Grant, 1963–1964; Honorary Research Fellow, Institute of Far Eastern Research, Chung Chi College, Hong Kong, 1963; Honorary Fellow, Institute of Oriental Studies, University of Hong Kong, 1964; Honorary Research Fellow, New Asia College Institute of Research, 1963–.

Panel Member, East-West Philosophers' Conferences, 1939, 1949, 1959. Member, Conference on Science, Philosophy and Religion, New York, 1944, 1945; Member, American Council of Learned Societies Committee on Far Eastern Studies, 1950–1953; Honorary Corresponding Associate, Asiatic Research Center, Korea University, 1959; Consultant on Chinese Studies, Pennsylvania-Maryland College group, 1962–1963, and New York State Department of Education, 1963.

Author of *Religious Trends in Modern China; Historical Charts of Chinese Philosophy; An Outline and an Annotated Bibliography of Chinese Philosophy*. Translator and compiler of *A Source Book in Chinese Philosophy*. Translator of *Instructions for Practical Living and other Neo-Confucian Writings by Wang Yang-ming; The Way of Lao Tzu, The Platform Scripture; Reflections on Things at Hand, a Neo-Confucian Anthology; the Basic Zen Buddhist Classic;* Editor with Charles A. Moore, *The Essentials of Buddhist Philosophy;* editor and author, with William Theodore de Bary and Burton Watson, *Sources of Chinese Tradition.* Contributor, *Philosophy East and West; China; Religion in the Twentieth Century; Radhakrishnan, Comparative Studies in Philosophy Presented in Honour of His Sixtieth Birthday; Essays in East-West Philosophy; Studies Presented to Hu Shih on His Sixty-fifth Birthday; The Concept of Man; A Study in Comparative Philosophy; Philosophy and Culture—East and West; Encyclopaedia Britannica; Journal of American Oriental Society; Journal of Asian Studies; Review of Metaphysics.* Associate Editor, *Lingnan Journal,* 1929–1936; Contributing Editor, *Philosophical Abstracts,* 1940–1947; Member, Board of Editors, *Philosophy East and West,* 1951–; Consulting Editor, *Tsing-hua University Journal of Chinese Studies,* 1955; Editor for Chinese Philosophy, *Encyclopedia of Philosophy,* 1963–.

MRS. SURAMA DASGUPTA

Reader in the Department of Philosophy, University of Lucknow, 1950.

M.A., 1930, and Ph.D., 1941, Calcutta University; Ph.D., Cambridge University, 1948.

Lecturer in a Degree College of Calcutta University, 1933–1945; Advanced Research Scholar, Research Department, Government Sanskrit College, 1931–1941.

Awarded the Government Shastri title from the Government Sanskrit College, 1939, and a Ghosh Travelling Fellowship, 1945.

Whitney Fulbright Professor to the University of Nebraska and the University of New Mexico, 1957–1958. Taught at Wellesley College, 1961–1962.

Member: American Philosophical Association, Eastern Division; Council for the Marathi Encyclopaedia of Philosophy, Poona; Sanskrit Literary Association, Lucknow; University Women's Federation, Lucknow Branch.

Author of *Development of Moral Philosophy in India*. Collaborated with the late Professor S. N. Dasgupta in the writing of the last three volumes of his *A History of Indian Philosophy* and edited some of his posthumous publications: *Religion and Rational Outlook; Fundamentals of Indian Art; A History of Indian Philosophy*, Vol. 5; *Aesthetics* (in Hindi) ; *History of the Religions of the World* (in press).

THOMÉ H. FANG

Professor of Philosophy, National Taiwan University.

Educated at the University of Nanking, Ohio State University, and the University of Wisconsin.

Associate Professor of Philosophy, National Wuchang University, 1924–1925; Professor of Philosophy, National Southeastern University, 1925–1927, the Central Institute of Political Sciences, 1927–1936, 1945–1948, the University of Nanking, 1927–1932, and National Central University, 1929–1948. Director of the Institute of Advanced Studies in Philosophy, National Central University, 1938–1948.

Visiting Professor of Philosophy, State University of South Dakota, 1959, and University of Missouri, 1960. Gave the 1960 Mead-Swing Lectures in Oberlin College, Ohio, and lectured at several other American colleges.

Awarded the Medal of Distinguished Service Professor by the Chinese Ministry of Education, 1956 and 1964.

Member of the Executive Committee, Chinese Philosophical Society, 1937–1948.

Principal writings (in Chinese) : *The Sentiment of Life and the Sense of Beauty; Essentials of Chinese Philosophy of Life; Science, Philosophy, and the Significance of Human Life—A Study in the History of European Ideas; Joint Studies in the Philosophy of Change* (in collaboration with Professor Li Cheng-kang) ; *Collected Poems (1938–1953)* ; *Philosophy of Hegel*, 2 vols. (in co-operation with various authors) ; (in English) : *Chinese View of Life: the Philosophy of Comprehensive Harmony*.

JOHN N. FINDLAY

Professor of Philosophy, King's College, University of London.

Educated in Pretoria, South Africa, and proceeded to Balliol College, Oxford, as Rhodes Scholar for the Transvaal, obtaining first class honours in the School of Literae Humaniores, 1926. Ph.D., University of Graz, 1933.

Taught in New Zealand (University of Otago, 1933–1934), South Africa (Rhodes University, 1945; Natal University, 1946–1948) and England (King's College, Newcastle-upon-Tyne, 1948–1951).

Visiting Professor at Carleton College, 1961, and the University of Texas, 1962. Lectured at Princeton University, Yale University, Columbia University, Brown University, Bryn Mawr College, Swarthmore College, Duke University, and many other universities in the United States, as well as in England, Switzerland, Austria, and Germany.

President, Aristotelian Society, 1955–1956; Vice-President, Aristotelian Society, 1956; Fellow of the British Academy since 1956.

Author of *Meinong's Theory of Objects and Values; Hegel: A Re-Examination; Values and Intentions; Language, Mind and Value,* and many articles in *Mind, Proceedings of the Aristotelian Society, Philosophy, Philosophical Quarterly, Philosophy and Phenomenological Research.*

MAX H. FISCH

Professor of Philosophy, University of Illinois.

A.B., Butler University, 1924; Ph.D., Cornell University, 1930.

Taught philosophy at Cornell University, 1926–1928, and at Western Reserve University, 1928–1943. Curator of Rare Books, Army Medical Library, 1942–1945; Chief of History of Medicine Division, 1946.

Fulbright Research Professor, University of Naples, 1950–1951; Visiting Professor of Philosophy, University of Chicago, 1955; Visiting Professor (Fulbright), Keio University (Tokyo), 1958–1959.

Matchette Lecturer, Purdue University, 1956; George Santayana Fellow, Harvard University, 1960.

Associate Member, Center for Advanced Study, University of Illinois, 1961–1963; Member, Administrative Board, International Association of Universities, 1950–1955; President, Western Division, American Philosophical Association, 1955–1956; Chairman, National Board of Officers, 1956–1958; Member of the Council, History of Science Society, 1951–1953; Delegate to the American Council of Learned Societies, 1955–1958.

Author, translator, editor, and reviewer of works in the history of philosophy, of science, and of medicine. Biographer of C. S. Peirce.

FURUKAWA TESSHI

Professor of Ethics, Tokyo University.

Graduated from the Imperial University of Tokyo, 1935. D. Litt., Tōhoku University, 1962.

University of Tokyo: Lecturer, 1946–1949; Associate Professor, 1949–1956; Professor, 1956—. Has also lectured at Tōhoku University, Okayama University, and Kumamoto University.

Director, Japanese Society for Ethics; Director, Japanese Society for Moral Education.

Member, Fourth East-West Philosophers' Conference, 1964.

Books (in Japanese): *A Study of Modern Japanese Thoughts; A Study of French Ethical Thoughts; History of Japanese Ethics; Idea of Yearning for the Heian Period and Its Tradition; Idea of Bushidō and Its Background; Heroes and Saints; Ethics for Young Peoples.* Editor: *Ethics, History of Japanese Thought, History of Moral Education in Japan, History of Ethics.* Also author of many articles in professional journals, such as, *East Asian Studies in Japan, Recent Trends of East Asian Studies in Japan, Philosophical Studies of Japan* (UNESCO publication, Tokyo).

WILLIAM ERNEST HOCKING

Alford Professor Emeritus, Harvard University.

A.B., 1901; A.M., 1902; Ph.D., 1904, Harvard University.

Honorary Degrees: L.H.D., William College, 1923; D.D., University of Chicago, 1933; Th.D., Glasgow University, 1933; L.L.D., Oberlin College, 1934; Duke University, 1941; Litt.D., Phil.D., University of Leiden, 1948.

Harvard Fellow in the universities of Göttingen, Berlin, and Heidelberg, 1902–1903. Taught at Andover Theological Seminary, 1904–1906, University of California, 1906–1908, Yale University, 1908–1914.

Lecturer in Philosophy, Princeton University, 1913–1914; Mills Professor, University of California, 1918–1919; Gifford Lecturer, Glasgow University, 1937–1939; Hibbert Lecturer, Oxford and Cambridge universities, 1938; Flint Lecturer, University of California, Los Angeles, 1946; William James Lecturer, Harvard University, 1947; Guest Professor, University of Leiden, 1947–1948; Lecturer at Munich and Erlangen, Bavaria, 1948.

Panel member, East-West Philosophers' Conference, 1959; Honorary Member, 1964.

Member: American Philosophical Association, American Philosophical Society, American Association for the Advancement of Science, American Oriental Association, East Asiatic Society, American Academy of Arts and Sciences, Aristotelian Society.

Among his more recent publications are: *Living Religions and a*

World Faith; What Man Can Make of Man; Science and the Idea of God; Freedom of the Press; The Coming World Civilization; The Meaning of Immortality in Human Experience; Strength of Men and Nations; Co-author, *Preface of Philosophy.*
Died in 1966.

HORI ICHIRŌ

Professor and Chairman, Department of the History of Religion, Tōhoku University; Professor of the History of Religion, Kokugakuin University; Lecturer of the History of Religion, University of Tokyo.

Educated at the Imperial University of Tokyo. D.Litt., University of Tokyo, 1954.

Member, National Institute for the Studies of Japanese Culture, 1939–1947; Professor of the History of Religion, Kokugakuin University and Lecturer of the History of Japanese Religion, University of Tokyo, 1948–1952; Associate Professor of the History of Religion, Tōhoku National University; Fourth East-West Philosophers' Conference, 1964.

Research Fellow of the Rockefeller Foundation, Harvard University, 1956–1957; Visiting Professor of the History of Religion, University of Chicago, 1957–1958; Research Fellow of the Rockefeller Foundation, Europe, 1958.

Awarded Honored Prize of the Mainichi Press for his book, *Japanese Folk-Beliefs,* 1952, and of the Japan Academy for his book, *A Study of the History of Japanese Folk Religions,* 1956.

Managing Director: Japanese Association of Religious Studies, Japanese Society of Ethnology, Japanese Folklore Society. Member of the Board of Trustees, Japanese Association of Indian and Buddhist Studies.

Among publications (in Japanese): *Essays on the History of Japanese Buddhism; Japanese Culture and Buddhism; Historical and Cultural Materials Concerning Japanese Buddhism; Biography and Evaluation of Dengyō Daishi; Japanese Folk-Beliefs; A Study of the History of Japanese Folk Religions; Social Roles of Japanese Religion; Control of the Life and Attitude of Japanese People by the Religions and Folk-ways.*

HSIEH YU-WEI

Professor of Philosophy and Dean of the Research Institute, New Asia College.

B.A., Soochow University, 1926; M.A., Harvard University, 1931.

Editor-in-chief, *Hsin Pao,* Batavia, Java, 1926–1929; Professor, National Kwangtung Law College, Canton, 1932–1937; Professor and Chairman of the Department of Philosophy, National Chekiang

University, 1937–1948; Editor-in-chief, *The Free Press,* Djakarta, Indonesia, 1949–1952; Editorial Director, *The Central Daily News,* Taipei, 1953–1954; Professor of Philosophy, National Chengchi University, 1954–1959.

Panel Member, East-West Philosophers' Conference, 1959.

Publications (in Chinese) : *An Introduction to Ethics; A Critical Exposition of Chief Contemporary Philosophical Works; Lectures on Philosophy; The Spirit of Chinese Culture; The True Meaning of Freedom; Mankind and Culture; On Whitehead's Philosophy; The Metaphysics of F. H. Bradley; On Hegel's Dialectic; The Logical Theory of F. H. Bradley; On Bertrand Russell's "Prejudice" and Western Philosophy; History of Western Philosophy,* Vol. 1.

KAWASHIMA TAKEYOSHI

Professor of Law, University of Tokyo.

Graduated from Imperial University of Tokyo, Faculty of Law, 1932; LL.D., University of Tokyo, 1959.

Visiting Professor, Stanford University, 1958–1959.

Director, Japanese Association of Private Law and Japanese Association of Sociology of Law; Councillor, Japanese Association of Ethnology and Agrarian History Society; Member, Research Committee of Sociology of Law (Subcommittee of the International Association of Sociology).

Member: Legislative Council of the Ministry of Justice and of the Central Council of Construction Industry of the Ministry of Construction.

Publications (in Japanese) : *Treatise on the Civil Code of the Republic of China; Familistic Structure of Japanese Society; Theory of the Law of Property; Structure of Law in the Theory of Sociology of Law; On the Contracts of Construction; The Study of Law as an Empirical Science; Dissolution of the Rights on Common Land; Sociology of Law; Modern Society and the Law; Treatise on Civil Code of Japan.* Also articles in English and Japanese.

KŌSAKA MASAAKI

President, Tokyo Gakugei University.

Graduated from Kyoto University, 1923; Ph.D. Kyoto University, 1940.

Taught at Kyoto Furitsu (Prefecture) College of Medicine, Tokyo Bunrika (Art and Science) University, Kyoto University, and Kansei Gakuin University. Director of the Center for Humanistic Studies, Kyoto University, 1941–1946. Dean, Faculty of Education, Kyoto University, 1955–1960.

Member: Central Advisory Council of Education; Board of Directors, Institute for Democratic Education; Board of Directors,

Philosophy of Education Association. President, Teacher's Training College Association.

Publications (in Japanese) : *Historical World; Kant; A Study of Mythology; Nishida Kitarō, His Life and Thought; From Kierkegaard to Sartre; Existential Philosophy; Modern Philosophy; Pragmatism; Philosophy of Nishida and Philosophy of Tanabe; History of Japanese Thought in the Meiji Era; Nishida Kitarō and Watsuji Tetsurō.*

CORNELIUS KRUSÉ

William Griffin Professor Emeritus, Wesleyan University.

Educated at Elmhurst College; Eden Seminary; B.D., 1915, A.M., 1917, Ph.D., 1922, Yale University; The Sorbonne and College of France, Paris. Honorary degrees: A.M., Wesleyan University, 1928; L.H.D., Lawrence College, 1952.

Lecturer, University of Illinois, summer school, 1924, 1929; Lecturer in Christian Ethics, Yale Divinity School, 1925; Visiting Professor in Philosophy of Religion, Yale University, 1942–1943; Acting Director, Honors College and Center for Advanced Studies, Wesleyan University, 1961–1962; Visiting Professor of Philosophy, Woman's College of the University of North Carolina, 1962–1963; Visiting Professor of Philosophy and Consultant for the Department of Humanities, University of Florida, Gainesville, 1963.

American Council of Learned Societies: Executive Director, 1947–1948, Chairman of the Board of Officers, 1949–1953; American Philosophical Association: Secretary-Treasurer, 1939–1949, President, 1947, Chairman of the National Board of Officers, 1947, 1959–1961, Chairman of the Committee on International Cultural Relations, 1948–1959; President, Inter-American Philosophical Society, 1956–1957.

On Cultural mission to Latin America under auspices of Coordinator's officer for Inter-American Affairs, June–November, 1943; Executive Director, Foreign Service of American Friends Service Committee, 1946–1947; U. S. specialist on mission to Latin America, Department of State, Program of International Educational Exchange, 1956 and 1958; Inter-American Congress of Philosophy: President, New York City, 1947, Chairman of North American Delegation, Mexico, 1950; Vice-President, International Congress of Philosophy, São Paulo, 1954; Vice-President, Congress of Inter-American Philosophical Society, Chile, 1956; Panel Member, East-West Philosophers' Conference, 1949, 1959.

Member: Institut Internationale de Philosophie, Paris; Societé Franco-Américaine de Philosophie, Paris; Associación Costarricense de Filosofía; Brazilian Philosophical Society (honorary).

Publications: *The Nature of Man; The Nature of Religious Experience;* Co-author: *Essays in East-West Philosophy and Essays in Honor of Douglas Clyde MacIntosh.*

Editor, *Proceedings of the American Philosophical Association,* 1937–1947; Member, editorial staff of *Philosophy and Phenomenological Research;* member, advisory board of *Handbook of Latin American Studies;* member, Board of Editors, *Philosophy East and West.*

GUNAPALA PIYASENA MALALASEKERA

High Commissioner for Ceylon in London; Emeritus Professor, University of Ceylon.

College, Panadura, Ceylon, 1918; M.A., Ph.D., D.Litt., University of London. D.Phil., (Honorary) Moscow University.

Vice-Principal, Ananda College, Colombo, 1921–1923; Principal, Nalanda Vidyalaya, Colombo, 1925–1927. Professor of Pali and Buddhist Civilization, University of Ceylon, from its inception to the time of appointment as the Ambassador for Ceylon to the USSR in 1957. Dean of the Faculty of Oriental Studies, University of Ceylon, for nine years.

Formerly Ambassador to Czechoslovakia and Poland, Minister of Ceylon to Romania; High Commissioner for Ceylon in Canada. Permanent Representative of Ceylon to the United Nations; Deputy Chairman, Ceylon Delegation to the United Nations Assembly sessions and to the General Assembly; Leader of the Ceylon Delegation to UNESCO, 1960. President: All Ceylon Buddhist Congress, 1939–1958, Ceylon Society of Arts, 1955–1959, World Fellowship of Buddhists, 1950–1958, Indian Philosophical Congress, 1957.

Panel Member, East-West Philosophers' Conference, 1949. Lectured widely in Europe, Asia, and the United States and participated in many East-West Symposia of UNESCO.

Among his publications are: *The Pali Literature of Ceylon; Dictionary of Pali Proper Names; The Buddha and His Teachings; Commentary on the Mahāvaṁsa; The Extended Mahāvaṁsa.* Editor-in-chief, *Encyclopaedia of Buddhism;* Editor of several Sinhalese translations in the field.

HAROLD E. McCARTHY

Professor of Philosophy, University of Hawaii.

B.A., 1937; M.A., 1939; Ph.D., 1947, University of California.

At the University of Hawaii since 1947.

Associate member, East-West Philosophers' Conference, 1949, Panel Member, 1959.

Author of numerous articles in learned journals.

Member, Board of Editors, *Philosophy East and West.*

RICHARD McKEON

Professor of Philosophy and Greek, University of Chicago.

B.A., 1920, M.A., 1920, Ph.D., 1928, Columbia University; "Diplôme d'Études Supérieures," The Sorbonne, 1923; "Élève Titulaire de l'École des Hautes Études," University of Paris, 1924.

Taught at Columbia University, 1925–1935; Dean of the Division of the Humanities, University of Chicago, 1935–1947.

Visiting Professor of History, University of Chicago; Visiting Professor, University of Arkansas, Baroda University, Yale University; Fulbright Fellow, University of Paris.

Member of U.S. delegation, General Conference of UNESCO, Paris, 1946, Mexico City, 1947, Beirut, 1948; Counselor, U.S. Embassy, Paris, 1947; former President, American Philosophical Association (Western Division), International Institute of Philosophy, Metaphysical Society of America; Member: American Society for Political and Legal Philosophy, Institut International de Philosophie Politique, Association for Symbolic Logic, American Society for Aesthetics, History of Science Society.

Publications include: *The Philosophy of Spinoza; Selections from Medieval Philosophers* (2 vols.); *The Basic Works of Aristotle;* Editor, *Democracy in a World of Tensions: A Symposium Prepared by UNESCO; Freedom and History: The Semantics of Philosophical Controversies and Ideological Conflicts; Thought, Action and Passion;* Co-author, *The Freedom to Read* and *The Edicts of Aśoka;* numerous articles in journals and symposium volumes.

STERLING M. McMURRIN

E. E. Ericksen Distinguished Professor of Philosophy, University of Utah.

A.B., 1936, A.M., 1937, University of Utah; Ph.D., University of Southern California, 1946; LL.D., University of Utah, Clark University, Delaware State College, University of Southern California; D.Litt., University of Puget Sound.

Visiting Scholar, Columbia University, Union Theological Seminary, 1952–1953; Ford Fellow in Philosophy, Princeton University, 1953.

Assistant Professor of Philosophy, University of Southern California, 1946–1948; Dean of the College of Letters and Science, University of Utah, 1954–1960; Academic Vice-President, University of Utah, 1960–1961.

United States Commissioner of Education; Member, National Commission for UNESCO, Board of Foreign Scholarships, National Culture Center Board, U.S. Delegation for several International Conferences; Chairman, Mountain States Regional Manpower Advisory Committee, Department of Labor.

Currently, Consultant to the Massachusetts Education Study; Member, Board of Trustees, Carnegie Foundation for the Advancement of Teaching; Member, Commission on Plans and Objectives for Higher Education of The American Council on Education.

Past Chairman, Mountain-Plains Philosophical Conference; Past President, Utah Conference on Higher Education; Member, Steering Committee for East-West Philosophers' Conference, 1964.

Lecturer and Seminar Moderator for the Aspen Institute of Humanistic Studies, 1955–.

Publications: Co-author, *A History of Philosophy* (2 vols.); Co-editor, *Contemporary Philosophy;* numerous monographs and articles on philosophy, religion, and education.

Y. P. MEI

Professor of Oriental Studies, Chairman of Chinese and Oriental Studies, Director of Center for Far Eastern Studies, State University of Iowa.

B.A., Oberlin College, 1924; Ph.D., University of Chicago, 1927. Studied at the University of Cologne, 1927–1928. Honorary degrees: LL.D., Oberlin College; L.H.D., Wabash College.

Yenching University, Peiping, 1928–1949: Professor of Philosophy, Dean of the College of Arts and Letters, Acting President.

Visiting Professor of Philosophy, University of Chicago, Indiana University, University of Cincinnati, Princeton University, Wabash College, Bowdoin College, Oberlin College.

Delivered Taft Memorial Lectures, University of Cincinnati, 1952; Tallman Foundation Lectures, Bowdoin College, 1953; Mahlon Powell Foundation Lectures, Indiana University, 1954; Franklin Machette Foundation Lectures, Purdue University, 1955.

Panel Member, East-West Philosophers' Conference, 1949; Member, Chinese Cultural Mission to U.S.; President, Oberlin-in-China; President, American Association of Teachers of Chinese Language and Culture, 1961–1962.

Author of *The Ethical and Political Philosophy of Motse; Motse, The Neglected Rival of Confucius;* articles in *Encyclopaedia Britannica, Encyclopedia Americana, Encyclopedia International, Encyclopedia of Philosophy, International Encyclopedia of the Social Sciences,* and such journals as *Chinese Culture, Tsing Hua Journal of Chinese Studies,* and *Harvard Journal of Asiatic Studies.* Member, Editorial Board, *Tsing Hua Journal of Chinese Studies.*

MIYAMOTO SHŌSON

Emeritus Professor of Buddhist Philosophy, Tokyo University.

M.A., Otani University, 1918; Ph.D., Oxford University, 1929; D.Litt., Imperial University of Tokyo, 1942.

Imperial University of Tokyo: Lecturer; Assistant Professor, 1928; Professor, 1942–1954; Emeritus Professor, 1954–. Professor, Waseda University, 1955–1964, and Komazawa University, 1955–. Visiting Professor, University of Chicago, 1958–1959.

Panel Member, East-West Philosophers' Conference, 1959.

Member, Science Council of Japan, 1954–1959; Chairman of the Directors, Japanese Association of Indian and Buddhist Studies, 1951–1965; Member, Executive Board, International Association for the History of Religions, 1955–1965; Executive Director, The Center of Religions, 1965–.

Publications (in Japanese): *Ultimate Middle and Voidness; Mahāyāna and Hīnayāna; Middle Way Thought and Its Development;* Editor, *A Study of the Formative History of Mahāyāna Buddhism;* Editor, *The Fundamental Truth of Buddhims.* Also many articles in English.

CHARLES A. MOORE

Senior Professor of Philosophy, University of Hawaii.

A.B., 1926, Ph.D., 1932, Yale University. Studied at Oriental Institute, University of Hawaii, 1936–1942; Banaras Hindu University, 1947–1948; Oxford University with Dr. Sarvepalli Radhakrishnan, 1948.

Instructor in Philosophy at Yale, 1933–1936; Department of Philosophy, University of Hawaii, since 1936.

Visiting Professor at Duke University, Cornell University, Boston University, and the University of Southern California.

Guggenheim Fellow and Watumull Foundation Associate, 1947–1948.

Director, East-West Philosophers' Conference, 1939, 1949, 1959.

Member: American Philosophical Association, the American Oriental Society, the Indian Philosophical Congress Association, the Association for Asian Studies.

Editor and Contributor: *Philosophy—East and West; Essays in East-West Philosophy; and Philosophy and Culture—East and West;* Co-editor, with Dr. S. Radhakrishnan, *A Source Book in Indian Philosophy,* and, with Wing-tsit Chan, Junjirō Takakusu's *The Essentials of Buddhist Philosophy;* Editor, *Philosophy East and West;* author of numerous articles for philosophical journals and symposium volumes.

Died in 1967.

T. R. V. MURTI

Professor of Philosophy and Chairman, Department of Philosophy, and Director, Centre for Advanced Study and Research in Indian Philosophy, Banaras Hindu University.

B.A., 1927, M.A., 1929, D.Litt., 1948; Śāstri, 1929, Banaras Hindu

University; Āchārya, Banaras Sanskrit College (now Sanskrit University), 1941.

Fellow and Lecturer, Indian Institute of Philosophy, Amalner, 1929–1936; Assistant Professor of Philosophy, Banaras Hindu University, 1936–1948; Professor of Philosophy, University of Ceylon, Colombo and Peradeniya, 1949–1953; Deputy for the Spalding Professor of Eastern Religions and Ethics, Oxford University, 1949–1950; Sayaji Rao Gaekwad Professor of Indian Civilization and Culture, Banaras Hindu University, 1953–1959; Vice-Chancellor, Sanskrit University, Banaras, 1962.

Visiting Professor of Indian Philosophy and Buddhism, Hebrew University, Jerusalem, 1958; Visiting Professor of Philosophy, Stanford University, 1960–1961; Visiting Professor of World Religions, Harvard University, 1963.

Member, Sanskrit Commission, Government of India, 1956–1957; Recipient of Padma Bhushan (Award of Distinction) by Government of India, 1959; General President, Indian Philosophical Congress, 1963.

Publications: *The Central Philosophy of Buddhism;* Co-author, *Ajñāna—The Theory of Ignorance;* General Editor, *Banaras Hindu University Darśana Series.*

WINFIELD E. NAGLEY

Professor of Philosophy and Chairman, Department of Philosophy, University of Hawaii.

B.A., University of Southern California, 1940; B.D., San Francisco Theological Seminary, 1943; Ph.D., University of Southern California, 1947.

Taught philosophy at Lewis and Clark College, 1941–1949; Washington State University, 1949–1951; and University of Hawaii, 1951–, Chairman, 1957–. Visiting Professor, San Francisco State College, 1962.

Associate Member, East-West Philosophers' Conference, 1949, Panel Member, 1959.

Fellow of the American Scandinavian Society; American Philosophical Association, Pacific Division.

Publications: articles in *Philosophy East and West* and other periodicals. Member, Board of Editors, *Philosophy East and West.*

NAKAMURA HAJIME

Professor of Indian and Buddhist Philosophy and Dean of the Faculty of Letters, University of Tokyo.

Graduated from the Imperial University of Tokyo, 1936; D.Litt., University of Tokyo, 1943.

President, Japan-India Society; Director, Japanese Association for Indian and Buddhist Studies; Director, Japanese Association for Religious Studies; Life Member, Bhandarkar Oriental Research Institute, Poona; Honorary Fellow, Government Sanskrit College, Calcutta.

Visiting Professor of Philosophy, Stanford University, 1951–1952; Visiting Professor of Religion, University of Florida, 1961; Senior Scholar, East-West Center, University of Hawaii, 1962; Visiting Professor of World Religions, Harvard University, 1963–1964; Summer Session Lecturer, University of Hawaii, 1959 and 1964. Lectured at the University of Michigan, Yale University, University of Chicago, Delhi University, Banaras Hindu University, Columbia University.

Delegate to Congress on Cultural Freedom in Asia, Rangoon, 1955; Delegate to the Buddhist Symposium sponsored by the Government of India, New Delhi, 1956; Delegate to the UNESCO-PAX ROMANA Conference, Manila, 1960; Tour of India at invitation of the Government of India, 1960; Panel Member, East-West Philosophers' Conferences, 1959, 1964.

Awarded the Imperial Prize by the Japan Academy, 1957, for *A History of Early Vedānta Philosophy* (4 vols.).

Publications include: *Ways of Thinking of Eastern Peoples.* In Japanese: *Selected Works of Hajime Nakamura* (10 vols.), *Comparative Thought.* Formerly editor of *The Bulletin of the Okurayama Oriental Research Institute* and of *Science of Thought;* Associate Editor, *Monumenta Nipponica;* Contributing Editor, *Journal of the History of Ideas* and *United Asia;* Member, Board of Editors, *Philosophy East and West.*

RAYMOND POLIN

Professor of Philosophy, The Sorbonne, University of Paris.

Ancien élève de l'École normale supérieure, Paris, 1931; Agrégé de Philosophie, Paris, 1934; Docteur, Paris, 1945.

Professor, the University of Lille, 1945–1961; Visiting Professor, University of Buffalo, 1953–1954; Columbia University, 1958–1959; Harvard University, 1963–1964.

Rockefeller Scholarship for research in political philosophy, 1960–1961.

Secrétaire général de l'Institut international de Philosophie politique.

Author of *La Création des valeurs; La Compréhension des valeurs; Du laid, du mal, du faux; Philosophie et Politique chez Thomas Hobbes; La Politique morale de John Locke; Introduction et traduction de: John Locke, Epistola de Tolerantia.*

KARL H. POTTER

Associate Professor of Philosophy, University of Minnesota.

B.A., University of California, Berkeley, 1950; M.A., 1952, Ph.D., 1955, Harvard University.

Fulbright Scholar in India, 1952–1953; Fulbright Research Fellow in India, 1959–1960; Research Fellowship, American Institute of Indian Studies, 1963–1964.

Teaching Fellow in Humanities, Harvard University, 1953–1955; Instructor in Philosophy, Carleton College, 1955–1956; Instructor in Philosophy, University of Minnesota, 1956–1957; Assistant Professor, 1957–1961, Associate Professor, 1961–.

Member: American Philosophical Association, Western Division; Association for Asian Studies; American Oriental Society; Bhandarhar Oriental Research Institute.

Publications include: *The Padārthatattvanirūpaṇam of Raghunātha Siromani; Presuppositions of India's Philosophies;* contributions to *Introducing India in Liberal Education* and *Resources for South Asian Area Studies in the United States;* articles in *Philosophy East and West, Journal of Philosophy, Philosophical Studies, Journal of Aesthetics and Art Criticism, Journal of Asian Studies.*

Book Review Editor for Indian Philosophy, *Philosophy East and West;* General Editor, *Encyclopedia of Indian Philosophies* (in press).

FAZLUR RAHMAN

Director, Central Institute of Islamic Research.

B.A., 1940; M.A., 1942, Punjab University; D.Phil., Oxford University, 1949.

Research Scholar, Punjab University, 1943–1946; Lecturer in Persian Studies, University of Durham, 1950–1958; Associate Professor of Islamic Studies, McGill University, 1958–1961; Visiting Professor, Central Institute of Islamic Research, 1961–1962.

Participated in Colloquium on Islamic Culture, Princeton, 1953, Lahore, 1958; delivered Presidential Address, Conference of the American Society for the Study of Religion, Michigan University, 1959; served as Panelist, Conference on American Foreign Policy, Colgate University, 1960; delivered six lectures, Institute of Higher Arab Studies, Cairo, and one lecture, Institute Fur Religionswissenschaft, Salzburg, 1962.

Director, National News Publications, Ltd., Pakistan; Member: National Press Trust of Pakistan; Advisory Panel for Education and Advisory Panel on Social Welfare of the Planning Commission, Government of Pakistan; Advisory Council of Islamic Ideology, Pakistan.

Publications: *Avicenna's Psychology; Prophecy in Islam; Islamic Methodology in History;* and Editor, *Avicenna's De Anima.*

P. T. RAJU

Retired University Professor of Philosophy and Psychology, University of Rajasthan; Professor of Philosophy and Indian Studies, The College of Wooster.

B.A., Allahabad University, 1928; M.A., 1931, Ph.D., 1935, Calcutta University; Sampūrṇa Madhyama, Śāstri, Banaras Sanskrit College.

Tata Visiting Professor of Philosophy, The Asia Institute, New York, 1949; Visiting Professor of Philosophy, University of California (Berkeley), 1950; Visiting Professor for Comparative Philosophy, University of Illinois, 1952–1953; Merton Guest-Professor, University of Maine, 1961–1962; Visiting Professor of Philosophy, University of Southern California, 1962; Gillespie Visiting Professor, The College of Wooster, 1962–1964.

Sir Hari Singh Foudation Lectures, Saugar University, 1956; Woodward Lecture, Yale University, 1950; Century Fund Lecture, Northwestern University, 1953; has also lectured at many European and American universities.

General President, All-India Philosophical Conference, 1958; General President, Indian Philosophical Congress, 1960; Panel Member, East-West Philosophers' Conferences, 1949, 1959, 1964.

Dean of the Faculty of Arts, University of Rajasthan, 1950–1953; Member, Commitee on Gandhian Life and Philosophy, Ministry of Education, India, until 1962 Participant in several international conferences.

Member: American Philosophical Association (Eastern and Western Divisions), American Oriental Society, Metaphysical Society of America, Association for Asian Studies, American Academy of Political and Social Science.

Awarded the Order of Merit, "Padma Bhūshan," by the President of India, 1958, "for contributions to East-West understanding at the philosophical level."

Author of nearly 150 articles in Indian, European, and American journals and the following books: *Thought and Reality: Hegelianism and Advaita; Idealistic Thought of India; Introduction to Comparative Philosophy; Indian Idealism and Modern Challenges;* Co-editor: *Comparative Studies in Philosophy* and *The Concept of Man: A Study in Comparative Philosophy.*

MIGUEL REALE

Professor, Law School, University of São Paulo.

Educated at Colégio Dante Alighieri. LL.D., University of São Paulo, 1934.

Director, Escola de Comércio Graça Aranha, 1934–1936; Teacher of philosophy, Inst. Paulista de Alta Cultura, 1936–1937; Visiting Professor at the University of Lisbon (1963).

Director, *review Panorama*, 1936–1937, *daly Ação*, 1936–1938; member, State Administrative Council, São Paulo, 1942–1945; Vice-President in Brazil, Partido Social Progressista, 1946; State Secretary of Justice and Interior, 1947; 1963–1964; Reitor of the University of São Paulo, 1949–1950; President of the Brazilian Institute of Philosophy—1950–1965; First President and Director of the "Interamerican Philosophical Society" (1954), Director of the "Revista Brasileira de Filosofia" (1950–1965).

Member: Inst. dos Advogados de São Paulo, Ordem dos Advogados do Brazil, "Inst. Argentino de Filosofia Juridica y Social," "Società Italiana di Filosofia del Diritto," "Sociedad Mexicana de Filosofia," "Accademia delle Scienze dell'Università di Bologna," Academia das Ciencias de Coimbra.

Author of (in Portuguese): *O Estado moderno, Formação da politica burgueza, Capitalismo International, Atualidades de um mundo antigo, Atualidades brasileiras, Fundamentos do direito, Filosofia do Direito, Horizontes do Direito e da História, A doutrina de Kant no Brasil, Filosofia em São Paulo, Teoria do Direito e do Estado, Pluralismo e Liberdade, Imperativos da Revolução de Março.*

CONSTANTIN REGAMEY

Professor of Indology, University of Fribourg and Professor of Slavic and Oriental Languages and Civilizations, University of Lausanne.

Educated at University of Warsaw (Indian Philology), Ph.D., 1936, and École des Hautes Études, Paris.

Privatdocent at Warsaw University, 1937–1939; Professor of General Linguistics, University of Fribourg, 1946–1963.

Delegate, Silver Jubilee of the Indian Philosophical Congress, 1950; Delegate, General Conferences of UNESCO, 1956, 1958; UNESCO Delegate, International Symposium on History of Eastern and Western Cultural Contacts, 1957; Panel Member, East-West Philosophers' Conference, 1959; Delegate, International Meeting of Composers, 1960. President, Swiss Society of Oriental Studies, 1961–

Active in the field of music as composer, musicographer, pianist, and critic.

Publications include: *Bibliographie, analytique des travaux concernants les éléments anaryens dans les langues et les civilisations de l'Inde; Three Chapters from the Samādhirājasūtra; Bhadramāyākāravyākarana; Considerations sur le systeme morphologique du tibetain litteraire; Buddhistische Philosophie: Bibliographische Einführung; East and West: Some Aspects of Historic Evolution; Die Religionen Indiens, Der Buddhismus Indiens, Die Religion Tibets; Comparison of the General Standpoint of Indian and European Philosophy;* Editor, *Etudes asiatiques;* and articles in scholarly journals.

S. K. SAKSENA

Professor of Philosophy, University of Hawaii.

B.A., 1925; M.A., 1927, Allahabad University; Ph.D., University of London, 1939.

Taught at the University of Agra and Delhi University; 1928–1947; Head of the Department of Philosophy, University of Saugar, 1954–1960.

Deputy Director (Editorial), Publications Division, Ministry of Information and Broadcasting of the Government of India, 1947–1954.

Visiting Professor of Indian Philosophy and Culture, University of Hawaii, 1950–1952. Lectured widely in Europe, Japan, and the United States.

Panel Member, East-West Philosophers' Conferences, 1959, 1964.

Author of *Nature of Consciousness in Hindu Philosophy,* articles in learned journals, and chapters in many symposium volumes. Member, Board of Editors, *Philosophy East and West;* formerly co-editor, *Indian Philosophical Quarterly.*

GREGG M. SINCLAIR

President Emeritus, University of Hawaii.

B.A., University of Minnesota, 1912; M.A., Columbia University, 1919. Honorary Degrees: LL.D., University of Minnesota, Ohio State University, Columbia University, University of California; H.H.D., University of Hawaii; D.Litt., Keio University.

Professor of English in Japan 1912–1915, 1923–1926. University of Hawaii: Professor of English, 1928–1942; Director, Oriental Institute, 1936–1940; President, 1942–1955.

Contributor of articles to various journals.

JOHN E. SMITH

Professor of Philosophy and Chairman, Department of Philosophy, Yale University.

B.A., 1942, Ph.D., 1948, Columbia University; B.D., Union Theological Seminary, 1945; LL.D., University of Notre Dame, 1964.

Taught at Barnard College, Columbia University, Vassar College, Union Theological Seminary, University of Michigan.

Dudleian Lecturer, Harvard University, 1960; Suarez Lecturer, Fordham University, 1963; Research Associate, Humanities, Princeton University.

Member, American Philosophical Association, American Theological Society, Aristotelian Society.

Author of *Royce's Social Infinite; Value Convictions and Higher Education; Reason and God; The Spirit of American Philosophy; The Philosophy of Religion;* Translator of Richard Kroner's *Kant's Weltanschauung;* Editor of *Treatise Concerning Religious Affections; Works of Jonathan Edwards,* Vol. 2. Member, The Editorial Board, *Monist* and *Journal of Religious Studies;* General Editor, Yale Edition, *Works of Jonathan Edwards.*

EDWARD W. STRONG

Chancellor, and Professor of Philosophy, University of California, Berkeley.

A.B., Stanford University, 1925; A.M., 1929, Ph.D., 1937, Columbia University.

Taught at City College of New York, 1927–1932, and at University of California, Berkeley. Chairman, Department of Sociology and Social Institutions; Associate Dean, College of Letters and Science; Chairman, Department of Philosophy, University of California, Berkeley.

American Philosophical Association: Chairman, National Officers Board, 1952; Pacific Division, Executive Committee member, 1939–1941; Secretary-Treasurer, 1945–1947; Vice-President, 1950; President, 1952. Member, Board of Directors, American Council on Education; Board of Advisers, Institute of World Affairs; Executive Committee of *Journal of the History of Philosophy.*

Author of *Procedures and Metaphysics;* Co-author, *University of California Publications in Philosophy,* Vols. 17–29; contributor to various journals.

DAISETZ T. SUZUKI

Emeritus Professor, Otani University; Director, Matsugaoka Bunko.

Educated at Tokyo Imperial University, 1891–1894. D.Litt., Otani University, 1933; LL.D. (honorary), University of Hawaii, 1959.

Taught at Gakushu-in, Tokyo Imperial University, and Otani University.

Lectured at various British universities under the auspices of the Japanese Foreign Ministry, 1936; University of Hawaii, 1949; Claremont College, 1950, 1951; as Rockefeller Foundation Lecturer at Yale, Harvard, Cornell, Princeton and other universities, 1950; Columbia University, 1951, 1952–1954, 1955–1957; University of Munich, 1953; Mexico City College, 1956; University of Mexico, 1957; and in many cities of Europe and the United States.

Elected member of the Japan Academy and awarded the Cultural Medal by the Emperor of Japan, 1949; received the Asahi Cultural Award, 1955; invited as State Guest of India, 1960; received the

Rabindranath Tagore Birth-Centenary Medal, Asiatic Society, Calcutta, 1964.

Member, East-West Philosophers' Conferences, 1939, 1949, 1959, 1964 (active and honorary); 13th Symposium of the Conference on Science, Philosophy and Religion, Columbia University, 1952; Eranos Conference, Ascona, Switzerland, 1953 and 1954; Conference on Zen and Psychoanalysis, Cuernavaca, Mexico, 1957; Massachusetts Institute of Technology Conference, "New Knowledge in Human Values," 1957.

His publications number over 125, among which are (in Japanese): *On "No-Mind"; Studies in the Pure Land Thought; Studies in the History of Zen Thought*, 2 vols.; *The Awakening of Japanese Spirituality; Bankei on the Unborn; The East and the West;* (in English): *Essays in Zen Buddhism*, 3 vols.; *Studies in the Laṅkāvatāra Sūtra; Manual of Zen Buddhism; An Introduction to Zen Buddhism; Living by Zen; Outlines of Mahāyāna Buddhism; Zen and Japanese Culture.* Editor, *The Eastern Buddhist*, 1921–1939; and many essays in learned journals.

Died in 1966.

T'ANG CHÜN-I

Dean of the Faculty of Arts, New Asia College.

Educated at Sino-Russian University, Peking University, and National Central University, 1925–1932.

Lecturer, West China Union University, 1937–1942; Associate Professor, 1942–1945, Professor of Philosophy, 1945–1949, National Central University.

Helped to found New Asia College, at which he has served as Dean since its beginning.

Panel Member, East-West Philosophers' Conference, 1959. Member, Philosophical Association of China and Oriental Idealistic Humanists Society; Adviser, Buddhistic Cultural Association.

Major publications (in Chinese): *Comparative Studies in Chinese and Western Philosophies; Reconstruction of the Moral Self; Experience of Human Life; Spiritual Values in Chinese Culture; Reconstruction of the Humanistic Spirit; Cultural Consciousness and Moral Reason* (2 vols.); *The Development of the Chinese Humanistic Spirit; Philosophy* (2 vols.).

TARA CHAND

Honorary Professor, Indian School of International Studies, Delhi.

Educated at Meerut College, Meerut; Muir Central College, Allahabad; and Queen's College, Oxford.

Member, Indian Parliament; Chairman, History of the Freedom Movement in India, New Delhi.

Kayastha Pathshala College: Professor of History, 1913–1918; Principal, 1925–1945. Allahabad University: Professor of Politics, 1945–1947; Vice-Chancellor, 1947–1948. Secretary, Hindustani Academy.

Secretary and Educational Adviser to the Government of India, 1948–1951; President, Indian History Congress; Indian Ambassador to Iran, 1951–1956.

Publications: *A Short History of the Indian People from the Earliest Times to the Present Day; History of the Freedom Movement in India; Influence of Islam on Indian Culture; Growth of Islamic Thought in India; State and Society in the Mughal Age;* Editor, *Sirr-i-Akbar* and *Gulzar-i-Hall.*

UEDA YOSHIFUMI

Professor of Buddhist Philosophy and Chairman, Department of Indic and Buddhist Studies, Nagoya University.

Graduated from Imperial University of Tokyo, 1933; D.Litt., University of Kyushu, 1948.

Professor, Ryukoku University, 1945–1949; Lecturer, Hiroshima University, 1952–1956; Hokkaido University, 1954; Kyoto University, 1957; Tōhoku University, 1961.

Director, Japanese Association of Indian and Buddhist Studies; Director, Japanese Association for Religious Studies.

Member, Fourth East-West Philosophers' Conference, 1964.

Publications (in Japanese): *A Study of the History of Buddhist Thought; On the Concept of "Karma" in Buddhism; On the Fundamental Structure of Mahāyāna Buddhist Thought; An Introduction to Yogācāra Philosophy;* and articles in learned journals.

W. H. WERKMEISTER

Professor and Director, School of Philosophy, University of Southern California, 1953–

Studied at the universities of Münster and Frankfurt, 1920–1923; Ph.D., University of Nebraska, 1927.

Instructor to Professor of Philosophy and Chairman of the Department, University of Nebraska, 1926–1953.

American Exchange Professor, University of Berlin, 1936–1937; Guest Lecturer, universities of Bonn, Cologne, Giessen, Hamburg, Jena, Konigsberg, Leipzig, Munich, Münster, 1937. Tully Cleon Knoles Lecturer, College of the Pacific, 1950; Visiting Lecturer, Harvard University, 1950–1951; Special Lecturer, University of Istanbul, 1956.

Panel Member, East-West Philosophers' Conference, 1959.

Member, American Philosophical Association, President, Pacific Division, 1964.

Publications: *A Philosophy of Science; The Basis and Structure of Knowledge; Introduction to Critical Thinking; A History of Philosophical Ideas in America; Outlines of a Value Theory; Theories of Ethics;* Editor, *Facets of the Renaissance; The Forest of Yggdrasil; Francis Bacon: His Career and His Thought; Theories of Value;* Editor, *The Personalist.* Contributor of articles to various professional journals.

JOHN C. H. WU

Professor of Asian Studies, Seton Hall University.

LL.B., Comparative Law School of China, Shanghai, 1920; J.D., Michigan University School of Law, 1921. Honorary degrees: LL.D., University of Oregon, Boston College, St. John's University; Litt.D., Rockhurst College.

Traveling Fellow, Carnegie Endowment for International Peace, the Sorbonne and Berlin University, 1921–1923; Research Scholar, Harvard Law School, 1923–1924; Professor of Law and, later, Principal, Comparative Law School of China, 1924–1940; Professor of Law, Seton Hall University School of Law, 1951–1961.

Judge, Chief Justice, and President, successively, of the Provisional Court, later, Special High Court, International Settlement of Shanghai, 1927–1929; Member, Legislative Body of National China, 1933–1946; Advisor, Chinese Delegation to the first General Assembly of the United Nations, 1945; Envoy Extraordinary and Minister Plenipotentiary of China to the Holy See, 1946–1949; Member, The Permanent Court of Arbitration, The Hague, 1957–   .

Rosenthal Lecturer, Northwestern University Law School, 1929; Research Fellow, Harvard Law School, 1930; Senior Visiting Professor of Chinese Philosophy, University of Hawaii, 1949–1951; Lecturer in Religion, Columbia University, 1964.

Panel Member, East-West Philosophers' Conference, 1959.

Honorary membership: American Academy of Arts and Sciences.

Among his publications are: Chinese versions of *The Psalms* and *The New Testament; Beyond East and West; The Interior Carmel; Fountain of Justice;* translator, *Tao Te Ching.* Managing editor, *T'ien Hsia Monthly,* 1935–1941.

Index

Absolute: in West, 9; in India, 47, 48, 51, 52, 53, 56, 59, 61, 212, 213; in Hegel, 59; in Buddhism, 67, 76, 204; for Royce, 493; in American philosophy, 495; *see also* Universal, *Brahman*

acitta, 81, 82, 88

action: in India, 57, 58, 209; *see also karma*

actuality: in Theravada Buddhism, 76

ādhyātmika, 49

Advaita Vedanta: 47, 55, 60, 62, 63n8, 125, 134, 135, 215, 355, 510, 556, 557, 558, 561; and individual, 51–52; and concept of inaction, 56; and freedom, 58, 211; and ignorance, 207; and God, 213

aggregates: in Buddhism, 67, 76

ahaṁkāra: "ego" or "mind" in Advaita Vedanta, 51; in Ramanujists, 53

Ājivikas: and soul, 203

Alexander, 458

Allport, Gordon, 92, 93

altruism, 95

Ambrose, St., 462

Amida Buddha, 77, 232, 234, 235, 242, 366

Amos: and individual in Hebraic tradition, 253

Analects of Confucius: 271, 274, 276, 277, 279, 280, 281, 337, 338, 399; on sincerity, 189; in Japan, 230

anattā, see anatman

anatman: in Buddhism, 68; in Vasubandhu, 81, 84, 88; *see also* non-self

ancestor worship: in China, 181; in Japan, 227, 239

animittam, 82

annihilation, 7

Anselm: 177; and the *Prosologium,* 267n6

apṛthaksiddhi: in Ramanujists, 54

Aquinas, Thomas: 87, 170, 177, 178n11, 267n8, 516; and God, 165; and the individual, 257–258, 318; and ethics, 323; and law, 463

arahant, 71

Aristotle: 77, 167, 173, 317, 463,

473, 516; and Thomas Aquinas, 257; and self-realization, 318; on reason, 323; social philosophy of, 413; concept of law, 456, 457

Asaṅga, 79, 86, 87, 88

Aśoka, 291, 352

Atlantic Charter, 72

Atman, 128, 134, 411, 509, 514

Atomists: on law, 456, 457

Augustine: 177, 462, 514, 515, 523; on the individual, 256–257

Avataṁsaka school: and Hua-yen, 39

awareness: in Buddhism, 73

axiology, 25

āyuth: and *karma,* 49

Bacon, Francis, 157

Being: in Confucianism, 25, 26; in Taoism, 30, 43; in Chuang Tzu, 31; in Wang Pi, 34; in Chinese Buddhism, 35; in Seng-chao, 36, 37

Benedict, Ruth, 364, 366

Bengal Vaiṣṇavism, 63n10

Bentham, Jeremy: on morality and utilitarianism, 320–321, 324; mentioned, 466

Bergson, Henri, 167, 289

Berkeley, 137n3

Bhagavad-gītā: 57, 63n2, 412, 427; *see also Gita*

Bhagāvata, 350

bhakti: 57, 419; *see also* emotion

Bhartṛhari: and the Grammarians, 128, 130, 132, 134, 135

Bhāskarites, 54, 55

Bhoga, 49

Bhūta-tathatā: 36; in Seng-chao, 37; in Hua-yen, 41

Bible: and concept of law, 463

Bodhidharma, 523, 526

bodhi-sattva, 87

Bradley, F. H., 493

Brahmā, 75, 211

Brahman: 47, 51, 53, 58, 59, 128, 130, 213, 216, 509, 514, 557, 558; and *mokṣa,* 206; *see also* Absolute

Brāhmaṇas, 349, 414, 508, 509, 510

Browne, Borden Parker, 494

Buber, Martin, 322

Buddha: in Hua-yen, 38, 40, 41; as an individual, 65; and individuality, 71; and morality, 72, 203; and